Sixth Edition

Teaching Children to Read

THE TEACHER MAKES THE DIFFERENCE

D. RAY REUTZEL
Utah State University

ROBERT B. COOTER, JR.
Bellarmine University

D1307176

Boston   Columbus   Indianapolis   New York   San Francisco   Upper Saddle River
Amsterdam   Cape Town   Dubai   London   Madrid   Milan   Munich   Paris   Montreal   Toronto
Delhi   Mexico City   Sao Paulo   Sydney   Hong Kong   Seoul   Singapore   Taipei   Tokyo

Vice President and Editor-in-Chief: Aurora Martínez Ramos
Senior Development Editor: Max Effenson Chuck
Editor: Erin K. L. Grelak
Editorial Assistant: Michelle Hochberg
Executive Marketing Manager: Krista Clark
Production Editor: Janet Domingo
Editorial Production Service: Omegatype Typography, Inc.
Manufacturing Buyer: Megan Cochran
Electronic Composition: Omegatype Typography, Inc.
Interior Design: Omegatype Typography, Inc.
Photo Researcher: Annie Pickert Fuller
Cover Designer: Linda Knowles

Credits and acknowledgments borrowed from other sources and reproduced, with permission, in this textbook appear on appropriate page within or below.

Chapter opening photos: pp. 2, 88, 212, 374, 456: Annie Fuller; p. 28: Bob Daemmrich Photography; p. 128: David Mager/Pearson Learning Group; p. 180: Shutterstock; pp. 256, 508: Thinkstock; p. 312: Krista Greco/Merrill; p. 422: Lori Whitley/Merrill.

Standards for Reading Professionals and Guiding Principles for Educators: Standards for Reading Professionals, reprinted with permission of the International Reading Association; Common Core Standards, © Copyright 2010. National Governors Association Center for Best Practices and Council of Chief State School Officers. All rights reserved; Response to Intervention, reprinted with permission of the International Reading Association.

Library of Congress Cataloging-in-Publication Data

Reutzel, D. Ray (Douglas Ray).
  Teaching children to read : the teacher makes the difference / D. Ray Reutzel, Robert B. Cooter, Jr.—6th ed.
        p.   cm.
  Includes bibliographical references and index.
  ISBN-13: 978-0-13-256606-3 (pbk.)
  ISBN-10: 0-13-256606-0 (pbk.)
 1. Reading (Elementary)   2. Reading (Elementary)—Language experience approach.   3. Language arts (Elementary)   I. Cooter, Robert B.   II. Cooter, Robert B.   III. Title.
  LB1573.R48   2012
  372.41—dc22

                                    2011004472

10 9 8 7 6 5 4 3 2 1   RRD-OH   15   14   13   12   11

www.pearsonhighered.com   ISBN-10:   0-13-256606-0
                             ISBN-13:   978-0-13-256606-3

For my wife, Pamela, my children and their spouses,
and my grandchildren, who are my life's inspiration.
To the many teachers and administrators who have also
inspired in me a passion for excellent instruction.

—DRR

For my first and best teachers—Toni and Bruce Cooter,
and for Mary, Catherine, and James Gooch.

—RBC

About the Authors

D. Ray Reutzel is the Emma Eccles Jones Distinguished Professor and Endowed Chair of Early Childhood Education at Utah State University. He has taught kindergarten, first grade, third grade, and sixth grade. Dr. Reutzel is the author of more than 185 refereed research reports, articles, books, book chapters, and monographs published in *The Elementary School Journal, Early Childhood Research Quarterly, Reading Research Quarterly, Journal of Literacy Research, Journal of Educational Research, Reading Psychology, Literacy Research and Instruction, Language Arts, Journal of Adolescent and Adult Literacy,* and *The Reading Teacher,* among others. He has received more than $7.5 million in research and professional development funding from private, state, and federal agencies including the Institute of Education Sciences and the U.S. Department of Education.

Dr. Reutzel is the past editor of *The Reading Teacher* and *Literacy Research and Instruction.* He is author or coauthor of several chapters published in the *Handbook of Classroom Management,* the *Handbook of Research on Literacy and Diversity,* and the *Handbook of Reading Research* (Vol. IV). Dr. Reutzel received the 1999 A.B. Herr Award from the College Reading Association for outstanding research and published contributions to reading education. Dr. Reutzel was given the John C. Manning Public School Service Award from the International Reading Association in May 2007 for his many years of working in schools with teachers and children. Dr. Reutzel has also served as past president of the College Reading Association/Association for Literacy Educators and Researchers and as a member of the board of directors of the International Reading Association from 2007 to 2010. Dr. Reutzel was inducted as a member of the Reading Hall of Fame in 2011.

Robert B. Cooter, Jr., currently serves as Ursuline Endowed Professor and dean of the Annsley Frazier Thornton School of Education at Bellarmine University in Louisville, Kentucky. Dr. Cooter served from 2006 to 2011 as editor of *The Reading Teacher,* the largest circulation literacy education journal worldwide. His research is focused exclusively on the improvement of literacy acquisition for children living in poverty. In 2008 Dr. Cooter received the A.B. Herr Award from the Association of Literacy Educators and Researchers for contributions to the field of literacy.

Earlier in his career Dr. Cooter served as an elementary classroom teacher and Title I reading specialist. In public school administration, Dr. Cooter served as the first "Reading Czar" (or associate superintendent) for the Dallas Independent School District. He was named Texas State Champion for Reading by the governor for development of the acclaimed Dallas Reading Plan for some 60,000 children. Dr. Cooter later designed and served as principal investigator of the Memphis Striving Readers Program, a $16 million middle school literacy research project funded by the U.S. Department of Education. In 2007 Dr. Cooter and colleagues J. Helen Perkins and Kathleen Spencer Cooter were recipients of the Urban Impact Award from the Council of Great City Schools for their work in high poverty schools.

Dr. Cooter has authored or coauthored over 20 books in reading education and more than 60 journal articles. His books include the bestselling *Strategies for Reading Assessment and Instruction,* used at over 200 universities; *The Flynt-Cooter Comprehensive Reading Inventory,* a norm-referenced classroom reading assessment with English and Spanish versions; and *Perspectives on Rescuing Urban Literacy Education: Spies, Saboteurs, and Saints.* He is currently completing work on a new book with his wife and colleague, Professor Kathleen Cooter, entitled *Urban Literacy Education: Helping City Kids in Regular and Special Education Classrooms.*

Dr. Cooter lives in Louisville, Kentucky, and enjoys family time on their houseboat, *Our Last Child,* with his bride, grandchildren, and golden retrievers. He sometimes appears in reunion with The George Washington Bridge Band, a Nashville-based rock group he cofounded and toured with during the 1960s and 70s.

Brief Contents

Contents

Part Two   Essentials of Reading Instruction   27

Developing Children's Oral Language
28

Early Reading Instruction: Getting Started with the Essentials 88

Contents

Phonics and Word Recognition: Learning to Read Words
128

STANDARDS for Reading Professionals and Guiding Principles for Educators   175

Reading Fluency
180

myeducationlab The Power of Classroom Practice / **A+RISE**   207

STANDARDS for Reading Professionals and Guiding Principles for Educators   208

Increasing Reading Vocabulary
212

Teaching Reading Comprehension 256

myeducationlab / A+RISE   305

Writing
312

Part Three   The Reading Teacher's Toolbox   373

Evidence-Based Programs, Interventions, and Standards for Reading Instruction
374

Assessment
422

Part Four Bringing It All Together in the Classroom 455

Effective Reading Instruction and Organization in Grades K–3 456

 502

Effective Academic Literacy Instruction in Grades 4–8
508

Why is high quality teacher education so critical for literacy teachers? Because research tells us it is the teacher who makes the difference in effective reading instruction. As a capable literacy teacher, you will need to think deeply about your teaching decisions in order to understand and meet the literacy needs of every student in your classes. That is a tall order, but this book will become your personal guide to help you succeed in doing so.

Teaching Children to Read: The Teacher Makes the Difference, Sixth Edition, emphasizes the essential nature of the teacher's role in literacy instruction. At the core of this new edition, we continue to assert the primacy of the role of teacher quality and effectiveness as the key to successful literacy instruction. We have thoroughly updated our previous five pillars of effective reading instruction, which provided a logical and consistent structure for closely examining the essential elements that well-prepared literacy teachers know, understand, and are able to implement in classrooms. In this new edition, we have added two additional pillars—Motivation and Engagement and Technology and New Literacies. By organizing every chapter around these seven pillars of effective instruction, the concept of the teacher as lynchpin in literacy instruction is reinforced and cemented. Using these seven pillars to ground your thinking about future teaching, you will be able to successfully develop and perform your vital role in helping all children become successful readers and writers.

Seven Pillars of Effective Instruction

Teacher Knowledge

This new edition thoroughly examines how teacher knowledge can lead to informed instructional decision making. Purple headings, figures, and tables mark the chapter sections that cover the central element of teacher knowledge. Material in the purple section of each chapter gives you the foundational, evidence-based knowledge you need to understand in order to assure you are well prepared as an informed literacy decision maker.

Classroom Assessment

The role of assessment, highlighted in royal blue, is integral to high quality, effective instruction and is part of informed instruction as covered in the sixth edition. Because you, the teacher, must be able to gauge your students' development of literacy skills to make informed instructional decisions, the blue assessment section is designed to help you make important determinations about student progress and intervention selections.

Evidence-Based Teaching Practices

Effective, evidence-based teaching practices, highlighted in turquoise, are richly described in this new edition. This section lays out practical intervention strategies and approaches for teaching essential literacy skills and strategies. Great teachers have a large assortment of effective tools in their instructional toolboxes, helping every child to reach their literacy potential.

Response to Intervention (RTI)

This section, highlighted in green, guides teachers toward ways to differentiate the instruction, monitor the effectiveness of that instruction, and then adapt the instruction based on progress-monitoring data as found in many renditions of Response to Intervention (RTI) models. It is clear to any teacher who has spent more than five seconds in today's classrooms that students come to school with diverse learning needs. Your goal must be to help all the students in your classroom succeed, including students who struggle because English is not their first language or because they have learning disabilities or other special needs.

Motivation and Engagement

This pillar of effective, evidence-based instruction is a new feature in the sixth edition. In this section, highlighted in gold, you are provided with specific strategies to help students get motivated to learn to read and to remain engaged in the process throughout the year. Motivation has been shown to be among the most important considerations in students' willingness to persist and put forth the necessary effort to learn to read and then love to read. Research evidence has been mounting over the past decade about the importance of motivation. Teachers need to know about and use various strategies to motivate their students to become and stay engaged in learning to read and reading to learn.

Technology and New Literacies

As we discuss in this section, highlighted in orange, teachers in today's classrooms are teaching children who are more familiar with a MP3 players, cell phones, and computers than they may be with traditional printed reading materials. They text, Google, and navigate social media to stay connected to their peers and the world outside. Access to the World Wide Web and the vast information available to students in contemporary classrooms demands that teachers know about how to connect learning to read to technologies and new literacies. Students will spend as much or more time reading materials presented or accessed through newer technologies than they will reading published print materials. In this new section, we provide teachers with a primer on new technologies that may be useful in teaching various essential elements of learning to read and reading to learn to today's plugged-in students. For those of you who are as well-versed in technology as your students, our strategies will help you harness your knowledge and experience and bring it to your teaching and student learning.

Family and Community Connections

The value of establishing durable relationships with children's caregivers and other community resources is clarified and amplified in red sections of the sixth edition. Here we provide recommendations for creating and nurturing important connections between the school classroom and community resources. The goal in the red sections of the chapters is to help you communicate with parents and other caregivers, including day care and other educational providers, and involve them in students' ongoing literacy success.

Text Organization

In preparing the sixth edition of *Teaching Children to Read,* we have presented information teachers need to develop into master literacy teachers. We believe that a foundation in scientific research evidence and a necessary acquaintance with classroom experience are pivotal to informing teacher decision making. Building on new evidence (National Early Literacy Panel, 2008) about the importance of oral language development as a foundation for reading success led to substantial updates for the chapter on oral language. This new understanding of the needs of early learners led naturally to the inclusion of an expanded section in Chapter 3 on learning the alphabetic principle and letter name learning, concepts about print, and phonemic awareness. Flowing from these updates the essential elements of effective, evidence-based reading instruction are covered in detail.

With that in place, we build on the chapter-by-chapter topical focus on assessment with a full chapter dedicated to the topic, including a focus on meeting contemporary guidelines of Race to the Top, a federal mandate for improving student and school literacy progress, and state Common Core Standards.

We then turn our attention to the reality of today's reading classrooms and the programs and standards teachers are asked to examine and follow. Lastly, because classroom organization and management are important considerations in setting up literacy programs, we offer you insight into the observations and recommendations we have made to K–8 teachers to help them prepare and organize their literacy materials to meet students' developmental needs.

New to This Edition

NEW! Two new pillars of effective reading instruction—*Motivation and Engagement* and *Technology and New Literacies*—have been added to the previous edition's five pillars of effective reading instruction.

NEW! Greatly expanded coverage of working with English learners includes important information about the particular learning needs of English learners plus methods for assessment and instruction.

NEW! An updated Chapter 4, "Phonics and Word Recognition," gives teachers exceptionally clear examples of explicit blending and segmenting lessons associated with effective phonics instruction. This instruction helps students to decode monosyllable and multisyllabic words, making phonics lessons clear enough for even the most difficult-to-teach students.

NEW! Heavily revised Chapter 7, "Teaching Reading Comprehension," includes new effective reading comprehension strategies that give teachers the tools to boost students' reading comprehension through effective instruction. This chapter also includes new coverage of brain research and its impact on reading comprehension.

NEW! Chapter 9, "Evidence-Based Programs, Interventions, and Standards for Reading Instruction," updates the standards for reading instruction and introduces students to core reading program features and purposes. It also helps readers become acquainted with evidence-based effective programs using the What Works Clearinghouse evidence base.

NEW! Chapter 11, "Effective Reading Instruction and Organization in Grades K–3," serves as a highly useful, step-by-step guide to teaching reading and planning a classroom from before the school year begins through the first day, week, month, and year.

NEW! Discussion on how to work with and benefit from the knowledge base and experience of reading coaches.

NEW! A major focus on—and new lesson examples for—explicit instruction of reading skills, strategies, and concepts gives teachers a way to "think aloud" and provide students with clear, routine, systematic, and highly useful reading strategies that lead to reading success.

NEW! Motivation is addressed as a key learning factor with chapters that include new sections with strategies aimed at stimulating interest and increasing motivation, based on up-to-the-moment research findings.

NEW! Marginal A+RISE® Teaching Strategies align with relevant concepts in the main body of the text and give teachers quick, research-based strategies for targeting their instruction and making content accessible for all students, including English language learners.

NEW! End-of-chapter tables and marginal notes align text with IRA, Common Core, and RTI standards.

MyEducationLab

In *Preparing Teachers for a Changing World,* Linda Darling-Hammond and her colleagues point out that grounding teacher education in real classrooms—among real teachers and students and among actual  examples of students' and teachers' work—is an important, and perhaps even an essential, part of training teachers for the complexities of teaching in today's classrooms. MyEducationLab is an online learning solution that provides contextualized interactive exercises, simulations, and other resources designed to help develop the knowledge and skills teachers need. All of the activities and exercises in MyEducationLab are built around essential learning outcomes for teachers and are mapped to professional teaching standards. Utilizing classroom video, authentic student and teacher artifacts, case studies, and other resources and assessments, the scaffolded learning experiences in MyEducationLab offer pre-service teachers and those who teach them a unique and valuable education tool.

For each topic covered in the course you will find most or all of the following features and resources.

Connection to National Standards

Now it is easier than ever to see how coursework is connected to national standards. Each topic on MyEducationLab lists intended learning outcomes connected to the appropriate national standards. All of the activities and exercises in MyEducationLab are mapped to the appropriate national standards and learning outcomes as well.

Assignments and Activities

Designed to enhance student understanding of concepts covered in class and save instructors preparation and grading time, these assignable exercises show concepts in action (through video, cases, and/or student and teacher artifacts). They help students deepen content knowledge and synthesize and apply concepts and strategies they read about in the book. (Correct answers for these assignments are available to the instructor only under the Instructor Resource tab.)

Building Teaching Skills and Dispositions

These learning units help students practice and strengthen skills that are essential to quality teaching. After presenting the steps involved in a core teaching process, students are given an opportunity to practice applying this skill via videos, student and teacher artifacts, and/or case studies of authentic classrooms. Providing multiple opportunities to practice a single teaching concept, each activity encourages a deeper understanding and application of concepts, as well as the use of critical thinking skills.

A+RISE

A+RISE®, developed by three-time Teacher of the Year and administrator Evelyn Arroyo, gives new teachers in grades K–12 quick, research-based strategies that get to the "how" of targeting their instruction and making content accessible for all students, including English language learners.

A+RISE® Standards2Strategy™ is an innovative and interactive online resource that offers new teachers in grades K–12 timely research-based instructional strategies that:

- Meet the linguistic needs of ELLs as they learn content.
- Differentiate instruction for all grades and abilities.
- Offer reading and writing techniques, cooperative learning, use of linguistic and nonlinguistic representations, scaffolding, teacher modeling, higher order thinking, and alternative classroom ELL assessment.
- Provide support to help teachers be effective through the integration of listening, speaking, reading, and writing along with the content curriculum.
- Improve student achievement.
- Are aligned to Common Core Elementary Language Arts standards (for the literacy strategies) and to English language proficiency standards in WIDA, Texas, California, and Florida.

Literacy Portraits

Year-long case studies of second graders—complete with student artifacts accompanying each video clip, teacher commentary, and student and teacher interviews—track the month-by-month literacy growth of five second graders. You'll meet English learner Rakie, struggling readers Rhiannon and Curt-Lynn, bilingual learner Michael, and grade-level reader Jimmy, and travel with them through a year of assessments, word study instruction, reading groups, writing activities, buddy reading, and more.

Lesson Plan Builder Activities

The Online Lesson Plan Builder is a tool that helps familiarize new and prospective teachers with the steps of a lesson plan, providing them a concrete structure that accounts for all the necessary elements, and allowing them quick access to important components including state and national standards.

Look for activities on the MyEducationLab for your course that link directly into the Online Lesson Plan Builder. You'll see video of a classroom and be offered the opportunity to determine a goal and craft a lesson for the group, scaffolded as you do to remember to focus on specific learning outcomes, incorporate standards, and focus on the individual needs of learners.

IRIS Center Resources

The IRIS Center at Vanderbilt University (http://iris.peabody.vanderbilt.edu), funded by the U.S. Department of Education's Office of Special Education Programs (OSEP), develops training enhancement materials for pre-service and in-service teachers. The Center works with experts from across the country to create challenge-based interactive modules, case study units, and podcasts that provide research-validated information about working with students in inclusive settings. In your MyEducationLab course we have integrated this content where appropriate.

Simulations in Classroom Management

One of the most difficult challenges facing teachers today is how to balance classroom instruction with classroom management. These interactive cases focus on the classroom management issues teachers most frequently encounter on a daily basis. Each simulation presents a challenge scenario at the beginning and then offers a series of choices to solve each challenge. Along the way students receive mentor feedback on their choices and have the opportunity to make better choices if necessary. On exiting each simulation, students will have a clear understanding of how to address these common classroom management issues and will be better equipped to handle them in the classroom.

Study Plan Specific to Your Text

A MyEducationLab Study Plan is a multiple choice assessment tied to chapter objectives, supported by study material. A well-designed study plan offers multiple opportunities to fully master required course content as identified by the objectives in each chapter:

- *Learning Outcomes* identify the outcomes for the chapter and give students targets to shoot for as they read and study. Learning outcomes are aligned with IRA and Common Core Standards.
- *Multiple Choice Pre-Test and Post-Test Assessments* evaluate mastery of the content. These assessments are mapped to chapter objectives, and students can take the multiple choice quiz as many times as they want. Not only do these quizzes provide overall scores for each objective, but they also explain why responses to particular items are correct or incorrect.
- *Study Material: Review, Practice, and Enrichment* gives students a deeper understanding of what they do and do not know related to chapter content. This material includes text excerpts, activities that include hints and feedback, and interactive multimedia exercises built around videos, simulations, cases, or classroom artifacts.

Book Resources

The Book Resources site in MyEducationLab houses video clips that illustrate the text's effective practices in action.

Course Resources

The Course Resources section on MyEducationLab is designed to help students put together an effective lesson plan, prepare for and begin their career, navigate their first year of teaching, and understand key educational standards, policies, and laws. The Course Resources tab includes the following:

- The *Lesson Plan Builder* is an effective and easy-to-use tool that students can use to create, update, and share quality lesson plans. The software also makes it easy to integrate state content standards into any lesson plan.
- The *Preparing a Portfolio* module provides guidelines for creating a high-quality teaching portfolio.
- *Beginning Your Career* offers tips, advice, and other valuable information on
  - *Resume Writing and Interviewing:* Includes expert advice on how to write impressive resumes and prepare for job interviews.
  - *Your First Year of Teaching:* Provides practical tips to set up a first classroom, manage student behavior, and more easily organize for instruction and assessment.
  - *Law and Public Policies:* Details specific directives and requirements teachers need to understand under the No Child Left Behind Act and the Individuals with Disabilities Education Improvement Act of 2004.
- *The Longman Dictionary of Contemporary English Online* is the quickest and easiest way to look up any word while you are working on MyEducationLab.

Certification and Licensure

The Certification and Licensure section is designed to help students pass their licensure exams by giving them access to state test requirements, overviews of what tests cover, and sample test items. The Certification and Licensure tab includes the following:

- In the *State Certification Test Requirements* students can click on a state and will then be taken to a list of state certification tests.
- Students can click on the *Licensure Exams* they need to take to find
  - Basic information about each test
  - Descriptions of what is covered on each test
  - Sample test questions with explanations of correct answers
- Students can see the tests in the *National Evaluation Series* by Pearson, learn what is covered on each NES exam, and access sample test items with descriptions and rationales of correct answers. They can also purchase interactive online tutorials developed by Pearson Evaluation Systems and the Pearson Teacher Education and Development group.
- Students can purchase *ETS Online Praxis Tutorials* developed by ETS and the Pearson Teacher Education and Development group. Tutorials are available for the Praxis I exams and for select Praxis II exams.

Visit **www.myeducationlab.com** for a demonstration of this exciting new online teaching resource.

Acknowledgments

We owe a great deal of credit to the many teachers, parents, and children in the classrooms we have visited over several editions and with whom we continually try out new ideas and strategies. The insights we gain from teachers and learners across the nation profoundly influence our understanding of how children successfully learn to read. We are especially thankful for the support of our professional colleagues at our home institutions and across the nation. Those who have reacted to our evolving ideas have offered many hints for improvement. We appreciate your wisdom and advice.

We also wish to express our gratitude to our reviewers for this edition: Janeen A. Kelly, Washoe County Schools, and Michelina Manzi, University of Wisconsin Oshkosh.

We are deeply grateful to Heather Garrison for providing excellent instructors' materials and a first-rate study plan on MyEducationLab, which provides thought-provoking questions and activities that promote the essential skills students need to be effective practitioners in the classroom.

Part One

Introduction

I

Effective Reading Instruction: The Teacher Makes the Difference

Effective Reading

1

Instruction

THE TEACHER MAKES THE DIFFERENCE

Teacher Knowledge

Classroom Assessment

Evidence-Based Teaching Practices

Response to Intervention (RTI)

Chapter Questions

- Why invest in teacher quality and effectiveness?

- How have political trends influenced reading instruction in our schools?

- What is reading?

- What is the primary ingredient in the recipe for every child's reading success?

- What are the seven pillars of effective reading instruction?

Key Terms

Illiteracy

Aliteracy

Reading reform

Literacy coach

Professional development

Teacher knowledge

Classroom assessment

Evidence-based instruction

Classroom management

Response to Intervention (RTI)

Motivation

New literacies

Motivation and Engagement

Technology and New Literacies

Family and Community Connections

Vignette: Becoming a Teacher

Selena is a college junior preparing to become an elementary school teacher. Her upcoming class on teaching children to read is not just another college class, but represents for her the real beginning of her teacher preparation and an eventual teaching career. Without doubt, teaching children to read will be the centerpiece of her classroom instructional program. Selena recalls fondly her own first-grade teacher, Mrs. Roberts, who introduced her to the world of books and reading. Selena hopes she will be a "Mrs. Roberts" to the many children she will teach over the course of her career.

Of the several professors who teach the required course on teaching children to read, Selena chose Dr. Favio's class. With many years of successful teaching experience in public schools, Professor Favio is known for her rigorous, evidence-based, hands-on instructional methods that get her students ready for their first year of teaching. She begins the course on the first day by asking students to read a scenario printed on the cover of the course syllabus:

> On one occasion, Frank Smith (1985), a well-known literacy expert who had never taught a child to read in a classroom, was confronted with a daunting question by a group of exasperated teachers: "So, what would you do, Dr. Smith, if you had to teach a room full of 30 five-year-olds to read?" Dr. Smith's response was quick and decisive. He first indicated that children learn to read from people—and the most important of these people are teachers. As teachers, you need to comprehend the general processes of how children develop and learn and the specific processes whereby children learn to read.

After the students finish reading the quote, Dr. Favio continues with a question clearly intended to provoke discussion: "How did *you* learn to read? What do you remember about learning to read? Who helped you? Turn to your neighbor, introduce yourself, and share your thoughts in response to these questions." Immediately the room fills with the buzz of students sharing their memories about how they learned to read. Selena shares her memories with her "elbow partner," Terrence. She tells him how she was first introduced to books by her mom and grandma. "Did they ever read *Curious George* books to you?" asks Terrence. "These books were my favorite!"

After a few minutes of discussion, Dr. Favio asks the class to share some of their memories, which she records on a whiteboard at the front of the classroom.

- Little kids learn to read from someone who reads to them.
- I learned to read from my older sister.

- I remember writing letters and asking my mother what they spelled.
- I had a favorite book I memorized because my grandmother read it to me over and over again.
- I remember my teacher reading a great big book to us in kindergarten called *Mrs. Wishy Washy*. I loved that book!
- I watched *Sesame Street*, *Barney*, and *Reading Rainbow*. I learned the letters and some words from watching TV.

Next, Dr. Favio asks her students to define what it means *to read*. She tells them to take one minute of think time and then share ideas with their elbow partners. Selena remembers how she struggled learning phonics. Terrence remarks, "Well, I agree that beginning reading should help children decode words using phonics, but I don't see how you can call it 'reading' if you don't understand what you are reading. I mean, I can call out all of the words in my geology textbook, but *understanding* what they mean is another thing. For me, that takes some work!"

Dr. Favio invites comments from the class and records statements about the meaning of reading:

- I think reading is when you sound out letters to make words.
- Reading involves understanding what's on the page. (Terrence's contribution)
- I learned to read from little books that used the same pattern over and over again like the *Three Billy Goats*.
- Learning phonics is the first part of reading and comprehension is the last.
- Reading is about learning information that makes you smarter.
- Reading is the ability to put together what you already know with what the author wants you to learn.

Dr. Favio brings the discussion to a conclusion at this point. "While these are critical issues for all teachers to reflect upon, when we look at research evidence there can be no doubt that the teacher's knowledge about teaching and learning and the skill to put this knowledge into practice make the greatest difference in whether or not a young child learns to read. And because reading is, in a very real way, the gateway to social justice, your role as a reading teacher has the potential of changing lives and, therefore, our society."

That, thinks Selena to herself, *is why I have chosen to become a teacher.* ■

Becoming a Master Teacher of Reading

● ● ●

IRA Standards for Reading Professionals: Standard 1, Elements 1.1, 1.2, 1.3

Response to Intervention: Expertise

Reading is the skill that makes virtually all other learning possible. For instance, at Oxford University in England, the oldest university in the English-speaking world, for nine centuries graduates have been described as "reading" their chosen subject or field of study. Of course, Oxford students like all other students from preschool through college engage in all sorts of additional learning activities, but clearly reading is the primary instrument. Thus, the teaching of reading is something we must get right if our students are to have the world of learning opened to them.

In our 60-plus combined years of service as teachers, we have come to understand that master teachers of reading have a unique skill set. For one thing, they are readers themselves. They read for pleasure and personal growth and in the process serve as great role models to their young charges. Master teachers know that you can't "sell" what you don't do.

Great reading teachers, like other accomplished professionals, keep up with cutting-edge developments in their field. They regularly read professional journals like *The Reading Teacher* or the *Journal of Adolescent and Adult Literacy* to learn about the latest research-based classroom practices. Almost surprisingly, we have seen that many master teachers are just a bit unsatisfied with their own knowledge or skill levels in spite of their tremendous success with student learning. They constantly seek out new ideas from colleagues and professional development opportunities that help them support children in becoming strong readers. We also know that master reading teachers see reading instruction as equal parts art and science. Though skills must indeed be taught, they believe that teaching reading is far more than simply teaching skills.

Shutterstock

Consider the piano teacher who must teach her young pupil how to make music. The student must learn to read sheet music and then translate that information into pleasing notes from the instrument. Although teaching the skill of reading music is critical to training new musicians, time must also be spent helping students learn techniques for interpreting the written script while appreciating and taking pride in the tunes they can perform. Similarly, the reading teacher's task is to teach students how to translate alphabetic symbols on a page into the language and ideas shared by great authors. As with a fine piano, there is richness and opportunity in the instruments of reading: books, graphic novels, online readings, and much more.

In the early grades, we introduce young children to reading with fictional allies like Bill Martin's Brown Bear (1990) and Bridwell's (1985) big red dog Clifford. As students grow as readers we enlist Shel Silverstein's poetry and even J. K. Rowling's adventures of Harry Potter and his friends. Throughout all levels of reading development, master teachers likewise bring in great nonfiction sources so that students hone their reading skills while learning about interesting subjects like dinosaurs, weather, and the origin of the universe. In this way master reading teachers are able to help their young charges transform squiggles on a page of paper into something rich and exciting.

We begin our learning experience in this chapter by first talking about the current state of reading instruction. Part of becoming a master reading teacher is to understand our historical roots, so we begin there. In the balance of the chapter we consider the fundamental characteristics of effective reading instruction.

A Brief History of Current Trends in Reading Instruction

Many would agree that the ability to read is a critical factor in living a healthy, happy, and productive life. In fact, the ability to read has been declared "a civil right" by the National Right to Read Foundation (2001). The ability to read and read well makes many life choices possible in a democratic society. Conversely, nonreaders and poor readers are often hindered in their career paths from taking full advantage of services and opportunities for themselves or their families, or in thoroughly accessing their rights and exercising their responsibilities as citizens.

Inability to Read: "A National Health Risk"

In recent years the *inability to read* has been listed as a health risk by the National Institutes of Health (NIH), an agency of the federal government. Designating *reading disability* or the *inability to read* as a national threat was based on the discovery of the many devastating and far-reaching effects that reading failure has on the quality of individuals' lives. To clearly understand the full impact that reading failure can have, we offer the following quote from *The 90% Reading Goal* by Fielding, Kerr, and Rosier (1998):

> The most expensive burden we place on society is those students we have failed to teach to read well. The silent army of low readers who move through our schools, siphoning off the lion's share of administrative resources, emerge into society as adults lacking the single prerequisite for managing their lives and acquiring additional training. They are chronically unemployed, underemployed, or unemployable. They form the single largest identifiable group of those whom we incarcerate, and to whom we provide assistance, housing, medical care, and other social services. They perpetuate and enlarge the problem by creating another generation of poor readers. (pp. 6–7)

Today, literacy is viewed as a "tool" for achieving economic, social, and personal goals. Helping students become fully literate is seen as a remedy for a host of social ills. Stretching across a period of the past three decades, **illiteracy**—the inability to read—has been identified as a significant factor related to myriad social problems including poverty, crime, and social dependency. Add to this those who have the ability to read but are reluctant, called **aliteracy,** and the size and scope of the problems associated with failure to read are magnified in today's society.

Government leaders and worldwide corporations have come to recognize the potential of literacy to transform lives, address social maladies, and bolster sagging economies. Many business leaders today complain that workers enter the marketplace unprepared to successfully engage in the range of increasingly complex and technologically based literacy tasks required in a changing national and global economy. This has led in recent years to legislative action in the United States aimed at improving literacy learning.

Political Responses to the Literacy Crisis

Why has literacy instruction in our schools become such a political issue? Actually, contentious debates about the "best" ways of teaching reading and writing in the

United States and Canada have been ongoing for nearly 150 years. From phonics to whole word approaches to skills-based programmed readers to whole language advocacy, the pendulum of literacy education approaches has swung back and forth between various viewpoints. In the past, however, debates about literacy policy and practice were largely confined to professionals within the educational community.

Current reform efforts arguably took root during the Reagan administration in the 1980s, when Secretary of Education Terrel Bell's blue-ribbon panel issued a report on the state of education. Entitled *A Nation at Risk* (U.S. Department of Education, 1983), the report defined education in U.S. schools to be at risk—in some ways equal to a national security threat. With the publication of this report, public suspicions began to run high about the trustworthiness of the educational establishment to make the necessary fixes to education in the United States. It also started the gradual process toward making educational changes based on research evidence rather than the popularity of trendy commercial programs that often resulted in unproven and ineffective teaching practices (American Federation of Teachers, 1999; National Research Council, 2001).

In the mid-1990s, President Clinton led an effort to improve literacy education and student learning through the Goals 2000: Educate America Act (U.S. Department of Education, 1994). President Clinton strongly supported increased professional development in literacy education and also urged the implementation of a nationwide testing program in reading and mathematics to assess whether national goals were being reached. Simultaneously, in 1995 the National Assessment of Education Progress (NAEP) released data showing a measurable *decline* in fourth-grade reading achievement across the nation.

By the late 1990s public opinion and politicians had determined that literacy instruction was in dire need of reform. But this time, decisions on teaching literacy had to be grounded in research evidence. **Reading reform** was first to take shape in The Reading Excellence Act (U.S. Department of Education, 1998). Funded and approved under the Clinton administration, it contained federal funding specifically targeted to underachieving and high-poverty school populations where lagging reading achievement needed immediate attention. It was clear that politicians would no longer allow decisions about something as socially, politically, and economically powerful as literacy to be the sole purview of the education profession.

With the election of President George W. Bush in 2000, literacy reform policy continued to gather momentum. With bipartisan support in the U.S. Congress, reform efforts were furthered by Senator Edward Kennedy's and President Bush's joint efforts to reauthorize the Elementary and Secondary Education Act of 1964, which resulted in a sweeping education reform bill known as No Child Left Behind (2001). Within this legislation, scientific or evidence-based reading research became the gold standard for making instructional decisions. Furthermore, the belief that early reading instruction should include early, systematic, explicit phonics instruction was transformed into law.

The No Child Left Behind legislation passed with one of the largest bipartisan affirmative vote margins on record since 1964. This federal intervention into state and local education provided federal funds to states in the form of Reading First grants along with a long menu of unfunded mandates to cement the reforms begun in the mid-1990s. Some saw the new NCLB legislation as federal intrusion into states' rights because functions of government not expressly mentioned in the U.S. Constitution should belong to the states, including education policy. As time went along Reading First was tainted by the scandalous if not illegal actions of some individuals operating in the U.S. Department of Education. Among the accusations were reports of certain vendors receiving "non-compete" contracts in preferential inside deals. Some ruefully mused that NCLB seemed to be an idea that might have been created by Mother Teresa, except that it was implemented by stormtroopers. Needless to say, enthusiasm for many legitimate advances in literacy education was blunted as these scandals came to light.

In 2008, after years of mixed results across the nation and billions of tax dollars expended, the Institute of Education Sciences (IES), a research division of the U.S. Department of Education, issued a report on Reading First, the federal literacy initiative. Their findings showed that students attending schools in Reading First reform programs performed no better on assessments of reading comprehension than did students in nonparticipating schools (Gamse, Jacob, Horst, Boulay, & Unlu, 2008). As a consequence, funds to support Reading First and efforts to provide professional development to classroom teachers in high-poverty, low-performing schools were cancelled by the U.S. Congress.

The historic presidential election of 2008 swept Barack Obama's change agenda into the White House and the halls of political power. Literacy continued to be seen as a means to solve personal, social, and economic problems, as illustrated by the words of President Obama (2005) on the importance of literacy and reading instruction.

> I believe that if we want to give our children the best possible chance in life, if we want to open doors of opportunity while they're young and teach them the skills they'll need to succeed later on, then one of our greatest responsibilities as citizens, as educators, and as parents is to ensure that every American child can read and read well.
>
> Reading is the gateway skill that makes all other learning possible, from complex word problems and the meaning of our history to scientific discovery and technological proficiency. In a knowledge economy where this kind of learning is necessary for survival, how can we send our kids out into the world if they're only reading at a fourth-grade level?"

As of the writing of this edition, the U.S. Congress is considering the reauthorization of the 1964 Elementary Secondary Education Act to replace the 2001 No Child Left Behind Act. In addition, under the leadership of Secretary of Education Arne Duncan, the teaching of literacy is a major plank in many states' plans to access funds under a new federal initiative called Race to the Top.

In addition, Congress is presently moving forward a literacy bill entitled the Literacy Education for All, Results for the Nation (LEARN) Act. This law would restore and enhance earlier funding to states to infuse evidence-based reading instruction practices into low-achieving and high-poverty schools.

One clear message teachers might take away from this brief recitation of recent historical developments is the value of literacy to our nation. It is indeed a national priority.

What Is Reading?

Learning educational terms, what these terms mean, and how to use them when communicating with colleagues in the field is essential for becoming a professional teacher. The term *reading* has been used for many years in a narrow sense to refer to a set of print-based decoding and rudimentary thinking skills necessary to remember a text (Harris & Hodges, 1981). On the other hand Snow, Burns, and Griffin provide a more expanded definition:

> Reading is a complex developmental challenge that we know to be intertwined with many other developmental accomplishments: attention, memory, language, and motivation, for example. Reading is not only a cognitive psycholinguistic activity but also a social activity. (1998, p. 15)

Nowadays our understanding of the reading act has been broadened to include the visual, analytical, and technological skills necessary to acquire information from digital video, handheld data assistants, computers, wireless reading devices, cell phones, or other technological learning devices (Hobbs, 2005; Malloy, Castek, & Leu, 2010; Messaris, 2005). Add to this broadened definition of reading the idea that the visual, analytical, and technological skills needed for acquiring information today are expanding. Students are challenged to use new reading skills shaped by the increasingly diverse social or cultural settings found in schools, homes, communities, businesses, groups, or in virtual social settings such as wikis, Ning social networks, and blogs (August & Shanahan, 2006; Morgan & Smith, 2008; Tracey & Morrow, 2006). As a result, the term *reading* is currently interpreted far more broadly and encompasses the learning of a complex set of strategies, skills, concepts, and knowledge enabling individuals to understand visual and print-based information presented in a variety of media or technological formats. The goal of reading instruction, then, is to empower readers to learn, grow, and participate in a vibrant and rapidly changing information-based world.

Learning to read is not a simple task and can be a struggle for many children, not to mention adults who must relearn the skill. In her book titled *My Stroke of Insight,* Dr. Jill Bolten Taylor (2006), a highly recognized brain neurologist, documented her difficulty in recovering the ability to read after suffering a stroke in her mid 30s. For her, reading was the most difficult skill she had to relearn.

As children begin the difficult, multifaceted process of learning to read, they need to acquire a set of skills, concepts, and strategies with the help and guidance of an effective teacher. In order to eventually read efficiently and purposefully, children must skillfully comprehend text, conceptually integrate information constructed from text into one's world knowledge network, and strategically solve real-world problems with print, whether presented in more traditional forms or technology-based formats. On the way to reaching the ultimate goal of reading comprehension (Kintsch, 2004)—that is, understanding the author's message and using what is learned for discovery in novel situations—students must acquire a set of reading skills or tools to get off to an early good start. As a current or future teacher of reading, do not underestimate the importance of initial or early reading skills, concepts, and strategies such as the following in making possible the achievement of reading with comprehension.

- Hearing and being able to manipulate individual sounds in spoken words (known as *phonemic awareness*)
- Recognizing and identifying a variety of upper- and lowercase printed alphabet letters
- Grasping concepts about how printed language looks and works
- Increasing oral language (speaking) vocabularies

- Understanding that sounds in spoken language "map" onto letters in written language
- Decoding words with accuracy, speed, and expression

Shanahan (2006) and others (e.g., Durkin, 1966) indicate that the earliest desire and ability to learn to read often grow out of a child's initial curiosity with writing letters and words at home. Consequently, writing very often represents not only the beginning point in many a young child's journey to learn to read but the finish line as well. As young children become increasingly aware of letters and words in the world around them, they may eventually ask how to write their names or spell other personally significant words or concepts (e.g., a pet's name or the name of a relative). When children are able to write letters and words, the "cognitive footprint," also called the *memory trace*, left in the brain is deep and long lasting—much longer lasting than those engendered by mere letter or word recognition alone. Similarly, when children can string words together to construct meaning as found in a written story, they have "comprehended" text at a deeper and longer-lasting level. In a very real sense, children's understanding of what they read is deepened and cemented when they write about it.

As children learn to write, they must also learn a set of early skills, concepts, and strategies similar to those in reading to help them on their way to achieving the ultimate goal of writing instruction—composition. To acquire initial proficiency in writing, young children need to acquire skills, concepts, and strategies such as the following:

- Handwriting (forming legible upper- and lowercase letters)
- Understanding and using mechanical conventions such as punctuation, headings, paragraph indents, and the like
- Learning to "encode" words and thoughts into print (i.e., spelling words, labeling pictures, writing sentences)

As you can readily see, it would be most difficult and terribly ineffective to separate reading from writing or writing from reading in an effective reading instruction program (Tierney & Shanahan, 1991).

Teachers Make the Difference

Here's a question for you to consider: *What is the primary ingredient in the recipe for every child's reading success?* Answer: An effective classroom teacher who has the ability to teach reading to a group of children who have a variety of abilities and needs (Snow, Griffin, & Burns, 2005; Strickland, Snow, Griffin, Burns, & McNamara, 2002). This fact was documented in 1985 in the National Academy and Institute of Education's landmark report, *Becoming a Nation of Readers: The Report of the Commission on Reading*. In this now classic report, commission members concluded that teacher knowledge, skill, and competence are absolutely essential in helping all learners become strong readers.

> An *indisputable* [italics added] conclusion of research is that the quality of teaching makes a considerable difference in children's learning. Studies indicate that about 15 percent of the variation among children in reading achievement at the end of the school year is attributable to factors that related to the skill and effectiveness of the teacher. In contrast, the largest study ever done comparing approaches to beginning reading

found that about 3 percent of the variation in reading achievement at the end of the first grade was attributable to the overall approach of the program. Thus, the prudent assumption for educational policy is that, while there may be some "materials-proof" teachers, there are no "teacher-proof" materials. (Anderson, Hiebert, Scott, & Wilkinson, 1985, p. 85)

From experience we know, and parental attitudes confirm, that "It all comes down to the teacher," since they [parents] are notorious for competing to get their children into classes taught by the current faculty stars of the school! And why shouldn't they? There is nothing in this world that can replace the power of a great classroom teacher (Strickland et al., 2002, p. 4).

In a national survey by Haselkorn and Harris (2001), 89 percent of Americans responded that it is very important to have a well-qualified teacher in every classroom. The poorest children and the most powerless families often receive the least our educational system has to offer (NCTAF, 2006)—what Jonathan Kozol (1991) once labeled "savage inequalities." More recently, Secretary of Education Arne Duncan declared anew that every student has a right to a highly qualified and effective classroom teacher (U.S. Department of Education, 2009).

In a national study of 1,000 school districts, Ferguson (1991) found that every additional dollar spent on more highly qualified teachers netted greater improvement in student achievement than did any other use of school resources. In fact, research also suggests that teachers influence student academic growth more than any other single factor, including families, neighborhoods, and the schools students attend (Rowan, Corretini, & Miller, 2002; Sanders & Rivers, 1996). Successful schools that produce high student reading and writing achievement test scores, regardless of socioeconomic status or the commercial program used to provide reading and writing instruction, have teachers who are knowledgeable and articulate about their work (McCardle & Chhabra, 2004; Mosenthal, Lipson, Torncello, Russ, & Mekkelsen, 2004).

A fairly recent addition to school literacy instruction is a specialist called a reading or **literacy coach.** Jane Moore (2004), a literacy coach in Dallas, once remarked, "even Cinderella had a coach." Much like for athletes, reading/literacy coaches help classroom teachers reflect on, plan, and improve their instructional skills to enhance student reading achievement and motivation (Burkins, 2009; Toll, 2007). Recent research has demonstrated that teachers who receive **professional development** that includes formal instruction coupled with classroom support from a reading literacy coach achieve measurably greater reading improvement in classrooms (Neuman & Cunningham, 2009).

● ● ●

IRA Standards for Reading Professionals: Standard 1, Elements 1.1, 1.2, 1.3; Standard 2, Elements 2.1, 2.2, 2.3

Response to Intervention: Instruction, Responsive Teaching and Differentiation; Assessment; Collaboration; Systemic and Comprehensive Approaches

What Do Reading Teachers Need to Know and Do? The Seven Pillars of Effective Reading Instruction

The remainder of this book is dedicated to those who want to learn what they need to know and be able to do to become effective teachers of reading. Drawn from decades of research describing the practices of exemplary reading teachers in elementary schools (e.g., Pressley, Allington, Wharton-McDonald, Collins-Block, &

Morrow, 2001; Risko, Roller, Cummins, Bean, Block, Anders, & Flood, 2008), we have learned what teachers know and do in their classrooms to become highly effective instructors of reading.

Because the research on effective reading instruction is extensive, we have attempted, as good teachers do, to make the complex simple. We know that in doing so we can increase the comprehensibility of our message. Conversely, we recognize that in making the complex simple we risk trivializing important issues around which there may be disagreement and misunderstandings. However, given the task of assisting novice and practicing teachers alike, we have opted to reduce the complexity of teaching reading to a simple organizational structure that represents the findings of research in seven distinct yet interrelated groupings we refer to as the "seven pillars" of effective reading instruction (Figure 1.1). These pillars provide a framework for highly effective reading instruction like the pillars that support great buildings.

As part of our structural approach, we have organized many of the succeeding chapters of this book around the seven pillars of effective reading instruction. Each pillar is given a particular color reflected in the table of contents, the chapter opener, and the headings within the text. This framework is based on our finding that readers learn best from a book that has a consistent and easily discernable organization and structure. We also hope that you, our readers, will construct your own knowledge of effective reading instruction using these seven pillars. To begin, we briefly describe the basis for each of the seven pillars of effective reading instruction.

Figure 1.1

The Seven Pillars of Effective Reading Instruction

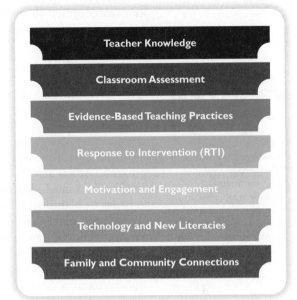

Pillar One: Teacher Knowledge

Decades of educational research confirm the importance of **teacher knowledge** to the quality of instruction offered to students. For example, evidence-based research has verified the basic skills that must be learned in order to read and the approximate order in which these skills should be taught. Effective teachers approach their instruction with this important knowledge in mind.

More broadly, research reveals the beneficial impact of teacher knowledge on the quality of their instruction and student learning. Dating back to the seminal work of Coleman (1966) in *Equality of Educational Opportunity* and continuing to more current documents such as the Education Trust's (2008) *Achievement in America,* researchers and policy makers alike have argued that improved teacher knowledge is our best hope in closing the achievement gap.

In fact, we now understand that what teachers know and do in classrooms matters even more than past research on teacher quality might have predicted (Duffy, 2004). Research conducted over the last two decades has suggested that differences in teacher classroom performance explain 15 to 20 percent of variation in student achievement (Anderson et al., 1985; Carlisle, Phelps, Rowan, & Johnson, 2006; Ferguson, 1991; Sanders, 1998; Scheerens & Bosker, 1997). Indeed, once children enter school, teachers influence student academic growth more than any other single factor including families, neighborhoods, and the schools that students attend (Darling-Hammond, 2006; Rowan et al., 2002; Sanders & Horn, 1994).

In order to teach reading and writing, teachers need to acquire research-based knowledge about student development in reading and writing processes and effective reading instruction practices.

Pillar Two: Classroom Assessment

Click on A+RISE—WIDA ELP Standard Strategies in the MyEducationLab (www.myeducationlab.com) for your course. Next, select the Strategy Card Index tab, scroll to Classroom Assessments for grades K–5, and select the Alternative ELL Assessments: Introduction strategy.

The ultimate goal of classroom assessment is to inform instruction. Assessments provide real-time student information so that teachers can make decisions about "next steps" for continuing student learning using effective teaching strategies. **Classroom assessment** refers to the observations, record keeping, and ongoing performance measures that a teacher uses to gather information about each student's reading progress (Afflerbach, 2007; Flippo, 2003).

Teachers must identify which reading abilities each child has already developed in order to plan instruction targeting those she has not. Effective reading teachers are able to quickly assess each student's knowledge, create instructional roadmaps of what children know, and then teach students according to what they are ready to learn next. Effective reading assessment happens in classrooms *before, during,* and *after* instruction has taken place. Assessment is essential for making sure every student receives appropriate instruction and then verifying that learning has taken place.

Classroom assessments help us examine students' literacy *processes* as well as the *products* they create when using these processes. Reliable, valid, and efficient reading assessment tools and careful analyses of data (McKenna & Stahl, 2009; Reutzel & Cooter, 2011) are necessary to support effective reading instruction. Teachers also need to know how to judge the quality of assessment tools as well as how to administer and interpret scores and data obtained from a variety of assessment tools.

Teachers often design, in collaboration with peers, their own well-thought-out assessment plans to achieve the goals of an effective reading instruction program. Teachers need to consider the purposes for each assessment, testing conditions, and how much time is available to collect and, most especially, to analyze assessment data to inform, shape, and adapt later teaching. Effective reading teachers think about how to infuse their assessment efforts seamlessly into classroom reading instruction to minimize the amount of time taken away from instruction, often using informal data-gathering strategies during whole-group, small-group, and individual instruction. More recently, many teachers have employed computer software and technology like personal data assistants (PDAs) to collect and analyze assessment data "on the run" during instruction (McKenna, Labbo, Kieffer, & Reinking, 2006; Wepner, Valmont, & Thurlow, 2000).

Pillar Three: Evidence-Based Teaching Practices

Once teachers create ongoing assessment profiles for students, locating each on the literacy development continuum and determining what each is ready to learn next, they must then link student learning needs to effective teaching strategies to advance their achievement. There is substantial research evidence on preferred ways of teaching each of the essential reading skills, concepts, and strategies necessary for success in learning to read and write. Great teachers have an abundance of tools in their instructional toolbox to ensure that every child is helped to reach his or her full potential when learning to read.

One of the earliest reports describing the need for **evidence-based instruction** in reading was sponsored by the National Academy of Sciences and the National Research Council. A panel of prominent reading and education experts convened to review existing research studies in order to determine which skills, concepts, and strategies need to be taught to prevent students from falling into early reading difficulties or eventual reading failure. Their report, *Preventing Reading Difficulties in Young Children* (Snow et al., 1998), was followed by a companion document, *Starting Out Right: A Guide to Promoting Children's Reading Success* (Burns, Griffin, & Snow, 1999) to make their findings more easily accessible to parents and teachers. In these twin reports, the National Research Council spelled out essential reading instruction components that must be taught to prevent early reading failure.

At around the same time, in direct response to a congressional mandate to examine the status of "scientific" research on teaching reading, the *Report of the National Reading Panel, Teaching Children to Read* (National Reading Panel, 2000), was jointly published by the National Institutes of Child Health and Human Development, the National Institutes of Health, and the U.S. Department of Education. Similar to the *Preventing Reading Difficulties* report, a companion document titled *Put Reading First: The Research Building Blocks for Teaching Children to Read* (Armbruster, Lehr, & Osborn, 2001) was distributed in order to disseminate widely the findings of the National Reading Panel (2000) report to parents and educators.

More recently, the National Early Literacy Panel (2008) issued *Developing Early Literacy: Report of the National Early Literacy Panel*. This report examined the research evidence supporting the acquisition of early literacy skills, concepts, and strategies for students' later reading achievement in elementary and secondary schools.

We now know that highly effective reading instruction programs focus on (1) classroom management, (2) teaching instructional essentials, (3) designing print-rich and highly interactive classroom environments, and (4) supporting reading with evidence-based techniques.

Classroom Management.   One of the most fundamental characteristics of effective instruction is the teacher's ability to manage the classroom (Evertson & Weinstein, 2006; Morrow, Reutzel, & Casey, 2006). The term **classroom management** refers to the ability of a teacher to organize, direct, and supervise the classroom environment so that effective student learning is made possible (Snow et al., 2005). Excellent classroom management (Reutzel, Morrow, & Casey, 2009) requires teachers to know and use a complex set of strategies to accomplish tasks such as the following:

- Allocate classroom space for multiple uses
- Supply and arrange classroom materials
- Communicate expectations and rules clearly within a positive classroom climate
- Employ effective instructional practices
- Train students effectively in classroom routines and procedures
- Establish a predictable and familiar daily schedule

A supportive and well-thought-out classroom management plan is integral to achieving the goals of an effective reading instruction program and is addressed in greater depth in Chapters 11 and 12.

Click on A+RISE—
Literacy Strategies in the
MyEducationLab (www.
myeducationlab.com) for
your course. Next, select
the Strategy Card Index tab,
scroll to English Language
Learners, and
select the Cumu-
lative Semantic
Map strategy.

Teaching Instructional Essentials.   The following aspects of literacy have been documented as instructional essentials in the aforementioned federal research reports (Burns et al., 1999; National Early Literacy Panel, 2008; National Reading Panel, 2000):

- Oral language development
- Concepts of printed language
- Letter name knowledge and production
- Sight word recognition
- Phonemic awareness
- Phonics
- Fluency
- Vocabulary
- Comprehension
- Writing/spelling

Designing Print-Rich Classroom Environments.   When planning print-rich, highly interactive classroom environments, teachers assess, arrange, and demonstrate the use of literacy tools and materials available in the classroom. Providing children access to various kinds and difficulty levels of print materials is a large part of provisioning and arranging literacy tools and materials (e.g., story and information books, poetry, graphic novels, maps, posters, etc.) in print-rich classroom environments (Neuman, 1999; Neuman & Celano, 2001, 2006).

Effective reading teachers treat classroom walls as creative palettes for designing both asthetically pleasing but also instructionally useful displays for student work, instructional charts, and other information. The design and maintenance of a classroom library, the grouping and accessibility of reading and writing tools in the classroom, written invitations and encouragements displayed on walls, and directions on how to participate in upcoming literacy events are just a few of the many considerations for teachers to become accomplished environmental designers and managers (Hoffman, Sailors, Duffy, & Beretvas, 2004; Wolfersberger, Reutzel, Sudweeks, & Fawson, 2004).

Supporting Reading with Evidence-Based Techniques.   The final essential component of an evidence-based reading instructional program is, not surprisingly, evidence-based reading support. Evidence-based support for high-quality reading instruction includes such practices as the following:

- Engaging in volume reading and writing in school and out on a regular basis
- Using various media and technologies to increase world knowledge
- Modeling reading and writing strategies for children and encouraging them to use these strategies to generate, process, and interact with text
- Connecting literature study to content learning in other curriculum areas (i.e., science, math, and history)
- Providing systematic, explicit, and sustained concept, skill, and strategy instruction in each of the essential elements of reading instruction

Pillar Four: Response to Intervention (RTI)

Response to Intervention (RTI) models of instructional delivery (Fuchs, Fuchs, & Vaughn, 2008; Lipson & Wixson, 2009) are becoming an increasingly popular evidence-based approach to meet the diverse needs of students. RTI models incorporate many of the excellent practices that have previously been described in research on instruction.

When using RTI models, all students are initially screened to determine their progress in achieving established literacy benchmark skills, objectives, and standards. Students who are shown in initial screening assessment to be on track in their literacy development continue to receive core reading instruction, called "Tier 1" developmental reading instruction. For students having difficulty, Tier 2 reading interventions are intended to fill in learning gaps as quickly as possible and return students to core (i.e., developmental) reading instruction. If Tier 2 instructional intervention fails to accelerate or positively affect a student's literacy learning, then Tier 3 evidence-based interventions are used with greater frequency and delivered in even smaller groups or individually until the student shows a positive response. In our discussions of RTI, we include the various forms of differentiated instruction that can be included in Tiers 2 and 3.

RTI models encourage teachers to integrate high-quality evidence-based instruction and frequent use of reliable and valid assessments in a systematic way to serve the needs of diverse learners. See Figure 1.2 for the RTI framework. A wonderful online tutorial for those just learning about RTI is found at Vanderbilt University's IRIS Center (http://iris.peabody.vanderbilt.edu/index.html).

Figure 1.2

Response to Intervention (RTI) Model

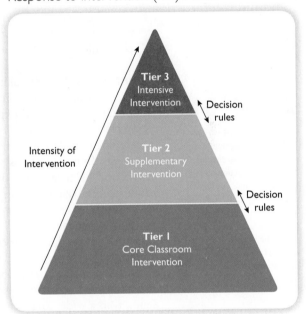

Differentiating Instruction.   Great teachers are able to differentiate instruction in order to meet every child's diverse learning needs, including English learners (ELs). As one example, in many school districts English is not the first language for a large percentage of students. Students may speak Spanish, Chinese, Korean, Arabic, Hmong, or other languages in their homes. In these instances, teachers need to discover a variety of ways to help students learn to read and write in English as a second language (August & Shanahan, 2006).

It has been estimated that up to 20 percent of students come to school having various learning differences, such as attention deficit disorder (ADD), dyslexia, cognitive challenges (i.e., "slow learners"), oral language deficiencies, or behavioral disorders (BD). The goal for teachers is to help *all* students succeed in learning to read. Differentiating reading instruction is essential if we are to help every child achieve.

Excellent reading teachers provide instruction that is responsive to the *specific* needs of every child based on ongoing assessment findings. How one goes about adapting reading instruction to address students' evolving needs is of critical importance for all teachers (Reutzel & Cooter, 2011). Today's teachers need abilities such as the following to provide effective instruction for diverse learners:

- Facility with a variety of assessment tools for multiple purposes and techniques for translating student data into effective teaching plans

- Knowledge of teaching interventions that make use of multiple instructional strategies because we know that one size does *not* fit all
- Understanding of multiple organizational and classroom management techniques

A workable model for many teachers is to begin with a simple, limited, and manageable small-group instructional system, placing children with similar abilities and needs for instruction in groups numbering four to eight. Over time and with experience, these same teachers can gradually expand their practice using a range of instructional strategies to include the following:

- Daily intensive, small-group, teacher-guided reading instruction in appropriately challenging text levels
- The use of student-selected books and other readings at appropriate reading levels
- Sensibly selected classroom spaces, often called *learning centers,* for independent practice of previously taught concepts, strategies, and skills accompanied by clear rules, directions, schedules, and familiar routines

Culturally Sensitive Reading Instruction.   Another important aspect of providing effective reading instruction is a recognition of cultural diversity. Students bring to school differing cultural experiences that, when recognized by the teacher, can be used as strengths to leverage learning of the school curriculum (Au, 2010). Although the empirical or data-based evidence for culturally sensitive instruction is only now emerging, doing so makes sense. Au (2010) recommends that classroom reading instruction balance competition and cooperation in classroom activities. She also advocates analyzing reading lessons to determine possibilities for classroom dialogue in small groups or pairs.

Finally, teachers should teach students how to discuss topics with one another appropriately in the classroom through modeling and dialogic routines (e.g., "This is how I say it. Now you say it."). Use of Response to Intervention (RTI) models and culturally sensitive instruction, when implemented well, help teachers consider ways to make their instruction responsive to the needs of ELs, struggling readers, and students from a wide range of differing cultural perspectives (Optiz, 1998).

Pillar Five: Motivation and Engagement

Gambrell and Marinak (2009) have referred to **motivation** as a key "pillar" of effective reading instruction not addressed in the National Reading Panel report (2000). Wigfield (1997) describes motivation as a complex of interrelated social and emotional dimensions that influence children's choices to engage in reading:

- *Efficacy.* The sense that "I can do this"
- *Challenge.* Easy and more difficult tasks
- *Curiosity.* The desire to know or find out
- *Involvement.* Active, intentional control of one's thinking
- *Importance.* Personal value or worth
- *Recognition.* Praise, certificates, awards, and so on
- *Grades.* A specific form of recognition in schools
- *Interaction.* Working cooperatively with others
- *Competition.* Working to win or be the best
- *Compliance.* Working to avoid punishment or negative recognition
- *Enjoyment.* Seeking the pleasurable and avoiding the difficult

A+RISE

Click on A+RISE—WIDA ELP Standard Strategies in the MyEducationLab (www.myeducationlab.com) for your course. Next, select the Strategy Card Index tab, scroll to Language and Content for grades 6–12, and select the Language and Content Development strategy.

Turner and Paris (1995) reduce this motivation construct to what they call the six Cs: (1) choice, (2) challenge, (3) control, (4) collaboration, (5) constructing meaning, and (6) consequences.

1. *Choice* does not mean that students are free to choose any text in the world to read. To offer choice, for instance, may mean choosing from two different information books on rocks and rock formations. When students know that they can make *some* choices, they are more willing to persist and remain engaged while reading.

2. *Challenge* can encourage increased reading motivation and engagement. Turner and Paris (1995) suggest that the common attitude that children prefer "easy" reading text materials over more difficult or challenging texts is just not supported in research. In fact, children enjoy a sense of being challenged.

3. *Control* involves sharing how texts and tasks in the classroom are presented with students to promote greater engagement in reading. Children need to feel and sense that they have an integral role to play while reading a text.

4. *Collaboration* requires that students discuss, interact, and work together with each other and their teachers to construct the meanings of texts. Collaboration results in greater student insight into the thinking processes of others as they learn new information from texts. Focused conversations also enhance reading comprehension by adding multiple understandings about text information to enhance individual comprehension.

5. *Constructing meaning* is a process of conscious selection, control, and use of various strategies while engaged in reading a text. The National Reading Panel (2000) found sufficient scientific support for implementing a number of comprehension strategies in classrooms (presented in Chapter 7).

6. *Consequences* is a concept that refers to the expectations stated and the resulting outcomes if expectations are not met. For example, if the expected outcome involves completing or participating in an open rather than a deterministic task, such as contributing to a discussion rather than getting the "right" answers to questions on a worksheet, then students interpret their failures in comprehension differently. When seeking correct or "right" answers, they often feel that they just do not have enough ability (Turner & Paris, 1995). On the other hand, if through discussion they detect that they missed some important element in the text, they often view this failure as the result of improperly selecting or applying effective comprehension strategies rather than not being "smart enough" or "not having the ability."

As a fundamental part of providing effective reading instruction, research clearly demonstrates the power of motivation on student reading achievement. In a 2004 study reported by Guthrie and Humenick, motivation accounted for 17 to 40-plus percentile points on standardized achievement tests of students' reading abilities. Such increases from the mean performance on reading achievement tests demonstrate that student motivation is among the most powerful determiners of students' future reading achievement.

Pillar Six: Technology and New Literacies

New literacy studies (NLS) has been defined as "the skills, strategies, and insights necessary to successfully exploit the rapidly changing information and communication technologies that continuously emerge in our world" (Leu, 2002, p. 310). Thus, NLS has to do with how literacy practices are linked to people's lives, identities,

Click on A+RISE—WIDA ELP Standard Strategies in the MyEducationLab (www.myeducationlab.com) for your course. Next, select the Strategy Card Index tab, scroll to Language and Content for grades 6–12, and select the Cooperative Learning Roles strategy.

and social affiliations (Compton-Lilly, 2009). A great deal of NLS research focuses on children's interactions with technological texts and views these interactions as meaningful and purposeful (Compton-Lilly, in press). Most notable is the ongoing work of the New Literacies Research Team (NLRT) at the University of Connecticut and Clemson University.

Findings about computer-assisted instruction (CAI) drawn from a meta-analysis of 42 studies have found that primary-grade children's overall learning experience is enhanced using CAI over conventional teaching approaches for acquiring a variety of beginning reading skills. The new literacies research group at the University of Connecticut has shown that online reading requires the development of a set of comprehension strategies: (1) reading online to generate a problem or question from one's social context, (2) reading to locate information online, (3) reading to critically evaluate information online, (4) reading to synthesize information online from multiple sources, and (5) reading to communicate and exchange information online with others.

According to these researchers, online reading comprehension strategies function in a manner similar to phonic and phonemic awareness skills in offline reading comprehension. If one cannot decode words accurately and effortlessly offline, comprehension becomes very difficult. But online, if you cannot read to locate and critically evaluate information, it becomes very difficult to answer the question or solve the problem that initially motivated one's online reading. Online reading comprehension can be supported by helping students learn to evaluate the accuracy and validity of information claims found during online reading (Mokhtari, Kymes, & Edwards, 2008).

McKenna and colleagues (2007) recommend the use of new technology for a variety of purposes, from crafting multimedia reports to presenting sight word lessons to first-grade students. **New literacies** (NLs) present many opportunities for engaging, interactive demonstrations of literacy skills, concepts, and strategies. NLs offer varied socially mediated opportunities for students to work together through e-mail, blogs, or instant messaging to conduct research and create project reports from the large amount of free materials readily available over the Internet. NLs also extend the teacher by offering students technologically driven practice of reading skills, concepts, and strategies via CD, DVD, and online media and "virtual" teachers. Reading teachers today will need to learn how to use and seamlessly integrate NLs into their daily reading and writing instruction.

Pillar Seven: Family and Community Connections

It has been said that 80 percent of student learning occurs outside of school. We know from research, for instance, that children who have been read to a great deal before entering kindergarten have a much stronger language base and are far more likely to succeed in reading (Snow et al., 1998). Parents and many involved others in the child's extended family and community are often interested in helping children develop as readers—*if* they know what to do. Thus, teachers can add great power to a child's literacy learning program by educating the adults in their lives in proven reading development strategies that make sense in our busy world.

Reading teachers in the twenty-first century no longer have the luxury of viewing home involvement as merely a good or even an important idea. There is now substantial agreement among literacy researchers and master teachers that parents can make powerful contributions to their children's success in early literacy learning

(Dickinson & Tabors, 2001; Paratore, 2003). Therefore, teachers who can reach out to parents and homes are vital to young children's progress in learning to read successfully. For example, in a large-scale federally funded study of 14 schools in Virginia, Minnesota, Colorado, and California, teachers, administrators, and parents were interviewed, surveyed, and observed to determine the characteristics of effective schools and classroom teachers. As described in *Beating the Odds in Teaching All Children to Read* (Taylor, Pearson, Clark, & Walpole, 1999), a key school-level factor clearly associated with the most effective schools in teaching at-risk children to read successfully was outreach to homes and parents. According to the researchers

> The four effective schools made a more concerted effort to reach out to parents than the other schools. Efforts included conducting focus groups, written or phone surveys, and having an active site council on which parents served. (p. 2)

These findings were echoed in research from a major urban school district in a high-poverty environment. In *Perspectives on Rescuing Urban Literacy Education*, R. Cooter (2004) described results of a privately funded "failure analysis" to learn what teachers must know and be able to do to reverse the 76 percent reading failure rate for the district's third graders. Five "pillars" or instructional supports, the report concluded, were necessary to ensuring reading success—one of which was family and community involvement. "Most parents help their children at home [with reading] if they know what to do; thus, teachers must be supported in their efforts to educate families in ways they can help their children succeed in the home" (p. 22).

There are many examples of excellent family literacy programs that may serve as models for teachers as they make plans to reach out to families. Project FLAME (Family Literacy Aprendiendo, Mejorando, Educando), a program designed for parents and children learning English, is one example of a nationally recognized family literacy program (Rodriquez-Brown, Fen Li, & Albom, 1999; Rodriquez-Brown & Meehan, 1998; Shanahan, Mulhern, & Rodriquez-Brown, 1995). Other examples include the Intergenerational Literacy Project (ILP) (Paratore, 2003) and Project EASE (Jordan, Snow, & Porche, 2000), in which parents significantly influenced their children's early literacy development prior to school and substantially benefited their children's early reading progress once in school.

Effective teachers of reading focus on building strong, sturdy, and easily traversed bridges between the classroom and the homes of the children they serve in order to help every child have a successful experience in learning to read and write.

Summary

We return full circle to our earlier question: *What is the primary ingredient in the recipe for every child's reading success?* We hope that by now you understand the significant role you will play or are now playing in the reading success of each and every child you teach. You are the hero in every child's literacy learning drama. Research confirms that your knowledge and skill in the teaching of reading is incredibly important.

A common myth about teachers goes something like this: "Those who can, do. Those who can't, teach."

Another equally distasteful myth alleges that "Teachers are born, not made." Neither could be further from the truth. Teachers today must understand a great deal about how children develop and learn generally, how they develop and learn to read specifically, and how to assess and adapt instruction in a classroom filled with diversity. Today's teachers are expected to know more and do more than teachers at any other time in our history. Teachers must master and put into practice a body of knowledge related to language development, children's literature, curriculum standards, classroom management, and evidence-based instruction practices. They must be able to assess students' strengths and needs, plan effective instruction that focuses on the essential elements of reading instruction, and ensure that every child makes adequate yearly progress so that no child fails to achieve his or her potential. In the end, the expert teaching of reading requires some of the best minds and talent to be found in our nation!

Field and Classroom Applications

- Read *Using Research and Reason in Education: How Teachers Can Use Scientifically Based Research to Make Curricular and Instructional Decisions* (Stanovich & Stanovich, 2003). Working with other members of a small group, list ten reasons why teachers should rely on the results of research evidence to inform their instructional and curricular choices. Share your group's list with the rest of the class. Collapse all of the small-group charts into a single class chart.
- Read "Beginning Reading Instruction: The Rest of the Story from Research" at www.nea.org/reading/images/beginningreading.pdf. Compile a list of research-supported practices in reading instruction in addition to those found in the *Report of the National Reading Panel: Teaching Children to Read* (National Reading Panel, 2000).

- Organize into small research groups. Select a grade level from kindergarten to third grade. Read *Starting Out Right: A Guide to Promoting Children's Reading Success* (Burns, Griffin, & Snow, 1999). Prepare a class presentation on student accomplishments in reading and writing at the grade level you selected.
- Read the Executive Summary of the *Developing Early Literacy* report from the National Early Literacy Panel, available at www.nifl.gov/earlychildhood/NELP/NELPreport.html. In small groups, prepare a brochure or pamphlet that explains to parents, teachers, and school administrators the best early predictors for success in learning to read. Share your pamphlet with your class or with parents at your first open house.

Recommended Resources

Print Resources

Armbruster, B. B., Lehr, F., & Osborn, J. (2001). *Put reading first: The research building blocks for teaching children to read.* Washington, DC: U.S. Department of Education. Available at www.nifl.gov/partnershipforreading/publications/reading_first1.html

August, D., & Shanahan, T. (2006). *Developing literacy in second-language learners: Report of the National Literacy Panel on language-minority children and youth.* Mahwah, NJ: Lawrence Erlbaum Associates.

Burns, M. S., Griffin, P., & Snow, C. E. (1999). *Starting out right: A guide to promoting children's reading success.* Washington, DC: National Academy Press.

National Early Literacy Panel. (2008). *Developing early literacy: Report of the National Early Literacy Panel.* Jessup, MD: National Institute for Literacy. Available at www.nifl.gov/earlychildhood/NELP/NELPreport.html

National Institute of Child Health and Human Development. (2000). *Report of the National Reading Panel: Teaching children to read.* Washington, DC: Author. Available at www.nationalreadingpanel.org/Publications/researchread.htm

Pressley, M. (2002). *Beginning reading instruction: The rest of the story from research.* Washington, DC: National Education Association. Available at www.nea.org/reading/images/beginningreading.pdf

Pressley, M. (2003). A few things reading educators should know about instructional experiments. *The Reading Teacher, 57*(1), 64–71.

Shanahan, T. (2003). Research-based reading instruction: Myths about the National Reading Panel Report. *The Reading Teacher, 56*(7), 646–654.

Slavin, R. E. (2003, February). A reader's guide to scientifically-based research. *Educational Leadership, 60*(5), 12–16.

Snow, C. E., Burns, M. S., & Griffin, P. (1998). *Preventing reading failure in young children.* Washington, DC: National Academy Press.

Snow, C. E., Griffin, P., & Burns, M. S. (2005). *Knowledge to support the teaching of reading: Preparing teachers for a changing world.* San Francisco, CA: Jossey-Bass.

Stanovich, P. J., & Stanovich, K. E. (2003). *Using research and reason in education: How teachers can use scientifically based research to make curricular and instructional decisions.* Washington, DC: National Institute for Literacy. Available at www.nifl.gov/partnershipforreading/publications/pdf/Stanovich_Color.pdf

U.S. Department of Education. (2001). *No Child Left Behind.* Washington, DC: Author. Available at www.ed.gov/index.jhtml

U.S. Department of Education. (2003). *Identifying and implementing educational practices supported by rigorous evidence: A user-friendly guide.* Washington, DC: Coalition for Evidence-Based Policy. Available at www.ed.gov/rschstat/research/pubs/rigorousevid/guide.html

Web Resources

www.reading.org
> Issues of *The Reading Teacher* and the *Journal of Adolescent and Adult Literacy*

www.nationalreadingpanel.org
> The National Reading Panel report (2000), available free

www.nifl.gov/earlychildhood/NELP/NELPreport.html
> The National Reading Panel report (2008), available free

http://iris.peabody.vanderbilt.edu/index.html
> IRIS Center at Vanderbilt University online tutorial for RTI

www.newliteracies.uconn.edu
> NLRT comprehensive website, including video cases, a team blog, articles, and many other valuable resources for teachers interested in learning more about new literacies

Go to Topic 10, Organization and Management, in the MyEducationLab (www.myeducationlab.com) for your course, where you can:

- Find learning outcomes for Organization and Management along with the national standards that connect to these outcomes.
- Complete Assignments and Activities that can help you more deeply understand the chapter content.
- Apply and practice your understanding of the core teaching skills identified in the chapter with the Building Teaching Skills and Dispositions learning units. (optional)
- Examine challenging situations and cases presented in the IRIS Center Resources. (optional)
- Access video clips of CCSSO National Teachers of the Year award winners responding to the question "Why Do I Teach?" in the Teacher Talk section. (optional)
- Check your comprehension on the content covered in the chapter by going to the Study Plan in the Book Resources for your text. Here you will be able to take a chapter quiz, receive feedback on your answers, and then access Review, Practice, and Enrichment activities to enhance your understanding of chapter content. (optional)

Go to the Topic A+RISE in the MyEducationLab (www.myeducationlab.com) for your course. A+RISE® Standards2Strategy™ is an innovative and interactive online resource that offers new teachers in grades K–12 just in time, research-based instructional strategies that:

- Meet the linguistic needs of ELLs as they learn content.
- Differentiate instruction for all grades and abilities.
- Offer reading and writing techniques, cooperative learning, use of linguistic and nonlinguistic representations, scaffolding, teacher modeling, higher order thinking, and alternative classroom ELL assessment.
- Provide support to help teachers be effective through the integration of listening, speaking, reading, and writing along with the content curriculum.
- Improve student achievement.
- Are aligned to Common Core Elementary Language Arts standards (for the literacy strategies) and to English language proficiency standards in WIDA, Texas, California, and Florida.

STANDARDS
for Reading Professionals and Guiding Principles for Educators

IRA STANDARDS FOR READING PROFESSIONALS

Standard 1: Foundational Knowledge

Element 1.1

Candidates understand major theories and empirical research that describe the cognitive, linguistic, motivational, and sociocultural foundations of reading and writing development, processes, and components, including word recognition, language comprehension, strategic knowledge, and reading–writing connections.

Element 1.2

Candidates understand the historically shared knowledge of the profession and changes over time in the perceptions of reading and writing development, processes, and components.

Element 1.3

Candidates understand the role of professional judgment and practical knowledge for improving all students' reading development and achievement.

Candidates use instructional approaches, materials, and an integrated, comprehensive, balanced curriculum to support student learning in reading and writing.

RESPONSE TO INTERVENTION

6. Expertise

All students have the right to receive instruction from well-prepared teachers who keep up to date and supplemental instruction from professionals specifically prepared to teach language and literacy (IRA, 2000).

- Teacher expertise is central to instructional improvement, particularly for students who encounter difficulty in acquiring language and literacy. RTI may involve a range of professionals; however, the greater the literacy difficulty, the greater the need for expertise in literacy teaching and learning.
- Important dimensions of teachers' expertise include their knowledge and understanding of language and literacy development, their ability to use powerful assessment tools and techniques, and their ability to translate information about student performance into instructionally relevant instructional techniques.

- The exemplary core instruction that is so essential to the success of RTI is dependent on highly knowledgeable and skilled classroom teachers (IRA, 2003).
- Professionals who provide supplemental instruction or intervention must have a high level of expertise in all aspects of language and literacy instruction and assessment and be capable of intensifying or accelerating language and literacy learning.
- Success for culturally and linguistically diverse students depends on teachers and support personnel who are well prepared to teach in a variety of settings. Deep knowledge of cultural and linguistic differences is especially critical for the prevention of language and literacy problems in diverse student populations.
- Expertise in the areas of language and literacy requires a comprehensive approach to professional preparation that involves preservice, induction, and inservice education. It also requires opportunities for extended practice under the guidance of knowledgeable and experienced mentors.

What Do Reading Teachers Need to Know and Do? The Seven Pillars of Effective Reading Instruction

IRA STANDARDS FOR READING PROFESSIONALS

Standard 1: Foundational Knowledge

Candidates understand the theoretical and evidence-based foundations of reading and writing processes and instruction.

Foundational knowledge is at the core of preparing individuals for roles in the reading profession and encompasses the major theories, research, and best practices that share a consensus of acceptance in the reading field. Individuals who enter the reading profession should understand the historically shared knowledge of the profession and develop the capacity to act on that knowledge responsibly. Elements of the Foundational Knowledge Standard set

expectations in the domains of theoretical and practical knowledge, and in developing dispositions for the active, ethical use of professional knowledge. Expectations are founded on the concept of a profession as both a technical and moral enterprise, that is, competent performance for the betterment of society.

Elements 1.1, 1.2, 1.3 (See previous)

Standard 2: Curriculum and Instruction

The Curriculum and Instruction Standard recognizes the need to prepare educators who have a deep understanding and knowledge of the elements of a balanced, integrated, and comprehensive literacy curriculum and have developed expertise in enacting that curriculum. The elements focus on the use of effective practices in a well-articulated curriculum, using traditional print, digital, and online resources.

Element 2.1

Candidates use foundational knowledge to design or implement an integrated, comprehensive, and balanced curriculum.

Element 2.2

Candidates use appropriate and varied instructional approaches, including those that develop word recognition, language comprehension, strategic knowledge, and reading–writing connections.

Element 2.3

Candidates use a wide range of texts (e.g., narrative, expository, and poetry) from traditional print, digital, and online resources.

RESPONSE TO INTERVENTION

1. Instruction

RTI is first and foremost intended to prevent problems by optimizing language and literacy instruction.

- Whatever approach is taken to RTI, it should ensure optimal instruction for every student at all levels of schooling. It should prevent serious language and literacy problems through increasingly differentiated and intensified assessment and instruction and reduce the disproportionate number of minority youth and ELLs identified as learning disabled.
- Instruction and assessment conducted by the classroom teacher are central to the success of RTI and must address the needs of all students, including those from diverse cultural and linguistic backgrounds. Evidence shows that effective classroom instruction can reduce substantially the number of students who are inappropriately classified as learning disabled.
- A successful RTI process begins with the highest quality core instruction in the classroom—that is, instruction that encompasses all areas of language and literacy as part of a coherent curriculum that is developmentally appropriate for preK–12 students and does not underestimate their potential for learning. This core instruction may or may not involve commercial programs, and it must in all cases be provided by an informed, competent classroom teacher.
- The success of RTI depends on the classroom teacher's use of research-based practices. As defined by IRA (2002), *research based* means "that a particular program or collection of instructional practices has a record of success. That is, there is reliable, trustworthy, and valid evidence to suggest that when the program is used with a particular group of children, the children can be expected to make adequate gains in reading achievement."
- Research on instructional practices must provide not only information about what works, but also what works with whom, by whom, in what contexts, and on which outcomes. The effectiveness of a particular practice needs to have been demonstrated with the types of students who will receive the instruction, taking into account, for example, whether the students live in rural or urban settings or come from diverse cultural and linguistic backgrounds.
- Research evidence frequently represents the effectiveness of an instructional practice on average, which suggests that some students benefited and others did not. This means that instruction must be provided by a teacher who understands the intent of the research-based practice being used and has the professional expertise and responsibility to plan instruction and adapt programs and materials as needed (see also principle 6, Expertise).
- When core language and literacy instruction is not effective for a particular student, it should be modified to address more closely the needs and abilities of that student. Classroom teachers, at times in collaboration with other experts, must exercise their best professional judgment in providing responsive teaching and differentiation (see also principle 2).

2. Responsive Teaching and Differentiation

The RTI process emphasizes increasingly differentiated and intensified instruction or intervention in language and literacy.

- RTI is centrally about optimizing language and literacy instruction for particular students. This means that differentiated instruction, based on instructionally relevant assessment, is essential. Evidence shows that small-group and individualized instruction are effective in reducing the number of students who are at risk of becoming classified as learning disabled.
- Instruction and materials selection must derive from specific student–teacher interactions and not be constrained by packaged programs. Students have different language and literacy needs, so they may not respond similarly to instruction—even when research-based practices are used. No single approach to instruction or intervention can address the broad and varied goals and needs of all students, especially those from different cultural and linguistic backgrounds.
- The boundaries between differentiation and intervention are permeable and not clearcut. Instruction or intervention must be flexible enough to respond to evidence from student performance and teaching interactions. It should not be constrained by institutional procedures that emphasize uniformity.

3. Assessment

An RTI approach demands assessment that can inform language and literacy instruction meaningfully.

- Assessment should reflect the multidimensional nature of language and literacy learning and the diversity among students being assessed. The utility of an assessment is dependent on the extent to which it provides valid information on the essential aspects of language and literacy that can be used to plan appropriate instruction.
- Assessments, tools, and techniques should provide useful and timely information about desired language and literacy goals. They should reflect authentic language and literacy activities as opposed to contrived texts or tasks generated specifically for assessment purposes. The quality of assessment information should not be sacrificed for the efficiency of an assessment procedure.
- Multiple purposes for assessment should be clearly identified and appropriate tools and techniques employed. Not all available tools and techniques are appropriate for all purposes, and different assessments—even in the same language or literacy domain—capture different skills and knowledge. Particular care should be

taken in selecting assessments for ELLs and for students who speak an English dialect that differs from mainstream dialects.

- Efficient assessment systems involve a layered approach in which screening techniques are used both to identify which students require further (diagnostic) assessment and to provide aggregate data about the nature of student achievement overall. Initial (screening) assessments should not be used as the sole mechanism for determining the appropriateness of targeted interventions. Ongoing progress monitoring must include an evaluation of the instruction itself and requires observation of the student in the classroom.
- Classroom teachers and reading/literacy specialists should play a central role in conducting language and literacy assessments and in using assessment results to plan instruction and monitor student performance.
- Assessment as a component of RTI should be consistent with the *Standards for the Assessment of Reading and Writing* developed jointly by the International Reading Association and the National Council of Teachers of English (2010).

4. Collaboration

RTI requires a dynamic, positive, and productive collaboration among professionals with relevant expertise in language and literacy. Success also depends on strong and respectful partnerships among professionals, parents, and students.

- Collaboration should be focused on the available evidence about the needs of students struggling in language and literacy. School-level decision-making teams (e.g., intervention teams, problem-solving teams, RTI teams) should include members with relevant expertise in language and literacy, including second-language learning.
- Reading/literacy specialists and coaches should provide leadership in every aspect of an RTI process—planning, assessment, provision of more intensified instruction and support, and making decisions about next steps. These individuals must embody the knowledge, skills, and dispositions detailed for reading specialists in IRA's (2003) *Standards for Reading Professionals* (and the accompanying revised role definitions from August 2007).
- Collaboration should increase, not reduce, the coherence of the instruction experienced by struggling readers. There must be congruence between core language and literacy instruction and interventions. This requires a shared vision and common goals for language and literacy instruction and assessment, adequate time for communication and coordinated planning among general education and specialist teachers, and integrated professional development.
- Involving parents and students and engaging them in a collaborative manner is critical to successful implementation. Initiating and strengthening collaborations among school, home, and communities, particularly in urban and rural areas, provides the basis for support and reinforcement of students' learning.

5. Systemic and Comprehensive Approaches

RTI must be part of a comprehensive, systemic approach to language and literacy assessment and instruction that supports all preK–12 students and teachers.

- RTI needs to be integrated within the context of a coherent and consistent language and literacy curriculum that guides comprehensive instruction for all students. Core instruction—indeed, all instruction—must be continuously improved to increase its efficacy and mitigate the need for specialized interventions.
- Specific approaches to RTI need to be appropriate for the particular school or district culture and take into account leadership, expertise, the diversity of the student population, and the available resources. Schools and districts should adopt an approach that best matches their needs and resources while still accomplishing the overall goals of RTI.
- A systemic approach to language and literacy learning within an RTI framework requires the active participation and genuine collaboration of many professionals, including classroom teachers, reading specialists, literacy coaches, special educators, and school psychologists. Given the critical role that language development plays in literacy learning, professionals with specialized language-related expertise such as speech-language pathologists and teachers of ELLs may be particularly helpful in addressing students' language difficulties.
- Approaches to RTI must be sensitive to developmental differences in language and literacy among students at different ages and grades. Although many prevailing approaches to RTI focus on the early elementary grades, it is essential for teachers and support personnel at middle and secondary levels to provide their students with the language and literacy instruction they need to succeed in school and beyond.
- Administrators must ensure adequate resources and appropriate scheduling to allow all professionals to collaborate.
- Ongoing and job-embedded professional development is necessary for all educators involved in the RTI process. Professional development should be context specific and provided by professional developers with appropriate preparation and skill to support school and district personnel. Professional expertise is essential to improving students' language and literacy learning in general as well as within the context of RTI (see also principle 6).

Part Two

Essentials of Reading Instruction

Developing Children's Oral Language

2

Teacher Knowledge	Classroom Assessment	Evidence-Based Teaching Practices	Response to Intervention (RTI)
What Do Teachers Need to Know About Oral Language?	Assessing Children's Oral Language Development and Use	Principles of Effective Oral Language Instruction	Tier 2 Adaptations

Chapter Questions

■ When considering the theories of oral language development, which do you feel best explains your own viewpoint?

■ What are three ways you could assess students' oral language development in your classrooms? Be sure to include an assessment of mean length of utterance (MLU).

■ In thinking about the strategies presented in this chapter's Pillar 3 section for developing children's oral language, which do you feel are best suited to core instruction for all learners and which might you reserve for assisting students with less developed oral language? Are some strategies equally useful in both situations?

■ What are the six guiding principles to providing effective oral English language instruction for English learners (ELs)? With a partner, identify a strategy exemplifying how you might implement these principles in your classroom.

■ Why are joint productive activities (JPA) so effective for increasing students' oral language competence?

■ How might the technologies and new literacy strategies described in this chapter be used to boost students' social studies and mathematics vocabularies?

■ What are some research-proven ways that parents can help their child develop robust oral language vocabularies?

Key Terms

Oral language

Expressive language

Receptive language

Phonology

Intonation

Stress

Juncture

Rime

Onset

Phoneme

Phonemic awareness

Orthography

Grapheme

Alphabetic principle

Phonics

Morphology

Morpheme

Syntax

Grammar

Semantics

Schema theory

Pragmatics

Dialect

Behaviorist theory

Innatist theory

Constructivist theory

Social interactionist theory

Zone of proximal development (ZPD)

Internalization

Modeling

Guided practice

Independent practice

Mean length of utterance (MLU)

Language functions

Forms of language

Language fluency

Talking protocols

Instructional conversation

Rule of five

Joint productive activity (JPA)

Electronic talking books (ETB)

Dialogic reading

Motivation and Engagement	Technology and New Literacies	Family and Community Connections
Motivation and Engagement in Oral Language Development	Technology and New Literacies for Oral Language Development	How Family and Community Connections Encourage Oral Language Development

Vignette: A Trip to the Zoo . . . and a *Hairy* Question

It is a beautiful spring morning in Mr. Cantwell's kindergarten class at Adams Elementary School. Earlier in the week, Mr. Cantwell, a second-year teacher, had taken the children on a field trip to a local petting zoo to learn about baby animals. Continuing the unit on life cycles of young animals including birds, insects, fish, and mammals, this morning Mr. Cantwell is reading books aloud and talking with the children about mammals. After reading and discussing several baby mammal books, the class makes a language experience chart based on what they learned at the zoo. As the children dictate their ideas aloud, Mr. Cantwell records the comments onto the chart using a different colored marker to identify each child's contribution.

When ready to contribute, children make the gesture Mr. Cantwell established on the first day of school signaling a request to speak—a hand placed over the mouth, meaning, in his words, "O Great One, I have something to say." (None of this waving hands in the air stuff!) Mr. Cantwell calls on a bright-eyed little boy named Jamal, who blurts out, "Mammals are born alive."

"That's very good," says Mr. Cantwell, as he writes the words *born alive* on the chart.

"Austin, what do you know about mammals?"

Austin thoughtfully replies, "Mammals don't hatch from eggs like birds and bugs."

"Way to go. Excellent thinking!" Mr. Cantwell adds *egg* to the chart.

Amalia is nearly ready to explode when called on. "Mammal moms feed their babies milk."

"Wow! You children are so smart! Amalia, you are absolutely right. Good job!" Mr. Cantwell adds *milk* to the language experience chart.

Rosa chimes in next: "Mammals have hair!" Mr. Cantwell writes *hair* on the chart.

Braxton, when recognized, removes his hand from his mouth and asks, "Mr. Cantwell, are boys mammals, too?"

Pointing to key words on the chart as he speaks, Mr. Cantwell responds, "Why, yes, they are, Braxton. Think about it. Boys are born alive; they don't hatch from eggs like birds and bugs, their mothers feed them milk when they are little, and they have hair. Why do you ask if boys are mammals, Braxton?"

"Well," replies Braxton, "I was just wondering because my grandpa doesn't have any hair. He's bald!"

Mr. Cantwell smiles and patiently explains that Braxton's grandpa is a mammal because when he was younger he used to have hair and that when boys become men they sometimes lose the hair on their heads. Mr. Cantwell notices a few of the children leaning forward to check their teacher for early signs of this mysterious hair loss some men experience. ■

Oral language is the foundation of learning to read and write (Roskos, Tabors, & Lenhart, 2009). As illustrated by this classroom story, teachers frequently assist children with their attempts to discover meaning from their own experiences and words. Young children often misinterpret words or ideas they do not fully understand, like the child who recites the Pledge of Allegiance saying *invisible* rather than *indivisible* and *liverty* rather than *liberty*. Understanding children's language development is important because **oral language,** the spoken form of communication, has been shown to be strongly related to children's early reading success and in predicting their ability to comprehend what they read (Dooley, 2010; National Early Literacy Panel, 2008). As Pinnell and Jaggar (2003) conclude, "Oral language is the foundation not only of learning and schooling but of our living together as people of the world. . . . Oral language development is inextricably related to literacy development" (p. 881).

In this chapter, we discuss the origins of oral language, ways to assess student oral language, and how teachers and family members can expand children's language meanings and structure.

Teacher Knowledge

What Do Teachers Need to Know About Oral Language?

Research confirms that a rich and extensive oral language foundation is critical to the later development of reading and writing (Dickinson & Tabors, 2001; Hart & Risley, 1995, 2002; National Institute for Literacy, 2010; Scarborough, 2001). Children must be relatively fluent in oral language use to communicate effectively with the teacher and with other students in the classroom and in life (Pinnell, 1998; Pinnell & Jaggar, 2003). Oral language paves the way for learning reading skills such as phonemic awareness, the alphabetic principle, phonics, decoding, and reading comprehension. In fact, oral language ability is the bedrock foundation on which all future literacy learning is built (Scarborough, 2001; Shanahan, 2006; Smith, 2001; Vukelich & Christie, 2009).

In January of 2009, an extensive review of existing scientific research was published, entitled *Developing Early Literacy: Report of the National Early Literacy Panel (NELP)*. Among the questions the National Early Literacy Panel (NELP) hoped to answer was the degree to which oral language development contributes to later literacy learning. Their initial findings about the correlation between oral language learning and later reading and writing development were somewhat surprising in that a strong relationship did not seem indicated. But after NELP examined oral language more completely they discovered that complex oral language skills like listening comprehension, grammar, and learning word meanings are strongly related to higher reading achievement (Westburg, 2010).

As Allington and Cunningham (1996) put it, children who come to school with thousands of "words in their head"—words they can hear, understand, and use in

● ● ●
IRA Standards for Reading Professionals: Standard 1, Elements 1.1, 1.2, 1.3; Standard 6, Element 6.2

Common Core Standards: Speaking and Listening: K–5, Comprehension and Collaboration (items 1, 6)

Response to Intervention: Expertise

their daily lives—are already on the path to learning success. Similarly, children who have small listening and speaking vocabularies—those who come from what might be termed "language-deprived backgrounds"—must receive immediate attention if they are to have any real chance at reading success (Dockrell, Sylva, Huxford, & Roberts, 2009; Johnson, 2001; National Research Council, 1998).

What Is Language?

Language is essentially an agreed-on "symbol system." People who share a common vocabulary are able to understand each other when they speak. Oral language is used in human society to represent our full range of knowledge, experiences, and emotions. All humans use language as a tool for getting their needs met, for learning, for thinking, for problem solving, and for sharing ideas and feelings.

Language is both expressive and receptive. **Expressive language** requires the *sender* of a message to "encode" or to put his or her thoughts into a symbolic form. Expressive language most often takes the form of spoken or written words but may also be represented visually through gestures, art, pictures, video, or dramatization. Thus, the size of one's oral language vocabulary can directly affect verbal expression and writing capacity (Dyson, 1983). **Receptive language** requires the *receiver* of a message to "decode" or unlock the code of the spoken or written communication used by the sender in order to understand the message.

The structure of language is typically divided into six interrelated components, as shown in Table 2.1:

1. Phonology
2. Orthography
3. Morphology
4. Syntax
5. Semantics
6. Pragmatics

You might be asking, "Do I really need to know all of this information about language to effectively teach children to read?" In short, yes! Research over the past decade has shed new light on how teachers' knowledge of language structure relates to their students' success (Cunningham, Perry, Stanovich, & Stanovich, 2004; Moats, 1994).

Phonology: Sounds in Spoken Words.   **Phonology** is a component of language that refers to sounds in speech. Phonology includes both *prosodic features* or what we sometimes call "speaking with expression," as well as the *articulatory units* or elements of speech such as individual sounds, syllables, and words (Snow, Burns, & Griffin, 1998).

Prosodic or expressive spoken language is described by features such as intonation, stress, and juncture. **Intonation** refers to how one's voice rises or falls in speaking. For example, vocal pitch usually drops at the end of a statement. (We use a period in writing so that the reader "hears" that drop.) On the other hand, vocal pitch generally rises at the end of a question. (In writing, of course, we use the question mark so the reader "hears" that rise in pitch.) **Stress** refers to speech intensity—the loudness or softness of spoken words. For example, a speaker who wants to emphasize a particular point will articulate a word or phrase more loudly.

Table 2.1

Six Components of Language Structure

Component	Concepts	Examples
Phonology	*Prosodic Features* • Pitch • Juncture • Stress	Expression • Highness or lowness of speech • Pauses within or between words • Emphasis or intensity of speech
	Articulated Speech Units • Words • Syllables • Onset • Rime • Phonemes	Spoken words and parts of words *duck, college, elephant* *win-dow, Mc-Don-ald's* *r, t, sl, pl, ch, str* *an, un, ick, ake, on* /s/, /r/, /t/, /m/, /ae/, /ə/

Orthography	*Grapheme*
	Phoneme
	*Grapheme–Phoneme
	  Correspondence*
		Written symbols/letters
		Spoken sounds
		The means by which spoken sounds are represented by
		  specific letters

Morphology	*Morpheme* • Free • Bound • Derivational • Inflected • Compound	Smallest unit of meaning *ball, peninsula, chain* *anti, pre, ology, bio* *rust* → *rusty* *big, bigger, biggest, walk* → *walked* *wallpaper, cowboy, towboat*
Syntax	*Grammar* • Parts of speech • Sentence structure • Sentence combining • Cohesion • Word order	System of rules for language verbs, nouns, adjectives, adverbs The dog ran after the bone. The dog ran. The cat ran. The dog and cat ran. *because, therefore, but, or, and* The dog ran *vs.* Dog the ran
Semantics	*Meaning* • Words • Connected language	To signify or represent an idea, concept, or action How many meanings are there for the word *run*? jokes, songs, books, stories
Pragmatics	*Purpose* • Instrumental • Regulatory • Interactional • Personal • Heuristic • Imaginative • Representational • Divertive • Authoritative • Perpetuating	Using language to satisfy human needs or to represent human situations To get one's needs met To control the behavior of others To establish relationships with others To share oneself with others To seek answers to questions To make believe To communicate information For humor and recreation For contracts, statutes, laws, rules For journals, diaries, notes, personal histories
	Variation • Dialect	Changes in language forms and function resulting from geographical and cultural influences *apartment* vs. *flat* *morning* vs. *mawnin'* *Yo!* vs. *Hey!* vs. *Hello!*

(In writing, an exclamation point may be used.) **Juncture** refers to the time between words; note, for example, the difference between "I scream" and "ice cream."

Articulatory features of spoken language include words, syllables, and phonemes. We assume that most of our readers are familiar with the spoken concept of *word*. Most people understand syllables too, but how words are divided into syllables may not be as clearly understood. All words in spoken English are made up of at least one syllable. A single syllable can also be a word. For example, the single-syllable spoken words *sat, run, dot,* and *cat* are both words and syllables. Of course, many spoken words contain more than one syllable. For example, *window* contains /win/ and /dow/.

Every syllable in English must contain a rime. A **rime** is defined as the vowel sound and every other sound that follows the vowel sound in a spoken syllable. The spoken words *an, it, a, of,* and *I* all contain a rime that includes the vowel sound (/a/, /e/, /i/, /o/, or /u/) and the other sounds that follow the vowel sound. Some spoken syllables may also contain an onset. An **onset** is defined as all sounds in a spoken syllable that come before the vowel sound. For example, *str*—/s/-/t/-/r/—in *street* or /f/ in *fit* are onsets.

A **phoneme** is the smallest unit of sound in a spoken word (Piper, 1998). The spoken word *wake* contains three phonemes: /w/, /ā/, and /k/. The word *wake* differs by only one phoneme from the words *wade* (/w/, /ā/, /d/) and *make* (/m/, /ā/, /k/), thus showing how changing a single phoneme can alter meaning. Linguists estimate that spoken English is composed of 44 speech sounds.

An abundance of research over the past two decades has shown that young children who are aware of phonemes in spoken words, as well as alphabet letters and their associated sounds are more likely to succeed in early reading and writing (Burns, Snow, & Griffin, 1998; National Early Literacy Panel, 2008; National Reading Panel, 2000). Students' awareness of phonemes is called **phonemic awareness.** It seems that young children benefit more from early phonics instruction and are able to create "invented spellings" (e.g., TRK for *truck*) in early writing if they have phonemic awareness (Armbruster, Lehr, & Osborn, 2001; Burns, Griffin, & Snow, 1999).

Orthography: Connecting Letters and Sounds.   **Orthography** refers to spelling patterns used in English, linking letters (graphemes) to sounds (phonemes) in spoken language (Snow, Griffin, & Burns, 2005). Orthography includes punctuation and graphic features such as directionality, orientation, configuration, word length, style such as cursive or manuscript, nonalphabetic symbols, and letter patterns as ways of representing meaning in texts. Readers use these features strategically to construct meaning (Arya, Wilson, & Martens, 2009, pp. 224–225). A **grapheme** is a printed or visual symbol, usually a letter such as *a, r, m, s,* or *o,* that represents a phoneme. Because English is an alphabetic language, its spelling or orthographic structure is represented by 26 letters or graphemes that relate in somewhat predictable ways to the 44 spoken sounds, or phonemes.

To understand orthography, teachers and students must know how the 44 speech sounds are matched with or "mapped" onto the 26 alphabet letters. English has a less predictable relationship between sounds and letters than many other languages. In languages like Spanish, French, and German, letters and corresponding sounds form one-to-one matches of sound to symbol with few or no exceptions. On the other hand, the 44 sounds of spoken English can be spelled using more than 500 letters or letter combinations! Not surprisingly, this can make learning to read and write in English a challenge.

Knowing that speech sounds and letters link to one another, sometimes called the **alphabetic principle,** is a critical insight that young children must achieve in learning to read and write (National Reading Panel, 2000). When students have grasped the alphabetic principle, research has shown they will be able to grasp the relationships between letters and sounds, or **phonics,** which can lead to significant increases in reading and writing achievement, especially for children of poverty (National Reading Panel, 2000). With these facts in mind, highly effective teachers offer very explicit instruction on the alphabetic principle and phonics (Williams, Phillips-Birdsong, Hufnagel, Hungler, & Lundstrom, 2009).

Morphology: The Building Blocks of Meaning in Words. **Morphology** refers to breaking words apart in order to study word structures that create meaning (Athans & Devine, 2010; Carlisle, 2004). Some people mistakenly believe that a word is the smallest unit of meaning in language; however, it is not the word but rather the **morpheme** that comprises the smallest unit of meaning. Morphemes can be either free or bound. A free morpheme stands alone as a word having meaning. Words like *ball, peninsula,* and *chain* consist of a single morpheme. A bound morpheme, on the other hand, although an equally meaningful unit of language, must be connected to another morpheme. Examples include *-ocracy, -ante,* and *bio-,* as well as other prefixes and suffixes like *re-, -ed,* and *-es.* In many words, one bound morpheme attaches to another bound morpheme—for example, *bio-* and *-ology,* which together form the word *biology.* Sometimes a bound morpheme (*anti-*) connects with a free morpheme (*thesis*) to form a new word (*antithesis*). Compound words are single words created by joining two free morphemes together in various ways (e.g., *bathroom, wallpaper, deerskin, bluebird*).

Linguists also classify some morphemes as inflected or derivational. Inflected morphemes are added suffixes or meaningful word endings, such as *-s, -ed, -ing,* and *-est.* Derivational morphemes are made by adding a letter to or changing letters within a word, thereby changing the part of speech. For example, changing *rust* to *rusty* by adding a *y* to the noun *rust* changes the word to an adjective.

When children first enter preschool, they are still developing morphological understanding. Word study is critical in the early years (pre-K through second grade) and is strongly related to early word reading ability (Baumann, Edwards, Boland, Olejnik, & Kame'enui, 2003; Carlisle, 2004). Word study lays the groundwork for all elementary reading and becomes even more important through students' secondary schooling.

Syntax and Grammar: The "Rule Book" of Language. **Syntax** involves an understanding of how words are combined into larger language structures, especially sentences. Many people use the term *grammar* as nearly synonomous with *syntax,* and we will do so here for the sake of simplicity. **Grammar** is defined as a rule system for describing the structure or organization of a language. Thus, English grammar is a system of rules for describing the structure or organization of the English language. Each language has its own syntax, grammatical system, structure, or organization.

The term *grammar* may conjure up visions of learning the names of the parts of speech, whereas *syntax* connotes the ways words are strung together to communicate meaning without necessarily identifying all the parts of speech involved. Proper use of syntactic rules results in the production of grammatically acceptable phrases and sentences in speech and writing. In short, knowledge of syntax involves an understanding of the system of rules for organizing words to communicate. Using accepted word order in language is important because it relates to how meaning (comprehension) is constructed. Suppose you were to read or hear the following:

> A is saying individual the is our aloud ability our in rarely purposes respond reader the silently only skill upon our is word of called conducted reading reading it. Most by is private fluent that for element of to to use course one each to. (Chapman & Hoffman, 1977, p. 67)

Although each word can be understood in isolation, the meaning of the passage is unclear because the word order is jumbled. When correct word order is restored, meaning is easier to construct:

> The ability to respond to each individual word by saying it aloud is, of course, only one element in reading. It is a skill that the fluent reader is rarely called upon to use. Most of our reading is conducted silently for our own private purposes. (Chapman & Hoffman, 1977, p. 67)

Syntactic, or grammatical, knowledge also enables readers to predict what comes next in a sentence or phrase. For example, read the following sentence.

> Hopalong Hank is the name of my green pet _____.

Even young children will fill in the blank with a noun. Although children may not be able to state a grammatical rule that accounts for the fact that a noun follows an adjective in a phrase, they are competent enough to know that only certain kinds of words are allowed in the blank. Moffet (1983) learned through his research that by the time children enter school they have mastered basic grammar and syntax. Moffet further discovered that young children can use their basic grammar and syntax knowledge to help them identify words in reading and to select grammatically correct phrases and sentences in writing.

On the other hand, English learners (ELs) may find the syntax of English quite different from that of their primary language. As teachers, we need to be aware of this fact and clearly model for children English syntax using full sentences in our spoken language.

Semantics: Connecting Past Experiences to Reading. **Semantics** involves connecting one's background experiences, knowledge, interests, attitudes, and perspectives with spoken or written language to construct meaning (Anderson & Pearson, 1984; Kintsch & Kintsch, 2005; Rumelhart, 1980). Essentially, our total collection of prior experiences and knowledge are connected in the mind in a vast network of related concepts and events. The belief that new knowledge is connected to related ideas one already knows is known as **schema theory** (the plural of *schema* is *schemas* or *schemata*). This enormous quantity of our stored memories is perhaps best seen in the vocabulary words we know. As we encounter new experiences in life, we store this new information in our minds by connecting new words to our known words. Helping students expand their schemas is a critical role for teachers of English-only students speaking their first language (L1) and learners of English as a second language (L2) alike (Rance-Roney, 2010).

The labeling of new knowledge and experiences with words provides a shared system for language users when a message is communicated to or comprehended from someone else (Kintsch & Kintsch, 2005). Prior knowledge and experiences, or the lack thereof, can affect our understanding of language in many ways. For example, read the following passage taken from an experiment conducted by Bransford and Johnson (1972). You may have prior knowledge about the content of the text but be unable to retrieve (remember) your stored knowledge (Kintsch & Kintsch, 2005).

> If the balloons popped the sound wouldn't be able to carry since everything would be too far away from the correct floor. A closed window would also prevent the sound from carrying, since most buildings tend to be well insulated. Since the whole operation depends upon a steady flow of electricity, a break in the middle of the wire would also cause problems. Of course, the fellow could shout, but the human voice is not loud enough to carry that far. An additional problem is that a string could break on the instrument. Then there could be no accompaniment to the message. It is clear that the best situation would involve less distance. Then there would be fewer potential problems. With face to face contact, the least number of things could go wrong. (p. 719)

Did you experience difficulty in understanding the content or topic of this excerpt? If you did, you are not alone. Bransford and Johnson's (1972) experimental subjects had great difficulty connecting the content of this passage to anything they already knew. Pause for a moment and try to make a mental note of your best guess about the meaning of this passage. Then turn the page and look at the picture in Figure 2.1. Finally, go back and reread the passage.

After your first reading, were you able to recognize that the passage was a modernized version of the Romeo and Juliet serenade? Or did you think the passage was about physics or electricity? Were you thinking about someone making a phone call? Although you could understand all the language in the passage, there was not enough information provided to allow you to retrieve knowledge you had stored in your mind to comprehend its meaning. However, once you were able to retrieve the correct schema, you were able to figure out the passage's meaning.

Here's another interesting fact: When you encounter new language, your brain will often modify your existing knowledge network (schema) to "rewire itself" to accommodate new learning into permanent schema structures, referred to in science as *neuroplasticity* (Draganski et al., 2006). For example, as you read the following sentences, pause after each one and think about what you see in your mind. Then move on to the next sentence and do the same. At each point, make note of which schema or "file folder" of knowledge and experiences your brain is retrieving to construct meaning.

> John was on his way to school.
> He was terribly worried about the math lesson.
> He thought he might not be able to control the class again today.
> It was not a normal part of a janitor's duties. (Sanford & Garrod, 1981, p. 114)

Did you notice a change in your understanding of the passage as you stopped each time? Did your schema selection (i.e., the direction your comprehension took) change with each sentence:

1. From a young boy on his way to school
2. Who was worried about his math class and lesson
3. To that of a concerned teacher
4. And finally a worried janitor?

The more you know about a topic or event, the clearer a written message becomes (Pearson, Hansen, & Gordon, 1979). However, researchers have also found that if prior knowledge is *contrary* to the information being heard or read, the result may

Figure 2.1

The Romeo Scene

be decreased understanding (e.g., Alvermann, Smith, & Readence, 1985; Collins-Block & Pressley, 2002; Reutzel & Hollingsworth, 1991).

Sometimes writers purposely create an initial misunderstanding. Suppose someone told you that the world was flat rather than round, as in Tom Friedman's book (2005) titled *The World Is Flat!* You might tend to dismiss Friedman as some kind of nut for thinking the Earth is flat when you know good and well from past learning this is not true. But if you later discovered that Mr. Friedman crafted his title to grab readers' attention and to point out that twenty-first-century governments and societies must realize that we are all economically connected as never before and must adapt to this "flattening" of world economies, then your schema for a "flat" world would be changed.

Finally, one's point of view or perspective can influence what is understood from language. Goetz, Reynolds, Schallert, and Radin (1983), for example, found that people who read a test passage from the perspective of a burglar recalled very different details from those who were told to read it from the perspective of a burglary victim. It is clear, then, that our prior knowledge, experiences, and perspectives help us anticipate and interpret meaning in language. The more we experience both directly and vicariously, the more our schemas expand. And the more we use our schemas, the easier it is for us to retrieve our past knowledge and understand spoken or written language (Draganski et al., 2006).

Pragmatics: Using Language to Get What We Need.   The study of how language is used in society to satisfy the needs of human communication is called **pragmatics.** Hymes (1964) defined *pragmatics* as knowing how language works and is used in one's culture. In other words, children's and adults' language-related knowledge, habits, and behaviors are directly influenced by the culture or society in which they live and interact.

M. A. K. Halliday (1975) described three pragmatic language functions in our day-to-day lives: ideational, interpersonal, and textual. F. Smith (1977) expanded Halliday's three aspects of pragmatic language functions into ten purposes for which language may be used, as shown in Figure 2.2 and discussed in more detail later in this chapter.

As children interact with their environment and other people, they discover that language is power! They learn that they can sometimes control the actions of others through language. They learn that language can be used to get what they want and need. In short, they learn that language is a potent tool that serves a wide variety of purposes. Once children understand the many uses for oral language in their lives, they begin to also see the purposes of written language. In fact, success in reading depends very much on the degree to which the language children encounter in their

Figure 2.2

Pragmatic Language Functions

1. *Instrumental:* "I want." (Getting things and satisfying material needs.)
2. *Regulatory:* "Do as I tell you." (Controlling the attitudes, behaviors, and feelings of others.)
3. *Interactional:* "Me and you." (Getting along with others, establishing relative status.) Also, "Me against you." (Establishing separateness.)
4. *Personal:* "Here I come." (Expressing individuality, awareness of self, pride.)
5. *Heuristic:* "Tell me why." (Seeking and testing world knowledge.)
6. *Imaginative:* "Let's pretend." (Creating new worlds, making up stories, poems.)
7. *Representational:* "I've got something to tell you." (Communicating information, descriptions, expressing propositions.)
8. *Divertive:* "Enjoy this." (Puns, jokes, riddles.)
9. *Authoritative/contractual:* "How it must be." (Statutes, laws, regulations, and rules.)
10. *Perpetuating:* "How it was." (Records, histories, diaries, notes, scores.)

From "The Uses of Language" by F. Smith, 1977, *Language Arts, 54*(6), p. 640. Copyright 1977 by the National Council of Teachers of English.

early speaking and reading experiences mirror one another (Pinnell & Jaggar, 2003; Watson, 2001).

Great teachers realize that children must have experiences with quality literature, extended discussions about important topics in their reading, and opportunities to write and respond to literature for reading success (Morrow & Gambrell, 2001). It is in this setting that children begin to make the critical connections between oral and written language uses. When texts connect to children's oral language experiences, they discover that written and oral language are mirror forms of language serving similar purposes.

Dialect, or speech variations associated with various geographic regions or ethnic groups, also impact children's ability to understand and use the sounds of spoken English. Regional speech differences are reflected in word choices, as in "We are getting ready to go" versus "We are fixin' to go." Even grammatical changes can be found in dialects—regional or cultural—that reflect unique cultural expression (Kynard, 2008). For example, grammatical changes such as "He be goin'" for "He is going" might be heard in some African American communities. Thus, language variation is evidence of how language is used in various cultures and regions of the nation.

Children reared in the Midwest are not always accustomed to the way speech sounds and words are produced in the South or Northeast of the United States, and vice versa. So a child living in the Midwest who is taught by a teacher from the South might experience some difficulty in perceiving that teacher's speech sounds and understanding his or her word choice. Consequently, teachers (1) must be aware that everyone speaks in a particular dialect and (2) therefore need to develop sensitivity to the differences between their particular articulations of spoken sounds and words and those of their students.

How Do Children Develop Oral Language?

There are essentially four major views on how children gain oral language ability: (1) behaviorist, (2) innatist, (3) constructivist, and (4) social interactionist. We have found that all of these views help to explain one or more aspects of how children acquire and use oral language.

The Behaviorist View of Oral Language Development.   Behaviorists believe that oral language is learned through conditioning and shaping processes that involve a stimulus and a reward or a punishment. Recall from your study of psychology the concept of stimulus–response training, one of the principles of behaviorism. Behaviorists contend that human role models in an infant's environment provide the stimuli and responses (i.e., rewards or punishments) that shape the learning of oral language. Parents' and other caregivers' speech tends to act as the stimulus in the social/cultural speech environment. When baby imitates the sounds or speech of adult models, she receives praise and affection as rewards. Thus, the **behaviorist theory** of language development states that infants learn oral language from other human role models through a process involving stimulation/modeling, imitation, rewards, punishment, and practice.

However, behaviorist theories of language development fail to answer a number of important questions associated with children's language acquisition. For example, if a parent is hurried, inattentive, or not present when the child attempts speech, then rewards for the desired speech responses are not always provided. Thus, if baby's language learning were only motivated by rewards, speech attempts would cease where regular rewards (the parent's smile or other responses) are absent.

Another problem with the behaviorist theory of oral language acquisition centers on the fact that young children do not simply imitate other human speech. Imitation implies certain behaviors. For example, when mother says, "Baby, say 'Mama,'" baby does not imitate or echo Mama by saying, "Baby, say 'Mama.'" Even in the earliest stages of language acquisition, children are not mere echo chambers. They are processing language meaning and sorting out the relevant from the irrelevant. Behaviorist theories of language learning fail to account for this kind of selective or strategic cognitive processing.

Behaviorist language acquisition theories also do not account for words and sounds invented by infants. For example, one girl we know used to call a sandwich a "weechie" even though no one in her home called a sandwich by any such name. Another failure of behaviorist theories to fully explain oral language development is the "jargon" that often emerges between identical twins and no one else. Although behaviorist theories may explain to some extent the role of the social environment and the importance of role models in shaping children's language learning, they seem incomplete. Arguments that counter behaviorist language acquisition theories include the following (Piper, 1998):

- Examples of regression in pronouncing sounds and words previously pronounced correctly
- Evidence of novel forms of language not modeled by others
- Inconsistency of reinforcement or rewards provided
- Learning the use and meanings of abstract words
- Uniformity of language acquisition in humans
- Uniqueness of human language learning

The Innatist View of Oral Language Development.   A second view of oral language development is referred to as **innatist theory,** which holds that language learning is natural for human beings. In short, babies enter the world with a biological propensity (inclination)—an inborn device as it were—to learn language. Lenneberg (1964) refers to this human built-in device for learning language as the *language acquisition device* (LAD). Thus, the innatist theory explains to some degree how children can generate or invent language they have never heard before.

Chomsky (1974, 1979) maintained that children use the language acquisition device to create an elaborate rule system for inventing complex and interesting speech. Put another way, just as wings allow birds to fly, LAD allows infant humans to speak. Although the innatist theory provides what appears to be a believable explanation for some aspects of oral language acquisition, researchers have failed to discover supporting evidence. Menyuk (1988) wrote, "Despite the apparent logic of this position, there is still a great deal of mystery that surrounds it" (p. 34). Innatist language acquisition theories have been countered by the following observations (Piper, 1998).

- The timing of language learning varies greatly within cultures.
- Feedback from other language users affects language acquisition.
- Environment shapes the language learned and how much language is learned.

The Constructivist View of Oral Language Development.　The first **constructivist theory** of oral language development emerged from the work of Jean Piaget (1959). Piaget believed that language development is linked to cognitive development (i.e., thought processes and abilities). Even though he contended that cognition and language operate independently of each other, Piaget believed that language development is deeply rooted in the development of cognition or thinking and that concept or cognitive development precedes the development of language ability (Cox, 2002).

Cox (2002) offers the following summary of the stages of language development, using (as was the case with Piaget) her own children as examples. These stages are presented with Piaget's cognitive stages noted as well, with age ranges in parentheses.

1. *Preverbal*—Piaget's *Sensorimotor Stage* (0–2 years). Preverbal language, from birth to 6 months, is characterized by crying and babbling. Approximation of others' speech also occurs. From 12 to 18 months, children repeat one-syllable sounds, typically beginning with consonant phonemes, such as "na-na-na-na." First "words" such as *Da-da, Ma-ma,* and *bye-bye* begin to appear.

2. *Vocabulary and True Language*—Piaget's *Preoperational Stage* (2–7 years). From 18 months to 2 years of age, children become skillful at naming things in their environment, with one-word utterances called *holophrases* that communicate a complex set of needs or ideas. They then move to two-word sentences, called *telegraphic speech,* as they grow in their ability to employ very simple sentences. Children 3 to 4 years of age continue using simple sentences and also begin trying compound sentences; they understand present and past tenses, but overgeneralize sometimes (e.g., *goed* for *went*); they understand concepts like *few* and *many, first* and *second;* and they may have a speaking vocabulary of up to 1,500 words. Children at this stage are still quite egocentric and do not always use words correctly—like Rob, who after fake-coughing a few moments said, "I have a carburetor stuck in my throat!" From ages 4 to 7 years, children's sentences grow in terms of both length and complexity. They commonly use grammatically correct sentences, learn the rudiments of reading and writing, and expand their speaking vocabularies to between 3,000 and 8,000 words.

3. *Logical and Socialized Speech*—Piaget's *Concrete Operational Stage* (7–11 years). During this stage, children's speech becomes more adult-like. Language is essentially mastered, although linguistic skills continue to grow in complexity. At ages 7 and 8, children use more symbolic language, often expressing concepts (e.g., *courage, freedom, time, seasons*). From 8 to 10 years, their language becomes more flexible, and they are able to engage in abstract discussions, facilitate and nurture less developed language users, and expand ideas into lengthy discourse. Children respond to questions more logically and often use language to establish and cement relationships.

4. *Abstract Reasoning and Symbolism*—Piaget's *Formal Operations Stage* (11–15 years and beyond). At this stage, children's speech becomes, at least in function and form, indistinguishable from adult speech. As with abstract thought, some learners seem to never quite reach this level of sophistication, which is why we have inserted the phrase "and beyond" as a caveat.

Two key assertions in Piaget's constructivist theory are that (1) children move through cognitive stages at fairly predictable times and (2) external influences, such as schooling, have very little effect on their evolution. In other words, children progress through these stages according to a biologically determined timetable, and external influences (e.g., parents and teachers) have very little effect on the pace of growth. These notions are very much at odds with the social interactionist perspective.

The Social Interactionist View of Oral Language Development.   One's environment and interactions with the people in it play a critical role in the development of language according to social interactionist explanations of oral language development. **Social interactionist theory** assumes that language development is greatly influenced by physical, social, and, of course, linguistic factors (Cox, 2002). Lev Vygotsky (1986, 1990) demonstrated that adult interactions with children could not only assist in language development, but could also change the pace of language learning (a point Piaget eventually embraced in his later years).

Vygotsky assessed cognitive development in terms of how well a child could perform a specific task *in collaboration with others*. The difference between what a child can do alone and in collaboration with others is what Vygotsky called the **zone of proximal development** (ZPD). Smith (1988) describes it this way: "Everyone can do things with assistance that they cannot do alone, and what they can do with collaboration on one occasion they will be able to do independently on another" (pp. 196–197). For a ZPD to be useful, there must be a joint task that creates a learning situation for learner/expert interaction. The "expert" (who has more experience and skill doing the assigned task) can then use different strategies to help the learner succeed in the learning situation (Tharpe & Gallimore, 1988). Instead of withholding certain tasks from a child until a particular stage of cognitive development is reached, as suggested by Piaget (1955), Vygotsky (1978) argued that once the zone of proximal development is identified, teachers, parents, or more advanced peers should help a learner perform a task he or she is not capable of doing alone. With much practice and support, the learner will ultimately master the new task.

Vygotsky (1978) also explained that learners internalize language activities, like reading and writing, by going through a three-stage process. **Internalization,** as Vygotsky called it, begins with the learner observing others as they perform a language task. For example, a child who continually asks for the same book to be read aloud again and again by an experienced reader is studying what the reader is doing and learning some of reading's most basic structures. The experienced reader is **modeling** the skill. Modeling can be performed by the teacher or another student who has mastered the desired skill. The next stage of internalization begins when the learner mimics the language task, like a child pretending to read a book aloud when she is really only looking at the pictures and repeating what was read aloud to her on previous occasions. These first attempts by a novice at performing a task with support from an expert are termed **guided practice.** The third stage of internalization comes when a learner, after benefiting from a great deal of skillful instruction and guided practice, is able to perform a

Figure 2.3

Teaching Model Based on Vygotsky's Theory

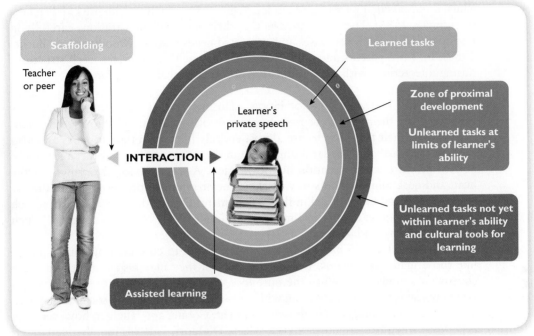

From Slavin, *Educational Psychology*, 4th ed., p. 50. © 1994 by Pearson Education, Inc. Reprinted by permission of Pearson Education, Inc.

specific reading task without further help. In teaching we refer to this final stage of learning as **independent practice.** Examples of this stage of internalization are shown in the developmental reading and writing descriptions found later in this chapter. Internalization and the zone of proximal development are depicted in Figure 2.3.

The idea that social interaction plays a significant role in developing a child's cognitive growth and language ability is extremely relevant to current trends in reading instruction. If children are immersed in reading and writing early in their schooling experience and receive support from peers and adults while they are learning, they will begin to internalize more mature reading and writing behaviors.

The Developmental Stages of Oral Language Development

Teachers need to be aware that children develop oral language in stages. Recognizing the average rates of children's oral language development allows teachers to help scaffold or structure improved language skills and assist children in reaching higher levels of knowledge. Bear in mind that oral language developmental rates can vary dramatically among children.

Parents' Baby Talk: One Way of Getting Attention.   Many parents use a special type of speech commonly called "baby talk" with their infants up to about 24 months of age (Stern & Wasserman, 1979). Characteristics of baby talk include higher pitch and special intonation patterns. Studies have shown that infants respond best to high-pitch levels and to varied rhythms in speech (Gopnik, Meltzoff, & Kuhl, 1999; Kearsley, 1973; Kessen, Levine, & Wendrich, 1979). Other research has shown that

Click on A+RISE—WIDA ELP Standard Strategies in the MyEducationLab (www.myeducationlab.com) for your course. Next, select the Strategy Card Index tab, scroll to Language and Content for grades K–5, and select the Listening and Speaking Descriptors strategy.

the ways infants react to adult speech affect the subsequent speech and behavior of their adult caretakers. In fact, adults usually use shorter speech patterns with significant periods of pausing to encourage the infant to respond (Gleason, 1989). Thus, it appears that parents and adult caregivers intuitively are intense kid watchers (Goodman, 1986). They seem to structure their speech demonstrations carefully in response to the child's responses and suspected needs (Harste, Woodward, & Burke, 1984). In short, parents and adult caregivers change their normal speech structures during interactions with their infants to encourage verbal interaction.

The First 12 Months: A Time for Hope.   During the first 2 months of life, babies cry to indicate their need to be fed, changed, or otherwise attended to in some manner. Because their tiny mouths are almost entirely filled with their tongues and also because the vocal cords are still quite high in the throat, children at this age are unable to produce much variation in vocalization. As time passes, the growth of the head and neck allows infants to vary their vocalizations to produce sounds already responded to and experienced in the environment. During this early stage of speech development, young infants also make what linguists call "vegetative sounds," such as burps, coughs, and sneezes.

From about 2 to 5 months of age, babies begin to coo, uttering sounds much like those made by pigeons. During this period, they may also begin to vary the consonant sounds attached to the pure /oo/ vowel sound typical of cooing, which typically seems to take place, along with sustained laughter, during social and speech interactions with caregivers in the environment. Cooing and laughter, however, may also occur when baby is alone or even asleep. D'Odorico (1984) has discovered that during this period, babies develop three distinct types of crying associated with three distinct needs: (1) a need for comfort, (2) a need for attention, or (3) a need for rescue from distress. Speech developments at this stage seem to provide great pleasure and even a sense of relief and encouragement for parents and caregivers.

From 6 months to 1 year of age, babies enter a period of oral language development called *vocal play* or *babbling*. This stage of growth is marked by the ability to utter single syllables containing a consonant sound followed by a prolonged vowel sound, such as "maa maa." Although many other syllables (e.g., "laa laa") may be uttered during this period of development, only a few will be retained into the next stage (e.g., "Ma-ma" and "Da-da"), primarily because their use seems to bring a quick, delighted reaction from parents or adult caregivers. It is also during this period of speech development that children begin saying single words (holophrases), sounds, or invented words to represent complete ideas (Au, Depretto, & Song, 1994; Gleason, 1989). For example, an 11-month-old may point to a picture of a cow and squeal in delight "Mooooo!" This same child may point at the sink and say, "Wa wa," indicating that he or she wants a drink of water.

From 1 to 2: By Leaps and Bounds.   Language expands rapidly during the second year of development. Children continue to approximate the speech of their parents to the point of duplicating their gestures and intonation patterns. Children in this stage continue to make hypotheses about the rules that govern language use, and they try out and refine these rules as they use language. During this year, toddlers achieve a significant linguistic milestone when they begin to put two words together. These words typically are selected from the large, open classes of nouns, verbs, and adjectives. Because these two-word utterances sound much like the condensed speech of a telegram, linguists have called this stage of speech development *telegraphic speech*. Typical utterances of the telegraphic type include "Mommy down!" or "Go potty?"

One recognizes readily how these seemingly cryptic two-word speech patterns can communicate an entire complex idea or need.

From 2 to 3: What Does It Mean When I Say No?

Oral language development continues to progress rapidly during the third year. The broken and incomplete nature of telegraphic speech begins to give way to more complex and natural forms of speaking. The use of descriptives such as adjectives and adverbs dramatically increases (Fields & Spangler, 2000; Glazer, 1989; Morrow, 2005).

One linguistic discovery made by the 2-year-old is the effect of negation. For many months the child has heard the word *no*. Although over time she has learned what "No-no" means for her behavior, she has yet to understand what *no* implies for the behavior of others. When asked, "Does baby want an ice cream cone?" she automatically responds, "No!" But when she discovers that the ice cream cone (to which she had said "No") is denied, she begins to cry. Over time, the 2-year-old learns what *no* means and how it affects the behavior of others. In a sense, children at this age begin to establish their own identity—separate from others in their environment—and the "No!" response is evidence of this. Use of the words *no* and *not* signals an important change in young children's language development.

From 3 to 4: The Why Years.

By age 3, children begin using complex sentences that include prepositions, pronouns, negatives, plurals, possessives, and interrogatives. Children at this age have a speaking vocabulary of between 1,000 and 1,500 words (Morrow, 2005). Also at this age, children begin to make analogical substitutions in their speech, meaning the overgeneralization by analogy of a language rule, which often results in using incorrect substitute words in speech. For example, a child may say, "Mom, will you put my boots on my foots?" In this case, the child has overgeneralized the rule for pluralizing nouns by adding an *-s* to the irregular noun *foot*. Analogical substitutions also occur when changing verbs to their past tense form. For example, Lee rushes into the house and yells, "Daddy, come quick. I digged up that mean bush with flowers and thorns on it!" Language "errors" such as these reveal the language rules children have been internalizing and how they go about refining their language hypotheses.

During this fourth year of oral language development, children begin to transform basic sentence structures into interrogative sentences (questions). At earlier stages, children indicate that questions are being asked by making statements ending with rising intonation patterns. Thus, questions are framed without the use of interrogatives or by transforming basic sentence structures. However, by the time the child is 3, parents have become well acquainted with the interrogative "Why?"

For statements that appear perfectly obvious to adults, the 3-year-old will typically begin a repeated line of questioning: "Why? Why? Why?" After several answers get this same response, parents realize they are trapped in a linguistic situation from which it is nearly impossible to escape with dignity. Bill Cosby once offered a simple solution that we tried on our own 3-year-old children with reasonable success: You ask "Why?" first! Regardless of the questioning nature of the 3-year-old, language development during this stage is an exciting experience for parents and caregivers.

From 4 to 6: Years of Growth and Refinement.

At 4 years of age, children seem to have acquired most of the elements of adult language (Morrow, 2001). Vocabulary and syntactical structures continue to increase in variety and depth. Children at this age possess a vocabulary of about 2,500 words, which by age 6 will have grown to 6,000 words (Clark, 1993; Johnson, 2001; Norton & Norton, 2003). Some children at age 4 or 5 continue to have trouble articulating the /r/ and /l/ sounds and the /sh/ at the ends of words, although the vast majority of children are 90 to 100 percent intelligible by age 4.

According to Seefeldt and Barbour (1986), adults find the way in which children of this age group use language imaginative and amusing. We certainly concur with these observations. For example, Cody, son of one of the authors, has provided many examples of imaginative and generative language. On one occasion, with his hard-earned money, Cody purchased several plastic clips for his belt. He could hang his flashlight and plastic tools on these clips and make believe he was a workin' man. When Cody's father saw these clips, he inquired, "Cody, what are those things on your belt?" The child responded, "Those are my *hookers*, Dad!"

Teachers also encounter creative descriptions. For example, on entering the world of school, kindergarten children often discover a genre of speech known as "toilet talk" or "curse words." One day, a young boy overheard his kindergarten teacher reprimanding some other boys for using inappropriate language. Sometime later during the day, his teacher overheard him discussing taboo words: "She means those words your daddy uses when he gets real mad!"

Understanding the development of oral language in children can be a source of increased enjoyment for parents and teachers. Knowing how children develop language helps adults recognize and appreciate the monumental achievement of learning to speak—especially when it occurs so naturally and in a space of just six short but very important years.

What Does Research Say About the Relationship Between Oral Language and Reading?

Deficits in oral language can ultimately limit a child's learning of reading and writing (Hart & Risley, 1995, 2002; National Early Literacy Panel, 2008). This is true whether the child is a first or second language learner (e.g., Biemiller, 2006; Pinnell & Jaggar, 2003; Scarborough, 2001). Language deficits also are the most common root causes for referrals to special education (Warren, 2001). Research shows that children with weak oral language abilities tend to (1) have small vocabularies characterized by lots of short words repeated often, (2) make frequent use of nonspecific words, and (3) employ fewer complex sentences and less elaboration (Biemiller, 2006; Greenhalgh & Strong, 2001; Paul, 2001; Wiig, Becker-Redding, & Semel, 1983).

Viewed from another perspective, research confirms that good readers "bring strong vocabularies and good syntactic and grammatical skills to the reading comprehension process" (Lyon, 1999, p. 10; see also Athans & Devine, 2010). We also know that early and intensive intervention with children having underdeveloped language can enhance literacy learning (Dickinson & Tabors, 2001; Warren & Yoder, 1997).

Effects of Poverty on Oral Language and Reading Development

Poverty, a condition in which individuals or entire groups do without resources (Payne, 1998), is highly correlated with underdeveloped oral language. Children born into poverty are often denied exposure to many language-growing experiences that are common to children from more affluent families, from a trip to Taco Bell or McDonald's, to participating in youth clubs, to going on summer vacations. Because the working poor often have to maintain several jobs just to make ends meet, parents frequently have little or no time to interact with their children.

The poorly developed oral language among children in poverty negatively affects their school experience. According to the 2002 report of the National Assessment of Educational Progress (NAEP) for reading, children from poverty scored significantly lower in reading proficiency than their more affluent counterparts. These children are often at greatest risk of failing in school and eventually dropping out.

In Hart and Risley's (1995, 2002) landmark research, they recorded every word spoken at home between parents and children in 42 families from various socioeconomic status (SES) backgrounds for 2½ years. These families were categorized according to SES as professional, working class, or welfare level. In comparing language interactions between professional-level (SES) parents and their children versus welfare-level parents' interactions, data revealed the following:

- Professional parents spent more than 40 minutes daily interacting with their young children whereas welfare parents spent 15 minutes each day.
- Professional-level parents verbally responded to their children 250 times per hour, as compared to welfare-level parents, who verbally responded 50 times per hour.
- Professional-level parents approved and encouraged their children's actions an average of 40 times per hour. Welfare-level parents approved and encouraged their children's actions an average of four times per hour.
- In their interactions, professional families usually spoke more than 3,000 words per hour as compared to 500 words per hour in welfare homes.
- Access to oral language in both quantity and quality was so consistent within levels that the differences in children's language experience were enormous by age 3.

Results showed that children in professional families experience 42 million words compared to 26 million words for children in working-class families and only 13 million words for welfare family children. In professional families, the extraordinary volume of verbal exchanges and exposure to many different words—greater richness of nouns, modifiers and past-tense verbs—suggest a language culture focusing on symbols and analytic problem solving. In welfare families, the fewer verbal exchanges focused more on the teaching of socially acceptable behavior: obedience, politeness, and conformity. The volume of early oral language interactions between parents and children and particularly the language interactions of parents and children with regard to the books parents read to or with their children are major predictors of later reading success (Dickinson & Tabors, 2001; National Early Literacy Panel, 2008; Watson, 2001).

The implications from these research findings seem clear. Children born into high poverty circumstances need early, intensive, and systematic language development. The earlier the better. It is not that children from poverty are less able to learn; rather it is a matter of exposure to conversations (not one-way directives) with others using more and more sophisticated words. As teachers of reading we must find ways to infuse new language into our curricula with dialogue and instructional conversations.

English Learners and Vocabulary Development

Teaching language-minority students to read and write well in English is an important and urgent challenge in our nation's schools. In the spring of 2002, the Institute of Education Sciences selected a panel of experts to review the research on ways to improve literacy learning for English learners (ELs). After four years of study, their work was published in a volume entitled *Developing Literacy in Second-Language Learners: Report of the National Literacy Panel on Language-Minority Children and Youth* (August & Shanahan, 2006). As they began their work, the magnitude of need in the United States was illuminated by the following statistics.

- A large and growing number of students came from homes where English was not the primary language. In 1979, there were 6 million language-minority students; by 1999, this number had more than doubled to 14 million students.
- Most language-minority students were not faring well in U.S. schools. For the 41 states reporting, only 18.7 percent of English-language learners scored above the state-established norm for reading comprehension.
- Whereas 10 percent of students who spoke English at home failed to complete high school, the percentage was three times higher (31%) for language-minority students who spoke English and five times higher (51%) for language-minority students who spoke English with difficulty. (August & Shanahan, 2006, p. 1)

ELs who experience slow vocabulary development often develop problems in reading comprehension at earlier grade level than their English-only peers and are more at risk of being diagnosed incorrectly as learning disabled (August, Branum-Martin, Cardenas-Hagan, & Francis, 2009; August, Carlo, Dressler, & Snow, 2005). Thus, it is very important indeed for ELs to receive early oral vocabulary development in English to lay the foundation for later reading and writing development.

It is almost surprising that a study by Diane August and her colleagues (2006) suggests that for bilingual students to become or stay proficient in English, parental use of English in the home is not required. This may be due to English learners having the benefit of immersion at home in the first language, while at school and in the larger community they are immersed in English.

There is a growing body of research suggesting strategies for helping ELs gain robust oral vocabularies. Curriculums must be carefully designed by school districts and refined by knowledgeable teachers in the classroom. Among the design concerns for developers are the following:

- Helping ELs identify high-utility words in their native language that are similar in English
- Ensuring that ELs know the meanings of basic words
- Providing sufficient review with practice and reinforcement for new words

In early work by August and Pease-Alvarez (1996) at the National Center for Research on Cultural Diversity and Second Language Learning, they were able to identify several attributes of effective programs serving English learners. These factors still seem particularly valid in light of their congruence with findings by the National Early Literacy Panel (2008). The researchers hasten to add that these attributes should be seen more as a framework for constructing and evaluating programs for ELs, rather than as a checklist.

1. A core curriculum for all students that is aligned with rigorous content standards
2. Rich academic programming consistent with rigorous content standards
3. Equal access to high-quality learning resources
4. A school curriculum designed to accommodate a range of abilities, knowledge, skills, and first- and second-language proficiencies
5. A schoolwide curriculum inclusive of other cultures and languages

Oral Language Is the "Great Predictor"

In 2010 the latest *Nation's Report Card* was released by the U.S. Department of Education (National Center for Education Statistics, 2010). Conducted as part of the ongoing National Assessment of Educational Progress, this report examines how well school children have progressed in reading achievement since 1999. In short, the results are uninspiring, if not dismal. Over the previous decade almost no literacy improvement has been registered in spite of billions of taxpayer dollars invested nationally in No Child Left Behind and local school district initiatives.

We seem to have hit a glass ceiling of sorts in reading development in the United States. For example, in fourth grade only 33 percent of children are reading at the Proficient level (on grade level) or higher. That statistic is mirrored in eighth grade with only 32 percent reading on grade level or higher. Although there are many possible causes for this ceiling effect one factor seems to be at the heart of many of our literacy issues—oral language development, or the lack thereof.

Oral language is the "great predictor" of reading and other academic skill development. Children who spend their early years participating in a good deal of rich dialogue with parents, older siblings, and daycare professionals typically grow expansive vocabularies (Hoff-Ginsberg, 1991, 2006; Pancsofar & Vernon-Feagans, 2006). Vocabulary expansion is sometimes measured by the number of complex words learned and mean length of utterance (MLU)—the average number of words spoken in a statement.

For children growing up in poverty circumstances as well as children in low-interaction homes, oral language grows much more slowly. Hart and Risley (1995), whose research we highlighted earlier, found that the "vocabulary gap" for children living in poverty begins by age 3. In low-interaction homes, children acquire only two new words per day compared to children in average-interaction homes, who gain five words per day—more than double. And children living in high-interaction homes gain a whopping nine words per day! The advantage for children growing up in verbally interactive homes continues throughout schooling such that high-knowledge third graders typically have vocabularies about equal to the lowest-performing twelfth graders (Hart & Risley, 1995).

Teachers *Can* Make a Difference

The good news is that teachers have the opportunity to make a positive difference for children coming to school with inadequate oral language vocabularies. Through careful language assessment and responsive evidence-based instruction delivered in a conversation-rich classroom environment, even the most language-deprived children can grow their vocabularies exponentially. Teachers can lay a proper foundation for helping all children become proficient readers and writers.

●●●
IRA Standards for Reading Professionals: Standard 3, Elements 3.1, 3.2, 3.3

Common Core Standards: Speaking and Listening: K–5, Comprehension and Collaboration (items 1–3), Presentation of Knowledge and Ideas (items 4–6); Speaking and Listening: Grades 6–12, Comprehension and Collaboration (items 1–3), Presentation of Knowledge and Ideas (items 4–6)

Response to Intervention: Assessment

Classroom Assessment

Assessing Children's Oral Language Development and Use

Oral language assessment can be a challenging undertaking because, as Walter Loban (1976) once said, "no published tests measure power over the living language, the spoken word" (p. 1). What part of oral language should one assess? Are any of the following worthwhile indicators to measure?

- The breadth and depth of children's oral language vocabularies
- Each child's mean length of utterance (MLU)
- Children's ability to retell stories
- Children's use of language in classrooms and on the playground
- Children's acquisition of the language structures previously described in this chapter
- Results of using procedures for English learners in English only or also in their primary language

The answer to this set of possibilities is that all are worthwhile measures. Realistically, however, teachers rarely have the time or resources necessary to engage in all of these types of oral language assessment. Many currently published oral language tests are expensive and time-consuming. On the other hand, teachers can and should assess children's oral language as part of the everyday classroom environment (Smith, 2001).

To help you with the assessment process, we recommend two free and widely available oral language assessment tools we find useful. A teacher using these two instruments can quickly gauge children's expressive language development.

- Teacher Rating of Oral Language and Literacy (TROLL). This tool allows teachers to simultaneously assess children's expressive (spoken) oral language along with their early reading and writing development.
- Get It, Got It, Go!—Picture Naming Test. This is a reliable and valid assessment of children's expressive (spoken) oral language.

We also favor a third instrument, the Oral Language Acquisition Inventory (OLAI), which can be used to assess children's acquisition of oral language structures and components (Gentile, 2003). In the next few pages we describe these useful tools. Before concluding Pillar 2: Classroom Assessment for this chapter, we offer a final "rule of thumb" assessment for quickly assessing students' mean length of utterance (MLU) as another indicator of oral language.

Teacher Rating of Oral Language and Literacy (TROLL)

Click on A+RISE—WIDA ELP Standard Strategies in the MyEducationLab (www.myeducationlab.com) for your course. Next, select the Strategy Card Index tab, scroll to Classroom Assessments for grades K–5, and select the Alternative ELL Assessments: Introduction strategy.

As we have seen, children must develop strong oral language skills to learn to read and write effectively (Shanahan, 2006). According to Dickinson, McCabe, and Sprague (2003), the TROLL rating system measures skills critical to speaking and listening in today's classrooms. The TROLL can be used to track children's progress in language and literacy development, to inform curriculum, and to encourage communication between parents and teachers. Oral language skills relevant to later literacy development include the ability to tell stories, to use talk while pretending during play, and to vary vocabulary usage (Dickinson & Tabors, 2001).

The TROLL assessment compares favorably to formal and more costly oral language assessments such as the well-established Peabody Picture Vocabulary Test (PPVT-III), a measure of receptive (listening) vocabulary. In about 5 minutes and with no special training, teachers themselves can index what trained researchers would spend roughly 25 to 30 minutes per child assessing (Dickinson, McCabe, & Sprague, 2003).

To administer the TROLL you will need a copy of the rating form (see Figure 2.4) for each student you plan to observe. Although no formal training is required to

Figure 2.4

Teacher Rating of Oral Language and Literacy (TROLL)

LANGUAGE USE

1. How would you describe this child's willingness to start a conversation with adults and peers and to continue trying to communicate when he or she is not understood on the first attempt? Select the statement that best describes how hard the child works to be understood by others.

1	2	3	4
Child almost never begins a conversation with peers or the teacher and never keeps trying if unsuccessful at first.	Child sometimes begins conversation with either peers or the teacher. If initial efforts fail, he or she often gives up quickly.	Child begins conversations with both peers and teachers on occasion. If initial efforts fail, he or she will sometimes keep trying.	Child begins conversations with both peers and teachers. If initial efforts fail, he or she will work hard to be understood.

2. How well does the child communicate personal experiences in a clear and logical way? Assign the score that best describes this child when he or she is attempting to tell an adult about events that happened at home or some other place where you were not present.

1	2	3	4
Child is very tentative and offers only a few words, requires you to ask questions, has difficulty responding to questions you ask.	Child offers some information, but information needed to really understand the event is missing (e.g., where or when it happened, who was present, the sequence of what happened).	Child offers information and sometimes includes the necessary information to understand the event fully.	Child freely offers information and tells experiences in a way that is nearly always complete, well sequenced, and comprehensible.

3. How would you describe this child's pattern of asking questions about topics that interest him or her (e.g., why things happen, why people act the way they do)? Assign the score that best describes the child's approach to displaying curiosity by asking adults questions.

1	2	3	4
To your knowledge, the child has never asked an adult a question reflecting curiosity about why things happen or why people do things.	On a few occasions the child has asked adults some questions. The discussion that resulted was brief and limited in depth.	On several occasions the child has asked interesting questions. On occasion these have led to an interesting conversation.	Child often asks adults questions reflecting curiosity. These often lead to interesting, extended conversations.

4. How would you describe this child's use of talk while pretending in the house area or when playing with blocks? Consider the child's use of talk with peers to start pretending and to carry it out. Assign the score that best applies.

1	2	3	4
Child rarely or never engages in pretend play or else never talks while pretending.	On occasion the child engages in pretending that includes some talk. Talk is brief, may only be used when starting the play, and is of limited importance to the ongoing play activity.	Child engages in pretending often and conversations are sometimes important to the play. On occasion child engages in some back-and-forth pretend dialogue with another child.	Child often talks in elaborate ways while pretending. Conversations that are carried out "in role" are common and are an important part of the play. Child sometimes steps out of pretend play to give directions to another.

5. How would you describe the child's ability to recognize and produce rhymes?

1	2	3	4
Child cannot say if two words rhyme and cannot produce a rhyme when given examples (e.g., *rat, cat*).	Child occasionally produces or identifies rhymes when given help.	Child spontaneously produces rhymes and can sometimes tell when word pairs rhyme.	Child spontaneously rhymes words of more than one syllable and always identifies whether words rhyme.

6. How often does child use a varied vocabulary or try out new words (e.g., heard in stories or from teacher)?

1	2	3	4
Never	Rarely	Sometimes	Often

continued

Figure 2.4

Continued

7. When child speaks to adults other than you or the teaching assistant, is he or she understandable?

1	2	3	4
Never	Rarely	Sometimes	Often

8. How often does child express curiosity about how and why things happen?

1	2	3	4
Never	Rarely	Sometimes	Often

Language Use Subtotal (   )

READING

9. How often does child like to hear books read in the full group?

1	2	3	4
Never	Rarely	Sometimes	Often

10. How often does child attend to stories read in the full group or small groups and react in a way that indicates comprehension?

1	2	3	4
Never	Rarely	Sometimes	Often

11. Is child able to read storybooks on his or her own?

1	2	3	4
Does not pretend to read books	Pretends to read	Pretends to read and reads some words	Reads the written words

12. How often does child remember the storyline or characters in books that he or she heard before either at home or in class?

1	2	3	4
Never	Rarely	Sometimes	Often

13. How often does child look at or read books alone or with friends?

1	2	3	4
Never	Rarely	Sometimes	Often

14. Can child recognize letters? (Choose one answer.)

1	2	3	4
None of the letters of the alphabet	Some of them (up to 10)	Most of them (up to 20)	All of them

15. Does child recognize his or her own first name in print?

1	2
No	Yes

16. Does child recognize other names?

1	2	3	4
No	One or two	A few (up to four or five)	Several (six or more)

17. Can child read any other words?

I	2	3	4
No	One or two	A few (up to four or five)	Several (six or more)

18. Does child have a beginning understanding of the relationship between sounds and letters (e.g., the letter b makes a buh sound)

I	2	3	4
No	One or two	A few (up to four or five)	Several (six or more)

19. Can child sound out words that he or she has not read before?

I	2	3	4
No	Once or twice	One-syllable words often	Many words

Reading Subtotal (   )

WRITING

20. What does child's writing look like?

I	2	3	4
Only draws or scribbles	Some letter-like marks	Many conventional letters	Conventional letters and words

21. How often does child like to write or pretend to write?

I	2	3	4
Never	Rarely	Sometimes	Often

22. Can child write his or her first name, even if some of the letters are backward?

I	2	3	4
Never	Rarely	Sometimes	Often

23. Does child write other names or real words?

I	2	3	4
No	One or two	A few (up to four or five)	Several (six or more)

24. How often does child write signs or labels?

I	2	3	4
Never	Rarely	Sometimes	Often

25. Does child write stories, songs, poems, or lists?

I	2	3	4
Never	Rarely	Sometimes	Often

Writing Subtotal (   )

Writing Subtotal	( ) (out of 24 possible)
Oral Language Subtotal	( ) (out of 32 possible)
Reading Subtotal	( ) (out of 42 possible)
Total TROLL Score	( ) (out of 98 possible)

use the TROLL instrument, it is most effective if teachers know about how language and literacy develops. The TROLL requires only 5 to 10 minutes of observation per child and need not disrupt classroom activities.

You can use information yielded by the TROLL to inform your teaching. The instrument identifies children who show evidence of serious oral language developmental delays and those who may need formal assessment by speech professionals, as well as children who are showing high levels of literacy development and could benefit from additional challenges. By completing the TROLL several times over the course of a year, you can track the progress of all your students' oral language development.

Finally, you can combine results for all your students to determine which students need additional oral language experiences and which are in need of more systematic instruction. For example, if all of your students score relatively low on asking questions, you will want to begin providing numerous opportunities to listen and ask questions during the daily routine in your classroom.

Get It, Got It, Go!—Picture-Naming Test

The Get It, Got It, Go! Individual Growth and Development Indicators (IGDI) are a set of several standardized, individually administered measures of early language and literacy development. The Picture-Naming Test (PN) was specifically designed to assess children's expressive (speaking) language development at ages 3 to 5 by asking them to look at picture cards drawn from their home, classroom, and community environments. An example can be found in Figure 2.5. Throughout this test, children are directed to look at pictures and name each.

A Get It, Got It, Go! free data reporting service is also available on the Internet, but users must enter their own data. Using this Internet-based system, teachers can enter assessment data directly into the Get It, Got It, Go! database and generate class reports as often as desired. However, the Picture Naming Test has not yet become available in Spanish. Missal and McConnell (2004) report reliability and validity data for the IGDI Picture Naming test that show a strong correlation with the Peabody Expressive Vocabulary Test, a standard oral language assessment tool widely accepted and used by school psychologists. Free Picture Naming Test directions, picture cards, and scoring forms are all available on the Internet at http://ggg.umn.edu. Directions for administration of the Picture Naming Test are shown in Figure 2.6.

The Oral Language Acquisition Inventory (OLAI)

The Oral Language Acquisition Inventory (OLAI), the third oral language assessment instrument we discuss, is a commercially available test developed to provide teachers key information to help English learners and children of poverty achieve oral language proficiency and literacy. The pre-K–3 version of the OLAI was constructed after analyzing nearly 2,000 oral dictations by 60 first-grade children during their Reading Recovery lessons. The common sentence structures drawn from sampling these oral dictations included (1) simple sentences, (2) sentences containing prepositional phrases, (3) sentences containing two phrases or clauses linked by a conjunction,

Figure 2.5

Sample Card from the Picture Naming Test: Get It, Got It, Go!

Front

Back

fish

From the Center of Early Education and Development, University of Minnesota. Reprinted with permission.

Figure 2.6

Directions for Administration of the Picture Naming Test

Remember
- This is a timed, 1-minute task. Be sure to use your stopwatch!
- Shuffle cards prior to each administration.
- Separate correctly named pictures into one pile and incorrectly named or skipped pictures into another pile.
- Follow directions below *exactly* as written.
- Read aloud all words in bold.

Standardized Procedure
1. Say, "**Now we're going to look at some other pictures. This time, name them as fast as you can!**"
2. Start the stopwatch and immediately show the first card to the child.
3. If the child does not respond within 3 seconds, point to the picture and say: "**Do you know what that is?**" or "**What's that?**"
4. If the child still does not respond within an additional 2 seconds, show the next card.
5. As soon as the child names a picture, show the next card.
6. After *1 minute,* STOP showing cards to the child. Record the total number of correctly named pictures on the appropriate form.

From the Center of Early Education and Development, University of Minnesota. Reprinted with permission.

(4) sentences containing two phrases or clauses linked by a relative pronoun, and (5) sentences containing two phrases or clauses linked by an adverb.

The Oral Language Acquisition Inventory is an informal repeated measure assessment that "provides teachers, in a short period of time, information related to the most common language structures children control in their expressive speech. It helps identify stages of linguistic development for instruction" (p. vi). The inventory is published by Dominie Press, Inc., and can be found at the following Web address: http://plgcatalog.pearson.com. Test materials include an accompanying curriculum guide for teachers—the *Pre-K–3 Oracy Instructional Guide*—that features oral language experiences and instruction related to strengths and weaknesses revealed by administration of the inventory.

A "Rule of Thumb" for Determining Children's Mean Length of Utterance (MLU)

Children's **mean length of utterance** (**MLU**) refers to the average number of words spoken in a verbal statement. MLU has been studied for many years by researchers worldwide as a predictor of later language development (e.g., Murray, 1990; Peterson, Carta, & Greenwood, 2005; Saaristo-Helin, 2009). Although researchers have sophisticated ways of measuring MLU, Kathleen Cooter (2006) suggests a simple "rule of thumb" method teachers can use to decide whether classroom interventions are needed to expand students' oral language. Based on the work of Murray (1990) and Peterson and colleagues (2005), the rule of thumb for gauging MLU can be condensed into the following equation:

Age = MLU

Thus, a 4-year-old should normally produce statements averaging four words or more. An 8-year-old should speak in statements averaging eight or more words, and so on. In the Pillar 3 section, we share simple but effective ways of expanding students' MLU through oral language activities. In so doing you will discover reciprocal benefits in language learning, especially in writing development.

Evidence-Based Teaching Practices

Principles of Effective Oral Language Instruction

●●●

IRA Standards for Reading Professionals: Standard 2, Elements 2.1, 2.2, 2.3; Standard 4, Elements 4.1, 4.2, 4.3; Standard 5, Elements 5.1, 5.2, 5.3

Common Core Standards: Speaking and Listening: K–5, Comprehension and Collaboration (items 1–3), Presentation of Knowledge and Ideas (items 4–6); Speaking and Listening: Grades 6–12, Comprehension and Collaboration (items 1–3), Presentation of Knowledge and Ideas (items 4–6)

Response to Intervention: Instruction, Responsive Teaching and Differentiation, Systemic and Comprehensive Approaches

Oral language knowledge is directly related to reading development and is the primary tool for learning. Nevertheless it continues to be practically ignored in the elementary school curriculum (Pinnell & Jaggar, 2003). Teachers must provide oral language instruction at all levels, and a research-based framework for oral language instruction is urgently needed. However, we have found very little research available for guiding the development of a curricular framework for effective oral language instruction. So what are we to do?

In the absence of a strong research base to support oral language curriculum development, we have taken as our guide the language instructional framework proposed by Dutro and Moran (2003), comprising three interrelated components:

1. Language functions
2. Forms of language
3. Language fluency

Language functions may be best defined as real-world and classroom-based oral language practice. Table 2.2 summarizes how pragmatics (the study of language in use) forms the basis of the oral language instruction conceptual framework.

Children also need oral language instruction that focuses attention on the **forms of language,** which Dutro and Moran (2003) identify as vocabulary, verb tense, parts of speech, and sentence structure. As stated earlier in this chapter, the teacher's knowledge of the components of language strongly influences children's oral language development. Just as an artist must understand how various paints and painting surfaces function to create an appealing image, so must a teacher understand the way English works in its various forms (Fillmore & Snow, 2000; Moats, 2000; Snow, Griffin, & Burns, 2005). Teachers must also understand the general sequence of how children acquire oral language. Knowledge of words that are both rich and varied is critical to developing a child's language proficiency and to later reading and writing success (Dutro & Moran, 2003).

Language fluency is defined by Dutro and Moran as varying the ways oral language can be used. For example, one reads aloud a folktale in a different way than a math story problem. Being able to use oral language in different ways certainly takes training and practice. Therefore, children need to experience a wide range of settings, purposes, and tasks for developing fluent oral language, such as understanding the different functions of conversational and academic language, for example. For this reason, supportive elementary classrooms provide a wide range of oral language practice and performance activities to teach, use, and refine children's oral language functions and forms. One example is **talking protocols** (Cooter & Cooter, in press),

Table 2.2

A Pragmatics-Based Conceptual Framework for Oral Language Instruction

Pragmatic Category	Function Served	Oral Language Instruction Strategies and Activities
Instrumental	I want; I need.	Dramatic play: "House," "Store," "Hospital" Interviews
Regulatory	Do as I tell you!	Simon Says Copy Cat
Interactional	Let's talk together.	Telephone conversations Face-to-face conversations
Personal	It's all about me.	Introductions Me Box Me Book Show and Tell
Heuristic	Tell me why?	Persuasion Discussions Debates
Imaginative	Let's pretend . . .	Dramatization Puppetry Storytelling Wordless picture books
Representational	Let me tell you how to . . .	Treasure hunt Following directions
Divertive	That's funny!	Jokes Riddles Singing songs
Authoritative	This is how it has to be!	Following the rules Role play justice system
Perpetuating	Let me tell you about how it used to be.	Pick a photograph Memorable moments

in which students are taught how to "use their words" more effectively in commonplace situations ("This is how I say it . . . Now you say it").

We believe Dutro and Moran's (2003) framework for oral language instruction is theoretically consistent and defensible for two reasons. First, the functions or pragmatics of language reflect the real purposes for which human beings learn and use language in their daily lives. Second, the demand for children to understand increasingly complex forms of language increases as they progress through the grades and largely determines their later academic success. The question becomes how to enhance children's oral language learning.

Promoting Oral Language Learning with Instructional Conversations

Elementary schools and classrooms should offer ample opportunities for real conversations. Unlike classrooms of old that saw children sitting silently in rows doing

A+RISE

Click on A+RISE—WIDA ELP Standard Strategies in the MyEducationLab (www.myeducationlab.com) for your course. Next, select the Strategy Card Index tab, scroll to Language and Content for grades K–5, and select the Language Acquisition and Content Knowledge strategy.

seatwork, twenty-first-century classrooms are buzzing with activity and productive oral language is encouraged. As K. S. Cooter (2006) asserts, "*Learning* is noisy, *death* is silent!" So, you ask, how do you tell the difference between productive conversations and activity versus chaos?

Roland Tharp and his colleagues at the Center for Research on Education, Diversity, and Excellence (CREDE) describe five standards for effective pedagogy (i.e., teaching and learning) (CREDE, 2010). They were developed by teachers and researchers interested in helping "students at risk of educational failure due to cultural, language, racial, geographic, or economic factors . . . [but] are effective with both majority and minority students in K–16 classrooms across subject matters, curricula, cultures, and language groups" (CREDE, 2010, p. 1).

The fifth CREDE standard, "Emphasizing Dialogue over Lectures," offers insights into the thinking behind productive instructional conversations and ways teachers can achieve them. **Instructional conversations** (CREDE, 2010) include the following characteristics:

- They involve teacher–student dialogue instead of lecture.
- They are especially focused on key areas like math, science, and social studies.
- They are explicitly goal directed.
- They are typically conducted in small-group discussions.

Several indicators of instructional conversation offered by CREDE to help teachers better understand what they may do to promote these exchanges are shown in Figure 2.7.

At the heart of instructional conversations (IC) is the understanding that all learning is social. When you think about it, all learning is interactive and uses language—both in spoken (with people) and written forms (with text). Of course, the essential part of IC is listening (Bakhtin, 1982).

Figure 2.7

CREDE Indicators of Instructional Conversation

The teacher:
- Arranges the classroom to accommodate conversation between the teacher and a small group of students on a regular and frequent basis
- Has a clear academic goal that guides conversation with students
- Ensures that student talk occurs at higher rates than teacher talk
- Guides conversation to include students' views, judgments, and rationales using text evidence and other substantive support
- Ensures that all students are included in the conversation according to their preferences
- Listens carefully to assess levels of students' understanding
- Assists students' learning throughout the conversation by questioning, restating, praising, encouraging, and so on
- Guides the students to prepare a product that indicates the instructional conversation's goal was achieved

From *The Five Standards for Effective Pedagogy*. Reprinted by permission of the Center for Research on Education, Diversity and Excellence (CREDE). Available at http://credeberkeleyedu/standards/standards.html

Oral Language Instructional Strategies

Perhaps the most important question elementary teachers ask us is "How do we *teach* listening and speaking vocabulary?" In the next section, we present key strategies and activities for enhancing children's oral language development using a pragmatics-based conceptual framework. We begin with instructional strategies focused on instrumental uses of oral language.

Instrumental Oral Language Instruction: Interviews

Recall that the instrumental function of language relates to meeting personal needs, which usually involves requesting information or services from others. Interviewing is an engaging oral language activity that helps children meet personal needs by refining their ability to ask questions and make requests of others (Tompkins, 2011), either in formal or informal formats. During informal interviews, children ask questions and make requests of others in day-to-day classroom settings. Informal interviews might be conducted during the first week of school with students working as partners to interview each other. The interview can be modeled initially by the teacher in the large group, asking questions such as the following:

What is your name?

What is your favorite food?

What is your favorite game or sport?

What do you like to do for fun?

What do you want to be when you grow up?

If you could go anywhere in the world, where would you go?

An effective way to introduce children to formal interviewing in the intermediate years is to share with them videos of recorded interviews or to have them watch real-time interviews on television. Discuss with children the purpose of the interview and the kinds of questions that were asked. Point out that good interview questions require more than a yes or no response and that effective questions prompt people to give information, state their opinions, and express their feelings.

Children should be taught how to plan and conduct effective formal interviews through teacher modeling of the process. First, an interview time and location should be arranged that is convenient for the interviewee and free from distractions. The types and sequence of questions to be asked should be carefully planned in a brainstorming process modeled by the teacher. Questions selected for the interview can be written on 3 × 5 note cards, which can be ordered and reordered until an effective sequence is achieved.

Next, the teacher should model how to conduct the actual interview. The school principal or a community member might be invited to class to act as the interviewee. Students should learn how to greet the person being interviewed, how to properly introduce themselves, and how to request permission to take notes or record the interview on video or audio. They should be taught how to politely and respectfully respond to their interviewee's answers. The teacher should also model how to end the interview by thanking the interviewee.

A natural follow-up to the formal interview activity is to have students share the results of their interviews with an audience. They might be invited to deliver an oral

Figure 2.8

Rule of Five

report about the interview to the class or to record their report on video for playback to the class at a later time.

Teaching children interviewing skills helps them develop their ability to ask good questions and listen for answers. These basic skills are essential to obtaining information or services they might need.

The Rule of Five.   In all language development dialogues, it is good to remind students that when they are the "interviewee" they have the responsibility when called on to respond in full sentences. Some teachers like to implement the **rule of five** (Cooter & Cooter, in press) to challenge students to speak in ever-increasing and complex statements. The rule of five simply states, "I speak in complete sentences." Sometimes a graphic is printed on large poster board and laminated with a giant hand having each of the words "I speak in complete sentences" written on a finger (see Figure 2.8). At Getwell Elementary School in Memphis, Tennessee, the principal and staff painted a similar graphic on several of their hallway walls with the inscription "We speak in complete sentences" as a reminder to everyone in the building to use complete statements. Reportedly their writing scores on the state test increased dramatically in just 1 year as a result of their students thinking, speaking, and writing in complete sentences.

Regulatory Oral Language Instruction: Giving and Following Commands

You will recall from earlier in this chapter that the regulatory language function focuses on using language to manage the behavior of others. Two classic and engaging activities that provide experience with the regulatory functions of oral language are "Simon Says" and "Copycat."

In playing "Simon Says," children learn both the receptive and expressive facets of regulatory oral language. As Simon, children learn to give commands to others. As participants in the game, they learn to listen and follow commands. For this activity, someone is chosen to be Simon, and the remaining players are the recipients of Simon's commands. The game has two simple rules: (1) If Simon gives a command prefaced by "Simon says," players are to follow the command, but (2) if Simon gives a command without first saying "Simon says," players should *not* follow the command. For example, if Simon says, "Jump up and down," players would do nothing. On the other hand, if Simon says, "Simon says, 'Touch your nose,'" players would touch their noses. Participants are eliminated from the game when they do not listen carefully to what Simon says. The last person remaining in a round becomes Simon in the next round.

In the game "Copycat," players are to say exactly—or copy—what the "top cat" says. Children can be asked to copycat a word, a phrase, a sentence, or several connected sentences. This activity usually begins with the teacher in the role of "top cat" for the first few minutes of play, after which the teacher chooses a student to take over. As the game progresses, the role of "top cat" is assumed by each player.

Both of these oral language activities help children develop skills in awareness, structure, and use of regulatory words, phrases, and connected language.

Interactional Oral Language Instruction: "Phone" and Small-Group Conversations

The interactional language function focuses on using oral language to talk or interact with others. The activity we call "Phone" requires two battery-operated telephones (which can be purchased at toy stores and often resemble cellular phones). It is helpful if the teacher develops a series of direction cards that give examples of phone calls for different purposes. For example, one card might require the student to make a phone call to tell his or her parent about a school event. One student plays the role of the student; a second student plays the role of the parent. Another card might direct the student to call a classmate to invite him or her to a birthday party. Other possible phone conversations in the elementary classroom are shown in the following partial list of ideas:

Ordering pizza

Reporting a fire to the fire station

Arranging a party at a local bowling alley

Informing the police about an escaped boa constrictor in your backyard

Inviting a friend to come over to watch a DVD or video

Calling a grandparent who lives far away

Like other oral language instructional activities, phone conversations are most successful when initially modeled by the teacher and several students. After demonstrating a few phone conversations focusing on telephone etiquette, the teacher can invite students to practice conversations with their classmates. Initial guided practice should be supervised by the teacher; later, students can work independently. Throughout their practice on the telephone, students can be encouraged to learn how to begin and end conversations, how to respond politely, and how to listen actively.

Children also learn to use oral language effectively when they have guidance and support while engaging in small-group conversations. Such conversations usually begin with someone asking a question or making a comment. Responses to the initial question or comment follow, with members of the conversational group taking turns asking other questions or expanding on the comments of others. Again, children should be taught the skills of polite, active listening and respectful responding. They should also learn that good conversations do not focus on only one of the speakers or put others down.

Conflict in conversations is inevitable, and students need to learn how to resolve such conflict peacefully. The teacher might model how people can agree to disagree with one another or how humor can "defuse" a tense conversational situation. Students also need to be taught acceptable ways to end a small-group conversation, perhaps by asking questions such as "Is that about it?" or "What do you think: Have we said all we can on this?"

The following list of prompts shows a few of the possibilities for small-group conversations:

Talking about characters in a book

Sharing what students like to do for fun after school

Reviewing what students have learned today in school

Examining current events in the news or on TV

Planning what students will do during recess time that day

Discussing the lunch menu and students' favorite foods

Personal Oral Language Instruction: "About Me!"

The personal language function focuses on using oral language to tell others about oneself and one's interests. A daily time set aside in many classrooms to use oral language for personal reasons is found in the time-honored activity called "Show and Tell." Children bring favorite objects to school and tell their classmates what the object is, how they obtained it, why they like it, and what they do with it. Although some teachers may think of this daily ritual as "Bring and Brag," "Show and Tell" daily time is ideal for bridging the home and school cultures. Here again, teacher modeling is paramount in teaching students to use language to share what they bring to class and to listen and respond appropriately. "Show and Tell" guidelines for speakers and listeners might include the following:

Speakers

Tell us about what you brought today.

Tell us how or where you got it.

Tell us why it is important to you.

Tell us what you do with it.

Tell us about one of the experiences you've had with it.

Listeners

Listen.

Pay attention.

Ask questions.

Thank the speaker for sharing.

Say something nice about the speaker or his or her presentation.

As an alternative to "Show and Tell," students might create and share a "Me Box." Each day a child is given a decorated "Me Box" to take home and bring back the next day. The outside of the "Me Box" has clear acrylic picture frames on all four sides, along with pictures from home representing "When I Was Little," "My Name," "My Family," and "My Favorite Thing to Do." Inside the "Me Box," students should place no more than six meaningful pictures or objects they want to share with the class. A student sharing his or her "Me Box" with the class begins by discussing the outside of the box and then proceeds to the objects and pictures inside. The rules for sharing are very similar to those for speaker and listener during "Show and Tell." Children enjoy telling others about who they are and what they like, and they appreciate having their classmates express interest. With both "Show and Tell" and the "Me Box," children have daily opportunities to share information about who they are in a personal way with the teacher and their peers in the classroom.

Heuristic Oral Language Instruction: Explaining and Convincing

The heuristic language function focuses on using oral language to debate, explain, and convince. The ability to use oral language to persuade others is a critical language function. Two oral language activities well suited to supporting its development are debates and TV commercials.

Debates are most engaging when children are enthused about a current issue. When children participate in debates, they learn how to use oral language to articulate their points of view and persuade others. In debates, students in grades 3 to 6 determine an issue or problem for discussion, which might emerge from books the teacher has read aloud, from current events, or from real classroom experience. For example, one issue that might provoke a debate is the preference among some students for more than one vegetable in school hot lunch offerings. Children on either side of the issue move to different areas of the room; children who choose not to take sides remain in their seats and become the judges for the debate, determining which side's argument is most persuasive.

The teacher acts as moderator of the debate. To begin, the teacher asks one child from the supporting side of the issue under debate and then a child from the opposing side to come up to the front of the class in turn, indicate his or her position on the issue, and then comment on or explain that position. Depending on the amount of time allotted to the debate, several children can present their views. After the time has run out, the teacher asks the judges to vote either by a show of hands or a written ballot on which "team" has won the debate.

To prepare children to be successful in debates, teachers might show several televised examples. Children should also be taught how to argue effectively: this is helpful not only for debaters, but also for those children who serve as judges. Tompkins (1998) recommends that children be taught to use a rubric for evaluating debates, such as the version found in Figure 2.9.

Figure 2.9

Debate Rubric

Resolved: There should be more than one vegetable choice in school lunches for students attending Sage Mountain School.

Rating Code: 1–5; 5 = highest, 1 = lowest

	Appearance	Delivery	Factual information	Keeping to the point	Persuasiveness	Teamwork	Participation in rebuttal	Total
Pro								
Shawn Meeks	___	___	___	___	___	___	___	___
Giana Zientek	___	___	___	___	___	___	___	___
Aaron Bailey	___	___	___	___	___	___	___	___
Con							Total	___
Melanie Spooks	___	___	___	___	___	___	___	___
Whitney Laws	___	___	___	___	___	___	___	___
Luke Winder	___	___	___	___	___	___	___	___
							Total	___

Based on Tompkins, G. E., *Language Arts: Content and Teaching Strategies*, 5th ed., p. 58. © 2002. Adapted by permission of Pearson Education, Inc.

Another effective oral language activity for developing students' skill in explaining and persuading is producing television commercials. To begin this activity, students learn about several propaganda techniques (see Table 2.3).

We have found that the teaching of propaganda or persuasion techniques is much more effective when these are illustrated using multiple examples, such as magazine advertisements, radio spots, and TV commercials. Students can reinforce their knowledge about propaganda methods by creating a series of posters identifying and explaining specific techniques and giving examples from magazine advertisements and/or TV commercials.

Once several propaganda techniques have been taught, we suggest dividing students into TV commercial production groups, with no more than four students per group. Groups select a propaganda technique to implement in making their commercial, develop a script, and collect props and other materials for production. After

Table 2.3

Propaganda Techniques

Name	Characteristics	Example
1. Snob appeal	Makes us want a product because superior or wealthy people have it. Association with a small, exclusive group.	L'Oreal Haircolor: Because I'm worth it. BMW: The ultimate driving machine.
2. Name calling	Creates a feeling of dislike for a person or product by associating it with something disliked or undesirable. May appeal to hate and fear. Asks people to judge without first examining the evidence.	My opponent is a tax-spending liberal! My opponent is a flip-flop man who cannot make up his mind. He changes his mind with the breeze! How could anyone follow such a weak-willed flip-flopper? In a campaign speech to a logging company, the Congressman referred to his environmentally conscious opponent as a "tree hugger."
3. Glittering generalities	Uses broad general statements, whose exact meanings are not clear. Appeals to emotions of love, generosity, brotherhood. Words suggest ideals such as truth, freedom, and the American way.	Be all that you can be . . . in the Army. Our world-class employees and their commitment to innovative ideas continue to drive our success in today's fast-paced business environment.
4. Plain folks	Identifies the person or product with the average person. Politicians may try to win confidence by appearing to be like the good folks in your town.	Motel 6: We'll leave the light on for you. Wendy's "Where's the beef?" campaign.
5. Transfer	Creates a good or bad impression by associating a product or person with something respected or not respected. The feeling for the symbol is supposed to transfer to the new product or person.	Texaco ad: You can trust your car to the man who wears the star. Hanes Underwear: Wait 'til we get our Hanes on you.
6. Testimonial	A respected person, such as a movie star or athlete, recommends a product and suggests that you buy it because he or she used it.	Brooke Shields: Know what comes between me and my Calvins? Nothing. Indy 500 Michael Schumacher's Choice: Omega Speedmaster Automatic. Life cereal: Hey, Mikey! He likes it.
7. Bandwagon	Follow the crowd and buy what everyone else is buying, or vote for the winner.	The Pepsi Generation. The president says, "We must unite in the fight against terrorism."

From Norton, Donna E., *The Effective Teaching of Language Arts*, 6th edition, © 2004, p. 149. Adapted by permission of Pearson Education, Inc., Upper Saddle River, NJ.

groups have rehearsed their commercial several times, they perform it in front of the video camera. When all of the commercials have been recorded, students view them and identify the propaganda technique used.

Imaginative Oral Language Instruction: "Let's Pretend"

The imaginative language function finds expression in using oral language for pretend or fantasy play. Dramatizing a story from a book is an excellent expressive oral language development activity that is a favorite among children. We have found several alternatives for dramatizing a story, whether it is one children have heard before or one they themselves have composed during play. Although many children are too shy to speak up in front of their peers, they open up when they use puppets to talk in their place. There are many types of puppets, from simple finger, paper bag, sock, paper cup or plate, and stick puppets, to more elaborate, commercially produced puppets. Teachers can demonstrate how to make a puppet character come alive by using a distinct voice and interesting actions. Flannel board cut-out characters can also be used to tell stories, and wordless picture books can stimulate children to fabricate stories based on illustrations.

The key elements to model for children when telling stories are found in narrative structures: setting, characters, problem, goal, events, and resolution. Younger children need to know that a good story has a beginning, middle, and end. To help children internalize the structure and language associated with storytelling, teachers need to read aloud traditional tales such as *The Little Red Hen, The Three Little Pigs, Goldilocks and the Three Bears, The Three Billy Goats Gruff,* and *Jack and the Beanstalk.*

Children develop greater ability to use oral language when they have many opportunities to retell and dramatize stories using props such as dress-up clothes, puppets, and flannel board cut-out characters (Tompkins, 2010). In Figure 2.10 we show a variety of puppets children can make for dramatizing stories from books they have read or that they have composed on their own.

Figure 2.10

Types of Puppets Students Can Make

From Tompkins, Gail E., *Language Arts: Patterns of Practice,* 6th edition, © 2005, p. 375. Reproduced by permission of Pearson Education, Inc., Upper Saddle River, NJ.

Representational Oral Language: Instructions and Directions

The representational language function focuses on using oral language to give others instructions for performing a task successfully or directions to find a location. Treasure hunts are ever-popular activities for developing these abilities, as in the following example:

- Hide two "treasure chests" (boxes containing granola bars) in two locations.
- Pair students with partners; show the first child in each pair where one of the treasure chests is hidden.

- Mark the starting place for the treasure hunt with an "X."
- Have the first child in each pair give oral directions for finding the treasure to the other child.
- Once the second child in the pair finds the treasure, have the children exchange roles.
- Show the second child the location of the other "treasure chest," and direct partners to return to the starting spot. The second child then gives oral directions to the first.

Another excellent activity for developing skill in giving oral directions can be conducted in small groups.

- Decide on a task, such as making instant chocolate pudding. Arrange four to six children into two groups of two to three students each.
- Blindfold one of the groups of students, and have them give oral directions for carrying out the task to the other students, who are not blindfolded.
- The members of the group carrying out the task must follow the oral directions exactly as given by the blindfolded students. For the task to be carried out successfully, the students in the blindfolded group must first discuss the directions they wish to give so that they are complete and sequential.
- On another day, the two groups can exchange roles in carrying out another activity (e.g., making a peanut butter and jelly sandwich).

Divertive Oral Language Instruction: "That's Funny!"

The divertive language function points to the use of oral language for enjoyment, amusement, and recreation—using language as a diversion. Children love to tell jokes and riddles. In fact, they love telling jokes and riddles so much they will go to great lengths to find as many willing listeners as they can! To help children develop both a repertoire of jokes and riddles as well as the ability to tell them well, teachers need to read aloud a variety of joke and riddle books, such as those show in Figure 2.11. After reading aloud to the large group, the teacher can invite students to "turn to a neighbor" and tell her or him a favorite joke or riddle.

For older children, "pundles" and "sniglets" are wonderfully rich divertive oral language activities. "Pundles" are configurations of letters, lines, and symbols used to spell out familiar words and phrases. (See, for example, *Pundles* or *Pundles II* by Bruce and Greg Nash [1980, 1983]). A "pundle" for the familiar breakfast cereal Cheerios might be represented as shown to the left.

A "sniglet" is a word that does not appear in the dictionary, but should. The listing of "sniglets" in Figure 2.12 from the website http://bertc.com/sniglets.htm was originally drawn from the very popular book *Sniglets* by Rich Hall (1984).

Singing humorous songs is another means by which elementary-aged students can share in divertive oral language. One of our favorite humorous songbooks is *A Prairie Home Companion Folk Song Book* by Garrison Keillor, Jon Pankake, and Marsha Pankake (1988). As children build up a store of jokes, riddles, and other humorous language, provide opportunities for them to share these with the class. "Joke, Song, or Riddle of the Day" is a favorite activity in many classrooms. Jokesters, singers, and riddlers are given an opportunity to tell their joke or riddle or sing their song with a microphone and karaoke box. Regardless of the activity, children should have opportunities to share in humorous oral language activities regularly in the elementary classroom.

Figure 2.11

Children's Jokes and Riddles Sources

Children's Joke and Riddle Websites

www.kidsjokes.co.uk
www.brownielocks.com/jokes.html
www.fun4children.com

Children's Joke and Riddle Books

Bonham, T. (1997). *The Treasury of Clean Children's Jokes.* Broadman & Holman Publishing, ISBN 080546364X.

Cerf, B. (1999). *Riddles and More Riddles* (Beginner Books). Random House, ISBN 0679889701.

Dahl, M. (2003). *A Book of Rhyming Riddles.* Picture Window Books, ISBN 1404802274.

Dahl, M. (2002). *The Everything Kids' Joke Book: Side-Splitting, Rib-Tickling Fun.* Adams Media Corporation, ISBN 1580626866.

Davis, J. (1997). *Garfield's Book of Jokes and Riddles.* Troll Communications, ISBN 0816742901.

Hills, T. (2000). *Knock-Knock—Who's There?: My First Book of Knock Knock Jokes.* Little Simon, ISBN 0689834136.

Horsfall, J. (2003). *Kids' Silliest Jokes.* Sterling Publishing Company, ISBN 1402705980.

Keillor, G. (2000). *Pretty Good Jokes.* Highbridge Publishing, ISBN 1565113683.

Keller, C. (2004). *Kids' Bathroom Book: Riddles.* Sterling Publishing Company, ISBN 1402717105.

Keller, C. (1997). *The Little Giant Book of Knock-Knocks.* Sterling Publishing Company, ISBN 0806981083.

Krull, K. (2003). *You Must Be Joking! Lots of Cool Jokes, Plus 17½ Tips for Remembering, Telling, and Making Up Your Own Jokes.* Cricket Books, ISBN 0812626613.

Lederer, R. (1996). *Pun and Games: Jokes, Riddles, Rhymes, Daffynitions, Tairy Fales, and More Wordplay for Kids.* Chicago Review Press, ISBN 1556522649.

Leno, J. (2005). *How to Be the Funniest Kid in the Whole Wide World (or Just in Your Class).* Simon & Schuster Children's Publishing, ISBN 1416906312.

Mauterer, E. (2005). *Laugh Out Loud: Jokes and Riddles from* Highlights for Children. Boyds Mills Press, ISBN 1590783484.

McCory, Martin, J. (2004). *Vocabulary-Boosting Jokes and Riddles.* Scholastic Professional Books, ISBN 0439542561.

O'Donnell, R. (1997). *Kids Are Punny: Jokes Sent by Kids to* The Rosie O'Donnell Show. Warner Books, ISBN 0446523232.

Peterson, S., Walton, R., Walton, A., & Schultz, S. (Eds.). (2004). *Ivan to Make You Laugh: Jokes and Novel, Nifty, and Notorious Names.* Carolrhoda Books, ISBN 1575056593.

Phillips, B. (2001). *Extremely Good Clean Jokes for Kids.* Harvest House Publishers, ISBN 0736903097.

Phunny, U. R. (2004). *Animal Jokes.* Buddy Books, ISBN 1591976200.

Rosenbloom, J. (2004). *696 Silly School Jokes and Riddles.* Sterling Publishing Company, ISBN 140271095X.

Rosenbloom, J. (1999). *Great Book of Riddles and Jokes.* Sterling Publishing Company, ISBN 0806999342.

Thomas, Lyn. (2004). *Ha! Ha! Ha!: 1,000+ Jokes, Riddles, Facts, and More.* Maple Tree Press, ISBN 1897066120.

Weintraub, A. (2005). *Everything Kids' Gross Jokes Book: Side-Splitting Jokes That Make Your Skin Crawl.* Adams Media Corporation, ISBN 1593374488.

Weitzman, I. (2000). *Jokelopedia.* Workman Publishing Company, ISBN 0761112146.

Figure 2.12

Examples of "Sniglets"

- *Accordionated* (ah kor' de on ay tid)—*adj.* Being able to drive and refold a road map at the same time.
- *Orosuctuous* (or oh suk' chew us)—*adj.* Being able to hold a glass to one's face by sheer lung power.
- *Pigslice* (pig' slys)—*n.* The last unclaimed piece of pizza that everyone is secretly dying for.
- *Tilecomet* (tyl kom' it)—*n.* the piece of toilet paper that clings to your foot after you've left a public restroom.

Authoritative Oral Language Instruction: Now Hear This!

The authoritative language function focuses on using oral language to provide others with important information or to enforce rules, statutes, laws, and ordinances. Because children are often reminded about rules for behavior in class, on the playground, and in the lunchroom, authoritative language is a daily experience at school. Invite children to listen for oral language during the day that is used to remind them of class or school rules. At the end of the day, share the reminders of school and class rules they have heard. Brainstorm with students places outside of school where authoritative oral language is used, such as in homes, stores, courtrooms, police stations, and so on. We have also found it effective to have students dramatize authoritative roles: a police officer informing a child that she should cross the street at a marked crosswalk, a lunchroom worker or teacher telling a child what to do before he can leave the lunchroom to go out to recess, a parent telling a child she can watch TV only after her homework is finished.

A less frequent authoritative oral language opportunity is to have students give oral reports about experiences they have had, books that someone read to them, or TV programs or movies they have watched. Modeling for children how to give well-presented oral reports and then having them engage in oral reporting is an excellent way to help them learn to use authoritative oral language.

Perpetuating Oral Language Instruction: Remember This!

The perpetuating language function employs oral language to tell others about historical events that are worthy of preserving and being passed on to others. Gordon (2001) offers two excellent activities that support the perpetuating function of oral language: "Memorable Moments" and "Pick a Picture."

The teacher makes a set of "Memorable Moments" cards featuring story starters similar to those in Figure 2.13. Next, he or she models choosing a card and telling a story from his or her past that uses the story starter on the card. Student storytellers follow suit.

Figure 2.13

"Memorable Moments" Story Starter Cards

The happiest moment of my life was _____.

I was terrified when _____.

You won't believe this, but _____.

The worst day of my life began _____.

Late last night, _____.

The best day of my life began _____.

It all started when _____.

I was so embarrassed when _____.

How was I to know that _____?

The funniest thing that ever happened to me was _____.

I expected it to happen, and it did _____.

The saddest thing I ever saw was _____.

The "Pick a Picture" oral language activity uses a similar process. The teacher collects a boxful of old personal and magazine photographs, old postcards, greeting cards, and newspaper photographs. Next, she or he models choosing an old photograph or other item from the box and telling a story from her or his past experiences that connects in some way to the photo, postcard, or greeting card. Children are invited to follow suit, telling stories from their own lives.

Response to Intervention (RTI)

Tier 2 Adaptations

IRA Standards for Reading Professionals: Standard 5, Elements 5.1, 5.2, 5.3

Common Core Standards: Speaking and Listening: K–5, Comprehension and Collaboration (items 1–3), Presentation of Knowledge and Ideas (items 4–6); Speaking and Listening: Grades 6–12, Comprehension and Collaboration (items 1–3), Presentation of Knowledge and Ideas (items 4–6)

Response to Intervention: Responsive Teaching and Differentiation, Collaboration, Systemic and Comprehensive Approaches

Differentiating instruction is essential if we are to help every child succeed. In the previous section, we reviewed a number of instructional strategies that can serve as "core" oral language instruction for all students. We saw how these activities and strategies could be used both in whole- and small-group situations and as part of instructional conversations (CREDE, 2010).

Under guidelines for implementing Response to Intervention (RTI), Reutzel and Cooter (2011) explain that Tier 2 interventions are intended to fill learning gaps as quickly as possible and return students to core (i.e., developmental) literacy instruction. They are usually delivered at least three times per week in small-group settings *in addition* to regular classroom instruction. Frequent and regular progress-monitoring assessment is used to determine the success of Tier 2 interventions with students. All instructional interventions must be documented and offered for a substantial amount of time (e.g., a minimum of 8 weeks). If Tier 2 instructional intervention fails to accelerate or positively impact a student's literacy learning, then Tier 3 evidence-based interventions are attempted with greater frequency and delivered in even smaller groups or individually until the student shows a positive response.

Resources and Programs Focused on Oral Language Development

RTI Tier 2 interventions are oftentimes offered by the classroom teacher, but in the case of oral language development (especially in early grades), instruction is frequently provided by a Title I specialist, special educator, or speech therapist. We highlight briefly several resources and programs focused on oral language development available to teachers and learning specialists for Tier 2 interventions.

Peabody Language Development Kits (Revised). The Peabody Language Development Kits (PLDK) (Dunn, Smith, Dunn, & Horton, 2002) are sets of language development materials for levels pre-K through grade 3. These popular kits, which have been available since the 1960s and were frequently used in the early Headstart programs, are still widely used in special education and other programs. The kits feature oral language and cognitive development activities using durable, inviting materials and puppets that lead children in a variety of activities including brainstorming and problem-solving techniques. Though research evidence of the effectiveness of PLDK is sparse, this program remains popular in schools worldwide.

The Headstart REDI Program. In March of 2009 the U.S. Department of Education's What Works Clearinghouse (WWC) concluded that the Headstart REDI Program meets rigorous standards for program effectiveness in language development (Bierman et al., 2008), using the following methods and goals:

- Aims to improve preschoolers' language development, literacy skills, and social-emotional development
- Is delivered using brief lessons, "hands-on" extension activities, and specific instructional strategies
- Includes interactive book reading, "Sound Games," and an alphabet center to foster language development and emergent literacy skills
- Uses the Preschool PATHS curriculum to promote preschoolers' friendship skills, understanding of emotions, social problem-solving skills, and self-control
- Provides teachers with training and ongoing mentoring and support

Let's Talk About It! An oral language and reading and writing program for grades K to 3 from Mondo Publishing (www.mondopub.com), Let's Talk About It! takes a structured approach to build students' oral language and develop their ability to understand basic print concepts. Let's Talk About It! is used in many urban school districts as a Tier 2 language intervention for at-risk English speakers and English learners.

English Learners: Important Considerations

Effectively teaching English learners (ELs) to read and write well in English is an important responsibility in today's elementary schools. A growing number of students come from homes where English is not the primary language or where children are exposed to limited amounts of oral language usage (Hart & Risley, 1995). According to the National Literacy Panel Report on Language-Minority Children and Youth (August & Shanahan, 2006), in 1979 there were 6 million language-minority students; by 1999, the number of EL students had swelled to 14 million. The panel concluded,

> Language-minority students who cannot read and write proficiently in English cannot participate fully in American schools, workplaces or society. They face limited job opportunities and earning power. Nor are the consequences of low literacy attainment in English limited to individual impoverishment. U.S. economic competitiveness depends on workforce quality. Inadequate reading and writing proficiency in English relegates rapidly increasing language-minority populations to the sidelines, limiting the nation's potential for economic competitiveness, innovation, productivity growth, and quality of life. (August & Shanahan, 2006, p. 1)

Dutro and Moran (2003) offer six excellent principles for providing effective oral English language instruction for English learners (ELs). These general principles extend far beyond the EL population of oral language learners and provide excellent suggestions for planning and adapting oral language instruction for children of poverty and other diverse language learners who struggle. By applying the following six principles, teachers can develop high levels of oral language ability among young learners.

- Build on students' prior knowledge of both language and content
- Create meaningful contexts for functional use of language

- Provide comprehensible input and model forms of language in a variety of ways connected to meaning
- Offer a range of opportunities for practice and application so as to develop fluency
- Establish a positive and supportive environment for practice, with clear goals and immediate corrective feedback
- Reflect on the forms of language and the process of learning

Activating and building on children's prior knowledge is essential. Gersten and Baker (2000) say that strategic use of *some* native language terms and phrases can help address specific problems in connecting new knowledge to students' existing knowledge and language abilities. When creating meaningful contexts for diverse learners to develop oral language, moving from the concrete to the abstract is another principle of importance. Whether children are learning a first or second language, the use of visuals, objects, diagrams, labels, simulations, gestures, and dramatization of situations and roles are extremely helpful for early language learners (Gersten & Baker, 2000; Marzano, 1998).

Another principle for teaching English learners involves teacher and peer modeling within a "communicative context" (Long, 1991). Such instruction involves clear modeling, slower pacing, information presented in smaller chunks, and frequent checking for understanding and feedback. Also, modeling is best if it occurs in relation to specific or defined tasks such as applying for a job, talking to the doctor, renting an apartment, or buying food at the store.

Working cooperatively in the classroom offers increased opportunities for children to use language purposefully and appropriately. Moran (1996) suggests that small-group work that is cooperative in nature increases the incentives for children to use oral language more often in more appropriate ways. Also, small-group work encourages children to help one another by providing corrective feedback in positive and constructive ways that involve little risk (Lightbrown & Spada, 1999).

Finally, for oral language development to flourish, children need to feel that the classroom is a safe place for risk taking when trying to use new language patterns (Krashen, 1985). Dutro and Moran (2003) also emphasize that, even though classrooms should be safe for trying out new language, teachers should provide clear communication about learning goals and offer positive corrective feedback so that students can improve.

●●●

IRA Standards for Reading Professionals: Standard 5, Element 5.2

Common Core Standards: Speaking and Listening: K–5, Comprehension and Collaboration (items 1–3), Presentation of Knowledge and Ideas (items 4–6); Speaking and Listening: Grades 6–12, Comprehension and Collaboration (items 1–3), Presentation of Knowledge and Ideas (items 4–6)

Response to Intervention: Instruction

Motivation and Engagement

Motivation and Engagement in Oral Language Development

Motivation for oral language always grows out of a person's need to communicate. In the classroom it is our goal to orchestrate authentic and *stimulating* situations for students to dialogue with us and/or their peers about new knowledge. Dialogic learning is the linchpin for successful teaching and learning. Two of the most motivational dialogic activities we have experienced are the joint productive activity (JPA) and the instructional conversation (IC) (CREDE, 2010). Both have long records of research support that have been documented by The Center for Research on

Figure 2.14

Indicators of Joint Productive Activity

The teacher:
1. Designs instructional activities requiring student collaboration to accomplish a joint product
2. Matches the demands of the joint productive activity to the time available for accomplishing them
3. Arranges classroom seating to accommodate students' individual and group needs to communicate and work jointly
4. Participates with students in joint productive activity
5. Organizes students in a variety of groupings, such as by friendship, mixed academic ability, language, project, or interests, to promote interaction
6. Plans with students how to work in groups and move from one activity to another, such as from large-group introduction to small-group activity, for clean-up, dismissal, and the like
7. Manages student and teacher access to materials and technology to facilitate joint productive activity
8. Monitors and supports student collaboration in positive ways

Education, Diversity, and Excellence (CREDE) at the University of California–Berkeley. Earlier we presented the CREDE indicators for teachers implementing instructional conversations, so we now add to your teacher's toolbox with the indicators for JPAs (see Figure 2.14).

Click on A+RISE—WIDA ELP Standard Strategies in the MyEducationLab (www.myeducationlab.com) for your course. Next, select the Strategy Card Index tab, scroll to Language and Content for grades K–5, and select Motivational Strategies.

Joint Productive Activity (JPA)

CREDE (2010) research supports the belief that learning occurs in powerful ways when experts (i.e., teachers, more skilled peers) and learners work together for a common goal. Thus they are therefore motivated to assist one another. Working together in a **joint productive activity** promotes discussion and language learning in the context of new knowledge. This kind of "mentoring" and "learning in action" is potent throughout grades pre-K to 12.

In traditional classrooms there is generally very little joint work going on from which common understandings and clarification can grow. However, in classrooms using joint productive activities the interaction between teacher and students helps create a common context for learning. This is especially important when the teacher and the students are not of the same background (CREDE, 2010). Joint productive activities and dialogue promote the highest level of language learning by connecting core subject concepts and everyday ideas to help young thinkers understand their world.

An example of a JPA for a group (3–5) of first-grade students who have been learning about the seasons might look something like the following (read orally by the teacher and provided in print):

> Your assignment is to think about what we have learned about the four seasons and create a poster with pictures and words answering the following:
>
> - Name the four seasons
> - How does the weather change in each season?
> - What are some of the holidays for each season?
> - What is the season for each of your birthdays?
> - How do you dress differently for each season?
>
> You have 30 minutes to prepare your poster to present to the class, and everyone MUST agree to all of your answers.

An example of a JPA for a group (3–5) of fifth-grade students who have been learning about aviation might be presented in the following format:

Aviation in America

Time Limit: 40 minutes

YOUR TASK: Using your book and library resources create a timeline of important aviation milestones.

1. Describe the airplanes of each era and some of their characteristics such as size, airspeed, and so on, as well as innovations.
2. Be sure to include aircraft used for commercial and military purposes.
3. Remember, you have forty (40) minutes to complete your timeline and descriptions. You will present your product to the class. Remember, you must all agree on the conclusions you present.
4. When you are done, evaluate each of your colleagues' performance on this task using the rubric below. Be sure to evaluate yourself so as to keep things anonymous!

In the example we ask students to evaluate one another using a rubric for joint productive activities. Although you will probably want to create your own rubric, we offer one as a model from the work of K. S. Cooter and R. Cooter (in press) as an example (See Figure 2.15). The form students can use for evaluating each other (one for each student) is presented in Figure 2.16.

Figure 2.15

Joint Productive Activity Rubric

4 Thorough Understanding
- Consistently and actively works toward group goals
- Is sensitive to the feelings and learning needs of all group members
- Consistently and actively contributes knowledge, opinions, and skills
- Values the knowledge, opinions, and skills of all group members and encourages their contributions
- Is obviously thoroughly prepared for class and knowledgeable about topic

3 Good Understanding
- Works toward group goals without prompting
- Contributes knowledge, opinions, and skills without prompting
- Shows sensitivity to the feelings of others
- Is well prepared for class and knowledgeable about topic

2 Satisfactory Understanding
- Works toward group goals with occasional prompting by others
- Contributes to the group with occasional prompting by others
- Shows sensitivity to the feelings of others
- Has read/prepared adequately but lacks thorough preparation

1 Needs Improvement
- Works toward group goals only when prompted/asked by others
- Contributes to the group only when prompted/asked by others
- Needs occasional reminders to be sensitive to the feelings of others
- Has not prepared thoroughly for the class; lacks knowledge needed for full participation

Figure 2.16

JPA Evaluation Form

JPA Assignment _____ Date _____

Students in group and score on JPA rubric

1. _____ _____
2. _____ _____
3. _____ _____
4. _____ _____
5. _____ _____

Technology and New Literacies for Oral Language Development

A number of new technologies can stimulate oral language growth in students. Our continuing goal as teachers and researchers is to find technologies that are accessible and relatively inexpensive (same thing, really). In considering technologies and new literacy programs for nurturing oral language growth for all students it helps to remember the following three fundamental student needs:

- Opportunities to discuss their new learning from challenging content in collaboration with others (Vygotsky, 1986, 1990)
- Temporary structure, also called *scaffolding* (Bruner, 1978; McGee & Ukrainetz, 2009), that helps students construct new language and knowledge
- Challenging tasks that advance student understanding to more complex levels (CREDE, 2010)

In this section we highlight some of the more promising alternatives for increasing students' oral vocabularies with these three factors in mind: discussion opportunities, scaffolding, and challenging tasks. As ever, we have studied the research base to determine which programs and tools seem to produce the most effective results.

Headsprout Early Reading

According to What Works Clearinghouse (2009, October, p. 1), Headsprout Early Reading (www.headsprout.com) is an Internet-based supplemental early literacy curriculum that includes eighty 20-minute animated stories, with the first 40 designed for prekindergarten age students. The episodes are designed to teach phonemic awareness, phonics, fluency, vocabulary, and comprehension. The program adapts to a child's responses and provides supplemental instruction and review when a child does not choose the correct answer. Some of the benefits to teachers and students of using Headsprout Early Reading include the following:

- Individualized, adaptive instruction for individual students
- Built-in assessment reports
- Quick implementation requires very little professional development

Of the technology-supported programs reviewed by What Works Clearinghouse in 2010, Headsprout Early Reading had the highest oral language improvement index rating (+22 percentile points) for students using the program. However, this is based on only one study that met WWC's strict standards for research.

Words and Concepts

Words and Concepts (www.laureatelearning.com) is a computer software program intended to strengthen oral language skills and "concept comprehension" in six units: vocabulary, categorization, word identification by function, word association, concept of same, and concept of different. Words and Concepts is designed for use by adults and children with varying special needs, including language-learning deficits.

Each of the Words and Concepts programs uses a core vocabulary of 40 nouns in six related language units. Many of the activities feature three levels of difficulty.

In 2007 What Works Clearinghouse (WWC) analyzed existing research evidence of the effectiveness of Words and Concepts for improving oral language. Results were somewhat positive with an average improvement index rating of +4 percentile points when used with economically disadvantaged children.

WhisperPhone

If you are like us, you remember as a child creating a kind of telephone using cans and string. The WhisperPhone seems to us to be a little like a modern-day version. This clever device has a phone-like headset so that when children speak they are able to hear themselves (solo headset) or another child speaking when connected with a kind of hose (duet).

WhisperPhone might be used as a motivation for students working in pairs to have "telephone conversations" about new topics they are learning, practice oral reading using readers' theatre or radio play scripts, or review new vocabulary on word walls.

www.whisperphone.com

Electronic Talking Books (ETB)

One of the methods to grow student vocabularies is through read-aloud activities. Though it is always desirable for teachers to conduct read-alouds, it is not always possible. One way to make read-alouds more available to students is with **electronic talking books** or **ETB** (Oakley & Jay, 2008; Pearman, 2008). ETBs are texts on CD-ROM or available over the Internet featuring not only the written word but also hypertext options for narration, animations, music, or video; some allow readers to highlight a word or sentence and have the computer explain (or pronounce) the highlighted content (Reutzel & Cooter, 2011). Some ETBs also include sound effects and "hot spots" for further learning. Not only are ETBs great for helping early and emergent readers increase their oral vocabulary through listening, they can be especially helpful for students having limited motivation to read. Recent research has also shown ETBs to be a valuable tool for reading home assignments (Oakley & Jay, 2008). In Web Tools You Can Use in the Classroom we share with you some online links to examples of ETBs.

To use ETBs in challenging ways that encourage word learning and dialogue, perhaps in a listening center equipped with a computer, begin by introducing the text selection to the whole group and explain any important key concepts and vocabulary followed by a brief discussion. Remember to "sell" the students on each selection so they will be motivated to listen carefully. In Pearman's (2008) study, students were also informed that they would be expected to *retell* what they remembered from the text selection; this increases attention by letting them know of the challenge in this task. Following the listening and/or reading of the ETB, ask students to retell what they remember from the selection to a partner. Use prompt questions such as "Pretend you are telling your partner about what you just read and they have not read

WEB TOOLS YOU CAN USE IN THE CLASSROOM

Promoting Oral Language Development with ETBs

- Woodlands Junior School: www.woodlands-junior.kent.sch.uk/Games/educational/onlinestory.html#talk
- Read On Audio Stories (audio stories for elementary school children): www.beenleigss.eq.edu.au/requested_sites/audiostories/index.html
- Ziptales (subscripton needed): www.ziptales.com.au
- CBeebies Stories (for younger children): www.bbc.co.uk/cbeebies/stories
- Awesome Talking Library (Awesome Talkster can turn any web page into an ETB, with text highlighting): www.awesomelibrary.org/Awesome_Talking_Library.html

this selection." If they seem to leave out important information, have their partner prompt the "reteller" again, saying "What else do you remember?" or "Can you tell me more?"

Family and Community Connections

How Family and Community Connections Encourage Oral Language Development

●●●

IRA Standards for Reading Professionals: Standard 4, Elements 4.1, 4.2, 4.3

Common Core Standards: Speaking and Listening: K–5, Comprehension and Collaboration (items 1–3), Presentation of Knowledge and Ideas (items 4–6); Speaking and Listening: Grades 6–12, Comprehension and Collaboration (items 1–3), Presentation of Knowledge and Ideas (items 4–6)

Response to Intervention: Collaboration

Parents are their children's first teachers, and homes are children's first schools where the foundations of oral language development are established (Biemiller, 2006). Parents who talk while playing with their children or who take time to engage in rich mealtime conversations, perhaps using rare (infrequent and mature) vocabulary words during their interactions, provide many of the essential elements for developing oral language (Dickinson & Tabors, 2001; Snow, Scarborough, & Burns, 1999; Watson, 2001). More than three decades of research, unfortunately, indicates that most parents spend very little time having real conversations with their children. Our goal as teachers, then, is to buttress language development at school with ways of teaching parents how they can help children at home through conversations.

Parent Read-Alouds

Perhaps the most effective practice for developing children's oral language at home is for parents to read books aloud to their children regularly and provide access to books and other print materials in the home (Dickinson & Tabors, 2001; Straub, 2003). Reading books aloud to children should be an important part of each day's family and home routine. Reading aloud before going to bed at night is a wonderful way for parents and children to bond; it is also helpful in settling children down for a good night's sleep. It is, however, a mistake for teachers to assume that because parents can read for their own purposes, they know how to effectively interact with their child around the reading of a book. Straub and DeBruin-Parecki (2003) note that many parents were not read to as children themselves. Teachers can help train these parents with the following two guidelines for effective parent–child read-alouds.

1. *Books should be read aloud interactively.* This means readers should stop to discuss parts of the text, the storyline, information, or a picture during the reading. In fact, evidence (Dickinson & Tabors, 2001) suggests that interaction is the most important part of making reading aloud effective! An interactive parent–child read-aloud starts with a brief introduction and discussion of the book that helps children recall their background knowledge and personal experiences with the topic or theme of the book. Background knowledge can be built through field trips, movie viewing, or searching for pictures and information on the Internet or in books. When reading aloud, parents should stop at various points in the book to ask the child open-ended questions. They should invite children to inquire about concepts they do not understand and help them make connections between the text read and their own life experiences. Parents should be sure that an adequate amount of time is allowed for discussion during and after the reading. Too often, parents talk too much, rush through the reading, and do not allow sufficient time for their listeners to express themselves or their ideas.

2. *Look for books that provide children information about their world.* Young children love fiction (stories), but they also love nonfiction—books about real facts, objects, and events such as butterflies, magnets, weather, and transportation (Mohr, 2003). Information books help children grow new concept knowledge and vocabulary (listening and speaking).

Taking parent training one step further, we have created a list of the "dos and don'ts" of reading aloud based on Trelease's (1995) *The New Read-Aloud Handbook* (see Figure 2.17).

Dialogue Reading for Parents Having Limited English or Reading Ability

Teachers, particularly those serving in rural or urban areas, will sometimes discover that some of their students' parents have limited English or reading abilities. Nevertheless, there are some research-proven strategies these parents can be taught to help their children develop oral language.

A mother's mean length of utterance (MLU), the average number of words spoken together, is predictive of her child's later language development (Cooter, 2006; Murray, 1990; Reutzel & Cooter, 2011). As parents speak in longer word chains—sentences that are longer and more complex—children tend to imitate and create longer sentences, too. Vocabulary becomes more complex and expressive as well.

Research on increasing a child's mean length of utterance (MLU) provides some valuable insights for teachers who are coaching language-limited parents.

- Parents who speak or question using complete sentences are more likely to have children who respond in longer word chains or longer utterances (Peterson et al., 2005).

Figure 2.17

Dos and Don'ts of Reading Aloud

DO

- Begin reading to children as early in their lives as they can be supported to sit and listen.
- Use rhymes, raps, songs, chants, poetry, and pictures to stimulate oral language development, listening, and interaction with others.
- Read aloud to children at least 10–15 minutes daily, more often if possible.
- Set aside a time for daily reading aloud in the family's schedule.
- Read picture books to all ages, but gradually move to reading longer books without pictures as well.
- Vary the topics and genre of read-aloud selections.
- Read books that stretch children's intellectual and oral language development.
- Allow plenty of time for interaction before, during, and after the reading.
- Read aloud with expression and enthusiasm.
- Add another dimension to reading by occasionally using hand movements or puppets or by dressing up in costume.
- Carry a book with you at all times to model your love of books and reading.

DON'T

- Don't read aloud too fast.
- Don't read aloud books children can read independently—give a "book talk" instead!
- Don't read aloud books and stories you don't enjoy yourself.
- Don't read aloud books and stories that exceed children's emotional development.
- Don't continue reading a book you don't like. Admit it, and choose another.
- Don't impose your interpretations and preferences on children.
- Don't confuse quantity with quality.
- Don't use reading aloud as a reward or punishment.

Based on Trelease (1995).

- Parents who read books or talk through books that are both narrative and manipulative—books that children can touch, pull, or handle—can increase their children's questions and length and number of utterances (Kaderavek & Justice, 2005).
- Simply giving children models and opportunities for lengthening and elaborating their sentences significantly increases their oral language abilities (Farrar, 1985; Remaly, 1990).

In an article titled "When Mama Can't Read: Counteracting Intergenerational Illiteracy," K. S. Cooter (2006) offers a proven strategy parents can use with their children to help increase their MLU: **dialogic reading.** Although often thought of as simple picture book reading, dialogic reading actually transfers the book's oral language responsibility to the child, who leads a dialogue with the parent around the pictures he or she chooses. Some of the original dialogic reading research was conducted by Whitehurst, Falco, and Lonigan (1988) and replicated many times in the ensuing years, each time with results that are educationally and statistically significant (Huebner, 2001; Huebner & Meltzoff, 2005; Scarborough & Dobrich, 1994; Whitehurst, Arnold, & Epstein, 1994).

Any picture book with illustrations that effectively tell the story is suitable for dialogic reading. Examples we often use to demonstrate this strategy are *Flossie and the Fox* (McKissack, 1986) and *Chicken Sunday* (Polacco, 1992). Either fiction or nonfiction books are appropriate, but we favor a heavy diet of nonfiction books for improving language and vocabulary. It is recommended that the text be read aloud first to the child, but sending home a cassette tape recording (and player) of the teacher reading the book aloud will do just fine. The child leads the conversation with the parent, focusing on and responding to the pictures in the book. The parent should be open to the child's remarks, using "what" questions or rephrasing and extending the child's utterances, while remaining at all times the follower in the dialogue. As one child put it, "I talk the book." The parent can be helped to learn how to engage the child in this child-led dialogue as well. The American Library Association, for instance, hosts parent training sessions and can help teachers locate trainers throughout the nation in their Every Child Ready to Read @ Your Library program (for more information, see their website at www.ala.org).

Picture book dialogic reading seems to yield the best results in improving the length of children's sentences (Cooter, 2006; Whitehurst et al., 1988). Vocabulary becomes more complex and expressive as well. Sometimes just adding gestures is valuable. Mothers who point as they talk establish joint attention and help children learn object names.

Huebner (2000) found that parents must be *taught* to use a book in this language-rich manner. Parents without training typically resort to the more traditional page turning and labeling of pictures with their children. This can lead to parents who are increasing their efforts to read to their children at home, but the quality or nature of the reading has not changed.

Parents with limited English literacy skills can easily partner with their child in dialogic reading in that the book itself is a tool in the parent–child dialogue.

Summary

Oral language is the foundation for all learning in school and out. Teaching oral language effectively may mean the difference between success in school and life for many children, especially those at risk due to poverty. To teach oral language effectively, teachers must understand six interrelated components of language structure: (1) phonology, (2) orthography, (3) morphology, (4) syntax, (5) semantics, and (6) pragmatics. Teachers also need to understand theories and the developmental trajectory of language acquisition in the early years of children's lives. Each theory of language acquisition—behaviorist, innatist, constructivist, and social interactionist—explains some facet of how children learn to speak their native language and other languages as well. Children's language acquisition follows a fairly predictable path in its development throughout the early years of life if children receive support for doing so. These stages were each discussed in broad descriptive terms in this chapter. However, when children do not receive this support in the early years, they begin school with a tremendous deficit in oral language that often translates into later school frustration and failure.

Adequately assessing children's oral language development is desirable but impractical due to expense in terms of time and money. Several simple, reliable, and inexpensive oral language assessments were described in this chapter to help teachers get a reasonable handle on children's oral language growth. An instructional framework was presented based on the pragmatics of language use for teaching elementary school children oral language. Within this framework several effective and motivating instructional strategies were described to develop oral language within each of ten different pragmatic language categories. Finally, we offered some thoughts on how to differentiate oral language instruction to meet diverse student learning needs as well as how to connect the teaching of oral language in the classroom to families and the larger community. Woven together, these elements will help you, the teacher, to become much more effective in planning and providing rich and focused oral language instruction in your elementary school classroom.

Field and Classroom Applications

- Divide into groups of four to six students. Refer to Table 2.1, Six Components of Language Structure. With your group, make a poster featuring examples of the six components of language.
- Read Chapter 9, pages 191–216, of Hart and Risley's (1995) *Meaningful Differences in the Everyday Experience of Young American Children*. Pair with another student in the class. Share five important ideas you learned from reading this chapter with your partner. As a class, discuss the significant concerns, issues, and problems raised in this chapter and what classroom teachers can do. Develop a list of oral language instruction dos and don'ts based on your discussion.
- Work with a partner in identifying the propaganda techniques used in several magazine or television advertisements. Join with another pair of students to jigsaw your findings in groups of four. Collaborate with another group of four students to achieve consensus on the propaganda techniques employed in the advertisements examined by each group.
- Design a motivational joint productive activity (JPA) for a second-grade class relating to a topic from the science curriculum in your state. Be sure it satisfies at least three of the CREDE indicators for JPAs.
- First, decide on a grade level that is of most interest to you. Next, construct a comparison grid showing each of the instructional tools described under the Pillar 6 section on technology and new literacies and how they might be used for developing oral language around the subject areas of social studies and mathematics literacy.

Recommended Resources

Print Resources

Athans, S. K., & Devine, D. (2010). *Fun-tastic activities for differentiating comprehension instruction, grades 2–6.* Newark, DE: International Reading Association.

August, D., & Shanahan, T. (2006). *Developing literacy in second-language learners: Report of the National Literacy Panel on language-minority children and youth.* Mahwah: NJ: Lawrence Erlbaum.

Cooter, K. S. (2006). When mama can't read: Counteracting intergenerational illiteracy. *The Reading Teacher, 59*(7), 698–702.

CREDE. (2010). *The CREDE five standards for effective pedagogy and learning: Instructional conversation.* Berkeley, CA: The Center for Research on Education, Diversity & Excellence (CREDE). Available at http://crede.berkeley.edu/research/crede/instruc_conv.html

National Early Literacy Panel. (2009). *Developing early literacy: Report of the National Early Literacy Panel (NELP).* Washington, DC: National Institute for Literacy. Available at www.nifl.gov/publications/pdf/NELPReport09.pdf

Web Resources

http://crede.berkeley.edu/
   CREDE: The Center for Research on Education, Diversity & Excellence

www.ala.org
   Every Child Ready to Read @ Your Library program

http://plgcatalog.pearson.com
   Oral Language Inventory

http://ggg.umn.edu
   Picture Naming Test

http://bertc.com/sniglets.htm
   Sniglets

The Power of Classroom Practice

www.myeducationlab.com

Go to Topic 11, Struggling Readers, and Topic 12, English Language Learners, in the MyEducationLab (www.myeducationlab.com) for your course, where you can:

- Find learning outcomes for Struggling Readers and English Language Learners along with the national standards that connect to these outcomes.
- Complete Assignments and Activities that can help you more deeply understand the chapter content.
- Apply and practice your understanding of the core teaching skills identified in the chapter with the Building Teaching Skills and Dispositions learning units. (optional)
- Examine challenging situations and cases presented in the IRIS Center Resources. (optional)
- Access video clips of CCSSO National Teachers of the Year award winners responding to the question "Why Do I Teach?" in the Teacher Talk section. (optional)
- Check your comprehension on the content covered in the chapter by going to the Study Plan in the Book Resources for your text. Here you will be able to take a chapter quiz, receive feedback on your answers, and then access Review, Practice, and Enrichment activities to enhance your understanding of chapter content. (optional)

Go to the Topic A+RISE in the MyEducationLab (www.myeducationlab.com) for your course. A+RISE® Standards2Strategy™ is an innovative and interactive online resource that offers new teachers in grades K–12 just in time, research-based instructional strategies that:

- Meet the linguistic needs of ELLs as they learn content.
- Differentiate instruction for all grades and abilities.
- Offer reading and writing techniques, cooperative learning, use of linguistic and nonlinguistic representations, scaffolding, teacher modeling, higher order thinking, and alternative classroom ELL assessment.
- Provide support to help teachers be effective through the integration of listening, speaking, reading, and writing along with the content curriculum.
- Improve student achievement.
- Are aligned to Common Core Elementary Language Arts standards (for the literacy strategies) and to English language proficiency standards in WIDA, Texas, California, and Florida.

STANDARDS

for Reading Professionals and Guiding Principles for Educators

IRA Standards for Reading Professionals

Standard 1: Foundational Knowledge

Candidates understand the theoretical and evidence-based foundations of reading and writing processes and instruction.

Element 1.1

Candidates understand major theories and empirical research that describe the cognitive, linguistic, motivational, and sociocultural foundations of reading and writing development, processes, and components, including word recognition, language comprehension, strategic knowledge, and reading–writing connections.

Element 1.2

Candidates understand the historically shared knowledge of the profession and changes over time in the perceptions of reading and writing development, processes, and components.

Element 1.3

Candidates understand the role of professional judgment and practical knowledge for improving all students' reading development and achievement.

Candidates use instructional approaches, materials, and an integrated, comprehensive, balanced curriculum to support student learning in reading and writing.

Standard 6: Professional Learning and Leadership
Element 6.2

Candidates display positive dispositions related to their own reading and writing and the teaching of reading and writing, and pursue the development of individual professional knowledge and behaviors.

Common Core Standards

Speaking and Listening: K–5

Comprehension and Collaboration

1. Prepare for and participate effectively in a range of conversations and collaborations with diverse partners, building on others' ideas and expressing their own clearly and persuasively.

6. Adapt speech to a variety of contexts and communicative tasks, demonstrating command of formal English when indicated or appropriate.

Response to Intervention

6. Expertise

All students have the right to receive instruction from well-prepared teachers who keep up to date and supplemental instruction from professionals specifically prepared to teach language and literacy (IRA, 2000).

- Teacher expertise is central to instructional improvement, particularly for students who encounter difficulty in acquiring language and literacy. RTI may involve a range of professionals; however, the greater the literacy difficulty, the greater the need for expertise in literacy teaching and learning.
- Important dimensions of teachers' expertise include their knowledge and understanding of language and literacy development, their ability to use powerful assessment tools and techniques, and their ability to translate information about student performance into instructionally relevant instructional techniques.

- The exemplary core instruction that is so essential to the success of RTI is dependent on highly knowledgeable and skilled classroom teachers (IRA, 2003).
- Professionals who provide supplemental instruction or intervention must have a high level of expertise in all aspects of language and literacy instruction and assessment and be capable of intensifying or accelerating language and literacy learning.
- Success for culturally and linguistically diverse students depends on teachers and support personnel who are well prepared to teach in a variety of settings. Deep knowledge of cultural and linguistic differences is especially critical for the prevention of language and literacy problems in diverse student populations.

IRA Standards for Reading Professionals

Standard 3: Assessment and Evaluation

Element 3.1

Candidates understand types of assessments and their purposes, strengths, and limitations.

Element 3.2

Candidates select, develop, administer, and interpret assessments, both traditional print and electronic, for specific purposes.

Element 3.3

Candidates use assessment information to plan and evaluate instruction.

Common Core Standards

Speaking and Listening: K–5

Comprehension and Collaboration

1. Prepare for and participate effectively in a range of conversations and collaborations with diverse partners, building on others' ideas and expressing their own clearly and persuasively.

2. Integrate and evaluate information presented in diverse media and formats, including visually, quantitatively, and orally.

3. Evaluate a speaker's point of view, reasoning, and use of evidence and rhetoric.

Presentation of Knowledge and Ideas

4. Present information, findings, and supporting evidence such that listeners can follow the line of reasoning and the organization, development, and style are appropriate to task, purpose, and audience.

5. Make strategic use of digital media and visual displays of data to express information and enhance understanding of presentations.

6. Adapt speech to a variety of contexts and communicative tasks, demonstrating command of formal English when indicated or appropriate.

Note on range and content of student speaking and listening

To build a foundation for college and career readiness, students must have ample opportunities to take part in a variety of rich, structured conversations—as part of a whole class, in small groups, and with a partner. Being productive members of these conversations requires that students contribute accurate, relevant information; respond to and develop what others have said; make comparisons and contrasts; and analyze and synthesize a multitude of ideas in various domains.

New technologies have broadened and expanded the role that speaking and listening play in acquiring and sharing knowledge and have tightened their link to other forms of communication. Digital texts confront students with the potential for continually updated content and dynamically changing combinations of words, graphics, images, hyperlinks, and embedded video and audio.

Speaking and Listening: Grades 6–12

The grades 6–12 standards . . . define what students should understand and be able to do by the end of each grade. They correspond to the College and Career Readiness (CCR) anchor standards below by number. The CCR and grade-specific standards are necessary complements—the former providing broad standards, the latter providing additional specificity—that together define the skills and understandings that all students must demonstrate.

Comprehension and Collaboration

1. Prepare for and participate effectively in a range of conversations and collaborations with diverse partners, building on others' ideas and expressing their own clearly and persuasively.

2. Integrate and evaluate information presented in diverse media and formats, including visually, quantitatively, and orally.

3. Evaluate a speaker's point of view, reasoning, and use of evidence and rhetoric.

Presentation of Knowledge and Ideas

4. Present information, findings, and supporting evidence such that listeners can follow the line of reasoning and the organization, development, and style are appropriate to task, purpose, and audience.

5. Make strategic use of digital media and visual displays of data to express information and enhance understanding of presentations.

6. Adapt speech to a variety of contexts and communicative tasks, demonstrating command of formal English when indicated or appropriate.

Response to Intervention

3. Assessment

An RTI approach demands assessment that can inform language and literacy instruction meaningfully.

- Assessment should reflect the multidimensional nature of language and literacy learning and the diversity among students

being assessed. The utility of an assessment is dependent on the extent to which it provides valid information on the essential aspects of language and literacy that can be used to plan appropriate instruction.

- Assessments, tools, and techniques should provide useful and timely information about desired language and literacy goals. They should reflect authentic language and literacy activities as opposed to contrived texts or tasks generated specifically for assessment purposes. The quality of assessment information should not be sacrificed for the efficiency of an assessment procedure.

- Multiple purposes for assessment should be clearly identified and appropriate tools and techniques employed. Not all available tools and techniques are appropriate for all purposes, and different assessments—even in the same language or literacy domain—capture different skills and knowledge. Particular care should be taken in selecting assessments for ELLs and for students who speak an English dialect that differs from mainstream dialects.

- Efficient assessment systems involve a layered approach in which screening techniques are used both to identify which students require further (diagnostic) assessment and to provide aggre-gate data about the nature of student achievement overall. Initial (screening) assessments should not be used as the sole mechanism for determining the appropriateness of targeted interventions. Ongoing progress monitoring must include an evaluation of the instruction itself and requires observation of the student in the classroom.

- Classroom teachers and reading/literacy specialists should play a central role in conducting language and literacy assessments and in using assessment results to plan instruction and monitor student performance.

- Assessment as a component of RTI should be consistent with the *Standards for the Assessment of Reading and Writing* developed jointly by the International Reading Association and the National Council of Teachers of English (2010).

Principles of Effective Oral Language Instruction

IRA Standards for Reading Professionals

Standard 2: Curriculum and Instruction

The Curriculum and Instruction Standard recognizes the need to prepare educators who have a deep understanding and knowledge of the elements of a balanced, integrated, and comprehensive literacy curriculum and have developed expertise in enacting that curriculum. The elements focus on the use of effective practices in a well-articulated curriculum, using traditional print, digital, and online resources.

Element 2.1

Candidates use foundational knowledge to design or implement an integrated, comprehensive, and balanced curriculum.

Element 2.2

Candidates use appropriate and varied instructional approaches, including those that develop word recognition, language comprehension, strategic knowledge, and reading–writing connections.

Element 2.3

Candidates use a wide range of texts (e.g., narrative, expository, and poetry) from traditional print, digital, and online resources.

Standard 4: Diversity
Element 4.1

Candidates recognize, understand, and value the forms of diversity that exist in society and their importance in learning to read and write.

Element 4.2

Candidates use a literacy curriculum and engage in instructional practices that positively impact students' knowledge, beliefs, and engagement with the features of diversity.

Element 4.3

Candidates develop and implement strategies to advocate for equity.

Standard 5: Literate Environment
Element 5.1

Candidates design the physical environment to optimize students' use of traditional print, digital, and online resources in reading and writing instruction.

Element 5.2

Candidates design a social environment that is low risk and includes choice, motivation, and scaffolded support to optimize students' opportunities for learning to read and write.

Element 5.3

Candidates use routines to support reading and writing instruction (e.g., time allocation, transitions from one activity to another, discussions, and peer feedback).

Common Core Standards

Speaking and Listening: K–5
Comprehension and Collaboration (See previous)
Presentation of Knowledge and Ideas (See previous)

Speaking and Listening: Grades 6–12
Comprehension and Collaboration (See previous)
Presentation of Knowledge and Ideas (See previous)

Response to Intervention

1. Instruction

RTI is first and foremost intended to prevent problems by optimizing language and literacy instruction.

- Whatever approach is taken to RTI, it should ensure optimal instruction for every student at all levels of schooling. It should prevent serious language and literacy problems through increasingly differentiated and intensified assessment and instruction and reduce the disproportionate number of minority youth and ELLs identified as learning disabled.
- Instruction and assessment conducted by the classroom teacher are central to the success of RTI and must address the needs of all students, including those from diverse cultural and linguistic backgrounds. Evidence shows that effective classroom instruction can reduce substantially the number of students who are inappropriately classified as learning disabled.
- A successful RTI process begins with the highest quality core instruction in the classroom—that is, instruction that encompasses all areas of language and literacy as part of a coherent curriculum that is developmentally appropriate for preK–12 students and does not underestimate their potential for learning. This core instruction may or may not involve commercial programs, and it must in all cases be provided by an informed, competent classroom teacher.
- The success of RTI depends on the classroom teacher's use of research-based practices.
- Research on instructional practices must provide not only information about what works, but also what works with whom, by whom, in what contexts, and on which outcomes. The effectiveness of a particular practice needs to have been demonstrated with the types of students who will receive the instruction, taking into account, for example, whether the students live in rural or urban settings or come from diverse cultural and linguistic backgrounds.
- When core language and literacy instruction is not effective for a particular student, it should be modified to address more closely the needs and abilities of that student.

2. Responsive Teaching and Differentiation

The RTI process emphasizes increasingly differentiated and intensified instruction or intervention in language and literacy.

- RTI is centrally about optimizing language and literacy instruction for particular students. This means that differentiated instruction, based on instructionally relevant assessment, is essential.

- Instruction and materials selection must derive from specific student–teacher interactions and not be constrained by packaged programs. Students have different language and literacy needs, so they may not respond similarly to instruction—even when research-based practices are used. No single approach to instruction or intervention can address the broad and varied goals and needs of all students, especially those from different cultural and linguistic backgrounds.

5. Systemic and Comprehensive Approaches

RTI must be part of a comprehensive, systemic approach to language and literacy assessment and instruction that supports all pre-K–12 students and teachers.

- RTI needs to be integrated within the context of a coherent and consistent language and literacy curriculum that guides comprehensive instruction for all students.
- Specific approaches to RTI need to be appropriate for the particular school or district culture and take into account leadership, expertise, the diversity of the student population, and the available resources. Schools and districts should adopt an approach that best matches their needs and resources while still accomplishing the overall goals of RTI.
- A systemic approach to language and literacy learning within an RTI framework requires the active participation and genuine collaboration of many professionals, including classroom teachers, reading specialists, literacy coaches, special educators, and school psychologists. Given the critical role that language development plays in literacy learning, professionals with specialized language-related expertise such as speech-language pathologists and teachers of ELLs may be particularly helpful in addressing students' language difficulties.
- Approaches to RTI must be sensitive to developmental differences in language and literacy among students at different ages and grades. Although many prevailing approaches to RTI focus on the early elementary grades, it is essential for teachers and support personnel at middle and secondary levels to provide their students with the language and literacy instruction they need to succeed in school and beyond.

Tier 2 Adaptations

IRA Standards for Reading Professionals

Standard 5: Literate Environment **Elements 5.1, 5.2, 5.3** (See previous)

Common Core Standards

Speaking and Listening: K–5
Comprehension and Collaboration (See previous)
Presentation of Knowledge and Ideas (See previous)

Speaking and Listening: Grades 6–12
Comprehension and Collaboration (See previous)
Presentation of Knowledge and Ideas (See previous)

Response to Intervention

2. Responsive Teaching and Differentiation (See previous)

4. Collaboration

RTI requires a dynamic, positive, and productive collaboration among professionals with relevant expertise in language and literacy. Success also depends on strong and respectful partnerships among professionals, parents, and students.

- Collaboration should be focused on the available evidence about the needs of students struggling in language and literacy. School-level decision-making teams (e.g., intervention teams, problem-solving teams, RTI teams) should include members with relevant

expertise in language and literacy, including second-language learning.

- Reading/literacy specialists and coaches should provide leadership in every aspect of an RTI process—planning, assessment, provision of more intensified instruction and support, and making decisions about next steps.
- Collaboration should increase, not reduce, the coherence of the instruction experienced by struggling readers.

5. Systemic and Comprehensive Approaches
(See previous)

Motivation and Engagement in Oral Language Development

IRA Standards for Reading Professionals

Standard 5: Literate Environment

Element 5.2 (See previous)

Common Core Standards

Speaking and Listening: K–5
Comprehension and Collaboration (See previous)
Presentation of Knowledge and Ideas (See previous)

Speaking and Listening: Grades 6–12
Comprehension and Collaboration (See previous)
Presentation of Knowledge and Ideas (See previous)

Response to Intervention

1. Instruction (see previous)

Technology and New Literacies for Oral Language Development

IRA Standards for Reading Professionals

Standard 5: Literate Environment

Element 5.1

Candidates design the physical environment to optimize students' use of traditional print, digital, and online resources in reading and writing instruction.

Common Core Standards

Speaking and Listening: K–5
Comprehension and Collaboration (See previous)
Presentation of Knowledge and Ideas (See previous)

Speaking and Listening: Grades 6–12
Comprehension and Collaboration (See previous)
Presentation of Knowledge and Ideas (See previous)

Response to Intervention

1. Instruction (See previous)

IRA Standards for Reading Professionals

Standard 4: Diversity
Elements 4.1, 4.2, 4.3 (See previous)

Common Core Standards

Speaking and Listening: Grades K–5
Comprehension and Collaboration (See previous)
Presentation of Knowledge and Ideas (See previous)

Speaking and Listening: Grades 6–12
Comprehension and Collaboration (See previous)
Presentation of Knowledge and Ideas (See previous)

Response to Intervention

4. Collaboration

RTI requires a dynamic, positive, and productive collaboration among professionals with relevant expertise in language and literacy. Success also depends on strong and respectful partnerships among professionals, parents, and students.

- Collaboration should be focused on the available evidence about the needs of students struggling in language and literacy. School-level decision-making teams (e.g., intervention teams, problem-solving teams, RTI teams) should include members with relevant expertise in language and literacy, including second-language learning.

- Involving parents and students and engaging them in a collaborative manner is critical to successful implementation. Initiating and strengthening collaborations among school, home, and communities, particularly in urban and rural areas, provides the basis for support and reinforcement of students' learning.

Early Reading **3**
Instruction
GETTING STARTED WITH THE ESSENTIALS

Teacher Knowledge	Classroom Assessment	Evidence-Based Teaching Practices	Response to Intervention (RTI)
Early Reading Concepts, Skills, and Strategies	Early Reading Classroom Assessment	Evidence-Based Early Reading Instruction Practices	Differentiating and Adapting Early Reading Instruction

Chapter Questions

- What are three early reading essentials?

- What criteria would you use to assess students' phonological and phonemic awareness?

- If you designed an instructional program for helping children learn letter names, what would it include?

- What are at least two ways in which early reading instruction can be accommodated for struggling readers and English learners?

- What are two ways teachers can motivate young students to learn to read?

- What are three technologies that can be used to support early readers as they learn to read?

- What are three programs of family literacy that have been researched to help schools and families support early readers?

Key Terms

Reading readiness

Emergent literacy

Print concepts

Phonemic awareness

Phonological awareness

Onset

Rime

Letter name knowledge

Oral blending

Oral segmenting

Motivation and Engagement	Technology and New Literacies	Family and Community Connections
Motivation and Engagement of Early Readers	Technology and New Literacies for Early Readers	Family and Community Support for Early Readers

Vignette: Inviting Them In

(Note: The following is based on an event that happened in a classroom attended by one of the authors as a child.)

Ms. Allen looked over her new class of kindergarten children at Emerson School. It was Thursday of the first week of school, and she was seeing the first signs of children becoming comfortable with their new and strange environment. To be sure, some of the children were practically pros—the ones who had attended the neighborhood preschool. But most of the 22 youngsters had not had that opportunity: They were from working-class families or from poverty, and preschool had not been an option for many of them in their small, rural town.

The one child Ms. Allen was most determined to reach today was Charles. On the first day, right after being walked to the school's front door by his mom, Ms. Jefferson, Charles fled school and actually beat his mom home. This may have been an indication that, in Charles's mind, school was not a great place to be.

On the second day of school, the principal phoned Ms. Jefferson and asked her to please come back to school and see her son. When she arrived at Principal Henderson's office, he asked her to look out the back window, which faced the playground. There Ms. Jefferson saw Charles . . . happily walking along the four-foot-high stone wall at the perimeter of the schoolyard about a hundred yards away. He had evidently gone straight to the wall at the opening bell. "You think he's a little reluctant about coming to school?" the principal asked with a grin. After much coaxing by his mother, Charles stoically took his place in Ms. Allen's class that day and was there again this morning.

Ms. Allen's goal was to make Charles feel at home at all costs. Perhaps a good way to achieve that goal, she told herself, was to help him feel some success in early reading. Later that day, when she was able to have all of the children working at stations, she called Charles aside for a little one-on-one assessment. "Charles," Ms. Allen began, "I'm so happy I have you in my class this year. I can tell you are very smart and you'll probably be one of my kindergarten leaders!" She gave Charles a genuine smile as she spoke and the lad beamed.

Ms. Allen continued by laying an index card between them. On it she had written his name in block letters. "Do you know what this says?"

"That's my name, Ms. Allen!" Charles responded with pride.

"That's right! I knew you were a reader the first day I saw you." Charles smiled, but she saw some puzzlement in his face. A reader?

"Yes," she said, anticipating his puzzlement. "One of the very first steps in becoming a reader is to know your own name when you see it. Good job!"

Charles relaxed slightly and Ms. Allen could see the tension starting to ebb. She had him! Next Ms. Allen asked, "Charles, can you tell me what any of the letters are in your name?"

Charles responded by pointing and saying, "This is *c*." He glanced up for affirmation.

"Correct!" said Ms. Allen. "What other letters do you know?"

Skipping over *h* and *a*, Charles confidently proclaimed, "This letter is *r*. It says *rrrrrrr*. My mom taught me that!"

"Your mom is a great teacher, Charles," said Ms. Allen. He nodded his agreement.

After continuing with this exercise, and then later with a short phonemic awareness and letter-naming test, Ms. Allen concluded her 10-minute session saying, "Charles, I am so pleased with how much you know about sounds and letters. You know so many! This year we will learn together all of the sounds and letters, and before you know it, you'll be able to read just about any book you want! How's that sound?"

"I like that, Ms. Allen." Charles returned her smile. He went back to his center activity, this time with a little more spring in his step. I think Charles will be just fine, thought Ms. Allen. ▪

Teacher Knowledge

Early Reading Concepts, Skills, and Strategies

Primary-grade teachers like Ms. Allen know well how to assess and teach the essentials of beginning reading instruction. Nested in a classroom environment resplendent with great books, where children engage in abundant amounts of reading and writing, there are essential skills, concepts, and strategies young children must learn to become readers. Not only do young children need to have books read aloud, print displayed around the room, and abundant opportunities to write, but they also need to have a teacher like Ms. Allen, who knows what is important to teach young children to get them off to a good start.

Over many decades, research has been converging on what pre-K, kindergarten, and primary grade teachers need to know—and children need to learn—in order to make progress in early reading instruction. In this chapter, we focus our attention on three of these essential beginning reading concepts, skills, and strategies: phonological and phonemic awareness, letter name knowledge, and print concepts.

IRA Standards for Reading Professionals: Standard 1, Elements 1.1, 1.3; Standard 2, Elements 2.1, 2.2, 2.3

What Is Early Reading and How Do Young Children Become Readers?

The question "What is early reading?" or perhaps more appropriately, "What should early reading instruction include?" has been at the heart of a long and continuing debate in the early childhood and elementary school teaching profession. In the late 1920s and early 1930s, early reading was thought to be the result of reading readiness (Smith, 2002). The concept of **reading readiness** distinguished readiness for reading from a general readiness for learning. During the reading readiness era of early reading instruction, researchers attempted to determine a threshold or point in time at which children could be taught to read with the greatest success rates. In practice, however, the concept of reading readiness often led to teachers withholding reading and writing instruction from young children until they were thought to be "ready" for reading.

In the early 1970s, the definition of early reading as "reading readiness" was challenged by a new concept. **Emergent literacy** is a term that implies children are becoming literate beginning at birth and continue to develop as literate beings throughout life. However, emergent literacy, like its predecessor philosophy, reading readiness, has been challenged in recent years.

Many of those who embraced the concept of emergent literacy believed that because literacy learning began at birth and extended throughout life, children learned to read and write as naturally as they learned to speak. As a result, some educators and teachers during the whole language era in the 1980s and early 1990s spurned the direct teaching of essential beginning reading skills. Many of the teachers who subscribed to a whole language philosophy of early reading instruction thought it was only necessary to "immerse" children in print by reading aloud to them or provide students informal experiences with books, literature, and opportunities to write (Goodman, 1986; Smith, 1985; Tunnell & Jacobs, 1989). This extreme whole language view became largely discredited when, in the mid-1990s, the 1994 National Assessment of Educational Progress (NAEP) found that large numbers of school children were failing to learn to read "proficiently" at grade level (Reutzel & Mitchell, 2005).

An overwhelming sense of frustration in the nation and within the profession of education itself led the U.S. Congress and then-President Clinton to appoint a National Reading Panel (NRP) to determine based on scientific evidence the most effective methods for teaching young children to read. The National Reading Panel (2000) found sufficient evidence to support five essentials of early reading instruction:

1. Phonemic awareness
2. Alphabetics (to include letter knowledge and phonics instruction)
3. Fluency
4. Vocabulary
5. Comprehension

Many educators and scholars over the past decade since the publication of the NRP report (2000) have sharply criticized the panel's findings as being too narrow in scope (Allington, 2002, 2006; Garan, 2002; Pressley, 2002). However, like NRP member T. Shanahan (2004), we find it difficult indeed to imagine early reading instruction without these five essentials.

Following release of the National Reading Panel's report, a second panel was commissioned to further study emergent reading. Their report, titled *Developing Early Literacy: Report of the National Early Literacy Panel*, examined early skills and abilities that predicted young children's (birth to age 5) later reading, writing, and spelling abilities. They also investigated the efficacy of programs, interventions, and instructional approaches that are linked to students' later outcomes in reading, writing, and spelling. Also of interest to the Early Literacy Panel were environments and settings shown to either inhibit or enhance students' literacy learning, as well as parenting and child characteristics linked to later literacy achievement.

Skills, concepts, and abilities found to be predictive of young students' later reading, writing, and spelling achievement include the following:

1. *Alphabet knowledge.* Knowledge of the names and sounds associated with printed letters
2. *Phonological awareness.* The ability to detect, manipulate, and analyze the auditory aspects (sounds) of spoken language, including words, syllables, and phonemes

3. *Rapid automatic naming (RAN) of letters or digits.* The ability to rapidly recognize and name a series of letters or digits
4. *Rapid automatic naming (RAN) of objects or colors.* The ability to recognize items or colors in a set of pictures of objects
5. *Writing letters of one's name in isolation*
6. *Phonological memory.* The ability to remember and repeat spoken information for a short period of time
7. *Concepts about print and print conventions*
8. *Oral language production and comprehension.* The ability to understand aspects of spoken language, including grammar and vocabulary
9. *Visual processing.* The ability to match or discriminate visually presented symbols

In addition, the National Early Literacy Panel (2008) found that phonics, or code-focused programs, book sharing, programs for parents to use at home, and oral language enhancement instruction help develop young students' oral language skills. Code-focused programs that directed children's attention on learning how to unlock the alphabetic code best predicted young students' later literacy growth. Age, race, and socioeconomic status (SES) did not seem to alter the effectiveness of the literacy interventions identified by the National Early Literacy Panel (2008).

Evidence clearly indicates that although some children appear to emerge into reading and writing effortlessly, this emergence rarely occurs naturally. Instead, young children's success in early reading is largely dependent on knowledgeable teachers who understand and teach early reading essentials to young children. Strickland and her colleagues echoed this finding when in 2002 they pointed out that not all children were succeeding as early readers, which, they believed, reaffirmed the need for improved early reading instruction and intervention.

Children's early literacy success, or failure, steers their academic course for years to come. In a document titled *Teaching Reading IS Rocket Science,* the American Federation of Teachers (1999) concluded that "the rate of reading failure for some groups [e.g., African-American, Hispanic, Native American] is 60 to 70 percent" (p. 9). Research also indicates that a pattern of school failure starts early and then often persists throughout a child's school career. Juel (1988) found that there is approximately a 90 percent chance that a child who is a poor reader in first grade will be a poor reader in fourth grade.

The evidence at hand today indicates that early reading is a developmental process that requires intentional, systematic, and explicit instruction by a knowledgeable teacher. Research on early reading development focuses principally on two large categories of reading instruction: word recognition and comprehension (Lomax & McGee, 1987; Morris, Bloodgood, Lomax, & Perney, 2003; Rasinski, 2003; Stahl, 2004). This early reading developmental process is represented in Figure 3.1.

Figure 3.1

Early Reading Developmental Processes

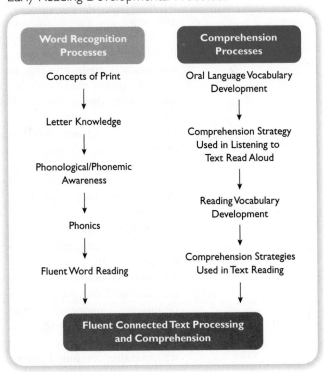

What Does Research Say About the Essentials of Early Reading Instruction?

Some children enter school already knowing a great deal about how books work, whereas others do not (e.g., Burns, Griffin, & Snow, 1999; Early Childhood–Head Start Taskforce, 2002; Reutzel, Young, Fawson, Morrison, & Wilcox, 2003; Yaden & Templeton, 1986). Some children know the difference between a word and a letter; others know where a story begins in a book; and others have had little access to books and few guided experiences with print (Neuman, 1999; Neuman & Celano, 2001). Concepts associated with printed language, such as directionality (reading left to right, top to bottom), concepts of word or letter, book handling, voice–print matching, and punctuation, are known as **print concepts** (also *concepts about print*) and are an essential part of early reading development for many beginning readers.

Research also shows that young children must develop phonological and **phonemic awareness** to succeed in learning to read (e.g., Adams, 2001; Armbruster, Lehr, & Osborn, 2001; National Reading Panel, 2000). Phonological and phonemic awareness involve the conceptual understanding that spoken language can be broken down into smaller units such as sentences, phrases, words, syllables, onsets, rimes, and phonemes (sounds). We know from the work of Marilyn Adams (2001) that children's **phonological awareness** begins with a perception of individual words in spoken language, followed by discernment of the syllables within words. Next, children become aware that syllables are made up of **onsets** (all the sounds in the syllable *before* the vowel) and **rimes** (the vowel sound in a syllable and everything following it). Third, young children become conscious of individual sounds, or phonemes, in spoken language. Finally, children develop the ability to manipulate (delete and substitute) individual sounds in spoken words. From these research findings, the teacher of reading realizes that children's awareness of spoken language progresses from the whole (ideas shared through speech) to the parts (individual words, syllables, onsets and rimes, and then phonemes).

In addition to phonological and phonemic awareness, the National Reading Panel (2000) and the National Early Literacy Panel (2008) point out the equally important contribution that **letter name knowledge** makes to early reading success, the NRP noting that "correlational studies identified PA [phonemic awareness] and letter knowledge as the two best school-entry predictors of how well children will learn to read during the first 2 years of instruction" (p. 7). The Early Childhood–Head Start Taskforce (2002), in a report titled *Teaching Our Youngest*, added, "Children who enter kindergarten knowing many letter names tend to have an easier time learning to read than do children who have not learned these skills" (p. 21). Burns, Griffin, and Snow (1999), in a document for the National Research Council titled *Starting Out Right*, listed "recognizes and can name all uppercase and lowercase letters" (p. 85) as one of several desirable kindergarten outcomes with regard to reading instruction. Finally, Stage, Sheppard, Davidson, and Browning (2001) found that letter naming fluency, or accurate and effortless letter naming ability, is a unique predictor of children's reading fluency at the end of first grade. Thus, letter name recognition is an essential skill to be taught and learned in early reading instruction. Taken together, research evidence clearly points out that print concepts, phonological/phonemic awareness, and letter name knowledge are critical stepping stones toward early reading success.

Recent research reported by Piasta and Wagner (2010) found that reading instruction that combined other early literacy skills and concepts such as oral language, print concepts, and phonological/phonemic awareness with attention to alphabet learning, had the greatest effect on students' later literacy growth. We talk more about how to apply this finding in your classroom later in the chapter.

Classroom Assessment

Early Reading Classroom Assessment

There are many purposes for conducting early reading assessment (Miesels & Piker, 2001). For most elementary classroom teachers, reading assessment is used to monitor students' progress and to inform the teacher's instructional decisions. Given these twin purposes for early reading assessment, the natural question to ask next is "*Which* early reading skills should teachers assess?" We would answer with the following list:

● ● ●
**IRA Standards
for Reading
Professionals:**
Standard 3, Elements 3.1,
3.2, 3.3

**Response to
Intervention:**
Assessment

- Oral language vocabulary and development
- Concepts about print
- Phonological and phonemic awareness
- Letter name knowledge
- Sight word recognition
- Phonics knowledge
- Listening comprehension

Many tools are available for assessing these essentials of early reading instruction, and we recommend that our readers obtain a copy of our companion book, *Strategies for Reading Assessment and Instruction: Helping Every Child Succeed,* 4th edition (Reutzel & Cooter, 2011) if more assessment tools are needed than we are able to provide here.

Assessing Concepts About Print (CAP)

In recent years, researchers and research reports have emphasized the importance of print concepts for success in early reading (Burns, Griffin, & Snow, 1999; Clay, 2000a; Early Childhood–Head Start Taskforce, 2002; Hiebert, Pearson, Taylor, Richardson, & Paris, 1998; Lomax & McGee, 1987; McGee & Richgels, 2003; Morris et al., 2003; Reutzel et al., 2003; Yaden & Templeton, 1986). Unfortunately, not all young children have had equal access to printed language in their everyday experiences, homes, and communities (Neuman, 1999; Neuman & Celano, 2001). Teachers need to know how well their children understand print concepts. We explain one informal classroom assessment, the Metalinguistic Interview, and one commercially published assessment, the Concepts About Print Test (Clay, 2000a, b), for examining young students' print concepts.

The Metalinguistic Interview.   The metalinguistic interview is an informal measure of young children's print concepts. It consists of a set of questions designed to assess children's understanding of academic or instructional language—the language teachers use in instruction as they talk about printed text. Young children often do not have a clear understanding of many of the common academic or instructional terms used in beginning reading instruction, such as *alphabet, letter, word,* and *sentence* (Clay, 1966; Denny & Weintraub, 1966; Downing, 1970, 1971–1972; Reid, 1966).

Knowledge of these terms is most likely linked to how well children understand and respond to early reading instruction. Academic or instructional language terms and concepts assessed in the metalinguistic interview include the following:

- Concept of a single letter, word, or sentence
- Directionality L → R (left to right), T → D (top/down), and so on
- Punctuation
- How to differentiate uppercase and lowercase letters
- Terms such as the *front* and *back* of a book or the *pages* inside

Any children's trade book or literature book containing both pictures and print may be used to administer a metalinguistic interview. For kindergarten assessment, locate a book that has print (no more than three sentences) on one page and a full-page picture on the facing page. A scoring sheet can easily be constructed by duplicating Figure 3.2.

Begin your assessment by seating the child comfortably next to you. Hand the child a picture book such as *The Gingerbread Man* (Schmidt, 1985) or *The Little Red Hen* (McQueen, 1985) upside down, with the spine of the book facing the child. Once the child has taken the book, say that the two of you are going to read the book together. Go through the list of interview questions and tasks listed in Figure 3.2. Mark responses on your copy of the figure.

When scoring a metalinguistic interview, write 0 or 1 following each of the 20 items. Scores on the interview range from a low of 0 to a high of 20. Carefully examine which items were missed in order to determine potential areas for print concepts instruction.

Figure 3.2

The Metalinguistic Interview

1. "What are books for? What do books have in them?" _____
2. "Show me the front cover of the book. Show me the back cover of the book." _____
3. "Show me the title of the book." _____
4. "Show me the author's name." _____
5. "Open the book to where I should begin reading." _____
6. "Show me which way my eyes should go on the page when I begin reading." _____
7. "Show me the last line on the page." _____
8. Begin reading the book. At the end of the first page ask, "Where do I go next?" _____
9. "Show me where to begin reading on this page. Will you point to the words with your finger as I say them?" _____
10. "Show me a sentence on this page." _____
11. "Show me the second word in a sentence on this page." _____
12. "Show me a word." _____
13. "Show me the first letter in that word." _____
14. "Show me the last letter in that word." _____
15. "Show me a period on this page." _____
16. "Show me a question mark on this page." _____
17. Show the child a quotation mark and ask, "What is this? What is it used for?" _____
18. Ask the child to put his fingers around a word. _____
19. Ask the child to put his fingers around a letter. _____
20. Ask the child to point to an uppercase letter and then a lowercase letter. _____

Correct responses are given a 1 score. Incorrect responses are scored 0.

Total Score _____

The Concepts About Print Test.   The Concepts About Print Test (CAP), developed by Marie Clay (1972, 2000b), is a commercially published instrument used to assess children's knowledge of concepts about printed or written language such as letter, word, sentence, directionality, text versus picture, and punctuation. The CAP test makes use of four small test-like booklets, two published in 1972, titled *Sand* and *Stones*, and two published in 2000, titled *No Shoes* and *Follow Me, Moon*. All four are read aloud by the teacher in working with individual students. We suggest that *Sand* and *Stones* be used for pre- and posttesting in kindergarten, and *No Shoes* and *Follow Me, Moon* be used for pre- and posttesting during first grade.

Directions for administering, scoring, and interpreting the Concepts About Print Test are found in Clay's (2000a) book, *Concepts About Print: What Have Children Learned About the Way We Print Language?*

Print concepts assessed in the CAP test include the following:

- Front of book
- Proper book orientation to begin reading
- Beginning of book
- Print, rather than pictures, carries the message
- Directional rules of left to right
- Top to bottom on a page
- Return sweep to the beginning of a line of print
- Matching spoken words with written words
- Concepts of first and last letters in a word
- Mapping spoken word and letter order onto print
- Beginning and ending of a story
- Punctuation marks
- Sight words
- Identifying printed letters, words, and upper- versus lowercase letters

In order to adequately test children's print concepts, the *Sand, Stones, No Shoes,* and *Follow Me, Moon* booklets make use of some rather unusual features. For example, at certain points the print or pictures in the test-like booklets are upside down, letter and word order are changed or reversed (*saw* for *was*), line order is reversed, and paragraph indentions are removed or inverted. Because of the somewhat tedious nature of this test and its tasks, children need to be tested in a calm environment by an examiner with whom they have a trusting relationship. The CAP test has established a long and excellent record as valid and reliable when used in conjunction with other tools in assessing beginning reading skills, concepts, and strategies in the early years (Denton, Ciancio, & Fletcher, 2006).

Assessing Phonemic Awareness

Researchers and research reports have long demonstrated the importance of young students' phonemic awareness for getting reading off to a good start (Adams, 1990, 2001; Adams, Foorman, Lundberg, & Beeler, 1998; Bear, Templeton, Invernizzi, & Johnston, 2008; Blevins, 1997, 1998; Goswami, 2000, 2001; National Reading Panel, 2000; Snow, Burns, & Griffin, 1998). It is estimated that roughly 20 percent of young children lack phonemic awareness (Blevins, 1997). Though phonemic awareness is no "magic cure" for preventing or fixing all reading problems (Shanahan, 2003b), it is certainly an essential component of early reading instruction (Shaywitz & Shaywitz, 2004). Two critical skills for young children to acquire in relation to phonemic awareness are oral blending and segmenting (Yeh, 2003). **Oral blending** refers to the ability to put spoken sounds together to say a word. **Oral segmenting** refers to stretching out a spoken word and being able to say each sound heard in the word. To help teachers assess young students' phonemic awareness, we present two assessment tools—one each for assessing oral blending and segmenting abilities.

Auditory Blending Test. Much like Roswell and Chall's Auditory Blending Test (1963), the auditory blending test (ABT), an informal assessment tool, requires students to say a word after hearing its individual sounds slowly articulated by the teacher. In other words, teachers say the word using segmented sound units (i.e., *m-an* or *sh-i-p*) and the child responds by blending the sounds mentally and then saying the word—*man* or *ship*. According to Griffith and Olson (1992), the ability to manipulate sounds in this way to blend the word from its segmented form demonstrates a high level of phonemic awareness. Yeh (2003) found that blending is one of two phonemic awareness tasks that cause kindergarten children to reach high levels of early reading achievement.

To administer an ABT, prepare a list of 30 words divided into three sets of 10 as follows (see Figure 3.3):

- The first 10 words should be two-phoneme words.
- The second set of 10 words should be three- to four-phoneme words that are divided before the vowel, demonstrating the onset and rime—for example, *c* (onset) -*ap* (rime).
- The third set of 10 words should be three- to four-phoneme words that are segmented completely—for example, *ch-i-p*.

Begin administering the ABT by telling the child that you will be stretching words out by saying the sounds in them slowly. Model several of these stretched words for the child and blend the words you have stretched. For example, stretch the word *s-i-t*. Then say the word: *sit*. Do this several times. Next, stretch a word and ask the child to tell you the word. Once this has been accomplished, say that you are going to play a game in which you say a stretched-out word and the child is to answer the question you will then ask: "What am I saying?" According to Yopp's (1988) research, kindergarten children should achieve a mean score of 66 percent, or correctly identify 20 out of the 30 target words.

Figure 3.3

Auditory Blending Test Sample Word List

at	l-ap	l-o-ck
two	t-ip	s-t-e-m
in	m-an	b-ea-k
if	st-ate	h-i-de
be	b-ox	c-a-sh
as	sc-ab	m-i-c-e
sea	r-ug	sh-ee-t
now	m-ind	f-r-o-g
go	th-ink	j-u-m-p
sew	p-ig	t-ur-key

Phoneme Segmenting Test. Yeh (2003) found that segmenting is the second phonemic awareness ability enabling kindergarten children to reach high levels of early reading achievement. In a phoneme segmenting test (PST), students are asked to listen to and isolate sounds in spoken words. The ability to isolate the sounds in spoken words is an excellent indication of whether a child will profit from initial phonics instruction, especially as pertaining to early spelling and writing development. The test should comprise 15 words consisting of three phonemes each. Target sounds in the beginnings, middles, and ends of the words should be like those shown in Figure 3.4.

The teacher begins by modeling how phonemes can be pronounced, showing how *sit* starts with /s/, *hike* has the /ī/ sound in the middle, and *look* ends with the /k/ sound. Next, the teacher tells the child they are going to play a quick game together: "I will say a word, and then you tell me the sound you hear in a certain place in the word, such as the beginning, the middle, or the end." As an example, the teacher might say, "*Slam.* Say the sound at the end of the word *slam.*" The child would respond correctly by articulating the /m/ sound.

The teacher should record each student's responses. According to Yopp's (1988) research, young children should achieve a mean score of 9 percent, or one to two correct responses out of 15 target words, at the beginning of kindergarten. By the end of kindergarten, young children should be able to segment words into individual sounds and represent these sounds with written letters, producing short words like *man, fun,* or *sit.*

Assessing Letter Name Knowledge

Recall earlier that we discussed the significance of recognizing and being able to name the letters of the alphabet in early reading acquisition. The National Reading Panel (2000) identifies letter name knowledge as one of the two best predictors and the National Early Literacy Panel (2008) identifies letter name knowledge as the single best predictor of early reading achievement. The letter naming task shown here, which is based on the work of Marie Clay (1993), can be used to determine whether young children can identify the letters of the alphabet.

Teachers begin this assessment by first reproducing a randomized alphabet letter display like the one shown in Figure 3.5 on a sheet of paper or chart paper. Next, the teacher explains that they are going to find out which letters of the alphabet the student can name. The teacher then points to the letters on the randomized letter display chart, beginning at the top of the display working left to right and line by line to the bottom of the display. The teacher uses a photocopy of the randomized letter display to mark the letters the child correctly names. The teacher then reverses the process, naming letters and asking the child to point to them out in the randomized letter display. The teacher also records this information.

Most young children should be able to identify 100 percent of the letters by the end of kindergarten. However, students who have little familiarity with letters at the beginning of kindergarten may perform poorly on this task. Fluency of letter naming is also related

Figure 3.4

Auditory Phoneme Segmenting Test Sample Word List

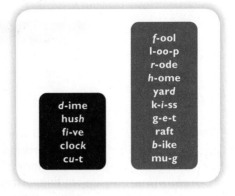

Click on A+RISE—WIDA ELP Standard Strategies in the MyEducationLab (www.myeducationlab.com) for your course. Next, select the Strategy Card Index tab, scroll to Phonics for grades K–5, and select the Letter Patterns strategy.

Figure 3.5

Randomized Alphabet Letter Display

to students' later reading achievement (Piasta & Wagner, 2010). The DIBELS Letter Naming Fluency (LNF) test is a quick and reliable test for determining students' letter naming fluency.

Evidence-Based Teaching Practices

Evidence-Based Early Reading Instruction Practices

● ● ●

IRA Standards for Reading Professionals: Standard 2, Elements 2.1, 2.2, 2.3; Standard 5, Elements 5.1, 5.2, 5.3

Common Core Standards: Reading: K–5, Key Ideas and Details (item 1)

Response to Intervention: Instruction; Systemic and Comprehensive Approaches

Children who get off to a good start in early reading rarely fall behind. Those who do fall behind tend to stay behind for the rest of their academic lives (Burns, Griffin, & Snow, 1999; Fielding, Kerr, & Rosier, 1998). It is imperative, then, that early reading instruction be evidence based so that all children have an equal opportunity to get off to a great start.

Effective early reading instruction has been the focus of several lines of research over the past two decades. This research has focused on teacher knowledge and the instructional elements and practices that lead to student achievement in early reading (August & Shanahan, 2006; Block, Oakar, & Hurt, 2002; Morrow, Tracey, Woo, & Pressley, 1999; National Early Literacy Panel, 2008; National Reading Panel, 2000; Pressley, Allington, Wharton-McDonald, Collins-Block, & Morrow, 2001; Taylor, Pearson, Peterson, & Rodriguez, 2005).

In addition to our insistence that teachers must focus early reading instruction on the "nonnegotiables" for children to succeed, such as phonemic awareness and letter name recognition, we also freely acknowledge that many other conditions must be present in classrooms for young children to flourish in early reading instruction. For instance, Morrow and her colleagues (1999) identified several characteristics of effective early reading instruction by studying the practices of exemplary first-grade reading teachers in New Jersey. All of these teachers produced exceptional reading achievement in their classrooms, which were happy places—communities of learning founded on the principles of respect, cooperation, and high expectations for hard work and achievement. The classrooms were rich with access to printed materials for reading and print production supplies for writing.

These exemplary teachers understood that in order to meet the diverse needs of their students, they were called on to employ multiple instructional strategies involving the whole group, small groups, partners, and one-to-one instruction. The early reading essentials—phonemic and phonological awareness, concepts about print, and letter name and sound knowledge—were explicitly and systematically taught. Children were immersed in abundant teacher-guided reading practice with feedback using appropriately selected texts: authentic literature, leveled books, decodable books, and big books. They read books aloud to students, especially information books but also storybooks. Their instruction was carefully planned, but these teachers also responded spontaneously to "teachable moments" as they occurred in the daily routines of the classroom. Exemplary early reading teachers were consistent in their expectations, student training, and daily execution of classroom management procedures, routines, and schedules.

Learning activities were engaging, varied, and involved children actively, often playfully. Instruction took a variety of forms: writing activities, shared reading and writing, reading aloud, modeled or shared writing, interactive writing, word study, word analysis, reading performances, guided reading, and independent reading and writing. Students often acquired content knowledge in themed cycles or units of study focused on exciting topics in social studies, science, and mathematics. Finally, exemplary teachers were students themselves, always seeking opportunities to learn how to teach early reading more effectively in grade-level team meetings, in professional development training sessions, and at professional conferences.

Much of what these researchers found (Morrow et al., 1999) forms a kind of template for the remainder of this chapter and the remaining chapters of our book.

The Essentials of Early Reading Instruction

Effective early reading instruction focuses on teaching young children the essential skills, concepts, and strategies necessary for developing fluent, expressive, and strategic reading. As discussed previously, these essentials include (1) oral language development, (2) concepts about print, (3) phonological and phonemic awareness, (4) letter name and sound knowledge, (5) sight word recognition, (6) phonics knowledge, (7) vocabulary, and (8) comprehension. We will confine our discussion of early reading instructional strategies in this chapter to print concepts, phonological and phonemic awareness, and letter name and sound knowledge. For each of these three, we will offer effective instructional strategies for introducing and reinforcing these concepts. We begin with instruction in print concepts.

Print Concepts Instruction

An understanding of print concepts can be divided into three distinct aspects of print: (1) functional purposes, (2) mapping elements, and (3) technical conventions (Clay, 2000a; Taylor, 1986).

Functions of Print.   Children learn early that written language, like oral language, is useful for a variety of purposes. Halliday's (1975) landmark research describes how oral and written language functions in our daily lives. The purposes children and adults have for using language can be divided into three categories: (1) conceptual, or expressions of one's thoughts; (2) interpersonal, or intimate/social interactions; and (3) factual, or information communication. Smith (1977) expanded on Halliday's theories about purposes for which language can be used, proposing ten functions of language, whether oral or written (Smith, 1977, p. 640): instrumental, regulatory, interactional, personal, heuristic, imaginative, representational, divertive, authoritative/contractual, and perpetuating. Children make use of oral language for varied purposes in their lives, at least in a subconscious way. As you help students become aware of these oral language functions, they will readily apply this knowledge in their written language as well.

Mapping Speech onto Print.   The ability to match or "map" speech sounds onto printed symbols or letters develops rather slowly. Some researchers believe that the ability to map speech sounds onto printed language and knowledge of the sound–symbol code, or phonics knowledge, may develop simultaneously (Lomax & McGee, 1987). Important concepts for students to learn include the following.

1. Speech can be written down and read. What is written down can also be spoken.
2. Print is in our environment in the form of signs and logos.

3. The message of a text is constructed from the print rather than from the pictures.
4. Written language uses different structures (see Halliday, 1975, and Smith, 1977, mentioned above) than spoken language.
5. The length of a spoken word is usually related to the length of the written word.
6. One written word equals one spoken word.
7. Correspondences exist between spoken sounds and written symbols.
8. Using context and other language-related clues can help readers construct meaning and identify words.

Mapping speech onto print helps students become successful readers and benefit from further experiences with written language (Reutzel, Oda, & Moore, 1989). For some readers, failing to acquire an understanding of mapping principles can slow their progress in reading and writing development (Clay, 1991; Ehri & Sweet, 1991; Johns, 1980).

Technical Aspects of Print.   The rules or conventions that govern written language constitute the technical aspects of print and include directionality (left to right/top to bottom progression across and down the page in reading), spatial orientation, and instructional terms used in classrooms to refer to written language elements. Because many of these technical concepts are commonsense matters for adults, it is little wonder that sometimes teachers and parents mistakenly assume that children already understand them. There is, however, ample evidence that knowledge of the technical aspects of written language is an important part of learning to read and write (Clay, 1979; Day & Day, 1979; Denton et al., 2006; Downing & Oliver, 1973; Johns, 1980; Meltzer & Himse, 1969; Morris et al., 2003; Reutzel et al., 2003). The technical aspects of print are summarized in Table 3.1.

Strategies for Teaching Young Children Concepts About Print

Lomax and McGee (1987) discovered that students' concepts of print have a direct relationship with learning letter name knowledge. Concept of word has been shown to interact with young students' abilities to spell using beginning and ending consonants and their ability to segment spoken words into phonemes (Morris et al., 2003).

Table 3.1

Technical Aspects of Print Concepts

Ordinal	Visual Clues Embedded in Books and Print	Location Concepts
• First, second, third, etc.	• Cover, spine, pages	• Top
• Beginning	• Margins, indentations	• Bottom
• Last	• Spacing	• Left
• Book	• Print size	• Right
• Paragraph	• Punctuation	• Beginning (front, start, initial)
• Sentence		• Middle (center, medial, in between)
• Word		
• Letter		

The National Early Literacy Panel (2008) found that students' concepts about print were moderately associated with young students' later reading achievement.

In recent studies on alphabet learning, Piasta and Wagner (2010) found that alphabet learning coupled with print concepts instruction is associated with young students' later literacy growth. Unlike many early literacy concepts and skills, print concepts are best learned implicitly in the context of examining and processing text rather than taught explicitly in isolated lessons. Reutzel, Oda, and Moore (1989) found that students learned concepts of print best when immersed in text, with the teacher guiding and pointing out print concepts in a shared reading of a big book where students could see them operating on the content.

Using Environmental Print to Teach Print Concepts.   Researchers have examined the value of using environmental print to teach children print concepts and have consistently shown it to be useful in initiating children's awareness of print in their world (Kuby & Aldridge, 1994; Neuman & Roskos, 1993; Orellana & Hernandez, 1999; Proudfoot, 1992; Reutzel et al., 2003; Vukelich, 1994; West & Egley, 1998). Environmental print is not only useful for giving children experiences with print that they see in the world outside of the classroom, but it can also help build children's confidence in their ultimate ability to learn to read (Reutzel et al., 2003).

The term *environmental print* refers to print that is frequent and commonly accessible in children's community, school, and home environments. Examples include signs in the school building and on school grounds, such as STOP, EXIT, and NO SMOKING. Other examples of environmental print include signs on, in, and around businesses and stores, and on products children and families commonly consume, such as McDonald's, Cheerios, Diet Coke, and so forth. To use environmental resources for teaching print concepts to early readers, you will need to gather product labels and logos. One strategy for adapting environmental print to teach print concepts involves creating "I Can Read" books. Titles for environmental print "I Can Read" books might include "My Favorite Foods," "I Spy: Signs I See," "A Trip to the Supermarket," and "My Favorite Things."

To prepare students for creating their own "I Can Read" books, present a read-aloud book that will serve as a template. If the selected topic is "Going Shopping," you might choose Lobel's *On Market Street* (1981). After selecting a template book, gather environmental print and product labels that can be used in the children's "I Can Read" books.

To present a lesson focused on the theme of "Going Shopping," read the template book *On Market Street* aloud to students, pausing to discuss each of the items the main character purchases while shopping on Market Street. After reading, tell students they are going to make their own "Going Shopping" book using *On Market Street* as a pattern. Model for students how to select different products for inclusion in their books: They must select an item whose name is indicated on the product label and begins with the alphabet letter on the bottom of the page. For example, the page featuring an *A* might be matched with an All detergent label or an Alphabits cereal label. You may want to pick just a few, perhaps no more than five to ten, familiar letters the children have been learning to include in the Going Shopping books. Once you have explained and modeled the process, children can be invited to create their own "I Can Read" *On Market Street* (Lobel, 1981) book by selecting product labels from a classroom collection or from several copied pages of product labels they can cut out. This is just one example of how children can use print they often recognize in their world to learn more about print concepts such as words and letters, matching letters, and so on.

You might also create a bulletin board featuring the 26 letters of the alphabet with an area for each letter where product logos can be displayed. Involve students in collecting, sharing, and displaying the print they read in their environment. One quick caution, however: Be sure to tell children that before they can remove a label from something at home, they need to get a parent's or caregiver's permission. It is most annoying to open a can without a label expecting to find corn and discovering refried beans!

Using Shared Reading Experiences to Teach Print Concepts. Shared reading, or what is sometimes called the *shared book experience,* is a way to model with very young readers how readers look at, figure out, and understand print. Shared reading is a logical and evidence-based context to teach young students print concepts (daCruz-Payne, 2005; Reutzel et al., 1989). During shared reading, the teacher typically uses a large-print text with a group of children, rather than a traditional-sized book with an individual child (Slaughter, 1993). In a shared book experience, children and teachers must be able to look at the print simultaneously. As noted, this requires that the print be enlarged so that every child can see it and process it with teacher guidance (Barrett, 1982; daCruz-Payne, 2005). When selecting big books, be sure the print is large enough for children to see from 20 feet away. Shared reading books should have literary merit, engaging content (both fiction and nonfiction), and high interest. Illustrations in shared reading books should augment and expand on the text. Books chosen for shared reading should also put reasonable demands on younger readers' capabilities. However, the number of unknown words in a book selected for shared reading should not overwhelm students.

Begin a shared book experience by inviting children to look at the book cover while you read the title aloud. Display and discuss the front and back covers of the book; point out certain features of the cover and title page, such as the author and illustrator names, publisher, and copyright date. Read the book with "full dramatic punch, perhaps overdoing a little some of the best parts" (Barrett, 1982, p. 16). While reading the story, invite children to join in reading any repeated or predictable words or phrases. They positively love doing this! At key points during shared read-

Michael Newman/PhotoEdit

ing, pause to encourage children to predict what is coming next in the story and to explain their predictions. ("That's an interesting prediction. What made you think that?") After reading, invite children to share their responses to the story. Ask them to talk about their favorite parts and connect the story to their experiences. Discuss how well they were able to predict and participate.

Once a shared reading book has been presented, you might select something from the print in the book to examine in a print concept reading. For example, in *The Carrot Seed* (Krauss, 1945), which is available in big book format, you might decide that students should understand the print concept of *word*—the visual detail that printed words are separated by spaces on either side. To direct students' attention to the spaces between the words in the text, you might use two-inch lengths of wax-covered string called *wikki stiks*. These adhere to the pages of a book without leaving a residue. During the lesson, engage students in the second reading of a text, pointing to and talking about the spaces between words. Insert wikki stiks between the words on the first page of the text and then count the words. Turn to the next page of the text, and invite a child to come forward and place wikki stiks between the words. This time, direct the whole class to count the words with you. This process of sharing the identification and counting of words on pages is repeated for the rest of the book. Eventually, ask volunteers to place the wikki stiks between words independently and to count words without your assistance.

We have found that teachers need the following tools to teach print concepts during a shared reading experience in their classroom.

- Large-print text
- Post-it notes
- Highlighting tape
- Pointer
- Fixed and sliding print frames
- Lap-sized whiteboard
- Word and sentence strips
- Chart or big book easel
- Pocket charts

Print concepts that might be the focus of shared reading experiences with big books or enlarged print on the whiteboard, chart paper, or computer projector include the following:

- The print carries the message, not the picture.
- Books have fronts and backs.
- The reader must be properly oriented to the print.
- The reader must know where to begin reading.
- Text is read left to right, top to bottom.
- Voice can be matched to print.
- Concept of *word*: A word is a unit of meaning.
- Concept of *letter*: A letter is a symbol for a sound.
- Concept of *first* and *last:* These words indicate sequence.
- Letters are written in both uppercase and lowercase.
- Some words can be reversed, such as *was* and *saw* or *not* and *ton.*
- Print has certain required characteristics.
- Punctuation carries meaning.

The teacher can use a variety of techniques during shared readings to direct children's eyes to the print concepts of interest. Smooth pointing underneath print on a page demonstrates for children that (1) print, not picture, is how the message of reading is carried, (2) one begins reading at a particular point on a page, and (3) one reads left to right, sweeping the eye back across the page to the next line and proceeding from top to bottom. Word-by-word pointing underneath print demonstrates for children (1) concept of word and (2) voice–print matching, sometimes called *finger-point reading*. When selecting a pointer to be used for print concept instruction, it is important to remember that it is the print children are to look at—not the pointer. Elaborate and distracting pointers—those with footballs, trees, moons, and snowmen on the ends—often deflect children's attention from print. The best pointers are simple. A plain wooden dowel approximately two feet in length with a black or white rubber tip or pencil eraser tip will hold students' attention without distracting them from the task at hand.

Another technique for directing children's eyes during shared reading to the print on the page is to use fixed or sliding print frames as shown in Figure 3.6. Sticky notes might also be used as shown in Figure 3.7. Some teachers have found that colored, transparent highlighter tape and arrows are useful in directing the eyes of young students to the features of print under study. Others create sentence strips or word and letter cards featuring text from a shared reading; these materials are then displayed to the group and become the focal point for instruction in print concepts.

Phonological and Phonemic Awareness Instruction

Adams (1990) reminds us that a child's level of phonemic awareness on entering school "may be the single most powerful determinant of the success he or she will experience in learning to read" (p. 304). Research reported by the National Reading Panel (2000) and the National Early Literacy Panel (2008) affirms the strength of the

Figure 3.6

Page from The Little Red Hen

Figure 3.7

Page from The Gingerbread Man

predicted relationship between learning to read and students' phonemic awareness. We begin our discussion of phonological and phonemic awareness by answering a most important question: What do the terms *phonological awareness* and *phonemic awareness* mean? If you are going to teach these essentials, then you must know what they are and what they are not. Phonological awareness is an umbrella term that includes hearing and manipulating larger parts of spoken language such as words, syllables, rhyming elements in syllables, and alliteration (Armbruster, Lehr, & Osborn, 2001; National Reading Panel, 2000; Snow, Burns, & Griffin, 1998). For example, the word *willow* has two syllables and rhymes with *pillow*. Phonemic awareness, in contrast, refers to the ability to focus on and manipulate phonemes (roughly equivalent to individual sounds) in spoken words (National Reading Panel, 2000, p. 2–10). For example, the word *rope* has three individual phonemes: /r/, /o/, and /p/.

One common misunderstanding among practicing educators is that phonological awareness and phonemic awareness are synonymous. Clearly, this is not so. Phonological awareness is a much broader term that pertains to hearing and manipulating units of spoken language larger than a single phoneme, such as words, syllables, and rhyming elements. Phonemic awareness pertains specifically to the ability to hear and manipulate individual or single phonemes in spoken words and syllables.

Another common misunderstanding is that phonemic awareness is the same thing as phonics. Not so. As we have just discussed, phonemic awareness is the understanding that spoken words are made up of individual speech sounds, or what are called *phonemes*. Phonics, on the other hand, is the understanding that letters and letter combinations are used in print to *represent* phonemes in spoken language and can be blended together to create spoken words from printed language. In other words, phonemic awareness does not involve the use of written symbols but rather refers to hearing spoken sounds. We often refer to phonemic awareness as *phonics-in-the-dark*, meaning one can hear sounds but sees no letters in the dark. Phonics, on the other hand, involves seeing written symbols, hearing spoken sounds, and making connections between the two.

One thing is certain: Building children's phonemic awareness will help them understand phonics concepts and develop phonics skills later on. The reason is simple, really. When students are phonemically aware and can hear individual sounds (phonemes) in spoken words, learning that letters or letter combinations represent sounds in speech makes perfect sense—because there is a relationship between many spoken sounds and individual letters.

According to Adams (1990), the path to phonemic awareness is "top down." It begins with awareness of spoken words, then moves to an awareness of syllables within spoken words, and then to an awareness of smaller units within spoken syllables called onsets and rimes. Recall from earlier in the chapter that onset involves the sounds in syllables that come before the vowel, as the /w/ sound in the syllable *win*. The rime includes the vowel sound and every other sound that follows it, as with *-in* (/i/-/n/) in the syllable *win*.

Adams (1990) describes how the movement from phonological to phonemic awareness occurs developmentally, in ascending order of difficulty.

1. Step one involves becoming aware of spoken words. Surprising as it may seem, research suggests that children neither naturally think of spoken language as a string of individual words nor understand words as individual units of meaning. When children listen, they attend to the full meaning of an utterance—and this meaning is only available after the meanings of the individual words have been combined automatically and without conscious attention.

Click on A+RISE—Literacy Strategies in the MyEducationLab (www. myeducationlab.com) for your course. Next, select the Strategy Card Index tab, scroll to Word Study, and select the Beginning Sounds Picture Sort strategy.

2. Step two in developing phonemic awareness involves becoming aware of spoken syllables. An awareness of syllables in words constitutes an essential link between the seemingly natural ability of many young children to hear similarities between initial word sounds and ending rhyming elements in words and the more sophisticated ability to hear and recognize individual phonemes.

3. Step three involves becoming aware of phonemes. Remember that syllables divide into two primary parts: the onset and the rime. Once a spoken word is broken down into syllables and then into onset and rime, children need to be able to identify each sound or phoneme in spoken syllables and words. Phonemic awareness occurs when teachers focus students' attention on individual sounds in spoken words.

Numerous studies have confirmed the effectiveness of several kinds of learning activities that help children develop phonological and phonemic awareness, helping students who come to school without this knowledge to develop this awareness and thus acquire important predictor skills of later reading success (Adams, 1990; Blevins, 1997; National Early Literacy Panel, 2008).

According to Armbruster, Lehr, and Osborn (2001), children can demonstrate their phonological awareness in a number of ways.

- Identifying and making rhymes orally
  Hickory, dickory *dock,*
  The mouse ran up the *clock.*
- Identifying and working with syllables in spoken words
  I can tap out the sounds in *kindergarten:* kin-der-gar-ten.
- Identifying and working with onsets and rimes in spoken syllables or one-syllable words
  The first sound in *tall* is /t/,
  and the last part is *–all.*
- Identifying and working with individual phonemes in spoken words
  The first sound in *dog* is /d/.

Next we discuss evidence-based categories to use in selecting learning activities related to developing children's phonemic awareness.

- *Phoneme isolation.* Recognizing individual sounds in words
  Teacher: What is the first sound in *boy?*
  Student: The first sound in *boy* is /b/.
- *Phoneme identity.* Hearing the same sound in different words
  Teacher: What sound is the same in *boy, bake,* and *butter?*
  Student: The first sound /b/ is the same.
- *Phoneme categorization.* Recognizing the word having a different sound in a group of three or four words
  Teacher: Which word doesn't belong? *run, rake, toy*
  Student: *Toy* doesn't belong because it begins with /t/.
- *Phoneme blending.* Understanding how to listen to phonemes spoken separately and then blend them together to form a word
  Teacher: What is this word? /m/ /a/ /k/
  Student: /m/ /a/ /k/ is *make.*
- *Phoneme segmentation.* Breaking a spoken word into its separate phonemes while tapping or counting on the fingers each sound
  Teacher: Say the sounds you hear in the word *cup* slowly.
  Student: *Cccccccc uhhhhhhhh pppppppp.*

Teacher: How many sounds did you count in *cup?*

Student: *Cup* has three sounds.

- *Phoneme deletion.* Recognizing that a phoneme can be removed from a spoken word and that part of the word remains

  Teacher: If I take away the sound /b/ in the word *brook,* what word is left?

  Student: *Brook* without /b/ is *rook.*

- *Phoneme addition.* The ability to create a new word by adding a phoneme

  Teacher: If I add the sound /s/ to the end of the word *tree,* what new word would I have?

  Student: *Tree* with /s/ added to the end would be *trees.*

- *Phoneme substitution.* Replacing a phoneme in a spoken word to create a new word

  Teacher: The word is *run.* Change /n/ to /t/. What's the new word?

  Student: The new word is *rut.*

Matching the Instructional Sequence to the Developmental Difficulty of Phonological and Phonemic Awareness Tasks. In phonological and phonemic awareness instruction, teaching should move from the simplest concepts toward the more complex. Figure 3.8 shows that the starting point is helping students understand that spoken words are made up of individual speech sounds. Word-stretching activities such as "rubber banding" can help students begin to hear word parts, such as each word in a compound word. For example, the compound word *clothespin* consists of two sound units familiar to children—*clothes* and *pin.* Young children are able to catch on quickly that compound words like *baseball, flagpole, sailboat,* and *rainbow* are just two smaller words "glued" together. They can hear and segment the two spoken words easily. If compound words are chosen so that each word part is a one-syllable word that carries a meaning students easily understand, both the sound and meaning connections can be understood at once by most students. Learning simple segmenting and blending with compound words is the first major jump from phonological awareness toward phonemic awareness.

Syllables are the next speech unit for students to orally segment and blend in this instructional sequence. This next step moves students from simply segmenting smaller words in compound words to dividing words by sound units that seem more abstract. Clapping or counting syllables heard in words like *window* and *kindergarten* helps them to segment sound elements (i.e., *win-dow, kin-der-gar-ten*). Blending activities are also effective: "I will say the first part of a word, and then the rest of the word—*sha . . . dow.* Then I will say the whole word blended together—*shadow.*

Figure 3.8

Sequence of Development and Instruction for Phonemic Awareness

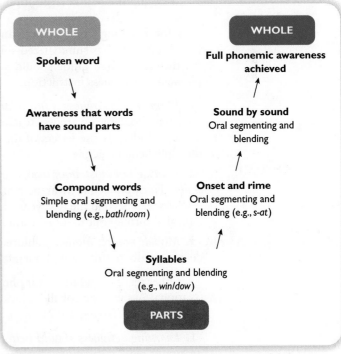

From *Sequence of Development and Instruction for Phonemic Awareness* by R. B. Cooter, Jr., D. R. Reutzel, and K. S. Cooter, 1998, unpublished paper.

Next, I will say the first part of a word and then the rest of the word—*win . . . dow.* Now you say the word as a whole."

Blending syllables is one way to help children along the path from phonological to phonemic awareness, but segmenting is also important. Consider the following segmenting sequence: "I will say the whole word—*shadow.* Next, I will stretch the word to count the speech parts—*ssshhhaaa dooo.* I count two. Now you try it. I will say the whole word—*mustache.* Now, let's stretch the word together and clap the speech parts—*mus tache.* How many times did we clap?" Yeh (2003) found that instructional time in kindergarten is best spent on blending and segmenting tasks rather than on rhyming tasks to develop phonemic awareness that will impact reading acquisition.

The next phonological awareness level calls for segmenting and blending onsets and rimes. As noted earlier, an onset is the part of a syllable that comes before the vowel; the rime is the rest (Adams, 1990, p. 55). For example, in the word *sat*, *s* is the onset and *-at* is the rime. Similarly, in the first syllable of the word *turtle*, *t* is the onset and *-ur* is the rime. This activity is easily done in the context of poetry (teaching *rimes* with *rhymes*).

Segmenting and blending spoken words sound by sound is the most abstract task and is the first and only level of phonemic awareness. Segmenting individual sounds in spoken words is a necessary precursor to children's developing the ability to spell words in writing. Blending, on the other hand, is a necessary precursor to children's developing the ability to blend or "sound out" words in reading. The difference is that we blend individual sounds to say whole words whereas we segment whole words into individual sounds.

The final phonemic awareness skills to be taught help children use phonemic blending and segmenting in more sophisticated and fun ways. At this point students are ready for phoneme manipulation activities such as the phonemic categorization, deletion, addition, and substitution tasks described earlier.

Tips for Planning Phonological and Phonemic Awareness Instruction.   Blevins (1997, pp. 7–8) has summarized some important points that teachers of kindergarten through second grade should keep in mind as they plan for phonological and phonemic awareness instruction.

   1. *Phonemic awareness is not related to print.* Oral and aural (listening) activities are what phonemic awareness teaching and learning are all about. Once children can name and identify the letters of the alphabet, they are ready to move into learning the alphabetic principle.

   2. *Many, if not most, poor readers in the early grades have weak phonemic awareness skills.* Thus, phonemic awareness may be an important issue (on a limited basis) for teachers well beyond the K–2 years. Indeed, phonemic awareness training may well be indicated throughout K–12 education for students considered "remedial" readers.

   3. *Model, model, model!* Children need to see you, their teacher, and other students actually performing phonemic awareness activities.

Other recommendations for phonemic awareness activities include the following (National Association for the Education of Young Children [NAEYC], 2009; Yopp, 1992; Yopp & Troyer, 1992).

   1. *Learning activities should help foster positive feelings toward learning through an atmosphere of playfulness and fun.* Drill activities in phonemic awareness should be avoided, as should rote memorization.

2. *Interaction among children should be encouraged through group activities.* Language play seems to be most effective in group settings.

3. *Curiosity about language and experimentation should be encouraged.* Teachers should react positively when students engage in language manipulation and should do so themselves occasionally. We like to read familiar stories aloud using spoonerisms to alert children to phonemic elements in spoken language. A spoonerism exchanges initial sounds in two words, for example, "Once upon a time, deep in the woods, there lived a family of *bee threars* (three bears)." Almost always children will hear these changes and want to correct the teacher's reading!

4. *Teachers should be prepared for wide differences among students in their acquisition of phonemic awareness.* Some children will catch on quickly, whereas others will need a great deal of guided practice. Teachers should avoid making quick judgments about children based on how they perform in phonemic awareness activities. In Figure 3.9 we summarize the levels of language through which phonological and phonemic awareness develop, the developmental sequence of tasks, and examples of those tasks.

Finally, research yields several important cautions for phonological and phonemic awareness instruction. First, the National Reading Panel (2000) advises teachers not to assume that *all* children need phonological and phonemic awareness (PPA) instruction. Rather, teachers should begin by assessing what young children may already know about PPA to be able to target instruction to meet students' needs. Second, research has determined that PPA instruction should require approximately 18 total hours of instruction for most children during their primary-grade years. This means that PPA instruction should occur in rather quick lessons of no more than 5 to 7 minutes over several months in kindergarten and first grade. It may be necessary in some cases of diagnosed need to review PPA instruction in second grade. Third, the National Reading Panel (2000) found that phonemic awareness instruction, especially focused on blending and segmenting, as shown in Figure 3.9, works best when combined with letter naming and phonics instruction and presented in small-group settings.

Letter Name Instruction

Recall that the National Reading Panel (2000) found that the two best predictors of early reading achievement are (1) letter name knowledge and (2) phonemic awareness. The National Early Literacy Panel (2008) found that letter name knowledge, including letter sound knowledge, is the single best predictor of later reading success in the primary grades. Other researchers have found that letter name knowledge is a unique predictor of first-grade reading achievement (Stage et al., 2001). Consequently, in kindergarten and early first grade, teachers need to be concerned with developing fluent letter recognition—perception that is both rapid and accurate.

Many teachers ask whether there is an evidence-based optimal order for teaching the alphabet letters. The answer to this question is no. Some educators prefer to teach the letters in the order of the alphabet. This approach allows children to link the letters of the alphabet to their learning of alphabetical order, which children accomplish by singing the alphabet song, viewing and having their attention drawn to an alphabet frieze displayed on the walls of the classroom, and listening to alphabet books read aloud. On the other hand, some educators prefer to explicitly teach letter names and sounds as a way to get children quickly into blending and spelling words using phonics. These teachers usually select one to three vowels along with some

Figure 3.9

Overview of Phonemic Awareness

Developmental Level Tasks	Phonological Awareness →			Phonemic Awareness →		Phonemic Awareness with Phonics →	
Linguistic Levels	Word → Awareness	Syllables →	Onset and Rime →	Single Sound →	Blending →	Segmenting →	Manipulation
Introduced (Approx.)	Pre → K		K review first 5 weeks of 1st grade	K–1st Grade		1st Grade	
Instruction Sounds Like	Model how many words heard in this sentence: *The cat runs quietly.* (4)	Model how many syllables heard in this word: *skateboard* (2) or *windy* (2)	Model what the sound(s) is/are before the vowel in this syllable: *sit* (/s/) Model what the sound unit is, including the vowel and the sounds after the vowel in a syllable *sit* (-it)	Model how many sounds heard in this word: *sit* (3)	Model what word we say when we blend the sounds /m/ + /a/ + /n/ (man)	Model individual sounds heard in the word *sit* (/s/ /i/ /t/)	Model manipulating sounds in words by taking the /k/ sound off *cat* (-at). Model manipulating sounds in words by substituting the /t/ sound for the /s/ sound in the words *son* (ton)
Child's Response Looks Like	• Count • Clap • Manipulate markers	• Count • Clap • Manipulate markers	• Recognize • Manipulate	Count sounds they heard (not letters)	Elongate the sounds, getting faster each time	• Count • Clap	• Delete sound to make new word • Substitute sound(s) to make new word
Helpful Hints	The dog ran 1 2 3	Best to start with compound words— *cowboy* 1 2	Use word families, rhyming words, alliteration *s + at* *w + in / d + ow*	*W i n d o w* 5 sounds (6 letters)	Clap when it's fast enough to be a word: *man*	Use a rubber band to "stretch" the word *c - a - t* /k/ /a/ /t/	*cat - /k/ = at* *ton - /t/ + /s/ = son*

Total: 18 hours of instruction unless indicated otherwise via assessment.

high-frequency consonants to teach initially, moving through the remaining letters of the alphabet in order of their frequency. To review comparative letter frequencies in words, we recommend that teachers consult the list compiled by Fry (2004), as shown in Table 3.2.

Still other teachers prefer to teach children to recognize alphabet letters by beginning instruction with students' names, as recent research has shown this to be a powerful source of motivation for learning letter names among 4-year-olds (Justice, Pence, Bowles, & Wiggins, 2006). An excellent classroom resource for teaching children letter name and sound recognition using children's names is Krech's *Fresh and Fun: Teaching with Kids' Names* (2000).

In our work with kindergarten and early first-grade children, especially those from poverty circumstances, we have found that flash cards featuring letters and the alphabet frieze (i.e., the display of uppercase and lowercase letters) above the chalkboard are insufficient to develop young students' letter naming and letter sound fluency. We have found that for kindergarten and early first-grade children to identify letter names accurately and quickly, they also need to *search* to find specific letters in a variety of print displays such as those found in small, easy-to-read books. They also need to *write* letters as their teachers dictate them (National Early Literacy Panel, 2008). To help you teach letter recognition more effectively, we provide examples of each of these processes—letter name and sound instruction, letter searching, and letter writing—as well as offering some evidence-based advice about the pacing of letter recognition instruction and review cycles.

Recognizing Letters.   To help children recognize alphabet letters (both uppercase and lowercase) quickly and accurately, we recommend teachers avoid relying solely on the alphabet frieze displayed in the classroom. Depending exclusively on this block print or script display of uppercase and lowercase letters found in nearly every classroom in the nation for practicing letter recognition is not recommended for one important reason. Children recall their knowledge of alphabetical order to help them recognize the letters in the alphabet frieze. For example, if you were to point to the letter *A* in the alphabet frieze, children would identify it accurately and quickly because this letter is at the beginning of alphabetical order. However, point to the letter *V* in the alphabet frieze, and note that children are slower in responding and less accurate in their identification. Careful observation will also reveal that children subvocalize, or say under their breath, the letters in alphabetical sequence, matching each to the order in the alphabet frieze. Hence, practicing letters in this fashion is excellent for learning alphabetical order, but not for recognizing nonsequential letters of the alphabet. When teaching letter recognition, teachers should present letters for practice tasks in random order so that learners rely on the physical characteristics of the letter rather than its place in the alphabet to identify it.

Young children enjoy matching activities. Create decks of letter cards using letters you have focused on; be sure each letter appears more than once. Deal out several cards to students, and have them match letters. This activity can be played in a way similar to the old favorite, "Go Fish!" Each of several players is dealt five letter cards. The remaining letter cards become the draw pile. The first player asks for a card—for example, "Do you have the letter *p*?" Another player with that letter card in his or her hand must give it to the player requesting it. If the player gets a pair, he

Table 3.2

Vowels and Consonants Ranked by Frequency

Vowels	Consonants
Short i—*pill*	r
Short a—*cat*	t
Short e—*get*	n
Schwa r—*girl*	s
Long o—*rope*	l
Long e—*me*	c
Short u—*cup*	d
Short o—*pot*	p
Long a—*ate*	m
Long u—*tune*	b
Long i—*like*	f
Broad a—*are*	v
Broad o—*for*	g
ou—*out*	h
oo—*look*	k
oi—*oil*	w
ai—*fair*	th
	sh
	ng
	ch
	x
	z
	j
	qu
	wh
	y

Click on A+RISE—Literacy Strategies in the MyEducationLab (www.myeducationlab.com) for your course. Next, select the Strategy Card Index tab, scroll to Word Study, and select the Working with Names to Teach the Alphabet strategy.

or she lays the pair on the table. If the other players do not have the letter requested, they say, "Go fish!" The first player takes a card from the draw pile and the next player gets to take a turn. The game is finished when a player is able to match all of the letter cards in his or her hand.

Searching for Letters.   One engaging way for students to search for letters is to play an adaptation of the game "I Spy." Required materials are several copies of the same book and an overhead transparency and washable ink overhead pen for each student. Tell students to place the transparency over the selected book page. Direct students to look carefully at the print on the page. Start the game by saying, "I spy with my little eye _____." Fill in the blank with a letter that occurs several times on the page—for example, "five lowercase *m*s." To increase the challenge of the game, tell children you will set a timer for 1 minute. Challenge them to accurately and quickly mark with the overhead pen on the transparency all of the *m*s on the page in the time allotted. Once children have learned a few letters, they can assume the role of "spy." The process can be repeated using different letters on the same page.

Writing Letters.   An important practice for ensuring that children can identify uppercase and lowercase alphabet letters quickly and accurately is through writing (National Early Literacy Panel, 2008). We use a game called "Beat the Clock." This game requires that children have paper and pencil or, better yet, a gel board or whiteboard and dry erase markers for writing. Set a timer for 3 minutes. Tell students, "Write an uppercase *b*." Count off 10 seconds and then say, "Write a lowercase *m*." Continue the process with a variety of letters until the timer alarm sounds. Then have students show you their letters. Make brief notes about each student's performance on the dictation task. Then tell students, "Let's see if we can beat the clock." This time, count off 9 seconds between each letter dictated. This slightly faster pace challenges children to write the dictated letters more quickly, yet legibly and accurately. A simple graph can be created for each child showing his or her times across rounds of the game.

The Pacing of Letter Name Instruction.   We recommend teaching a new letter each day in kindergarten. In 2006, H. Pashler presented an initial series of research studies detailing how instructional pacing and multiple reviews distributed over time maximize what he called "reducing forgetting." Pashler and his colleagues have since demonstrated in several published research reports the desirability of distributed review and spacing effects for reducing forgetting (Cepeda, Coburn, Rohrer, Wixted, Mozer, & Pashler, 2009; Cepeda, Pashler, Vul, Wixted, & Rohrer, 2006; Cepeda, Vul, Rohrer, Wixted, & Pashler, 2007). To optimize memory for learning information and reduce forgetting, these researchers have described what they call the "law of 10/20." This law of 10/20 proposes that if one wants to remember something, whether colors, dates, letters, words, math facts, or other information for 6 months or more, then a spaced review should take place at intervals of 10 to 20 percent of the time period for which the item is to be remembered. Because 6 months is equivalent to 183 days, the law of 10/20 suggests that a complete review of the 26 letters taught in the first 5 weeks of school should occur at intervals of 10 to 20 percent of 183 days, or every 18 to 36 days. Reviewing all of the 26 letters every 5 weeks falls within the 10 to 20 percent range. There is no question that letters are best learned through distributed practice and review rather than from massed practice.

Pashler's 10/20 rule goes against the grain for many kindergarten teachers for whom a letter a week is the traditional practice. However, five letters a week can be taught quickly over time, with spaced reviews every 5 weeks for a total of seven review cycles in the kindergarten year. Such teaching is far more effective in helping children learn to quickly and accurately identify their alphabet letters (Jones & Reutzel, in press). An example letter name lesson that can be used in pre-K to first-grade classrooms is shown in Figure 3.10.

Figure 3.10

Teaching Letter Names and Sounds for Young Learners

Lesson Objective: Students will learn the name, sound, and write the symbols for the upper- and lowercase letter *T/t*.

Supplies:
Bag of mixed alphabet letters
Washable markers and lapboards
Copies of enlarged print page
Highlighter tape

Explanation: Tell children, "Today boys and girls you will be learning to name, say the sound of, and write the upper- and lowercase letter *t*. Learning the letter name, sound, and how to write upper- and lowercase letter *t* will help you to read and write many new words."

Letter Name Identification: "This is the capital letter *T*." (Write and show the uppercase form of the letter *t*.) "This is the lowercase letter *t*." (Write and show the lowercase form of the letter *t*.) "Let's practice naming this letter. What is this letter? *T*." (Point in different order to upper- and lowercase letter *T/t* at least three times.)

Letter Sound Identification: "The letter *t* makes the /t/ sound. Say the /t/ sound with me . . . /t/, /t/, /t/. What is the sound of the letter *t*? /t/." (Point to upper- and lowercase letter *T/t* at least three times asking students to make the sound of the letter.)

Sort the Letters: "Here are some examples of uppercase *T* and lowercase *t* mixed in this bag" (6–8 upper- and lowercase *T/t* magnetic letters, foam letters, or die cuts). "We need to sort these letters into upper- and lowercase categories." (Begin with a closed sort and in subsequent review lessons use an open sort.) "I'll put each letter on the board and if it is an uppercase letter *T*, you say 'Uppercase *T*.' If it is a lowercase letter *t*, say 'Lowercase *t*.'" Place letters on whiteboard one at a time for students to identify and sort.

Find the Letters: "Now, let's see how many letter *t*s we can find on this page." (Be sure to pick short pages of enlarged print with no more than four lines of print. Run a pointer underneath the words in each line of print.) "When you see the pointer on a letter *t*, point to the *t*." (Call on one student to come up and place a piece of highlighter tape over the letter *t* on the enlarged print page.)

Write the Letter: Name and demonstrate the proper formation of the uppercase *T*. Say something such as "The uppercase letter *T* starts at the top of the line and goes straight down to the bottom of the line. Then make a straight line across the top. (Down and across the top.)" Next name and demonstrate the proper letter formation of the lowercase *t*. Say something such as "The lowercase letter *t* also starts at the top of the line and goes straight down to the bottom of the line. Next, make a line that crosses the other line between the middle and top of the line. (Down and cross.)"

Pass out whiteboards, gel boards, or lapboards and ask students to take letter dictation. Ask students to write three to six dictated lower- and uppercase *T/t* letters and also quickly review other letters learned. Have students write and cover their letters. Then ask them to show you using a choral response mode the letter they wrote. Using a sticky note or clipboard, notice which students show successful written dictated letters and which may need additional help in small-group settings.

Differentiating and Adapting Early Reading Instruction

● ● ●

IRA Standards for Reading Professionals: Standard 4, Elements 4.1, 4.2, 4.3; Standard 5, Element 5.3

Response to Intervention: Responsive Teaching and Differentiation

As teacher educators, we have worked for over three decades with teachers and children in very diverse schools, including urban, rural, suburban, affluent, middle-class, and high-poverty situations. In this section we first consider general adaptations to instruction that apply in most classrooms and then conclude with special considerations for differentiating instruction for English learners (ELs).

Struggling Readers

Children who struggle learning early reading concepts need more instructional time and more repetitions or "doses" of instruction (Shanahan, 2003a). Supplemental differentiated instruction may fall under Response to Intervention (RTI) Tier 2 guidelines, in which interventions are intended to fill in learning gaps as quickly as possible and return students to core (i.e., developmental) literacy instruction. Tier 2 interventions are delivered at least three times per week in small-group settings *in addition* to regular classroom instruction. Frequent and regular progress-monitoring assessment is used to determine the success of Tier 2 interventions with students (Reutzel & Cooter, 2011).

Maintaining students' time-on-task, or student engagement, during reading instructional time is another critical feature of differentiated instruction. Struggling readers often remain more engaged when they are instructed in pairs, small groups, or one-to-one teaching situations (Mathes et al., 2005; O'Connor, Harty, & Fulmer, 2005). Increasing struggling readers' on-task reading behaviors can also be enhanced by the following:

- Increasing the pacing of instruction so that learning is "just within reach"
- Reviewing skills, strategies, and concepts at regular intervals (more dosing)
- Reducing transition time between daily learning activities
- Involving key personnel such as special educators, Title I teachers, and English-as-a-second-language (ESL) teachers to help increase small-group reading instructional opportunities within the classroom.

Some schools also provide before-school, after-school, and summer reading programs to increase instructional time for struggling readers.

All learners, especially struggling readers, benefit from structure and routine. This means that their daily schedule should be predictable and have few unannounced or unexpected changes. Assigned early reading practice tasks should be clearly and explicitly explained.

Early intervention to catch reading problems before they become insurmountable has been shown in many studies to have the greatest impact on student outcomes (Ramey & Ramey, 2006). Instruction offered to struggling readers needs to be *targeted* to their needs; it needs to be clear and explicit, provide "scaffolding" (i.e., structured learning experiences) over time, and occur every day in the "relentless pursuit of success" (Duffy, 2004). Struggling readers also benefit from peer tutoring.

Struggling readers require more feedback from teachers and peers. They need to know exactly what they are doing well and precisely where they need to focus their attention to do better. Generic feedback such as "Gee, that was really good!" will not be of much help to struggling readers (National Reading Panel, 2000; Reutzel, 2006). Explicit feedback like "Your phrasing was very good because you paused at the commas and stopped at the periods in each sentence" or "You read every word on the page accurately" is far more meaningful. Constructive criticism should also be specific: "When a sentence ends in a period, you need to lower your voice and stop at the period like this." or "You need to compare the words you say to what is written on the page."

Finally, struggling readers are helped when schoolwide assessment occurs and when the approach to reading instruction is consistent across and within grades (Taylor, Pearson, Clark, & Walpole, 1999; Taylor et al., 2005; Wonder-McDowell, Reutzel, & Smith, in press). Successful schools that help struggling readers succeed have well-articulated schoolwide assessment, instructional approaches, and curricula that all teachers use and honor. Remember: For struggling readers, *acceleration of learning* is the paramount goal. Struggling readers need to make larger gains each month to catch up to their peers in reading. Failure to do so can cause them to re-main behind in school and in attaining life's opportunities (Fielding et al., 1998; Juel, 1988). But most of all, good reading instruction has the potential to help all young children succeed (August & Shanahan, 2006).

Some Special Considerations for English Learners (ELs)

Research suggests that all young students, including those from differing cultural backgrounds or for whom English is a second language, learn early literacy skills in much the same way (August & Shanahan, 2006; Fitzgerald, Armendum, & Gutherie, 2008). However, English learners (ELs) are faced with a dual literacy-learning task. In addition to absorbing the characteristics of written language, they must also learn an unfamiliar oral language in a sometimes unfamiliar cultural context. Just like mainstream students, ELs can vary in their phonemic awareness as well as in general language awareness and abilities.

For some children the written system of their home language and culture may not use an alphabet like English. Chinese students, for example, read single symbols that represent whole phrases in their native language; Arabic students read from right to left in theirs.

According to Cummins (1981), there are two types of language proficiency: basic interpersonal communication skills (BICS), oral language learned through informal conversations, which takes ELs generally 2 years to achieve, and cognitive academic language proficiency (CALP), oral language related to academic content knowledge, which takes ELs 5 to 7 years to achieve.

English learners, especially those from many Asian backgrounds, need teach-ers to help them learn to hear differences between the phonemes in their primary language and those that are different or new in English (Fitzgerald et al., 2008). For example, children whose home language is Japanese may have difficulty telling the difference between *r* and *l* sounds because these sounds do not exist in Japanese.

One important insight from research is that letter name learning for many ELs proceeds along the same path as English-only speaking students (Trieman, Levin, & Kessler, 2007). In China, for example, many young children are taught the let-ters of the Greek alphabet rather than traditional Chinese symbols or logographs in early reading. Consequently, letter name learning seems to develop similarly to English-speaking students during early reading instruction. However, little research has been reported on differences in ELs' concepts about print acquisition during the stage of early reading development. As a result, teachers would do well in the absence of evidence to the contrary to provide ELs with the same high-quality concepts about print instruction as English-speaking students. Finally, we want to note that required instructional time in many states, especially in reading, has been doubled for ELs.

Motivation and Engagement of Early Readers

● ● ●

IRA Standards for Reading Professionals: Standard 5, Elements 5.1, 5.2

Pressley and colleagues (2003) note that primary-grade teachers can change learning for the better every minute of every day by flooding the classroom with books. Access to books is essential for motivating young readers. Neuman (1999) notes that many young children from high-poverty circumstances do not have equal access to a variety of books in their homes, schools, and public libraries. Furthermore, young children living in high-poverty environments experience books read aloud to them far less than children in more affluent homes and schools (Adams, 1990). For example, it has been estimated that young children living in high-poverty environments are read to out of storybooks about 25 hours before entering school, as compared to 1,000+ hours of reading aloud to children in nonpoverty homes (Adams, 1990; Heath, 1983; Teale, 1986). If young children are going to develop the motivation necessary to sustain them through the often difficult early stages of reading development, they will need to experience many and varied read-alouds from books that are of high interest to them.

Read Aloud with Expository Books

We encourage elementary teachers to read aloud to their students for at least 20 to 30 minutes each day (in total) from interesting expository (nonfiction) books as well as storybooks to boost interest and build vocabulary knowledge. Duke (2000) asserted years ago that teachers need to be sure that young children have opportunities to experience read-alouds from a wide variety of book genres ranging from information to storybooks during their earliest years in school.

Mohr (2003) found that first graders greatly prefer information books over many other available book genres such as storybooks. When given a wide range of book genres, languages, topics, and characters to choose from, 84 percent of the first-grade children in Mohr's (2003) study selected a single information book in English with photographs of spiders and other real insects and animals. Reading aloud from information books provides students with rich conceptual learning opportunities as well (Neuman, 2001; Smolkin & Donovan, 2001). It is beyond doubt that reading aloud books to young children helps them to develop a love for what can be learned and experienced from reading books.

Student Interests and Choice Matter

More recently, Edmunds and Bauserman (2006) learned from 831 pre-K to fifth-grade students what motivated them to read. For narrative books, book characteristics (pictures, book covers, humor, action-packed plots), personal interests, and choice were most motivating. For expository books, young students indicated that the knowledge gained, choice, and personal interests were keys to motivation. The intersection of both text types, narrative and expository, indicted that appealing to students' interests and giving them choice are shared motivating factors.

This finding confirms the earlier six Cs of reading motivation found by Turner and Paris (1995), indicating that *choice* leads naturally to students' pursuing books to be read from areas of interest. Choice also relates to students' willingness to explore the world of print through writing. Writing is often the first indicator of a child's interest in print (Clay, 1975). Children as young as 1 year have been found to experiment with writing to create "messages" for others (Baghban, 1984; Lancaster, 2001). Young children quickly learn that lines and scribbles carry meaning. Sharing thoughts and getting one's needs met through writing is important to young children and so they begin to modify their writing to more closely resemble the written text they experience in their environment. For many young children, writing is the way into reading (Bissex, 1980; Clay, 2002; Durkin, 1966; Hansen, 1987). In terms of test scores, choice increases students' reading comprehension and achievement by a whopping 1.2 standard deviations, or roughly the equivalent of 40+ percentile points on a standardized test (Guthrie & Humenick, 2004).

Click on A+RISE—WIDA ELP Standards Strategies in the MyEducationLab (www.myeducationlab.com) for your course. Next, select the Strategy Card Index tab, scroll to Language and Content for Grades K–5, and select the Motivational strategies.

Technology and New Literacies

Technology and New Literacies for Early Readers

Many of today's young children have been exposed to print, written letters, and sounds in spoken language through some of the readily available forms of technology and media found in many homes, preschools, and primary-grade classrooms. Many, if not most, young children have access to a television set in their homes and classrooms. Familiar reading- and writing-oriented television programs for young children include *Sesame Street, WordGirl, Super Why!,* and *Reading Rainbow.* These PBS programs provide young students with exposure to words, oral language, rhymes, books read aloud, printed letters and words, and many other print and oral language–related exposures to the essential elements of early literacy.

Most classroom teachers today have access to CD-ROM or audio recorders and players. Children can follow along with books read aloud by these devices in order to have semi-guided experiences in hearing books read aloud (Bus, de Jong, & Verhallen, 2006). Recent developments in speech recognition software have made many easy-to-read books, including decodable books, available via computer and Internet technologies for young students. One excellent program with advanced speech recognition software called Reading Assistant, Expanded Edition, allows young students to hear story and information books read aloud at a variety of reading levels (Adams, 2006). As the books are read aloud each word on the page is highlighted to simulate someone pointing to each word as it is pronounced. Children can also read along with the book and the highlighting and create recorded accounts of their own oral reading. If they have trouble with a word, a simple click of the mouse will activate the computer to pronounce the word for the student. See the Web Tools box on the next page for programs you can use in the classroom.

IRA Standards for Reading Professionals: Standard 2, Element 2.3

Common Core Standards: Reading: K–5, Integration of Knowledge and Ideas (item 7); Writing: K–5, Production and Distribution of Writing (item 6)

WEB TOOLS YOU CAN USE IN THE CLASSROOM

Early Literacy Programs

To support today's digital learners, the following technology-based early literacy websites, software, and media are essentials in reaching, teaching, and motivating young students to learn to read and write in early literacy classrooms.

- To view the Scientific Learning Reading Assistant, go to www.scilearn.com/products/reading-assistant/rademo.php?f=ra-K-5.

- Other Internet-based resources for letter-naming games, word games, books read aloud, and other early literacy activities can be found for free at http://pbskids.org/lions and www.learningplanet.com/act/abcorder.asp.

- Free and purchasable early literacy activities for supporting young students as they learn to read and write can be found at www.starfall.com. Teachers of young children have found this website to be a veritable treasure trove of easy-to-read books, both decodable and leveled, learning games, and ABC getting-ready-to-read activities.

- Children love to sit at the computer and play free games and activities on the Leapfrog website at www.leapfrog.com. The same company produces and markets low-cost computer toys with a variety of built-in early literacy learning games and activities that can be used to support young learners at home and school.

- For other early literacy technology resources and websites, we recommend that teachers go to the Literacy Web at www.literacy.uconn.edu/littech.htm, sponsored by the University of Connecticut literacy technology research team.

Family and Community Connections

Family and Community Support for Early Readers

●●●

IRA Standards for Reading Professionals: Standard 4, Elements 4.1, 4.2, 4.3

Response to Intervention: Collaboration

As young children learn to read, parent involvement is a critical component of an effective classroom reading program (DeBruin-Parecki & Krol-Sinclair, 2003; Enz, 2003). One successful approach for teaching parents how to implement effective early literacy activities in the home is called Project EASE (Early Access to Success in Education). Research has shown that children whose parents were trained in Project EASE to implement structured activities to improve their children's early literacy knowledge at home demonstrated statistically significant gains over those of control group students on measures of both language and literacy growth (Jordan, Snow, & Porche, 2000). The data also indicate that the more parents participated in using the literacy activities in Project EASE, the better their children performed. One finding of significance is that the children who began the project with the lowest scores on language and literacy made the greatest gains.

Project EASE states four goals:

1. All students should have a strong beginning to their educational career.
2. Each student should have a plan to meet his or her individual needs.
3. Parents are integral to the success of their children in reading.
4. Early efforts will yield long-range success in school.

Effective schools and classrooms do not operate in isolation. Young children's early reading success requires the combined efforts of both home and school (DeBruin-Parecki & Krol-Sinclair, 2003). Literacy development plays a critical role in assuring academic success (Fielding et al., 1998; Snow, Burns, & Griffin, 1998).

The parent component of Project EASE includes scripted and structured activities that address the critical early reading components of vocabulary development, decoding, narrative and information text reading, and others. These structured lessons require parents to be highly engaged in helping their child develop reading ability. The creators of Project EASE indicate that the parent activities are designed to foster "de-contextualized" language skills such as decoding that not only support early reading behaviors but also reading fluency in later years.

Parents are asked to commit to five monthly parent education sessions with follow-up weekly parent–child activities or lessons that are available on the Project EASE website. Parents can attend these educational sessions at different times depending on how their child's school sets them up. For example, morning, afternoon, or evening sessions may be set up to correspond with kindergarten schedules and allow at least one session for working parents. Typically, the parent education sessions for Project EASE begin in October and continue until April of the kindergarten year. Title I aides and other school staff have been used to facilitate the parent education component and assist in the classroom on the designated Project EASE parent education days. Each session includes (1) parent education, (2) modeled activities for parent and child, and (3) structured weekly activities completed at home. Parents are invited to participate in kindergarten classroom activities after attending the parent educational sessions.

Parent–child activities focus on five monthly topics that have been shown to significantly impact early reading development: (1) storybook reading, (2) working with words, (3) letter recognition and sound awareness, (4) retelling family narratives, and (5) talking about the world (using information books). Each of the five parent activity units contains background information for parents, parent education session information, at-school activities, at-home activities, book titles, and flash cards. These five parent involvement activities, available at the Project EASE website, have been shown to successfully build beginning print skills by establishing strong letter recognition and sound awareness. Other activities such as storybook and information book readings, retellings, and so on have been shown to positively influence children's reading comprehension.

Project EASE is just one of many possible parent involvement programs for early reading success. There are several others, including Project FLAME (Shanahan, Mulhern, & Rodriguez-Brown, 1995), the Intergenerational Literacy Project (ILP) (Paratore, 2003), the Parent Project (Vopat, 1994), and Keeping Up with Children (Brooks et al., 2002). No early reading instructional program can be considered comprehensive and complete without serious attention given to the use of a parent and community involvement program.

Summary

In this chapter we learned how young children take their first steps in becoming readers. Part of our journey in this chapter was to learn about the developmental stages young readers typically go through as beginning readers.

Phonological and phonemic awareness, print concepts, and letter recognition are but a few of the early skills learned as children move through literacy development stages. We also saw how the twin skills of segmenting and blending spoken words become the bedrock supporting future phonics, decoding, and spelling instruction.

Next, we presented several important assessment tools that help teachers monitor student progress in early reading development. For example, we learned how to use the Metalinguistic Interview and the Concepts About Print Test for assessing and supervising children's emerging understanding about how print works. Finally, we discussed how to monitor children's acquisition of letter recognition and letter-naming ability.

We followed the discussion of assessing early reading essential skills with a detailed description of how to teach children phonological and phonemic awareness, concepts about print, and letter recognition. We stressed the importance of explicit, systematic instruction for each of these early reading essential skills through teachers' informed and systematic application of a variety of effective, evidence-based instructional strategies.

We described specific adaptations of instructional interventions and necessary accommodations for meeting young children's diverse reading and writing learning needs, including increased time allocations, small-group differentiated reading instruction, classroom structure and routine, providing specific feedback, early intervention, knowledge and concept development, and schoolwide assessment.

We discussed how books, especially information books, read aloud to children as they learn about reading and writing essentials can motivate them to want to learn to read. We also discussed the need to provide children with a choice of interesting books for reading aloud and for their own learning.

We provided information about various technologies and new literacies that will not only motivate young learners but also provide them guided practice as they learn to read. Using digital technologies, even in the earliest stages of reading and writing development, will be necessary as this generation of learners emerge into a fully digitized communication society at home and in the workplace.

Finally we presented information dealing with one evidence-based program, Project EASE, among several for supporting young readers' early development in the home and broader community.

Field and Classroom Applications

- Work with a partner. Teach one another a 3- to 5-minute phonemic awareness lesson focused on phoneme blending, segmenting, or manipulation.
- Administer the Concepts About Print Test (Clay, 2000a) to a young student in kindergarten or early first grade. Discuss insights you have gained from administering this test. How would you apply these insights in selecting appropriate strategies for teaching print concepts?
- Working in pairs of students, visit and write a review of a website mentioned in this chapter or one that is recommended at www.literacy.uconn.edu/littech.htm. Share your findings about these websites with your classmates.
- Get together with a small group of your colleagues to create a "Community of Scholars." Your task is to assume the role of a school district leader and create a job description for a highly qualified primary teacher (grades K–2). Describe the required knowledge and skills the teacher you will hire must possess using information learned in this chapter. By the way, assume that this teacher may one day have your own child in his or her classroom!
- In your class, using the lesson framework in Figure 3.10, prepare and teach a letter-naming lesson to a peer or in a school classroom. Share your experience with your teacher preparation or professional development peers. Discuss ways in which this sample lesson could be improved.

Recommended Resources

Print Resources

Adams, M. J. (1990). *Beginning to read: Thinking and learning about print—a summary.* Urbana, IL: Center for the Study of Reading.

Armbruster, B. B., Lehr, F., & Osborn, J. (2001). *Put reading first: The research building blocks for teaching children to read.* Washington, DC: U.S. Department of Education. Available at www.nifl.gov/partnershipforreading/publications/reading_first1.html

Burns, M. S., Griffin, P., & Snow, C. E. (Eds.). (1999). *Starting out right: A guide to promoting children's reading success.* Washington, DC: National Academy Press.

DeBruin-Parecki, A., & Krol-Sinclair, B. (2003). *Family literacy: From theory to practice.* Newark, DE: International Reading Association.

Dickinson, D. K., & Tabors, P. O. (2001). *Beginning literacy with language.* Baltimore: Paul H. Brookes.

Edmunds, K. M., & Bauserman, K. L. (2006). What teachers can learn about reading motivation through conversations with children. *The Reading Teacher, 59*(5), 414–424.

McKenna, M. C., Walpole, S., & Conradi, K. (2010). *Promoting early reading: Research resources, and best practices.* New York: Guilford Press.

Prior, J., & Gerard, M. R. (2004). *Environmental print in the classroom: Meaningful connections for learning to read.* Newark, DE: International Reading Association.

Strickland, D. S. (2010). *Essential readings on early literacy.* Newark, DE: International Reading Association.

Vaughn, S., & Linan-Thompson, S. (2004). *Research-based methods of reading instruction, grades K–3.* Alexandria, VA: Association for Supervision and Curriculum Development.

Venn, E. C., & Jahn, M. D. (2004). *Teaching and learning in preschool: Using individually appropriate practices in early childhood literacy instruction.* Newark, DE: International Reading Association.

Web Resources

https://dibels.uoregon.edu/measures/lnf.php
The DIBELS Letter Naming Fluency (LNF) test, a quick and reliable test for determining students' letter-naming fluency

http://gseweb.harvard.edu/~pild/projectease.htm
Four goals of Project EASE (Early Access to Success in Education), a parent–child early intervention program to promote early literacy for kindergarten children

www.heinemann.com/authors/699.aspx
Information about Marie Clay's works

The Power of Classroom Practice
www.myeducationlab.com

Go to Topic 2, Emergent Literacy, in the MyEducationLab (www.myeducationlab.com) for your course, where you can:

- Find learning outcomes for Emergent Literacy along with the national standards that connect to these outcomes.
- Complete Assignments and Activities that can help you more deeply understand the chapter content.
- Apply and practice your understanding of the core teaching skills identified in the chapter with the Building Teaching Skills and Dispositions learning units. (optional)
- Examine challenging situations and cases presented in the IRIS Center Resources. (optional)
- Access video clips of CCSSO National Teachers of the Year award winners responding to the question "Why Do I Teach?" in the Teacher Talk section. (optional)
- Check your comprehension on the content covered in the chapter by going to the Study Plan in the Book Resources for your text. Here you will be able to take a chapter quiz, receive feedback on your answers, and then access Review, Practice, and Enrichment activities to enhance your understanding of chapter content. (optional)

Go to the Topic A+RISE in the MyEducationLab (www.myeducationlab.com) for your course. A+RISE® Standards2Strategy™ is an innovative and interactive online resource that offers new teachers in grades K–12 just in time, research-based instructional strategies that:

- Meet the linguistic needs of ELLs as they learn content.
- Differentiate instruction for all grades and abilities.
- Offer reading and writing techniques, cooperative learning, use of linguistic and nonlinguistic representations, scaffolding, teacher modeling, higher order thinking, and alternative classroom ELL assessment.
- Provide support to help teachers be effective through the integration of listening, speaking, reading, and writing along with the content curriculum.
- Improve student achievement.
- Are aligned to Common Core Elementary Language Arts standards (for the literacy strategies) and to English language proficiency standards in WIDA, Texas, California, and Florida.

STANDARDS
for Reading Professionals and Guiding Principles for Educators

IRA Standards for Reading Professionals

Standard 1: Foundational Knowledge

Candidates understand the theoretical and evidence-based foundations of reading and writing processes and instruction.

Foundational knowledge is at the core of preparing individuals for roles in the reading profession and encompasses the major theories, research, and best practices that share a consensus of acceptance in the reading field. Individuals who enter the reading profession should understand the historically shared knowledge of the profession and develop the capacity to act on that knowledge responsibly. Elements of the Foundational Knowledge Standard set expectations in the domains of theoretical and practical knowledge, and in developing dispositions for the active, ethical use of professional knowledge. Expectations are founded on the concept of a profession as both a technical and moral enterprise, that is, competent performance for the betterment of society.

Element 1.1

Candidates understand major theories and empirical research that describe the cognitive, linguistic, motivational, and sociocultural foundations of reading and writing development, processes, and components, including word recognition, language comprehension, strategic knowledge, and reading–writing connections.

Element 1.3

Candidates understand the role of professional judgment and practical knowledge for improving all students' reading development and achievement.

Candidates use instructional approaches, materials, and an integrated, comprehensive, balanced curriculum to support student learning in reading and writing.

Standard 2: Curriculum and Instruction

The Curriculum and Instruction Standard recognizes the need to prepare educators who have a deep understanding and knowledge of the elements of a balanced, integrated, and comprehensive literacy curriculum and have developed expertise in enacting that curriculum. The elements focus on the use of effective practices in a well-articulated curriculum, using traditional print, digital, and online resources.

Element 2.1

Candidates use foundational knowledge to design or implement an integrated, comprehensive, and balanced curriculum.

Element 2.2

Candidates use appropriate and varied instructional approaches, including those that develop word recognition, language comprehension, strategic knowledge, and reading–writing connections.

Element 2.3

Candidates use a wide range of texts (e.g., narrative, expository, and poetry) from traditional print, digital, and online resources.

Response to Intervention

6. Expertise

All students have the right to receive instruction from well-prepared teachers who keep up to date and supplemental instruction from professionals specifically prepared to teach language and literacy (IRA, 2000).

- Teacher expertise is central to instructional improvement, particularly for students who encounter difficulty in acquiring language and literacy. RTI may involve a range of professionals; however, the greater the literacy difficulty, the greater the need for expertise in literacy teaching and learning.
- Important dimensions of teachers' expertise include their knowledge and understanding of language and literacy development, their ability to use powerful assessment tools and techniques, and their ability to translate information about student performance into instructionally relevant instructional techniques.

- The exemplary core instruction that is so essential to the success of RTI is dependent on highly knowledgeable and skilled classroom teachers (IRA, 2003).
- Professionals who provide supplemental instruction or intervention must have a high level of expertise in all aspects of language and literacy instruction and assessment and be capable of intensifying or accelerating language and literacy learning.
- Success for culturally and linguistically diverse students depends on teachers and support personnel who are well prepared to teach in a variety of settings. Deep knowledge of cultural and linguistic differences is especially critical for the prevention of language and literacy problems in diverse student populations.
- Expertise in the areas of language and literacy requires a comprehensive approach to professional preparation that involves preservice, induction, and inservice education. It also requires opportunities for extended practice under the guidance of knowledgeable and experienced mentors.

IRA Standards for Reading Professionals

Standard 3: Assessment and Evaluation

Candidates use a variety of assessment tools and practices to plan and evaluate effective reading and writing instruction.

Element 3.1

Candidates understand types of assessments and their purposes, strengths, and limitations.

Element 3.2

Candidates select, develop, administer, and interpret assessments, both traditional print and electronic, for specific purposes.

Element 3.3

Candidates use assessment information to plan and evaluate instruction.

Response to Intervention

3. Assessment

An RTI approach demands assessment that can inform language and literacy instruction meaningfully.

- Assessment should reflect the multidimensional nature of language and literacy learning and the diversity among students being assessed. The utility of an assessment is dependent on the extent to which it provides valid information on the essential aspects of language and literacy that can be used to plan appropriate instruction.
- Assessments, tools, and techniques should provide useful and timely information about desired language and literacy goals. They should reflect authentic language and literacy activities as opposed to contrived texts or tasks generated specifically for assessment purposes. The quality of assessment information should not be sacrificed for the efficiency of an assessment procedure.
- Multiple purposes for assessment should be clearly identified and appropriate tools and techniques employed. Not all available tools and techniques are appropriate for all purposes, and different assessments—even in the same language or literacy

domain—capture different skills and knowledge. Particular care should be taken in selecting assessments for ELLs and for students who speak an English dialect that differs from mainstream dialects.

- Efficient assessment systems involve a layered approach in which screening techniques are used both to identify which students require further (diagnostic) assessment and to provide aggregate data about the nature of student achievement overall. Initial (screening) assessments should not be used as the sole mechanism for determining the appropriateness of targeted interventions. Ongoing progress monitoring must include an evaluation of the instruction itself and requires observation of the student in the classroom.
- Classroom teachers and reading/literacy specialists should play a central role in conducting language and literacy assessments and in using assessment results to plan instruction and monitor student performance.
- Assessment as a component of RTI should be consistent with the *Standards for the Assessment of Reading and Writing* developed jointly by the International Reading Association and the National Council of Teachers of English (2010).

IRA Standards for Reading Professionals

Standard 2: Curriculum and Instruction

Elements 2.1, 2.2, 2.3 (See previous)

Standard 5: Literate Environment

Candidates create a literate environment that fosters reading and writing by integrating foundational knowledge, instructional practices, approaches and methods, curriculum materials, and the appropriate use of assessments.

Element 5.1

Candidates design the physical environment to optimize students' use of traditional print, digital, and online resources in reading and writing instruction.

Element 5.2

Candidates design a social environment that is low risk and includes choice, motivation, and scaffolded support to optimize students' opportunities for learning to read and write.

Element 5.3

Candidates use routines to support reading and writing instruction (e.g., time allocation, transitions from one activity to another, discussions, and peer feedback).

Common Core Standards

Reading: K–5

Key Ideas and Details

1. Read closely to determine what the text says explicitly and to make logical inferences from it; cite specific textual evidence when writing or speaking to support conclusions drawn from the text.

Response to Intervention

1. Instruction

- A successful RTI process begins with the highest quality core instruction in the classroom—that is, instruction that encompasses all areas of language and literacy as part of a coherent curriculum that is developmentally appropriate for preK–12 students and does not underestimate their potential for learning. This core instruction may or may not involve commercial programs, and it must in all cases be provided by an informed, competent classroom teacher.
- The success of RTI depends on the classroom teacher's use of research-based practices. As defined by IRA (2002), *research based* means "that a particular program or collection of instructional practices has a record of success. That is, there is reliable, trustworthy, and valid evidence to suggest that when the program is used with a particular group of children, the children can be expected to make adequate gains in reading achievement."
- Research evidence frequently represents the effectiveness of an instructional practice on average, which suggests that some students benefited and others did not. This means that instruction must be provided by a teacher who understands the intent of the research-based practice being used and has the professional expertise and responsibility to plan instruction and adapt programs and materials as needed (see also principle 6, Expertise).
- When core language and literacy instruction is not effective for a particular student, it should be modified to address more closely the needs and abilities of that student. Classroom teachers, at times in collaboration with other experts, must exercise their best professional judgment in providing responsive teaching and differentiation (see also principle 2).

5. Systemic and Comprehensive Approaches

RTI must be part of a comprehensive, systemic approach to language and literacy assessment and instruction that supports all preK–12 students and teachers.

- RTI needs to be integrated within the context of a coherent and consistent language and literacy curriculum that guides comprehensive instruction for all students. Core instruction—indeed, all instruction—must be continuously improved to increase its efficacy and mitigate the need for specialized interventions.
- Specific approaches to RTI need to be appropriate for the particular school or district culture and take into account leadership, expertise, the diversity of the student population, and the available resources. Schools and districts should adopt an approach that best matches their needs and resources while still accomplishing the overall goals of RTI.
- A systemic approach to language and literacy learning within an RTI framework requires the active participation and genuine collaboration of many professionals, including classroom teachers, reading specialists, literacy coaches, special educators, and school psychologists. Given the critical role that language development plays in literacy learning, professionals with specialized language-related expertise such as speech-language pathologists and teachers of ELLs may be particularly helpful in addressing students' language difficulties.
- Approaches to RTI must be sensitive to developmental differences in language and literacy among students at different ages and grades. Although many prevailing approaches to RTI focus on the early elementary grades, it is essential for teachers and support personnel at middle and secondary levels to provide their students with the language and literacy instruction they need to succeed in school and beyond.
- Administrators must ensure adequate resources and appropriate scheduling to allow all professionals to collaborate.
- Ongoing and job-embedded professional development is necessary for all educators involved in the RTI process. Professional development should be context specific and provided by professional developers with appropriate preparation and skill to support school and district personnel. Professional expertise is essential to improving students' language and literacy learning in general as well as within the context of RTI (see also principle 6).

Differentiating and Adapting Early Reading Instruction

IRA Standards for Reading Professionals

Standard 4: Diversity

Candidates create and engage their students in literacy practices that develop awareness, understanding, respect, and a valuing of differences in our society.

Element 4.1

Candidates recognize, understand, and value the forms of diversity that exist in society and their importance in learning to read and write.

Element 4.2

Candidates use a literacy curriculum and engage in instructional practices that positively impact students' knowledge, beliefs, and engagement with the features of diversity.

Element 4.3

Candidates develop and implement strategies to advocate for equity.

Standard 5: Literate Environment
Element 5.3 (See previous)

Response to Intervention

2. Responsive Teaching and Differentiation

The RTI process emphasizes increasingly differentiated and intensified instruction or intervention in language and literacy.

- RTI is centrally about optimizing language and literacy instruction for particular students. This means that differentiated instruction, based on instructionally relevant assessment, is essential. Evidence shows that small-group and individualized instruction are effective in reducing the number of students who are at risk of becoming classified as learning disabled.
- Instruction and materials selection must derive from specific student–teacher interactions and not be constrained by pack-

aged programs. Students have different language and literacy needs, so they may not respond similarly to instruction—even when research-based practices are used. No single approach to instruction or intervention can address the broad and varied goals and needs of all students, especially those from different cultural and linguistic backgrounds.

- The boundaries between differentiation and intervention are permeable and not clearcut. Instruction or intervention must be flexible enough to respond to evidence from student performance and teaching interactions. It should not be constrained by institutional procedures that emphasize uniformity.

Motivation and Engagement of Early Readers

IRA Standards for Reading Professionals

Standard 5: Literate Environment   **Elements 5.1, 5.2** (See previous)

Technology and New Literacies for Early Readers

IRA Standards for Reading Professionals

Standard 2: Curriculum and Instruction   **Element 2.3** (See previous)

Common Core Standards

Reading: K–5

Integration of Knowledge and Ideas

7. Integrate and evaluate content presented in diverse media and formats, including visually and quantitatively, as well as in words.

Writing: K–5

Production and Distribution of Writing

6. Use technology, including the Internet, to produce and publish writing and to interact and collaborate with others.

Family and Community Support for Early Readers

IRA Standards for Reading Professionals

Standard 4: Diversity   **Elements 4.1, 4.2, 4.3** (See previous)

Response to Intervention

4. Collaboration

RTI requires a dynamic, positive, and productive collaboration among professionals with relevant expertise in language and literacy. Success also depends on strong and respectful partnerships among professionals, parents, and students.

- Collaboration should be focused on the available evidence about the needs of students struggling in language and literacy. School-level decision-making teams (e.g., intervention teams, problem-solving teams, RTI teams) should include members with relevant expertise in language and literacy, including second-language learning.

- Collaboration should increase, not reduce, the coherence of the instruction experienced by struggling readers. There must be congruence between core language and literacy instruction and interventions. This requires a shared vision and common goals for language and literacy instruction and assessment, adequate time for communication and coordinated planning among general education and specialist teachers, and integrated professional development.
- Involving parents and students and engaging them in a collaborative manner is critical to successful implementation. Initiating and strengthening collaborations among school, home, and communities, particularly in urban and rural areas, provides the basis for support and reinforcement of students' learning.

Phonics and 4
Word Recognition
LEARNING TO READ WORDS

Teacher Knowledge	Classroom Assessment	Evidence-Based Teaching Practices	Response to Intervention (RTI)
What Teachers Need to Know to Teach Phonics	Assessing and Monitoring Student Progress in Learning Phonics	Effective Phonics Instruction	Meeting the Needs of Diverse Learners in Phonics Instruction

Chapter Questions

- What are two processes children need to learn to recognize words?

- How do effective teachers assess students' word recognition?

- What does research show as the best ways of teaching phonics?

- Who has difficulty learning phonics and what can be done to assist them?

- What are some ways teachers can engage students in learning phonics?

- How can technology be used to enhance phonics instruction?

- What strategies can parents use to help their children learn phonics skills?

Key Terms

Phonics

Graphophonemic knowledge

Decoding

Word recognition

Alphabetic principle

Consonant blends

Consonant clusters

Consonant digraphs

Vowel digraphs

Diphthongs

Structural analysis

Morphemes

Segmenting

Sight words

Interactive strategies

Motivation and Engagement	Technology and New Literacies	Family and Community Connections
Motivation and Engagement Strategies for Teaching Phonics	Using Technology and New Literacies to Enhance Phonics Instruction	How Family and Community Connections Can Foster Phonics Development Outside the Classroom

Vignette: Mr. Bill and Emily

Mr. Bill, as his students like to call him, is a second-grade teacher beginning his third year of teaching at Doolittle Elementary in downtown Chicago. As is his practice, Mr. Bill conducts a number of short assessments in the first 2 weeks of school to get a better handle on where his students are in their reading development and to help in planning small-group instruction. While his students are engaged in independent work, Mr. Bill invites Emily, apparently one of his more precocious readers, to join him in the reading center. He had asked her to pick a favorite book or two and show him her "very best reading."

"Emily," asks Mr. Bill, "what book did you choose to share with me today?"

Emily proudly holds up a copy of *The Summer of the Swans* by Betsy Byars and says, "I'm ready to show you my very best reading, Mr. Bill."

"Go for it!" responds Mr. Bill. "Let's do it! Pick out a page and show me your very best reading." He then turns on the audio recorder.

Emily opens her book to page 46, where she had placed her bookmark, and begins reading. At one point, Emily reads tentatively: "'Already he had started shhh–aaakkk–ing, shaking his head again, all the while waaa–chh–ing the swans gliding across the dark water.'" Emily looks up for a reaction from her teacher.

Mr. Bill says, "I like how you said the sounds for the letters in that word and blended them. Well done! Let's continue."

Emily reads, "'Sss–kwint–ing, squinting!'" then quickly looks up with a mix of anticipation and dread in her eyes.

"Right again! You're quite a reader, Miss Emily!" says Mr. Bill. Emily beams at her teacher's words of praise.

When Emily's recitation is finished, she looks up, obviously hoping for some sign of approval from the room's best reader. Mr. Bill says, "Emily, I've already noticed this year how much you enjoy poetry." When Emily nods, Mr. Bill says, "Me, too! I love poetry that rhymes and also tells a story. One of my favorite poems is by a man named Pek Gunn. He was from Tennessee and liked to tell stories from his childhood."

Mr. Bill continues. "Pek Gunn wrote a poem called *June Bug on a String* that talks about how children a hundred years ago used to catch June bugs. They're bugs kind of like bumblebees, except they don't sting. Kids would tie a thread around a June bug and then let it fly around while they held the string and watched."

"That sounds mean," responds Emily.

"I see your point. But they didn't hurt the bug—they just watched it fly slowly around."

"I guess that's okay," says Emily. "As long as they let the June bug go after they played awhile."

"They did. The point of the poem is that whoever holds the string in life is in control. So, the child in the poem holding the string was in control!"

"Mr. Bill, I see what you mean. But what are you trying to tell me?" Emily queries.

"Only this. When I see how well you are coming along with your reading, I see a girl who is getting control over reading like a grown-up! This year we are going to learn new ways to make sure that, whenever you come to a new word in a book, you'll be able to pronounce that new word as fast as lightning. That way, you will be the one holding the string. You'll be in control of reading all the time!" ■

Teacher Knowledge

What Teachers Need to Know to Teach Phonics

What do you think of when you hear the word *phonics?* Does it call to mind the familiar phrase *"Sound it out"*? If so, you're not alone! But the truth is there is much more to learning to unlock the code of written language than you may think. An understanding of how students learn phonics and other decoding skills is essential for effective word recognition assessment and instruction. In this chapter, we take a close look at what the evidence base says about what children must know and be able to do to effectively "decode" words using phonics. In addition, we will learn about how to help students commit high-frequency words to memory or teach what we call *sight words*.

IRA Standards for Reading Professionals: Standard 1, Elements 1.1, 1.2, 1.3

Response to Intervention: Expertise

What Is Phonics?

Phonics is defined as a teaching method that relates spoken sounds to written symbols in systematic and predictable ways (letter–sound relationships or **graphophonemic knowledge**) and how this knowledge can be used by readers to decode words in print (Burns, Griffin, & Snow, 1999; Rasinski & Padak, 1996). Before we go further in this discussion of phonics, let's clarify the difference between two important concepts: decoding and word recognition.

Decoding has to do with the phonics skills students learn and apply that help them to figure out the pronunciation of an unfamiliar word in print. This is what the old phrase, "Sound it out," meant. When a reader sees a new word in print (for example, *start*), he or she must be able to identify each letter in sequence left-to-right, match a speech sound to each letter, and then blend together the string of speech sounds represented by the letters of the word *start* to pronounce the word correctly. Decoding skills are also sometimes referred to as *word attack skills* or *word identification* because the purpose is to break the code of written words and translate the letters, affixes, syllables, and so forth into a spoken word.

Word recognition, on the other hand, has to do with instantly identifying words as wholes, without resorting to analyzing words letter by letter and blending sounds to access an approximate pronunciation. It is possible for a student to use decoding skills to pronounce a word in print, yet not be able to connect the pronunciation of the word to its meaning, thereby saying a word but not recognizing its meaning. For instance, a child may well be able to use decoding skills to pronounce the word *mordant,* yet have no idea what the word means. By the way, do *you* know the meaning of the word *mordant?* If not, then you now know the difference between decoding or saying a word (the ability to pronounce a word in print—*mordant* is pronounced *more/dent*), and word recognition (the ability to instantly identify a word and simultaneously understand its meaning).

Learning the Alphabetic Principle

The early steps in becoming aware of the alphabetic nature of spoken and printed language begin when children notice, either on their own or with help, that spoken words are made up of individual speech sounds called *phonemes.* By developing an awareness of phonemes in words, children learn to hear smaller parts of spoken words. Next in the learning sequence comes an awareness of printed alphabet letters in books and other print materials in their environment.

Learning the **alphabetic principle** means that children develop an understanding that specific letters or letter combinations represent specific speech sounds in spoken words—for example, the awareness that the *rrrrrr* sound is represented by the letter *r* every time you see that letter in print. Understanding that the English language, both spoken and written, relies on an understanding of the alphabetic principle is a major step toward learning to decode words using phonics. It is a critical conceptual connection about the relationship of spoken language to written language that young children must acquire to benefit from phonics instruction provided in elementary school classrooms. Primary-grade teachers (pre-K–3) teach students the following:

- Speech is made up of individual speech sounds (phonemes).
- Print is represented using the 26 letters of the English alphabet.
- Spoken sounds (phonemes) are represented by specific letters (graphemes) and letter combinations.

In summary, when children are able to combine their phonemic awareness with letter name knowledge, they attain a new conceptual understanding that letters and sounds in spoken words connect in systematic ways. Called the alphabetic principle (Byrne & Fielding-Barnsley, 1989), this understanding is absolutely necessary for almost all students to make progress in their reading development, particularly when it comes to benefiting from classroom phonics instruction, which requires knowledge of the alphabetic principle to be effective.

Phonics for Teachers

Over the years, surveys conducted by the International Reading Association (IRA) have found that "phonics instruction" is one of the most hotly debated issues in the field of reading education. Before we plunge into an "executive briefing" for teachers about phonics and other related decoding concepts, we invite you to take a short pretest to find out what you already know—or what you need to know—about phonics. Complete the *Phonics Quick Test* (Figure 4.1) before reading further. The results may surprise you!

Now that you have assessed your own phonics knowledge, let's take a look at major elements of phonics instruction that you will need to know as a teacher. We begin with consonant letters and sounds—*b, c, d, f, g, h, j, k, l, m, n, p, q, r, s, t, v, x,* and *z.* Then we discuss the vowel letters and sounds—*a, e, i, o, u* and sometimes *y* and *w.*

Figure 4.1

The Phonics Quick Test

Phonics Quick Test*

1. The word *charkle* is broken into syllables between _____ and _____. The *a* has an _____-controlled sound, and the *e* is _____.
2. In the word *small*, *sm-* is known as the onset and *-all* is known as the _____.
3. The *ch* in the word *chair* is known as a _____ .
4. The letter *c* in the word *city* has a _____ sound and in the word *cow* has a _____ sound.
5. The letters *bl* in the word *blue* are referred to as a consonant _____.
6. The underlined vowels in the words *author*, *spread*, and *blue* are know as vowel _____.
7. The words *tag*, *run*, *cot*, and *get* fit which vowel pattern? _____
8. The words *glide*, *take*, and *use* fit the _____ vowel pattern.
9. The word part *work* in the word *working* is known as a _____.
10. The word part *-ing* in the word *working* is known as a _____.
11. Teaching students the meanings of prefixes, suffixes, and root words to help them better understand word meanings is part of word attack skills known as _____.
12. Writers often provide _____, which help readers discover the meaning of unknown words in print.

*Answers to the *Phonics Quick Test* are found at the end of this chapter, on p. 173.

Consonant Letters and Sounds

The most reliable starting point for phonics instruction is the teaching of consonants, which more consistently represent single phonemes when compared to vowel sounds and letters. However, not all consonants are created equal—some are much more stable than others. The most consistently stable consonants and their sounds are listed in Table 4.1. We also share in Table 4.2 some of the not-very-consistent consonants, which should not be taught until after students acquire consistent letter–sound phonics mastery of the stable consonants. Only once they have done so should teachers gradually introduce the fact that some consonant letters represent more than one consonant sound, such as the letters *c* and *g*.

The C Rule. The letter *c* is an irregular consonant because it can represent more than one phoneme or speech sound. It can be used for two phonemes that are already represented by the letters *k* and *s*. As authors, we have oft contemplated starting a petition drive to eliminate the letter *c* due to its redundancy with the letters *k* and *s* anyway! Until then, however, readers should know how *c* functions to represent the two sounds normally association with *k* and *s*. In general, when *c* is followed by the letters *a*, *o*, or *u*, it represents the sound we associate with the letter *k*, also known as the *hard c* sound. Some examples are the words *cake*, *cosmic*, and *cute*. On the other hand, *c* can sometimes represent the sound associated with the letter *s*. This is referred to as the *soft c* sound, which is usually produced when *c* is followed

Table 4.1

Most Consistent Consonants

Sound	Letter–Sound Matching (Percentage of Use in English)	Example
/v/	v (99.5%)	vault
/d/	d (98%)	doll
/h/	h (98%)	hall
/b/	b (97%)	ball
/n/	n (97%)	not
/r/	r (97%)	road
/t/	t (97%)	tell
/p/	p (96%)	put
/m/	m (94%)	Molly
/l/	l (91%)	lost

Table 4.2

Some Not-Very-Consistent Consonants

Sound	Letter–Sound Matching (Percentage of Use in English)	Examples
/g/	g (88%), gg, gh	good, egg, ghost
/f/	f (78%), ff, ph, lf	fun, staff, phone, wolf
/k/	c (73%), cc, k (13%), ck, lk, q	can, stucco, rock, Chuck, chalk, bisque
/s/	s (73%), c (17%), ss	some, cent, stress
/j/	g (66%), j (22%), dg	giraffe, jelly, judge
/y/	i (55%), y (44%)	onion, yell
/z/	z (23%), zz, s (64%)	zip, jazz, easy

by *e, i,* or *y.* Examples of the soft *c* sound are found in the words *celebrate, circus,* and *cycle.*

The G Rule.   English uses *g* as the key symbol for the phoneme we hear in the word *get* (Hull, 1989, p. 35). This letter is irregular, having both a soft and a hard sound. The rules are the same as for the letter *c.* When *g* is followed by the letters *e, i,* or *y,* it represents a soft *g* or /j/ sound, as with the words *gently, giraffe,* and *gym.* If *g* is followed by the letters *a, o,* or *u,* then it usually represents the hard or regular sound, as with the words *garden, go,* and *gum.*

Once children know about these two exceptional consonants, they should be introduced to other consonant variations that will be encountered as they learn to blend letter sounds together to say words. These include consonant blends or clusters and consonant digraphs.

Consonant Blends or Clusters.   Combinations of two or more consonant letters whose sounds can be blended together such that each consonant is still pronounced (*bl, fr, sk, spl*) are referred to as **consonant blends** (2 letters) or **consonant clusters** (3 or more letters). Examples of words containing consonant blends and clusters are shown in the following list:

   bl—black, block, blast, blur, oblige, nimbly

   fr—frost, fruit, afraid, befriend, leapfrog, refresh

   sk—sky, skunk, outskirts, desk, task

   spl—splash, splat, split, splotch

Consonant Digraphs.   Two consonant letters that represent only one distinct speech sound (*th, sh, ch, wh, gh, ck, ng*) are called **consonant digraphs,** as in the following examples:

   ch—children, change, merchant, search, which, branch

   th—thank, author, both, that, mother, smooth

   ng—sling, gang, long, fang, hung, wrong

Vowel Letters and Sounds

Unlike consonant letters, which are the most reliable starting point for phonics instruction, vowel letters are highly variant in representing sounds in spoken language. At the simplest level, most teachers are familiar with long and short vowel sounds. These variant speech sounds, represented by five to seven vowel letters, can be written using 96 different letter combinations. In explaining vowels, teachers need to be cautious in overloading young students with too many technical linguistic terms and definitions. For example, when teaching about long and short vowels, it may be useful to simplify the terminology by saying that vowel letters usually represent a sound (short) and the name (long) of the vowel letters. Thus, telling children that a vowel letter can represent its sound and name when blending certain word patterns is a simple way of helping them gain insights into the variant sounds that are represented by vowel letters. However, vowels, unlike consonants, are even more unreliable in representing a single phoneme (sound) to grapheme (letter) relationship, as noted by the 96 combinations used in English. Once students learn that vowels can represent the sounds associated with their names and sounds, they encounter vowel letter combinations that are quite challenging. These include vowel digraphs, diphthongs, the schwa, and *r*-controlled vowel sounds, as briefly explained in the following subsections.

Vowel Digraphs. Combinations of two vowel letters together in words representing only one distinct speech sound (*ee, oo, ie, ai*) are called **vowel digraphs.** The usual rule is "When two vowels go walking, the first one does the talking," but this is not always so. The following examples show words containing vowel digraphs.

> *ee*—eel, sleep, week, three, spree
>
> *ea*—head, each, threat, heaven
>
> *oa*—houseboat, oak, coat, loaf, toad

Diphthongs. Combinations of two vowels together in words producing a single, glided sound (*oi* in *oil, oy* in *boy*) are known as **diphthongs,** as in the examples that follow:

> *ow*—down, flower, crowd, towel, how, bow, avow
>
> *oi*—oil, voice, exploit, soil, void, typhoid
>
> *ou*—out, hour, doubt, our, around, count

Schwa. Some vowel letters produce the *uh* sound (like the *a*'s in *America*). The schwa is represented by the backward upside-down *e* symbol: ə. Vowel letters can represent the schwa sound. Also, explosive consonants like *p* blended with the letter sound of *l* can combine to produce a schwa sound even when no vowel letter is represented, as in the word *simple*. The following examples show words containing the schwa sound.

> *a*—about, ago, several, canvas, china, comma
>
> *e*—effect, erroneous, happen, children, label, agent
>
> *o*—other, mother, atom, riot, second, objection
>
> no vowel letter—simple, apple, subtle (the schwa sound *uh* is heard between the *p* and the *l*)

r–Controlled Vowels. Vowels that appear before the letter *r* are usually neither long nor short but tend to be overpowered or "swallowed up" by the /r/ sound. Examples include *person, fir, car, player, neighborhood,* and *herself.*

Word Patterns

It may be useful at this point to discuss word patterns that give relatively reliable cues about which of the variant sounds a vowel letter may represent when found in words. Certain combinations of consonants (C) and vowels (V) in syllables produce consistent vowel sounds. We begin with the CVC and CV word patterns followed by the VCe and CVVC word patterns.

The CVC Pattern. When a vowel comes between two consonants in a syllable, it usually represents what is referred to as a *short* vowel sound. Examples of words following the CVC pattern include *sat, ran, let, pen, win, fit, hot, mop, sun,* and *cut.*

The CV Pattern. When a consonant is followed by a vowel, the vowel usually produces a long sound. This is especially easy to see in two-letter words such as *be, go,* and *so.*

The VCe (Final Silent e) Pattern. When two vowels appear in a word and one is an *e* at the end of the word, the first vowel is generally long and the final *e* is silent. Examples include *cape, rope,* and *kite.*

Vowel Digraphs (CVVC). When two vowels come together in a word, the first vowel usually carries what is referred to as a *long* sound and the second vowel is silent. This occurs especially often with the *oa, ee,* and *ay* combinations. Some examples are *toad, fleet,* and *day.* As noted previously, a common slogan used by teachers to help children remember this generalization is "When two vowels go walking, the first one does the talking."

Onset and Rime

Because many vowel letters and vowel letter combinations are not as consistent in English as we would like, teachers can show children other levels of word patterns that are somewhat more reliable. Adams (1990) states that linguistic researchers have found an instructionally useful alternative form of decoding words involving the use of onsets and rimes. An onset is that part of a syllable that comes before the vowel; the rime is the rest of the syllable (Adams, 1990, p. 55). Although all syllables must have a rime, not all have an onset. The following are a few examples of onsets and rimes in words.

Word	Onset	Rime
a	—	a
in	—	in
aft	—	aft
sat	s-	-at
trim	tr-	-im
spring	spr-	-ing

One may wonder about the usefulness of onset and rime in the classroom, at least as far as decoding instruction is concerned. First, some evidence indicates that children are better able to identify the spellings of rimes than of individual vowel sounds (Adams, 1990; Barton, Miller, & Macken, 1980; Blevins, 1997; Moustafa, 1997; Treiman, 1985). Second, children as young as 5 and 6 years of age can transfer by analogy what they know about the pronunciation of one word to another that has the same rime, such as *call* and *ball* (Adams, 1990). In a way, children are learning to use analogies from known rime patterns to pronounce new or novel words with that same rime pattern—what is called learning phonics by analogy. Third, although many vowels represent single phonemes unreliably, even irregular vowel sounds seem to remain stable within rimes. For example, the *ea* vowel digraph is quite consistent within rimes, with the exceptions of *-ear* in *hear* compared to *bear* and *-ead* in *bead* compared to *head* (Adams, 1990). Finally, there is evidence supporting the utility of learning and using rimes in early decoding instruction (Goswami & Bryant, 1990). Nearly 500 primary-level words can be derived through the following set of only 37 rimes (Adams, 1990; Blachman, 1984):

-ack	-at	-ide	-ock	-ain	-ate
-ight	-oke	-ake	-aw	-ill	-op
-ale	-ay	-in	-or	-all	-eat
-ine	-ore	-ame	-ell	-ing	-uck
-an	-est	-ink	-ug	-ank	-ice
-ip	-ump	-ap	-ick	-ir	-unk
-ash					

The application of using onset and rime to decode and write words almost seems obvious. Many students will find it easier to identify new words in print by first noting familiar rimes within words. Spelling efficiency may also be increased as rimes are matched with onsets to construct "invented" spellings. (We prefer to call them "temporary" spellings so that children and parents understand that we intend to develop students' ability to generate conventional or correct spellings later on through instruction.)

One teacher remarked that the easiest way to teach rimes is through using *rhymes* as a part of early phonological awareness instruction. She was exactly right! Children learn many otherwise laborious tasks through rhymes, songs, chants, and raps, any of which can contain rhyming words that are very useful to teachers. For example, a teacher may wish to use an excerpt like the following from the book *Taxi Dog* by Debra and Sal Barracca to emphasize the *-ide* and *-ill* rimes. The rimes are noted in bold type for easy identification by the reader.

> It's just like a dream,
> Me and Jim—we're a team!
> I'm always there at his s**ide**.
> We never stand st**ill**,
> Every day's a new thr**ill**—
> Come join us next time for a r**ide**!* (p. 30)

Another potentially useful insight for teachers of phonics involves another way of dividing syllables for the purpose of blending sounds in syllables to pronounce words, called *body-coda*. Body and coda are the opposite way of dividing a syllable as compared to onset and rime. The *body* is the first part of a syllable including the vowel sound and the *coda* is what is left. For example, consider the syllable *fun* (remembering that single syllables can also be words). The body in *fun* is *fu* and the coda is *n*. Rather than using onset and rime to say *f* and then *un*, body-coda would have students blend the parts of a syllable as *fu* and then *n*. Recent research has demonstrated that young children can blend syllable parts more fluently when using body and coda than with onset and rime (Murray, Brabham, Villaume, & Veal, 2008).

Table 4.3

The Thorndike–Lorge Magazine Count of High-Frequency Words

Word	Frequency of Use	Cumulative Percentage of Use
1 the	236,472	.0515
2 and	138,672	.0817
3 a	117,222	.1072
4 to	115,358	.1323
5 of	112,601	.1568
6 I	89,489	.1763
7 in	75,253	.1926
8 was	58,732	.2055
9 that	55,667	.2176
10 it	52,107	.2290
11 he	49,268	.2397
12 you	42,581	.2490
13 for	39,363	.2576
14 had	34,341	.2651
15 is	33,404	.2723
16 with	32,903	.2795
17 her	31,824	.2884
18 she	31,087	.2932
19 his	30,748	.2999
20 as	30,693	.3066
21 on	30,244	.3132
22 at	26,250	.3189
23 have	24,456	.3242
24 but	23,704	.3292
25 me	23,364	.3345

Sum = 1,535,783

Total number of words = 4,591,125

From Thorndike, E. L., & Lorge, I. (1944). *The Teacher's Word Book of 30,000 words*. New York: Columbia University.

Word Recognition: Teaching High-Frequency Sight Words

Learning to decode words fluently and without a great deal of cognitive effort will get most children about 50 percent of the way toward automatic and fluent word recognition. But there is another group or corpus of words called *high-frequency words* that must be recognized by sight without letter-by-letter decoding analysis. Learning to "see and say" or instantly recognize a group of high-frequency words by sight will get young students the other 50 percent of the way toward the goal of effortless and automatic word recognition. Once word recognition is an effortless and fluent process, students' attention and thinking are freed up to make the comprehension of text possible, which, although not automatically guaranteed, becomes possible with instruction in comprehension strategies.

High-frequency words are by definition those words that occur most often in printed texts. For example the word *the* occurs roughly 5 percent of the time in running English texts at almost any level of difficulty. Imagine it, once children can effortlessly recognize the word *the*, they have mastered 5 percent of all the reading they will ever do! Researchers have long been interested in counting the relative frequency with which certain words in English appear in print. In 1944, Thorndike and Lorge conducted a 4.5 million word frequency count taken from American magazine articles. These researchers found that there was a list of 25 words that accounted for 1.5 million words in the total word frequency count of 4.5 million words. This means that a list of 25 high-frequency words will account for roughly 33 percent of the words an adult American would read in printed texts such as magazines, newspapers, and so on. A listing of these 25 highly frequent words is found in Table 4.3.

What's more, many of the words on this list are irregular words, meaning that they are not easily decodable. For instance, imagine blending the sounds of letters to pronounce the word *the*. Either one would blend the letter sounds /t/ /h/ /ē/ or perhaps say the consonant digraph /th/ and then blend that with the sound /ē/. However, blending these sounds together does not get one to the conventional pronunciation of *the*. Thus, the word *the* is best learned by focusing attention of students on how the word "looks" and committing it to memory through repetitious exposures of various types (what is called learning the word "by sight").

More recently a group of researchers has found that a group of 107 high-frequency words comprises 50 percent of all the words that one would normally encounter when reading English texts (Zeno, Ivens, Millard, & Duvvuri, 1995). This listing of the 107 high-frequency words (which includes the 25 words in the Thorndike-Lorge list as well) that should be taught by sight or recognized instantly without further analysis is found in Table 4.4. Imagine how knowing these 107 words instantly, by sight, would affect students' reading fluency. They would instantly know how to say 1 out of every 2 words they would encounter in English texts! A process for teaching children to recognize high-frequency words by sight will be thoroughly presented later on in this chapter.

Although there are many more "relatively" high-frequency words that young students will eventually commit to memory or sight through volume reading, explicitly teaching more than the 107 words listed in Table 4.4 shows a clear diminishing return for the investment of time—sometimes referred to as a *cost to benefit analysis*. Zeno and colleagues (1995) showed that in order to learn 65 percent of typically occurring words in English texts students would have to commit to memory 930 words, or about 823 more words to get an additional 15 percent return rate on the 50 percent rate already achieved by learning the 107. Thus, learning an additional 100 words through explicit sight word lessons would increase students' reading fluency by a mere 2 percent. Consequently, once the 107 frequently occurring words

Click on A+RISE—WIDA ELP Standard Strategies in the MyEducationLab (www.myeducationlab. com) for your course. Next, select the Strategy Card Index tab, scroll to Phonics for grades K–5, and select the Portable Word Wall strategy.

Table 4.4

Zeno et al. High-Frequency Word List

the	as	but	about	your	how	also	back
of	are	by	up	which	than	down	where
and	they	were	said	do	two	make	know
to	with	one	out	then	may	now	little
a	be	all	if	many	only	way	such
in	his	she	some	these	most	each	even
is	at	when	would	no	its	called	much
that	or	an	so	time	made	did	our
it	from	their	people	been	over	just	must
was	had	there	them	who	see	after	
for	I	her	other	like	first	water	
you	not	can	more	could	new	through	
he	have	we	will	has	very	get	
on	this	what	into	him	my	because	

From Zeno, S. M., Ivens, S. H., Millard, R. T., & Duvvuri, R. (1995). *The Educator's Word Frequency Guide.* Reprinted by permission of Touchstone Applied Science Associates, Inc.

have been learned by sight, time is better spent on helping children learn additional sight words through reading everyday books that contain these "relatively" high-frequency words in running English texts.

Structural Analysis: A Tool for Recognizing Multisyllabic Words

Another strategy readers use to decode unfamiliar words in print is called **structural analysis.** Rather than attacking words on the letter–phoneme level or on the onset and rime or body and coda levels, this kind of word recognition applies a reader's knowledge of memorized, meaningful word parts that are often added to base words, or what some people call *root* words.

Here's how it works. A reader encounters an unfamiliar word (that is, a word that is recognized when heard but is not familiar in print), usually a multisyllabic word—let's say the word *unbelievable.* Our reader in this example has heard and read the base or root word *believe* dozens of times in conversations and in books (e.g., in sentences like "Yes, I believe you" or "I believe that all children should have a nice birthday party") and immediately recognizes the base or root word. Moreover, the prefix *un-* has been explicitly taught in class along with other familiar prefixes such as *re-, be-, non-, anti-,* and so on. Also, the prefix *un-* is likewise very familiar to the reader from other words heard in conversation and encountered when learning to read, such as *untie, unreal,* and *unhook.* The student is able to infer from prior knowledge of meaningful word parts or prefixes that *un-* means something like "not" or "to reverse." Finally, the reader's attention focuses briefly on the suffix (and word) *-able* and its meaning and pronunciation, also deduced from prior knowledge of words like *workable* and previous teacher-directed explicit instruction on suffixes. In our example, then, the reader has found a way to both decode words and unlock word meanings at a level something larger than the sound–symbol level. Progressing from recognition and understanding of the root word (*believe*) to the prefix (*un-*) to the suffix (*-able*) led to successful word decoding and comprehension from the meanings of the word parts. Structural analysis couples decoding words with understanding word and word part meanings at a higher level. This is a particularly important strategy for children in second and third grade, during which multisyllabic words become more common and are decoded in chunks.

Words are made up of basic meaning units known as **morphemes,** which, as previously discussed, may be divided into two classes—bound and free. Bound morphemes are affixes that must be attached to a root word (sometimes called a *base word*) to have meaning. Prefixes and suffixes are bound morphemes (e.g., *pre-, un-, dis-, en-, inter-, extra-, -ed, -ies, -er, -ing*). Free morphemes (base words or root words) are meaning units that can stand alone and have meaning. The word *replay* has both a bound and free morpheme: *re-,* the bound morpheme (prefix) meaning "again," and *play,* the free morpheme that has meaning on its own. Sometimes two free morphemes combine to form a new compound word, such as *doghouse, outdoors, playground,* and *tonight.*

Teachers can help children begin to practice structural analysis of words in the same ways as they do onset and rime. The idea to get across to students is that whenever a good reader comes to a word she cannot identify through phonics alone, she sometimes looks within the word for a recognizable base (root) word and its accompanying prefix, suffix, or endings (Durkin, 1989; Lass & Davis, 1985). In other words, we tell our students to "look for something you know within the word."

Figure 4.2 shows selected examples of affixes adapted from *The Reading Teacher's Book of Lists* (Fry, Kress, & Fountoukidis, 2006). Teachers can also find lists of

Figure 4.2

Examples of Affixes

Prefixes

Prefix	Meaning	Example	Prefix	Meaning	Example
intro-	inside	introduce	ad-	to, toward	adhere
pro-	forward	project	para-	beside, by	paraphrase
post-	after	postdate	pre-	before	predate
sub-	under	submarine	per-	throughout	pervade
ultra-	beyond	ultramodern	ab-	from	abnormal
dis-	opposite	disagree	trans-	across	transatlantic

Suffixes

Suffix	Meaning	Example	Suffix	Meaning	Example
-ant	one who	servant	-ee	object of action	payee
-ist	one who practices	pianist	-ary	place for	library
-ence	state/quality of	violence	-ity	state/quality of	necessity
-ism	state/quality of	baptism	-ette	small	dinette
-s, -es	plural	cars	-ard	one who	coward
-kin	small	napkin	-ing	material	roofing

root words, prefixes, and suffixes easily accessible online at: www.betterendings.org/homeschool/Words/Root%20Words.htm. Note that once a student has pronounced a word, a series of additional cues may be used to confirm the word has been correctly pronounced and the meaning understood in context. Considering whether the word pronounced looks right, sounds right, makes sense, and fits with any visuals or pictures available to the student in the context of reading can help provide confirmation.

Putting It All Together: A Sequence for Phonics and Word Identification Skill Instruction

Most states and local school districts have either developed or purchased a core reading program (or *basal*) with a "scope and sequence" of reading skills to help teachers know which reading skills should be taught at each grade level. The primary value of a scope and sequence of skills is to help all teachers approach decoding instruction systematically among classrooms within a grade level and across grade levels in a school. Research has clearly shown that normally developing and, most especially, struggling students benefit from schools and teachers that follow a predetermined scope and sequence of skills when providing phonics instruction (National Reading Panel, 2000). A secondary value is that doing so also helps coordinate instruction across the state, which is especially useful in maintaining continuity in learning for highly transient students. Texas, California, Mississippi, Kansas, and Oklahoma are just a few states that have developed their own scope and sequence of reading skills. Evidence-based reading research allows us to suggest a general scope and sequence of early phonics and word recognition skills, as shown in Figure 4.3. The phonics

Figure 4.3

End-of-Year Benchmark Skills: K–3

Kindergarten End-of-Year Benchmarks for English and Spanish

DECODING AND WORD RECOGNITION

✓ Recognizes and names all uppercase and lowercase letters
✓ Knows that the sequence of written letters and the sequence of spoken sounds in a word are the same
✓ (Spanish only) Applies letter–sound knowledge of consonant–vowel patterns to produce syllables

SPELLING AND WRITING

✓ Writes independently most uppercase and lowercase letters
✓ Uses phonemic awareness and letter knowledge to spell independently (invented/temporary spelling)

ORAL READING

✓ Recognizes some words by sight, including a few common words

First Grade End-of-Year Benchmarks for English and Spanish

DECODING AND WORD RECOGNITION

✓ Decodes phonetically regular one-syllable words and nonsense words accurately
✓ (Spanish only) Decodes two-syllable words, using knowledge of sounds, letters, and syllables including consonants, vowels, blends, and stress

SPELLING AND WRITING

✓ (English only) Spells three- and four-letter words correctly
✓ Uses phonics to spell independently
✓ Uses basic punctuation and capitalization
✓ Uses graphic organizers to plan writing with guidance
✓ Produces a variety of types of compositions like stories, descriptions, journal entries, and so on
✓ (Spanish only) Recognizes words that use specific spelling patterns such as *r/rr, y/ll, s/c/z, q/c/k, g/j, j/x, b/v, ch, h, i/y, gue,* and *gui*
✓ (Spanish only) Spells words with two syllables using dieresis marks, accents, *r/rr, y/ll, s/c/z, q/c/k, g/j, j/x, b/v, ch, h,* and *i/y* accurately
✓ (Spanish only) Uses verb tenses appropriately and consistently

ORAL READING

✓ Reads aloud with fluency any text that is appropriate for the first half of grade 1
✓ Comprehends any text that is appropriate for the first half of grade 1
✓ Uses phonic knowledge to sound out unknown words when reading text
✓ Recognizes common, irregularly spelled words by sight

Second Grade End-of-Year Benchmarks for English and Spanish

DECODING AND WORD RECOGNITION

✓ Decodes phonetically regular two-syllable words and nonsense words
✓ (Spanish only) Decodes words with three or more syllables using knowledge of sounds, letters, and syllables including consonants, vowels, blends, and stress
✓ (Spanish only) Uses structural cues to recognize words such as compounds, base words, and inflections such as *-mente, -ito,* and *-ando*

SPELLING AND WRITING

✓ Spells previously studied words and spelling patterns correctly in own writing
✓ Represents the complete sound of a word when spelling independently
✓ Begins to use formal language patterns in place of oral language patterns in own writing
✓ Uses revision and editing processes to clarify and refine own writing with assistance
✓ Writes informative, well-structured reports with organizational help
✓ Attends to spelling, mechanics, and presentation for final products
✓ Produces a variety of types of compositions like stories, reports, correspondence, and so on
✓ Uses information from nonfiction text in independent writing
✓ (Spanish only) Spells words with three or more syllables using silent letters, dieresis marks, accents, verbs, *r/rr, y/ll, s/c/z, q/c/k, g/j, j/x, b/v, ch, h,* and *i/y* accurately

ORAL READING

✓ Reads aloud with fluency any text that is appropriate for the first half of grade 2
✓ Comprehends any text that is appropriate for the first half of grade 2
✓ Uses phonic knowledge to sound out words, including multisyllable words, when reading text
✓ Reads irregularly spelled words, diphthongs, special vowel spellings, and common word endings accurately

Third Grade End-of-Year Benchmarks for English and Spanish

DECODING AND WORD RECOGNITION

✓ Uses phonic knowledge and structural analysis to decode words

SPELLING AND WRITING

✓ Spells previously studied words and spelling patterns correctly in own writing
✓ Uses the dictionary to check and correct spelling
✓ Uses a variety of formal sentence structures in own writing
✓ Incorporates literary words and language patterns in own writing (elaborate descriptions, figurative language)
✓ Uses all aspects of the writing process in compositions and reports with assistance
✓ Combines information from multiple sources in written reports
✓ Suggests and implements editing and revision to clarify and refine own writing with assistance
✓ Reviews written work for spelling, mechanics, and presentation independently
✓ Produces a variety of written work (response to literature, reports, semantic maps)
✓ Uses graphic organizational tools with a variety of texts
✓ (Spanish only) Writes proficiently using orthographic patterns and rules such as *qu,* use of *n* before *v, m* before *b, m* before *p,* and changing *z* to *c* when adding *-es*
✓ (Spanish only) Spells words with three or more syllables using silent letters, dieresis marks, accents, verbs, *r/rr, y/ll, s/c/z, q/c/k, g/j, j/x, b/v, ch, h,* and *i/y* accurately

ORAL READING

✓ Reads aloud with fluency any text that is appropriate for the first half of grade 3
✓ Comprehends any text that is appropriate for the first half of grade 3

skills shown in the figure seem to be included in virtually all commercial or locally developed scope and sequence charts of reading skills.

Children who become proficient in these word recognition skills by the end of grade 3 and practice them regularly in academic and recreational reading will attain a high degree of later reading fluency. Note that these word recognition skills are appropriate for children learning to read in English and/or Spanish. We also include suggested phonics and word recognition skills for the closely related areas of spelling and writing.

● ● ●

IRA Standards for Reading Professionals:
Standard 3, Elements 3.1, 3.2, 3.3

Response to Intervention:
Assessment

Classroom Assessment

Assessing and Monitoring Student Progress in Learning Phonics

We have seen in this chapter that word identification skills proceed from grasp of the alphabetic principle to decoding single-syllable words to decoding multisyllabic words. In this section we present reliable and widely used assessment strategies used by effective teachers to determine students' reading instructional needs.

Figure 4.4

Alphabet Letter Display (Mixed-Case Letters)

From Cooter, Flynt, & Cooter, *Comprehensive Reading Inventory.* © 2007 by Pearson Education, Inc. Reproduced by permission of Pearson Education, Inc.

Letter-Naming Tests

A critical first step in helping children move from phonemic awareness to the alphabetic principle and then phonics instruction is letter naming (Piasta & Wagner, 2010). Accurate letter naming is important, but *automatic, rapid,* and *fluent* letter-naming ability is the end goal. Recognizing letters accurately but slowly will not free up sufficient cognitive attention capacity to allow decoding processes to proceed without laborious effort. In fact, children who become bogged down in decoding processes are largely obstructed from the possibility of comprehension. One widely used screening test for assessing fluent letter-naming ability is the DIBELS Letter Naming Fluency (LNF) test. One shortcoming of the test is that one may only find out whether a child can name a subset of alphabet letters rapidly in 1 minute. Consequently, we recommend that teachers augment the DIBELS LNF test with a letter-naming accuracy test as well.

Letter Name Accuracy Test. A test based on the work of Marie Clay (1993) helps teachers determine whether students can identify all upper- and lower-case letters of the alphabet. To administer this test, first reproduce the randomized alphabet letter display (shown in Figure 4.4) on a sheet of paper or chart paper to use in this exercise.

Invite a student to be seated next to you and explain that you would like to find out which letters of the alphabet he or she can name as you point to them on a chart. Begin pointing at the top of the alphabet letter display and working line by line and left to right to the bottom of the display, keeping letters below your line of focus covered. Using a photocopy of the display, mark which of the letters was correctly named. Next, ask the child to point to the letter you name in the display. Record this information. It is important that accuracy precede fluency. In view of this prerequisite, children should be able to name all of the upper- and lowercase letters with 100 percent accuracy before moving on to fluent or rapid letter naming.

DIBELS Letter Naming Fluency Test. The DIBELS Letter Naming Fluency (LNF) test is a standardized screening test, administered individually. It consists of a page of upper- and lowercase letters arranged in a random order, which is shown to an individual student. The student is asked to name as many letters as he or she can in 1 minute. Students should be told if they do not know a letter they will be told the letter. The LNF score is the number of letters a student names correctly in 1 minute. All information, including the test forms, for standardized administration of the DIBELS LNF test can be obtained free at https://dibels.uoregon.edu/measures/lnf.php. Students who perform in the lowest 20 percent of students in their class or school district, depending on the size of the unit administering the test, are considered at risk. An example of the LNF test probe is shown in Figure 4.5.

Figure 4.5

Sample DIBELS Letter Naming Fluency Test Probe

Probe 1									
c	c	N	u	Q	M	u	h	S	i
n	b	e	N	F	f	o	a	K	K
g	p	k	p	a	H	C	e	G	D
b	w	F	i	h	O	x	j	l	K
x	t	Y	q	L	d	f	T	g	v
T	V	Q	o	w	P	J	t	B	X
Z	v	U	P	R	I	V	C	I	W
R	J	m	O	z	D	G	y	U	Y
Z	y	A	m	X	z	H	S	M	E
q	n	j	s	W	r	d	s	B	I
r	A	E	L	c	c	N	u	Q	M

Total _____/110

High-Frequency Sight Word Reading Test

The ability to instantly recognize by sight a core set of highly frequent words, which may often be difficult to decode, has been discussed previously in this chapter. A quick and easy way to determine how many of the Zeno et al. (1995) 107 high-frequency words students can recognize instantly or by sight can be accomplished by creating flash cards of the 107 words or several scrambled printed lists of these same high-frequency words. As with letters, it is an important prerequisite that early readers, grades 1 to 2, learn to recognize these 107 words accurately, which, once accomplished, should be followed by testing for fluent recognition. A general rule of thumb is that students should be able to recognize 60 words in 1 minute or one word per second to have sufficiently automatic access to these sight words to facilitate fluent reading. If students do not know the words accurately, teacher-directed lessons should focus on the unrecognized words, including seeing and reading these words in books and running texts. We also encourage the writing and spelling of these 107 sight words to help students develop automatic or instant word recognition.

The Consortium on Reading Excellence (CORE) Phonics Survey

The CORE Phonics Survey is a quick, easy-to-administer, and affordable phonics screening or diagnostic test, costing approximately $40 for a product that can be copied for use within a school. Taking approximately 10 minutes to administer, it is considered by teachers a user-friendly test. Because of this and because it assesses phonics concepts identified in the NRP Report (2000) as important, the CORE phonics survey has gained much popularity with educators. The test is composed of two subtests: *Alphabet Skills and Letter Sounds* and *Reading and Decoding Skills*. In the alphabet subtest, the CORE Phonics Survey investigates a student's knowledge of upper- and lowercase letter names as well as consonant and long and short vowel sounds. In the Reading and Decoding Skills subtest, the survey looks at a student's knowledge of short vowels in CVC words, consonant blends with short vowels, *r*-controlled vowels, short vowel digraphs and trigraphs, long and variant vowel spellings, low-frequency variant vowel and consonant spellings, and multisyllabic word decoding.

Student scores on the CORE Phonics Survey are reliable, ranging from a rating of .73 for the first subsection to .96 on the second subsection. Examples of items on the CORE Phonics Survey are shown in Figure 4.6. The survey can be administered

Figure 4.6

Items on the CORE Phonics Survey

Alphabet Skills and Letter Sounds

Part A   Letter names—uppercase

Say to the student: *Can you tell me the names of these letters?* If the student cannot name three or more consecutive letters, say: *Look at all of the letters and tell me which ones you do know.*

```
D   A   N   S   X   Z   J   L   H
T   Y   E   C   O   M   R   P   W
K   U   G   B   F   Q   V   I
              _____ /26
```

Part B   Letter names—lowercase

Say to the student: *Can you tell me the names of these letters?* If the student cannot name three or more consecutive letters, say: *Look at all of the letters and tell me which ones you do know.*

```
d   a   n   s   x   z   j   l   h
t   y   e   c   o   m   r   p   w
k   u   g   b   f   q   v   i
              _____ /26
```

Part C   Consonant sounds

Say to the student: *Look at these letters. Can you tell me the sound each letter makes?* Be sure to ask if he or she knows of another sound for the letters g and c. If the sound given is correct, do not mark the Record Form. If it is incorrect, write the sound the student gives above each letter. If no sound is given, circle the letter. If the student cannot say the sound for three or more consecutive letters, say: *Look at all of the letters and tell me which sounds you do know.*

```
d   l   n   s   x   z   j
t   y   p   c   h   m   r
k   w   g   b   f   q   v
              _____ /21
```

From "Assessing Reading: Multiple Measures," 2008, Arena Press. Used by permission of Arena Press and CORE, Inc.

by classroom teachers with a minimum of training at the cost of copying once the CORE Phonics Survey Assessment has been purchased for a school. Scores indicate where students have gaps in their understanding of phonics concepts and decoding skills so that teachers can target future instruction to meet students' needs in individual or small-group formats.

The Running Record

It is important that teachers follow students' phonics and word attack skills development throughout the year. The most widely used method for doing so is called the running record. Let's take a quick look at how running records came about.

From the earliest days of formal reading instruction, the ability to decode words in print has been viewed as essential (Reutzel & Cooter, 2011). In 1915, for example, William S. Gray published the *Standardized Oral Reading Paragraphs* for grades 1

Part D   Vowel sounds

Ask the student: *Can you tell me the sounds of each letter?* If the student names the letter, count it as the long vowel sound. Then ask: *Can you tell me another sound for the letter?* The student should name the short vowel sound.

e __ __   i __ __   a __ __   o __ __   u __ __

l = long sound   s = short sound

Record "l" on the first line for the long sound (letter name) and "s" for the short sound on the second line. If the student makes an error, record the error over the letter.

_____ /5   Long vowel sounds (count the number of l's above)

_____ /5   Short vowel sounds (count the number of s's above)

Reading and Decoding

For Parts E through K students must read both real and pseudowords (made-up words). For the real word lines, tell the student: *I want you to read each line of words aloud.* If the student cannot read two or more of the real words in each line, do not administer the line of pseudowords; go to the next set of items. Before asking the student to read the line of pseudowords, say: *Now I want you to read some made-up words. Do not try to make them sound like real words.* When using this assessment as a specific skills test or screening measure, do not discontinue testing if a student does not do well on one of the items in Parts F through K. Instead, move to the next item and continue testing.

Part E   Short vowels in CVC words

____ /5	sip	mat	let	bun	hog	(real)
____ /5	rut	fit	bat	hot	set	(real)
____ /5	nop	sut	dit	pem	fap	(pseudo)
____ /15						

Part F   Consonant blends with short vowels

____ /5	stop	trap	quit	spell	plan	(real)
____ /5	silk	fast	sank	lump	held	(real)
____ /5	nask	dilt	qued	cang	dran	(pseudo)
____ /15						

through 8, which focused on oral reading errors and reading speed exclusively. In the 1930s and 1940s, Durrell (1940) and Betts (1946) discussed at length the value of studying oral reading errors as a way to inform reading instruction. These and other writings began the development of assessment methods for analyzing oral reading errors.

Marie Clay (1972), in her manual *The Early Detection of Reading Difficulties,* sought to formalize methodology for teachers conducting decoding assessments. Clay's running records for analyzing oral reading errors proved to be functional for many classroom teachers. A New Zealand educator and former president of the International Reading Association, Clay described the running record as an informal assessment procedure with high reliability (.90 on error reliabilities) that informs teachers regarding students' decoding development.

The procedure for maintaining a running record is not difficult, but does require practice. In essence, the teacher notes everything the student says while reading a selected passage, including all words read correctly as well as all miscues (Wiener & Cohen, 1997). Clay recommends that three running records be obtained for each child on various levels of difficulty for initial reading assessment. Her criteria for oral reading evaluation are based on words correctly read aloud:

Independent Level (easy to read)	95–100% correct
Instructional Level (ideal for teaching)	90–94% correct
Frustration Level (too difficult)	89% or less correct

Running records in Clay's method are taken using books on different reading levels; student errors (miscues) can be recorded on a sheet of paper. In recent research (Fawson, Ludlow, Reutzel, Sudweeks, & Smith, 2006), it was found that reliable scores are obtained when teachers take three running records within the same reading level of text and average the three scores. Teachers should observe the following guidelines for generating running records:

1. Gather passages from a number of reading materials in a variety of reading levels. Each reading level should be represented by three passages; passages should be 100 to 200 words in length (for early readers, texts may fall below 100 words).

2. Have the student read the passage one or two times orally before you begin the running record.

3. Sit alongside while the student reads so that both of you can see the page of text. Mark a check mark on a sheet of blank paper for each word the student says correctly. Miscues (errors) should be recorded using the notations indicated in Figure 4.7. Figure 4.8 shows an example of a running record based on a passage from the Flynt-Cooter Reading Inventory for the Classroom (Flynt & Cooter, 2004).

Understanding Miscues: MSV Analysis. Clay (1985) developed a way of interpreting miscues for her widely acclaimed Reading Recovery program, a method commonly referred to as MSV analysis. This interpretive strategy enables you to examine miscues and determine whether the student uses primary cueing strategies on encountering new words—meaning cues (M), syntax cues (S), or visual cues (V). The following summary of Clay's ideas is taken from the work of Flynt and Cooter (2004).

• *Meaning (Semantic—Does it make sense?)* In reviewing each miscue, consider whether the student is using meaning cues in the attempt to identify the word. Context clues, picture cues, and information from the text are examples of possible meaning cues.

Figure 4.7

Notating Miscues in a Running Record

Reading Behavior	Notation	Explanation
Accurate Reading	✓✓✓✓✓✓	*Notation:* A check is noted for each word pronounced correctly.
Self-Correction	✓✓✓✓ attempt / word in text SC	The child corrects an error himself. This is not counted as a miscue. *Notation:* "SC" is the notation used for self-corrections.
Omission	——— / Word in text	A word or words are left out during the reading. *Notation:* A dash mark is written over a line above the omitted word(s) from the text.
Insertion	Word inserted / ———	The child adds a word that is not in the text. *Notation:* The word inserted by the reader is placed above a line and a dash placed below it.
Student Appeal and Assistance	——— A / Word from text	The child is "stuck" on a word he cannot call and asks (verbal or nonverbal) the teacher for help. *Notation:* "A" is written above a line for "assisted" and the problem word from the text is written below the line.
Repetition	✓✓✓ R ✓✓✓	Sometimes children will repeat words or phrases. These repetitions are not scored as an error, but are recorded. *Notation:* Write an "R" after the word repeated and draw a line back to the point where the reader returned.
Substitution	Substituted word / Word from text	The child says a word that is different from the word in the text. *Notation:* The student's substitution word is written above a line under which the correct word from text is written.
Teacher Assistance	——— / Word from text T	The student pauses on a word for 5 seconds or more, so the teacher says the word. *Notation:* The letter "T" is written to the right of a line that follows the word from text. A blank is placed above a cross-line to indicate that the student didn't know the word.

Figure 4.8

Running Record Example

Student Paco (Grade 2)	
Title The Pig and the Snake	
One day Mr. Pig was walking to	✓ ✓ ✓ ✓ ✓ ✓ ✓
town. He saw a big hole in the	✓ ✓ $\frac{sam}{saw}$ | sc ✓ ✓ ✓ ✓ ✓
road. A big snake was in the	✓ ✓ $\frac{=}{big}$ ✓ ✓ ✓ ✓
hole. "Help me," said the snake,	✓ ✓ ✓ $\frac{ouT}{—}$ ✓ ✓ ✓
"and I will be your friend." "No, no,"	✓ ✓ ✓ ✓ ✓ $\frac{—}{friend}$ | A ✓ ✓
said Mr. Pig. "If I help you get	✓ ✓ ✓ ✓ ✓ ✓ ✓ ✓
out you will bite me. You're	✓ ✓ ✓ R ✓ ✓ ✓
a snake!" The snake cried and	✓ ✓ ✓ ✓ ✓ ✓
cried. So Mr. Pig pulled the	✓ ✓ ✓ ✓ $\frac{popped}{pulled}$ ✓
snake out of the hole.	✓ ✓ ✓ ✓ ✓
Then the snake said, "Now I am	✓ ✓ ✓ ✓ ✓ ✓ ✓
going to bite you, Mr. Pig."	✓ ✓ ✓ ✓ ✓ ✓
"How can you bite me after	✓ ✓ ✓ ✓ ✓ $\frac{—}{after}$ | T
I helped you out of the hole?"	✓ ✓ ✓ ✓ ✓ ✓ ✓
said Mr. Pig. The snake said,	✓ ✓ ✓ ✓ ✓ ✓
"You knew I was a snake	✓ ✓ ✓ ✓ ✓ ✓
when you pulled me out!"	✓ ✓ ✓ ✓ ✓

- *Syntax (Structure—Does it sound right?)* A rule system, or *grammar*, governs all languages. The English language is essentially based on a subject–verb grammar system. *Syntax* is the application of this subject–verb grammar system in creating sentences. The goal of studying syntax cues as part of your miscue analysis is to determine the extent to which the student unconsciously uses rules of grammar in attempting to identify unknown words in print. For example, if a word in a passage causing a miscue is a verb, determine whether the miscue is also a verb. Consistent use of the appropriate part of speech in miscues (a noun for a noun, a verb for a verb, articles for articles, etc.) is an indication that the student has internalized the rule system of English grammar and is applying that knowledge in attacking unknown words.

- *Visual (Graphophonic—Does it look right?)* Sometimes a miscue looks a good bit like the correct word. The miscue may begin with the same letter or letters—for example, *top* for *toy* or *sit* for *seat*. Or letter patterns in the miscue may match the text word (e.g., *introduction* for *introspection*). Use of visual cues is essentially the student's ability (or inability) to apply phonics skills.

Applying MSV thinking is fairly simple once you get the hang of it. In Figure 4.9 we return to the miscues noted in Figure 4.8 and conduct an MSV analysis on each. Do you see why each interpretation was made?

An Alternative Running Records System.   Flynt and Cooter (2004) developed an efficient and useful method of generating running records for classroom teachers, involving what they call a "miscue grid." It can be extremely effective when used with reading passages that are matched to student interests.

Figure 4.10 shows how miscues are noted on the left side of the grid over the text, which are then tallied in the appropriate columns to the right according to miscue type. This process expedites administration and enables teachers to identify error patterns for each oral reading. The grid method can easily be adapted for use with excerpts from any piece of literature.

Teachers should select passages representing a range of reading levels (or have students select the text to be read) one day prior to assessment so that the first 100 words can be transcribed onto the left-hand side of a blank grid patterned after the one shown in Figure 4.10. Audio record the student's oral reading so that it can be reviewed later for accuracy of transcription. Miscues should be noted in the left-hand column over the text facsimile using the symbols described earlier. After all miscues are noted, examine each and make a final determination about its type (mispronunciation, substitution, insertion, etc.). Then make a mark in the appropriate grid box on the right side of the form. Only one mark is made for each miscue. Once this process is completed, each column is tallied.

In Figure 4.10 you will note that the reader had two mispronunciations, four substitutions, and so on. When the student has read several passages for the teacher over a period of weeks and months, it becomes easy to identify error patterns—types of miscues that happen regularly—and to plan appropriate instruction for small groups or individuals.

If you decide to use the grid system, be sure to conduct an MSV analysis on each miscue to better understand which cueing systems the reader is using.

A Running Record Self-Assessment.   It is critical that all assessments be carried out with precision. When we are learning how to do a running record, which takes six or so practice sessions, it is helpful to have a way of judging for ourselves how we

Figure 4.9

Running Record with MSV Analysis

Student Paco (Grade 2)		E MSV	SC MSV
Title The Pig and the Snake			
One day Mr. Pig was walking to	✓ ✓ ✓ ✓ ✓ ✓ ✓		
town. He saw a big hole in the	✓ ✓ sam | sc / saw ✓ ✓ ✓ ✓ ✓		Ⓜ Ⓢ Ⓥ
road. A big snake was in the	✓ ✓ =/big ✓ ✓ ✓ ✓	m s v	
hole. "Help me," said the snake,	✓ ✓ ✓ ouT/_ ✓ ✓ ✓	Ⓜ Ⓢ v	
"and I will be your friend." "No, no,"	✓ ✓ ✓ ✓ ✓ _ | A / friend ✓ ✓	m s v	
said Mr. Pig. "If I help you get	✓ ✓ ✓ ✓ ✓ ✓ ✓ ✓		
out you will bite me. You're	✓ ✓ ✓ R ✓ ✓ ✓		Ⓜ Ⓢ Ⓥ
a snake!" The snake cried and	✓ ✓ ✓ ✓ ✓ ✓		
cried. So Mr. Pig pulled the	✓ ✓ ✓ ✓ popped/pulled ✓	Ⓜ Ⓢ Ⓥ	
snake out of the hole.	✓ ✓ ✓ ✓ ✓		
Then the snake said, "Now I am	✓ ✓ ✓ ✓ ✓ ✓ ✓		
going to bite you, Mr. Pig."	✓ ✓ ✓ ✓ ✓ ✓		
"How can you bite me after	✓ ✓ ✓ ✓ ✓ _ | _ / after | T	m s v	
I helped you out of the hole?"	✓ ✓ ✓ ✓ ✓ ✓ ✓		
said Mr. Pig. The snake said,	✓ ✓ ✓ ✓ ✓ ✓		
"You knew I was a snake	✓ ✓ ✓ ✓ ✓ ✓		
when you pulled me out!"	✓ ✓ ✓ ✓ ✓		

Figure 4.10

Sample of a Miscue Grid

	ERROR TYPES							ERROR ANALYSIS		
Hot Shoes	Mis-pronun.	Sub-stitute	Inser-tions	Tchr. Assist	Omis-sions	Error Totals	Self-Correct.	Meaning (M)	Syntax (S)	Visual (V)
The guys at the I. B. Belcher										
Elementary School ~~loved~~ _lived_ all the new sport		1				1		1	1	
shoes. Some ~~wore~~ _wear_ the "Sky High"		1				1		1	1	
~~made~~ _mobil_ by Leader. Others who		1				1				
couldn't afford Sky High would settle (sc)					2	2		1	1	
for a lesser shoe. Some liked the "Street							1			
Smarts" by Master, or the										
"Uptown-Downtown" by Beebop.										
The Belcher boys got to the point										
with their shoes that they could										
in-duh-fee identify their friends just by	1					1				
looking at their feet. But the boy who										
was the ~~envy~~ _enemy_ of the entire fifth		1				1		1	1	
grade was Jamie Lee. He had a							1			
pair of "High Five Pump 'em Ups"										
by ~~Superior~~ _sooner_. The only thing Belcher // (sc)	1				1	2		1	1	
boys loved as much as their										
shoes was basketball.										
TOTALS	2	4			3	9	2	5	5	

Summary of Reading Behaviors (Strengths and Needs)

are doing and make corrections as needed. If a literacy coach is available to help us with modeling and feedback, so much the better, but that is not always an available resource. R. Cooter and colleagues (Cooter, Mathews, Thompson, & Cooter, 2004) developed a self-assessment tool to help teachers with "fidelity of implementation" in administering running records. Their running record self-assessment is offered in Figure 4.11 for your use in the classroom.

Figure 4.11

Self-Assessment/Goal Continuum: Running Records

Directions: Using a red marker, draw a vertical line after the description on each row that best describes your current implementation of each aspect of running records. Using a yellow marker, indicate your end-of-the-year goal for each aspect.

Conventions: marking system					
I have never received training on a universal marking system.	I created my own marking system.	I use markings that can be interpreted by my grade level.	I use markings that can be interpreted by my school. Some markings can be universally read.	I use markings that can be interpreted by district teachers. Most markings can be universally read.	I use markings that can be interpreted universally by teachers.

Scoring: accuracy rate, error rate, self-correction					
I do not score running records.	I score for accuracy rate.	I use the conversion chart to score for accuracy rate to group my students.	I use the conversion chart to score for accuracy rate and error rate to group my students.	I use the conversion chart to calculate accuracy rate, error rate, and self-correction rate for grouping.	I use the conversion chart to calculate accuracy, error rate, and self-correction rates daily to inform my instruction.

Analysis: cueing systems (MSV)					
I do not analyze my running records.	I sometimes analyze errors on running records.	I analyze all errors on each running record.	I analyze all errors and self-corrections on each running record.	I analyze all errors and self-corrections for meaning, structure, and visual cues on each running record to guide and inform instruction.	I analyze all errors and self-corrections for meaning, structure, and visual cues on each running record. In addition, I look for patterns over time to further guide instruction.

Frequency					
I do not use running records.	I use running records two times a year, at the beginning and end of school.	I do running records occasionally throughout the year.	I do one running record on my struggling students once per 6 weeks.	I do one running record on all my students once per 6 weeks.	I perform running records daily so that each student is assessed every 6 weeks. My struggling students are done twice every 6 weeks.

From Cooter, R., Matthews, B., Thompson, S., & Cooter, K. "Searching for Lessons of Mass Instruction," *Reading Teacher, 58*(4), December 2004. Reprinted with permission of the International Reading Association.

Commercial Diagnostic Reading Tests

Teachers sometimes believe it necessary to assess an individual student's reading ability using norm-referenced measures. This often happens when new students move into a school district without their permanent records or when struggling readers are being considered for extra assistance programs such as Title 1 or special education services provided in inclusive classrooms. Here we describe for you one such measure, a diagnostic tool called the Woodcock Reading Mastery Tests—Revised (Woodcock, 1997; Woodcock, Mather, & Barnes, 1987).

The WRMT–R/NU (normative update) is a battery of six individually administered subtests intended to measure reading abilities from kindergarten through adult levels. Subtests cover visual–auditory learning, letter identification, word identification, word attack, word comprehension, and passage comprehension. The test's design aligns with a skills perspective of reading. The assessment is divided into two sections according to age and ability levels: readiness and reading achievement. The WRMT–R/NU reports norm-referenced data for both of its forms and offers insights into remediation. Results may be calculated either manually or by using the convenient scoring program developed for personal computers. The WRMT–R/NU is frequently used by teachers in special education and Title I reading programs.

Evidence-Based Teaching Practices

Effective Phonics Instruction

Research confirms that explicit and systematic phonics instruction is more effective than nonsystematic instruction or programs that ignore phonics instruction altogether (National Reading Panel, 2000). When delivered as part of a comprehensive reading program—one that includes expansive vocabulary instruction, reading practice in great books, and writing development—by a skillful teacher, phonics instruction can help children become enthusiastic lifelong readers.

Five Approaches to Phonics Instruction

Several approaches to explicit and systematic phonics instruction have found support in the research (National Reading Panel, 2000). These approaches are sometimes modified or combined within published "core" reading programs.

Synthetic Phonics Instruction. In synthetic phonics instruction, students learn how to change letters or letter combinations into speech sounds and then blend them together to form known words ("sounding out").

Embedded Phonics Instruction. The embedding of phonics instruction in texts selected for reading can result in a more implicit approach that relies to a large extent on incidental learning (National Reading Panel, 2000, p. 8). This learning can become more focused by following a predetermined scope and sequence of phonics instruction and then selecting specific books for reading in which the instructed phonics element appears frequently to optimize practice.

Analogy-Based Phonics Instruction. A variation of onset and rime instruction that encourages students to use their knowledge of word families to identify new words

IRA Standards for Reading Professionals: Standard 2, Elements 2.1, 2.2, 2.3; Standard 5, Elements 5.1, 5.3

Common Core Standards: Reading K–5: Key Ideas and Details (item 1)

Response to Intervention: Instruction; Systemic and Comprehensive Approaches that have the same word parts. For example, students learn to pronounce *light* by applying their prior knowledge of the *-ight* rime from three words they already know: *right, might,* and *night.*

Analytic Phonics Instruction. In a variation of the previous two approaches, students study previously learned whole words to discover letter–sound relationships. For example, *Stan, steam,* and *story* all include the *st* word element (*st* is a consonant blend).

Phonics-Through-Spelling Instruction. Students segment spoken words into phonemes and write letters that represent those sounds to spell the words. For example, *rat* can be segmented sound by sound, left to right in sequence representing each sound heard with the related letter. This approach is often used as part of a process writing program called invented spelling.

Effective Strategies for Teaching Phonics

Imagine the following exchange between a teacher and a child. "Teacher, how do you read this word (pointing to a word in a book)?" "Sound it out!" says the teacher. When saying this familiar phrase, "Sound it out," many teachers believe they are teaching children how to effectively unlock unfamiliar words through decoding. If a child asks again, the teacher may say the phrase with a bit more emphasis—*Sound it out!* Sometimes, teachers will resort to a line of decoding questioning to help children discover decoding strategies. "What is the first letter? What sound does that make? What is the second letter? What sound does that make?" And so forth. Some teachers actually encourage children to use checking and confirmation clues to avoid the act of decoding words. "Look at the picture. What would make sense here? Did that sound right? Did that look right?" Only when these fail to help a child figure out an unknown word does the teacher encourage the student to look carefully at the word and decode it. With such methods, children don't learn how to decode nor do they practice decoding strategies with sufficient support, guidance, and consistency to become expert at the process. Think about it; how good would you get at anything if you failed to practice the skill you wanted to learn?

Click on A+RISE—WIDA ELP Standard Strategies in the MyEducationLab (www.myeducationlab.com) for your course. Next, select the Strategy Card Index tab, scroll to Phonics for grades K–5, and select the Big Book Phonics strategy.

Blending. One of the most important skills for readers to learn is how to blend the sounds of letters in words to gain approximate pronunciations that can be matched to words represented in their speaking vocabularies. The blending process is anything but intuitive and is seldom discovered by young or even adult learners without specific, sustained, and explicit teacher explanation, modeling, and guided practice. The blending process occurs on two different levels: sequential and hierarchical. In sequential blending of single-syllable words, the reader scans each letter of a word moving from left to right, saying the associated sound of each letter and blending the letter sounds together to say the word. To teach readers how to sequentially blend letters and sounds to pronounce single-syllable words, teachers must be very explicit in modeling and guiding students' practice in applying the strategy. For example, consider the following explicit lesson for teaching students a sequential blending strategy.

Explanation. Today we will be learning how to blend the sounds of letters to say words. Blending the sounds of letters to say words is a very important part of learning how to read unfamiliar words. Blending words to read is one of the important things you will learn in kindergarten and first grade to help you learn about many other things in school and in life.

Modeling.   I will model for you how to blend the sounds of letters in words. Here is a word—*fan.* I want to blend the sounds of the letters to say the word. To blend the letter sounds in this word I begin with the first letter in the word—*f* (point to the letter). I think to myself, this is the letter *f* and I know that the sound that this letter makes is /f/. So, I say /f/. I look at the second letter in the word—*a* (point to the letter). I need to learn a hint about three-letter words with a vowel letter in the middle. The hint says that the middle vowel letter in a three-letter word makes its sound. So I think to myself, this letter *a* makes the /a/ sound. I say /a/. Then I say the first sound in the word, /f/, and then the second sound in the word, /a/. Next I look at the third letter in the word—*n* (point to the letter). I think to myself, this is the letter *n* and I know that the sound this letter makes is /n/. Then I say the first sound in the word, /f/, and then the second sound in the word, /a/, and last the third sound in the word, /n/. Then I say the three sounds in order again a little faster like this, /f/ /a/ /n/. I say them again even faster. I listen as I say them faster and begin to blend the sounds together to hear a word. The word I hear when I say the sounds in order fast is *fan.*

Students can be greatly helped to understand this strategy of sequential blending through the use of a graphic organizer such as Figure 4.12.

Students practice, with teacher guidance, many more single-syllable CVC words using this strategy until they are able to blend CVC words independently with accuracy and fluency. After accomplishing sequential blending of CVC words, sequential blending of single-syllable words continues with the introduction of consonant digraphs, blends, and clusters as well as vowel digraphs and diphthongs along with *r*-controlled vowels and VCe word patterns. The process remains the same: Scan words for known patterns and then begin blending the letter sounds left to right through the word to say the word. Once children understand and practice the sequential blending strategy, they become very able to apply it to many of the words they read in kindergarten and first grade.

Beginning in second grade, teachers need to help students understand the second type of blending—hierarchical blending—used to decode multisyllabic words. The

Figure 4.12

Graphic Organizer Showing Sequential Blending of CVC Words

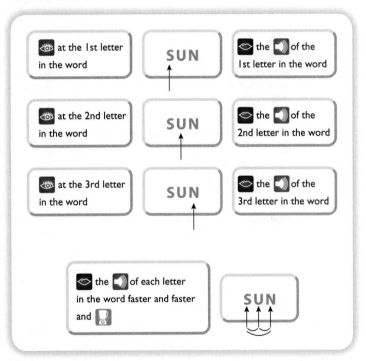

name comes from the hierarchical nature of the blending process. Begin by dividing a whole word into pronunciation units around the vowels that signal the number of syllables. Blending then moves from syllables back to the familiar sequential blending process within syllables and then back up to the level of blending syllables to say the word. Thus, hierarchical blending moves through levels of a multisyllabic word—word to syllables to letters to syllables to word again. To teach readers how to hierarchically blend letters and sounds to say multisyllable words, one must be very explicit. For example, consider the following lesson for teaching students hierarchical blending.

Explanation.   Today we will be learning how to blend parts of words to say big words. Blending the parts of words to say big words is a very important part of learning how to read. Reading is one of the important abilities you will learn in school to help you discover many other things in school and life.

Modeling.   I will model for you how to blend the parts of words to say big words. Here is a word—*confirm*. I want to blend the parts of the word to say a big word. To blend the parts of this word I look for the vowels. (Model underlining the vowels in the word.) Once I have found the vowels in the word, I break the word into parts around the vowels. Never divide double vowels, such as *oi, ai, oa,* and *ee,* or consonant digraphs, such as *ph, ch, wh, th,* and *sh.* We can divide between double consonants that are not consonant digraphs.

In the word *confirm* there are two vowels—*o* and *i.* So, if I divide this word around the vowels *o* and *i* and between two consonants that are not a consonant digraph, I could divide the word *confirm* as *con/firm.* To say this big word, I say the sound for each letter in the first word part /c/–/o/–/n/. Then I blend the three sounds to say the word part—*con.* Next I say each letter sound in the second word part—/f/–/i/–/r/–/m. Then I blend the four sounds to say the word part—*firm.* Last, I say the two word parts—*con* and *firm.* When I blend these two word parts together I say the word—*confirm.*

Students can be greatly helped to understand this strategy of hierarchical blending through the use of a graphic organizer such as Figure 4.13.

Students practice, with teacher guidance, many more multisyllable words, beginning with two- and three-syllable words and then progressing to four- and five-syllable words that do not use prefixes or suffixes. Next, teach students prefixes and suffixes explicitly and place a listing of common affixes on the classroom wall. Then provide guided practice in the hierarchical blending strategy for words containing known prefixes and suffixes (e.g., *na/tion*) until students are able to blend multisyllabic words independently with accuracy and fluency. Once children understand and practice the hierarchical blending strategy, they become comfortable with decoding many of the "big" words they were once almost scared to read in second grade and beyond. In fact, our experience has been that once children learn to use the hierarchical blending strategy fluently, they have the confidence to decode almost any word of any length!

Segmenting.   Imagine once again an exchange between a teacher and a student who wants to write or spell a word. "Teacher, how do you write the word *fast?*" Many teachers use the very same instructional phrase to help students spell words as they did to help them blend words in reading—*Sound it out!* Unfortunately, these teachers do not recognize the obvious. They are applying the same method—*Sound it out*—to instruct children in two different, reverse processes—

Figure 4.13

Hierarchical Blending Strategy for Decoding Multisyllabic Words

Look for the vowels in the word and underline them—
eleph<u>a</u>nt

▼

Break the word into chunks around the vowels
(*Note:* Never divide double vowels—
for example, *oi, ai, oa, ee*—or consonant diagraphs—for
example, *ph, ch, wh, th, sh.* We can divide between double
consonants that are not consonant digraphs.)—
e/leph/ant or *el/e/phant* or *e/le/phant*

▼

Blend the letter sounds in the first chunk—
e or *el*

▼

Say the chunk

▼

Blend the letter sounds in the second chunk—
leph or *e* or *le*

▼

Say the chunk

▼

Blend the first and the second chunk—
eleph or *ele*

▼

Blend the letter sounds in the third chunk—
ant or *phant*

▼

Say the chunk

▼

Blend the first, second, and third chunks—
e/leph/ant or *el/e/phant* or *e/le/phant*

▼

Say the word—
elephant

blending letter sounds to say words and segmenting spoken words into sounds to spell written words.

One of the most important strategies that writers and spellers can learn is how to segment words into sounds and represent those spoken sounds with letters to write approximate spellings of the words represented in one's speaking vocabulary. Like the blending process, **segmenting** is not intuitive for young or even adult learners and requires explicit explanation, specific modeling, and sustained guided practice. Like the blending process, the segmenting process occurs on sequential and hierarchical levels. In sequential segmenting of single-syllable words, the writer stretches out the sounds in a spoken word, listens for and counts each sound in the spoken word from beginning to end, and then writes a letter for each sound that is heard in the stretched out word to spell the word. In order to teach writers how to sequentially segment sounds in words to spell single-syllable words, one must be very explicit. For example, consider the following explicit lesson for teaching students sequential segmentation.

Click on A+RISE— Literacy Strategies in the MyEducationLab (www. myeducationlab.com) for your course. Next, select the Strategy Card Index tab, scroll to Word Study, and select the Phonemic Segmentation with Elkonin Boxes strategy.

Explanation.   Today we will be learning how to segment words into sounds to spell words. Segmenting the sounds in spoken words to write words is a very important part of learning how to spell unfamiliar words. Segmenting spoken words to spell is one of the important abilities you will learn in kindergarten and first grade to help you write about the many other things you will discover in school and in life.

Modeling.   I will model for you how to segment the sounds in spoken words to spell words. Listen to the word as I say it—*sit.* (Say the word *sit.*) I want to segment the sounds in this word to spell the word. To segment the sounds in this word, I stretch the word out or say it very slowly like this—*sssssssss–iiiiiii–t.* Next, I count how many sounds I hear and make a blank on my paper for each sound I hear in the word *sit.* (Write three blanks on the board.) I stretch the word to hear the first sound—/s/—and I think to myself, this is the sound that goes with the letter *s.* So I write an *s* in the first blank. Next, I listen to the second sound in the word *sit.* I stretch the word again—*sssss–iiiii.* I stretch the word to hear the second sound–/i/—and I think to myself, this is the sound that goes with the letter *i.* So I write an *i* in the second blank. Finally, I listen to the third sound in the word *sit.* I stretch the word again—*ssssss–iiiii–t.* I stretch the word to hear the third sound—/t/—and I think to myself, this is the sound that goes with the letter *t.* So, I write a *t* in the third blank. This is how I segment sounds in words to write words I don't know how to spell.

Students can be greatly helped to understand this strategy of sequential segmentation through the use of a graphic organizer such as shown in Figure 4.14.

Students practice, with teacher guidance, many more single-syllable CVC words using this strategy until they are able to segment CVC words

Figure 4.14

Sequential Segmenting Strategy Chart

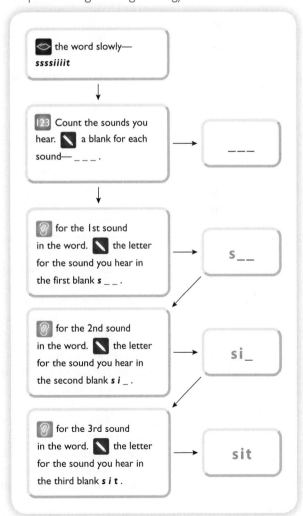

independently with accuracy and fluency. After accomplishing sequential segmenting of CVC words, sequential segmenting of single-syllable words continues with the introduction of consonant digraphs, blends, and clusters as well as vowel digraphs and diphthongs along with *r*-controlled vowels and VCe word patterns. The process remains the same: Stretch spoken words to hear individual sounds, segment, count, write blanks for the sounds heard in words, and finally write a letter for each sound to spell the word. Once children understand and practice the sequential segmentation strategy, they can apply it to many of the words they want to use in their in kindergarten and first grade writing.

Beginning in second grade, teachers should begin teaching the second type of segmenting—hierarchical segmenting—to help students write or spell multisyllabic words. Similar to blending, hierarchical segmenting moves from words to syllables to letters and back again. Hierarchical segmenting begins by stretching a whole word into pronunciation units or spoken syllables and then to the familiar sequential segmentation process within syllables to write the word. Teaching writers how to hierarchically segment multisyllable words requires very explicit teaching. For example, consider the following explicit lesson for teaching students hierarchical segmenting.

> **Explanation.**   Today we will be learning how to segment words into sounds to spell words. Segmenting words to write big words is a very important part of learning how to write. Writing and spelling are important abilities you will learn in school to help you write about the things that you will discover in school and life.
>
> **Modeling.**   I will model for you how to segment a word to spell big words. Here is a word—*macaroni*. I want to segment the word to spell this big word. To segment the parts of this word, I stretch the word into pronounceable units or syllables—*mac/a/ro/ni*. I hear four syllables or pronunciation units. The first syllable or pronunciation unit I hear is *mac*. I stretch this syllable out slowly—*mmmm–aaaa–k*. I hear three sounds so I write three blanks for the first syllable. Next I listen for the first sound—*mmm*. I think about this sound and write the letter that I know represents this sound—*m*. Next, I listen for the second sound in the syllable *mac*. I hear the second sound—*aaaaa*. I write the second sound's letter—*a*. I listen to the third sound in the syllable *mac*. I hear the sound and write the letter *k*. In the second syllable I hear the sound "uh" and write the letter *a*. In the third syllable I hear two sounds—*rrrrrooooo*. I write down two more blanks and write the letter I hear in the first sound in this syllable—*r*. Then I listen for the second sound and write the letter for the sound I hear—*o*. Finally, I stretch the last syllable of the word—*nnnnneeee*. I write two blanks after stretching the sounds in this syllable. The first sound is *nnnn*, so I write the letter *n*. The final sound is *eeee* so I write the letter *e*. Now I have the spelling *makarone*. I look at this spelling to see if it looks like the word as I have seen it. If not, I check it using a dictionary or spell check. (Model this process of checking in a dictionary or spell check.)

Students can be greatly helped to understand this strategy of hierarchical segmenting through the use of graphic organizers such as Figure 4.15.

Students practice, with teacher guidance, many more multisyllable words from two- up to four- and five-syllable words without prefixes or suffixes. Then, teach prefixes and suffixes explicitly if this has not already taken place. Provide guided practice in this strategy with known prefixes and suffixes until students are able to segment multisyllabic words independently with accuracy and fluency. With this strategy, they become willing to attempt writing and spelling most of the words they encounter in second grade and beyond.

As previously noted, decoding or analyzing words constitutes about 50 percent of the word recognition process; the other 50 percent of words are the common words often referred to as **sight words,** also discussed earlier in this chapter. Next we describe an effective strategy for teaching beginning readers to commit to memory a series of 107 sight words that comprise half of all the words an adult reader encounters in reading materials written at the readability level of the general population.

Effective Strategies for Teaching High-Frequency Sight Words

To teach children a strategy for committing high-frequency sight words to memory accurately and fluently without sound–symbol analysis, we have drawn on the work of E. Horn (1919) and P. Cunningham (1980). But before discussing this strategy, we want to address the issue of pacing high-frequency sight word instruction.

In 2006, H. Pashler presented an initial series of research studies funded by the Institute of Education Sciences, U.S. Department of Education, detailing how instructional pacing and multiple distributed reviews maximize what he called "reducing forgetting." He and his colleagues have since demonstrated in several published papers the desirability of distributed review and spacing effects for reducing forgetting (Cepeda, Coburn, Rohrer, Wixted, Mozer, & Pashler, 2009; Cepeda, Pashler, Vul, Wixted, & Rohrer, 2006; Cepeda, Vul, Rohrer, Wixted, & Pahsler, 2007). To optimize memory for learning sets of information and reducing forgetting, these researchers have conceptualized the law of 10/20.

Serial lists of unrelated information items such as state capitals, state names, days of the week, months of the year, and sight words are examples of the types of memory sets these researchers tested to investigate the optimal review cycle necessary to remember memory set items for up to 6 months. The law of 10/20 indicates that if one wants to remember something for 6 months or more, then a spaced review of the items taught should take place at intervals of 10 and 20 percent of the time period of half a year (183 days) or every 18 to 36 days. The law of 10/20 has demonstrated that learning "constrained" (finite) memory sets occurs *optimally* when these items are learned quickly enough to facilitate a distributed practice and review every 18 to 36 days.

Figure 4.15

Hierarchical Segmenting Strategy for Spelling Multisyllabic Words

Say the word slowly by stretching it out and listen for and count the number of syllables in the word—*complete.*

▼

Write down big blanks for the number of syllables— _____ _____—*complete.*

▼

Segment the first syllable into sounds by saying and stretching the syllable slowly— *cccc/uh/mmm.*

▼

Write three blanks for the first syllable: __ __ __ .

▼

Listen for the first sound in the syllable and write the letter—*c* or *k.*

▼

Listen for the next sound in the syllable and write the letter—/ə/—*a, o,* or *u.*

▼

Listen for the next sound in the syllable and write the letter—*m.*

▼

Segment the second syllable into sounds by saying and stretching the syllable slowly—*pp/lll/eeee/t.*

▼

Write four blanks for the second syllable: __ __ __ __ .

▼

Listen for the first sound in the syllable and write the letter—*p.*

▼

Listen for the next sound in the syllable and write the letter—*l.*

▼

Listen for the next sound in the syllable and write the letter—*e.*

▼

Listen for the last sound in the syllable and write the letter—*t.*

▼

Check the spelling—*complet* or *komplet*—using a dictionary or spell check.

Using the law of 10/20 as a guide, an optimal instructional pacing and review of 25 sight words in the Thorndike-Lorge high-frequency word list, considered appropriate for kindergarten, would involve immediately implementing the 18- to 36-day cycle in a sight-word-a-day approach to instructional pacing. For kindergarten teachers following this pace, all 25 high-frequency sight words would be taught within a 5-week period, allowing for a possible seven distributed review cycles throughout the typical 180-day school year.

To then complete the 107 sight words in first grade would require teaching the remaining 82 words. Using the law of 10/20 as a guide, an optimal instructional pacing and review of the remaining 82 words in the Zeno et al. (1995) high-frequency word list on an 18- to 36-day cycle demands a pace of two to three sight words a day. In this approach, typically for first grade (or for other grades as a review), all 82 high-frequency sight words would be taught within a 7-week period, allowing for a possible five distributed review cycles in the 180-day school year.

With such methods, teachers are applying the research showing that high-frequency sight words are best remembered as a result of distributed practice over time rather than from a single massed or continuous presentation. A week focused on remembering a single set of high-frequency sight words and then moving to another set of words without regular distributed review cycles will not be as effective.

Another effective strategy for teaching students to remember high-frequency sight words involves word recognition instruction. Many teachers will remember Horn's (1919) strategy for remembering word spellings from elementary school.

- See the word.
- Say the word.
- Spell the word.
- Write the word.
- Check the word.

P. Cunningham (1980) elaborated on this basic memory strategy for word spellings when she created the "drastic strategy" for remembering what she called "four-letter words" that were difficult to decode, highly frequent, and had broad meanings that were difficult to remember, such as *were, with, that,* or *what*. The drastic strategy as described by Cunningham (1980) adds elements of oral language use, cutting words into letters and spelling, as well as highlighting words in written contexts and writing words from dictation.

A lesson plan for a high-frequency sight word lesson related to the drastic strategy is found in Figure 4.16. The steps are appropriate for a whole class or a small group of students. During dictation time writing the word *the*, have the students use

Figure 4.16

High-Frequency Sight Word Lesson

Explanation. Today we will be learning how to remember words we read and write often. Remembering words we read and write often is a very important part of learning how to read and write. Being able to read and write words we see often is one of the many important abilities you will learn in school to help you discover things in school and life.

Modeling. I will model for you how to remember a word we read and write often. To remember a word I read and write often I use a memory strategy. For example if I want to remember the word *the* I would go through the following steps to put that word into my memory.

1. See the word—*the*
2. Say the word—*the*
3. Spell the word—*t-h-e*
4. Visualize the word (take a picture in your mind)—*the*
5. Cover the word—*the*
6. Verbally spell the word—*t-h-e*
7. Uncover and check the word—*the*
8. Look at the word again and verbally spell the word—*t-h-e*
9. Cover the word—*the*
10. Write the word—*the*
11. Uncover and check the word—*the*
12. Cut up the word *the* on a 3 × 5 index card, mix and manipulate letters of the word to spell the word (2–3 times), checking the spelling after each time.
13. Find the word *the* in print such as a copied book page or newspaper and color or highlight.
14. Write the word *the* three times.

Figure 4.17

The High-Frequency Sight Word Strategy

lapboards, whiteboards, or other type of writing surface and ask for choral responses in which students show their dictations after each word or group of words. Watch for students who copy from others and make quick notes about those who are not able to write words from dictation for follow-up instruction. An instructional chart for displaying this strategy for committing high-frequency words to memory is found in Figure 4.17.

Teaching students to recognize words fluently essentially boils down to repeatedly modeling and having students use the three strategies—blending, segmenting, and sight word memorization—as presented in this section on effective phonics and word recognition instruction. If teachers will explicitly teach and then guide students in the practice and use of phonics and word recognition strategies in reading decodable, leveled, and appropriately challenging trade books as well as in their writing, they will probably develop students who read and write words accurately and fluently, making comprehension of text possible.

Click on A+RISE—WIDA ELP Standard Strategies in the MyEducationLab (www.myeducationlab.com) for your course. Next, select the Strategy Card Index tab, scroll to Phonics for grades K–5, and select the Mad Three Minutes strategy.

Meeting the Needs of Diverse Learners in Phonics Instruction

● ● ●

IRA Standards for Reading Professionals: Standard 4, Elements 4.1, 4.2

Response to Intervention: Responsive Teaching and Differentiation

There are many reasons that children may have difficulty learning phonics and other word identification skills. If students have not developed phonemic awareness, knowledge of letter names, and an understanding of concepts of print, learning phonics and sight words will be more difficult. Research also suggests that most students who experience reading difficulties may also have deficits in oral language, language comprehension, and background knowledge (Snow, Burns, & Griffin, 1998; Stanovich & West, 1989). These deficits are particularly acute among children living in poverty. Other factors that affect the learning of phonics include challenges faced by English learners (ELs), children who are less cognitively able ("slow learners"), and those with attention deficit disorder (ADD), dyslexia, auditory disability, or language impairment affecting sound perception. In this section we offer strategies for meeting the needs of many of these learners.

Interactive Strategies for Struggling Readers

Vellutino and Scanlon (2002) developed and field-tested a sequence of instruction for struggling readers called **interactive strategies.** This approach for providing differentiated instruction appears to be adapted in part from the Reading Recovery model originally developed by Marie Clay (2003). Students are first assessed using the formats described in this chapter to determine student sight word or phonics/decoding knowledge gaps needing instructional attention. Next students are grouped together according to their identified gaps. Interactive strategies for struggling readers comprise the following series of five "lessons" in an intervention format. Walpole and McKenna (2004) recommend this sequence as providing "strategic integration" of new decoding skills.

1. *Five minutes of rereading familiar texts.* Repeated oral readings of familiar texts is an effective way to improve word identification skills and automaticity in decoding (National Reading Panel, 2000). Daily rereading of familiar or decodable texts orally can be a powerful reinforcement in phonics acquisition.

2. *Five minutes of phonics instruction.* This focused and intensive instruction is designed to fill students' gaps in phonics knowledge and decoding skills, based on diagnosed individual needs using a reliable and valid phonics assessment. In the research by Vellutino and Scanlon (2002), students received short, focused "bursts" of instruction and practice in such areas as phonemic awareness, alphabet recognition, phonics, studying word families (onset and rime), and producing spelling patterns.

3. *Ten minutes of reading and applying decoding skills to new text.* Children read a new text each day on their instructional reading level (90–95 percent correct word identification). Before reading, the teacher introduces the text in an enticing way (sometimes referred to as a "book talk"). As the child reads the text aloud, the teacher may intervene to offer prompts when the child encounters an unknown

word. Some teachers have found that using decodable books containing the phonics element under review prior to reading in instructional-level texts offers additional scaffolding of phonics skills in the context of reading.

4. *Five minutes of word work using high-frequency words in isolation.* We have long been proponents of students keeping personal word banks in which they save high-frequency words on small plain or lined index cards (e.g., *was, the, run, are, and, there, this,* etc.). In the interactive strategies model, students spend 5 minutes each day practicing the identification of high-frequency words and others selected by the teacher. These practice sessions can be conducted easily with students working in pairs.

5. *Five minutes of writing.* In the final step of the interactive strategies model, teachers begin (as they always should for any practice activity) with building background or activating students' prior experiences related to the current task. The writing activity may involve dictation by the teacher or student, spelling practice with the target words, or sentence writing according to criteria established by the teacher.

The interactive strategies described here form a useful instructional format for providing targeted Tier 2 instruction in small groups of students who share gaps in sight word and decoding knowledge, as would be suggested in a Response to Intervention (RTI) model (Fuch, Fuchs, & Vaughn, 2008).

Helping Students with Dyslexia

Dyslexia is defined by the International Dyslexia Association (2006) as a specific learning disability, neurological in origin, that is characterized by difficulties with accurate and/or fluent word recognition and by poor spelling and decoding abilities. These difficulties typically result from a deficit in the phonological component of language that is often unexpected in relation to other cognitive abilities and the level of effective classroom instruction provided. Secondary consequences may include problems in reading comprehension and reduced reading experience that can impede growth of vocabulary and background knowledge. Many people who are dyslexic are of average to above-average intelligence.

Recommended instruction for students with dyslexia typically involves individualized, intensive, multisensory (i.e., visual, tactile, auditory, kinesthetic) methods and writing and spelling components. Remedial teaching of phonics for dyslexic students may include direct instruction in phonics and structural analysis.

It is recommended that instruction for students with dyslexia be individualized to meet their specific learning needs. Materials used should be matched to each student's individual ability level. Following are key recommendations of the International Dyslexia Association (IDA):

- *Linguistic.* Instruction should be aimed at insuring fluency with the patterns of language in words and sentences.
- *Meaning-based.* All instruction should lead to an emphasis on comprehension and composition.
- *Multisensory.* The simultaneous use of two or more sensory pathways (auditory, visual, kinesthetic, tactile) during presentation and practice are often effective.
- *Phonemic awareness.* It can be beneficial to offer instruction that reteaches students to detect, segment, blend, and manipulate sounds in spoken language.

- *Explicit direct instruction.* Phonics instruction should be systematic (structured), sequential, and cumulative, and presented in a logical sequential plan that fits the nature of language (alphabetic principle), with no assumption of prior skills or language knowledge.

English Learners

Recently, the *Report of the National Literacy Panel on Language-Minority Children and Youth* (August & Shanahan, 2006) was released, shedding new light on the reading instruction needs of English learners (ELs). For example, the report found evidence-based reading research to confirm that focusing instruction on key reading components—phonemic awareness, decoding, oral reading fluency, reading comprehension, vocabulary, and writing—has clear benefits. The researchers went on to say that differences due to children's second-language proficiency make it important to adjust instruction to meet the needs of all second-language learners.

Another finding was that language-minority students who become literate in their first language are likely to have an advantage in the acquisition of English literacy. This finding was supported by studies demonstrating that language-minority students taught in both their native language and English performed, on average, better on English reading measures than language-minority students instructed only in English. Unfortunately, it is often difficult for large school districts to find enough well-qualified bilingual teachers to serve these children.

This important study makes it clear that phonics instruction is critical to English learners and must be delivered by a knowledgeable teacher.

Other research specifically concerns native Spanish speakers, who are the most rapidly growing population of ELs in many states. Some basic similarities and differences between English and Spanish languages may cause some problems in the learning of phonics. Table 4.5 shows a few points for you to consider in planning phonics instruction with ELs, adapted from Honig, Diamond, and Gutlohn (2000). Happily, most phonics generalizations in English and Spanish are the same. If anything, Spanish is far more phonically consistent than English.

Table 4.5

Phonics for Spanish Speakers

Sound	Explanation	Examples
/s/	This sound is spelled with *s* in English and Spanish.	English: *seed, secret* Spanish: *semilla, secreto*
/m/	This sound is spelled with *m* in English and Spanish.	English: *map, many* Spanish: *mapa, mucho*
Spanish *e*	The letter *e* in Spanish has the long *a* sound, as in *eight.*	
/ch/	In Spanish, the digraph *ch* also make the /ch/ sound. However, *ch* only appears in the beginning or medial positions in Spanish.	English: *church, each* Spanish: *chico, ocho*
/sh/	The *sh* digraph does not exist in Spanish. Sorting new words with *sh* and *ch* will be helpful. Be sure to also focus on the meaning of each word.	

Motivation and Engagement Strategies for Teaching Phonics

Engaging students' attention and sustained practice through play and games, according to Harris (2009), is not all that new and may even be instinctual. This is also true of learning literacy skills, including gaming in virtual environments or computer gaming (Owston, Wideman, Ronda, & Brown, 2009). Game-based learning (Jackson, 2009) has been shown to produce motivational effects in learners that most teachers can only dream about.

IRA Standards for Reading Professionals: Standard 5, Element 5.2

Motivating Students with Games

We have found that even simple board games and the other games described in this section are motivating for students who need phonics practice to make progress in decoding and word recognition (Harris, 2009).

Letter–Sound Cards.   Intended as prompts, letter–sound cards can help students remember individual and combination (i.e., digraphs and blends) letter sounds that have been introduced during mini-lessons or other teachable moments. You will need to have a word bank for each child (children's shoe boxes, recipe boxes, or other small containers in which index cards can be filed), alphabetic divider cards to separate words, index cards, and colored markers.

The idea is to provide students with their own word cards on which you (or they) have written a key letter sound or sounds on one side and a word that uses that sound on the other. Whenever possible, it is best to use nouns or other words that can be depicted with a picture, so that, for emergent readers, a drawing can be added to the side having the word (as needed). Two examples are shown in Figure 4.18.

Phonics Fish (or Foniks Phish?) Card Game.   We have previously discussed the children's card game "Fish" (sometimes called "Go Fish") for matching activities. This review activity helps students use their growing awareness of phonics sounds and letter patterns to construct word families

Figure 4.18

Letter–Sound Card Examples

From Reutzel and Cooter, *Strategies for Reading Assessment and Instruction,* 4th ed., p. 185. © 2011 by Pearson Education, Inc. Reprinted by permission of Pearson Education, Inc.

(i.e., groups of words having the same phonetic pattern). It can be played in small groups, at a learning center with two to four children, or during reading groups with the teacher.

You will need a deck of word cards. The words can be selected from the students' word banks or chosen by the teacher or parent/teaching assistant from among those familiar to all students. The word cards should contain ample examples of at least three or four phonetic patterns that you wish to review (e.g., beginning consonant sounds, *r*-controlled vowels, clusters, digraphs, rime families, etc.).

Before beginning the game, explain which word families or sound patterns are to be used. Next, explain the rules of the game.

1. Each child will be dealt five cards.
2. The remaining cards (deck of about 50) are placed facedown in the middle of the group.
3. Students find any matching pairs in their hands and set them faceup.
4. Taking turns in a round-robin fashion, each child tries to match his or her remaining cards by asking any other child if he or she is holding a word having a particular sound or pattern. For example, if one of the included patterns is the /sh/ sound, the first student may say something like "Juanita, do you have any words with the /sh/ sound?" Juanita must hand over an /sh/ card if she has it. If she does not have any word cards with that pattern, she says, "Go Fish!" The student asking the question then draws a card from the deck.
5. The first student to get rid of all his or her cards wins the game.

Click on A+RISE—WIDA ELP Standard Strategies in the MyEducationLab (www.myeducationlab.com) for your course. Next, select the Strategy Card Index tab, scroll to Phonics for grades K–5, and select the Puzzle Cards strategy.

Stomping, Clapping, Tapping, and Snapping Sound. Helping children hear syllables in words enables them to segment sounds. This knowledge can be used in myriad ways to improve writing or spelling, increase awareness of letter combinations that produce specific speech sounds, and apply knowledge of onsets and rimes. All these skills and more enable students to sound out words in print more effectively. Many teachers have found success in helping children hear syllables by clapping them out when reading nursery rhymes: "Mar-y had a lit-tle lamb, lit-tle lamb, lit-tle lamb."

We prefer to use rhyming poetry, songs, chants, or raps for these syllabication activities. With an enlarged version produced for an overhead projector, a big book version, or simply rewriting the text on large chart paper with a watercolor marker, first model-read the enlarged text aloud in a normal cadence for students. Reread the selection, again at a normal cadence, inviting students to join in as they wish. Next, explain that you will reread the selection, but this time you will clap (or snap, stomp, etc.) the syllables in the words. (*Note:* If you have not already explained the concept of syllables, you will need to do so at this point.) Finally, invite students to clap (or make whatever gesture or sound you have chosen) as you reread the passage.

Tongue Twisters. Many students enjoy word play. Tongue twisters can be a wonderful way of reviewing consonants (Cunningham, 1995) in a way that is fun for students. We have found that tongue-twister activities can combine reading and creative writing processes to help children deepen their understanding of phonic elements. There are many traditional tongue twisters in published children's literature that may be used. However, we find that children enjoy creating their own tongue twisters. All you need to do is decide which sounds or letter pattern families are to be the focus.

Cunningham (2008) suggests that you begin by simply reciting some tongue twisters aloud and inviting students to join in. We recommend that you produce two or three examples on chart paper and post them on the wall as you introduce the concept of tongue twisters. For example, you might use the following.

Silly Sally sat in strawberries.

Peter Piper picked a peck of pickled peppers.
If Peter Piper picked a peck of pickled peppers,
Then how many peppers did Peter Piper pick?

Peter Piper panhandles pepperoni pizza,
With his pint-sized pick-up he packs a peck of pepperoni pizzas,
For Patti, his portly patron.

Simple Simon met a pieman going to the fair,
Said Simple Simon to the pieman,
"Let me taste your wares!"
Said the pieman to Simple Simon,
"Show me first your penny!"
Said Simple Simon to the pieman,
"I'm afraid I haven't any."

Children especially love it when teachers create tongue twisters using names of children in the class, such as the following example:

Pretty Pam picked pink peonies for Patty's party.

Challenge students to create their own tongue twisters to "stump the class." It may be fun to award students coupons that can be used to purchase take-home books for coming up with clever tongue twisters.

Creating Nonsense Words

Some teachers actually wince at the thought of having students decode or identify nonsense words because they have been told that all reading should make sense. Well, when it comes to blending the syllables in multisyllabic words this is not always true. Students can learn phonics principles by blending sounds into nonsense syllables and then blending these nonsense syllables to pronounce multisyllable words. The appeal of nonsense words has already been discovered by many popular poets, such as Shel Silverstein and Jack Prelutsky, who have tapped into children's fascination with word play in their very creative poetry. For instance, when Silverstein speaks of "gloppy glumps of cold oatmeal," we all understand what he means, even though *glumps* is a nonsense word. Having students create nonsense words and then apply them to popular poetry is a motivating way to help them practice phonic patterns.

First decide which phonic sound or letter pattern family you wish to emphasize. For instance, it may be appropriate to review the letter–sound families represented by the word endings *-ack, -ide, -ing,* and *-ore*. You will also need books of poetry or songs with rhyming phrases, chart paper or overhead transparencies, and markers.

As with all activities, begin by modeling what you expect students to do. On a large sheet of chart paper or at the overhead projector, write the word family parts that you wish to emphasize (for this example, *-ack, -ide, -ing,* and *-ore*). Illustrate how you can convert the word parts into nonsense words by adding a consonant, consonant blend, or consonant digraph before each one, as shown here.

-ack	-ide	-ing	-ore
gack	spide	ging	zore
splack	mide	zwing	glore
chack	plide	shing	jore

In the next phase of the demonstration, select a poem or song that rhymes and review it with students (using enlarged text for all of your modeling). Next, show students a revised copy of the song or poem in which you have substituted nonsense words. The following example is based on the song "I Know an Old Lady Who Swallowed a Fly." We show only the first verse here in both original and transformed versions, but you could use the entire song, substituting a nonsense word in each stanza.

Original Verse

I know an old lady who swallowed a fly,
I don't know why,
she swallowed the fly,
I guess she'll die.

Nonsense-Word Version

I know an old lady who swallowed a *bly,*
I don't know why,
she swallowed the *bly,*
I guess she'll die.

Learning phonics in a gaming environment that is carefully structured and selected to support and fill students' phonics knowledge gaps and provide extended practice in blending, segmenting, and recognizing words is clearly part of an effective evidence-based reading instructional program.

Technology and New Literacies

Using Technology and New Literacies to Enhance Phonics Instruction

● ● ●

IRA Standards for Reading Professionals: Standard 2, Element 2.3; Standard 5, Element 5.1

Common Core Standards: Reading: K–5, Integration of Knowledge and Ideas (item 7); Writing: K–5, Production and Distribution of Writing (item 6)

Gambrell (2007) argues that technology is the way that many of today's "digital learners" engage to decode and recognize words in print. Twenty-first-century teachers are increasingly instructing students who are more wired than they are, having been drenched in digital environments from birth onward (Hughes, 2010). Fortunately, teachers today have ready access to computers connected to the Internet that provide easy and free access to phonics and decoding lessons and word recognition teaching materials. Many schools also have computer projectors and document cameras that can bring online material to larger groups. In addition, computer programs with interactive gaming environments for students to work with words in decoding and word recognition activities are increasingly found on school computers. Examples include the Leap Frog Didj game system and the Leapster Learning System (online at http://store.leapfrogschoolhouse.com/SchoolHouse.jsp). See Web Tools You Can Use in the Classroom for more online phonics programs.

Finally, many classrooms now have "smart boards" that allow teachers to work from the front of the class and interact with students' computers to highlight, type, write by hand, and otherwise operate directly on the computer image on students' screens. Programs like PowerPoint can also enhance sight word lessons by adding movement, as a sight word might fly in from the left, drop from the top, or disintegrate to add more spice to learning.

WEB TOOLS YOU CAN USE IN THE CLASSROOM

Phonics and Word Recognition

The following websites offer useful, creative, and pedagogically sound letter, phonics, decoding, and word recognition lesson plans, materials, games, and so on.

- For tools and resources, go to First School Years at www.firstschoolyears.com.
- Reading Rockets furnishes a variety of technologies and ideas for helping to teach reading at www.readingrockets.org.
- BBC Words and Pictures offers tools for teaching phonics at www.bbc.co.uk/schools/wordsandpictures.
- EdHelper.com provides word lists and sound lists at www.edhelper.com/phonics/Phonics.htm.
- Softschools.com presents activities and games to engage students in learning phonics at www.softschools.com/language_arts/phonics.
- Readinga-z.com has a wide array of resources that help teach children to read at www.readinga-z.com.

Many other Internet sites provide phonics instructional materials and decodable books for reading practice that are available for a single subscription price for teachers or may be purchased as a school license.

Family and Community Connections

How Family and Community Connections Can Foster Phonics Development Outside the Classroom

The Public Library Association (www.pla.org) and the Association for Library Service to Children conduct a joint project known as Every Child Ready to Read @ Your Library. In this section we describe some of this project's excellent ideas. We have worded them in language you might use with parents. The activities listed below are arranged, like our benchmark skills, from easiest to most difficult. It is wisely recommended that parents be sure that their children can perform tasks at the simpler level before moving on to a higher level.

IRA Standards for Reading Professionals: Standard 4, Elements 4.1, 4.2, 4.3

Response to Intervention: Collaboration

Words from Pictures

Have your child glue pictures cut from donated magazines onto paper. Ask him or her tell a "story" about the picture as you write it down. You can teach new words at this time, but be sure to draw the child's attention to the printed word. After the story is written, go back and take turns "reading" the story to each other. Collect these pictures and stories and make them into a book that can be looked at again and again.

Nursery Rhymes

A somewhat lost tradition in the United States is reading nursery rhymes to children. Hearing rhymes helps children later learn rimes (and onsets), so read nursery rhymes to your child. After he or she can say a rhyme and is very familiar with it, practice counting the words in one sentence at a time. Focus on hearing like sounds in words and how the sounds look in print.

Rhyming Picture Cards

Create picture cards with words beneath and practice categorizing the rhyming words. If your child has trouble matching rhyming words, provide help by drawing attention to the fact that words that rhyme have the same sound at the end. For example, *cat* and *rat* rhyme because they both have the *-at* sound at the end; *clock* and *block* both have the *-ock* sound (emphasize the ending that makes the words rhyme when saying them). Adding some examples that do not rhyme may help your child understand (e.g., *clock* and *ball* do not rhyme because they have different ending sounds).

Silly Words

Make up "silly" words by changing the first letter in a known word. Play a game of seeing how many silly words you and your child can create and then ask whether or not the silly word is a real word. To play this game at the easiest level, you should make up several words by changing the first sound (e.g., *cook—sook, book, wook, took*) and then asking whether or not each is a real word. At a more advanced level, you can model and ask your child to change the first sound in a word to make another word. For example, say: "My word is *be* and the new sound is /*m*/." (Say the sound, not the word.) "What is the new word?" *(Me.)* There are many familiar words in which the first sound can be changed to make a new word *(light–night, boat–goat, pail–sail, cat–rat, ball–wall).*

Many states have established their own collaborative websites featuring valuable information about family involvement in early reading development. For instance, you can find many more activities like these online at www.ala.org/ala/pla/plaissues.

Summary

In this chapter we have learned about how young students learn to decode and instantly recognize words. We have looked at phonics instruction, in which concepts such as digraphs, diphthongs, *r*-controlled vowels, and the schwa help teachers understand and teach the system of sounds and letters in English and other alphabetically represented words in print. In addition, we learned about sight words—words that are highly frequent in printed language but often difficult to decode and remember because they often have unusual spellings and abstract meanings. Having examined both phonics and sight words as part of the word recognition process, we then learned about a variety of assessments that classroom teachers can use to diagnose, screen, and monitor student progress and growth in phonics knowledge, including letter names, phonics concepts, decoding skills, reading miscues in a running record, and memory for a core of 107 highly frequent sight words.

Next we discussed three major strategies for teaching students to recognize and decode words: blending, segmenting, and memorizing sight words. Each process used to recognize and understand words was described in detail.

We also learned how to modify phonics and word recognition instruction to meet the diverse needs of struggling readers, dyslexic readers, and English learners.

This was followed by a discussion of word learning and phonics games as motivation for learning to decode and recognize words. We then looked at technology applications—of phonics and word recognition computer games, especially programs for digital learning systems and instructional Internet sites. Finally, we discussed several word recognition activities parents can use at home to help their children learn sight words and practice decoding strategies with a variety of texts.

To conclude this chapter, we reiterate the fact that that although some children may emerge into reading and writing without systematic, explicit phonics and word recognition instruction, it is rare. Instead, the National Reading Panel (2000) advises teachers that students who are taught phonics explicitly and systematically learn to read more quickly and with fewer missteps than those who aren't taught phonics or who are taught phonics incidentally. This same evidence base shows that teaching explicit, systematic phonics to children living in poverty increases the magnitude of learning and reading achievement by 50 percent. Effective teachers understand the importance of teaching students to instantly recognize a core of high-frequency sight words in addition to explicitly teaching phonics concepts and decoding strategies for recognizing words accurately and effortlessly. Mastering these abilities sets the stage for another critical ability called reading fluency.

Field and Classroom Applications

- Conduct a library and Internet search for decodable and leveled books that could provide students practice with sight words, phonics concepts, and decoding strategies. Prepare an annotated bibliography of your sources to share with your colleagues.

Phonics Quick Test

1. The word *charkle* is broken into syllables between ___r___ and ___k___. The *a* has an ___r___ -controlled sound, and the e is ___silent___.
2. In the word *small*, *sm-* is known as the onset and *-all* is known as the ___rime___.
3. The *ch* in the word *chair* is known as a ___consonant digraph___.
4. The letter *c* in the word *city* has a ___soft___ sound and in the word *cow* has a ___hard___ sound.
5. The letters *bl* in the word *blue* are referred to as a consonant ___blend___.
6. The underlined vowels in the words *author*, *spread*, and *blue* are known as vowel ___digraphs___.
7. The words *tag, run, cot,* and *get* fit which vowel pattern? ___CVC___
8. The words *glide, take,* and *use* fit the ___VCE___ vowel pattern.
9. The word part *work* in the word *working* is known as a ___root or base word, or free morpheme___.
10. The word part *-ing* in the word *working* is known as a ___suffix or bound morpheme___.
11. Teaching students the meanings of prefixes, suffixes, and root words to help them better understand word meanings is part of word attack skills known as ___structural analysis___.
12. Writers often provide ___context clues___, which help readers discover the meaning of unknown words in print.

- Locate the website for your state's education department. Print out the scope and sequence of recommended phonics, decoding skills, and sight words to be taught. Compare this list to the curriculum guide or map from the school district in which you plan to carry out your internship (student teaching). Using this information, prepare a "Comprehensive Decoding Checklist" to use in profiling each child's decoding abilities. This will be useful to you later, when we discuss reading assessment in this text. More importantly, you will have created a valuable tool for informing your teaching.

- Develop a PowerPoint slide presentation on the steps of the sight word teaching strategy presented in this chapter. Share this PowerPoint file with your college class. Use this file as a template for teaching sight words when you enter the classroom.

- Through your college or university teacher preparation program, find a teacher who will allow you to perform running records on two of his or her students. Analyze your findings using MSV analysis. Be sure to do three running records on each level of difficulty with each child as recommended by research cited in this chapter.

- Prepare a lesson plan for teaching the blending or segmenting words strategies presented in this chapter. Teach this lesson in a classroom associated with your practica work or in your own classroom. Write a reflection paragraph on how the lesson went and how you might change or improve it when you next teach the blending or segmenting strategy.

- Obtain a copy of the CORE Phonics Survey. Request permission to enter a classroom to administer the survey to at least one student. Write a two-paragraph summary of the results, indicating the student's phonics strengths and any gaps requiring future targeted instruction.

Recommended Resources

Print Resources

American Federation of Teachers. (1999). *Teaching reading is rocket science: What expert teachers of reading should know and be able to do.* Washington, DC: Author.

Beck, I. L. (2006). *Making sense of phonics: The hows and whys.* New York: Guilford Press.

Burns, M. S., Griffin, P., & Snow, C. E. (1999). *Starting out right: A guide to promoting children's reading success.* Washington, DC: National Academy Press.

Cooter, R. B., Matthews, B., Thompson, S., & Cooter, K. S. (2004). Searching for lessons of mass instruction? Try reading strategy continuums. *The Reading Teacher, 58*(4), 388–393.

Cunningham, P. M. (2008). *Phonics they use: Words for reading and writing* (5th ed.). Boston: Pearson/Allyn & Bacon.

Fry, E. B., Kress, J. E., & Fountoukidis, D. L. (2006). *The reading teacher's book of lists* (5th ed.). San Francisco, CA: Jossey-Bass.

Leu, D. J., Kinzer, C. K., Wilson, R. M., & Hall, M. A. (2006). *Phonics, phonemic awareness, and word analysis for teachers: An interactive tutorial* (8th ed.). Upper Saddle River, NJ: Pearson/Merrill/Prentice Hall.

National Institute for Literacy. (2003). *Put reading first: The research building blocks for teaching children to read.* Washington, DC: National Institute for Literacy at Ed Pubs. Available at www.nifl.gov/partnershipforreading.

Reutzel, D. R., & Cooter, R. B. (2011). *Strategies for reading assessment and instruction: Helping every child succeed* (4th ed.). Boston: Pearson/Allyn & Bacon.

Web Resources

www.fcrr.org/SCASearch
  Florida Center for Reading Research

www.knowledgeadventure.com/reading-games.htm
  Knowledge Adventure

http://store.leapfrogschoolhouse.com/SchoolHouse.jsp
  Leapster Learning System

www.firstschoolyears.com
  First School Years

www.readingrockets.org
  Reading Rockets

PEARSON myeducationlab™
The Power of Classroom Practice
www.myeducationlab.com

Go to Topic 3, Phonemic Awareness/Phonics, in the MyEducationLab (www.myeducationlab.com) for your course, where you can:

- Find learning outcomes for Phonemic Awareness/Phonics along with the national standards that connect to these outcomes.
- Complete Assignments and Activities that can help you more deeply understand the chapter content.
- Apply and practice your understanding of the core teaching skills identified in the chapter with the Building Teaching Skills and Dispositions learning units. (optional)
- Examine challenging situations and cases presented in the IRIS Center Resources. (optional)
- Access video clips of CCSSO National Teachers of the Year award winners responding to the question "Why Do I Teach?" in the Teacher Talk section. (optional)
- Check your comprehension on the content covered in the chapter by going to the Study Plan in the Book Resources for your text. Here you will be able to take a chapter quiz, receive feedback on your answers, and then access Review, Practice, and Enrichment activities to enhance your understanding of chapter content. (optional)

A+RISE

Go to the Topic A+RISE in the MyEducationLab (www.myeducationlab.com) for your course. A+RISE® Standards2Strategy™ is an innovative and interactive online resource that offers new teachers in grades K–12 just in time, research-based instructional strategies that:

- Meet the linguistic needs of ELLs as they learn content.
- Differentiate instruction for all grades and abilities.
- Offer reading and writing techniques, cooperative learning, use of linguistic and nonlinguistic representations, scaffolding, teacher modeling, higher order thinking, and alternative classroom ELL assessment.
- Provide support to help teachers be effective through the integration of listening, speaking, reading, and writing along with the content curriculum.
- Improve student achievement.
- Are aligned to Common Core Elementary Language Arts standards (for the literacy strategies) and to English language proficiency standards in WIDA, Texas, California, and Florida.

STANDARDS
for Reading Professionals and Guiding Principles for Educators

IRA Standards for Reading Professionals

Standard 1: Foundational Knowledge

Candidates understand the theoretical and evidence-based foundations of reading and writing processes and instruction.

Element 1.1

Candidates understand major theories and empirical research that describe the cognitive, linguistic, motivational, and sociocultural foundations of reading and writing development, processes, and components, including word recognition, language comprehension, strategic knowledge, and reading–writing connections.

Element 1.2

Candidates understand the historically shared knowledge of the profession and changes over time in the perceptions of reading and writing development, processes, and components.

Element 1.3

Candidates understand the role of professional judgment and practical knowledge for improving all students' reading development and achievement.

Candidates use instructional approaches, materials, and an integrated, comprehensive, balanced curriculum to support student learning in reading and writing.

Response to Intervention

6. Expertise

All students have the right to receive instruction from well-prepared teachers who keep up to date and supplemental instruction from professionals specifically prepared to teach language and literacy (IRA, 2000).

- Teacher expertise is central to instructional improvement, particularly for students who encounter difficulty in acquiring language and literacy. RTI may involve a range of professionals; however, the greater the literacy difficulty, the greater the need for expertise in literacy teaching and learning.
- Important dimensions of teachers' expertise include their knowledge and understanding of language and literacy development, their ability to use powerful assessment tools and techniques, and their ability to translate information about student performance into instructionally relevant instructional techniques.
- The exemplary core instruction that is so essential to the success of RTI is dependent on highly knowledgeable and skilled classroom teachers (IRA, 2003).

- Professionals who provide supplemental instruction or intervention must have a high level of expertise in all aspects of language and literacy instruction and assessment and be capable of intensifying or accelerating language and literacy learning.
- Success for culturally and linguistically diverse students depends on teachers and support personnel who are well prepared to teach in a variety of settings. Deep knowledge of cultural and linguistic differences is especially critical for the prevention of language and literacy problems in diverse student populations.
- Expertise in the areas of language and literacy requires a comprehensive approach to professional preparation that involves preservice, induction, and inservice education. It also requires opportunities for extended practice under the guidance of knowledgeable and experienced mentors.

IRA Standards for Reading Professionals

Standard 3: Assessment and Evaluation

Candidates use a variety of assessment tools and practices to plan and evaluate effective reading and writing instruction.

Element 3.1

Candidates understand types of assessments and their purposes, strengths, and limitations.

Element 3.2

Candidates select, develop, administer, and interpret assessments, both traditional print and electronic, for specific purposes.

Element 3.3

Candidates use assessment information to plan and evaluate instruction.

Response to Intervention

3. Assessment

An RTI approach demands assessment that can inform language and literacy instruction meaningfully.

- Assessment should reflect the multidimensional nature of language and literacy learning and the diversity among students being assessed. The utility of an assessment is dependent on the extent to which it provides valid information on the essential aspects of language and literacy that can be used to plan appropriate instruction.
- Assessments, tools, and techniques should provide useful and timely information about desired language and literacy goals. They should reflect authentic language and literacy activities as opposed to contrived texts or tasks generated specifically for assessment purposes. The quality of assessment information should not be sacrificed for the efficiency of an assessment procedure.
- Multiple purposes for assessment should be clearly identified and appropriate tools and techniques employed. Not all available tools and techniques are appropriate for all purposes, and different assessments—even in the same language or literacy

domain—capture different skills and knowledge. Particular care should be taken in selecting assessments for ELLs and for students who speak an English dialect that differs from mainstream dialects.

- Efficient assessment systems involve a layered approach in which screening techniques are used both to identify which students require further (diagnostic) assessment and to provide aggregate data about the nature of student achievement overall. Initial (screening) assessments should not be used as the sole mechanism for determining the appropriateness of targeted interventions. Ongoing progress monitoring must include an evaluation of the instruction itself and requires observation of the student in the classroom.
- Classroom teachers and reading/literacy specialists should play a central role in conducting language and literacy assessments and in using assessment results to plan instruction and monitor student performance.
- Assessment as a component of RTI should be consistent with the *Standards for the Assessment of Reading and Writing* developed jointly by the International Reading Association and the National Council of Teachers of English (2010).

Effective Phonics Instruction

IRA Standards for Reading Professionals

Standard 2: Curriculum and Instruction

Candidates use instructional approaches, materials, and an integrated, comprehensive, balanced curriculum to support student learning in reading and writing.

Element 2.1

Candidates use foundational knowledge to design or implement an integrated, comprehensive, and balanced curriculum.

Element 2.2

Candidates use appropriate and varied instructional approaches, including those that develop word recognition, language comprehension, strategic knowledge, and reading–writing connections.

Element 2.3

Candidates use a wide range of texts (e.g., narrative, expository, and poetry) from traditional print, digital, and online resources.

Standard 5: Literate Environment

Candidates create a literate environment that fosters reading and writing by integrating foundational knowledge, instructional practices, approaches and methods, curriculum materials, and the appropriate use of assessments.

Element 5.1

Candidates design the physical environment to optimize students' use of traditional print, digital, and online resources in reading and writing instruction.

Element 5.3

Candidates use routines to support reading and writing instruction (e.g., time allocation, transitions from one activity to another, discussions, and peer feedback).

Common Core Standards

Reading: K–5

Key Ideas and Details

1. Read closely to determine what the text says explicitly and to make logical inferences from it; cite specific textual evidence when writing or speaking to support conclusions drawn from the text.

Response to Intervention

1. Instruction

- A successful RTI process begins with the highest quality core instruction in the classroom—that is, instruction that encompasses all areas of language and literacy as part of a coherent curriculum that is developmentally appropriate for preK–12 students and does not underestimate their potential for learning. This core instruction may or may not involve commercial programs, and it must in all cases be provided by an informed, competent classroom teacher.
- The success of RTI depends on the classroom teacher's use of research-based practices. As defined by IRA (2002), *research based* means "that a particular program or collection of instructional practices has a record of success. That is, there is reliable, trustworthy, and valid evidence to suggest that when the program is used with a particular group of children, the children can be expected to make adequate gains in reading achievement."
- Research evidence frequently represents the effectiveness of an instructional practice on average, which suggests that some students benefited and others did not. This means that instruction must be provided by a teacher who understands the intent of the research-based practice being used and has the professional expertise and responsibility to plan instruction and adapt programs and materials as needed (see also principle 6, Expertise).
- When core language and literacy instruction is not effective for a particular student, it should be modified to address more closely the needs and abilities of that student. Classroom teachers, at times in collaboration with other experts, must exercise their best professional judgment in providing responsive teaching and differentiation (see also principle 2).

5. Systemic and Comprehensive Approaches

RTI must be part of a comprehensive, systemic approach to language and literacy assessment and instruction that supports all preK–12 students and teachers.

- RTI needs to be integrated within the context of a coherent and consistent language and literacy curriculum that guides comprehensive instruction for all students. Core instruction—indeed, all instruction—must be continuously improved to increase its efficacy and mitigate the need for specialized interventions.
- Specific approaches to RTI need to be appropriate for the particular school or district culture and take into account leadership, expertise, the diversity of the student population, and the available resources. Schools and districts should adopt an approach that best matches their needs and resources while still accomplishing the overall goals of RTI.
- A systemic approach to language and literacy learning within an RTI framework requires the active participation and genuine collaboration of many professionals, including classroom teachers, reading specialists, literacy coaches, special educators, and school psychologists. Given the critical role that language development plays in literacy learning, professionals with specialized language-related expertise such as speech-language pathologists and teachers of ELLs may be particularly helpful in addressing students' language difficulties.
- Approaches to RTI must be sensitive to developmental differences in language and literacy among students at different ages and grades. Although many prevailing approaches to RTI focus on the early elementary grades, it is essential for teachers and support personnel at middle and secondary levels to provide their students with the language and literacy instruction they need to succeed in school and beyond.
- Administrators must ensure adequate resources and appropriate scheduling to allow all professionals to collaborate.
- Ongoing and job-embedded professional development is necessary for all educators involved in the RTI process. Professional development should be context specific and provided by professional developers with appropriate preparation and skill to support school and district personnel. Professional expertise is essential to improving students' language and literacy learning in general as well as within the context of RTI (see also principle 6).

IRA Standards for Reading Professionals

Standard 4: Diversity

Candidates create and engage their students in literacy practices that develop awareness, understanding, respect, and a valuing of differences in our society.

Element 4.1

Candidates recognize, understand, and value the forms of diversity that exist in society and their importance in learning to read and write.

Element 4.2

Candidates use a literacy curriculum and engage in instructional practices that positively impact students' knowledge, beliefs, and engagement with the features of diversity.

Response to Intervention

2. Responsive Teaching and Differentiation

The RTI process emphasizes increasingly differentiated and intensified instruction or intervention in language and literacy.

- RTI is centrally about optimizing language and literacy instruction for particular students. This means that differentiated instruction, based on instructionally relevant assessment, is essential. Evidence shows that small-group and individualized instruction are effective in reducing the number of students who are at risk of becoming classified as learning disabled.
- Instruction and materials selection must derive from specific student–teacher interactions and not be constrained by pack-

aged programs. Students have different language and literacy needs, so they may not respond similarly to instruction—even when research-based practices are used. No single approach to instruction or intervention can address the broad and varied goals and needs of all students, especially those from different cultural and linguistic backgrounds.

- The boundaries between differentiation and intervention are permeable and not clearcut. Instruction or intervention must be flexible enough to respond to evidence from student performance and teaching interactions. It should not be constrained by institutional procedures that emphasize uniformity.

IRA Standards for Reading Professionals

Standard 5: Literate Environment

Element 5.2

Candidates design a social environment that is low risk and includes choice, motivation, and scaffolded support to optimize students' opportunities for learning to read and write.

IRA Standards for Reading Professionals

Standard 2: Curriculum and Instruction

Element 2.3 (See previous)

Standard 5: Literate Environment

Element 5.1 (See previous)

Common Core Standards

Reading: K–5

Integration of Knowledge and Ideas

7. Integrate and evaluate content presented in diverse media and formats, including visually and quantitatively, as well as in words.

Writing: K–5

Production and Distribution of Writing

6. Use technology, including the Internet, to produce and publish writing and to interact and collaborate with others.

How Family and Community Connections Can Foster Phonics Development Outside the Classroom

IRA Standards for Reading Professionals

Standard 4: Diversity

Elements 4.1, 4.2 (See previous)

Element 4.3

Candidates develop and implement strategies to advocate for equity.

Response to Intervention

4. Collaboration

RTI requires a dynamic, positive, and productive collaboration among professionals with relevant expertise in language and literacy. Success also depends on strong and respectful partnerships among professionals, parents, and students.

- Collaboration should be focused on the available evidence about the needs of students struggling in language and literacy. School-level decision-making teams (e.g., intervention teams, problem-solving teams, RTI teams) should include members with relevant expertise in language and literacy, including second-language learning.
- Collaboration should increase, not reduce, the coherence of the instruction experienced by struggling readers. There must be congruence between core language and literacy instruction and interventions. This requires a shared vision and common goals for language and literacy instruction and assessment, adequate time for communication and coordinated planning among general education and specialist teachers, and integrated professional development.
- Involving parents and students and engaging them in a collaborative manner is critical to successful implementation. Initiating and strengthening collaborations among school, home, and communities, particularly in urban and rural areas, provides the basis for support and reinforcement of students' learning.

Reading Fluency

Teacher Knowledge	Classroom Assessment	Evidence-Based Teaching Practices	Response to Intervention (RTI)
Describing Reading Fluency	Classroom Fluency Assessment	Effective Evidence-Based Teaching Strategies That Enhance Fluency	Differentiating Reading Fluency Instruction for Diverse Learners

Chapter Questions

Key Terms

- If you were asked to describe a fluent reader to someone who isn't a teacher, what would you say?

- What would you do to quickly and efficiently take the "fluency pulse" of your students?

- What are seven characteristics of effective evidence-based fluency instruction and practice?

- How would you address an inaccurate and slow reader's deficiencies when designing an individual intervention to increase reading fluency?

- What are two reading fluency performance strategies that can motivate students to improve reading fluency?

- What are three technological tools or programs that can support students' reading fluency development?

- How can busy parents help their children practice to improve reading fluency at home?

Reading fluency

Automaticity

Reading rate

Prosody

Repeated readings

Wide reading

Unison reading

Echo reading

Antiphonal reading

Reading in rounds

Partner reading

Scaffolded silent reading (ScSR)

Neurological impress method (NIM)

Readers' theatre

Radio reading

Motivation and Engagement	Technology and New Literacies	Family and Community Connections
Motivation and Engagement Strategies That Promote Fluency	Using Technology and New Literacies to Promote Reading Fluency	How Family and Community Connections Can Help Students Improve Reading Fluency

Vignette: Assessing Reading Fluency

Michelle, a second-grade student, settles in next to Mrs. Chang for a 1-minute reading sample. Mrs. Chang hands her the second-grade passage and sets a timer. "Michelle, I am glad to spend some time today listening to you read. Are you ready?" queries Mrs. Chang.

"Yes, I think so," answers Michelle.

"I want you to read the passage aloud as quickly as you can without making mistakes. Do you understand?"

"Yes, Mrs. Chang, I understand," replies Michelle.

"Okay, then. When I say 'Start,' you may begin reading."

Michelle nods and clears her throat.

"Start!" says Mrs. Chang.

Michelle begins reading. "My Friend. I have a new friend at school. She can't walk so she uses a wheelchair to get around. She comes to school in a special van . . ." When Michelle finishes the reading, Mrs. Chang praises her: "Michelle, you are reading very fluently. You read quickly enough for a second grader, made only two errors, had expression in your voice, and read more than a word at a time!"

Michelle beams with pride. "Thanks," she says quietly.

"Can you tell me what you remember from the pages you read?"

"I think so," responds Michelle.

When Michelle finishes retelling what she can remember, Mrs. Chang praises her again.

"Would you like to add anything to what you remember from your reading?" she questions.

"Uh-huh."

Mrs. Chang listens while Michelle adds one more remembered detail to her oral retelling.

"Michelle, I'm going to ask you a few questions about what you have just read. I would like for you to answer the questions as best you can."

"Okay," responds Michelle.

Mrs. Chang probes Michelle's comprehension of the passage with a few well-chosen questions to see if she remembers more than she has retold.

That afternoon, Mrs. Chang looks at the record she made of Michelle's earlier oral reading. With 95 percent accuracy, Mrs. Chang knows that decoding this text wasn't a problem for Michelle. She had timed Michelle's reading and calculated her reading rate in words read correctly per minute (wcpm). She now compares Michelle's wcpm to a chart showing expected oral reading rate ranges by grade level. Michelle scores near the 75th percentile for her grade level. Next, Mrs. Chang reviews the oral reading expression rating scale she had filled out right after listening to Michelle read. Michelle averaged three out of four points on expression, pacing, smoothness, and phrasing using this rating scale as a measure. Finally, Mrs. Chang carefully reviews what she wrote down while listening to Michelle's oral retelling of the pages she had read aloud. Michelle remembered the major ideas and more than half of the details in the passage, evidencing her comprehension of the text. All things considered, Michelle has performed well. There is no doubt in Mrs. Chang's mind that Michelle is making good progress toward the goal of becoming a fluent reader. ■

Teacher Knowledge

Describing Reading Fluency

To begin, teachers need to understand how reading fluency is described. **Reading fluency** is characterized by (1) accurate, effortless, and automatic (requiring little conscious attention) word identification; (2) age- or grade-level-appropriate reading speed or rate; (3) suitable use of volume, pitch, juncture, and stress (expressive or prosodic features) in the voice; and (4) correct text phrasing or "chunking." In addition, most reading experts would agree that fluent readers also simultaneously comprehend what they read (Samuels, 2007). There is a high degree of agreement among researchers about these elements defining fluent reading (Allington, 2001; Juel, 1991; National Reading Panel, 2000; Richards, 2000; Samuels & Farstrup, 2006).

IRA Standards for Reading Professionals: Standard 1, Elements 1.1, 1.2, 1.3

Response to Intervention: Expertise

Fluent readers decode the words in text accurately and effortlessly, reading with correct volume, phrasing, appropriate intonation, and at a reasonably rapid rate indicating that reading has become "automatic." By reading aloud effortlessly with speed, accuracy, and proper expression, a fluent reader's mind is free to focus on comprehension of text. The top half of Figure 5.1 presents a model reflecting the automaticity of fluent readers.

On the other hand, less fluent readers struggle through text in a labored, word-by-word manner. They focus most of their attention on decoding or figuring out how to pronounce the words, so reading comprehension suffers. The bottom half of Figure 5.1 shows how comprehension can be virtually ignored when readers devote most of their mental energies to decoding. Fluency is therefore crucial in reading because it provides a much-needed bridge between word recognition and reading comprehension (National Reading Panel, 2000; Rasinski, 1989; Reutzel & Hollingsworth, 1993; Samuels & Farstrup, 2006).

Figure 5.1

A Model of Fluent Reading

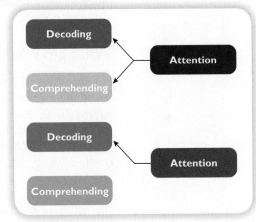

Adapted from Chall, 1967.

How Do Children Develop Reading Fluency?

How readers become fluent has been the focus of many years of research and theory development (Jenkins, Fuchs, Van den Broek, Espin, & Deno, 2003; Kame'enui & Simons, 2001; National Reading Panel, 2000; Rasinski, Reutzel, Chard, & Linan-Thompson, 2010; Stahl, 2004; Wolf & Katzir-Cohen, 2001). Perhaps the most prominent hypothesis devised to explain reading fluency is the LaBerge and Samuels (1974) theory of automatic information processing, or **automaticity** theory. This popular and well-researched explanation of how reading fluency develops proposes that the human mind functions in some ways like a computer, with input (letters and words) sequentially entered into the CPU (mind of the reader). Although computers and humans have some capacity to perform more than one task at a time (called *multitasking*), each computer and human mind is limited in its ability to process or pay attention and must often shift resources from one job to another. If one job requires a large portion of the available computer's processing (or the mind's attention) capacity, then capability for another job is limited.

The term *automaticity* implies that human minds of readers, like computers, are limited in ability to shift attention between the processes of decoding (sounding out words) and comprehending (thinking about the meaning of the author's message in the text). If readers are too bogged down in decoding the text, they will not be able to focus on the job of comprehending the author's message. Particularly in the earliest stages of reading development, the relationship between fluency and comprehension is relatively high (Paris, Carpenter, Paris, & Hamilton, 2005).

An example of automaticity in action can be seen in the skill of riding a bike. Novice bike riders focus so intently on balancing, turning the handlebars, and pedaling that they sometimes fail to attend to other important tasks like direction and potential dangers. Similarly, a reader who is a poor decoder focuses so much attention on phonics and other sounding out strategies that little brainpower is left for comprehending. When this happens the reading act, like an overloaded computer or a novice bike rider, "crashes." In contrast, children who are accomplished bike riders can pedal without hands, carry on a conversation with a friend, dodge a pothole in the road, and chew gum at the same time. Like the accomplished bike rider, fluent readers can rapidly shift attention and focus on the author's message because decoding no longer demands the lion's share of their attention capacity. LaBerge and Samuels's theory of automaticity predicts that if reading can occur automatically without too much focus or effort devoted to the decoding process, then reading comprehension, although not guaranteed, is at least made possible (Samuels, 2006).

What Do We Know from Research About Reading Fluency?

For many years, reading fluency has been acknowledged as an important goal in becoming a proficient and strategic reader (Allington, 1983, 1984, 2001; Klenk & Kibby, 2000; National Reading Panel, 2000; Opitz & Rasinski, 1998; Rasinski, 2000; Rasinski & Padak, 1996; Rasinski et al., 2010). With the publication of the *Report of the National Reading Panel* in 2000, teaching, practicing, and assessing reading fluency became a clear focal point for reading instruction in many elementary school classrooms.

The history of fluency instruction in reading has been somewhat sporadic, characterized by periods of focused attention followed by periods of benign neglect (Rasinski, 2006a). Prior to and during the early part of the twentieth century, oral reading ability and performance were highly valued as a cultural asset (Rasinski, 2006a; Smith, 2002). As the emphasis shifted away from ideas of vocal performance, research disclosed that reading silently seems to hold an advantage for readers in terms of reading rate and comprehension (Huey, 1908), an idea reinforced by the knowledge that most adult readers engage almost exclusively in silent reading as opposed to oral reading (Rasinski, 2003).

Allington (1983) noted that fluency instruction has often been neglected in reading programs, a deficiency highlighted in a large-scale study of fluency achievement in U.S. education by the National Assessment of Educational Progress. The findings indicated that "44% of fourth grade students tested were disfluent *even with grade-level stories that the student read under supportive testing conditions*" (National Reading Panel, 2000, p. 3–1; emphasis added). The analyses and findings in the National Reading Panel report (2000) about effective fluency practice have once again put an emphasis on the importance of oral reading practice—at least in the earliest stages of fluency development.

The National Reading Panel's (2000) analysis of the fluency studies showed that fluency practice is most effective when (1) the reading practice is oral; (2) it involves repeated readings of a text (more than three readings); and (3) students receive guidance or feedback from teachers, parents, volunteers, and peers (pp. 3–11). However, the panel was unable to locate sufficient evidence showing a positive impact for independent silent reading practice on students' reading fluency acquisition. From these findings and new information about oral versus silent reading for younger students (Wright, Sherman, & Jones, 2010), we have concluded that younger students will likely benefit far more from repeated oral reading practice with feedback during the early stages of reading fluency acquisition, instruction, and practice than from silent reading.

There is little research available about how expression and intonation affect fluency or comprehension (Dowhower, 1991; Rasinski et al., 2010; Reutzel, 2006). Most measures of expression in the reading literature make use of informal scales (Rasinski, 2003; Zutell & Rasinski, 1991) that ask teachers to make judgments about the prosodic features of oral reading rather than more exacting prosodic measures similar to those used by speech–language pathologists.

Stahl (2004) and Stahl and Heubach (2006) reported investigations of the effects of fluency-oriented reading instruction (FORI) using two variations of reading practice: monitored, wide silent reading practice compared to oral repeated readings with feedback. A control group was also used in these studies to determine the results of each approach compared to a baseline of second-grade readers. They found that both repeated oral readings with feedback and wide silent readings with monitoring produced results that were superior to the control group performance. Moreover, the two variations—oral readings with feedback and wide silent readings with monitoring—were roughly equivalent to one another, suggesting that "the increased amount of reading and the support given during the reading are what underlie the success of the two approaches" (p. 205). This finding has been confirmed in other studies (Kuhn, 2005; Kuhn & Woo, 2008).

Hasbrouck and Tindal (2006) conducted a study of oral fluency reading rates that spanned grades 1 through 8. Reading rate norms were adjusted for accuracy using the metric words correct per minute (wcpm). Their research suggests, for instance, that children ought to be able to read about 56 wcpm by the end of first grade (Hasbrouck & Tindal, 2006). Rates for other grades and ages will be discussed later in this chapter as they relate to assessing oral reading fluency.

At present, research is somewhat unclear about which levels of text should be used for optimal fluency practice and instruction. Kuhn and Stahl (2000) recommend the use of "instructional-level text" (90–95% of words correctly identified) for fluency instruction and practice. Stahl and Heubach (2006) argue that the appropriate text level for any given student's reading fluency practice should be related to the amount of support readily available to the student: when there is less available support, the level of text difficulty can be easier, but when there is more available support, the text difficulty can be more challenging, even up to and including the frustration level.

Fluency, much like reading comprehension, needs to be developed across all text types, such as poetry, narrative, and expository texts. An ability to read narrative or poetry texts fluently does not necessarily imply an ability to read information or expository texts with similar ability.

Even though most research indicates that fluency practice and instruction are essential components of high-quality reading instruction in the elementary years (Stahl,

2004), it can be overdone. In one short-term study, Anderson, Wilkinson, and Mason (1991) reported that too much attention and time spent on developing fluency, especially when the emphasis is largely focused on accuracy and rate, may detract from students' ability to comprehend text. The National Reading Panel (2000) found in its review of fluency instruction that lessons ranging in length from 15 to 30 minutes show positive effects on students' fluency development.

Finally, research on fluency has generally demonstrated a strong relationship between fluency development in the early grades and children's later reading comprehension (Paris et al., 2005). Recent studies show, however, that this relationship between fluency and comprehension is transitory, diminishing over time. Some educators believe that fluency is the key that unlocks the door to comprehension. But this is only partially true. Fluency may *unlock* the door, but it does not *open* the door to reading comprehension. Rather, it is best to think of fluency as a necessary but insufficient element for children to comprehend what they read. To comprehend, children must be more than fluent. They must learn how to select and use a variety of cognitive strategies to help them understand text (Pressley, 2000, 2006).

Classroom Assessment

Classroom Fluency Assessment

● ● ●

IRA Standards for Reading Professionals: Standard 3, Elements 3.1, 3.2, 3.3

Response to Intervention: Assessment

Assessing reading fluency has, for many years, focused somewhat exclusively on how quickly students can orally read a given text (Hiebert & Reutzel, 2010), a measure known as **reading rate.** More recently, reading teachers have used words correct per minute (wcpm) to measure reading speed. Although wcpm is one indicator of fluent oral reading, it is *only* one. As noted at the beginning of this chapter, to adequately assess fluency, teachers should consider at least four different components: (1) accurate and effortless decoding of text; (2) reading rate or speed; (3) use of volume, stress, pitch, and juncture (prosodic markers); and (4) mature phrasing or "chunking" of text.

Teachers have in recent years begun to discuss how they might more efficiently and authentically assess reading fluency (Kuhn & Stahl, 2000). Most teachers feel that paper-and-pencil assessment tools, such as standardized reading tests, are inadequate or at least incomplete measures of reading fluency. Another significant issue for many teachers today is obtaining valid and reliable estimates of reading rates appropriate for children of differing ages and grades.

One of the simplest and most useful means of collecting reading fluency data in today's classrooms is the 1-minute reading sample (Rasinski, 2003), a method typical of the approach used in curriculum-based measurements (CBM) such as the Oral Reading Fluency Test (ORF) drawn from the Dynamic Indicators of Basic Early Literacy Skills (DIBELS) battery (Good & Kaminski, 2002).

To administer a 1-minute reading test, teachers need a grade-level text of between 200 and 300 words, a cooking timer with an alarm or a stopwatch, and a pencil for marking the text. Children are asked to read aloud the grade-level passage for 1 minute. Words omitted, substituted, or hesitations of more than 3 seconds are scored as errors. Words self-corrected within 3 seconds are scored as accurate. After 1 minute, the student stops reading. The teacher subtracts the total number of errors from the number of words read by the student to obtain a score of words correct per minute (wcpm). This number constitutes the student's reading rate. Using more than one passage helps to control for any text-based or genre-type differences or variations. However, if standardized passages are used, such as from published sources of

CBM materials (e.g., DIBELS, Reading Fluency Monitor, AimsWEB), a score from a single passage is considered valid (Hintze & Christ, 2004). The final wcpm score can then be compared to the ORF norms (see Table 5.1) for making screening, diagnostic, or progress-monitoring decisions. By using words correct per minute (wcpm),

Table 5.1

Grades 1–8 Oral Reading Fluency Norms

Grade	Percentile	WCPM Fall	WCPM Winter	WCPM Spring
1	90	XX	81	111
	75	XX	47	82
	50	XX	23	56
	25	XX	12	28
	10	XX	6	15
2	90	106	125	142
	75	79	100	117
	50	51	72	89
	25	25	42	61
	10	11	18	31
3	90	128	146	162
	75	99	120	137
	50	71	92	107
	25	44	62	78
	10	21	36	48
4	90	145	166	180
	75	119	139	152
	50	94	112	123
	25	68	87	98
	10	45	61	72
5	90	166	182	194
	75	139	156	168
	50	110	127	139
	25	85	99	109
	10	61	74	83
6	90	177	195	204
	75	153	167	177
	50	127	140	150
	25	98	111	122
	10	68	82	93
7	90	180	192	202
	75	156	165	177
	50	128	136	150
	25	102	109	123
	10	79	88	98
8	90	185	199	199
	75	161	173	177
	50	133	146	151
	25	106	115	124
	10	77	84	97

Count 5546 3496 5335

WCPM: Words correct per minute

Adapted from Hasbrouck, J., & Tindal, G. (2006). "Oral Reading Fluency Norms: A Valuable Assessment Tool for Reading Teachers." *The Reading Teacher, 59(7)*, 636–645; Behavioral Research & Teaching (2005, January). Oral Reading Fluency: 90 Years of Assessment (BRT Technical Report No. 33), Eugene, OR: Author.

reading rate is corrected for the accuracy of the reading. The new ORF norms align closely with those published in 1992 and also closely match the widely used DIBELS norms for fall, winter, and spring.

If you want to use the DIBELS oral reading fluency test to augment 1-minute fluency samples you take during the year, the full directions for administering the ORF measure are available at the DIBELS website (http://dibels.uoregon.edu). After registering as a user, one can download grade-level passages along with administration and scoring procedures.

Assessing Expressive Reading

Reading fluency is not just described as accurate reading at an age-appropriate rate. It also includes reading that is appropriately expressive. To augment 1-minute reading sample measurements of accuracy and rate, Rasinski (2003) provides the Multidimensional Fluency Scale (see Figure 5.2). This rating tool offers more extensive and reliable information about four additional components of fluent reading: (1) volume and expression, (2) phrasing, (3) smoothness, and (4) pace. This recent revision of Zutell and Rasinski's (1991) original Multidimensional Fluency Scale (MFS) adds a reliable and valid assessment of reading volume and expression. Zutell and Rasinski (1991) report a .99 test-retest reliability coefficient for the original MFS.

To administer the Multidimensional Fluency Scale, teachers take a 1-minute reading sample as previously described and fill in the required ratings using a paper copy of the MFS. The MFS can also be used to rate group performances such as plays, readers' theatre, and radio readings (Reutzel & Cooter, 2011).

Student Self-Assessment of Reading Fluency

The purpose of explicit fluency instruction is to teach students to self-assess their fluency after reading, such as with a simple assessment rubric containing the elements of oral reading fluency shown in Figure 5.3. Once students have self-assessed and identified areas of strength and weakness using the rubric in Figure 5.3, they are taught to select and apply an appropriate fluency "fix-up" strategy (see Figure 5.4) to improve their fluency in future practice sessions.

Finally, teachers take 1-minute oral readings of the passages children have been practicing. The teacher then charts or graphs the words correct per minute (wcpm) for younger children, whereas children in grades 2 or 3 can chart or graph the number of words read correct per minute themselves. Students set reasonable goals, usually two to four more words read correctly per minute the next week, trying to better their own reading rate and cut down on errors with each successive assessment. Also, students are encouraged to improve their **prosody,** or vocal inflections, as fluent reading is not strictly confined to reading rate and accuracy (Dowhower, 1987; Hudson, Lane, & Pullen, 2005; Rasinski, 2006b; Reutzel & Hollingsworth, 1993). Figure 5.5 illustrates a tracking graph for charting a student's progress across several 1-minute reading samples.

Some teachers draw a blue line indicating the minimum wcpm needed to maintain grade-level reading rate and use red lines to show the student's actual performances. As an illustration of the power of graphing progress, one second-grade student happily noted the fact that his red line was above the blue line: "Oh, I better slow down; I've gone over the blue line!" All students, especially struggling readers, find it greatly reinforcing to see visible evidence of their reading fluency improvement.

Click on A+RISE—WIDA ELP Standard Strategies in the MyEducationLab (www.myeducationlab. com) for your course. Next, select the Strategy Card Index tab, scroll to Fluency for grades K–5, and select the Partner Fluency Check strategy.

Figure 5.2

Multidimensional Fluency Scale

Use the following scale to rate reader fluency on the five dimensions of accuracy, expression and volume, phrasing, smoothness, and pace.

A. Accuracy

1. Word recognition accuracy is poor, generally below 85%. Reader clearly struggles in decoding words. Makes multiple decoding attempts for many words, usually without success.
2. Word recognition accuracy is marginal: 86–90%. Reader struggles with many words. Many unsuccessful attempts at self-correction.
3. Word recognition accuracy is good: 91–95%. Reader self-corrects successfully.
4. Word recognition accuracy is excellent: 96–100%. Self-corrections are few but successful, as nearly all words are read correctly on initial attempt.

B. Expression and Volume

1. Student reads with little expression or enthusiasm. Reads words as if simply to get them out. Little sense of trying to make text sound like natural language. Tends to read in a quiet voice.
2. Student reads with some expression. Begins to use voice to make text sound like natural language in some areas of the text, but not others. Focus remains largely on saying the words. Still reads in a voice that is quiet.
3. Student's reading sounds like natural language throughout the better part of the passage. Occasionally slips into expressionless reading. Voice volume is generally appropriate throughout the text.
4. Student reads with good expression and enthusiasm throughout the text. Sounds like natural language. Reader is able to vary expression and volume to match his or her interpretation of the passage.

C. Phrasing

1. Monotonic with little sense of phrase boundaries; frequent word-by-word reading.
2. Student uses frequent two- and three-word phrases, giving the impression of choppy reading; improper stress and intonation that fails to mark ends of sentences and clauses.
3. Student reads in mixture of run-ons, with mid-sentence pauses for breath and possibly some choppiness; reasonable stress/intonation.
4. Reading is generally well-phrased, mostly in clause and sentence units, with adequate attention to expression.

D. Smoothness

1. Student reads with frequent extended pauses, hesitations, false starts, sound-outs, repetitions, and/or multiple attempts.
2. Student experiences several "rough spots" in text, where extended pauses, hesitations, etc., are more frequent and disruptive.
3. Reader experiences occasional breaks in smoothness caused by difficulties with specific words and/or structures.
4. Generally smooth reading with some breaks, but word and structure difficulties are resolved quickly, usually through self-correction.

E. Pace (during sections of minimal disruption)

1. Slow and laborious.
2. Moderately slow.
3. Uneven mixture of fast and slow reading.
4. Consistently conversational.

Figure 5.3

Assessment Rubric of the Elements
of Oral Reading Fluency

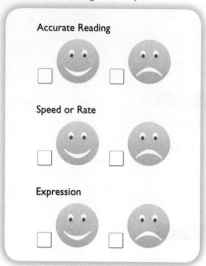

Figure 5.4

Fluency Fix-Up Strategies for Oral Reading Fluency Elements

Accuracy
1. Slow down your reading speed.
2. Look carefully at the words and the letters in the words you didn't read correctly on the page.
3. Think about if you know this word or parts of this word. Try saying the word or word parts.
4. Make the sound of each letter from left to right and blend the sounds together quickly to say the word.
5. Listen carefully to see if the word you said makes sense.
6. Try rereading the word in the sentence again.
7. After saying the word, use pictures to help you make sure you have the right word.
8. If the word still doesn't make sense, ask someone to help you.

Rate
1. Adjust your reading speed to go slower when the text is difficult or unfamiliar, or you need to read to get detailed information.
2. Adjust your reading speed to go faster when the text is easy or familiar, or you are reading to just enjoy the book.

Expression
1. Try to read three or more words together before pausing, stopping, or taking a breath.
2. Take a big breath and try to read to the comma or end punctuation without stop-ping for another breath.
3. Be sure to raise or lower your pitch when you see punctuation marks at the ends of sentences.

Figure 5.5

Tracking Graph for 1-Minute Reading Rate

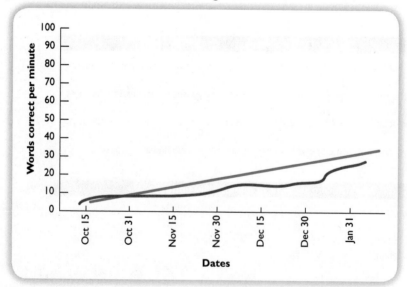

From Reutzel and Cooter, *Strategies for Reading Assessment and Instruction: Helping Every Child Succeed,*
Figure 14.6 "Rate and Accuracy Tracking Graphs," p. 424. © 2007 by Pearson Education, Inc. Reprinted by
permission of Pearson Education, Inc.

Effective Evidence-Based Teaching Strategies That Enhance Fluency

We begin our discussion of evidence-based teaching practices in reading fluency by elaborating on seven characteristics of effective evidence-based fluency instruction and practice.

Characteristics of Effective Fluency Instruction

Explicit Instruction.   Hoffman (2003) asserts that teachers should "work to develop the meta-language of fluency with . . . students, which includes concepts of expression, word stress, and phrasing" (p. 6). Students need to understand the following:

- The importance of fluency as a goal in becoming successful readers
- What fluency is
- The academic language or terms used by teachers and researchers to describe fluency, so that they too can think and talk specifically about fluency as a concept and skill with peers and teachers
- The meta-language of fluency to be able to examine and regulate their own reading fluency as an independent reader
- The importance of developing an awareness of the various elements of fluency in order to effectively monitor and fix them if necessary to improve their fluency
- How to use fluency fix-up strategies and understand the varying purposes of fluency in order to self-regulate and improve it

As classroom teachers, we must not only facilitate reading fluency practice but also cultivate a deeper appreciation among students of the importance of fluency as a personal goal of reading improvement. Equally important, we need to develop students' understanding of what we mean when we say that reading is fluent so they can make fixes when it isn't going along as it should (Rasinski, Blachowicz, & Lems, 2006; Rasinski et al., 2010; Reutzel, 2006; Worthy & Broaddus, 2002).

Model Reading Fluency.   Expose students to rich and varied models of fluent oral reading. Also occasional modeling of nonfluent oral reading seems to alert struggling and less attentive students' attention to the specific characteristics of fluent reading that are sometimes transparent or taken for granted when teachers only model fluent oral reading. In other words, some students need to know what fluency *is* and *is not* to achieve clarity on the concept of fluency and its attendant characteristics (Reutzel, 2006). When parents, teachers, or siblings spend significant amounts of time reading aloud to children while modeling fluent (and sometimes nonfluent) oral reading, children learn the behaviors of fluent readers as well as the elements of fluent oral reading. Many researchers have documented the significant impact of modeling on the acquisition of fluency in reading (Rasinski, 2003; Rasinski et al., 2006; Rasinski et al., 2010; Reutzel, 2006; Stahl, 2004).

Reading Practice.   Good readers are given more opportunities to read connected text for longer periods of time than are students having reading problems. This dilemma led Allington (1977) to ask, "If they don't read much, how are they ever

●●●
IRA Standards for Reading Professionals: Standard 2, Elements 2.1, 2.2, 2.3; Standard 5, Elements 5.1, 5.3

Response to Intervention: Instruction; Systemic and Comprehensive Approaches gonna get good?" The National Reading Panel (2000) among others has emphasized the need for children to experience regular, daily reading practice (Allington, 2002; Krashen, 2002).

Access to Appropriately Challenging Reading Materials.

Proficient readers spend more time reading appropriately challenging texts than students having reading problems (Gambrell, Wilson, & Gnatt, 1981). Reading appropriately challenging books with instruction and feedback may help proficient readers make the transition from word-by-word reading to fluent reading. Meanwhile, poorer readers often spend more time with reading materials that are relatively difficult, denying them access to texts that could help them develop fluent reading skills.

Research has yet to determine the level of frustration students can tolerate during oral practice even with immediate assistance available (Hiebert & Reutzel, 2010). Menon and Hiebert (2005) and Hiebert and Fisher (2006) found that texts for supporting early readers' fluency development need to be controlled to contain fewer unfamiliar words than is typical in many beginning reading texts as well as to maintain a balance between high-frequency words and decodable words. When children read in such texts, they made weekly gains of over 3.4 words correct per minute (Menon & Hiebert, 2005). Carefully selected texts, in a very real way, are the scaffolding teachers use to support students' reading fluency practice (Brown, 1999). Teachers need to not only increase the volume of students' reading but do so with appropriately designed and controlled texts in the early stages of fluency development (Hiebert & Fisher, 2006).

Use of Oral and Silent Reading.

The *Report of the National Reading Panel* (2000) indicated the ample scientific evidence supporting reading practice for fluency that included the following elements: (a) oral reading, (b) repeated reading of the same text, and (c) feedback and guidance during and after reading of a text. On the other hand, silent reading of self-chosen books without monitoring or feedback did not have substantial scientific evidence to support its exclusive use for reading practice across elementary grades. Recent experimental research suggests that silent, wide reading (across genre or text types) with monitoring seems to produce equivalent or better fluency gains in second- and third-grade students when compared to oral repeated readings (Hiebert & Reutzel, 2010; Kuhn & Schwanenflugel, 2006; Pikulski & Chard, 2005; Reutzel, Fawson, & Smith, 2008; Stahl, 2004). There is mounting evidence that the old practice of sustained silent reading (SSR), in which the teacher reads as a model for children, is giving way to a new model of silent reading practice that incorporates book selection instruction, student monitoring and accountability, and reading widely (Hiebert & Reutzel, 2010; Kelley & Clausen-Grace, 2006; Kelley & Clausen-Grace, 2010; Kuhn, 2005; Reutzel, Jones, Fawson, & Smith, 2008).

Monitoring and Accountability.

For many years, teachers believed that sitting and reading a book silently provided modeling sufficient to promote students' desires and abilities to read. This has never been demonstrated to be the case. In recent years, Bryan, Fawson, and Reutzel (2003) have reported that monitoring disengaged readers with quick stop-in visits to listen to oral reading and discuss a piece of literature during silent reading has a beneficial effect on their engagement during silent reading. This finding coincides with earlier findings by Manning and Manning in 1984. Furthermore, having children account for their fluency practice by reading into a computer to create a digital audio file for a teacher has a positive impact on fluency growth (Reutzel, 2006; Reutzel, Jones, et al., 2008).

Wide and Repeated Reading.   There is considerable evidence that repeated reading of the same text leads to automaticity—fast, accurate, and effortless word recognition (Dowhower, 1991; National Reading Panel, 2000; Manning, Lewis, & Lewis, 2010). However, once automaticity is achieved, reading widely seems to provide the necessary ingredient to move students' fluency from automaticity to comprehension (Kuhn, 2005; Kuhn & Woo, 2008). Thus, it is important that after achieving grade-level automaticity, a student be encouraged to read widely as well as repeatedly to develop connected text comprehension (Kuhn, 2005; Kuhn & Schwanenflugel, 2006; Pikulski & Chard, 2005; Reutzel, 2006; Stahl, 2004). From the currently available evidence (Wright et al., 2010), this occurs in second or third grade for some children whereas others may need to continue to read texts repeatedly until they achieve automaticity at grade level in the intermediate years.

An awareness of these seven characteristics of effective fluency instruction and practice can help you, the teacher, create optimal conditions for students to become fluent readers.

Evidence-Based Teaching Strategies

Fluency instruction time is wisely divided unequally between needed explicit instruction about fluency and lots of reading practice. Students need sustained and regular practice to become more fluent readers. Explicit fluency instruction enhances this process by helping students gain awareness of how to improve their own reading fluency, with or without feedback from others. As a result, we recommend that at least 70 percent of allocated fluency instruction time be spent on practice, with no more than 30 percent spent on explicit instruction of the elements of fluent reading. Different aspects of fluency should be explored in explicit instruction. The following elements of fluency need to be clearly modeled, explained, and taught:

- Inaccurate reading versus accurate reading
- Reading too fast or slow versus reading "just right"
- Reading without phrasing—two or three words or word-by-word reading—versus reading with phrasing
- Reading without expression in a monotone versus reading with appropriate pitch and stress and suitable breaks, pauses, or stops
- Reading too loud or soft versus reading with just the right volume

Having formulated a scope and sequence of fluent reading elements to be taught, teachers need to develop explicit fluency lessons around these concepts, skills, and strategies of fluent reading. To help you do this, we have created a template fluency lesson on the concept of phrasing in Figure 5.6.

We suggest 5 to 9 minutes of explicit lessons to develop understanding of fluency or the meta-language of fluency. After these brief lessons, teachers should provide roughly 15 to 20 minutes per day of effective fluency practice—either oral or silent—depending on grade level and student reading development. Fortunately, there are many effective ways to develop students' reading fluency through practice.

Repeated Readings.   Teachers should engage students in **repeated readings** of oral passages to enhance reading fluency (Dowhower, 1987; Samuels, 1979). Although it might seem that reading a text again and again leads to boredom, it can actually have just the opposite effect. Success is never boring to students.

Figure 5.6

Fluency Instruction Explicit Lesson Plan

Objective. Students will be able to read "A Very Important Day" with appropriate phrasing.

Supplies. Book copies; markers (red, yellow, green, blue); document camera; student books for choral unison reading.

Text Types. Narrative ( ) Information Books ( ) Poetry ( ) Hybrid (X)

Explain. What is to be taught: Today, boys and girls, we will be learning about phrasing when we read. Important parts of phrasing are reading to the punctuation without pausing or stopping. Marks on the page called punctuation marks (point to) help us to know when we need to pause or stop. When we come to punctuation, we need to remember to raise or lower our pitch as we read. Pitch is how high or low the sounds are that we make with our voices (demonstrate high and low pitch).

Why it is important to learn: Phrasing in reading is important because it helps you and your listeners understand and enjoy the story.

When/Where will it be used: Phrasing is always an important part of reading.

Modeling. How you think about this or do it.

Appropriate Model: First I am going to read this page with good phrasing, paying attention to what the punctuation tells me to do, such as pause or stop. Please look at the page on the board. Notice that I have colored each punctuation mark with a different color to help you see them more clearly. Red is for periods, which tell us to stop and lower our pitch. Yellow is for commas, which tell us to take a quick breath, lowering our pitch, and then we read on. Blue is for exclamation points, which tell us to stop and raise our pitch. Green is for quotation marks. Quotation marks mean someone is talking, so we change our voice to sound like someone else. Follow what I read with your eyes. Listen very carefully to see if I stop or pause with each punctuation mark.

Inappropriate Model: Next I am going to read this page with poor phrasing paying no or little attention to what the punctuation tells me to do. I won't pause or stop. Please look at the page on the board. Notice that I have colored each punctuation mark with a different color to help you see them more clearly. Follow what I read with your eyes. Listen very carefully and watch to see where I should have stopped or paused at the punctuation.

Brief Discussion. Find out what the children have observed.

Brief Whole-Group Practice. Whole group: Now that I have shown you how and how not to read this page, let's practice with echo reading. This means I read the phrase first and you echo me. We will begin reading this page all together. (Point) Watch my pen so that we can all stay together. Reminder: Phrasing when we read means to read to the punctuation without pausing or stopping.

Individual or Partner Practice. Now students, it is time to practice with your partner. On my count of three, please move your chairs next to your partner. After you are seated next to your partner, partner one will read and partner two will listen and give feedback. Once this is completed, switch roles. Partner two reads and partner one listens and gives feedback.

In the beginning, texts selected for repeated readings should be short, predictable, and easy. For expository (nonfiction) texts, you might want to use an easy summary of an upcoming unit of study. This not only helps students improve reading speed and accuracy, but also previews important new vocabulary. When students attain adequate speed and accuracy with easy selections, the length and difficulty of texts can gradually be increased.

Repeated readings expand the total number of words students can recognize instantaneously. They also help improve students' comprehension and oral elocution (performance) with each succeeding attempt. Better performance quickly leads to increased confidence in reading aloud and positive attitudes toward the act of reading. Additionally, because high-frequency words (*the, and, but, was,* etc.) occur in literally all reading situations, the increase in automatic sight word knowledge developed through repeated readings transfers far beyond the practiced texts.

Wide Oral Reading. As a counterbalance to repeated readings, **wide reading** involves students with different text types (narrative, expository, and poetic) across a range of genres (fantasy, fairy tales, myths, science fiction, historical fiction, series books, autobiographies, diaries, journals, logs, essays, encyclopedia entries, information books). To ensure that students read widely, many teachers find a reading genre wheel useful (Figure 5.7).

Children are required to read one selection from each genre represented on the wheel during a specified period of time determined by the teacher. Children usually color in each genre wheel section as they complete it. In wide oral reading, children read aloud and receive support, guidance, feedback, and monitoring from a peer, a tutor, or the teacher. Some teachers encourage children to read aloud quietly, using a PVC pipe fluency phone.

Recent research studies conducted by Stahl, Bradley, Smith, Kuhn, Schwanenflugel, Meisinger, and colleagues (2003) and Kuhn (2005) suggest wide readings of different texts may be as effective as repeated readings of the same text for second grade readers, if not more so. Stahl and colleagues (2003) found that a wide-reading group significantly outperformed a repeated-reading group. In a separate study of small-group fluency instruction focused on struggling second-grade readers, Kuhn (2005) found that wide oral reading of different titles and genres resulted in equivalent gains in fluency when compared with repeated oral reading on several measures, including number of words read in isolation, correct words per minute in context, and expressive reading measures. In addition, the wide oral reading group performed better on answering both implicit and explicit textual questions to assess comprehension than did the oral repeated reading group.

Figure 5.7
Reading Genre Wheel

From Reutzel, D. R., & Fawson, P. C., *Your Classroom Library: Ways to Give It More Teaching Power.* Reprinted by permission of Scholastic, Inc.

Ray Reutzel

Fluency Oriented Reading Instruction (FORI). Based on repeated reading research, fluency oriented reading instruction (FORI) is an integrated lesson framework for providing differentiated instruction and practice in fluency (Kuhn & Schwanenflugel, 2006; Stahl, 2004; Stahl, Heubach, & Cramond, 1997). FORI consists of

Click on A+RISE—
Literacy Strategies in the
MyEducationLab (www.
myeducationlab.com) for
your course. Next, select
the Strategy Card Index
tab, scroll to Fluency, and
select the Fluency
Oriented Oral
Reading (FOOR)
strategy.

three interlocking instructional steps: (1) a redesigned basal or core reading program lesson, (2) a free reading period at school, and (3) a home reading program. Research on the effects of FORI has shown children receiving FORI instruction significantly outperforming a control group (Stahl et al., 2003). Teachers need the following components to provide a FORI lesson:

- A core reading or basal reading program text
- An adequately appointed classroom library for free reading at school and home, with extension activities drawn from the core or basal reading program text
- A teacher-prepared graphic organizer of the text in the core or basal program
- A teacher-prepared audio recording for assisted reading practice

On the first day of a FORI reading lesson, the teacher begins by reading the core reading program story or text aloud to the class. Following the reading, the students and teacher interactively discuss the text, placing reading comprehension upfront as a primary goal in reading any text. Following this discussion, the teacher explains important vocabulary words and uses graphic organizers and other comprehension activities focused around the story or text.

On the second day of a FORI reading lesson, teachers can choose to have students either echo read the core reading program text with the teacher or read only a part of the story repeatedly for practice with a partner or the teacher. Following this practice session on the second day, the core reading program story is sent home for the child to read with parents, older siblings, or other caregivers.

On the third and fourth days of a FORI lesson, children continue to practice while also participating in vocabulary and comprehension exercises based on the core reading text. On these two days, children also receive decoding instruction on difficult words in the core reading story or text.

On the fifth and final day of the FORI lesson, children are asked to generate a written response to the story to cement their comprehension of the text. In addition to the core program fluency instruction found in the FORI framework, teachers provide additional in-school free reading practice with instructional-level books that are read alone or with a partner for approximately 15 minutes a day at the beginning of the year, progressing to about 30 minutes by the end of the year. As a part of their homework in the FORI framework, children are also expected to read at home 15 minutes a day at least 4 days per week. This outside reading is monitored through the use of weekly reading logs turned in to the teacher (Stahl, 2004).

Choral Reading.   There are several formats for choral readings of text. Wood (1983) recommends both **unison reading,** in which everyone reads together, and **echo reading** (sometimes called *echoic reading*), in which the teacher or a student reads a passage aloud and then everyone else "echoes" by repeating it. Another method we have found useful is **antiphonal reading,** a type of choral reading derived from ancient monastic traditions, in which two groups take turns reading passages aloud (usually a sentence or two). Finally, we suggest a fourth option called **reading in rounds,** which, like singing in rounds, involves groups reading simultaneously but not in unison, starting at different times on a staggered schedule.

Partner or Paired Reading.   Putting students together in **partner reading** (also called *paired* or *buddy reading*) allows students who may be struggling to read aloud with more fluent partners. The partner models fluent reading in place of the teacher, providing useful feedback and helping with word recognition.

Click on A+RISE—WIDA
ELP Standard Strategies
in the MyEducationLab
(www.myeducationlab.com)
for your course. Next,
select the Strategy Card
Index tab, scroll to
Fluency for grades
K–5, and select
the Echo strategy.

Usually partners take turns reading aloud an assigned passage to one another, with the more developed reader going first, thus providing the model for fluent reading. The second reader then attempts the passage based on the partner's modeling. The more fluent reader offers feedback on how to achieve greater fluency, and the less fluent reader rereads the passage until he or she can do so independently. Readers of about the same ability are sometimes paired for this exercise, with the teacher providing the initial modeled reading and the two "buddies" then taking turns reading to each other and offering feedback until each can read the passage fluently.

Scaffolded Silent Reading (ScSR).   Reutzel, Jones, and Newman (2010) describe how **scaffolded silent reading (ScSR)** works. Students are encouraged to read widely from across a variety of genres using a reading genre wheel as in Figure 5.7. Students are asked to read one self-selected book from each slice of the reading genre wheel before returning to a previous genre. This approach ensures that students are reading widely. Students self-select an independent-level book of interest to them from a collection of leveled books displayed by genre in the classroom library. For example, students wanting to read a fairy tale will select a book from the fairy tale section of the classroom library that is at their level based on the colored dot on the back of the book indicating the text's reading level.

Children can be assisted in making appropriate selections using a strategy known as "Rule-of-Thumb" (ROT). Many teachers like to use a chart (see Figure 5.8) to show the steps in ROT.

The goal is for students to read a total of 15 to 20 minutes per day in their self-selected books chosen from various genres. As children read, the teacher circulates among them, randomly stopping and asking students to read aloud the book they have chosen. The teacher may ask the student some questions to measure comprehension or talk with the student about her or his goal for reading in the next few days. The teacher also discusses how students can share their reading with others, including posters, oral or written book reports, read-aloud performances of favorite passages, or other forms of expression. Teachers often give prompts like the following as part of their scaffolding:

- "I'd like you to draw me a picture of your favorite character when you finish reading this story."
- "Complete a story map poster showing setting, characters, problem, goals, events, and resolution."
- "I will want you to act out one of the characters when you finish and I'll see if I can guess which one it is!"

Click on A+RISE—WIDA ELP Standard Strategies in the MyEducationLab (www.myeducationlab.com) for your course. Next, select the Strategy Card Index tab, scroll to Fluency for grade K–5, and select the Echo Reading strategy.

Figure 5.8

Rule-of-Thumb Strategy for Choosing "Just Right" Books

1. Choose a book that looks interesting.
2. Open the book to any page that has lots of words on it.
3. Begin reading aloud or silently. When you come to a word you do not know, hold up your small finger.
4. If you come to another word you do not know, hold up your next finger. If you use up all of your fingers on one hand (and come to your thumb) on one page, then the book is too hard and you should put it back. Find another book you like just as well and repeat the ROT exercise to make sure it is just right for you.

As they finish reading their books, students color in the appropriate genres on their reading genre wheels, which lets the teacher know they are ready to share their responses.

Differentiating Reading Fluency Instruction for Diverse Learners

●●●

IRA Standards for Reading Professionals: Standard 4, Elements 4.1, 4.2

Response to Intervention: Responsive Teaching and Differentiation

Reading fluency has been used as a routine indicator for identifying struggling readers in classrooms over the past decade. Students who read inaccurately and too slowly according to established rate norms are classified as requiring additional interventions to increase their reading fluency. Although it can be used as an indicator light of reading problems, reading fluency does not indicate the origins of the problem. For teachers to design responsive interventions for fluency problems, they must learn how to quickly diagnose the origins of the difficulties. This can be accomplished by using what we call a "drill down" model of assessment (Figure 5.9) to inform the design and measurement of reading interventions intended to increase fluency.

An examination of the drill down model of reading fluency diagnosis in Figure 5.9 shows that fluency problems can be traced to one of two sources: word recognition or vocabulary/comprehension issues. Students who read inaccurately and slowly typically have problems with word recognition. On the other hand, students who read accurately but slowly are trying to comprehend what they read and may be hav-

Figure 5.9

Drill Down Model of Reading Fluency Diagnosis

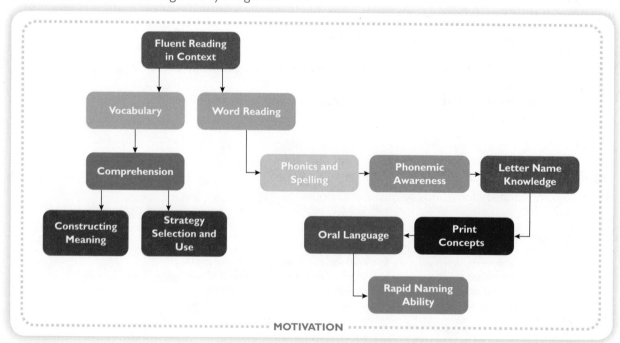

ing some difficulties doing so. Students who are reading accurately and slowly and understand what they are reading need assistance in taking control of their reading speed and increasing it in order to more efficiently process texts.

Struggling Readers

For those students who are struggling with reading fluency due to word recognition problems, there are typically two places where a classroom teacher can look. First, struggling students may not know core high-frequency sight words. Second, they may have gaps in their phonics knowledge that prevent them from efficiently applying blending strategies to decode one-syllable and multisyllabic words. Students who do not know the core sight words need extended practice with high-frequency words using a sight word memorization strategy. Students who struggle with decoding words accurately and quickly need to have their phonics knowledge assessed to locate their gaps in understanding. These students need to be taught the missing phonics elements and shown how to use this knowledge in a blending strategy for unlocking word pronunciations. It is also entirely possible that some students may be lacking both sight word and phonics knowledge and need instructional interventions for both.

Students who read accurately but slowly may be having troubles with vocabulary and comprehension. This can be determined by observing the students' reading errors and noting whether problems occur around words with rare or unfamiliar meanings rather than from pronunciation issues. Interventions for these students will need to focus on learning unfamiliar vocabulary terms or employing a range of comprehension strategies that will be addressed in later chapters of this text.

For students who read accurately but slowly and demonstrate comprehension of the text through answering teacher questions or providing fairly complete retellings of the content of a text, interventions need to focus on increasing their reading speed by setting goals to increase their measured reading rate gradually over time until they meet grade-level speed norms. A graph like Figure 5.5 can be used for this purpose.

One well-researched method of working with struggling readers who need to increase reading speed is called the **neurological impress method (NIM),** which involves a struggling student and a slightly more fluent student reader or a trained reading tutor in reading the same text aloud simultaneously (Heckelman, 1966, 1969). By employing unison reading, unlike the partner reading examples described earlier, NIM fosters gradual improvement in which, with time and practice, the model's voice gradually fades as the struggling student becomes more confident and reads louder than the model.

The use of multiple sensory systems during NIM is thought to "impress" on the struggling student the fluent reading patterns of the more capable model through direct example. It is assumed that exposing students to numerous examples of texts (read in a more sophisticated way than struggling readers could achieve on their own) will enable them to achieve automaticity in word recognition more naturally. This assumption stands to reason when viewed in light of advances in learning theory, especially those espoused by Vygotsky (1978).

Each NIM session is aimed at reading as much material as possible in 10 minutes. Reading material selected for the first few sessions should be easy, predictable text that makes sense for the reader. However, other more challenging materials that are on the student's normal guided reading level can eventually be added.

To use NIM, the student sits slightly in front and to one side of his or her partner as they hold the text. The more fluent reader moves her finger beneath the words as both partners read in near-unison fashion. Both try to maintain a comfortably brisk and continuous rate of oral reading. The more fluent reader's role is to keep the pace when the less proficient student starts to slow down. Pausing for analyzing unknown words is not permitted. The more fluent reader's voice is directed at her partner's ear so that words are seen, heard, and spoken simultaneously.

Because many struggling readers have not read at an accelerated pace before, their first efforts often sound like mumbling. Most less fluent readers typically take some time to adjust to NIM; however, within a few sessions they start to feel more at ease. Many struggling readers say they enjoy NIM because it allows them to read more challenging and interesting material like "good" readers.

At first, the more fluent reader's voice will dominate oral reading, but in later sessions it should be reduced gradually. This will allow the less fluent student to assume the vocal lead naturally. Usually three sessions per week are sufficient to obtain noticeable results. This routine should be followed for a minimum of 10 consecutive weeks (Henk, 1983).

NIM can also be adapted for group use (Hollingsworth, 1970, 1978). Here the teacher records 10 minutes of his or her own oral reading in advance. Individual students can read along with the audio while following the text independently, or the audio can be used in a listening center to permit the teacher to spend individual time with each student as others read along. Despite the convenience of the prerecorded format, teachers' and more fluent peers' one-to-one interactions with individual students result in a better instructional experience.

English Learners

Recent research has shown that ELs gain in reading fluency at roughly the same rate as first language learners and are benefited by similar instructional strategies as those we have discussed for helping typical, normally developing readers achieve greater reading fluency (August & Shanahan, 2006; Fitzgerald, Amendum, & Guthrie, 2008). Teachers who work with ELs need to determine whether they have any phonological or phonemic awareness gaps that would cause them to lag behind in word reading processes. If not, research indicates that they will make progress similar to native English speakers in reading fluency.

Modeling oral reading to ELs may be especially helpful if their parents do not yet read English. Assigning a capable reading buddy in the classroom may help alleviate this problem. It is important to read aloud to ELs, regardless of reading level, so that they can hear the rhythm of the English language as their brains actively process the new language. Grouping for ELs must be modified during the year, too. Groups with same-language speakers who are more fluent readers are helpful, as are groups where English-speaking peers model read-alouds.

Motivation and Engagement

Motivation and Engagement Strategies That Promote Fluency

● ● ●
IRA Standards for Reading Professionals: Standard 5, Element 5.2

Students will practice diligently and persevere if they know that their reading will be performed for an authentic audience. Performance reading has an additional benefit because students read aloud so that the teacher can monitor fluency growth and sustained reading engagement. Students prepare for a performance, regardless of format, by orally practicing the text to be performed until they can read it with maximum fluency. There are several ways this can be done that have found support in evidence-based research. Before we get to those, we will examine a very well-known approach that you should *not* use—round-robin reading.

Long ago, teachers commonly relied on round-robin reading as a means for listening to students read orally. Students would sit in a circle, and the teacher would call on a student to begin reading orally from a story in the basal reader while the other students would follow along. After the first student read a paragraph or two, the teacher would stop him or her and call on the next student to continue reading. This process was repeated until every child in the circle had a chance to read aloud.

Though the simplicity of round-robin is very appealing, research has revealed it to be far less effective than other available strategies for monitoring fluency development. The process can even have a negative impact on some children (Eldredge, Reutzel, & Hollingsworth, 1996). Round-robin reading fails to give children adequate opportunities for repeated readings before performing, defeats comprehension (i.e., when a student realizes the paragraph he'll be asked to read is three ahead of the current student in the "hot seat," he'll tend to look ahead and start silently reading his passage feverishly, hoping he won't "mess up" when it's his turn), and causes some students embarrassment if they are unable to read their paragraphs fluently. Our advice? Do not use round-robin in your classroom; there are better alternatives that will help you monitor fluency development, improve comprehension, and protect fragile egos in the process. Following are several activities that can be used for performance reading found to be effective in classrooms.

Perhaps the most successful performance reading strategy, in terms of the research (Griffith & Rasinski, 2004; National Reading Panel, 2000; Sloyer, 1982) is **readers' theatre,** which involves rehearsing and performing before an audience from a script that is rich with dialogue. The script itself may be taken from a book or, in the upper elementary or middle school grades, could be developed by a group of students working in collaboration as part of a literature response activity (Cooter & Griffith, 1989).

Stayter and Allington (1991) tell about a readers' theatre activity for which a group of heterogeneously grouped seventh-graders spent 5 days reading, rehearsing, and performing short dramas. After a first reading, students began to negotiate about which role they would read. More hesitant students were permitted to opt for smaller parts, but everyone was required to participate. As time passed, students critiqued each other's readings and made suggestions as to how they should sound (e.g., "You should sound like a snob"). The most common response in this experience was how repeated readings through drama helped them better understand the text. One student said, "The first time I read to know what the words are. Then I read to know what the words *say* and later as I read I thought about how to say the words. . . . As I got to know the character better, I put more feeling in my voice" (Stayter & Allington, 1991, p. 145).

Texts selected for readers' theatre are often drawn from oral traditions, poetry, or quality picture books designed to be read aloud by children. However, nonfiction passages can also be adapted for presentation. Selections should, whenever possible, be packed with action, have an element of suspense, and comprise an entire, meaningful story or nonfiction text. Also, texts selected for use in readers' theatre should contain sufficient dialogue to make reading and preparing the text a challenge as well as necessitate the involvement of several children as characters. Narrative texts

A+RISE

Click on A+RISE—Literacy Strategies in the MyEducationLab (www. myeducationlab.com) for your course. Next, select the Strategy Card Index tab, scroll to Fluency, and select the Readers' Theater strategy.

we have seen used in readers' theatre include Martin and Archambault's *Knots on a Counting Rope* (1987), Viorst's *Alexander and the Terrible, Horrible, No Good, Very Bad Day* (1987), and Barbara Robinson's *The Best Christmas Pageant Ever* (1988). Many readers' theatre scripts are available for free online at www.teachingheart.net/readerstheater.htm.

If a story is selected for reading, students should be assigned to read characters' parts. If poems are selected, students may read alternating lines or groups of lines. Readers' theatre in-the-round, in which readers stand around the perimeter of the room surrounding their audience, is a fun and interesting variation for both performers and audience.

Students will often benefit from a discussion prior to attempting a readers' theatre script for the first time. This discussion helps students make connections between their background experiences and the text to be read. Also, struggling readers usually profit from listening to a previously recorded performance of the text as a model prior to their initial reading of the script.

Hennings (1974) describes a simplified procedure for preparing readers' theatre scripts for classroom performance.

1. The text to be performed is read silently by individual students.
2. The text is read again orally, sometimes using choral reading in a group. After the second reading, readers either choose their parts, or the teacher assigns parts to them. We suggest that students be allowed to select their three most desired parts, write these choices on slips of paper, and submit them to the teacher. Teachers should do everything possible to assign one of these three choices.
3. After parts are assigned, the third reading is an oral reading from scripts. There may be several rehearsal readings as students prepare for the final reading or performance in front of the class or other audience.

Readers' theatre offers students a unique opportunity to participate in reading along with other, perhaps more skilled readers. Participating in the mainstream classroom with better readers helps students having reading problems feel a part of their peer group while providing them with ready models of good reading and demonstrating how good readers, through practice, become even better readers. Working together with other readers fosters a sense of teamwork, support, and pride in personal and group accomplishment.

Radio reading possesses all of the effective elements of practice in developing fluency we have just discussed. Radio reading (Greene, 1979; Optiz & Rasinski, 2008; Rasinski, 2003; Searfoss, 1975) is a variation on repeated reading and readers' theatre. We have found radio reading to be most effective with short selections from information texts threaded together into a single news broadcast performance script. In radio reading, each student is given a script to read aloud. Selections can be drawn from any print media, such as newspapers, magazines, or any print source that can be converted into a news story, such as short selections from articles or sections in information books. One student acts as the news anchor, while other students act in the roles of various reporters presenting the weather, sports, breaking news, and so on. Only the radio readers and the teacher have copies of the scripts. Because other students have no script to follow, minor word recognition errors will go unnoticed if the text is well presented. Struggling students enjoy radio reading from *Know Your World*. This publication is well suited for use in radio reading activities because the content and level of difficulty make it possible for older readers with fluency problems to read with ease and enjoyment. Short selections from information books on weather, volcanoes, spiders, sports figures, or any other topic can be presented as short reports by various reporters during the news broadcast. An example of a radio reading script on mummies in Egypt is found in Figure 5.10.

A script for the anchor may need to be written by students with help from the teacher to thread the various news reports together in a cohesive fashion. Once students have the radio reading script prepared for rehearsal, they gather materials for sound effects (police whistles, doors opening or shutting, people screaming, and so on).

Figure 5.10

Mummies Made in Egypt by Aliki

Radio reading script by
Dr. John A. Smith
Department of Elementary Education
Utah State University

Performers: Radio Newsperson 1 and Radio Newsperson 2

Radio Newsperson 1	We are here to report some very important information about mummies.
Radio Newsperson 2	We have learned that ancient Egyptians believed that a person would start a new life after he died. They believed that the person's soul would travel back and forth to a new world.
Radio Newsperson 1	They believed that the person's soul needed his body to come back to. That is why Egyptians preserved dead bodies as mummies.
Radio Newsperson 2	A mummy is a dead body, or corpse, that has been dried out so it will not decay. The earliest mummies were dried out naturally in the hot, dry sands of Egypt's deserts.
Radio Newsperson 1	Later, the Egyptians wrapped the mummies in cloth and buried them in wooden coffins or put them in tombs made of brick and stone.
Radio Newsperson 2	It took 70 days to prepare a mummy. First they took out the dead person's inner organs. They cut a hole in the mummy's side to remove the intestines. They pulled the dead person's brains out through the nose with metal hooks.
Radio Newsperson 1	The inner organs were kept in jars with a chemical called *natron* that dried out the body parts. After the inner organs were removed, embalmers also put natron inside the body to dry it out.
Radio Newsperson 2	After 40 days, the natron was removed from the body, and the body was cleaned with oils and spices.
Radio Newsperson 1	The body was packed with new chemicals to keep it dry. The mummy's eyes were closed, and the nose was stuffed with wax.
Radio Newsperson 2	The hole in the mummy's side was sewn up and the mummy was carefully wrapped with long strips of cloth.
Radio Newsperson 1	After the embalmers finished wrapping the mummy, they painted it to look like the person and then covered it with resin, a sticky substance that dried into a hard covering.
Radio Newsperson 2	When the mummy was finished, they made a coffin to put the mummy in for burial. The coffin was decorated with pictures of gods and magic spells to protect it. Jewels and other treasures were also put into the coffin.
Radio Newsperson 1	Finally, the mummy and its coffin were placed in a tomb made of brick and stone. The Egyptian pyramids are large tombs that are burial places for powerful Egyptian rulers.
Radio Newsperson 2	There would be an elaborate funeral parade. The mummy would be placed in the tomb, sometimes in a secret chamber. Then the tomb would be sealed shut for the mummy's eternal resting place.
Radio Newsperson 1	Thank you very much, and now back to our teacher.

Before performing a radio reading for an audience, students should rehearse their parts with a partner or the teacher until they gain confidence and can read the script with proper volume, accuracy, rate, phrasing, and expression. Emphasis is first placed on the meaning of the text segments so that the students can paraphrase any difficult portions of the text if needed during the presentation. Students are encouraged to keep ideas flowing in the same way a reporter or anchor does. After thorough rehearsal of the script with sound effects, the radio play is recorded on audio and played over the school's public address system into other classrooms.

Students who participate in reading performances found readers' theatre and other similar performance opportunities to be an engaging and motivating way to practice reading to fluent levels (Rasinski et al., 2010). From these results, one can reasonably conclude that engaging students in various forms of reading practice that culminate in reader performance of texts for an authentic audience is a significantly motivating approach for developing students' reading fluency.

IRA Standards for Reading Professionals: Standard 2, Element 2.3; Standard 5, Element 5.1

Common Core Standards: Reading: K–5, Integration of Knowledge and Ideas (item 7); Writing: K–12, Production and Distribution of Writing (item 6)

Technology and New Literacies

Using Technology and New Literacies to Promote Reading Fluency

© Ellen Senisi/The Image Works

In technology-assisted reading fluency practice, children read a book with the assistance of a fluently read model on a CD or computer-recorded audio file such as an MP3 file. Technology-assisted reading for fluency development is a solution to the problem teachers experience in arranging engaging and self-directed one-to-one fluency practice activities for students.

During a first reading using an audio file, children follow along in their own copy of the text, typically displayed on a computer screen. They are instructed to point to each word as the fluent model reads it aloud. Younger children who are practicing reading fluency with short books read aloud with the audio file model at least three but up to five times or until they can read the text fluently. Students who are reading longer texts listen to the entire piece once and then select a passage (usually 150–300 words) for repeated practice. Once they have read the passage repeatedly (three to five times), they read the passage to the teacher.

Teacher management of technology-assisted fluency centers is of great importance. For some students, listening to a CD or audio file presents an opportunity to engage in off-task behaviors—looking like readers but not engaging (Stahl, 2004). In other cases, however, computer-assisted reading practice has been found to be effective in improving reading fluency across a range of grade levels (National Reading Panel, 2000).

WEB TOOLS YOU CAN USE IN THE CLASSROOM

Improving Reading Fluency

Generally speaking, most of these computer programs use speech recognition software and immediate feedback as students read text aloud as it is presented on the computer screen. In recent years, a number of computer-based programs have been developed to provide students with repeated reading practice to develop reading fluency as measured by speed and accuracy.

- Read Naturally (www.readnaturally.com) engages students in repeated readings of paper or computer presented texts until a preset criterion is reached and then students are advanced to more difficult text levels to increase their rate and accuracy to eventually reach grade level performance norms.

- Charlesbridge Reading Fluency (www.charlesbridge.com/school/html/fluency.html) involves students in repeated readings using speech recognition software to assist students as they practice reading computer presented texts. Students' oral readings are recorded as audio files and are accessible for later analysis by the teacher.

Family and Community Connections

How Family and Community Connections Can Help Students Improve Reading Fluency

One effective way to connect reading fluency practice from the school to the home is by encouraging parents to use closed-caption television (Koskinen, Wilson, & Jensema, 1985; Neuman & Koskinen, 1992). Closed-caption TV has been found to be a particularly effective tool for motivating students who are learning English as a second language to improve reading fluency. Closed-caption television, which uses written subtitles, provides students with meaningful and motivating reading material. Parents should carefully select high-interest television programs. They may even want to record and preview programs before making final selections for captioned TV practice at home (Koskinen et al., 1985).

One advantage of captioned TV fluency practice is that it does not require busy parents to sit and read daily with their children at home. However, parents who want to increase their involvement in this practice have several options. For example, parents and children can record and watch a part of the captioned TV program together. Then parents can stop the program and ask the child to predict what will happen next. They continue viewing the program so that the child can check his or her predictions. Or after watching a closed-caption TV program, children can practice reading aloud along with the captions to parents. If necessary, both the auditory portion and the closed captioning can be played simultaneously to provide children with support. At some later point, children should be allowed to practice reading the captioning without the auditory portion of the program. Koskinen and her colleagues (1985) do "not recommend that the sound be turned off if this, in effect, turns off the children. The major advantage for using captioned television as fluency

IRA Standards for Reading Professionals: Standard 4, Elements 4.1, 4.2, 4.3

Response to Intervention: Collaboration

practice is the multisensory stimulation of viewing the drama, hearing the sound, and seeing the captions" (p. 6). Reading TV in English at home also helps parents of ELs who may not yet be fluent in English.

Summary

Fluency is the ability to read a text accurately with appropriate intonation and phrasing at an age-appropriate speed. Fluency instruction, because it helps readers achieve automatic decoding, provides the opportunity for readers to turn more of their mental energies toward comprehending the message of text.

Reading fluency can be developed through explicit teacher-led instruction, teacher modeling of fluency concepts, and student participation in a variety of effective ways to practice reading fluency such as guided oral repeated reading, wide oral and silent reading, choral reading, scaffolded silent reading, performance reading, and so on.

Fluency is further strengthened by engaging children in generous amounts of daily reading practice. Struggling readers and, in fact, all others benefit most from reading that provides feedback and monitoring in appropriately challenging texts. Monitoring and assessing children's development of oral reading fluency is important in effecting needed improvements. Careful tracking of students' oral reading progress should result from goal setting, which in turn can lead to incremental improvements in students' oral and silent reading fluency.

Field and Classroom Applications

- Develop a letter or brochure that could be sent home to parents giving information about using TV captioning and the research benefits for doing so.
- Give a child between ages 6 and 12 a grade-level book to read for 1 minute. Calculate the number of errors and the words correct per minute (wcpm). Then using the oral reading rates norms, describe whether this student's reading rate with accuracy is at, above, or below grade-level and time-of-year norms.
- Using the lesson plan in Figure 5.6 as a model, develop a lesson plan for teaching another element or aspect of reading fluency to a classroom of children.

- Go online to any search engine and type in "readers' theatre script" as a search term. Make a collection of free readers' theatre scripts available online for your future or current teaching file.
- Go online to one to the URLs listed at the end of this chapter. Order a trial or sample copy of Read Naturally or Insight's Reading Fluency software on a CD. Prepare a brief report for your university class on the strengths and weaknesses of one of these nationally available software programs designed to support classroom reading fluency acquisition.

Recommended Resources

Print Resources

Opitz, M. F., & Rasinski, T. V. (2008). *Good-bye round robin: 25 effective oral reading strategies* (2nd ed.). Portsmouth, NH: Heinemann.

Osborn, J., Lehr, F., & Hiebert, E. H. (2003). *Focus on fluency*. Honolulu, HI: Pacific Resources for Education and Learning. Available at www.prel.org.

Rasinski, T. V. (2003). *The fluent reader: Oral reading strategies for building word recognition, fluency, and comprehension*. New York: Scholastic.

Rasinski, T. V. (2009). *Essential readings on fluency*. Newark, DE: International Reading Association.

Rasinski, T. V., Blachowicz, C., & Lems, K. (2006). *Fluency instruction: Research-based best practices*. New York: Guilford Press.

Stahl, S. (2004). What do we know about fluency? In P. McCardle & V. Chhabra (Eds.), *The voice of evidence in reading research* (pp. 187–211). Baltimore: Paul H. Brookes.

Children's Literature

Archambault, J. (1987). *Knots on a counting rope.* New York: Holt.

Robinson, B. (1988). *The best Christmas pageant ever.* New York: Harper Collins.

Viorst, J. (1989). *Alexander and the terrible, horrible, no good, very bad day.* New York: Scholastic.

Web Resources

http://dibels.uoregon.edu
DIBELS

www.teachingheart.net/readerstheater.htm
Readers' Theater Scripts

www.readnaturally.com
Computer Based Programs: Read Naturally

www.charlesbridge.com/school/pdf/fluency
Computer Based Programs: Charlesbridge Reading Fluency Program

---

PEARSON
myeducationlab™
The Power of Classroom Practice
www.myeducationlab.com

Go to Topic 4, Fluency, in the MyEducationLab (www.myeducationlab.com) for your course, where you can:

- Find learning outcomes for Fluency along with the national standards that connect to these outcomes.
- Complete Assignments and Activities that can help you more deeply understand the chapter content.
- Apply and practice your understanding of the core teaching skills identified in the chapter with the Building Teaching Skills and Dispositions learning units. (optional)
- Examine challenging situations and cases presented in the IRIS Center Resources. (optional)
- Access video clips of CCSSO National Teachers of the Year award winners responding to the question "Why Do I Teach?" in the Teacher Talk section. (optional)
- Check your comprehension on the content covered in the chapter by going to the Study Plan in the Book Resources for your text. Here you will be able to take a chapter quiz, receive feedback on your answers, and then access Review, Practice, and Enrichment activities to enhance your understanding of chapter content. (optional)

Go to the Topic A+RISE in the MyEducationLab (www.myeducationlab.com) for your course. A+RISE® Standards2Strategy™ is an innovative and interactive online resource that offers new teachers in grades K–12 just in time, research-based instructional strategies that:

- Meet the linguistic needs of ELLs as they learn content.
- Differentiate instruction for all grades and abilities.
- Offer reading and writing techniques, cooperative learning, use of linguistic and nonlinguistic representations, scaffolding, teacher modeling, higher order thinking, and alternative classroom ELL assessment.
- Provide support to help teachers be effective through the integration of listening, speaking, reading, and writing along with the content curriculum.
- Improve student achievement.
- Are aligned to Common Core Elementary Language Arts standards (for the literacy strategies) and to English language proficiency standards in WIDA, Texas, California, and Florida.

STANDARDS
for Reading Professionals and Guiding Principles for Educators

IRA Standards for Reading Professionals

Standard 1: Foundational Knowledge

Candidates understand the theoretical and evidence-based foundations of reading and writing processes and instruction.

Element 1.1

Candidates understand major theories and empirical research that describe the cognitive, linguistic, motivational, and sociocultural foundations of reading and writing development, processes, and components, including word recognition, language comprehension, strategic knowledge, and reading–writing connections.

Element 1.2

Candidates understand the historically shared knowledge of the profession and changes over time in the perceptions of reading and writing development, processes, and components.

Element 1.3

Candidates understand the role of professional judgment and practical knowledge for improving all students' reading development and achievement.

Candidates use instructional approaches, materials, and an integrated, comprehensive, balanced curriculum to support student learning in reading and writing.

Response to Intervention

6. Expertise

All students have the right to receive instruction from well-prepared teachers who keep up to date and supplemental instruction from professionals specifically prepared to teach language and literacy (IRA, 2000).

- Teacher expertise is central to instructional improvement, particularly for students who encounter difficulty in acquiring language and literacy. RTI may involve a range of professionals; however, the greater the literacy difficulty, the greater the need for expertise in literacy teaching and learning.
- Important dimensions of teachers' expertise include their knowledge and understanding of language and literacy development, their ability to use powerful assessment tools and techniques, and their ability to translate information about student performance into instructionally relevant instructional techniques.
- The exemplary core instruction that is so essential to the success of RTI is dependent on highly knowledgeable and skilled classroom teachers (IRA, 2003).

- Professionals who provide supplemental instruction or intervention must have a high level of expertise in all aspects of language and literacy instruction and assessment and be capable of intensifying or accelerating language and literacy learning.
- Success for culturally and linguistically diverse students depends on teachers and support personnel who are well prepared to teach in a variety of settings. Deep knowledge of cultural and linguistic differences is especially critical for the prevention of language and literacy problems in diverse student populations.
- Expertise in the areas of language and literacy requires a comprehensive approach to professional preparation that involves preservice, induction, and inservice education. It also requires opportunities for extended practice under the guidance of knowledgeable and experienced mentors.

IRA Standards for Reading Professionals

Standard 3: Assessment and Evaluation

Candidates use a variety of assessment tools and practices to plan and evaluate effective reading and writing instruction.

Element 3.1

Candidates understand types of assessments and their purposes, strengths, and limitations.

Element 3.2

Candidates select, develop, administer, and interpret assessments, both traditional print and electronic, for specific purposes.

Element 3.3

Candidates use assessment information to plan and evaluate instruction.

Response to Intervention

3. Assessment

An RTI approach demands assessment that can inform language and literacy instruction meaningfully.

- Assessment should reflect the multidimensional nature of language and literacy learning and the diversity among students being assessed. The utility of an assessment is dependent on the extent to which it provides valid information on the essential aspects of language and literacy that can be used to plan appropriate instruction.
- Assessments, tools, and techniques should provide useful and timely information about desired language and literacy goals. They should reflect authentic language and literacy activities as opposed to contrived texts or tasks generated specifically for assessment purposes. The quality of assessment information should not be sacrificed for the efficiency of an assessment procedure.
- Multiple purposes for assessment should be clearly identified and appropriate tools and techniques employed. Not all available tools and techniques are appropriate for all purposes, and different assessments—even in the same language or literacy

domain—capture different skills and knowledge. Particular care should be taken in selecting assessments for ELLs and for students who speak an English dialect that differs from mainstream dialects.

- Efficient assessment systems involve a layered approach in which screening techniques are used both to identify which students require further (diagnostic) assessment and to provide aggregate data about the nature of student achievement overall. Initial (screening) assessments should not be used as the sole mechanism for determining the appropriateness of targeted interventions. Ongoing progress monitoring must include an evaluation of the instruction itself and requires observation of the student in the classroom.
- Classroom teachers and reading/literacy specialists should play a central role in conducting language and literacy assessments and in using assessment results to plan instruction and monitor student performance.
- Assessment as a component of RTI should be consistent with the *Standards for the Assessment of Reading and Writing* developed jointly by the International Reading Association and the National Council of Teachers of English (2010).

Effective Evidence-Based Teaching Strategies That Enhance Fluency

IRA Standards for Reading Professionals

Standard 2: Curriculum and Instruction

Candidates use instructional approaches, materials, and an integrated, comprehensive, balanced curriculum to support student learning in reading and writing.

Element 2.1

Candidates use foundational knowledge to design or implement an integrated, comprehensive, and balanced curriculum.

Element 2.2

Candidates use appropriate and varied instructional approaches, including those that develop word recognition, language comprehension, strategic knowledge, and reading–writing connections.

Element 2.3

Candidates use a wide range of texts (e.g., narrative, expository, and poetry) from traditional print, digital, and online resources.

Standard 5: Literate Environment

Candidates create a literate environment that fosters reading and writing by integrating foundational knowledge, instructional practices, approaches and methods, curriculum materials, and the appropriate use of assessments.

Element 5.1

Candidates design the physical environment to optimize students' use of traditional print, digital, and online resources in reading and writing instruction.

Element 5.3

Candidates use routines to support reading and writing instruction (e.g., time allocation, transitions from one activity to another, discussions, and peer feedback).

Response to Intervention

1. Instruction

- A successful RTI process begins with the highest quality core instruction in the classroom—that is, instruction that encompasses all areas of language and literacy as part of a coherent curriculum that is developmentally appropriate for preK–12 students and does not underestimate their potential for learning. This core instruction may or may not involve commercial programs, and it must in all cases be provided by an informed, competent classroom teacher.

- The success of RTI depends on the classroom teacher's use of research-based practices. As defined by IRA (2002), *research based* means "that a particular program or collection of instructional practices has a record of success. That is, there is reliable, trustworthy, and valid evidence to suggest that when the program is used with a particular group of children, the children can be expected to make adequate gains in reading achievement."
- Research evidence frequently represents the effectiveness of an instructional practice on average, which suggests that

some students benefited and others did not. This means that instruction must be provided by a teacher who understands the intent of the research-based practice being used and has the professional expertise and responsibility to plan instruction and adapt programs and materials as needed (see also principle 6, Expertise).

- When core language and literacy instruction is not effective for a particular student, it should be modified to address more closely the needs and abilities of that student. Classroom teachers, at times in collaboration with other experts, must exercise their best professional judgment in providing responsive teaching and differentiation (see also principle 2).

5. Systemic and Comprehensive Approaches

RTI must be part of a comprehensive, systemic approach to language and literacy assessment and instruction that supports all preK–12 students and teachers.

- RTI needs to be integrated within the context of a coherent and consistent language and literacy curriculum that guides comprehensive instruction for all students. Core instruction—indeed, all instruction—must be continuously improved to increase its efficacy and mitigate the need for specialized interventions.
- Specific approaches to RTI need to be appropriate for the particular school or district culture and take into account leadership, expertise, the diversity of the student population, and the available resources. Schools and districts should adopt an approach that best matches their needs and resources while still accomplishing the overall goals of RTI.

- A systemic approach to language and literacy learning within an RTI framework requires the active participation and genuine collaboration of many professionals, including classroom teachers, reading specialists, literacy coaches, special educators, and school psychologists. Given the critical role that language development plays in literacy learning, professionals with specialized language-related expertise such as speech-language pathologists and teachers of ELLs may be particularly helpful in addressing students' language difficulties.
- Approaches to RTI must be sensitive to developmental differences in language and literacy among students at different ages and grades. Although many prevailing approaches to RTI focus on the early elementary grades, it is essential for teachers and support personnel at middle and secondary levels to provide their students with the language and literacy instruction they need to succeed in school and beyond.
- Administrators must ensure adequate resources and appropriate scheduling to allow all professionals to collaborate.
- Ongoing and job-embedded professional development is necessary for all educators involved in the RTI process. Professional development should be context specific and provided by professional developers with appropriate preparation and skill to support school and district personnel. Professional expertise is essential to improving students' language and literacy learning in general as well as within the context of RTI (see also principle 6).

Differentiating Reading Fluency Instruction for Diverse Learners

IRA Standards for Reading Professionals

Standard 4: Diversity

Candidates create and engage their students in literacy practices that develop awareness, understanding, respect, and a valuing of differences in our society.

Element 4.1

Candidates recognize, understand, and value the forms of diversity that exist in society and their importance in learning to read and write.

Element 4.2

Candidates use a literacy curriculum and engage in instructional practices that positively impact students' knowledge, beliefs, and engagement with the features of diversity.

Response to Intervention

2. Responsive Teaching and Differentiation

The RTI process emphasizes increasingly differentiated and intensified instruction or intervention in language and literacy.

- RTI is centrally about optimizing language and literacy instruction for particular students. This means that differentiated instruction, based on instructionally relevant assessment, is essential. Evidence shows that small-group and individualized instruction are effective in reducing the number of students who are at risk of becoming classified as learning disabled.
- Instruction and materials selection must derive from specific student–teacher interactions and not be constrained by packaged programs. Students have different language and literacy

needs, so they may not respond similarly to instruction—even when research-based practices are used. No single approach to instruction or intervention can address the broad and varied goals and needs of all students, especially those from different cultural and linguistic backgrounds.

- The boundaries between differentiation and intervention are permeable and not clearcut. Instruction or intervention must be flexible enough to respond to evidence from student performance and teaching interactions. It should not be constrained by institutional procedures that emphasize uniformity.

Motivation and Engagement Strategies That Promote Fluency

IRA Standards for Reading Professionals

Standard 5: Literate Environment

Element 5.2

Candidates design a social environment that is low risk and includes choice, motivation, and scaffolded support to optimize students' opportunities for learning to read and write.

Using Technology and New Literacies to Promote Reading Fluency

IRA Standards for Reading Professionals

Standard 2: Curriculum and Instruction

Element 2.3 (See previous)

Standard 5: Literate Environment

Element 5.1 (See previous)

Common Core Standards

Reading: K–5

Integration of Knowledge and Ideas

7. Integrate and evaluate content presented in diverse media and formats, including visually and quantitatively, as well as in words.

Writing: K–12

Production and Distribution of Writing

6. Use technology, including the Internet, to produce and publish writing and to interact and collaborate with others.

How Family and Community Connections Can Help Students Improve Reading Fluency

IRA Standards for Reading Professionals

Standard 4: Diversity

Elements 4.1, 4.2 (See previous)

Element 4.3

Candidates develop and implement strategies to advocate for equity.

Response to Intervention

4. Collaboration

RTI requires a dynamic, positive, and productive collaboration among professionals with relevant expertise in language and literacy. Success also depends on strong and respectful partnerships among professionals, parents, and students.

- Collaboration should be focused on the available evidence about the needs of students struggling in language and literacy. School-level decision-making teams (e.g., intervention teams, problem-solving teams, RTI teams) should include members with relevant expertise in language and literacy, including second-language learning.
- Collaboration should increase, not reduce, the coherence of the instruction experienced by struggling readers. There must be congruence between core language and literacy instruction and interventions. This requires a shared vision and common goals for language and literacy instruction and assessment, adequate time for communication and coordinated planning among general education and specialist teachers, and integrated professional development.
- Involving parents and students and engaging them in a collaborative manner is critical to successful implementation. Initiating and strengthening collaborations among school, home, and communities, particularly in urban and rural areas, provides the basis for support and reinforcement of students' learning.

Increasing Reading Vocabulary 6

Teacher Knowledge	Classroom Assessment	Evidence-Based Teaching Practices	Response to Intervention (RTI)
What Does Research Tell Us About Vocabulary Learning?	How Can Teachers Effectively Assess Students' Vocabulary Knowledge?	Evidence-Based Instruction Practices for Increasing Vocabulary Knowledge	Tier 2 Vocabulary Instruction

Chapter Questions

- How do students acquire reading vocabulary?

- Name four types of vocabulary assessment and tools that may be used for each.

- What explicit instruction strategies can be employed to help students learn vocabulary? Can you describe incidental instructional strategies that may also help students learn new words?

- Which vocabulary instruction strategies are appropriate for Tier 2 instruction as a part of a Response to Intervention (RTI)?

- What lessons can teachers learn from the Lemony Snicket series for incidentally teaching new vocabulary word meanings?

- If you were to decide between digital jumpstarts or podcasts to weave technology into your vocabulary instruction, which would you choose? How might your choice change for use with struggling readers?

- How can "reading backpacks" be used to involve parents in their child's vocabulary learning?

Key Terms

Listening vocabulary
Speaking vocabulary
Reading vocabulary
Writing vocabulary
Word consciousness
Academic knowledge domain vocabulary
Screening assessments
Vocabulary definition
Word map
Before-and-after word knowledge self-rating
Directive context
Nondirective context
Misdirective context
Frayer Model
Word bank
Word walls
Academic word walls (AW^2)
Key vocabulary
Discovery words
Text talk
Morpheme triangle
Semantic map
Digital jumpstarts (DJs)
Reading backpack
Language workshop

Motivation and Engagement	Technology and New Literacies	Family and Community Connections
Teaching Vocabulary	Using Technology and New Literacies to Enhance Vocabulary Learning	Family and Community Connections That Enhance Vocabulary Learning

Vignette: Can You Hear Me Now?

(Authors' Note: To learn more about how to use joint productive activities with your class, go to http://crede.berkeley.edu and view "The Five Standards.")

It is November and Becky has only recently arrived at Hillview School from Pennsylvania. She likes living on the West Coast and has made a new friend, Katy, in her fourth-grade class. Katy has been asked to be Becky's personal docent for a few weeks by their teacher, Mr. Garcia, to help Becky feel comfortable in her new surroundings. Today is a great day for Katy-the-docent for two reasons. For one thing it is a stormy day.

"I positively *love* a good gulley-washer!" says Katy to Becky rather theatrically.

Not only that, today Mr. Garcia is having the students work in groups of four on a "joint productive activity" or JPA during science. Katy enjoys JPAs because she gets to work with a small group to solve a kind of puzzle as a team. When they finish, the group always gets to post their "findings" on chart paper for a Gallery Walk and also see how the other students solved the same task. Because Katy is Becky's docent, they get to be in the same group.

Katy and Becky are assigned to work with Alfred and Walker in their JPA group. (Their task sheet is on the following page.) After their group work and Gallery Walk are finished and they are at lunch, Katy asks Becky what she likes best about the JPA.

"I've never done anything like it!" replies Becky. "I'm not used to being allowed to actually *talk* in class like this. It was pretty great! I liked how we were able to decide together how to fill out the grid. Alfred had some ideas about cell phones I *never* would have thought of on my own. Also, Walker did a great job being our spokesperson for the Gallery Walk. I think I'd like to try being the spokesperson sometime."

"No problem," says Katy. "Mr. Garcia makes sure everyone gets a turn. Just let the rest of the group know when you want to try it. We'll all help you!" ■

●●●

IRA Standards for Reading Professionals:
Standard 1, Element 1.1

Common Core Standards: Language: K–12, Conventions of Standard English (items 1, 2), Knowledge of Language (item 3), Vocabulary Acquisition and Use (items 4–6)

Response to Intervention:
Expertise

Teacher Knowledge

What Does Research Tell Us About Vocabulary Learning?

It has been rightly said that vocabulary is the glue that holds stories, ideas, and content together, making comprehension accessible for children (Rupley, Logan, &

Joint Productive Activity

Can You Hear Me Now?

Comparing and Contrasting High-Tech Vocabulary

Time allowed: 45 minutes

Your Group's Task: Scan the article we have been reading together, "The Cell Phone Revolution," from *Invention & Technology* magazine to complete the "semantic feature analysis grid" below. In this chart you will compare and contrast the important ideas and characteristics of the words listed in the left-hand column. This activity should be done in the same way I modeled the example yesterday when we compared insects and animals.

Important things to remember from past JPAs:

1. All group members must agree on answers.
2. You should appoint a timekeeper to keep things moving. You will only have 45 minutes to complete this task. No exceptions.
3. Use a "six-inch voice" when you talk so you don't disturb the other groups.
4. No "side bar" conversations. Listen as each person talks; you might learn something!
5. Observe "equity of voice"; let everyone talk at least two times.

When your work is done, copy your semantic feature analysis grid onto the chart paper provided using the colored markers at your table. Vote for one of your group members to be the "champion" for the group to do a 1-minute presentation at the beginning of the Gallery Walk to explain your answers. If someone hasn't been champion for a group before, let them give it a go if they are ready.

Here is the semantic feature analysis grid for you to complete.

The Cell Phone Revolution

	Wireless	Makes this tool work	Early communications technology	People who use or have used this	Tool for two-way communication technology
cellular phone tower					
mobile phone					
transistor radio					
antenna					
silicon chip					
subscriber					
BlackBerry					
walkie-talkie					

Directions: After checking for the meanings of the vocabulary words in the left-hand column against the magazine article, "The Cell Phone Revolution," put a "0" in the appropriate box if the word and description do NOT go together, a "1" if the word partly matches, and a "2" if they go together well. If you have disagreement in your group, vote for a majority opinion before marking your response.

Nichols, 1998/99, p. 339). Children who come to school with thousands of words "in their head"—words they can hear, understand, and use in their daily lives—are already on the path to reading success whether they speak English as their native language or are English learners (Lervag & Auhrust, 2010). Conversely, children who have small listening, speaking, and reading vocabularies—who are from what could be termed "language-deprived backgrounds"—must receive immediate attention if they are to have any real chance at reading success (Johnson, 2001; National Research Council, 1998).

Words are the *captions,* you might say, that describe our life experiences (Reutzel & Cooter, 2011). An analysis of the domain of vocabulary instruction should first consider what the word means. The first definition of *vocabulary* in the *Random House Webster's Unabridged Dictionary* (Flexner, 2003) is "the stock of words used by or known to a particular people or group of persons." A subsequent definition is "the words of a language." Vocabulary instruction is defined as teaching word meanings and how one determines word meanings from an understanding of word parts and contextual clues when available. When clues are unavailable, then word meanings and word meaning learning strategies must be taught. Vocabulary development in humans, which goes on throughout life, can be enhanced in the classroom through explicit and incidental instruction. Except for the economically deprived or children with learning disabilities, most children acquire a vocabulary of over 10,000 words during the first 5 years of their lives (Smith, 1987). Most schoolchildren will learn between 2,000 and 3,600 words per year, though estimates vary from 1,500 to more than 8,000 (Clark, 1993; Johnson, 2001; Nagy, Herman, & Anderson, 1985). First-graders from high socioeconomic status (SES) populations have access to twice as many word meanings as children from lower SES groups (Graves, Brunetti, & Slater, 1982; Graves & Slater, 1987).

Vocabulary knowledge in reading is the "great predictor" of school success (Cooter, 2010). For example, we now know that vocabulary knowledge accounts for over 80 percent of the variance in students' reading comprehension test scores. In fact, for fourth-grade students, 70 percent of reading comprehension problems are related to a lack of vocabulary (National Research Council, 1998). Even though the need for robust vocabulary development in our students is obvious for developing fluent reading, there is currently little emphasis on instruction focused on the acquisition of vocabulary in schools and classrooms (Biemiller, 2001; Reutzel, 2010).

How Do Students Acquire New Vocabulary?

There are many sources for learning new word meanings. Some of them may surprise you. Students learn a great deal of their new vocabulary from conversations, independent reading, and even from the media. However, they do not learn new words from each source equally. To illustrate this point, Table 6.1 presents selected statistics revealing the provenance of rare words (i.e., new or unfamiliar words) found in various language and text sources commonly accessed by children and adults (Cunningham & Stanovich, 1998; Rasinski, 1998).

Are you surprised by any of these figures? How about the number of rare words used by college graduates in their conversations with friends compared to the number commonly found in comic books? Or for that matter, the number of uncommon words found in comic books compared to elementary children's books? Such findings help make the supporting case for students' daily reading in self-selected books—including nonfiction (e.g., science, social studies), comics, graphic novels, and popular magazines.

Table 6.1

Sources of Rare Words in Children's and Adults' Vocabulary Acquisition

Source	Number of Rare (Uncommon) Words per 1,000
Adult speech (expert testimony)	28.4
Adult speech (college graduates to friends)	17.3
Prime time adult television	22.7
Mister Rogers and Sesame Street	2.0
Children's books—preschool	16.3
Children's books—elementary	30.9
Comic books	53.5
Popular magazines	66.7
Newspapers	68.3
Adult books	52.7
Scientific article abstracts	128.0

Research on Vocabulary Learning

In reviewing research on vocabulary learning, one conclusion becomes crystal clear: *Reading comprehension and writing composition are dependent on word knowledge.* Indeed, all good readers and writers have a large store of word meanings they can access without significant effort or attention. So what do we know about vocabulary learning? To partially answer this question, we discuss in the following section key findings supported by research (e.g., Beck, McKeown, & Kucan, 2002; Johnson, 2001; Sanacore & Palumbo, 2009).

Vocabulary Is Built Through Language Interactions

Children who are exposed to vocabulary through conversations learn words they will need to recognize and comprehend while reading (Dickinson & Tabors, 2001). Burns, Griffin, and Snow (1999) explain early language acquisition in the following way:

> Vocalization in the crib gives way to play with rhyming language and nonsense words. Toddlers find that the words they use in conversation and the objects they represent are depicted in books—that the picture is a symbol for the real object and that the writing represents spoken language. In addition to listening to stories, children label the objects in books, comment on the characters, and request that an adult read to them. . . . Talking to adults is children's best source of exposure to new vocabulary and ideas. (p. 19)

Reading, and being read to, also increase vocabulary learning (Blewitt, Rump, Shealy, & Cook, 2009). Books give us challenging concepts, colorful description, and new knowledge and information about the world in which we live. Conversely, children who come to school with limited vocabularies as a result of either second-language learning or the effects of poverty (Cooter, 2003, 2010) struggle to take even their first steps in reading and understanding texts. Burns, Griffin, and Snow (1999) ask, "How can they understand a science book about *volcanoes, silkworms,* or *Inuits?* What if they know nothing of *mountains, caterpillars,* or *snow* and *cold climates?*" (p. 70). As teachers, we must make sure that every child is offered many educational opportunities to develop a rich and useful vocabulary.

Research Findings by the National Reading Panel.   To determine how vocabulary can best be taught and related to the reading comprehension process, the National Reading Panel (NRP) examined more than 20,000 research studies identified through electronic and manual literature searches. The studies reviewed suggest that vocabulary instruction does not necessarily lead to gains in comprehension *unless the methods used are appropriate to the age and ability of the reader.* Vocabulary is also learned incidentally through storybook reading or in listening to others read aloud. Preteaching word meanings before reading a text is also helpful.

Repeated Exposure.   Having the student discover words in various contexts appears to enhance vocabulary development. This may include word games, word wall activities, and reading high-interest supplemental texts.

The Four Types of Vocabulary

Although we often speak of vocabulary as if it were a single entity, it is not. Human beings acquire four types of vocabulary—in descending order according to size, listening, speaking, reading, and writing vocabularies. **Listening vocabulary,** the largest, is made up of words we can hear and understand. All other vocabularies are subsets of our listening vocabulary. The second-largest vocabulary, **speaking vocabulary,** is composed of words we use when we speak. Next is our **reading vocabulary,** those words we can identify and understand when we read. The smallest vocabulary is our **writing vocabulary**—words we use in writing. These four vocabularies are continually nurtured in the effective teacher's classroom.

Levels of Vocabulary Learning

As with most new learning, new vocabulary words and concepts are mastered by degree. Beck, McKeown, and Kucan (2002) describe three levels of vocabulary words: tiers 1, 2, and 3. In order to avoid confusing these tiers of vocabulary words with Tier 1, 2, and 3 Response to Intervention (RTI) terminology, we will refer to these three levels of vocabulary words to be learned as *basic speaking vocabulary* (Tier 1), *elaborated speaking vocabulary* (Tier 2), and *academic knowledge domain vocabulary* (Tier 3). Definitions for these three levels of vocabulary are presented in Table 6.2. These levels of vocabulary knowledge apply to each of the four types of vocabularies every individual possesses: listening, speaking, reading, and writing.

Levels of Word Learning

Research informs us about the number of words that need instruction found in individuals' basic speaking vocabularies. Estimates indicate that about 8,000 basic speaking vocabulary words need no instruction for most students (Beck et al., 2002). At the elaborated speaking vocabulary level there are about 7,000 words that require explicit instruction. Beck and colleagues (2002) recommend that we plan instruction for about 400 elaborated speaking vocabulary words per year to help students stay on track academically.

What Research Tells Us About Teaching Vocabulary

Most vocabulary is learned indirectly, but some vocabulary *must* be taught explicitly (Rupley, Blair, & Nichols, 2009). The following conclusions about indirect vocabu-

Table 6.2

Levels of Vocabulary Learning

Level Word Knowledge	Definition
Tier 1 Basic speaking vocabulary	Word meanings that are commonly learned in conversation and from accessible media sources (no instruction needed)
Tier 2 Elaborated speaking vocabulary	Word meanings that are "sophisticated synonyms" for words in the basic speaking vocabulary (e.g., *gigantic* vs. *big; fortunate* vs. *lucky);* relatively frequent in the speaking vocabularies of well-educated persons
Tier 3 Academic knowledge domain vocabulary	Word meanings that are learned within highly specialized knowledge domains such as botany, geography, medicine, and physics (*photosynthesis, peninsula, astereopis, quark*)

Adapted from Beck, I. L., McKeown, M. G., & Kucan, L. (2002). *Bringing Words to Life: Robust Vocabulary Instruction.* New York: Guilford Press.

lary learning and direct vocabulary instruction are of particular interest and value to classroom teachers (National Reading Panel, 2000):

- *Children learn the meanings of most words indirectly, through everyday experiences with oral and written language.* Children learn word meanings in conversations with other people. As they participate in conversations children often hear words repeated several times. The more conversations children have, the more words they learn.

  Another indirect way children learn words is by being read to. Reading aloud is especially powerful when the reader pauses to define an unfamiliar word and, after reading, engages the child in a conversation about the book using the word (Blewitt et al., 2009).

  The third way children indirectly learn new words is through reading. This is why many teachers believe that daily, independent reading practice sessions of 10 to 20 minutes are so critical (Krashen, 1993). Put simply, the more children read, the more words they'll learn. There is a caveat to mention on this point, however. Struggling readers are often incapable of sitting and reading on their own for extended periods of time. Many readers learn much more from practice reading when working with a "buddy."

- *Students learn vocabulary when they are explicitly taught individual word meanings and word learning strategies.* Explicit instruction helps students learn unfamiliar word meanings (Taylor, Mraz, Nichols, Rickelman, & Wood, 2009) such as those that represent complex concepts not part of students' everyday experiences (National Reading Panel, 2000). When teachers *preteach* new words that are associated with a text that students are about to read, better reading comprehension likewise results (Webb, 2009).

- *Developing word consciousness boosts vocabulary learning.* **Word consciousness** learning activities stimulate awareness and interest in words, their meanings, and their power. Word-conscious students enjoy words and are zealous about learning them. By modeling the use of sophisticated words, teachers can promote students' vocabulary growth and word consciousness (Lane & Allen, 2010).

  The keys to maximizing word consciousness are wide reading and extensive writing. When reading a new book aloud to students, call their attention to the way the author chooses her words to convey particular meanings. Imagine the fun you can have discussing some of the intense words used by Gary Paulsen (1987) in his novel *Hatchet* or the downright captivating word selection employed by J. K. Rowling (2009) in *Harry Potter and the Deathly Hallows*. Encourage your students to play with words by constructing puns or raps. Help students research a word's history and find examples of its usage in their everyday lives.

Which Words Should Be Taught?

Not all words are created equal, especially in terms of difficulty. As McKeown and Beck (1988) explain:

> The choice of which words to teach and what kind of attention to give them depends on a variety of factors, such as importance of the words for understanding the selection, relationship to specific domains of knowledge, general utility, and relationship to other lessons and classroom events. (p. 45)

Figure 6.1

The 60 Most Frequent Academic Knowledge Domain Words

analysis	contract	factors	legal	research
approach	create	financial	legislation	response
area	data	formula	major	role
assessment	definition	function	method	section
assume	derived	identified	occur	sector
authority	distribution	income	percent	significant
available	distribution	indicate	period	similar
benefit	economic	individual	policy	source
concept	environment	interpretation	principle	specific
consistent	established	involved	procedure	structure
constitutional	estimate	issues	process	theory
context	evidence	labor	required	variables
	export			

From Coxhead, A. "A New Academic Word List," *TESOL Quarterly, 34*(2), 213–238. Copyright 2000 by the Teachers of English to Speakers of Other Languages. Reproduced with permission of TESOL via Copyright Clearance Center.

Realistically, you will only be able to thoroughly teach about 10 per week, so you must choose words carefully. Focus your energy on high-utility words in literature selections (elaborated speaking vocabulary words) and words that are important to understanding the content selections you will be reading in class (academic knowledge domain vocabulary words).

Academic Knowledge Domain Vocabulary. The words used to represent the specialized concepts and ideas found in core subject area fields (i.e., mathematics, science, social studies, English/language arts) are referred to as **academic knowledge domain vocabulary.** Although each field of study has its own comprehensive list of academic vocabulary there are some commonly used across boundaries, though in different contexts. In a study of over 3.5 million running words of written academic text, Coxhead (2000) identified the 60 most frequently used words across disciplines (see Figure 6.1). These are of great utility to all learners and deserve our attention.

● ● ●

IRA Standards for Reading Professionals: Standard 3, Elements 3.1, 3.2, 3.3

Common Core Standards: Speaking and Listening: K–5, Comprehension and Collaboration (item 3); Speaking and Listening: Grades 6–12, Comprehension and Collaboration (items 2, 3); Language: Grades K–5, Conventions of Standard English (items 1,2), Knowledge of Language (item 3), Vocabulary Acquisition and Use (items 4–6)

Response to Intervention: Assessment

Classroom Assessment

How Can Teachers Effectively Assess Students' Vocabulary Knowledge?

To help you plan and evaluate learning you must consider tactics for assessing students' reading vocabulary knowledge (Berne & Blachowicz, 2008; Pearson, Hiebert, & Kamil, 2007). Dale Johnson (2001), a prominent researcher in the area of vocabulary instruction, explains three challenges in vocabulary assessment: (1) choosing *which* words to test, (2) determining what it means for a student to actually "know" a word, and (3) deciding how to reliably test vocabulary knowledge. In this section, we take a look at ways classroom teachers can do four types of assessments: screening assessments at the beginning of the school year or at the start of a unit of study, diagnostic assessments for students having special learning needs, progress-monitoring assessments, and outcome assessments once instruction has been concluded.

Screening Assessments

Screening assessments provide a critical first look at students' vocabulary knowledge. They should be quick but also provide reliable and valid data. Screening assessments help teachers place students into preliminary instructional groups based on their vocabulary knowledge and needs. Here is our "short list" of screening assessments for vocabulary knowledge we have found helpful.

Vocabulary Definition.   A teacher-constructed tool, **vocabulary definition** (Beck et al., 2002) can be used either as a whole-group screening assessment or for individual (one-on-one teacher and student) assessment. The idea is to identify key words to be learned and then ask students to complete a grid like Figure 6.2 in which they describe their knowledge of each word. Once students have completed this quick self-assessment, teachers can plot each student's results to create a profile similar to Figure 6.3. From this classroom profile small-group instruction can be planned based on student needs. Notice that individual student responses are rated in terms of how well students may know word meanings: *established, acquainted,* and *unknown.*

Click on A+RISE—WIDA ELP Standard Strategies in the MyEducationLab (www.myeducationlab.com) for your course. Next, select the Strategy Card Index tab, scroll to Classroom Assessments for grades K–5, and select the Alternative ELL Assessments: Introduction strategy.

Figure 6.2

Vocabulary Definition Student Sheet

Name   Betheny

Words	I know it well (Established)	I know something about it, and can relate it to something (Acquainted)	I do not really know this word (Unknown)
tyranny		A	
sensitive	E		
dubious			U
purport			U
revolution		A	
traitor		A	

Adapted from Beck, I. L., McKeown, M. G., & Kucan, L. (2002). *Bringing Words to Life: Robust Vocabulary Instruction.* New York: Guilford Press.

Figure 6.3

Vocabulary Definition Student Profile

Key Words	Shannon	Randy	Julie	Eddie	Betheny	Jake
tyranny	U	E	U	A	A	U
sensitive	E	E	A	A	E	A
dubious	A	A	U	U	U	U
purport	U	U	U	U	U	U
revolution	A	E	A	A	A	U
traitor	A	A	A	U	A	A

Key: U = Unknown, A = Acquainted, E = Established

Figure 6.4

Word Map

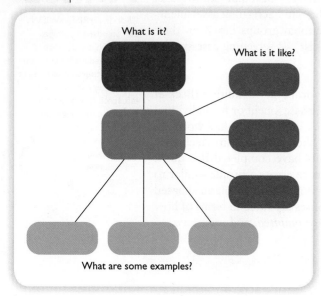

What is it?

What is it like?

What are some examples?

Word Map. A **word map** (Schwartz & Raphael, 1985; Stahl, Hare, Sinatra, & Gregory, 1991) is a kind of graphic rendering of a word's meaning. Word maps were found to be informative and easy to implement in urban middle schools serving underprivileged students in a federally funded research study (Cooter & Cooter, 2010). A good alternative to the word definition strategy described previously, word maps ask students to answer three important questions about target words: *What is it? What is it like? What are some examples?* Answers to these questions are valuable because they help children link the new word or concept to their prior knowledge and world experiences, a process known to have a beneficial effect on reading comprehension.

To get started, Cooter and Cooter (2010) recommend that you carefully review an upcoming unit of study in your core reading program or in content area studies (i.e., science, social studies, etc.). Identify the most important facts, terms, and concepts and select five to ten of these to use in your assessment. Prepare and administer the word map assessment to your students using one map for each word (see Figure 6.4). This will help you better understand the background knowledge students have about each word before you begin instruction. Use a word map summary sheet like the one shown in Figure 6.5 to summarize your students' results. A check mark indicates an acceptable response.

Before-and-After Word Knowledge Self-Ratings. Blachowicz and Fisher (2006) recommend the **before-and-after word knowledge self-rating** as an efficient way to survey student vocabulary knowledge. In introducing students to a new text, the teacher distributes to students before-and-after word knowledge self-rating forms

Figure 6.5

Word Map Summary Sheet

Key Terms	Background Knowledge Item	Shannon	Randy	Julie	Eddie	Betheny	Jake
1. republic	What is it?	✓					
	What is it like? (1)	✓	✓		✓	✓	
	What is it like? (2)						
	What is it like? (3)						
	Example 1	✓	✓	✓	✓		✓
	Example 2	✓			✓		
	Example 3						

Notes: For most of these students the term *republic* is either *unknown* or they are somewhat *acquainted* with the term. Two students, Shannon and Eddie, have nearly mastered it (i.e., have *republic* as an *established* term in their background knowledge).

with important vocabulary-building words from the text listed on the left. Using the three-level self-rating on the form, students can indicate not knowing a word (level 1), having heard the word (level 2), or being able to define and use the word (level 3). This rating system is congruent with research findings of the Partnership for Reading (2001) and the National Reading Panel (2000), which describe the three levels of vocabulary learning with the terms *unknown, acquainted,* and *established,* as in Figure 6.3. Figure 6.6 features a before-and-after word knowledge self-rating form completed by a student on a text with the theme of transportation.

Diagnostic Vocabulary Assessments

Diagnostic vocabulary assessments, which can be teacher constructed or commercially produced, provide in-depth information about each student's particular vocabulary knowledge and needs. These assessments are a bit more involved and take extra time to conduct. An educational psychologist, certified diagnostician, or bilingual specialist may be needed to administer some diagnostic tests due to the amount of time and/or special training required.

Perhaps the simplest way to conduct a quick diagnostic vocabulary assessment is using teacher-made flash cards. Flash cards can also be produced on a computer with a word-processing program. For recording purposes, you will also need a master list of the words to record each student's responses. "Flash" each card to the student, one at a time, and ask him to name the word. Allow about 5 seconds for the student to respond. Circle any words that the student does not know or that he mispronounces on the student's record form.

Formal Diagnostic Vocabulary Assessment Tools

Several commercially produced vocabulary tests are available for diagnostic purposes. They are often used by Title I reading specialists and special education faculty, but may be employed by classroom teachers who have appropriate training. We recommend four tests for assessing a student's word knowledge or *receptive vocabulary.* The first two are intended for native English speakers, and the other two are for students who speak Spanish as their first language and are learning to speak and read in English.

Peabody Picture Vocabulary Test, **Third Edition (PPVT–III).**　The PPVT–III (Dunn & Dunn, 1997) is a quickly administered instrument (11–12 minutes) that indicates the strength of a student's vocabulary knowledge compared to other students of the same age nationally. Results can help the teacher better understand the needs of students in terms of formal and informal vocabulary instruction. It is available in two parallel forms, Form III A and Form III B. Each form contains four training items followed by 204 test items divided into 17 sets of 12 items each. The sets are progressively difficult, a format referred to as a "power" test. Each item has four simple black-and-white illustrations arranged in a multiple-choice format. The examinee's task is to select the picture that best illustrates the meaning of a stimulus word presented orally by the examiner.

Expressive Vocabulary Test **(EVT).**　The EVT (Williams, 1997), which correlates well with the PPVT–III, is an untimed norm-referenced, individually administered assessment of expressive (speaking) and word retrieval (word memory) that takes about 15 minutes to complete. The EVT was developed and normed using the most recent U.S. census data for gender, race/ethnicity, region, and parent or self-education

Figure 6.6

Before-and-After Word Knowledge Self-Rating Form

	Before-Reading Word Knowledge		
Key Terms	I can define and use this word in a sentence. (Established) 3	I have heard this word before. (Acquainted) 2	I don't know this word. (Unknown) 1
mileage	X		
freight		X	
GPS		X	
passenger	X		
fossil fuel			X
ethanol			X
route			X
express		X	
destination		X	
ETA			X
alternative fuels			X

	After-Reading Word Knowledge			
Key Terms	Self-Rating (3, 2, 1)	Define	Use in a Sentence	Questions I Still Have About This Term
mileage	3	How far it is to a place you're going	The mileage from Salt Lake city to Provo is about 50 miles.	
freight	3	Things that are being shipped by a truck or by another way	Boxes on a truck are called freight.	
GPS	2	A kind of compass	A GPS can help me find my way home.	I can't remember what GPS means.
passenger	3	A person going somewhere in a vehicle	I was once a passenger in an airplane.	
fossil fuel	2	Makes a car run	Cars use fossil fuels to run the engine.	I don't know what *fossil* means.
ethanol	1			I can't remember anything about this. Did we really learn this?
route	3	How you are getting to a destination	I took a northern route to get to Canada.	
express	3	Getting something or someone to their destination quickly	I sent my package by FedEx overnight express.	
destination	3	Where you are going	My destination on my next trip is Boston.	
ETA	3	When you are getting somewhere	My estimated time of arrival or ETA is 9 a.m.	
alternative fuels	2	Like gas and diesel fuel	Some cars run on gas; others use diesel.	I think there may be other kinds, but I'm not sure.

level as a measure of socioeconomic status. This easy to administer test contains two types of items, labeling and synonym. For the 38 labeling items, the examiner points to a picture or a part of the body and asks a question. For the 152 synonym items, the examiner presents a picture and a stimulus word or words within a carrier phrase. The examinee is instructed to respond to each item with a one-word answer. Four unscored examples are presented, two before the labeling items and two before the synonym items. No reading or writing is required by the examinee.

***Test de Vocabulario en Imágenes Peabody* (TVIP).**   This test (Dunn, Lugo, Padilla, & Dunn, 1986) is an adaptation of an early version of the PPVT–III for native Spanish speakers. It takes about 10 to 15 minutes to administer and it measures Spanish vocabulary knowledge.

***Woodcock–Muñoz Language Survey* (WMLS).**   This test has English and Spanish forms (Woodcock & Muñoz-Sandoval, 1993). Teachers, particularly in urban centers, often have a large number of students who are learning English as a second language (ESL). The extent to which students have acquired a listening and speaking vocabulary in English is an important factor in reading instruction because reading is a language skill that depends on learners having a fairly strong English vocabulary. The WMLS is a widely respected instrument used throughout the United States. It takes about 20 minutes to administer, featuring two subtests: Oral Language and Reading/Writing.

Progress-Monitoring Vocabulary Assessments

Progress-monitoring assessments provide ongoing and timely feedback as to how well individual students are responding to your explicit teaching of word meanings. This allows you to continually reevaluate your instruction and make adjustments as needed. Most core reading programs adopted by school districts include progress-monitoring vocabulary assessments for key words in their units of study.

Outcome Assessments

Outcome assessments assist us in determining how effectively our reading program and teaching help students attain grade-level standards or benchmarks. These tests are usually administered to whole groups of students at one time (typically in the spring), but may be given individually when necessary. The following instruments are considered to be excellent examples in this area of reading assessment.

***The Woodcock–Johnson Tests of Achievement,* Third Edition (WJTA–III).**   The WJTA-III (Woodcock, McGrew, & Mather, 2001) is a norm-referenced, individually administered wide-range test of academic knowledge and skills. It is designed for ages 5 and up, including adults. Many areas are covered in the basic achievement test, with vocabulary included in the supplemental tests. The total test time varies, depending on which tests are administered.

***Iowa Tests of Basic Skills* (ITBS).**   The ITBS (Hoover, Dunbar, & Frisbie, 2005) is a popular standardized achievement battery used by school districts to provide information for improving instruction and by U.S. researchers to measure the effects of experimental education programs. Available for levels 5 through 14, the ITBS includes a vocabulary subtest measuring listening vocabulary. At the primary level students hear a word and sometimes they also hear the word used in a sentence. Then they choose one of three pictorial response options. The vocabulary test at levels 7 and 8 measures reading vocabulary. For each question, a pictorial or written stimulus (sentence) is followed by a set of written responses. Approximately equal numbers of nouns, verbs, and modifiers are tested at all levels.

Evidence-Based Teaching Practices

Evidence-Based Instruction Practices for Increasing Vocabulary Knowledge

● ● ●

IRA Standards for Reading Professionals: Standard 2, Elements 2.1, 2.2, 2.3; Standard 4, Elements 4.1, 4.2, 4.3; Standard 5, Elements 5.1, 5.2, 5.3

Common Core Standards: Speaking and Listening: K–5, Comprehension and Collaboration (items 1, 3), Presentation of Knowledge and Ideas (items 4, 6); Speaking and Listening: Grades 6–12, Comprehension and Collaboration (items 1, 3), Presentation of Knowledge and Ideas (items 4, 6); Language: K–5, Knowledge of Language (item 3), Vocabulary Acquisition and Use (items 4–6); Language: Grades 6–12, Conventions of Standard English (items 1, 2), Knowledge of Language (item 3), Vocabulary Acquisition and Use (items 4–6)

Response to Intervention: Instruction; Responsive Teaching and Differentiation; Systemic and Comprehensive Approaches

How can we help students increase their vocabulary knowledge? To answer this essential question for teachers, in this section we present some of the most successful research-backed methods.

Principles of Effective Vocabulary Instruction

We have developed a list of principles for effective vocabulary instruction from the research of such scholars as Stahl (1986), Rasinski (1998), and Coyne and colleagues (Coyne, McCoach, Loftus, Zirpoli, & Kapp, 2009). Consider these principles as you think about vocabulary strategies to use in your classroom.

Principle 1: Vocabulary Should Be Taught Both Explicitly and Incidentally. Children learn new words in two ways. First, they are taught basic definitions or information that helps them connect the new word to known words (i.e., elaboration). This step can be accomplished by simply providing the definition, by building semantic maps linking the known to the new, and through examining the target word in terms of its synonyms, antonyms, classification, root, and affixes.

On the foundation of explicit teaching, context helps readers choose the correct meaning for multiple-meaning words. The old adage that "experience is the best teacher" is certainly true in vocabulary learning. Much new vocabulary is learned through indirect, vicarious experience in daily reading of interesting and varied texts (Rasinski, 1998). Marilyn Jager Adams (1990) put it this way:

> The best way to build children's visual vocabulary is to have them read meaningful words in meaningful contexts. The more meaningful reading that children do, the larger will be their repertoires of meanings, the greater their sensitivity to orthographic structure, and the stronger, better refined, and more productive will be their associations between words and meanings. (p. 156)

Principle 2: Learning How to Construct Vocabulary from Rich Contexts Is Valuable. Context has to do with knowing the core definition of a word and understanding how that definition varies in different texts. For example, the word *run* is generally thought of as a verb meaning "to move swiftly." When looking for this simple word in the dictionary, one quickly realizes that the word *run* has approximately 50 definitions! Context helps the reader know which definition the author intends.

Principle 3: Effective Vocabulary Instruction Must Include Depth of Learning as Well as Breadth of Word Knowledge. Deep processing of vocabulary includes both relating new word meanings to other similar known word meanings (elaboration) as well as learning new concepts and the words that label these new concepts (expansion). Stahl (1986) defines three levels of processing for vocabulary instruction:

1. *Association processing.* Students learn simple associations through synonyms and word associations.
2. *Comprehension processing.* Students move beyond simple associations by doing something with the association, such as fitting the word into a sentence blank, classifying the word with other words, or finding antonyms.
3. *Generation processing.* Students use the comprehended association to generate a new or novel product (sometimes called *generative comprehension*). This could be a restatement of the definition in the student's own words, a novel sentence using the word correctly in a clear context, or a connection of the definition to the student's personal experiences.

Principle 4: Multiple Meaningful Exposures Are Important for Learning New Vocabulary. Vocabulary learning requires repetition (Coyne et al., 2009). To learn words thoroughly, students need to see, hear, and use words many times in different contexts (Rasinski, 1998). Providing students with multiple exposures in varied contexts appears to significantly improve reading comprehension.

Planning Vocabulary Instruction

Use the following suggestions to guide you in selecting words to teach and planning instruction in your classroom:

1. First, examine the type of text the children will be reading. Is it narrative or informational? Recalling the three levels of word knowledge discussed earlier—unknown, acquainted, and established (Partnership for Reading, 2001), develop a list of ten unknown and acquainted words to be taught during the week, two per day. Select elaborated speaking vocabulary words to teach if the children will primarily be reading narrative, literary texts. Select academic knowledge domain vocabulary words to teach if children will be reading informational, expository texts.

2. Read the text to determine the nature of the context in which each of the selected words appear. This will give you some insights into how much support and modeling you may need to provide. Reading contexts can be described as: *directive, nondirective,* or *misdirective.* A **directive context** gives clues, hints, and synonyms to help readers determine an approximate word meaning. If a word appears in a directive context, teach children how to use the information to determine an approximate word meaning. On the other hand, **nondirective context** only mentions the word without giving any clues to determine word meaning, whereas **misdirective context** gives clues that lead readers to false word meaning construction. Words that appear in nondirective or misdirective contexts are good candidates for your ten-word teaching list.

3. If you have English learners in your classroom, be sure to determine whether any Spanish–English cognates may help them in understanding English words. Consider the following example:

> *information* (English)
>
> *información* (Spanish)

A good source for finding English–Spanish cognates is *NTC's Dictionary of Spanish Cognates Thematically Organized* (Nash, 1999).

4. Okay, now that you have selected ten words to teach for an upcoming week, begin your preparations by looking up each word in a dictionary or glossary for a definition. Next, construct a "student-friendly" definition using your own words. If you have trouble doing this, try looking up the term online in Wikipedia. We like the

Collins Cobuild New Student's Dictionary (Cobuild Staff, 2002) as a resource that saves a lot of planning time.

Next, find the page where the word occurs in the story or subject area text and look at its context. List the textual clues and write the word in a sentence. Think about ways each word can be introduced to students in a rich and meaningful context. For example, you may be able to use pictures or video clips found online; you could list examples of the word in different contexts or find synonyms and antonyms in a thesaurus. Think about the characteristics or attributes of the word (roots, prefixes, suffixes) and how these could feature in your presentation.

You might decide to employ a graphic organizer known as the **Frayer Model** (Frayer & Klausmeir, 1969). This tool is a classic strategy that is not only useful for teacher preparation but also helps students understand new vocabulary and concepts in relation to what is already known. Frayer is especially useful for nonfiction terms or academic vocabulary because it presents essential and nonessential information related to the term, as well as examples and nonexamples (Reutzel & Cooter, 2011). For example, let's say the text you are using in a social studies lesson has the British word *tram* (the word *streetcar* would be used in the United States). In Figure 6.7 we share a completed Frayer Model for the word *tram*.

Vocabulary Instruction Activities and Tools

There are a number of activities and tools teachers can use in the classroom to help build students' vocabulary.

Word Banks.   A **word bank** is a tool to help students collect and review words. They can also be used as personal dictionaries or students can review the words in their banks to apply in their writing. A word bank can take many forms, from a student-constructed box to a file or notebook in which newly learned words are stored. In the early grades, teachers often collect small shoeboxes from local stores for this purpose. Students decorate the boxes to make them their own. In the upper grades,

Figure 6.7

Frayer Model Example for the Word *Tram*

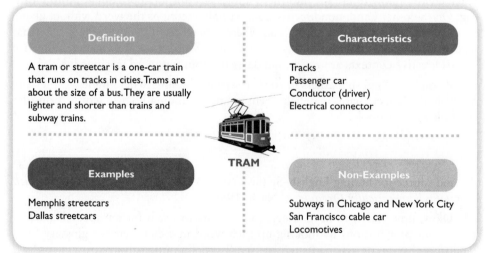

Adapted from Frayer, D., Frederick, W. C., & Klausmeir, H. J. (1969). *A Schema for Testing the Level of Concept Mastery* (Working Paper No. 16). Madison: University of Wisconsin. Wisconsin Research and Development Center for Cognitive Learning.

more formal-looking word banks—notebooks or recipe boxes—give an "adult" appearance.

Alphabetic dividers can be used at all levels to facilitate the quick location of word bank words. Alphabetic dividers in the early grades also help students rehearse and reinforce knowledge of alphabetical order. Figure 6.8 shows a sample word bank.

Word Walls. Many teachers use **word walls** to direct students' attention to words of all kinds—high-frequency words, important words in a content unit of study, or useful words for books they are reading (Cunningham, 2000). There are many possible types of word walls. In essence, you simply post important words on a section of wall, usually on butcher paper or a pocket chart, and categorize them according to your purpose (Reutzel & Cooter, 2011). **Academic word walls** (**AW**^{2}) (Cooter & Cooter, 2010) provide a variation on word walls for core subject area instruction (e.g., science, social studies, mathematics).

Word Walls Versus Word Wallpaper. In classrooms across America we have often seen fantastic examples of word walls used as potent learning tools—as resources for generating multiple meaningful exposures to new words, as opportunities for discussions around new concepts and terms in subject area studies, and as mechanisms to boost the learning of students from even the

Figure 6.8

Word Bank

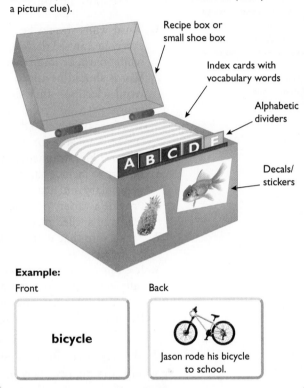

A word bank is a box in which children keep/file new words they are learning. The words are usually written in isolation on one side of the card, and in a sentence on the back of the card (usually with a picture clue).

Recipe box or small shoe box

Index cards with vocabulary words

Alphabetic dividers

Decals/stickers

Example:

Front

bicycle

Back

Jason rode his bicycle to school.

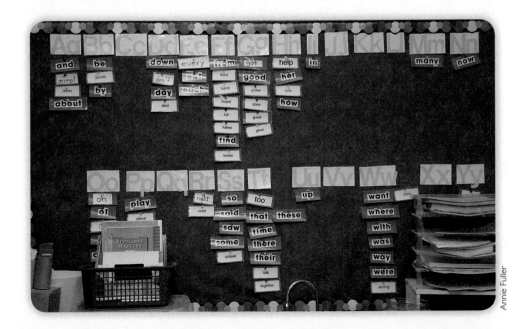

Annie Fuller

Click on A+RISE—WIDA ELP Standard Strategies in the MyEducationLab (www.myeducationlab.com) for your course. Next, select the Strategy Card Index tab, scroll to Vocabulary for grades K–5, and select the Vocabulary Mental Connections strategy.

most challenging life circumstances. As words are moved and sorted and discussed in fascinating ways, students can become enthusiastic wordsmiths. However, we have also seen word *wallpaper* instead of word *walls*—that is, words laminated in place and rarely noticed or used. In one case we saw a "word wall" pasted on the ceiling of a classroom! So how does one use a word wall to its best potential? Here are some guidelines adapted from Dade County Schools in Miami, Florida (Dade County Schools, 2010).

1. Word walls should be placed in a prominent location in the classroom where everyone can see the words. A blank section of wall, a moveable bulletin board, whiteboard, or large sheets of butcher paper are often used as media.
2. Words should be added gradually (five to ten per week), so be stingy with your word selection—they should be important examples that are frequently used in your texts.
3. Words may be printed on card stock with bold markers. Word cards should be easily removable for word sort and other activities with the class.
4. Remove high-frequency words when they are no longer needed.
5. Be sure to include the two levels of words discussed earlier—elaborated speaking vocabulary and academic knowledge domain vocabulary.
6. Provide a variety of review activities to ensure enough practice so that words are read and spelled instantly and automatically.
7. Make sure that word wall words are spelled correctly in any writing students complete.
8. It is fine to have more than one word wall. Many teachers eventually have separate word walls for reading, social studies, science, and mathematics.
9. Use word wall activities in 5- to 10-minute increments as opening routines for lessons, as closing routines, before lunch, and so forth.

Word Sorts. The purpose of doing word sorts is to get students to group, discuss, regroup, and discover new meanings of important vocabulary and word parts (prefixes, suffixes, etc.) in the texts you use. There are many ways words can be sorted and talked about with your students, and you may be able to invent some of your own, especially in specific subject areas (i.e., mathematics, science, social studies). Basic word sort strategies include the following:

- *Closed word sorts.* Closed sorts are teacher-directed activities in which students are told in advance the categories for sorting the new words. To provide multiple meaningful exposures to new words try using word hunting, which can be done by partners, with small groups, or in a learning center. Students go through familiar books, magazines, or websites and make a list of the words they find that match entries posted on the word wall. They then record their findings in a notebook giving the sentence and source where the word was found.

In subject area vocabulary instruction using an academic word wall (AW[2]), words may be sorted in many ways (e.g., concepts, events, and so forth). For example, one teacher presenting a unit of study about the discovery of North America had the following entries on his word wall: *Columbus, Nina, Indians, Vikings, danger, rough, Eric the Red, Pinta, corn, tobacco, disease, Spain, The New World, Santa Maria, Queen Isabella, forests.* Students were asked to do the following: "Read the following vocabulary words out loud with your partner. Then consider the following three word categories—People, The Voyage, and What They Discovered. Sort each word into its *best* category among those three choices and make a chart." This academic word wall (AW^2) sort when completed by students might look like the following:

Discovery of North America Vocabulary

People	The Voyage	What They Discovered
Columbus	Nina	New World
Vikings	Portugal	forests
Eric the Red	Santa Maria	corn
Queen Isabella	Pinta	tobacco
Indians	danger	disease
	rough	

- *Open word sorts.* Open sorts are student-directed activities in which they are free to group words from the word wall according to how they think they are related, providing their own labels for each group of words. The label may be an important concept in a unit of study, a relationship, or a common characteristic certain words share. For example, each student in a group might be asked to sort words on their word wall and give each grouping a name (category) without telling the other students their categories. The other people in the group will be asked to guess the categories created by each person and explain their guesses.

Example: A Student's Word Sort and Categories Identified (in parentheses)

dog	asparagus	apple	chair
cat	peas	orange	sofa
mouse	beans	banana	table
hamster	corn	apricot	cot
(Animal)	(Vegetable)	(Fruit)	(Furniture)

- *Speed sorts.* Using open or closed sorts, teachers can direct students to complete them within a certain amount of time (e.g., 1-minute sort, 2-minute sort). This is a great review or assessment tool. It is important to note that in each word sort activity, students should be expected to explain or justify why they think specific academic words belong under a label or category. This creates an opportunity for students to talk about the words, explore their meanings, and retell what they have learned.

There are a number of additional word sort activities that teachers can use to help build students' vocabularies. Some involve working in groups whereas others are individual activities.

Password. Divide the class into two teams. One person from each team sits in a chair in front of the class. Those two people receive a card with a vocabulary word from the AW^2. The first person gives a one-word clue to his team. If no one from the team can guess the word, the second person gives a clue to her team. This alternates back and forth until someone from one of the teams guesses the word, or until a specified number of clues have been given.

Drawing Pictures. Students draw pictures—but no words—on the board so that the students in the other group can guess the word or expressions they're trying to represent. This is a fun way to review some vocabulary and break up the class routine.

Key Vocabulary. As a category of words mainly for beginning or emergent readers in grades pre-K–1, Silvia Ashton-Warner, in her classic book *Teacher* (1963), describes **key vocabulary** as "organic"—words that emerge from the child's experiences. Ashton-Warner defines key vocabulary words as "captions" for important events in the child's life.

Children can be taught key vocabulary through a variety of direct instructional strategies. For example, the student meets with the teacher individually at an appointed time, or during a group experience, and indicates which words he or she would like to learn. The teacher might prompt: "What word would you like to learn today?" The child responds with a lexical word—*police, ghost, sing.* The teacher writes the word on an index card or a small piece of tagboard using a dark marker. The teacher directs the student to share the word with as many people as possible during the day. Later, the word is added to his or her writing folder or word bank for future use in writing.

Ashton-Warner found that the most common categories of key vocabulary children wanted to learn were (1) fear words (*dog, bull, kill, police*); (2) sex (as she called them) or affection words (*love, kiss, sing, darling*); (3) locomotion words (*bus, car, truck, jet*); and (4) a miscellaneous category generally reflecting cultural and other considerations (*socks, frog, beer, Disneyland, Dallas Cowboys*). Ashton-Warner (1963) refers to key vocabulary as "one-look words" because one look is usually all that is required for permanent learning to take place.

Click on A+RISE—
Literacy Strategies in the
MyEducationLab (www.
myeducationlab.com) for
your course. Next, select
the Strategy Card Index
tab, scroll to Vocabulary
for grades K–5,
and select the
More Mad Three
Minutes strategy.

Discovery Words.   During the course of a typical school day, students are exposed to many new words in their content studies. Words such as *experiment, algebra, social, enterprise, conquest, Bengal tiger, spider,* and *cocoon* find their way into students' listening and speaking vocabularies. Every effort should be made to add these **discovery words** to the word bank as they are discussed in their natural contexts. Such words often appear in student compositions.

Clap, Chant, Write—Introduction of New Words.   In this adaptation from Sigmon (1997), the teacher introduces five new words per week with the following activities: See the words, say the words, chant the words (snap, clap, stomp, cheer), write the words and check them together with the teacher, and trace around the words and check together with the teacher. Use the following procedure:

1. Have the students number a sheet of paper 1 through 5.
2. Place one of the five new academic word cards on the academic word wall. Say the word, use the word in a sentence, provide a picture clue if appropriate, and then have students write the word on their paper. Continue in this way with your four new additional words.
3. When all five words have been written, point to the words and have the students clap and chant the spellings of the words.
4. Students use a red pen, marker, or crayon to trace around the word.
5. On the following days of the week, the teacher practices the new word wall entries and reviews previous words with practice activities.

Hangman.   An old favorite game, Hangman is a simple (though perhaps somewhat morbid) vocabulary review activity. The following example is from a unit and word wall focusing on The Moon. The target word is *crater.*

1. On a whiteboard or chart paper, draw a "gallows" and spaces below it representing each letter of the target word (see following illustration).

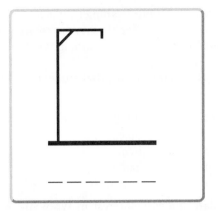

2. Say, "I'm thinking of a word on our academic word wall that has six letters and has something to do with an impact."

3. Students guess one letter at a time. As a correct letter is guessed, write the letter in the corresponding blank. For each incorrect guess, draw one part of a stick man in this order—head, body, one arm, then the next, and ending with each leg. If the whole body is drawn due to incorrect responses, the man is hanged (see below) and the teacher/partner supplies the correct answer. (*Note:* You can also play Hangman on the Internet by going to the fun website www.hangmangame.net.)

The possibilities for word sort activities are endless. One of the more popular resources for word sorts is the book series *Words Their Way* (Bear, Invernizzi, Templeton, & Johnston, 2007), and many more free activities can be found online at www.readwritethink.org.

Teaching Word Functions and Changes

Synonyms are words that have similar, but not exactly the same, meanings (Johnson & Pearson, 1984). No two words carry exactly the same meaning in all contexts. Thus, when teaching new words and their synonyms, teachers should provide numerous opportunities for students to see differences as well as similarities. As with all reading strategies, this is best done within the natural context of real books and authentic writing experiences.

One very productive way to get students interested in synonyms in the upper elementary grades is to teach them how a thesaurus can add variety and flavor to their writing. This tool is best used during the revising and editing stages of the writing process when students sometimes have problems coming up with descriptive language. For example, let's say a character in their story was tortured by hostile savages (sorry to be so violent in our example!), but the child writes that the victim felt "bad." If this word is targeted for thesaurus research, then the student might come up with synonyms for *bad* such as *in pain, anguished, in misery, depressed,* or *desperate.*

Following are several common words that students overuse and their synonyms as listed in a thesaurus.

good	big	thing
pleasant	vast	object
glorious	grand	item
wonderful	enormous	gadget
delightful	huge	organism

One way to stimulate students' interest in synonyms is to develop a modified cloze passage using an excerpt from a favorite book. In preparing the passage, replace targeted words with blanks that students will fill in with synonyms for the original text. The following excerpt from Eric Carle's *The Grouchy Ladybug* (1986) is well suited to this strategy.

> "Good morning," said the friendly ladybug.
> "Go away!" shouted the grouchy ladybug. "I want those aphids."
> "We can share them," suggested the friendly ladybug.
> "No. They're mine, all mine," screamed the grouchy ladybug.
> "Or do you want to fight me for them?"*

The teacher might delete the words *said, shouted, suggested,* and *screamed* and list them on the chalkboard along with possible synonyms and near synonyms, such as *hinted, greeted, growled, yelled, reminded, mentioned, pointed out,* and *offered.* Student rewrites might look something like the following:

> "Good morning," *greeted* the friendly ladybug.
> "Go away!" *growled* the grouchy ladybug. "I want those aphids."
> "We can share them," *hinted* the friendly ladybug.
> "No. They're mine, all mine," *yelled* the grouchy ladybug.
> "Or do you want to fight me for them?"*

Class discussions might look at how the use of different synonyms can alter meaning significantly, thus showing how synonyms have similar but not exact same meanings. For example, if we took the sentence

> "Go away!" *shouted* the grouchy ladybug.

and changed it to read

> "Go away!" *hinted* the grouchy ladybug.

it would be easy for children to understand how the author's message had been softened considerably. This "cross-training" with reading and writing experiences helps synonyms take on new relevance as a literacy tool in the hands of students.

Antonyms are word opposites or near opposites based on a shared characteristic. *Hard–soft* (density), *dark–light* (energy), and *big–small* (size) are examples of antonym pairs. Like synonyms, antonyms help students gain insights into word meanings. When searching for ideal antonym examples, teachers should try to identify word sets that are mutually exclusive or that completely contradict each other.

---

*From *The Grouchy Ladybug* by E. Carle. Copyright secured 1977 in countries signatory to International Copyright Union. Used by permission of HarperCollins Publishers.

Several classes of antonyms have been identified (Johnson & Pearson, 1984) that may be useful in instruction. One class is referred to as *relative pairs* or *counterparts* because one term implies the other. Examples include *mother–father, sister–brother, uncle–aunt,* and *writer–reader.* Other antonyms reflect a complete opposite or reversal of meaning, such as *fast–slow, stop–go,* and *give–take.* Complementary antonyms tend to lead from one to another, such as *give–take, friend–foe,* and *hot–cold.*

Antonym activities, as with all language-learning activities, should be drawn from the contexts of familiar books and student writing samples. Interacting with familiar text and clear meanings, children can easily see the full impact and flavor of different word meanings. Remember, in classroom instruction involving mini-lessons, teaching from whole text to parts (antonyms in this case) is key. Thus, if the teacher decides to develop an antonym worksheet for students, it should be drawn from a book that has already been shared (or will be shared) with the whole class or group. A fun book for this exercise is *Weird Parents* by Audrey Wood (1990), which could yield sentences like the following in which students supply antonyms for the underlined words.

1. There once was a boy who had <u>weird</u> (   ) parents.
2. In the <u>morning</u> (   ), the weird mother always walked the boy to his bus stop.
3. At twelve o'clock when the boy <u>opened</u> (   ) his lunchbox, he'd always have a weird surprise.*

Another activity to practice antonyms is to ask students to find words in their writing or reading for which they can think of antonyms. A student in sixth grade who reads *A Wrinkle in Time* (L'Engle, 1962) might create the following list of words from the novel and their antonyms.

Wrinkle Words	Antonyms
punishment	reward
hesitant	eager
frightening	pleasant

A student in third grade who writes a story about his new baby sister might select antonyms for some of the words he uses in his account.

Baby Story Words	Opposites
asleep	awake
cry	laugh
wet	dry

One way to assess students' ability to recognize antonyms is through multiple-choice and cloze exercises. The teacher should extract sentences from familiar text and have students select the correct antonym for a targeted word from among three choices. These choices might be (1) a synonym of the targeted word, (2) an unrelated word, and (3) the appropriate antonym. Following are two examples of this assessment technique that are based on *The Glorious Flight* (Provensen & Provensen, 1983).

1. Like a great swan, the *beautiful* (attractive, <u>homely</u>, shoots) glider rises into the air . . .
2. Papa is getting *lots* (<u>limited</u>, from, loads) of practice.

*From *Weird Parents* by Audrey Wood, copyright © 1990. Used by permission of Dial Books for Young Readers, a division of Penguin Young Readers Group, a member of Penguin Group (USA), Inc. 395 Hudson Street, New York, NY 10014. All rights reserved.

Of many possible classroom activities, the most profitable will probably be those in which students are required to generate their own responses. Simple recognition items, as with multiple-choice measures, do not require students to think critically in arriving at a correct response.

Activities That Support Incidental Vocabulary Learning

Reading aloud to students is an effective way to boost students' vocabulary development. We know that books, especially nonfiction, are almost twice as rich in rare words (elaborated speaking and academic knowledge domain vocabulary words) as adult conversation (Stahl & Nagy, 2006). It is most productive to read aloud texts that are above students' independent reading levels and at the leading edge of their listening vocabulary (Trelease, 2009). We also want to read aloud from a variety of text genres. One tool we like in planning for read-alouds is the genre wheel discussed in Chapter 5.

When reading aloud you should use **text talk.** There are six components to consider for "talking the text."

- *Selection of texts.* Discuss why you chose this text to share, and name the kind of text genre it represents.
- *Background knowledge.* Have a short discussion about anything within students' common background that may relate to what you will be reading.
- *Vocabulary.* Briefly introduce new vocabulary (elaborated speaking and academic knowledge domain vocabulary words). Pronounce and explain.
- *Initial questions.* Pose some questions about the content of the text to lead students' thinking. This will enhance their attention to key terms and increase comprehension. You may want to post your questions on the whiteboard.
- *Follow-up questions.* Revisit your initial questions and discuss what students learned. You may want to also pose some additional questions to further their thinking.
- *Pictures and concrete objects.* Use pictures and/or concrete objects that represent new vocabulary and concepts. The more concrete the experience, the easier it is for students to understand and retain information.

Helping Students Learn Words Independently

The ultimate task for teachers is to help students become independent word meaning learners. The ongoing learning of new vocabulary throughout life is unquestionably a key to continued self-education. In this section, we feature ways students can become independent learners of new words.

Word-Learning Strategies.   Students must determine the meanings of new words they encounter in reading. The teacher must help them develop effective word-learning strategies such as how to use dictionaries and other reference aids, how to apply information about word parts to figure out the meanings, and how to make inferences from context clues to determine word meanings.

Dictionaries and Other Reference Aids.   Students must understand how dictionaries, glossaries, and thesauruses can help broaden and deepen their knowledge of words. In preparation for using these tools, students must learn alphabetical order, ordinal language (i.e., first, second, third), and the function of guide words. The most helpful dictionaries and reference aids include sentences providing clear examples of word meanings in context.

Structural Analysis: Understanding Word Parts.   As previously discussed in Chapters 1 and 2, morphemes are the smallest parts of words that carry meaning. Free morphemes (or *base words*), stand alone as words and carry meaning. Bound morphemes—like prefixes and suffixes—must be attached to a free morpheme in order to carry meaning. Structural analysis was explained in Chapter 2 as a way to decode multisyllabic words. It involves gaining understanding of morphemes in order to comprehend the meanings of words. For example, learning the four most common prefixes in English (*un-, re-, in-, dis-*) can provide helpful meaning clues for about two-thirds of all English words having prefixes. They are relatively easy to learn because most prefixes have clear meanings (for example, *un-* means "not" and *re-* means "again") and are usually spelled the same way from word to word. Suffixes can often be a bit more challenging. For one thing, quite a few suffixes only change a word's part of speech and do not explain much (e.g., the suffix *-ness,* meaning "the state of," is not all that helpful in figuring out the meaning of *tenderness*).

Students should also learn about root words. About 60 percent of all English words have Latin or Greek origins (Partnership for Reading, 2001). Latin and Greek word roots are common in terms of science and social studies and also form a large share of the new words in students' content area textbooks.

A **morpheme triangle** (Winters, 2009) is a tool for helping students understand and apply their knowledge of word parts (see Figure 6.9). In a visual graphic with three defined spaces for thinking about three-syllable words, the teacher during

Figure 6.9

Morpheme Triangle for *Transported*

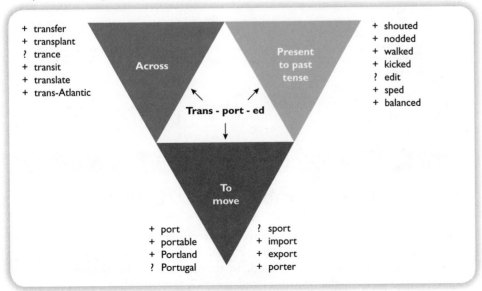

From Winters, R. (2009). "Interactive Frames for Vocabulary Growth and Word Consciousness," *The Reading Teacher, 62*(8), 685–690. Reprinted by permission of the International Reading Association.

instruction divides the word written at the center of the inverted triangle into its morphemes, saying each morpheme while visually splitting the word apart. The class begins thinking aloud about each word part, using the corners of the triangle for each morpheme. Students are asked to volunteer known words that contain the morpheme and each word is discussed and added to an emerging list in the space provided. After five to six words have been suggested, the teacher leads a discussion about possible meanings. When the group agrees on a shared meaning, plus signs are placed in front of words where the meaning seems appropriate. Question marks are inserted for words thought to be "imposters" and more follow-up discussion takes place to confirm the word part's meaning. Winters (2009) states that this willingness to question word meanings rather than assume that the "same spelling always equals same meaning" can be important for students' future word analyses.

Using Context Clues to Determine Word Meanings.   Context clues are indicators of the meaning of an unknown word found in the words, phrases, and sentences that surround the word. It is not an overstatement to say that the ability to use context clues is fundamental to acquiring a larger reading vocabulary. This is because most word meanings students learn incidentally occur from context. The following classroom example from *Put Reading First* (2001) demonstrates the use of context clues as a word-learning strategy.

An Example of Classroom Instruction

Using Context Clues

In a third-grade class, the teacher models how to use context clues to determine word meanings.

Student *(reading the text):* When the cat pounced on the dog, the dog jumped up, yelping, and knocked over a lamp, which crashed to the floor. The animals ran past Tonia, tripping her. She fell to the floor and began sobbing. Tonia's brother Felix yelled at the animals to stop. As the noise and confusion mounted, Mother hollered upstairs, "What's all that commotion?"

Teacher: The context of the paragraph helps us determine what *commotion* means. There's yelping and crashing and sobbing and yelling. And then the last sentence says, "as the noise and confusion mounted." The author's use of the words *noise* and *confusion* gives us a very strong clue as to what *commotion* means. In fact, the author is really giving us a definition there, because *commotion* means something that's noisy and confusing—a disturbance. Mother was right; there was definitely a commotion!

From National Institute for Literacy. (2001). *Put Reading First: The Research Building Blocks for Teaching Children to Read.* Available online at www.nifl.gov.

Response to Intervention (RTI)

Tier 2 Vocabulary Instruction

In the previous sections of this chapter we have focused on basic or "core" vocabulary instruction. In a Response to Intervention (RTI) model this type of teaching would be considered Tier 1 instruction. In this section we focus mainly on Tier 2 interventions that might be considered when Tier 1 vocabulary instruction is insufficient for some students to acquire new word meanings. Struggling readers are more likely to learn essential vocabulary if explicit instruction is part of the

● ● ●

IRA Standards for Reading Professionals: Standard 5, Elements 5.1, 5.2, 5.3

Common Core Standards: Speaking and Listening: K–5, Comprehension and Collaboration (items 1, 3), Presentation of Knowledge and Ideas (items 4, 6); Speaking and Listening: Grades 6–12, Comprehension and Collaboration (items 1, 3), Presentation of Knowledge and Ideas (items 4, 6); Language: K–5, Knowledge of Language (item 3), Vocabulary Acquisition and Use (items 4–6); Language: Grades 6–12, Conventions of Standard English (items 1, 2), Knowledge of Language (item 3), Vocabulary Acquisition and Use (items 4–6)

Response to Intervention: Responsive Teaching and Differentiation; Collaboration; Systemic and Comprehensive Approaches teacher's repertoire of teaching methods (Rupley et al., 2009). At the heart of explicit instruction are explanations, modeling or demonstrating, and guided practice coupled with gradual release to independence, a technique sometimes called *scaffolding*. We also know that student engagement and response are important keys to success (Taylor, et al., 2009). In this section we consider Tier 2 strategies that include both an explicit instruction component and active student engagement. Note that any of the strategies found in this chapter can be adapted for struggling readers as long as you are direct and explicit in your teaching. Direct instruction helps less proficient readers create mental scaffolding for support of new vocabulary and concepts.

The Vocabulary Cluster Strategy

It is especially important that students who struggle with reading use the context of the passage, their background knowledge, and the vocabulary they know to understand new words in print. This is true whether English is their second language or their first (as with students from language-deprived backgrounds). With the vocabulary cluster strategy, students are helped to read a passage, gather context clues, and then predict the meaning of a new word targeted for learning. Here's how it works.

You will need multiple copies of the text students are to read, an overhead transparency and projector, and erasable marking pens for transparencies. Select vocabulary you want to teach from the reading, which could be a poem, song, book excerpt (novel), or nonfiction passage. Prepare a transparency containing an excerpt from this text with sufficient context to help students predict what the unknown word might be. Delete the target words and replace them with blank lines, much the same as you would with a cloze passage. Figure 6.10 illustrates a passage prepared in this way along with a vocabulary cluster supporting the new word to be learned. This example is based on the book *Honey Baby Sugar Child*.

Through discussion, lead students into predicting what the unknown word might be. If the word is not already in students' listening vocabulary, you will be able to introduce the new word quite easily and effectively using the context and synonyms provided in the vocabulary cluster.

Figure 6.10

Vocabulary Cluster based on *Honey Baby Sugar Child*: Target Word *Twirl*

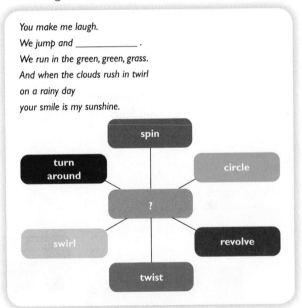

Text reprinted with the permission of Simon and Schuster books for Young Readers, an imprint of Simon and Schuster Children's Publishing, from *Honey Baby Sugar Child* by Alice Faye Duncan. Text copyright © 2005 Alice Faye Duncan.

Semantic Maps

A **semantic map** is essentially a kind of blueprint in which students sketch out or map what they know about a topic. Semantic maps help students relate new concepts to schemata and vocabulary already in the brain as they integrate new information and restructure existing information for greater clarity (Yopp & Yopp, 2000). Students who struggle with reading can use semantic maps prior to the act of

Figure 6.11

Semantic Map: Tennessee

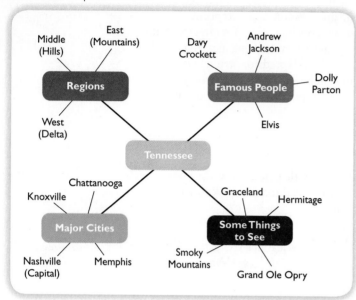

From Reutzel and Cooter, *Strategies for Reading Assessment and Instruction: Helping Every Child Succeed*, 3rd ed. © 2007 by Pearson Education, Inc. Reprinted by permission of Pearson Education, Inc.

reading to promote better recall (Sinatra, Stahl-Gemake, & Berg, 1984).

There are many ways to introduce semantic mapping to students, but the first time around it is best to use direct instruction followed up with a lot of teacher modeling and guided and independent practice.

The actual map is a type of graphic organizer in which a topic under discussion forms the center of a network of descriptors, concepts, and related categories. In introducing the process of mapping, begin with a topic familiar to the entire class, such as your home state. Write the topic on the board or an overhead transparency. Have students brainstorm categories of descriptors and concepts related to the topic and record their ideas. Connect these categories to the topic visually using bold or double lines. Students then brainstorm details that relate to these major categories. Connect details to categories with single lines. Figure 6.11 shows a semantic map for the topic "Tennessee."

Semantic maps (also called *webs*) can also relate to a story or chapter book students are reading. Figure 6.12 features an example (Reutzel & Cooter, 2011) of a

Figure 6.12

Semantic Map: "Guanina"

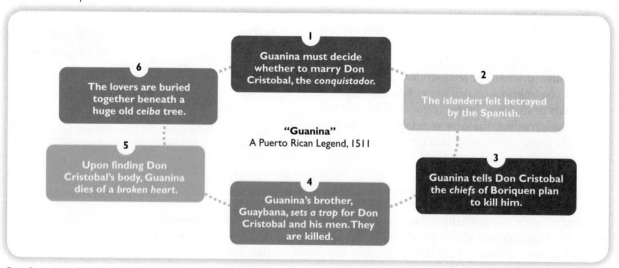

From Reutzel and Cooter, *Strategies for Reading Assessment and Instruction: Helping Every Child Succeed*, 3rd ed. © 2007 by Pearson Education, Inc. Reprinted by permission of Pearson Education, Inc.

semantic map from a story in the book *Golden Tales: Myths, Legends, and Folktales from Latin America* (Delacre, 1996).

Linking Multicultural Experiences with Vocabulary Development

Vocabulary development in spoken and written English is at the heart of literacy learning (Wheatley, Muller, & Miller, 1993). Because of the rich diversity found in U.S. classrooms, teachers need to consider ways of adapting the curriculum so that all students can learn to recognize and use appropriate and varied vocabulary. In this section, we consider three possible avenues proven to be successful in multicultural settings.

Link Vocabulary Studies to a Broad Topic or Novel.   We know that there is a limit to the number of words that can be taught directly and in isolation. Au (1993) tells us that students in multicultural settings learn vocabulary best if the new words are related to a broader topic. Working on vocabulary development in connection with students' exploration of content area topics is a natural way to learn new words and explore their various meanings.

Encourage Wide Reading at Independent Levels as a Vehicle for Vocabulary Development.   Reading for enjoyment on a daily basis helps to increase vocabulary. Teachers can help students become regular readers by assessing their reading interests and then locating books that fit them. Matching books with students is a simple way of encouraging the kinds of reading behaviors that pay dividends.

Implement the Village English Activity.   Delpit (1988) writes about a method of teaching Native Alaskan students new vocabulary that works well in many other multicultural settings. The Village English Activity respects and encourages students' home language while helping them see relationships between language use and social and professional realities in the United States (Au, 1993).

The Village English Activity begins with the teacher writing "Our Language Heritage" at the top of one side of a piece of poster board and "Standard American English" at the top of the other side. The teacher explains to students that in the United States people speak in many different ways, and this variety of languages makes our nation as colorful and interesting as a patchwork quilt. For elementary students, we think this would be a good time to share *Elmer* by David McKee (1990), a book about an elephant of many colors (called a "patchwork elephant") and how he enriched his elephant culture.

The teacher then explains that there are many times when adults need to speak in the same way so they can be understood, usually in formal situations. At such times, we speak Standard American English. When at home or with friends in our community, we usually speak the language of our heritage. It is like the difference between a picnic compared to a "dressed-up" formal dinner. The teacher writes phrases used in students' native dialect under the heading "Our Language Heritage" and notes and discusses comparative translations on the side labeled "Standard American English." These comparisons can be noted in an ongoing way throughout the year as part of a special word wall. The Village English Activity can be an engaging way to increase vocabulary knowledge while demonstrating appreciation for language differences.

IRA Standards for Reading Professionals: Standard 5, Element 5.2

Common Core Standards: Speaking and Listening: K–12, Presentation of Knowledge and Ideas (item 6)

Response to Intervention: Instruction

Click on A+RISE—WIDA ELP Standard Strategies in the MyEducationLab (www.myeducationlab.com) for your course. Next, select the Strategy Card Index tab, scroll to Vocabulary for grades K–5, and select the Mix and Match strategy.

IRA Standards for Reading Professionals: Standard 5, Element 5.1

Common Core Standards: Speaking and Listening: K–12, Comprehension and Collaboration (item 2), Presentation of Knowledge and Ideas (item 5); Language: K–12, Vocabulary Acquisition and Use (items 4, 6)

Response to Intervention: Instruction

Motivation and Engagement

Teaching Vocabulary

Vocabulary instruction is motivating when it is challenging, inventive, and playful. A recent article by Arter and Nilsen (2009) illustrates this point with the popular 13-book series Lemony Snicket. In fact, we encourage you to consider books like these for whole-class instruction to present clever and offbeat uses of words to open readers' eyes to the fun of word play. We fashioned the following lessons from Arter and Nilsen's analysis of Snicket's (a.k.a., Daniel Handler) technique.

1. *Provide readers multiple experiences with a word or a concept.* In *The Ersatz Elevator* (2000) Snicket explains that *ersatz* is "a word that describes a situation in which one thing is pretending to be another, the way the secret passageway the Baudelaires were looking at had been pretending to be an elevator" (p. 129). He also describes a villain as being *ersatz* for pretending to be a good person and calls a cable made of tied-together strips of cloth an *ersatz* rope. Finally, he advises readers who may be imagining a happy ending for the Baudelaires that their "imaginings would be *ersatz,* as all imaginings are" (p. 253) (Arter & Nilsen, 2009, p. 236).

2. *Help students see that words can be defined in quite different yet still correct ways.* Arter and Nilsen (2009) share another clever Snicket example of this truism: "In *The Hostile Hospital* (2001), Snicket plays with the difference between literal and figurative meanings when he has Esmé Squalor arrive at the hospital wearing 'a pair of shoes with stiletto heels.' Although dictionaries describe *stiletto heels* as 'a woman's shoe with a very long and narrow heel, each of Esmé's shoes 'is affixed with a small, slender knife where each heel should be' (p. 116)" (p. 236).

3. *Provide opportunities for creative activities around words.* As an alternative to completing vocabulary worksheets or activity pages, have students create and present Snicket-style definitions for important new vocabulary. This can take place in small-group work (joint productive activities) or involve creating products (such as poster presentations, PowerPoint slides, or interactive whiteboard presentations) that can be presented and discussed.

Technology and New Literacies

Using Technology and New Literacies to Enhance Vocabulary Learning

Digital Jumpstarts

Teacher-composed digital stories, or **digital jumpstarts (DJs)**, have been shown to help students, especially English learners, build vocabulary knowledge and factual background information (Rance-Roney, 2010). The University of Houston's website on digital storytelling explains, "Digital Storytelling is the practice of using computer-based tools to tell stories. As with traditional storytelling, most digital stories focus on a specific topic and contain a particular point of view. However, as the name implies, digital stories usually contain some mixture of computer-based images, text, recorded audio narration, video clips and/or music. Digital stories can vary in length, but most of the stories used in education typically last between two and ten minutes. In essence, DJs help teachers to create supplemental materials for instruction that focus on targeted vocabulary and concepts."

Digital jumpstarts use software such as iMovie for MacBook users or free, downloadable versions of Photo Story or Movie Maker for PC users that can unite still images, a narrator-teacher's voice, music, and sometimes video (Rance-Roney, 2010). Teachers begin by creating a script that provides background information and a schema for the topic and then introduces and repeats targeted vocabulary crucial to the topic. Next the teacher searches for images that support the script and introduces visual images connected to upcoming reading. Google Images (http://images.google.com) and Flickr (www.flickr.com) are great sources for these images. The "voice-over" reading of the script is added next, along with music (if desired). For examples of digital storytelling, links, and resources, go online to http://digitalstorytelling.coe.uh.edu.

Using Podcasts to Enhance Content Vocabulary Development

Podcasting borrows from the traditional radio broadcast concept and transforms it into portable digital media that people can subscribe to over the Internet to receive "shows" directly on their computer (Putman & Kingsley, 2009). Podcasts can then, if desired, be listened to on a portable music player like an MP3 player or iPod. Podcasts were first used for entertainment and in higher education settings, but have since become more common in school settings from kindergarten through high school as teachers use them to enhance learning. We see podcasting as a supplemental tool for vocabulary instruction that can enhance learning and student engagement.

To help teachers interested in trying podcasts for instruction, Putman and Kingsley (2009, p. 106) offer the following suggestions from their work in classrooms.

- *Don't rely on traditional definitions.* Use your own or have students develop their own and use them.

- *Include information that utilizes the words in context.* Periodically read portions of text that include the targeted vocabulary word.

- *Don't just lecture.* Keep the tone light and create podcasts that feel like conversations.

- *Make them interactive.* Students should have to stop the podcast periodically to process the information and complete a brief activity.

- *Be spontaneous.* Students are not going to listen to podcasts that are not interesting or motivating, so add sound effects or an occasional joke.

WEB TOOLS YOU CAN USE IN THE CLASSROOM

Digital Story Telling and Podcasts as Instructional Tools

Digital Story Telling

- For examples of digital storytelling links and resources, go to http://digitalstorytelling.coe.uh.edu.

- To embed images into your digital stories, go to Google Images at http://images.google.com and Flickr at www.flickr.com, both great sources for these images.

Podcasting Technology

- To learn to podcast, go to www.apple.com/ilife/tutorials/#garageband-podcast-51 for a tutorial regarding podcasting with Garageband, Apple's software for creating podcasts. See also www.apple.com/support/garageband/podcasts.

- Podcasting with Audacity, a tutorial for creating podcasts and free PC software for creating audio files used in podcasts, can be found at www.teachertube.com/view_video.php?viewkey=23dc8f4753bcc5771660.

- KidCast: Learning and Teaching with Podcasting, a blog and podcast by Dan Schmit at www.intelligenic.com/blog, can aid educators in learning to create and use podcasts in the classroom.

Web Tools You Can Use in the Classroom lists recommended resources to guide you through developing your own podcasts for vocabulary instruction.

IRA Standards for Reading Professionals: Standard 4, Elements 4.1, 4.2, 4.3

Common Core Standards: Speaking and Listening: K–12, Comprehension and Collaboration (item 1), Presentation of Knowledge and Ideas (items 4, 6); Language: K–12, Knowledge of Language (item 3)

Response to Intervention: Collaboration

Family and Community Connections

Family and Community Connections That Enhance Vocabulary Learning

There are a number of vocabulary-enhancing strategies teachers can use to involve family and community. Opportunities for learning can be found in family activities at home or in community events sponsored by the school.

Reading Backpacks

During our respective careers, we have gone back and forth between teaching in elementary classrooms and in teacher education programs. Some may think we have suffered a series of identity crises (especially our spouses), but we never tire of working with children and their families. Because our better halves are teachers themselves, they humor us. Teaching is the greatest profession on earth!

One of the mainstays of our instruction is the **reading backpack** strategy (Cooter, Mills-House, Marrin, Mathews, & Campbell, 1999; Reutzel & Cooter, 2007; Reutzel & Fawson, 1990). In this straightforward technique, a teacher provides one or more backpacks, perhaps with the school's name and mascot emblazoned on them, that are sent home at least once a week containing reading or writing activities to be completed by a child and parent. Many homes are without printed text of any sort, and reading backpacks can bring fresh opportunities for enjoyment and learning into the family's evening. They can also help parents in their efforts to do something constructive for their child's literacy development. We have used backpacks to send home a supply of trade books on a variety of topics on different reading levels matching the child's ability (in both English and Spanish), easy activities written on reusable laminated card stock, and materials for written responses to books (e.g., markers, colored paper, scissors, tape). Sometimes, if parents themselves are not literate, we have sent books accompanied by tape recordings and a tape player. Teacher-produced videotapes or DVDs demonstrating educational games parents can play with their children can also be sent home for special occasions.

In this section, we share a few backpack ideas you might consider for drawing families into the circle for developing reading vocabulary. In most cases these ideas are easy and inexpensive.

Newspaper Word Race.   Send home the following materials in the backpack:

- Two out-of-date newspapers
- Two copies listing target words you want the child to practice seeing and saying
- An egg timer
- Two highlighting markers
- Directions explaining the task

On a laminated instruction card to the parents, explain that they are to sit down at a table with their child and take one newspaper and highlighter for themselves and give one of each to the child. They should set the egg timer for 1 minute and then have a race to see how many of the target words they can find and circle in the newspaper with their highlighter. When they are finished, they should share with each other the words they found and read the sentence in which they appear. For beginning readers, the parent will sometimes need to read the sentences with words located by the student and then explain what the sentences mean. This process encourages meaningful verbal interaction between parent and child, which we consider very powerful for a child's verbal improvement.

Catalog Interviews.   In this backpack activity, the parent is given an imaginary $5,000 to spend in a shopping spree. The student conducts an interview to find out what the parent will purchase and why. Afterward, the student should write a short summary of what he or she learned from the interview. If $5,000 doesn't seem enough, offer a "million dollar bill." The student interviews family members to find out what they would do with such a fantastic sum. The student then writes about their responses.

The point here is to inspire real dialogue between the parent and student in which words are exchanged and discussed. As we saw earlier in this chapter, students add words to their listening and speaking vocabularies when they are engaged in two-way discussions (K. Cooter, 2006), which this activity helps to make happen. This backpack activity only needs a few supplies:

- A target words vocabulary card with words to be used in writing
- A catalog that may be used for inspiring joint writing between student and parent
- Directions explaining the task
- Writing supplies (paper, pencils)

Scrabble. If you are lucky in your garage sale junkets you may come across an old edition of the perennial favorite Scrabble for your reading backpacks. This is the quintessential vocabulary game, of course, and having students play Scrabble with their family will provide a splendid opportunity for word talk. A variation would be to send home with the board game a target words vocabulary card and indicate that every target word used by anyone playing the game earns an extra five points. For this backpack activity you will need the following:

- Scrabble game
- Target words vocabulary card with words to be used for bonus credit
- Directions explaining the task

Language Workshop: After-School Vocabulary-Building Activities

Townsend (2009) developed a voluntary after-school program for English learners (ELs) called the **language workshop**. Research-based sessions focus on increasing academic vocabulary knowledge (see Figure 6.2) and include collaborative, fast-paced, and highly interactive activities combined with elements of direct instruction and text-based discussions of the target words. As Townsend (2009) explains,

> In designing Language Workshop, we absolutely had to respond to needs for engagement and fun; a voluntary after-school program on academic vocabulary words without these components would not have yielded much student attendance. Each session involved direct instruction of words and discussions around words as they appeared in short pieces of informational text that were accompanied with many diagrams and pictures. (pp. 244–245)

Following are some of the activities found to be effective in the language workshop.

Picture Puzzlers. Because academic vocabulary can be quite abstract and may carry different meanings in different contexts, activities in which students are asked to match pictures to new target words can be a little confusing. Townsend (2009) illustrates these challenges using the word *function* as an example. He notes that this word is defined both as the purpose something has and as something working correctly.

Such definitions are nearly impossible to illustrate with a picture, but a picture of a computer working correctly (or incorrectly) provides an opportunity to discuss what it means when something is functioning. A picture of a household item such as a kitchen sponge or a screwdriver allows for a discussion of the functions of these items.

With picture puzzlers (Townsend, 2009) the teacher works each day with students to choose pictures with contexts that match target words and then use those pictures to prompt small-group and whole-class discussion. Picture puzzlers are consistent with reading research in that they provide students with visual cues, multiple exposures to new words in varied contexts, and opportunities to process and personalize word meanings.

Academic Taboo.   Based on the popular Hasbro game Taboo, the object of Academic Taboo is for one student to provide clues to get his team to say a target word or academic word wall term by describing it without using certain specified (closely related) words. For example, a student might have to get his team to guess the word *automobile* without using the words *car, vehicle,* or brand names (e.g., Chevrolet, Toyota). In Townsend's language workshop version of Academic Taboo players make game cards using the academic target words and other words from instructional texts and discussions. The group is divided into two teams, with one student from each group competing on every turn. Because academic vocabulary words are so abstract, they do not always include a list of related words that are banned from play (making it more like the Password game). In this case, students name as many clue words as they can in 1 minute. Academic Taboo is a fast-paced and highly interactive game that provides students with opportunities to think about word meanings and connections between words.

Summary

Dale Johnson (2001, pp. 41–48), an eminent researcher in the field of vocabulary development, provides valuable insights in his book *Vocabulary in the Elementary and Middle School.* From his writings, we know that word knowledge is essential for reading comprehension. Evidenced-based research tells us that vocabulary instruction should utilize motivational activities that link word learning to concept and schema development. We should also teach specific word learning strategies to our students, as well as strategies they can use on their own to understand unfamiliar words in print.

Wide reading should be encouraged and made possible in the classroom. Literally thousands of words are learned through regular and sustained reading. Time should be set aside each day for this crucial learning activity. As an example, Johnson (2001) advocated the use of a program called "Read-a-Million-Minutes" which was designed to foster wide reading throughout Iowa. All students set their own in-school and out-of-school reading goals that contribute to the school's goal.

Explicit instruction should be used to teach words that are necessary for passage comprehension. Considering how critical some words are for comprehending a new passage, teachers should not leave vocabulary learning to incidental encounters, but rather plan regular explicit vocabulary instruction lessons to make sure that new word meanings are learned as a part of every school day. Active learning activities yield the best results. According to research conducted by Stahl (1986), vocabulary instruction that provided only definitional information (i.e., dictionary activities) failed to significantly improve comprehension. Active learning opportunities such as creation of word webs, playing word games, and discussing new words in reading groups or literature circles, are far more effective in cementing new knowledge and improving comprehension.

We also know that students require a good bit of repetition to learn new words and integrate them into existing knowledge (schemas). In some cases, students may require as many as 40 encounters to fully learn new vocabulary. To know a word well means knowing what it means, how to pronounce it, and how its meaning changes in different contexts. Repeated exposures to the word in different contexts are key to successful vocabulary learning.

Students should be helped to develop independence in using vocabulary learning strategies. This includes the use of context clues, structural analysis (word roots, prefixes, suffixes), and research skills (use of the dictionary, thesaurus, etc.).

Finally, parents can help their children succeed in expanding concept and vocabulary knowledge by exposing them to new experiences and helping them to read about and discuss new ideas in the home.

Field and Classroom Applications

- Design a lesson plan introducing word walls to third-grade students. Be certain that the lesson includes rich literature examples, teacher–student interaction, and student–student discussion.
- As a joint productive activity, with a group of peers in your college class or in your school, review a local school district's curriculum guide for a specific grade level and select two topics or themes of study in either science or social studies. Plan and teach three word sort activities using relevant academic vocabulary to a group of children. How can you assess the effectiveness of your lessons?
- Develop and present a podcast for a unit of instruction in science that emphasizes the specialized vocabulary contained therein. This can be for a grade level of your choosing.
- Develop and administer a cloze test and a maze test to two different groups of children using a text they will be reading. Analyze your results. Afterward, interview several of the students from each group. Try to discover whether the "cloze" or the "maze" students felt they did well on the exercise. Does one group feel more positive when you use the given procedure? Why do you think that is?
- With two partners, fully develop five reading backpack family activities. Work with your cooperating classroom teacher to distribute your backpacks to five students. Once the backpacks return, interview the students to discover what happened at home and what they thought of the backpack activity. Send home a brief survey to parents as well if time permits.

Recommended Resources

Print Resources

Bear, D., Invernizzi, M., Templeton, S., & Johnston, F. (2007). *Words their way: Word study for phonics, vocabulary, and spelling instruction.* Boston: Pearson.

Cooter, K. S. (2006). When mama can't read: Counter-acting intergenerational illiteracy. *The Reading Teacher, 59*(7), 698–702.

Fry, E. B., Kress, J. E., & Fountoukidis, D. L. (2006). *The reading teacher's book of lists* (5th ed.). Hoboken, NJ: Jossey-Bass/Wiley.

Johnson, D. D. (2001). *Vocabulary in the elementary and middle school.* Boston: Allyn and Bacon.

Peregoy, S. F., & Boyle, O. F. (2001). *Reading, writing, & learning in ESL.* New York: Longman.

Web Resources

http://crede.berkeley.edu
   The CREDE Center at U.C. Berkeley: Information on Joint Productive Activities

www.hangmangame.net
   The Hangman Game

http://digitalstorytelling.coe.uh.edu
   Digital storytelling links and resources

http://images.google.com
www.flickr.com
   Google Images and Flickr; digital images that may be used in preparing PowerPoints and other teaching aids connected to upcoming reading assignments, etc.

www.readwritethink.org.
   Word sorts and many other vocabulary activities

www.apple.com/ilife/tutorials/#garageband-podcast-51
   Learning to Podcast (Apple)

www.apple.com/support/garageband/podcasts
   More support from Apple for podcasting

www.teachertube.com/view_video.php?viewkey=23dc8f4753bcc5771660
   Podcasting with Audacity: A Tutorial for PCs

www.intelligenic.com/blog
   KidCast: Learning and Teaching with Podcasting

The Power of Classroom Practice
www.myeducationlab.com

Go to Topic 5, Vocabulary, in the MyEducationLab (www.myeducationlab.com) for your course, where you can:

- Find learning outcomes for Vocabulary along with the national standards that connect to these outcomes.
- Complete Assignments and Activities that can help you more deeply understand the chapter content.
- Apply and practice your understanding of the core teaching skills identified in the chapter with the Building Teaching Skills and Dispositions learning units. (optional)
- Examine challenging situations and cases presented in the IRIS Center Resources. (optional)
- Access video clips of CCSSO National Teachers of the Year award winners responding to the question "Why Do I Teach?" in the Teacher Talk section. (optional)
- Check your comprehension on the content covered in the chapter by going to the Study Plan in the Book Resources for your text. Here you will be able to take a chapter quiz, receive feedback on your answers, and then access Review, Practice, and Enrichment activities to enhance your understanding of chapter content. (optional)

Go to the Topic A+RISE in the MyEducationLab (www.myeducationlab.com) for your course. A+RISE® Standards2Strategy™ is an innovative and interactive online resource that offers new teachers in grades K–12 just in time, research-based instructional strategies that:

- Meet the linguistic needs of ELLs as they learn content.
- Differentiate instruction for all grades and abilities.
- Offer reading and writing techniques, cooperative learning, use of linguistic and nonlinguistic representations, scaffolding, teacher modeling, higher order thinking, and alternative classroom ELL assessment.
- Provide support to help teachers be effective through the integration of listening, speaking, reading, and writing along with the content curriculum.
- Improve student achievement.
- Are aligned to Common Core Elementary Language Arts standards (for the literacy strategies) and to English language proficiency standards in WIDA, Texas, California, and Florida.

STANDARDS
for Reading Professionals and Guiding Principles for Educators

IRA Standards for Reading Professionals

Standard 1: Foundational Knowledge

Element 1.1

Candidates understand major theories and empirical research that describe the cognitive, linguistic, motivational, and sociocultural foundations of reading and writing development, processes, and components, including word recognition, language comprehension, strategic knowledge, and reading–writing connections.

Common Core Standards

Teachers should be familiar with the following standards.

Language: K–12

Conventions of Standard English

1. Demonstrate command of the conventions of standard English grammar and usage when writing or speaking.

2. Demonstrate command of the conventions of standard English capitalization, punctuation, and spelling when writing.

Knowledge of Language

3. Apply knowledge of language to understand how language functions in different contexts, to make effective choices for meaning or style, and to comprehend more fully when reading or listening.

Vocabulary Acquisition and Use

4. Determine or clarify the meaning of unknown and multiple-meaning words and phrases by using context clues, analyzing meaningful word parts, and consulting general and specialized reference materials, as appropriate.

5. Demonstrate understanding of word relationships and nuances in word meanings.

6. Acquire and use accurately a range of general academic and domain-specific words and phrases sufficient for reading, writing, speaking, and listening at the college and career readiness level; demonstrate independence in gathering vocabulary knowledge when encountering an unknown term important to comprehension or expression.

Response to Intervention

6. Expertise

All students have the right to receive instruction from well-prepared teachers who keep up to date and supplemental instruction from professionals specifically prepared to teach language and literacy (IRA, 2000).

- Teacher expertise is central to instructional improvement, particularly for students who encounter difficulty in acquiring language and literacy. RTI may involve a range of professionals; however, the greater the literacy difficulty, the greater the need for expertise in literacy teaching and learning.
- Important dimensions of teachers' expertise include their knowledge and understanding of language and literacy development, their ability to use powerful assessment tools and techniques, and their ability to translate information about student performance into instructionally relevant instructional techniques.
- The exemplary core instruction that is so essential to the success of RTI is dependent on highly knowledgeable and skilled classroom teachers (IRA, 2003).
- Professionals who provide supplemental instruction or intervention must have a high level of expertise in all aspects of language and literacy instruction and assessment and be capable of intensifying or accelerating language and literacy learning.
- Success for culturally and linguistically diverse students depends on teachers and support personnel who are well prepared to teach in a variety of settings. Deep knowledge of cultural and linguistic differences is especially critical for the prevention of language and literacy problems in diverse student populations.

IRA Standards for Reading Professionals

Standard 3: Assessment and Evaluation

Element 3.1

Candidates understand types of assessments and their purposes, strengths, and limitations.

Element 3.2

Candidates select, develop, administer, and interpret assessments, both traditional print and electronic, for specific purposes.

Element 3.3

Candidates use assessment information to plan and evaluate instruction.

Common Core Standards

Speaking and Listening: K–5
Comprehension and Collaboration

3. Evaluate a speaker's point of view, reasoning, and use of evidence and rhetoric.

Speaking and Listening: Grades 6–12
Comprehension and Collaboration

2. Integrate and evaluate information presented in diverse media and formats, including visually, quantitatively, and orally.

3. Evaluate a speaker's point of view, reasoning, and use of evidence and rhetoric.

Language: K–5
Conventions of Standard English

1. Demonstrate command of the conventions of standard English grammar and usage when writing or speaking.

2. Demonstrate command of the conventions of standard English capitalization, punctuation, and spelling when writing.

Knowledge of Language

3. Apply knowledge of language to understand how language functions in different contexts, to make effective choices for meaning or style, and to comprehend more fully when reading or listening.

Vocabulary Acquisition and Use

4. Determine or clarify the meaning of unknown and multiple-meaning words and phrases by using context clues, analyzing meaningful word parts, and consulting general and specialized reference materials, as appropriate.

5. Demonstrate understanding of word relationships and nuances in word meanings.

6. Acquire and use accurately a range of general academic and domain-specific words and phrases sufficient for reading, writing, speaking, and listening at the college and career readiness level; demonstrate independence in gathering vocabulary knowledge when considering a word or phrase important to comprehension or expression.

Response to Intervention

3. Assessment

An RTI approach demands assessment that can inform language and literacy instruction meaningfully.

- Assessment should reflect the multidimensional nature of language and literacy learning and the diversity among students being assessed. The utility of an assessment is dependent on the extent to which it provides valid information on the essential aspects of language and literacy that can be used to plan appropriate instruction.
- Assessments, tools, and techniques should provide useful and timely information about desired language and literacy goals. They should reflect authentic language and literacy activities as opposed to contrived texts or tasks generated specifically for assessment purposes. The quality of assessment information should not be sacrificed for the efficiency of an assessment procedure.
- Multiple purposes for assessment should be clearly identified and appropriate tools and techniques employed. Not all available tools and techniques are appropriate for all purposes, and different assessments—even in the same language or literacy domain—

capture different skills and knowledge. Particular care should be taken in selecting assessments for ELLs and for students who speak an English dialect that differs from mainstream dialects.
- Efficient assessment systems involve a layered approach in which screening techniques are used both to identify which students require further (diagnostic) assessment and to provide aggregate data about the nature of student achievement overall. Initial (screening) assessments should not be used as the sole mechanism for determining the appropriateness of targeted interventions. Ongoing progress monitoring must include an evaluation of the instruction itself and requires observation of the student in the classroom.
- Classroom teachers and reading/literacy specialists should play a central role in conducting language and literacy assessments and in using assessment results to plan instruction and monitor student performance.
- Assessment as a component of RTI should be consistent with the *Standards for the Assessment of Reading and Writing* developed jointly by the International Reading Association and the National Council of Teachers of English (2010).

Evidence-Based Instruction Practices for Increasing Vocabulary Knowledge

IRA Standards for Reading Professionals

Standard 2: Curriculum and Instruction

The Curriculum and Instruction Standard recognizes the need to prepare educators who have a deep understanding and knowledge of the elements of a balanced, integrated, and comprehensive literacy curriculum and have developed expertise in enacting that curriculum. The elements focus on the use of effective practices in a well-articulated curriculum, using traditional print, digital, and online resources.

Element 2.1

Candidates use foundational knowledge to design or implement an integrated, comprehensive, and balanced curriculum.

Element 2.2

Candidates use appropriate and varied instructional approaches, including those that develop word recognition, language comprehension, strategic knowledge, and reading–writing connections.

Element 2.3

Candidates use a wide range of texts (e.g., narrative, expository, and poetry) from traditional print, digital, and online resources.

Standard 4: Diversity

Element 4.1

Candidates recognize, understand, and value the forms of diversity that exist in society and their importance in learning to read and write.

Element 4.2

Candidates use a literacy curriculum and engage in instructional practices that positively impact students' knowledge, beliefs, and engagement with the features of diversity.

Element 4.3

Candidates develop and implement strategies to advocate for equity.

Standard 5: Literate Environment

Element 5.1

Candidates design the physical environment to optimize students' use of traditional print, digital, and online resources in reading and writing instruction.

Element 5.2

Candidates design a social environment that is low risk and includes choice, motivation, and scaffolded support to optimize students' opportunities for learning to read and write.

Element 5.3

Candidates use routines to support reading and writing instruction (e.g., time allocation, transitions from one activity to another, discussions, and peer feedback).

Common Core Standards

Speaking and Listening: K–5

Comprehension and Collaboration

1. Prepare for and participate effectively in a range of conversations and collaborations with diverse partners, building on others' ideas and expressing their own clearly and persuasively.

3. (See previous)

Presentation of Knowledge and Ideas

4. Present information, findings, and supporting evidence such that listeners can follow the line of reasoning and the organization, development, and style are appropriate to task, purpose, and audience.

6. Adapt speech to a variety of contexts and communicative tasks, demonstrating command of formal English when indicated or appropriate.

Speaking and Listening: Grades 6–12

Comprehension and Collaboration

1. Prepare for and participate effectively in a range of conversations and collaborations with diverse partners, building on others' ideas and expressing their own clearly and persuasively.

3. Evaluate a speaker's point of view, reasoning, and use of evidence and rhetoric.

Presentation of Knowledge and Ideas

4. Present information, findings, and supporting evidence such that listeners can follow the line of reasoning and the organization, development, and style are appropriate to task, purpose, and audience.

6. Adapt speech to a variety of contexts and communicative tasks, demonstrating command of formal English when indicated or appropriate.

Language: K–5

Knowledge of Language

3. (See previous)

Vocabulary Acquisition and Use

4. (See previous)

5. (See previous)

6. (See previous)

Language: Grades 6–12

Conventions of Standard English

1. Demonstrate command of the conventions of standard English grammar and usage when writing or speaking.

2. Demonstrate command of the conventions of standard English capitalization, punctuation, and spelling when writing.

Knowledge of Language

3. Apply knowledge of language to understand how language functions in different contexts, to make effective choices for meaning or style, and to comprehend more fully when reading or listening.

Vocabulary Acquisition and Use

4. Determine or clarify the meaning of unknown and multiple-meaning words and phrases by using context clues, analyzing meaningful word parts, and consulting general and specialized reference materials, as appropriate.

5. Demonstrate understanding of word relationships and nuances in word meanings.

6. Acquire and use accurately a range of general academic and domain-specific words and phrases sufficient for reading, writing, speaking, and listening at the college and career readiness level; demonstrate independence in gathering vocabulary knowledge when considering a word or phrase important to comprehension or expression.

Response to Intervention

1. Instruction

RTI is first and foremost intended to prevent problems by optimizing language and literacy instruction.

• Whatever approach is taken to RTI, it should ensure optimal instruction for every student at all levels of schooling. It should

prevent serious language and literacy problems through increasingly differentiated and intensified assessment and instruction and reduce the disproportionate number of minority youth and ELLs identified as learning disabled.

• Instruction and assessment conducted by the classroom teacher are central to the success of RTI and must address the needs of all students, including those from diverse cultural and linguistic backgrounds. Evidence shows that effective classroom instruction can reduce substantially the number of students who are inappropriately classified as learning disabled.

- A successful RTI process begins with the highest quality core instruction in the classroom—that is, instruction that encompasses all areas of language and literacy as part of a coherent curriculum that is developmentally appropriate for preK–12 students and does not underestimate their potential for learning. This core instruction may or may not involve commercial programs, and it must in all cases be provided by an informed, competent classroom teacher.
- The success of RTI depends on the classroom teacher's use of research-based practices.
- Research on instructional practices must provide not only information about what works, but also what works with whom, by whom, in what contexts, and on which outcomes. The effectiveness of a particular practice needs to have been demonstrated with the types of students who will receive the instruction, taking into account, for example, whether the students live in rural or urban settings or come from diverse cultural and linguistic backgrounds.
- When core language and literacy instruction is not effective for a particular student, it should be modified to address more closely the needs and abilities of that student.

2. Responsive Teaching and Differentiation

The RTI process emphasizes increasingly differentiated and intensified instruction or intervention in language and literacy.

- RTI is centrally about optimizing language and literacy instruction for particular students. This means that differentiated instruction, based on instructionally relevant assessment, is essential.
- Instruction and materials selection must derive from specific student–teacher interactions and not be constrained by packaged programs. Students have different language and literacy

needs, so they may not respond similarly to instruction—even when research-based practices are used. No single approach to instruction or intervention can address the broad and varied goals and needs of all students, especially those from different cultural and linguistic backgrounds.

5. Systemic and Comprehensive Approaches

RTI must be part of a comprehensive, systemic approach to language and literacy assessment and instruction that supports all preK–12 students and teachers.

- RTI needs to be integrated within the context of a coherent and consistent language and literacy curriculum that guides comprehensive instruction for all students.
- Specific approaches to RTI need to be appropriate for the particular school or district culture and take into account leadership, expertise, the diversity of the student population, and the available resources. Schools and districts should adopt an approach that best matches their needs and resources while still accomplishing the overall goals of RTI.
- A systemic approach to language and literacy learning within an RTI framework requires the active participation and genuine collaboration of many professionals, including classroom teachers, reading specialists, literacy coaches, special educators, and school psychologists. Given the critical role that language development plays in literacy learning, professionals with specialized language-related expertise such as speech-language pathologists and teachers of ELLs may be particularly helpful in addressing students' language difficulties.
- Approaches to RTI must be sensitive to developmental differences in language and literacy among students at different ages and grades. Although many prevailing approaches to RTI focus on the early elementary grades, it is essential for teachers and support personnel at middle and secondary levels to provide their students with the language and literacy instruction they need to succeed in school and beyond.

Tier 2 Vocabulary Instruction

IRA Standards for Reading Professionals

Standard 5: Literate Environment

Elements 5.1, 5.2, 5.3 (See previous)

Common Core Standards

Speaking and Listening: K–5
Comprehension and Collaboration

1. (See previous)

3. (See previous)

Presentation of Knowledge and Ideas

4. (See previous)

6. (See previous)

Speaking and Listening: Grades 6–12
Comprehension and Collaboration

1. (See previous)

3. (See previous)

Presentation of Knowledge and Ideas

4. (See previous)

6. (See previous)

Language: K–5
Knowledge of Language

3. (See previous)

Vocabulary Acquisition and Use

4. (See previous)

5. (See previous)

6. (See previous)

Language: Grades 6–12

Conventions of Standard English

1. (See previous)

2. (See previous)

Knowledge of Language

3. (See previous)

Vocabulary Acquisition and Use

4. (See previous)

5. (See previous)

6. (See previous)

2. Responsive Teaching and Differentiation (See previous)

4. Collaboration

RTI requires a dynamic, positive, and productive collaboration among professionals with relevant expertise in language and literacy. Success also depends on strong and respectful partnerships among professionals, parents, and students.

- Collaboration should be focused on the available evidence about the needs of students struggling in language and literacy. School-level decision-making teams (e.g., intervention teams, problem-solving teams, RTI teams) should include members with relevant

experience in language and literacy, including second-language learning.

- Reading/literacy specialists and coaches should provide leadership in every aspect of an RTI process—planning, assessment, provision of more intensified instruction and support, and making decisions about next steps.
- Collaboration should increase, not reduce, the coherence of the instruction experienced by struggling readers.

5. Systemic and Comprehensive Approaches (See previous)

Standard 5: Literate Environment

Element 5.2 (See previous)

Speaking and Listening: K–12

Presentation of Knowledge and Ideas

6. Adapt speech to a variety of contexts and communicative tasks, demonstrating command of formal English when indicated or appropriate.

1. Instruction

RTI is first and foremost intended to prevent problems by optimizing language and literacy instruction.

- Instruction and assessment conducted by the classroom teacher are central to the success of RTI and must address the needs of all students, including those from diverse cultural and linguistic backgrounds. Evidence shows that effective classroom instruction can reduce substantially the number of students who are inappropriately classified as learning disabled.
- The success of RTI depends on the classroom teacher's use of research-based practices.

- Research on instructional practices must provide not only information about what works, but also what works with whom, by whom, in what contexts, and on which outcomes. The effectiveness of a particular practice needs to have been demonstrated with the types of students who will receive the instruction, taking into account, for example, whether the students live in rural or urban settings or come from diverse cultural and linguistic backgrounds.
- When core language and literacy instruction is not effective for a particular student, it should be modified to address more closely the needs and abilities of that student.

Standard 5: Literate Environment

Element 5.1 (See previous)

Common Core Standards

Speaking and Listening: K–12

Comprehension and Collaboration

2. Integrate and evaluate information presented in diverse media and formats, including visually, quantitatively, and orally.

Presentation of Knowledge and Ideas

5. Make strategic use of digital media and visual displays of data to express information and enhance understanding of presentations.

Language: K–12

Vocabulary Acquisition and Use

4. (See previous)

6. (See previous)

Response to Intervention

1. Instruction

- Whatever approach is taken to RTI, it should ensure optimal instruction for every student at all levels of schooling. It should prevent serious language and literacy problems through increasingly differentiated and intensified assessment and instruction and reduce the disproportionate number of minority youth and ELLs identified as learning disabled.

- The success of RTI depends on the classroom teacher's use of research-based practices.
- Research on instructional practices must provide not only information about what works, but also what works with whom, by whom, in what contexts, and on which outcomes.

Family and Community Connections That Enhance Vocabulary Learning

IRA Standards for Reading Professionals

Standard 4: Diversity

Elements 4.1, 4.2, 4.3 (See previous)

Common Core Standards

Speaking and Listening: K–12

Comprehension and Collaboration

1. Prepare for and participate effectively in a range of conversations and collaborations with diverse partners, building on others' ideas and expressing their own clearly and persuasively.

Presentation of Knowledge and Ideas

4. Present information, findings, and supporting evidence such that listeners can follow the line of reasoning and the organiza-

tion, development, and style are appropriate to task, purpose, and audience.

6. Adapt speech to a variety of contexts and communicative tasks, demonstrating command of formal English when indicated or appropriate.

Language: K–12

Knowledge of Language

3. (See previous)

Response to Intervention

4. Collaboration

- Collaboration should be focused on the available evidence about the needs of students struggling in language and literacy. School-level decision-making teams (e.g., intervention teams, problem-solving teams, RTI teams) should include members with relevant experience in language and literacy, including second language learning.

- Involving parents and students and engaging them in a collaborative manner is critical to successful implementation. Initiating and strengthening collaborations among school, home, and communities, particularly in urban and rural areas, provides the basis for support and reinforcement of students' learning.

Teaching Reading 7
Comprehension

Teacher Knowledge	Classroom Assessment	Evidence-Based Teaching Practices	Response to Intervention (RTI)
What Is Reading Comprehension?	Assessing Reading Comprehension	What Are the Most Effective Ways to Teach Reading Comprehension?	Meeting Diverse Needs for Tiers 1 and 2 in Comprehension Instruction

Chapter Questions

What is reading comprehension, and what does research say about reading comprehension instruction?

How is reading comprehension assessed effectively?

What are evidence-based instructional practices or strategies for developing reading comprehension?

How can Tier 1 and Tier 2 comprehension instruction be adapted to meet the needs of diverse learners including English learners (ELs)?

How can literature circles play a role in improving motivation to learn comprehension skills?

What are some ways that the Internet can be used to support comprehension instruction?

How can families and communities support children's reading comprehension development?

Key Terms

Schema theory

Construction-integration theory

Multiple comprehension strategies

Benchmark standards

Metacognition

Story grammar

Unaided recall

Content approaches

Dialogic reading

Visualizing

Text features

Scaffolding

Input

Teaching modeling

Guided practice

Higher-order thinking

Question–Answer Relationships (QARs)

Questioning the author

Elaborative interrogation

Fix-up strategies

PARIS

Reciprocal teaching (RT)

Dialogic teaching

Reader response

Motivation and Engagement	Technology and New Literacies	Family and Community Connections
Motivation and Engagement Strategies for Teaching Reading Comprehension	Internet Reciprocal Teaching	Family and Community Connections That Enhance Students' Reading Comprehension

Vignette:
Breakthroughs to Comprehension

Since the beginning of the school year, Ms. Dewey has taught seven comprehension strategies to her students. She taught these strategies one at a time, using clear explanations and think-aloud modeling, and scaffolded her instruction so each student can use the strategies independently.

After the winter holiday break, Ms. Dewey decides to teach her second graders how to use the seven reading comprehension strategies in combination—as a "strategy family." To start this process, she produces seven posters, one for each strategy in the set of seven. She refers to these posters when she models for her students how to select comprehension strategies and use them during reading. Her posters are shown in the photo at the bottom of the page.

Ms. Dewey loves to read science books with her students, especially big books. And her students particularly enjoy reading science big books and participating in lessons using the "family" of seven comprehension strategies. For example, one day while videotaping a lesson for later review, Ms. Dewey records one little boy, Juan, saying enthusiastically, "I just love this stuff!" The class is reading a book about different frogs.

It has taken several years for Ms. Dewey to reshape comprehension instruction in her classroom and to see students achieve on much higher levels. In fact, she is always making adjustments to her teaching as she learns more about comprehension instruction and, most important, her students. As she listens to Juan's excited pronouncement, she echoes it, whispering to herself, "I love this stuff, too!" ■

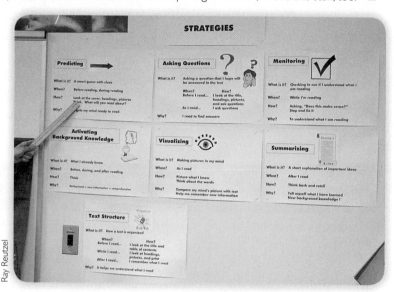

Ray Reutzel

Comprehension is the very heart and soul of reading. Although learning to translate letters into words is extremely important, understanding the author's message is what it's all about. From the very beginning, teachers help students construct meaning from print. But what is it that teachers like Ms. Dewey know that helps them develop good "comprehenders" in their classrooms?

Teacher Knowledge

What Is Reading Comprehension?

Early in the twenty-first century, reading comprehension research was summarized by two "blue ribbon" groups: the National Reading Panel (2000) and the RAND Reading Study Group (2002). The National Reading Panel (NRP) described reading comprehension thus:

> Comprehension is a complex process . . . often viewed as "the essence of reading." Reading comprehension is . . . *intentional thinking* during which meaning is constructed through interactions between text and reader. . . . The content of meaning is influenced by the text and by the reader's prior knowledge and experience that are brought to bear on it. (pp. 4–5)

Similarly, the RAND Reading Study Group (2002) noted that reading comprehension involves four components: (1) the reader, (2) the text, (3) the activity, and (4) the situational context (p. 1). The first three essential components—the reader, the text, and the task—occur within the fourth component of reading comprehension—the situational context. The *reader* is the one doing the comprehending, and the *text* is the reading material (stories, nonfiction selections, etc.). The *activity* refers to what kind of comprehension task, skill, strategy, or concept the reader is attempting to perform (e.g., discovering the author's main idea, understanding a sequence of events, or thinking about a character's intent in a story).

The *situational context* of reading comprehension can be thought of in at least two ways. First, the actual setting where reading occurs—at home, in a school classroom, the library, under a blanket at bedtime, and so on—affects how well one comprehends while reading. There is little doubt that children's reading comprehension is influenced by the setting in which they read. (Aren't you more focused and relaxed when reading alone at home than if called on to read during a college class?) Second, there is a social context associated with reading comprehension. In some cases, reading comprehension occurs individually, alone—a very limited social setting. In other cases, however, reading comprehension can be part of a vibrant social activity in which people—teachers, parents, and children—read a text together and jointly construct meaning through discussion. Lively interaction about a text in the company of others seems to be the optimal situational context to enhance students' reading comprehension (McKeown, Beck, & Blake, 2009).

IRA Standards for Reading Professionals: Standard 1, Elements 1.1, 1.2

Common Core Standards: Reading: K–5, Key Ideas and Details (items 1–3), Craft and Structure (items 4, 5), Integration of Knowledge and Ideas (items 7–9), Range of Reading and Level of Text Complexity (item 10); Reading: Grades 6–12, Key Ideas and Details (items 1–3), Craft and Structure (items 4–6), Integration of Knowledge and Ideas (items 7–9), Range of Reading and Level of Text Complexity (item 10)

Response to Intervention: Expertise

"Less Is More" in Comprehension Instruction

Dewitz, Jones, and Leahy (2009) found that commercial reading programs used by most school districts are not very effective in teaching reading comprehension. Such core reading programs must be used selectively and supplemented by a knowledgeable teacher if children are to reach their potential. For example, the National

Reading Panel (2000) recommends that teachers primarily focus on seven specific comprehension strategies supported by rigorous research (plus multiple-strategy instruction) whereas other researchers (e.g., Dymock & Nicholson, 2010) feel five is the magic number of strategies for intensive focus. But the curricula found in leading core reading programs today cover skills and strategies varying from 18 to 29 per program *per year!* Not only is this unnecessary and ineffective, but the large numbers of skills and strategies taught in core reading programs means that all get superficial treatment, often at a rate of one skill a week (Dewitz et al., 2009). As Dewitz and colleagues state:

> Our analysis of comprehension instruction in core reading programs demonstrates several shortcomings that may undermine their efficacy. First, the comprehension skills and strategies curricula are wide but not terribly deep. The structure of the curricula is often incoherent so that students and teachers do not know how skills and strategies relate to one another or how acquiring these sets of skills leads to becoming a better reader. (p. 120)

Later in this chapter's Pillar Three section, we review ways you can take control and supplement your core reading program to produce effective comprehension instruction for your students.

How Do Children Develop Reading Comprehension?

Research over the past 30 years has contributed greatly to our understanding of the thinking processes involved in reading comprehension. Surprisingly, however, little research has focused on the development of *young* children's comprehension (Reutzel, Smith, & Fawson, 2005).

Pressley (2000) describes the development of reading comprehension as a two-stage process, beginning with "lower processes" focused at the word level—such as word recognition (phonics, sight words), fluency (rate, accuracy, and expression), and vocabulary (word meanings). The second stage of reading comprehension development focuses on higher-order thinking—relating prior knowledge to text content and consciously learning, selecting, and controlling the use of several cognitive strategies for remembering and learning from text.

Schema Theory. Reading comprehension research over the years has been profoundly influenced by **schema theory**, a hypothesis that explains how information we have stored in our minds helps us gain new knowledge. The term *schema* (the plural is *schemata* or *schemas*) can be defined as a kind of storage cabinet in our brains with file folders containing different information about (1) concepts (chairs, birds, ships), (2) events (weddings, birthdays, school experiences), (3) emotions (anger, frustration, joy, pleasure), and (4) roles (parent, judge, teacher) drawn from our life experiences (Anderson & Pearson, 1984; Rumelhart, 1981). Researchers often think of our schemas as neural networks (i.e., "brain networks") of connected meanings (Collins & Quillian, 1969; Lindsay & Norman, 1977). Each schema is connected to other related schemas, forming a vast, interconnected network of knowledge and experiences. The size and content of an individual's schemas are influenced by personal experiences, both direct and vicarious. Therefore, younger children typically possess fewer, less well-developed schemas about a great many things than do mature adults. For example, Figure 7.1 represents a schema for birds that an elementary student might produce, showing it as a network of associated meanings.

Figure 7.1

Elementary Student's Schema

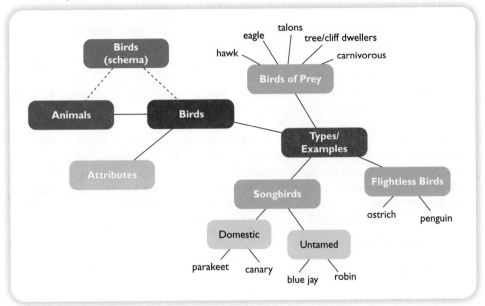

It turns out that representations of schemas as interconnected information networks in our brain are well documented in neuroscience (e.g., Christensen, 2010; Shonkoff & Phillips, 2000; Wang & Morris, 2010). Figure 7.2 shows how neural networks develop in the brain at three points in time: birth, 6 years of age, and 14 years (Shore, 1997). It demonstrates how the brain adds neurons (i.e., cells that processes and transmit information by electrical and chemical signals) and connects new information to what is already known by way of synapses (shown as lines connecting neurons—the dark "spots"). In short, when new learning occurs the brain changes, adding neurons and synapses.

We now know that synapses are created with astounding speed during the first 3 years of life, and for the rest of the first decade of life children's brains have twice as many synapses as adults' brains (Shore, 1997). As you study Figure 7.2, do you notice anything interesting about the brain networks at age 6 versus age 14? The 6-year-old's brain actually has more memory structures (schemas) than does the 14-year-old's. The explanation (from our novice understanding) is akin to the saying, "Use it or lose it." The 6-year-old absorbs new information much like a sponge does water. But it seems that between the ages of about 10 and 14 there is a great "shedding" of unused memory structures, a bit like a newly planted forest with many new saplings that gradually thin out, leaving only those trees getting sufficient sunlight to survive.

Neurologists used to think that this shedding process was not reversible—that you could add

Figure 7.2

Brain Schemas

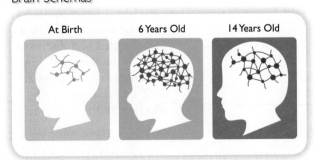

"branches" (synapses) to the existing trees (neurons) in the brain's forest, but that new trees could not be added. We now know this is not true. New learning structures (neurons and synapses) can be added, although it is more difficult the older one gets. That is why it seems to be much easier, for instance, to learn a second language when you are young than when you are in your 30s or 40s. It can be done with a lot of work, but it is not as easy as when you were, say, 5.

We believe that understanding schema theory, a fairly easy concept, and linking it to your teaching of comprehension are essential steps in providing high-quality instruction. Connecting new knowledge to what is already known provides the scaffolding students need to comprehend texts.

Construction-Integration Theory. What happens in our brains when the text or learning task becomes a bit more complicated? Kintsch (2004) developed the **construction-integration theory** to explain the complex thinking processes by which readers successfully understand a text. We briefly illustrate how this construction-integration process works using the story *The Carrot Seed* by Ruth Krauss (1945). We begin with a familiar series of statements from the text:

> A little boy planted a carrot seed.
> His mother said, "I'm afraid it won't come up."
> His father said, "I'm afraid it won't come up."
> His big brother said, "It won't come up."*

To understand these lines, we draw from our previous experiences with family members—parents and siblings. We also call up our memories of planting seeds or growing a garden. We read the next line:

> Every day the little boy pulled up the weeds around the seed and sprinkled the ground with water.

At this point, we focus in on the meaning of the actions taken by the little boy: pulling weeds and sprinkling the ground with water. This connects with our prior knowledge of planting seeds and growing things. We read the next two lines:

> But nothing came up.
> And nothing came up.

These two sentences lead us to make the prediction, in this case, that the outcome of planting a seed might be different than expected. Our motivation is to find out *why* the seed is not coming up—or to think, "Maybe it will."

According to Kintsch (2004), what the text is really all about—ideas, people, objects, or events—is remembered longest—for days, months, even years. In the case of *The Carrot Seed,* the process of planting, nurturing, and harvesting as well as persevering in the face of doubt are the information and messages that are stored for this story.

Processing of text by a reader occurs in cycles, usually clause by clause (just as we presented and discussed the story of *The Carrot Seed*), and it involves multiple and simultaneous thinking (cognitive) processes that eventually create memories. The cognitive processes are influenced by (1) the reader's knowledge about the text topic or message; (2) the reader's goals and motivations; (3) the reader's strategy selection and use; (4) the genre, type, and difficulty of the text; (5) the processing

---

*Text copyright © 1945 by Ruth Krauss. Used by permission of HarperCollins Publishers.

constraints of the reader's memory; and (6) the reader's ability to learn in and from a sociocultural context (group, classroom) if it is available when a text is processed (Kintsch, 2004; van Dijk, 1999).

Two phases of mental processing occur, then, for each clause the reader encounters in a text: (1) a construction phase and (2) an integration phase. The *construction phase* involves lower-level processes such as the following:

- Activating prior knowledge and experiences
- Retrieving word meanings
- Examining the surface and grammatical structure of the printed text
- Analyzing each clause into idea units called *propositions,* which include text elements, connecting inferences, and generalizations, that are formed into a coherent network of connected meanings (e.g., processing a sentence like "The student placed a tack on the teacher's chair" into the general memory that the student played a prank on his teacher) (Zwann, 1999)

During the second phase of processing meaning, the *integration phase,* ideas from the text are connected with what we already know, our prior knowledge, and new concepts that do not fit with the meaning of the text are deleted from our network knowledge.

What Does Research Say About Reading Comprehension Instruction?

In 1978, Dolores Durkin reported findings from her studies of reading comprehension instruction as taught by teachers using commercial reading programs (i.e., *basal* or *core* reading programs). After observing in both reading and social studies classrooms, Durkin concluded that the teachers spent very little time actually teaching children how to understand what they read. *In fact, less than 1 percent of total reading or social studies instructional time was devoted to the teaching of reading comprehension.* Unfortunately, researchers have concluded that the situation in today's schools has not improved appreciably over the past 30 years (Dewitz et al., 2009).

Research has shown that reading comprehension improves most when teachers provide explicit comprehension instruction to children (e.g., Dymock & Nicholson, 2010; Manyak & Bauer, 2008; McKeown et al., 2009; National Reading Panel, 2000). We support the following five research-supported strategies as the most critical keys for focused instruction:

1. Activating prior knowledge
2. Questioning
3. Analyzing text structure
4. Creating mental or visual images
5. Summarizing

The National Reading Panel, and other studies since, have also found that comprehension instruction is most effective when there is a great deal of text-focused dialogue among students (Kelley & Clausen-Grace, 2007, in press; Mills, 2009; Pressley, 2006). Research also indicates that teaching children how to use combinations of comprehension strategies as they read, or **multiple comprehension strategies** (McKeown et al., 2009), yields particularly strong results for improving children's reading achievement. Other research evidence points clearly to the need for teachers to help students apply comprehension strategies in a variety of text types (narrative and expository) and genres (fairy tales, realistic fiction, almanacs, encyclopedias, etc.) (Dymock & Nicholson, 2010). Thus, the key to successful instruction is delivering carefully structured learning activities that support children while they are developing the ability to use multiple comprehension strategies to understand what they read (McKeown et al., 2009; Pressley, 2006; Reutzel et al., 2005).

A Proposed Sequence for Reading Comprehension Instruction

It is important that teachers know and understand the minimum expected outcomes, or end-of-year **benchmark standards,** for comprehension development at each grade level, especially in the early years. This information becomes an essential roadmap for teachers to use in assessing each student's level of comprehension development. With this knowledge, you can plan instruction that best fits the needs of every child and that lays the groundwork for appropriate "next steps" in comprehension development. Of course, in the classroom you will discover students are at different places in their comprehension development, and you will need to plan small-group sessions each day for students having common needs. In this way, you can help all students continue learning in a systematic fashion. Figure 7.3 offers research-based end-of-year benchmark standards. Later in this chapter we provide specific assessment and teaching strategies related to these standards.

Figure 7.3

Benchmark Standards for Reading Comprension for Grades K–3

Kindergarten End-of-Year Benchmarks

✓ Uses new vocabulary and language in own speech
✓ Distinguishes whether simple sentences do or don't make sense
✓ Connects information and events in text to life experiences
✓ Uses graphic organizers to comprehend text with guidance
✓ Retells stories or parts of stories
✓ Understands and follows oral directions
✓ Distinguishes fantasy from realistic text
✓ Demonstrates familiarity with a number of books and selections
✓ Explains concepts from nonfiction text

First Grade End-of-Year Benchmarks

✓ Reads and comprehends fiction and nonfiction that is appropriate for the second half of grade 1
✓ Notices difficulties in understanding text
✓ Connects information and events in text to life experiences
✓ Reads and understands simple written directions
✓ Predicts and justifies what will happen next in stories
✓ Discusses how, why, and what-if questions in sharing nonfiction text
✓ Describes new information in own words
✓ Distinguishes whether simple sentences are incomplete or don't make sense
✓ Expands sentences in response to what, when, where, and how questions
✓ Uses new vocabulary and language in own speech and writing
✓ Demonstrates familiarity with a number of read-aloud and independent reading selections including nonfiction
✓ Demonstrates familiarity with a number of types or genres of text like storybooks, poems, newspapers, phonebooks, and everyday print such as signs, notices, and labels
✓ Summarizes the main points of a story

Second Grade End-of-Year Benchmarks

✓ Reads and comprehends both fiction and nonfiction that is appropriate for the second half of grade 2
✓ Rereads sentences when meaning is not clear
✓ Interprets information from diagrams, charts, and graphs
✓ Recalls facts and details of text
✓ Reads nonfiction materials for answers to specific questions
✓ Develops literary awareness of character traits, point of view, setting, problem, solution, and outcome
✓ Connects and compares information across nonfiction selections
✓ Poses possible answers to how, why, and what-if questions in interpreting nonfiction text
✓ Explains and describes new concepts and information in own words
✓ Identifies part of speech for concrete nouns, active verbs, adjectives, and adverbs
✓ Uses new vocabulary and language in own speech and writing
✓ Demonstrates familiarity with a number of read-aloud and independent reading selections including nonfiction
✓ Recognizes a variety of print resources and knows their contents (joke books, chapter books, dictionaries, atlases, weather reports, *TV Guide*, etc.)
✓ Connects a variety of texts to literature and life experiences (language to literacy)
✓ Summarizes a story including the stated main idea

Third Grade End-of-Year Benchmarks

✓ Reads and comprehends both fiction and nonfiction that is appropriate for grade 3
✓ Reads chapter books independently
✓ Identifies specific words or wordings that are causing comprehension difficulties
✓ Summarizes major points from fiction and nonfiction text
✓ Discusses similarities in characters and events across stories
✓ Discusses underlying theme or message when interpreting fiction
✓ Distinguishes between cause and effect, fact and opinion, and main idea and supporting details when interpreting nonfiction text
✓ Asks how, why, and what-if questions when interpreting nonfiction text
✓ Uses information and reasoning to examine bases of hypotheses and opinions
✓ Infers word meaning from roots, prefixes, and suffixes that have been taught
✓ Uses dictionary to determine meanings and usage of unknown words
✓ Uses new vocabulary and language in own speech and writing
✓ Uses parts of speech correctly in independent writing (nouns, verbs, adjectives, and adverbs)
✓ Shows familiarity with a number of read-aloud and independent reading selections, including nonfiction
✓ Uses multiple sources to locate information (tables of contents, indexes, available technology)
✓ Connects a variety of literary texts with life experiences (language to literacy)

From *Perspectives on Rescuing Urban Literacy Education: Spies, Saboteurs, and Saints* by Robert B. Cooter. Copyright 2004 Lawrence Erlbaum, via Copyright Clearance Center.

IRA Standards for Reading Professionals: Standard 3, Elements 3.1, 3.2, 3.3

Common Core Standards: Reading: K–5, Key Ideas and Details (items 1–3), Craft and Structure (items 4–6), Integration of Knowledge and Ideas (items 7–9), Range of Reading and Level of Text Complexity (item 10); Reading: Grades 6–12, Key Ideas and Details (items 1–3), Craft and Structure (items 4–6), Integration of Knowledge and Ideas (items 7–9), Range of Reading and Level of Text Complexity (item 10)

Response to Intervention: Assessment

Classroom Assessment

Assessing Reading Comprehension

Reading comprehension assessment is currently a topic of debate and some concern (Paris & Stahl, 2005). Reading comprehension, as we have already learned, is composed of several essential components: the reader, the text, the activity, and the social context. In this section we discuss comprehension assessments relating to two of these categories: assessing factors within the reader that affect comprehension and assessing students' knowledge of text features and structure.

Click on A+RISE—WIDA ELP Standard Strategies in the MyEducationLab (www.myeducationlab.com) for your course. Next, select the Strategy Card Index tab, scroll to Classroom Assessments for grades K–5, and select the Comprehension Level: ELL Assessments strategy.

Assessing Factors Within the Reader Affecting Comprehension

Teachers and researchers have known for many years that reading comprehension is positively affected when students are interested in the reading materials (Vlach & Burcie, 2010). Knowing how important student interest is in developing reading comprehension, many feel the first place to begin is assessing this factor. Figure 7.4 is an example of an interest inventory (Cooter, Flynt, & Cooter, 2007) for this purpose that we like to use as a game at the beginning of the school year, called "Twenty Questions." This assessment can be administered to the whole class at one time, in small groups, or individually.

Assessing Students' Use of Comprehension Strategies. **Metacognition** refers to two important concepts related to reading comprehension: (1) a reader's awareness of how well he or she is understanding the reading (such as when you have been

Figure 7.4

Twenty Questions: An Interest Inventory

Student's Name _____ Age _____

Date _____ Grade _____ Teacher/Examiner _____

Directions: *Ask the student the following questions to discover more about his or her interests that may be useful in selecting texts of interest during instruction. Record responses and observations that seem useful for instructional planning.*

Alternative Directions: *This inventory can also be group administered where students are capable of recording written responses. However, one-on-one interviews are preferable since nonverbal cues are often observed.*

1. If you were to win one million dollars in a contest, how might you use the money?
2. Do you like computer games? Which ones?
3. Do you use e-mail? Would you like me to send you an e-mail message sometime?
4. What are your favorite classes/subjects at school? Why?
5. What kinds of jobs do you think you might like to have when you are older?
6. Do you like to use computers? What do you like best?
7. Who are some famous people that you like? Why?
8. Name some of your favorite movies.
9. How much television do you watch each day? What are some of your favorite shows? Why?
10. What are some magazines that you like?
11. Name some of the best books you have read.
12. Do you ever read parts of the newspaper? Which parts? Do you like the comics section?
13. What kinds of books would you most like to read in the future?
14. What do you like best about your home?
15. What things in life bother you most?
16. Do you know how to use the Internet? If yes, what are some of your favorite websites?
17. Who is your favorite person in the world? Why?
18. Do you like sports? If so, which ones? Who are your favorite athletes?
19. What makes a person a good reader?
20. What causes a person to not be a good reader?

Examiner's Notes:

"reading" and realize your mind has wandered) and (2) a reader's ability to control his or her own thinking, including the use of comprehension strategies to improve or repair failing comprehension while reading (such as rereading a passage after realizing your mind had wandered) (Paris, Wasik, & Turner, 1991). For many readers, problems in comprehension result from failures related to one or both of these two important concepts.

The purpose of metacognitive assessment is to gain insight into how students select strategies for comprehending text and how well they regulate the status of their own comprehension as they read. For your classroom use, we have modified a survey developed by Pereira-Laird and Deane (1997) and call it the Student Comprehension Strategy Use Survey, or SCSUS (Reutzel & Cooter, 2011). Administered to groups, SCSUS scores provide insights into how well students select, apply, and regulate their use of comprehension strategies.

The Student Comprehension Strategy Use Survey shown in Figure 7.5 is suitable for most text selections. When administering this survey, be sure to include the following steps:

- Tell students that the SCSUS is not a test and there are no right or wrong answers.
- Direct students to fill in the personal information at the top of the survey.
- Read the directions aloud and ask children if they have any questions about the nature of the responses sought for each statement.
- Once you feel sure that students understand, instruct them to read each item and circle the number under the response that best represents their behavior in relation to each statement.
- When children finish, ask them to remain seated and to quietly read, write, or draw so as not to disturb others who are still completing the scale.

Scoring is accomplished by summing the response numbers circled and dividing by 15, the number of items in the SCSUS (i.e., Sum of individual responses/15 items), to produce the mean score.

- A mean score near 3 suggests strong selection, use, and self-regulation of comprehension monitoring strategies.

- A mean score near 2 indicates occasional selection and use of comprehension monitoring strategies. The pattern of responses should be carefully studied to see which strategies are in use and which are not to inform instructional planning for the future.

- A mean score near 1 indicates poorly developed selection, use, and self-regulation of comprehension monitoring strategies. These students need explicit teacher explanation of (1) comprehension monitoring strategies; (2) how, when, and why to use them; (3) teacher modeling of comprehension monitoring strategy use; and (4) guided practice applying selected strategies during the reading and discussion of stories in the classroom.

Assessing Students' Knowledge of Text Features and Structure

One key to effective comprehension instruction lies in accurately identifying the genres or text structures students are able to read effectively as well as those they have more difficulty comprehending (Reutzel & Cooter, 2011). To help teachers plan effective instruction, we have identified informal text structure assessments for both narrative and expository text types (Stahl, 2009).

Figure 7.5

Student Comprehension Strategy Use Survey

Name: _____ Grade: _____

Teacher: _____ School: _____

Directions: Read each item and circle the number of the word that best describes how often you do what is stated. Let's do number 1 together to make sure you understand how you are to respond to each item.

1. I read quickly through the story to get the general idea before I read the story closely.

Always	Sometimes	Never
3	2	1

2. When I come to a part of the story that is hard to read, I slow my reading down.

Always	Sometimes	Never
3	2	1

3. I am able to tell the difference between important story parts and less important details.

Always	Sometimes	Never
3	2	1

4. When I read, I stop once in a while to go over in my head what I have been reading to see if it is making sense.

Always	Sometimes	Never
3	2	1

5. I adjust the speed of my reading by deciding how difficult the story is to read.

Always	Sometimes	Never
3	2	1

6. I stop once in a while and ask myself questions about the story to see how well I understand what I am reading.

Always	Sometimes	Never
3	2	1

7. After reading a story, I sit and think about it for a while to check my memory of the story parts and the order of the story parts.

Always	Sometimes	Never
3	2	1

8. When I get lost while reading, I go back to the place in the story where I first had trouble and reread.

Always	Sometimes	Never
3	2	1

9. When I find I do not understand something when reading, I read it again and try to figure it out.

Always	Sometimes	Never
3	2	1

10. When reading, I check how well I understand the meaning of the story by asking myself whether the ideas fit with the other information in the story.

Always	Sometimes	Never
3	2	1

11. I find it hard to pay attention when I read.

Always	Sometimes	Never
3	2	1

12. To help me remember what I read, I sometimes draw a map or outline the story.

Always	Sometimes	Never
3	2	1

13. To help me understand what I have read in a story, I try to retell it in my own words.

Always	Sometimes	Never
3	2	1

14. I learn new words by trying to make a picture of the words in my mind.

Always	Sometimes	Never
3	2	1

15. When reading about something, I try to relate it to my own experiences.

Always	Sometimes	Never
3	2	1

Story Grammar Questioning. **Story grammar** is the rule system or necessary elements that make a story as well as the expected sequence for these elements. Researchers generally agree on the following elements and sequence in a story grammar: setting that includes the characters, problem, goal, events, and resolution. Research on story grammar questioning suggests that good readers have a well-developed understanding of story structure, whereas poor readers do not (Whaley, 1981). Therefore, using a story grammar to guide teacher questioning and self-questioning can help teachers and students to better assess understanding of story structure.

To prepare before conducting story grammar questioning, you will need a simple story to be read (aloud as a group or silently as individuals), a copy of a blank story grammar map (see Figure 7.6), and a set of questions allowing you to deal with each element shown in the story map (see Figure 7.7). (*Hint:* It is best if questions are sequenced in the order of the story map.) In our example we use *Jack and the Beanstalk*. Construct a story grammar map for the story as shown in Figure 7.6.

Next, write one question for selected major elements in the story grammar map, as shown by the example questions in Figure 7.7. Students can be asked, depending on their level of writing development, to answer the questions orally or in written form. Answers to each question are evaluated for accuracy and completeness. Story elements missed in the story grammar questioning should be stressed in future story discussions and/or in future explicit story structure instruction.

Later in this chapter we offer other models of questioning that can be used by students for self-monitoring or by teachers as comprehension assessments.

Figure 7.6

Story Grammar Map of *Jack and the Beanstalk*

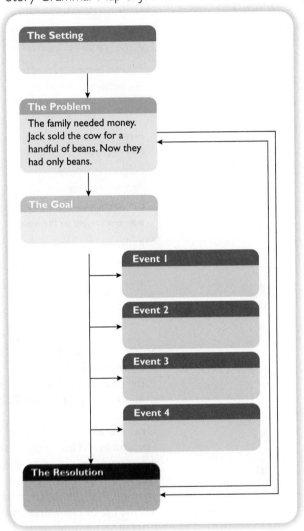

Figure 7.7

Story Grammar Questioning for *Jack and the Beanstalk*

Setting:	In the beginning of the story, why did Jack's mother want him to sell the cow?
Problem:	When Jack traded the cow for a handful of beans, what kind of a problem did this decision create for Jack and his mother?
Events:	When Jack climbed the beanstalk the first time, relate what happened to him.
	Why did Jack climb the beanstalk a second time?
Resolution:	At the end of the story, what had happened to Jack and his mother to solve the problem of trading the cow for a handful of beans?

Figure 7.8

Story Grammar Parsing of *The Carrot Seed*

Setting

A little boy planted a carrot seed.

Problem (getting the seed to grow)

His mother said, "I'm afraid it won't come up."
His father said, "I'm afraid it won't come up."
And his big brother said, "It won't come up."

Events

Every day the little boy pulled up the weeds around the seed and sprinkled the ground with water.

But nothing came up.

And nothing came up.

Everyone kept saying it wouldn't come up.

But he still pulled up the weeds around it every day and sprinkled the ground with water.

Resolution

And then, one day, a carrot came up just as the little boy had known it would.

Text from *The Carrot Seed* by Ruth Krauss (1945). Text copyright © 1945 by Ruth Krauss. Used by permission of HarperCollins Publishers.

Story Grammar Parsing. Type the text of the story onto a separate piece of paper for parsing. In this instance, parsing refers to dividing a story into four major and somewhat simplified story grammar categories: setting, problem, events, and resolution, as shown in Figure 7.8 about *The Carrot Seed* by Ruth Krauss (1945).

Oral Retellings: Assessing Narrative (Story) and Expository (Nonfiction) Text Structures. One of the most effective processes for finding out whether children understand what they read is to ask them to retell it (e.g., Brown & Cambourne, 1987; Gambrell, Pfeiffer, & Wilson, 1985; Lapp, Fisher, & Johnson, 2010; Morrow, 1985). To retell a story or information text, children must reconstruct the entire text, including the major elements, details, and sequence. In stories, children need to understand story structure, the story sequence, and important elements of the plot. In addition, they make inferences ("read between the lines") and note relevant details. Retelling an expository text involves reconstructing the content of the expository text into its main ideas and supporting details within the underlying organization of the text (compare/contrast, cause-effect, description, list, enumeration, etc.) Thus, oral expository text retellings help us assess students' comprehension of the content and text structure.

You will need the following supplies for capturing students' oral retellings of texts they have read:

- Blank audiotape (if you are using a cassette recorder)
- Portable audiocassette or digital recorder with an internal microphone
- Text selection (i.e., a brief story or information text selection)

Begin a text oral retelling by selecting a brief story or information selection for students to listen to (for grades K–1), to read aloud (grades 2 or 3), or to read silently (grades 4 and above).

Because the processes for obtaining and scoring oral retellings are different for narrative and expository text types, we will discuss each separately.

Obtaining and Scoring Narrative Oral Retellings. Oral story retellings may be elicited from children in a number of ways such as by pictures or verbal prompts related to the story. For example, as pictures of the story are flashed sequentially, the child is asked to retell the story as remembered from listening or reading. Or, as Morrow (1985, 2005) suggested, teachers prompt children to begin story retellings with a statement such as "A little while ago, we read a story called [name of story]. Retell the story as if you were telling it to a friend who has never heard it before." Other prompts for oral story retelling may be framed as questions:

- How does the story begin?
- What happens next?
- What happened to [the main character] when . . . ?
- Where did the story take place?
- When did the story take place?
- How did the main character solve the problem in the story?
- How did the story end?

Morrow (2005) recommends that teachers offer only general prompts such as those listed rather than ask about specific details, ideas, or a sequence of events from the story. Remember that when asking questions such as the prompts just listed, you are moving from free recall of text to a form of assisted recall. Incidentally, you should know that assisted recall of story text information is especially useful with struggling readers.

Another way to elicit oral story retellings from students is through **unaided recall,** in which students retell the story without picture or verbal prompts. As with a prompted retelling, ask the child to tell the story "as if she were telling it to someone who had never heard or read the story before." To record critical elements of the story structure included in the child's oral story retelling, use an audio recording and oral story retelling coding form like the one shown in Figure 7.9.

The information gleaned from an oral story retelling may be used to help you, the teacher, focus future instruction on enhancing students' understanding of narrative parts or story structure.

Obtaining and Scoring Expository Oral Retellings. Several researchers have found that children in the elementary grades are aware of and can be taught to recognize expository text structures like compare/contrast, cause-effect, description, and so forth (McGee, 1982; Williams, 2005). As with other text, retellings can show whether a child understands expository text (Duke & Bennett-Armistead, 2003; Lapp et al., 2010).

Expository text oral retellings may be obtained from children in the same ways as for narrative texts, such as pictures or verbal prompts from the text. Examples of verbal prompts during a retelling of expository text like *Is It a Fish?* (Cutting & Cutting, 2002) might include the following:

- Tell me more about . . .
- You said _____. Is there anything else you can tell me about . . .
- Tell me about gills.
- Tell me about fins.
- Tell me how fish move, look, or breathe.

Figure 7.9

Oral Story Retelling Coding Form

Student's name: _____   Grade: _____

Title of story: _____   Date: _____

General directions: Give 1 point for each element included, as well as for "gist." Give 1 point for each character named, as well as for such words as *boy, girl,* or *dog.* Credit plurals (*friends,* for instance) with 2 points under characters.

Setting

a. Begins with an introduction   _____
b. Indicates main character   _____
c. Names other characters   _____
d. Includes statement about time or place   _____

Objective

a. Refers to main character's goal or problem to be solved   _____

Events

a. Number of events recalled   _____
b. Number of events in story   _____
c. Score for events (a/b)   _____

Resolution

a. Tells how main character resolves the story problem   _____

Sequence

Summarizes story in order: setting, objective, episodes, and resolution.
(Score 2 for correct order, 1 for partial order, 0 for no sequence.)   _____

Possible score: _____   Student's score: _____

From Reutzel and Cooter, *Strategies for Reading Assessment and Instruction: Helping Every Child Succeed,* 4th ed. © 2011 by Pearson Education, Inc. Reprinted by permission of Pearson Education, Inc.

As previously mentioned, these types of assisted recall may be especially useful with struggling readers. Teachers can obtain expository text oral retellings from students with unaided recall in the same way as the narrative text, by asking the student to retell the information read "as if she were telling it to someone who had never heard or read the content of the book or text before." Once again, make an audio recording of the child's oral retelling to make it easier to double-check what you observe. Use an expository text retelling form similar to Figure 7.10, also based on *Is It a Fish?* (Cutting & Cutting, 2002). To score the quality of an unaided expository text oral retelling you might use a rating guide sheet like the one shown in Figure 7.11, which is based on the work of Moss (1997).

As you develop the ability to listen to expository text oral retellings, you may no longer need to use an audio recording and may simply make notes on the scoring sheet as to the features you hear included in the child's oral retelling.

Figure 7.10

Oral Expository Text Retelling Coding Form

Put a check mark by everything the child retells from his or her reading of the text.

_____ **Big Idea: A fish is an animal.**
_____ Detail: It has a backbone (skeleton inside).
_____ Detail: Most fish have scales.
_____ Detail: It is cold-blooded.

_____ **Big Idea: All fish live in water.**
_____ Detail: Some live in salt water.
_____ Detail: Some live in fresh water.
_____ Detail: Salmon and eels live in salt and fresh water.
_____ Detail: Salmon leave the sea to lay eggs in the river.

_____ **Big Idea: All fish breathe with gills.**
_____ Detail: All animals breathe oxygen.
_____ Detail: Some get oxygen from the air.
_____ Detail: Fish get oxygen from the water.
_____ Detail: A shark is a fish.
_____ Detail: Gills look like slits.
_____ Detail: A ray's gills are on the underside of its body.
_____ Detail: Rays breathe through holes on top of their head when they rest.

_____ **Big Idea: Most fish have fins to help them swim.**
_____ Detail: A sailfish has a huge fin that looks like a snail on its back.
_____ Detail: A (sting) ray waves its pectoral fin up and down.

Scoring:

Tally the marks for the big ideas and details. Place the total number in the blanks shown below.

Big Ideas _____ /4   Details:_____ /16   No. of Prompts _____

Sequentially Retold (Circle One):   Yes   No

Other ideas recalled including inferences: _____

From Reutzel and Cooter, *Strategies for Reading Assessment and Instruction: Helping Every Child Succeed,* 4th ed. © 2011 by Pearson Education, Inc. Reprinted by permission of Pearson Education, Inc.

Figure 7.11

A Qualitative Assessment of Student Retellings of Expository Texts

Rating Level	Criteria for Establishing a Level
5	Student includes all main ideas and supporting details, sequences properly, infers beyond the text, relates text to own life, understands text organization, summarizes, gives opinion and justifies it, and may ask additional questions. The retelling is complete and cohesive.
4	Student includes most main ideas and supporting details, sequences properly, relates text to own life, understands text organization, summarizes, and gives opinion. The retelling is fairly complete.
3	Student includes some main ideas and details, sequences most material, understands text organization, and gives opinion. The retelling is fairly complete.
2	Student includes a few main ideas and details, has some difficulty sequencing, may give irrelevant information, and gives opinion. The retelling is fairly incomplete.
1	Student gives details only, has poor sequencing, gives irrelevant information. The retelling is very incomplete.

From Moss, B. (1997). A Qualitative Assessment of First Graders' Retelling of Expository Text. *Reading Research and Instruction,* 37(1), pp. 1–13. Reprinted by permission.

What Are the Most Effective Ways to Teach Reading Comprehension?

● ● ●

IRA Standards for Reading Professionals: Standard 2, Elements 2.1, 2.2, 2.3; Standard 4, Elements 4.1, 4.2, 4.3; Standard 5, Elements 5.1, 5.2, 5.3

Common Core Standards: Reading: K–5, Key Ideas and Details (items 1–3), Craft and Structure (items 4–6), Integration of Knowledge and Ideas (items 7–9), Range of Reading and Level of Text Complexity (item 10); Reading: Grades 6–12, Key Ideas and Details (items 1–3), Craft and Structure (items 4–6), Integration of Knowledge and Ideas (items 7–9), Range of Reading and Level of Text Complexity (item 10)

Response to Intervention: Instruction; Responsive Teaching and Differentiation; Systemic and Comprehensive Approaches

The question as to the best ways of teaching reading comprehension is still somewhat open, but research points the way to methods found to be successful. However, our conclusions must remain tentative because new research is coming forward that challenges research findings of even just a few years ago.

Earlier in this chapter we shared four essential components of the RAND Reading Study Group's (2002) description of reading comprehension: (1) the *reader,* (2) the *text,* (3) the *activities or strategies,* and (4) the *situational context.* Because this and other research strongly support these attributes, we use the RAND logic to present our discussion of effective strategies that help the reader prepare for and succeed in reading comprehension.

Recently, researchers McKeown, Beck, and Blake (2009) found support for methods they call **content approaches** as an important part of the instructional picture. They describe content approaches as focusing student attention on the content of the text through open, meaning-based questions about the text. This seems consistent with findings by the What Works Clearinghouse (Institute of Education Sciences [IES], 2010) supporting such practices as **dialogic reading** in which comprehension instruction focuses student attention on text content through similar types of questions about the text. In short, having structured, collaborative dialogue around the content and vocabulary found in assigned texts is a powerful tool for improving reading comprehension. We will integrate selected dialogic strategies in this section for a broad view of comprehension instruction.

The Reader

According to the RAND Study Group's (2002) landmark research, effective reading comprehension considers student factors in instruction. Activating background knowledge and fostering interest and motivation for reading a given text is critical, whether the student is a native English speaker or an English learner (EL).

Activating Student Background Knowledge: Theme or Topic?   Activating students' background knowledge (i.e., opening the relevant schema "file folders" in children's brains) in preparation for reading is critical for promoting reading comprehension. Many core reading program or basal reader teacher's guides contain a section titled "Building Background for the Story" or "Building Background Knowledge." Unfortunately, the guidance offered in many core reading program teacher's editions for building students' background knowledge is often misleading.

> Analyses of several basal teachers' manuals show instances of problems in the prereading component. Some manuals suggest that teachers focus on tangential concepts that are irrelevant to the upcoming selection; sometimes the suggestion for presenting the concepts would encourage far-ranging discussions that could distract children from what is important. Even under the best conditions, the teachers' manuals may suggest concepts inappropriate for a specific group of children. (Beck, 1986, p. 15)

Sadly, Beck's findings a quarter century ago have been reverified in more recent research (Dewitz et al., 2009), but teachers *can* improve on what the publishing companies' core reading programs do not provide. For example, in presenting the story *The Ugly Duckling*, one teacher's manual focuses background knowledge activation on a discussion of the differences between ducks and swans. Although such a concept may be appropriate for an information text on these birds, it was not very helpful for *The Ugly Duckling.*

Background knowledge activation for stories should focus discussion on the message or theme rather than on a topic. For example, a teacher might ask students, "Have any of you ever experienced what it feels like to have someone not want to play with you? How did you feel when you were left out of a game?" These questions would be much more likely to help children remember the necessary background knowledge for interpreting the story of the ugly duckling than would examining the differences between ducks and swans. Thus, for fiction or narrative text, background knowledge activation should focus on evoking knowledge related to the theme or message of the story (e.g., exclusion or being left out because you are different).

On the other hand, for informational text (nonfiction or expository), background knowledge activation should focus on evoking knowledge from the particular domain or topic associated with the content of the text (e.g., migratory waterfowl or land formations).

Activating Student Background Knowledge: Telling Tales.   Stimulating "before reading" dialogue can help students draw on relevant past experience to improve all levels of comprehension. Telling Tales (Mills, 2009) is a prereading discussion activity in which students make predictions about the events in a text by drawing inferences from the visual elements. As ever, the teacher begins by modeling the strategy. Using a big book version or, if available, a document camera to project the pages, the teacher models how to make predictions about the content from the images found in the text. For example, the teacher might say, "The front cover has a large picture of a fishing boat, so I think that this is probably a nonfiction book." Next, students work in pairs to view images in the text. The first student might say, "I think this

Anthony Magnacca/Merrill Education

article is about a way scientists tag killer whales so they can follow them around in the ocean." The second student listens and then makes a prediction based on the next image. Students continue in this way, building on each other's predictions in a consistent and logical way. Students confirm or correct their predictions when they read the article (Mills, 2009).

Visualizing: Three-Step Frames. **Visualizing** uses the mind's capacity to imagine what is being communicated within a text. For example, many who read the first Harry Potter books (before viewing the movies) no doubt formed vivid images in their "mind's eye" when learning about Harry and his new friends. Visualizing helps to anchor new ideas in a reader's mind by connecting unfamiliar ideas and concepts to past experiences. Thus, students need to be encouraged to recall ideas in a visual way in appropriate reading contexts (Pressley, 2000).

Three-Step Freeze Frames is a visualizing activity that can be conducted during and after reading (Mills, 2009). Students working in pairs or small groups create a series of three pictures to retell events in a text using dramatic movement (without words—almost like pantomime). The following example from Mills shows how a small group of students introduced visualizing to their class, followed by some tips for teachers:

> [A]fter reading Aesop's fable, "The Hare and Tortoise," one student uses expressive postures and facial expressions to reenact the Hare running, falling asleep, and waking. At the same time, a second student could play the Tortoise who plods consistently three times. Other students in the group might be animals cheering as the Tortoise crosses the finish line. The students should use a range of heights—low, medium, and high—to create interest and should remember to face the audience when performing. Divide the class members into groups to plan, rehearse, and present their freeze frames. When presenting each performance, the teacher and class signal for the group to change postures by clapping. Class members offer an interpretation of each freeze frame, and the performing group clarifies the depicted events. (p. 327)

The Text

The quality of the text examples children experience in the books or texts we use in teaching comprehension is a consideration of principal importance. Text that is well organized has been shown by many researchers to have a positive impact on all students' comprehension (Donovan & Smolkin, 2002; McKeown, Beck, & Worthy, 1993; Seidenberg, 1989). As a teacher, you must select texts that provide clear examples of the **text features** and structures you are intent on teaching children to recognize and use to improve their comprehension.

What Are the Text Features We Should Teach? In Figure 7.12 we display text features suggested by researchers Kelley and Clausen-Grace (2010) for explicit teaching.

Teaching Text Structure. The text feature walk (Kelley & Clausen-Grace, 2010) is a dialogic activity wherein students working in small groups or pairs read and identify each feature and discuss what they think the text may be about. Students are asked to think about and have conversations about how the information relates to the main ideas of the text. This process helps students become familiar with the text's organization and recall relevant background knowledge related to the topic.

Discussing the text features helps students to frontload important vocabulary and concepts. This is especially helpful when the content has a good bit of new infor-

Figure 7.12

Common Text Features to Explicitly Teach Students

Name of Text Feature	Purpose of Text Feature
Title	Quickly tells the reader what information they will learn about.
Table of Contents	Shows students the different chapter or section titles and where they are located.
Index	Directs students where to go to find even more specific information on a topic, word, or person.
Glossary	Identifies important vocabulary words and their definitions.
Headings or Subtitles	Help the reader identify the main idea for that section of text.
Sidebar	Set apart from the main text, sidebars (usually located on the side or bottom of the page) elaborate on a detail (content) mentioned in the text.
Pictures or Captions	Show an important object or idea from the text.
Labeled Diagrams	Allow readers to see detailed depictions of an object from the text with labels that teach the important components.
Charts or Graphs	Represent and show data related to or elaborate on something in the main body of text.
Maps	Help a reader locate a place in the world that is related to text.
Cutaways	Allow readers to see inside something by dissolving part of a wall or to see all the layers of an object by bisecting it for viewing.
Inset Photos	Can show both a far-away view of something or an up-close shot to show minute detail.

mation and concepts. As students make predictions and talk about various features they are better able to anticipate new information.

Kelley and Clausen-Grace (2010) suggest guidelines for what we would consider to be a kind of joint productive activity for a text feature walk.

1. In your small group, choose one person to start by reading the first text feature.
2. That person names the text feature. (Is it a heading? Picture and caption? Map?)
3. That same person reads the text feature.
4. As a group, discuss any predictions, questions, and connections you have based on the text feature and discuss how you think it will relate to the main idea. Everyone should contribute.
5. Have a new person share the next text feature and repeat steps 2 through 4. Repeat until all text features have been discussed or the teacher calls time.

Finally, here are some tips for teachers offered by Kelley and Clausen-Grace (2010) for successful text feature walks:

- Select texts for which students have some background knowledge.
- Do not have students walk (read and discuss) through too much text at one time.
- Scaffold the pronunciation of new vocabulary words before students begin their discussion (sometimes multisyllabic words can intimidate students even though they may have schemas for the word or concept).
- Have students determine how the text feature walk improved their comprehension of the content.

Figure 7.13

Model of Effective Comprehension Instruction: Identifying and Using Text Structure

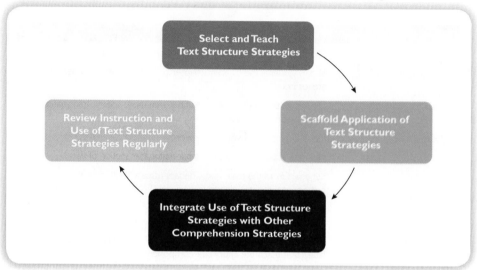

Text Structure and Using Graphic Organizers. A model for teaching children to use text structure is found in Figure 7.13.

To begin, text structure instruction should focus on the physical features that help students understand the way that an author has organized a text.

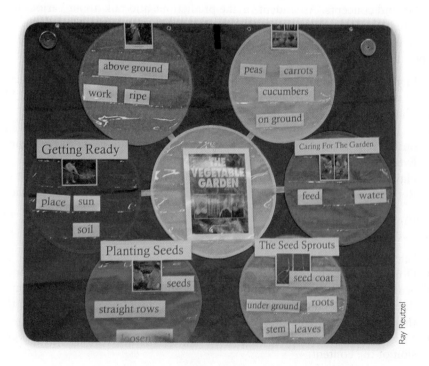

Ray Reutzel

- The table of contents
- Chapter headings and subheadings
- Paragraph organization such as topic sentence and signal words
- Visual insets or aids

Next, students can be helped to recognize the way the author has organized the text. For narrative texts, this means teaching explicitly the parts of a narrative or story grammar structure (National Reading Panel, 2000). For young children, this may begin with the concepts of a story having a beginning, middle, and end. Older children should be taught that a story has prototypical parts organized in a predictable sequence, including the setting, problem, goal, events, and resolution.

Teaching the structure of expository texts means explicitly teaching different text structures of time order, cause and effect, problem and solution, comparison, simple listing/enumeration, and descriptions. It appears that time sequence structures like the following are the easiest for younger students to understand.

- Counting books
- Days of the week
- Months of the year
- Step-by-step instruction, seasons, and so on

Another kind of structure is the question–answer format. In these types of expository structures, authors typically ask a question and then proceed immediately to answer the question in the very next sentence, paragraph, or page. After this type of text structure, in a developmental progression of difficulty, come information books that describe single topics such as frogs, sand, or chocolate.

In an information book structured by enumeration, the author lists a category of related concepts or objects such as reptiles, dogs, or the Pueblo Indians. Listing different types, examples, and aspects of a category are described as a *collection*. Compare and contrast or cause-effect expository text structures are the most challenging for young readers.

Effective text structure instruction requires that teachers provide short, frequent review opportunities for application of the text structure strategies taught. We have listed the characteristics of effective text structure instruction in Figure 7.14 and have chosen two types of text structures, narrative and expository, as examples to illustrate the kind of effective text structure instruction we present in this figure. We begin by focusing on effective text structure instruction with a selected narrative text.

Effective Narrative Text Structure Instruction. Begin by selecting an excellent example of a narrative text. This means we want to find a story text that exemplifies the clear and traditional use of story structure. For a text to qualify for selection, it must possess the traditional elements and follow the traditional sequence of elements in a story grammar:

Figure 7.14

Characteristics of Effective Text Structure Instruction

Select exemplars of various text types.

Focus initial instruction on physical features of text that help students understand organization:

- Table of contents
- Chapter headings
- Subheadings
- Paragraph organization
- Main idea and topic sentence location
  - Signal words
  - Typographic features
  - Spacing features
  - Visual insets

Teach children how to determine the way the author has organized or structured the text.

Teach children how to think about and visually represent the way the author has implicitly organized the text using graphic organizers.

Provide scaffolding or gradual release.

Activate and use text feature and text structure knowledge in regular review cycles.

Figure 7.15

Simple Story Structure Graphic Organizer

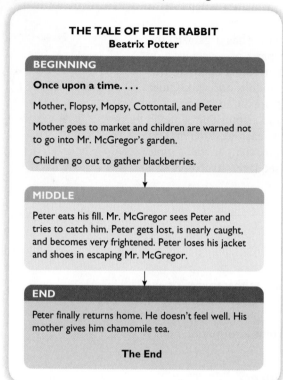

THE TALE OF PETER RABBIT
Beatrix Potter

BEGINNING

Once upon a time. . . .

Mother, Flopsy, Mopsy, Cottontail, and Peter

Mother goes to market and children are warned not to go into Mr. McGregor's garden.

Children go out to gather blackberries.

MIDDLE

Peter eats his fill. Mr. McGregor sees Peter and tries to catch him. Peter gets lost, is nearly caught, and becomes very frightened. Peter loses his jacket and shoes in escaping Mr. McGregor.

END

Peter finally returns home. He doesn't feel well. His mother gives him chamomile tea.

The End

setting, characters, problem, goal, events, and resolution. The familiar story *The Tale of Peter Rabbit* by Beatrix Potter (1986) is well-suited to our purpose.

Next, we carefully examine the physical features of our text: the title, the author, the illustrator, the title page, and that many stories begin with "Once upon a time" and end with "The End." *The Tale of Peter Rabbit* is well-suited for teacher modeling because of its clear paragraph structure. For example, when Peter saw Mr. McGregor, he was very frightened and the details of the paragraph clearly relate to actions and events that would support this major idea—the character's rushing all over, forgetting his way out, losing something in the tussle, and so on. This storybook also makes use of a great many signal words: *first, after, after a time, presently, suddenly,* and *at last.*

This book also makes good use of spacing and print arrangements. On the first page, ONCE UPON A TIME is printed in all capitals, as is THE END. Also on the first page, the four little rabbits' names—Flopsy, Mopsy, Cottontail, and Peter—are printed one name to a line with an increasing paragraph indent as each name is added to the list, resulting in a four-stair, step-shaped list. This print arrangement is used several times throughout the book as a visual indicator of a list.

In *The Tale of Peter Rabbit* the setting is clearly stated, including mention of the characters of Flopsy, Mopsy, Cottontail, Peter, and Mother. The problem is described when Mother Rabbit tells the children to stay away from Mr. McGregor's garden because their father had been caught and ended up in Mr. McGregor's pie. Peter, of course, decides he will test fate by straying away from his siblings into Mr. McGregor's garden. The tale chronicles Peter's many close calls and his multiple attempts to escape Mr. McGregor. The resolution occurs when Peter escapes from Mr. McGregor and goes home to his waiting Mother.

For younger children, a simple graphic organizer with beginning, middle, and end components can be used to convey implicit story structure. Older students can be presented with a more complex graphic organizer that includes setting, characters, location, time, problem, goals, events, and resolution. Two examples of graphic organizers are shown in Figures 7.15 and 7.16. Figure 7.15 shows *The Tale of Peter Rabbit* graphic organizer for teaching younger children story structure. Figure 7.16 shows *The Tale of Peter Rabbit* graphic organizer using story grammar logic for teaching older students story structure.

Once story structure is explicitly and thoroughly explained and modeled by the teacher, we turn our attention to the issue of scaffolding narrative text structure instruction effectively in the classroom. **Scaffolding,** also called the *gradual release of responsibility,* refers to students selecting and using strategies, beginning with high teacher control and involvement, moving to shared control and involvement between teachers and students, and finally to students' independent control over strategy selection and use (Dewitz et al., 2009). This process requires multiple lessons perhaps using a variety of storybooks.

Scaffolding Comprehension Instruction. The following sequence of lessons provides the steps that foment student learning.

- In the first lesson, the teacher does most of the explaining (**input**) as well as thinking aloud and representing the elements of story structure in a graphic organizer (**teacher modeling**).
- In the second and third lessons, the teacher might share the explaining of story structure, thinking aloud, and representing of the elements of story structure in the graphic organizer with students; the beginning of releasing responsibility to students, or **guided practice.**
- Finally, in remaining lessons, students do most of the explaining, thinking aloud, and representing of the elements of story structure in the graphic organizer with the expert guidance of the teacher.
- Later on, students are encouraged to make and use graphic organizers of story structure on their own (*independent practice*) to help them understand and remember the narrative texts with which they engage.

Effective Expository Text Structure Instruction. Here again, we begin by selecting an exemplary expository text, perhaps one within the information text genre. This means we want to find an expository text that makes clear and simple use of only *one* of the many expository text structures, such as problem–solution or question–answer. For a text to qualify for selection, it must utilize one and only one expository text structure throughout rather than a mix or variety of expository text structures, as many do.

A simple information text, *Sand* (Clyne & Griffiths, 2005), serves our purpose for teacher modeling. This book features an attractive appearance, clear layout, and interesting content for younger and even some older children.

To begin, we consider carefully the physical features of this expository text. We note several important physical features that we make a point of showing to and discussing with children, namely the title, the author, and postreading follow-up questions at the end of the book. Although not as rich in physical features as some expository books, *Sand* does evidence the use of a single text structure—question–answer—throughout. For example, the book begins with the question "What is sand?" The book also makes good use of spacing, print arrangements, and typographic features. "What is sand?" is printed on a single line at the top of the first page in bold typeface. The answer to the question is at the bottom of the page in regular typeface.

Every question in *Sand* appears at the top of the page in isolation in bold typeface. Answers are all placed on the bottom of the page in regular typeface and relate

Figure 7.16

Complex Story Structure Graphic Organizer

The Setting

Characters: Mother, Peter, Flopsy, Mopsy, Cottontail, and Mr. McGregor
Location: Rabbit home in a tree, the woods, and Mr. McGregor's garden
Time: Long ago

The Problem

Peter was not an obedient little rabbit who listened to his mother's warning. He went into Mr. McGregor's garden. Peter was seen by Mr. McGregor.

Goal

Escape from Mr. McGregor and get home again

Events/Attempts

Peter rushed all over the garden and lost his shoes trying to get away from Mr. McGregor.

Peter got caught on a gooseberry net by the large brass buttons on his new jacket. He lost his jacket.

Peter jumped into a watercan to hide from Mr. McGregor in the tool shed.

Peter found a locked gate but couldn't get out. He made his way back to where Mr. McGregor was working.

Peter squeezed under the gate and ran quickly home.

Resolution

Peter got home safely and went to bed. Mother gave him chamomile tea.

Figure 7.17

Graphic Organizer for Primary-Grade Readers (K–2)

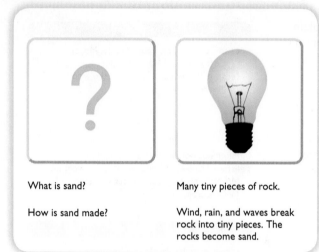

What is sand?

How is sand made?

Many tiny pieces of rock.

Wind, rain, and waves break rock into tiny pieces. The rocks become sand.

Figure 7.18

Graphic Organizer for Intermediate-Grade Readers (3–6)

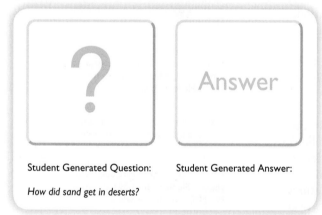

Student Generated Question:

How did sand get in deserts?

Student Generated Answer:

A+RISE

Click on A+RISE—WIDA ELP Standard Strategies in the MyEducationLab (www.myeducationlab.com) for your course. Next, select the Strategy Card Index tab, scroll to Comprehension for grades K–5, and select the Question Stems strategies.

to an illustrative photograph that helps answer the question. The book also uses black versus white type, depending on the background color of the page. This use of color leads readers' attention to the answers to the questions in physically obvious ways.

For younger children, a simple graphic organizer using icons along with print can be helpful. For older students, a more complex graphic organizer may include student-generated questions for which they will seek and retrieve answers through reading across a variety of other information texts on the topic of sand, rocks, and soil. Two examples of question–answer graphic organizers for the book *Sand* are shown in Figures 7.17 and 7.18. Figure 7.17 shows a *Sand* graphic organizer for teaching younger students this expository text structure. Figure 7.18 shows a *Sand* graphic organizer for teaching older students about question–answer expository text structure.

Similar to our narrative example, we turn our attention to the issue of scaffolding expository text structure instruction effectively in the classroom. This would require multiple lessons such as the one just described using a variety of expository books that implement question–answer text structure, such as *Bridges* (Ring, 2003), *How Do Spiders Live?* (Biddulph & Biddulph, 1992), and others.

The Activity

The third essential component in the RAND Reading Study Group's (2002) definition of reading comprehension is the activity. One of the chief comprehension activities for young readers is learning how to use comprehension strategies to improve their understanding and memory for text. We begin our discussion of comprehension strategies by focusing on one strategy that has long been a mainstay in elementary school classrooms: question asking and answering.

Questions are an integral part of life both in and out of school. In school, teachers ask questions to guide and motivate children's reading comprehension and to assess the quality of their reading comprehension after reading. We begin with some basic information about the levels of thought required by different kinds of questions.

Asking Questions at Differing Levels of Thinking. During the past several decades, a variety of questioning taxonomies—ordered lists of questions that tap different levels of human thought, such as Bloom's (1956), Barrett's (1972), and Taba's (1975) taxonomies—were published along with impassioned appeals for teachers to ask students more higher-order questions. Figure 7.19 illustrates Bloom's taxonomy in an

Figure 7.19

Bloom's Taxonomy

LITERAL (LOW LEVEL)

KNOWLEDGE—Identification and recall of information

Who, what, when, where, how?
Describe . . .

COMPREHENSION—Organization and selection of facts and ideas.

Retell _____ in your own words.
What is the main idea of _____?

INFERENTIAL LEVEL (HIGHER-ORDER THINKING)

APPLICATION—Use of facts, rules, principles

How is _____ an example of _____?
How is _____ related to _____?
Why is _____ significant?

ANALYSIS—Separation of a whole into component parts

What are the parts or features of _____?
Classify _____ according to _____
Outline/diagram/web _____.
How does _____ compare/contrast with _____?
What evidence can you list for _____?

SYNTHESIS—Combinations of ideas to form a new whole

What would you predict/infer from _____?
How would you create/design a new _____?
What might happen if you combined _____ with _____?
What solutions would you suggest for _____?

EVALUATIVE LEVEL (HIGHER-ORDER THINKING)

EVALUATION—Development of opinions, judgments, or decisions

Do you agree _____?
What do you think about _____?
What is the most important _____?
How would you prioritize _____?
How would you decide about _____?
What criteria would you use to assess _____?

easy-to-use format wherein teachers simply fill in the blanks with key words/concepts from an assigned text selection. The inferential and evaluative levels are considered **higher-order thinking** questions.

Much can be and will be argued about asking higher-order questions for some time into the future, but the fact is that students will need to answer a great many questions throughout their school life and beyond. Unfortunately, many students are not helped to develop effective strategies for answering or asking their own questions. Raphael and Pearson (1985) developed a strategy for teaching students how to answer questions asked of them called **Question–Answer Relationships (QARs)** (Raphael, 1982).

Question–Answer Relationships. Raphael (1982, 1986) and Raphael and Au (2005) describe four question–answer relationships that help children identify the connection between the type of question asked and the information sources necessary and available for answering it: (1) right there, (2) think and search, (3) author and me, and (4) on my own. Instruction using QARs begins by explaining that there are basically two places they can look for information: *in the book* and *in their head*. This concept should be practiced with students by reading aloud a text, asking questions, and having students explain or show where they would look to find their answers. Once students understand the two-category approach, expand the in-the-book category to include *right there* and *think and search*. The distinction between these two categories should be practiced under the guidance of the teacher using several texts and gradually releasing responsibility to students. Raphael (1986) suggests that older students be shown specific strategies for locating the answers to right there questions. These include looking in a single sentence or looking in two sentences connected by a pronoun. For think and search questions, students can be asked to focus their attention on the structure of the text (cause–effect, problem–solution, listing–example, comparison–contrast, and explanation).

Next, instruction is directed toward two subcategories in the in-my-head category: *author and me* and *on my own*. Here again, these categories can be practiced as a group by reading a text aloud, answering the questions, and discussing the sources of information. To expand this training, students can be asked to identify the types of questions asked in their basal readers, workbooks, content area texts, and tests as well as to determine the sources of information needed to answer these questions.

Students may be informed that certain types of questions are asked before and after reading a text. For example, questions asked before reading typically require that students activate their own prior knowledge. Therefore, questions asked before reading will usually be on my own questions. However, questions asked after reading will make use of information found in the text. Therefore, questions asked after reading will typically focus on the think and search and author and me types of questions.

Using the QAR question–answering training strategy is useful for at least two other purposes. First, it can help teachers examine their own questioning with respect to the types of questions and the information sources students need to use to answer their questions. Second, some teachers may find that by using QARs to monitor their own questioning behaviors, they are asking only right there types of questions (i.e., literal/low level questions in Bloom's taxonomy). This discovery should lead teachers to ask questions that require the use of more in my head questions.

Students can use QARs for self-questioning before and after reading. They may be asked to write questions for each of the QAR categories and answer these questions. Finally, Figure 7.20 shows

Figure 7.20

Core Question–Answer Relationships

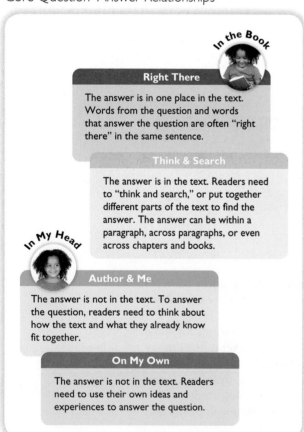

In the Book

Right There

The answer is in one place in the text. Words from the question and words that answer the question are often "right there" in the same sentence.

Think & Search

The answer is in the text. Readers need to "think and search," or put together different parts of the text to find the answer. The answer can be within a paragraph, across paragraphs, or even across chapters and books.

In My Head

Author & Me

The answer is not in the text. To answer the question, readers need to think about how the text and what they already know fit together.

On My Own

The answer is not in the text. Readers need to use their own ideas and experiences to answer the question.

From Raphael, T. E., & Au, K. H. (2005). QAR Enhancing comprehension and Test Taking Across Grades and Content Areas. *The Reading Teachers, 59*(3), pp. 206–221. Reprinted by permission of the McGraw-Hill Companies.

posters that can heighten children's and teachers' awareness of the types of questions asked and the information sources available for answering those questions.

Questioning the Author.   **Questioning the author** lessons attempt, in a sense, to engage students in a "conversation" with the author (McKeown, Beck, & Worthy, 1993). To begin, students are shown examples in information books and textbooks in which someone's ideas may not be written as well or as clearly as they might be. Next, the teacher prompts students as they read a book or textbook using a series of questions like the following:

- What is the author trying to tell you?
- Why is the author telling you that?
- Is it said so that you can understand it?

Asking children to search out answers to these questions in the text, or even supplemental online resources, encourages them to actively engage with the ideas in the text. As children encounter difficulties in understanding the text they are encouraged, again through teacher questioning, to recast the author's ideas in clearer language. Questions used for this purpose might include the following:

- How could the author have said the ideas to make them easier to understand?
- What would you say instead?

Asking children to restate the author's ideas causes them to grapple with the ideas and problems in a text. In this way, children engage with text in ways that successful readers use to make sense of complex ideas presented in texts.

Elaborative Interrogation.   **Elaborative interrogation** is well-suited to helping students generate and answer questions in information texts (Mills, 2009; National Reading Panel, 2000). By asking and answering their own questions, students link information together into a network of relationships (schemas) improving both understanding and memory for text information.

It is important that "why" questions be asked so as to orient students to search their prior knowledge for supporting the facts they need to learn—otherwise such questions will not enhance comprehension and memory for text. We apply the elaborative interrogation student-generated questioning strategy to a trade book titled *Ways of Measuring: Then and Now* (Shulman, 2001) in the model lesson shown in Figure 7.21.

The elaborative interrogation strategy has been shown to improve readers' comprehension of factual material ranging from elementary school ages to adult. It is recommended that teachers use elaborative interrogation to train students to begin asking their own questions to guide their search for meaning from information texts.

Comprehension Monitoring and Fix-Up Strategies

The National Reading Panel (2000) found that teaching students to monitor the status of their own ongoing comprehension to determine when it breaks down is one of a handful of scientifically supported, evidence-based comprehension instructional strategies. The act of monitoring one's unfolding comprehension of text is called *metacognition,* or sometimes *metacomprehension.* The ability to plan, check, monitor, revise, and evaluate one's unfolding comprehension is of particular importance in reading. If a reader fails to detect comprehension breakdowns, then she or he

Figure 7.21

Example of an Elaborative Interrogation Lesson

Purpose for Learning the Strategy: This strategy will help students relate their own experiences and knowledge to what they read in information texts. By using this strategy, they will improve their understanding of and memory for text information.

Objective: To learn to respond to statements in text as if they were stated as "why" questions.

Teacher Explanation and Modeling: This strategy is begun by the teacher reading a section of text aloud and modeling. The teacher reads the title of the book: *Ways of Measuring: Then and Now.* She asks herself: "Why are ways of measuring today different than in the past?" Her answer might include ideas about people not having scales, rulers, and measuring cups in the past. Next, she reads the sentence: "Long ago, people used their bodies to measure the length of things." She asks herself the "why" question: "Why did people use their bodies to measure things instead of something else?" She reads on: *"Arms and hands were always around when you needed them, and they couldn't get lost. But you can't weigh flour with a hand span, or measure oil with a cubit. For thousands of years, people used stones to weigh things. They used hollow gourds and shells to measure out amounts."* She asks herself: "Why did people in the old days use stones and gourds to measure?"

Guided Application: The teacher says: "Now let's use this strategy together. Manny, please read this statement aloud for the class." Manny reads: "'The old ways of measuring had some problems.'" The teacher forms a "why" question based on the statement. Then she says, "Mariann, please read this statement." Mariann reads: "'The metric system is used almost everywhere in the world except in the United States.'" The teacher generates a "why" question based on the statement: "Why doesn't the United States use the metric system?" She then invites students to use their background knowledge to respond to her question. The teacher says: "Now let's reverse roles." She reads aloud the next statement from the text. "'Using these measurement systems solves a lot of problems.' Who can put together a good 'why' question based on this statement?" Benji raises his hand. He asks, "Why do measurement systems solve problems?" Discussion ensues.

Individual Application: The teacher says: "I want you to read the rest of this book. When you get to the end of each page, pick one statement and write a 'why' question about it in your notebooks. See if you can answer the question from your own knowledge or experiences. If not, try using the book to answer your question. If neither source can answer your question, save it for our discussion of the book when we are all finished reading. Now, go ahead and read. If you forget what I want you to do, look at this poster for step-by-step directions." The teacher points to the poster at the front on the room on the board.

> *Using the Elaborative Interrogation Strategy*
> - Read each page carefully.
> - Stop at the end of each page and pick a statement.
> - Write a "why" question for the statement you pick in your reading notebooks.
> - Think about an answer to the "why" question using your own knowledge and experiences.
> - If you can, write an answer to your "why" question.
> - Read the pages again looking for an answer. Read on to another page to look for the answer.
> - If you can, write an answer to your "why" question.
> - If you can't write an answer to your "why" question, save it for our group discussion after reading.

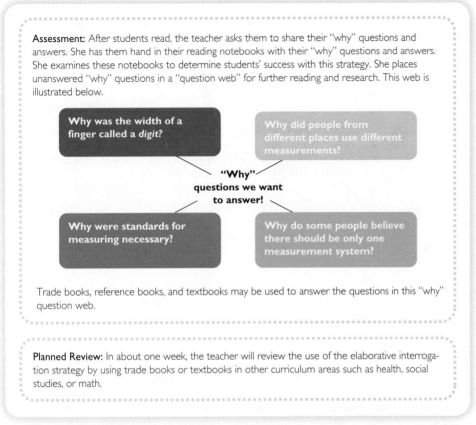

Assessment: After students read, the teacher asks them to share their "why" questions and answers. She has them hand in their reading notebooks with their "why" questions and answers. She examines these notebooks to determine students' success with this strategy. She places unanswered "why" questions in a "question web" for further reading and research. This web is illustrated below.

> Why was the width of a finger called a *digit*?

> Why did people from different places use different measurements?

"Why" questions we want to answer!

> Why were standards for measuring necessary?

> Why do some people believe there should be only one measurement system?

Trade books, reference books, and textbooks may be used to answer the questions in this "why" question web.

Planned Review: In about one week, the teacher will review the use of the elaborative interrogation strategy by using trade books or textbooks in other curriculum areas such as health, social studies, or math.

From Reutzel, D. R., Camperell, K., & Smith, J. A. (2002). Hitting the Wall: Helping Struggling Readers Comprehend. In C. Collins-Block, L. B. Gambrell, & M. Pressley (Eds.), *Improving Comprehension Instruction: Advances in Research, Theory, and Classroom Practice* (pp. 321–353). San Francisco: Jossey-Bass. Reprinted by permission.

will take no action to correct misinterpretations of the text. However, if a reader expects that text should make sense and has the ability to strategically self-correct comprehension problems, then reading can progress as it should. To teach an explicit comprehension strategy lesson, one can use a framework lesson plan, such as shown in Figure 7.22.

Click or Clunk. To help students develop the ability to monitor their own comprehension processes, Carr (1985) suggested a strategy called "click or clunk." This strategy urges readers to reflect at the end of each paragraph or section of reading by stopping and asking themselves if the meaning or message "clicks" for them or goes "clunk." If it clunks, the reader asks what is wrong and what can be done to correct the problem.

Fix-Ups. Although the ability to detect when comprehension breaks down is important, it is equally important to know which strategies to select in repairing broken comprehension and when to use them. Children should be introduced to the options available to them for repairing broken comprehension. Collins and Smith (1980)

Figure 7.22

Explicit Comprehension Monitoring Strategy Lesson Plan Template

Objective Children will monitor their own comprehension processes and use fix-up strategies to repair broken comprehension processes when necessary.

Supplies

- Exemplary story or information text

Explain

What

- Today, boys and girls, we are going to be learning about how to monitor or check our understanding or comprehension as we read. The first step in learning to monitor our understanding or comprehension as we read is to learn to stop periodically and ask ourselves a few simple questions like "Is this making sense? Am I getting it? Do I understand what this is about?"

Why

- We need to monitor our comprehension or understanding when we read because what we read should make sense to us. If it doesn't make sense, there is no point in continuing to read. Monitoring our comprehension while reading helps us to be aware of whether or not we understand or are making sense of what we read. We can just keep on reading if we understand, or stop and do something to help us understand if the text is not making sense to us.

When/Where

- Whenever we read, we should monitor or think about whether or not we are understanding or comprehending what we are reading.

Model

- I am going to read aloud the first two pages of our book *Volcano!* (Hunt, 2004). After reading the first two pages, I am going to stop and monitor my comprehension. I will think out loud about the questions I should ask when I stop to monitor my comprehension: "Is this making sense? Am I getting it? Do I understand what this is about?" I've written these monitoring steps (stop and question) on a poster to help me remember. I have also written the three comprehension-monitoring questions on the poster to help me remember. After thinking about these questions for a minute, I will answer the question with a yes or no. If my answer is yes, I will continue to read. If my answer is no, I will have to stop for now because I don't yet know what I should do when it doesn't make sense to me. Notice that I have also put YES and NO on our poster to help me know what to do when I answer yes or no to the three comprehension-monitoring questions. Okay. Here I go.

Volcano!

There are many volcanoes in the world.

About 1,500 of them are active.

That means that they are erupting, or they might erupt someday.

An erupting volcano is quite a sight!

Rocks and ash shoot up.

Lava races down.

Smelly gases fill the air.

(STOP!)

"Am I getting it? Is it making sense? Do I understand what this is about?" Yes, I think I do. There are loads of volcanoes all over. Some of them are active, meaning they might erupt. An example of an active volcano is Mt. Etna. When volcanoes erupt they send rocks, ash, lava, and gases into the air. So, if what I have read makes sense and I answer yes, I just keep on reading. After I read a few more pages, I should STOP to monitor my comprehension again.

(Repeat this cycle with a few more pages and one or two more stopping points for modeling.)

Scaffolding (ME, YOU & ME, YOU)

Whole Group (Me & You)

- Now that I have shown you how I STOP and monitor my comprehension, I want to share this task with you. Let's read three more pages. At the end of the three pages, I want you to call out, "STOP!" After I stop, I want you to ask me the three monitoring questions on our poster: "Is this making sense? Am I getting it? Do I understand what this is about?" I will answer YES or NO. If I answer yes, tell me what to do. If I answer no, then tell me I will have to quit reading until we learn what to do tomorrow. Okay. Here we go.

> Volcanoes come in different sizes and shapes. Some volcanoes have steep sides.
> They rise high above the land around them.
> Other volcanoes are very wide.
> Their sides are not so steep.
> This type of volcano may look like a regular mountain. But it isn't!
> **(STOP!)**

Small Group/Partners/Teams (Me & You)

- Now that we have shared the process of STOPPING and monitoring our comprehension as a group when we read, I want you to share this monitoring process with a partner. I am going to give you either the number 1 or the number 2. Remember your number. (Count heads by 1 and 2.) We are going to read three more pages in our story. At the end of the three pages, I want partner 1 to call out, "STOP!" Then I want partner 2 to ask partner 1 the three monitoring questions on our poster: "Is this making sense? Am I getting it? Do I understand what this is about?" Then partner 1 will answer the questions asked by partner 2 with a yes or no. If partner 1 answers yes, partner 2 says to keep on reading. If partner 1 answers no, then partner 2 says to quit reading until we learn what to do tomorrow. Okay, ready.

> Volcanoes can change the land quickly.
> In 1980, a volcano in the state of Washington erupted. Its top blew off with a roar.
> Mud raced down its sides.
> Trees crashed, and animals fled.
> But the land was not bare for long.
> The ash from volcanoes helps things grow.
> Today, Mount St. Helens is full of new life.
> **(STOP!)**

Individual (You)

- Today we have learned that when we read we should STOP every few pages and monitor our comprehension or understanding by asking ourselves three questions. Today, during small-group reading or in paired reading, I would like for you to practice monitoring comprehension with a friend or by yourself as you read. STOP every few pages and ask yourself the three questions on our poster. Then decide if you should keep on reading or quit reading and wait until tomorrow, when we will learn about what to do when what you read isn't making sense.

Assess

- Pass out a bookmark that reminds students to stop every few pages while reading and ask the three questions. List the three questions on the bookmark to remind students about them.

Reflect

- What went well in the lesson?
- How would you change the lesson?

Excerpted text from *Volcano!* by Jewell Hunt from Reading Power Works series, reprinted with permission from Sundance/Newbridge Educational Publishers, LLC.

suggest the following **fix-up strategies** for use by readers who experience comprehension failure:

- Ignore the problem and continue reading.
- Suspend judgment for now and continue reading.
- Form a tentative hypothesis, using text information, and continue reading.
- Look back or reread the previous sentence.
- Stop and think about the previously read context; reread if necessary.
- Seek help from the environment, reference materials, or other knowledgeable individuals.

To help students develop a sense for when to select these strategies, teachers may consider using a think-aloud modeling procedure. The teacher begins by reading part of a text aloud, and as she proceeds, comments aloud on her thinking. By revealing to students her thinking, the hypotheses she has formed for the text, and anything that strikes her as difficult or unclear, the teacher demonstrates for students the processes successful readers use to comprehend a text (Duffy, 2003). Next, the teacher reminds students of the click or clunk strategy. Gradually, she releases the responsibility for modeling metacognitive strategies to students during follow-up lessons on metacognitive monitoring. She displays the fix-up or repair strategies listed above along with the click-or-clunk strategy on a wall chart or poster in a prominent place in the classroom and draws students' attention to these strategies throughout the year.

Summarizing.   The purpose of summarizing is to extract and succinctly organize the "gist" of a text. Summarizing is important because it helps readers select and store relevant main ideas and details from their reading to form memory structures for text. Many readers do not spontaneously summarize their reading and, as a result, have poor understanding and recall of what they read (Brown, Day, & Jones, 1983).

To begin a lesson on summarizing, we recommend using an information trade book, a storybook, or content area textbook along with a chart displaying the steps for producing a summary based on the work of Hare and Borchordt (1984) featured in Figure 7.23. Distribute sufficient numbers of copies of the text to be read by the group. Have the students silently read the first few passages. Next, on an overhead transparency, model for students how you would use the five summary rules in Figure 7.23 to produce a summary. After modeling, direct students to finish reading the entire text. Divide the chalkboard into four sections. For example, if you are learning about an animal (say, alligators), your subcategories might be "Description," "Food," "Home," and "Interesting Facts." As the groups read, have students write facts on the chalkboard in each of the four sections.

Next, organize students into groups of five to work on summarizing together. Each student in the group is assigned to take charge of one of the five summary-writing rules shown in Figure 7.23. Circulate around the classroom to assist groups as needed. After reading the selection and working in their groups, students responsible for the topic statement rule in each group should read their topic statement aloud to the other students in the group. After that, have students discuss the facts they have listed at the board, erase duplicates, and restate the remaining main ideas and detail facts in complete sentences. You may want to have students use different colored transparency pens for each of the five summary rules to record their work in the groups. For example, green may be used for lists, red for eliminating unnecessary details, and so on. Share each group's summarizing processes and their summary statement(s) with the entire class on the overhead projector. Be sure to provide addi-

A+RISE

Click on A+RISE—WIDA ELP Standard Strategies in the MyEducationLab (www.myeducationlab.com) for your course. Next, select the Strategy Card Index tab, scroll to Comprehension, and select the Comparison Webs strategy.

Figure 7.23

Steps for Producing a Summary

1. *Collapse lists.* If there is a list of things, supply a word or phrase for the whole list. For example, if you saw *swimming, sailing, fishing,* and *surfing,* you could substitute *water sports.*
2. *Use topic sentences.* Sometimes authors write a sentence that summarizes the whole paragraph. If so, use that sentence in your summary. If not, you'll have to make up your own topic sentences.
3. *Get rid of unnecessary detail.* Sometimes information is repeated or is stated in several different ways. Some information may be trivial and unnecessary. Get rid of repetitive or trivial information. Summaries should be short.
4. *Collapse paragraphs.* Often, paragraphs are related to each other. For example, some paragraphs simply explain or expand on other paragraphs in a selection. Some paragraphs are more important than others. Join the paragraphs that are related. Important paragraphs should stand alone.
5. *Polish the summary.* When you collapse a lot of information from many paragraphs into one or two paragraphs, the resulting summary sometimes sounds awkward and unnatural. There are several ways to remedy this: add connecting words such as *like* or *because,* or write introductory or closing statements. Another method is to paraphrase the material. This will improve your ability to remember what you read and enable you to avoid plagiarism—using the exact words of the author.

From Marc, V. C., & Borchordt, K. M. (1984). Direct Instruction of Summarization Skills. *Reading Research Quarterly 20*(1), pp. 62–78. Reprinted with permission of the International Reading Association.

tional practice on summarizing throughout the year with other books and gradually release the task of summarizing using all five rules to students for independent use.

If students encounter difficulties initially using the five rules in Figure 7.23, we have found the following procedure by Noyce and Christie (1989) to be helpful. The teacher will need to model this process and then guide students as they apply it in their work. Noyce and Christie (1989) use the four easy steps listed here.

Step 1. Write a topic sentence, that is, one that summarizes the content in general terms. You need to either select one that the author has written or write your own.

Step 2. Delete all unnecessary or irrelevant sentences, words, and other information from the entire passage.

Step 3. After sorting all terms into categories, think of a collective term(s) for those things that fall into the same category.

Step 4. Collapse paragraphs on the same subject down to one when they are largely redundant.

The Situational Context

As we learned earlier in the first section of this chapter, the situational context of reading comprehension can be thought of in at least two ways. There is little doubt that children's reading comprehension is influenced by the *setting* in which one reads. Second, there is a *social context* associated with reading comprehension. In most classroom instruction, reading comprehension is best developed as a vibrant social activity in which people—teachers, parents, and children—read a text together and jointly construct meaning through discussion, what we have termed *dialogic* instruction. Lively discussion about a text in the company of others seems to be the optimal situational context to enhance students' reading comprehension (McKeown et al., 2009). In this section we add to our knowledge of dialogic instruction to maximize the social context of classrooms.

Cooperative/Interactive Comprehension Discussions. Research reported by the National Reading Panel (2000) found that cooperative, collaborative, and highly interactive discussions in which readers work together to learn comprehension strategies while interacting with each other and the teacher around a variety of texts is highly effective. There are multiple ways to create and sustain a cooperative and interactive classroom conducive to discussing texts. One effective approach for carrying on cooperative, collaborative, and highly interactive discussions of text to support reading comprehension instruction is called *text talk*.

Text Talk. Effective reading comprehension instruction, at least in the primary grades, is dependent on developing younger children's oral language vocabularies and language structures. Beck and McKeown (2001) have adapted their questioning-the-author strategy for intermediate grades for use in the early grades. They refer to this adaptation for simultaneously developing younger children's reading comprehension and oral language as text talk. Beck and McKeown (2001) recommend that teachers of younger students read aloud books that have stimulating and intellectually challenging content. Doing so allows younger students to grapple with difficult and complex ideas, situations, and concepts in text even when their word recognition abilities are quite limited.

Talk around texts should give students a chance to reflect, think, and respond beyond simple answers to simple questions. Talk should be analytic, requiring that students think deeply about the content of the text and the language (Dickinson & Smith, 1994). When they observed children talking about texts read aloud to them, Beck and McKeown (2001) found that children often talked about the pictures or related something from their background knowledge rather than focusing their attention and talk on the content of the text or the language in the text. Similarly, teachers' talk during read-aloud experiences in the classroom often focused on clarifying unfamiliar vocabulary by asking a question such as "Does anyone know what a tsunami is?" The other practice among teachers talking with children about text was to ask a question directly from the language, such as "When the little red hen asked the goose, the dog, and the cat for help, what did they say?" These types of interactions constrain children's construction of meaning for the whole text to local issues of understanding. Text talk was developed to help teachers further students' comprehension as well as to promote greater use of oral language in elaborated responses to text during discussion.

Text talk has six components: (1) selection of texts, (2) initial questions, (3) follow-up questions, (4) pictures, (5) background knowledge, and (6) vocabulary. For our discussion here, we will use the book *White Socks Only* by Evelyn Coleman (1996). This book has a challenging storyline that centers on the theme of racial discrimination. When reading this book, we can focus on several important text-related concepts, including fairness, equality, and social justice. To begin our text talk, we will construct a series of open-ended questions that we can use to initiate discussion with students at several points in the story:

- When Grandma was telling her story, she said, "I had two eggs hid in my pockets. Not to eat, mind you. But to see if what folk said was true." What do you think she was going to do with those eggs in her pocket?
- When Grandma got to the courthouse, she broke the egg against the horse's leg. Why do you think she did this?
- What do you think "frying an egg on cement" means?
- There was a sign on the water fountain that read "Whites only." What do you think Grandma thought this sign meant?

Next, we need to think of a few follow-up questions that will help children elaborate on their answers to our initial open-ended questions:

- Grandma couldn't understand why the white man pushed her away from the water fountain and asked her if she couldn't read. After all, she was wearing her white socks when she stepped up to the fountain to get a drink. Why was the white man mad at Grandma?
- Why did people move aside when the chicken man came into town?
- What was the fight about between the white man and the black people in the town?

After reading each page in the book displaying the drinking fountain with the sign "Whites Only," we would draw students' attention to the picture on these pages, asking them to explain what the sign means. We might ask questions: Why were the black people in this story ignoring the sign and stepping up to the drinking fountain to take a drink? What happened to Grandma when the chicken man showed up? Why did they take the sign "Whites Only" down?

Remember that rich, text-related discussions occur *before* showing pictures in text talks. Seeing the pictures after reading and discussing the text will take some getting used to for younger children, but they will soon come to expect it and pay greater attention to the linguistic and meaning content of the text. When children bring up their background knowledge in response to questions, teachers have found it best to acknowledge their comments by repeating back or rephrasing what the child has said and then moving discussion back to the text content.

An integral part of an effective text talk lesson is developing children's oral language vocabulary. Beck and McKeown (2001) recommend that vocabulary words be selected from the text that seem likely to be unfamiliar to young readers but that represent concepts they can identify with and use in normal conversation (p. 18). Words from our story, *White Socks Only*, that meet these criteria include *slinking, prancing, bandanna, fumbled*, and *snorted*. What seems to work best for vocabulary instruction is to create a chart of the words from the story along with their meanings, examples, and attributes. Then the teacher can keep track of the times during the day students read, say, or hear the words on the chart. Points can be awarded to individual students or teams for finding, saying, or hearing the words on the chart to create motivation for learning and using new vocabulary.

PARIS. The comprehension skills of retelling and summarizing information provide fertile ground for a virtual sea of talk in the classroom. Retelling involves selecting the most important information, making personal connections, and representing the information in a logical sequence. Summarizing requires choosing between significant and unimportant ideas. **PARIS** is a speaking activity used to combine five essential self-monitoring comprehension strategies: Predict, Ask questions, Retell, Infer, and Summarize (Mills, 2009).

As with all strategies, we want to provide scaffolding for gradual release of responsibility. The teacher begins by explaining and modeling each PARIS strategy with a text that is read aloud or viewed by the class using a document camera. Mills (2009) offers example questions and responses (see Table 7.1). Be sure to provide students with a sheet listing the PARIS strategies so they can record their shared responses when working in small groups.

Explain that before reading a text, students should begin with the first two strategies—*predict* and *ask questions*. Model using the book's cover, author's name, illustrations, headings, and other textual features for these first two steps. Next,

Table 7.1

PARIS Examples

Strategy	Example Question and Answer
Predict	Q: What do you think this text is about when you look at the cover? A: I think that the article is about a ferocious marsupial.
Ask questions	Q: What questions do you have when you look at the pictures? A: Why does the Tasmanian Devil have sharp teeth?
Retail	Q: What were the most important events (fiction) or information presented (nonfiction) in the text? A: It describes the appearance, habitat, breeding, and diet of the Tasmanian Devil.
Infer	Q: What can you infer from the information that is not directly stated in the text? A: Tasmanian Devils are nocturnal because the text states that they are awake during the night.
Summarize	Q: What was the main point of the text? A: The article gives information about an endangered native marsupial, the Tasmanian Devil.

From Mills, K. A. (2009). Floating on a Sea of Talk: Reading Comprehension Through Speaking and Listening. *The Reading Teacher, 63*(4), pp. 325–329. Reprinted with permission of the International Reading Association.

model using the last three strategies—*retell* the events, *draw inferences* from the information, and *summarize* the text, during and after reading the text. Mills (2009) likes to have students in her classroom summarize text selections in 66 words or less as a goal.

Multiple-Strategies Reading Comprehension Instruction

Although teaching comprehension strategies one at a time is an effective practice (Duffy, 2003; National Reading Panel, 2000), students also need to learn how to use several comprehension strategies at the same time when reading a variety of texts (e.g., Pressley, 2002; Reutzel et al., 2005).

Descriptive research by El-Dinary (2002) and Pressley, Gaskin, Wile, Cunicelli, and Sheridan (1991) showed that it can take up to 3 years of practice for students to effectively use multiple comprehension strategies. Research suggests there are three important conditions that need to be in place when teaching students to use multiple comprehension strategies during reading (El-Dinary, 2002; Palincsar, 2003).

First, teaching for self-regulation requires teachers to gradually scaffold the responsibility for determining what is worth knowing in a text or how the text might be interpreted. Second, multiple comprehension strategies instruction focuses on how one goes about making decisions about what is worth knowing in a text or how a text might be interpreted. It is important for teachers to understand and convey to students that learning reading comprehension strategies is a means to an end and not an end in and of itself. In summary, teaching multiple reading comprehension strategies requires a highly interactive, collaborative social setting for discussing text. Teachers need to promote independence through explicitly showing students how to select and apply each and every reading comprehension strategy in the set of multiple strategies. This means starting by teaching each strategy explicitly and then quickly moving to combine the use of the entire set of strategies when reading a text. Teachers need to explicitly and interactively model how to strategically coordinate multiple strategies while interacting around texts over time. And finally, teachers gradually release the responsibility and authority for using multiple strategies in collaborative settings to the students themselves while interacting over texts (El-Dinary, 2002; Palincsar, 2003). Reciprocal teaching is one strategy used by teachers as a way of helping children use multiple comprehension strategies.

Reciprocal Teaching. In 1984, Palincsar and Brown designed an instructional procedure called **reciprocal teaching** (RT) for students who struggled with comprehending text. RT makes use of a set of four reading comprehension strategies to enhance students' reading comprehension. The RT instructional process typically involves teachers and students in a discussion or dialogue about text. The purpose of the discussion is for teachers and students to work together to co-construct the meaning of the text (Palincsar, 2003). Any discussion between teachers and students is supported by the consistent application of the four RT comprehension strategies: (1) predicting, (2) question generating, (3) clarifying, and (4) summarizing.

When first using RT in the classroom, teachers explain and model the application of the four RT comprehension strategies while reading and thinking aloud over small text segments, usually paragraphs. Over time, however, teachers gradually progress to larger units of text and release the responsibility for using the four RT strategies independently to students. Prior to providing a classroom example of reciprocal teaching, we describe in a bit more detail the four RT strategies.

- *Predicting* requires that students make a "best guess" based on their background knowledge of the topic available to them from previewing a text. As we saw earlier, this information includes such variables as reading headings, chapter titles, pictures or illustrations, boxed items, and so on. When predicting, students usually anticipate what might happen next, the order that events may take, or even the knowledge or information they expect to be able to learn from reading a text. Using a graphic organizer to facilitate predictions has also been shown to have positive effects on students' predictions and comprehension of text (Meyers, 2006; Oczkus, 2003; Reutzel & Fawson, 1989, 1991).

- *Question generating* reinforces the summarizing strategy, according to one of RT's authors (Palincsar, 2003). Formulating appropriate questions is difficult, as we have previously discussed.

- *Clarifying*, according to Palincsar (2003), is a particularly important strategy for working with children who have come to believe that reading is all about saying the words correctly and who do not monitor their understanding of text. When children are taught to clarify the meaning of text, their attention is directed toward unknown vocabulary words, unclear referent terms, and unfamiliar concepts or text organizations. When they encounter difficulty understanding a text or term, they are taught to identify what is causing the problem and take affirmative steps to "fix up" their comprehension difficulties.

- *Summarizing* involves students in identifying, in proper sequence, the important ideas found within a text. They are asked to sort through many details and come up with the most important ideas through paraphrasing and integrating important ideas in sentences, paragraphs, and across the entire text. For example, if students have read a narrative text, they may summarize it by using story structure—setting, problem, events, and resolution. On the other hand, if students have read an expository text, they may summarize the important ideas by using headings, subheadings, and important related details in the proper sequence. Students need to pay attention to the most important ideas in the text as well as the order in which those ideas are

Figure 7.24

Wall Poster Display of the Four RT Comprehension Strategies

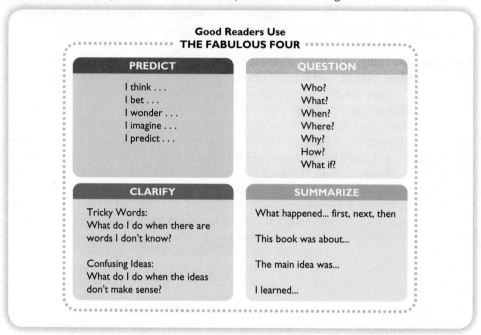

Adapted from "The Four Reciprocal Teaching Strategies," in *Reciprocal Teaching at Work* by L. D. Oczkus. Copyright © 2003 by the International Reading Association.

● ● ●

IRA Standards for Reading Professionals: Standard 5, Elements 5.1, 5.2, 5.3

Common Core Standards: Reading: K–5, Key Ideas and Details (items 1–3), Craft and Structure (items 4–6), Integration of Knowledge and Ideas (items 7–9), Range of Reading and Level of Text Complexity (item 10); Reading: Grades 6–12, Key Ideas and Details (items 1–3), Craft and Structure (items 4–6), Integration of Knowledge and Ideas (items 7–9), Range of Reading and Level of Text Complexity (item 10)

Response to Intervention: Responsive Teaching and Differentiation; Systemic and Comprehensive Approaches

presented. Research by Rinehart, Stahl, and Erickson (1986) has shown that summarizing improves students' reading comprehension of fiction and nonfiction texts.

We recommend that a poster or wall chart be produced and displayed showing the four RT comprehension strategies (see Figure 7.24).

Research on the effects of using reciprocal teaching found that using RT produced generally superior outcomes when compared to the other comprehension or reading instructional conditions (Rosenshine & Meister, 1994). And finally, Palincsar and Brown (1984) found that the collection of four strategies improved students' comprehension more than the use of any single strategy selected and used in isolation from among the four RT strategies.

Response to Intervention (RTI)

Meeting Diverse Needs for Tiers 1 and 2 in Comprehension Instruction

Many times it is necessary to adjust the reading comprehension strategies discussed in this chapter to meet the varied needs of students in your classroom. Here we are thinking about struggling readers, English learners (EL), and some who may have learning disorders. Sometimes these adaptations are done in small-group sessions as part of your Tier 1 instruction and at other times a more intensive Tier 2 approach is required with three extra supplemental sessions of 20 to 30 minutes each with weekly progress assessments. We urge you to consider the following recommendations for working with students who need extra help in reading comprehension:

- Ensure that students can decode your texts fluently to allow sufficient cognitive processing needed for comprehension. If the text is too difficult the student will spend too much time trying to sound out words and comprehension will be compromised.
- Use dialogic instruction and text features liberally to supplement understanding of text materials and strategy applications.
- Arrange flexible, cooperative grouping to allow all children to learn from and with others. Joint productive activities (JPA) are strongly encouraged.
- Focus on developing deep vocabulary and concept knowledge.
- Capitalize on students' interests and abilities (i.e., use their strengths to help overcome weaknesses).
- Provide increased teacher modeling and scaffolding and extended instructional time for struggling students. As one literacy coach says, "You have to *marinate* students in using new comprehension skills!"
- Remember that struggling readers need to have *more* encounters and experiences with informational text (Brozo, 2010).

Alternative Strategy Instruction for Tiers 1 and 2: Comprehension Under Construction

Researchers Dewitz and colleagues (2009) observed that strategy instruction outlined in core reading programs is wide but not deep, expansive but not unified. It is not surprising that many students struggle in reading comprehension and often require additional developmental instruction at the Tier 1 level, not to mention struggling readers who may require Tier 2 instructional support. In these situations it is always best that teachers offer concrete instruction so that students can better understand the comprehension strategies being taught.

Comprehension Under Construction (CUC) (Marcell, DeCleene, & Juettner, 2010) is small-group activity well-suited to teaching students to use reading comprehension strategy combinations in a concrete way. Lessons begin with the teacher adopting the role of foreman. The foreman's task is to survey the job site (i.e., activate students' background knowledge) and introduce the four workers who will help their group build shared comprehension. These workers—and their comprehension strategies—are described with job titles:

- The architect, who draws up the blueprint to *predict* what the building will look like
- The job inspector, who wears his "get-it goggles" to *clarify* better the meanings of words and ideas
- The electrician, who keeps the group "wired" with *questions* that provoke both big and little sparks
- The bricklayer, who cements understanding by connecting main ideas, brick by brick, into a cohesive *summary*

Props such as pictures, construction hats (with names attached), and tools add to student motivation and task commitment.

Implementation of Comprehension Under Construction (CUC) is done over several days and phases (Marcell, DeCleene, & Juettner, 2010). In the initial phase the teacher *models* the strategies using authentic literature. During the second stage, *collaboration,* hats are given to students along with personal "four-square blueprints" of the strategies. This is actually guided practice during which students become comprehension construction workers and improve their specialties. After students reach proficiency the foreman announces a "strategy switcheroo," and hats are exchanged so that students have many opportunities to practice the four strategies with teacher guidance until independence is reached.

The third phase is termed *reciprocal* and the group begins to function more independently. During this stage, hats are initially rotated on a lesson-to-lesson basis, as in a literature circle (discussed in the next section of this chapter). The four-square blueprint is now replaced by a "CUC sticky note" to be completed by students. The sticky notes serve as a running record of strategy implementation—artifacts that can be adhered to student folders. Over time, RTI-oriented data develops appropriate for problem-solving team discussions.

The final stage in the CUC, called *metacognition,* has students becoming independent contractors who carry their own comprehension toolboxes. Each CUC lesson ends with the query, "Who helped you most today? Was it the electrician? Why was this strategy helpful?"

Adapting Comprehension Instruction for English Learners

Over the last decade, a number of studies that have carefully examined young English learners' early reading in English have found convergence on a number of key points (Manyak & Bauer, 2008). For example, ELs from a variety of first languages can successfully develop beginning literacy skills in English regardless of limitations in English proficiency. Second, the early stages of ELs' reading development looks a lot like that of native speakers (NS) of English, with the same basic underlying factors of phonological awareness, letter identification, and decoding skills. Third, it appears that the same percentages of NSs and ELs have difficulties learning to read in English. Finally, explicit instruction has proven to be beneficial for the early English reading development of ELs. Taken together, we need to hold high expectations for ELs' learning of reading and writing skills in English.

At this point there seem to be few existing studies on comprehension instruction for ELs that offer examples of sound instructional practices (Shanahan & Beck, 2006). Nevertheless, it seems clear that comprehension instruction is critical to the long-term achievement of ELs.

Manyak and Bauer (2008) offer several principles to guide instruction for ELs summarized from extant research. First, research has demonstrated that ELs may comprehend more than they are able to communicate verbally in English. Thus we must not underestimate ELs' ability to read difficult texts and participate in higher-order comprehension activities and discussions. Second, learning new vocabulary through language-rich instruction is key in ELs' comprehension. Third, it has been established that using ELs' background knowledge (i.e., culturally familiar content) as a means for scaffolding to new text content learning boosts their comprehension.

Teachers should provide children with culturally familiar texts whenever possible. However, ELs will always face many texts with unfamiliar content, so it is critical that teachers implement prereading activities that build ELs' relevant background knowledge. An activity called synopsis text (Manyak & Bauer, 2008) is recommended for building background knowledge for ELs. First, identify key ideas from an upcoming text into a brief one- to two-paragraph synopsis. Students are asked to read the synopsis twice and then, working in pairs or small groups, identify three key points, one idea they find difficult to understand, and any unfamiliar words. Next, the groups write a question they have that relates to the upcoming reading. This familiarizes students with the content of the text and prompts them to anticipate new information (a schema-building activity).

Finally, approaches such as Beck and McKeown's (2006) questioning the author (discussed earlier) help ELs break down texts into small sections for discussions about meanings or to use fix-up strategies, providing them with opportunities for rich discussion.

Motivation and Engagement

Motivation and Engagement Strategies for Teaching Reading Comprehension

As mentioned in Chapter 1, Turner and Paris (1995) propose six Cs of motivation that promote student engagement in the act of reading and comprehending a text: (1) choice, (2) challenge, (3) control, (4) collaboration, (5) constructing meaning, and (6) consequences.

IRA Standards for Reading Professionals: Standard 5, Element 5.2

Response to Intervention: Instruction

1. *Choice* does not mean that students are free to select any text or to make up what they have read when asked about it. Choices are always bounded or limited. To offer choice may mean choosing to read from two different information books on rocks and rock formations. However, when children have the sense that they can make some choices about what to read and for which purposes, they are more willing to persist and remain intellectually engaged while reading.

2. *Challenge* is the second way in which we can encourage increased reading motivation and engagement to improve reading comprehension. Turner and Paris (1995) dispute the common notion that children prefer "easy" reading texts and tasks to more difficult or challenging material, noting that research supports the opposite conclusion—that students enjoy challenge. Of course, children are also motivated by success, so the text challenge must not become excessive to the point of frustration.

3. Sharing the *control* of texts and tasks in the classroom with the teacher through choice is associated with greater reading engagement. Students need to feel that they have an integral role to play while reading a text in order to take sufficient control of their own thinking processes.

4. *Collaboration* has been shown to be another strategy for which there is sufficient scientific evidence of benefit. Collaboration requires that students discuss, interact, and work together with each other and their teachers to construct the meanings of texts, what we have termed **dialogic teaching.** Collaborative discussions and interactions also elaborate the outcomes of the reading comprehension process by combining memories triggered from the reading of a text.

Click on A+RISE—WIDA ELP Standard Strategies in the MyEducationLab (www.myeducationlab.com) for your course. Next, select the Strategy Card Index tab, scroll to Comprehension for grades K–5, and select the Carousel strategy.

5. *Constructing meaning* is the very essence of reading comprehension instruction. This process requires the conscious selection, control, and use of various cognitive comprehension strategies while engaged in reading text.

6. *Consequences* are the final factor that leads students to increased motivation and reading comprehension. This concept refers to the nature of the outcomes expected within a specified amount of time. If the outcome expected is an open-ended rather than a closed-ended task, such as contributing to a discussion rather than getting the "right" answers to questions on a worksheet, students interpret their failures in comprehension differently. When seeking correct or "right" answers, they often feel that they just do not have enough ability (Turner & Paris, 1995). On the other hand, if through discussion they detect that they failed to pick up on some element in the text, they often view this failure as the result of insufficiently or improperly selecting or applying effective comprehension strategies.

Affective Responses: Interpreting and Elaborating Meaning

Discussion and dialogue are critical aspects of effective comprehension instruction (Gambrell & Almasi, 1996). One widely recognized and recommended approach to inspiring discussions about text is called **reader response,** which invites students to take a much more active role (Bleich, 1978; Rosenblatt, 1978, 1989, 2004).

Discussion about texts in small groups often takes place in literature circles or book clubs that lead students into grand conversations about books (Daniels, 1994; McMahon & Raphael, 1997; Peterson & Eeds, 1990; Tompkins, 2006). Grand conversations about books motivate students to extend, clarify, and elaborate their own interpretations of the text as well as to consider alternative interpretations offered by peers. It's a simple procedure to initiate a literature circle.

- Begin by selecting four or five books that will engender interest and discussion among students.
- Next, give a book talk on each of the four or five titles selected, enthusiastically presenting and describing each book to the students.
- Ask students to individually select their top three book choices for reading.
- Give students their first choices to the extent possible. If too many students want the same title, offer some second choices as you compile the assignment list.

This system works well, because students always know that they get to read a book of their own choosing. After books are distributed the next day, give the students a large block of uninterrupted time in class to read. At the beginning of the year, students can read about 20 minutes without undue restlessness. However, later in the year children can often sustain free reading for up to a full hour.

As students complete several hours of independent reading, each literature circle meets on a rotating basis for about 20 minutes with the teacher. Group members discuss and share their initial reactions to the book. We have found that meeting with one to two literature circles per day—with a maximum of 2 days independent reading between meetings—works quite well.

Based on the group discussion, an assignment is given to the group to extend the discussion of the book into their interpretive media (i.e., writing, art, drama, and so on). Each member of the literature circle works on this assignment before returning to the group for a second meeting. This sequence of reading and working on an extension response assignment repeats until the entire book is completed. We recommend that the first extension assignment focus on personal responses and connections with the book. Subsequent assignments can concentrate on understanding literary elements (i.e., characterization, point of view, story elements, role of the narrator). At the conclusion of the book, the literature circle meets to determine a culminating project (Reutzel & Cooter, 2000; Zarillo, 1989). This project captures the group's interpretation and feelings about the entire book as demonstrated in a mural, story map, diorama, character wanted poster, and so on.

There are many ways to invite students to respond to texts they read. One of the most common is to ask children to write in a response journal (Parsons, 1990). We have developed a listing of affective responses to text that represent concepts described by Rosenblatt (1978) in Figure 7.25.

Click on A+RISE—WIDA ELP Standard Strategies in the MyEducationLab (www.myeducationlab.com) for your course. Next, select the Strategy Card Index tab, scroll to Comprehension for grades K–5, and select the Venn Diagram, T-Chart strategy.

Figure 7.25

Alternative Affective Responses to Books

1. Prepare a condensed or simplified version of the text to read aloud to younger readers.
2. Draw a map of the journey of characters in a story.
3. Talk to your teacher or a peer about the book.
4. Make a "Wanted" poster for a character in the text.
5. Make a poster based on an information book.
6. Select a part of the book to read aloud to others.
7. Send a letter to your parents, a friend, or your teacher telling about a book and why they should read it.
8. Write a classified newspaper ad for a book.
9. Rewrite a story or part of a story as a readers' theatre.
10. Make overhead transparencies about the story to use on the overhead projector.
11. Make a PowerPoint slide computer presentation about an information book.
12. Make a character report card on your favorite character.
13. Make a passport application as your favorite character.
14. Write a "Dear Abby" column as your favorite character.
15. Write a missing persons report about a story character.
16. Draw a part of the book and ask others to tell about what part of the story is illustrated.
17. Write a newspaper headline for a book or story.
18. Write a newspaper report for a story character or about information you have learned in an information book.
19. Write to the author to describe your responses to a book.
20. Illustrate a book using a variety of art media or techniques.
21. Write a letter to the librarian suggesting why he or she should or should not recommend a book to someone.
22. Study about the author and write a brief biography.
23. Compose a telegram about the book to tell someone why he or she must read this book.
24. Write a TV commercial and videotape it.
25. Plan a storytelling session for kindergarten children.
26. Interview a story character and write the interview.
27. Compare and contrast characters, settings, or facts in a book using a Venn diagram.
28. Construct a game of Trivial Pursuit using facts in an information book.
29. Construct a game of Password using clues about characters or events in a story.
30. Compose an imaginary diary that might be kept by a book character.

IRA Standards for Reading Professionals: Standard 5, Element 5.1

Common Core Standards: Reading: K–5, Integration of Knowledge and Ideas (item 7); Reading: Grades 6–12, Integration of Knowledge and Ideas (item 7)

Response to Intervention: Instruction

Technology and New Literacies

Internet Reciprocal Teaching

Based on the well-established research on reciprocal teaching (Palincsar, 1986; Palincsar & Brown, 1984), Internet reciprocal teaching (Leu et al., 2008; Reinking & Castek, 2007;) was developed around the use of wireless laptop carts in the classroom. IRT is a very rich model of instruction that involves online informational texts; the reading, processing, and construction of students' own texts (using hypertext links, wikis, etc.) using varied online texts as sources; instruction offered by teachers many times in whole-class settings; student modeling of online comprehension strategies; a focus on questioning, locating, critically evaluating, synthesizing, and communicating strategies; a gradual release of responsibilities (scaffolding); and student collaboration and discussion.

Leu and colleagues (2008) developed through their research a three-phase model for Internet reciprocal teaching as a means for improving online reading comprehension.

- *Phase 1: Teacher-led instruction.* Students take part in teacher-led sessions to establish basic routines and Internet/computer skills (e.g., handling laptops or PCs, opening and closing programs, how to manage multiple windows). The teacher models online reading strategies as well as procedures to follow for group discussions.

- *Phase 2: Collaborative modeling of online reading comprehension strategies.* Teachers and students begin to share strategies for online reading comprehension. Small groups of students having a common problem often take the lead in sharing strategies for finding information they have discovered. These may relate to key curriculum standards or goals. One example offered by Leu and colleagues (2008) has the student groups being given three problems/questions to solve on the Internet:

> How high is Mt. Fuji in Japan?
>
> Find a different answer to the same question.
>
> Which answer do you think is most accurate and how did you determine that it was?

Students in each group are guided to discuss their solutions, exchanging reading comprehension strategies for locating information and critically evaluating information. Lessons are designed to minimize teacher talk and to maximize the time students are engaged with the task. An essential part of planning is setting aside time at the end of each lesson for students to debrief and to exchange strategies with the entire class after having already done so in their small groups (p. 9).

Phase 2 lessons move from highly structured to less structured over time as student competence and ability to work independently increases. Early lessons focus on the rudiments of locating and critically evaluating online information. Later, the emphasis shifts to using a variety of online tools (e.g., e-mail, wikis, blogs, Google docs, instant messaging).

- *Phase 3: Inquiry.* In this phase, students begin to move more into independent online inquiry linked to the curriculum standards. Much of the work by students is done independently and in small groups. Students also have the opportunity to decide on the most effective ways to share what they have learned. The teacher shifts to a role of helping individual students and groups find new ways of solving problems. This may involve working with students in other classrooms as well as their own homeroom.

Family and Community Connections That Enhance Students' Reading Comprehension

Although families usually do not have the expertise to provide explicit reading comprehension strategies instruction and guided practice, they can do a great deal to facilitate children's reading comprehension. For years now, Allington (2006) has insisted that children need to read a lot to get good at reading. Families are in an ideal position to facilitate wide reading and discussion of text. As teachers, we can provide families with both access to reading materials and structure for facilitating discussion and interaction around texts.

Richgels and Wold (1998) have designed the Three for the Road program to involve parents in choosing one or more books to read and discuss with their children at home from among three "leveled" books. These leveled books are placed in a backpack that is sent home to parents with their children. The three books selected in each backpack represent a variety of themes, including fantasy, comedy, math mania, adventure, ABCs, and sing-along. The three levels of books included in each backpack are at the "easiest," "in-between," and "most challenging" levels for the student's grade level. The backpack includes a letter to parents as shown in Figure 7.26. This letter may be easily adapted to suit the needs of parents and children in other grades.

●●●
IRA Standards
for Reading
Professionals:
Standard 4, Elements 4.1, 4.2, 4.3

Response to Intervention:
Collaboration

Figure 7.26

Parent Letter from Three for the Road

Dear First Grade Parents,

Beginning next week, the first graders will be taking home our "Three for the Road" backpacks. The packs are designed to foster enjoyment of children's literature and to nurture lifelong reading habits. We encourage your partnership in reading by sharing these stories and your responses together.

During the year, the A-B-C Pack, Adventure Pack, Comedy Pack, Fantasy Pack, Math Mania Pack, and Sing-Along Pack will rotate in the first grades. Your child will take a pack home once in the next 4 to 5 weeks. Please return the pack to school the next morning after you have helped your child recheck all of the contents on the inside pocket list. In this way, every child will have a chance to take home a class pack once each month.

Since your child may choose to read all or only some of the books included, please try to set aside a special reading time. First graders love to make choices about their reading and may ask a parent to read aloud, to read along with them, or to listen to them read alone. A black journal is also included for students' and parents' written comments and illustrations about meaningful characters or preferred story parts. Check the inside cover of the journal for parent and child response ideas. You may also choose how you would like to respond. Sock puppets are furnished to support language and literacy development. To encourage story responses, you may consider asking, "Which character seems most like the purple puppet?" Or your child may want to "role play" a favorite person or animal by making the puppet "talk" like the story character.

Whatever activities you choose, make this a relaxed and enjoyable experience in reading, from parent read-alouds to rereading children's favorite parts.

We thank you for your support and hope you enjoy our Three for the Road packs!

Your Partners in Reading at _____ School.

From Richgels, D. J., & Wold, L. S. (1998). Literacy on the Road: Back Packing Partnerships Between School and Home. *The Reading Teacher, 52*(1), pp. 18–29. Reprinted with permission of the International Reading Association.

Parents are given several ways to respond to and discuss the books with their children within each themed backpack. Child responses can include writing or drawing about (1) whatever they want in relation to the book, (2) their favorite part, (3) how the book reminded them of something else, or (4) how these three books were alike or different. Parents can also respond by writing and drawing about something of interest to them in the books or something they learned with their child from this activity.

Summary

Comprehension is intentional thinking during which meaning is constructed through interactions between texts and readers. Comprehending a text involves two phases—construction and integration. In phase one of this process, the reader constructs meaning from text and in the second phase integrates this newly constructed knowledge into the existing prior knowledge network.

Monitoring and assessing children's development of comprehension is an important activity to help you, the teacher, select appropriate comprehension strategy instruction and other supports.

Reading comprehension is developed through activating and adding to students' background knowledge, offering explicit teacher-led comprehension strategy instruction, and by helping students coordinate a set or family of comprehension strategies to construct meaning through rich discussions and interactions around a variety of text structures and genres. Struggling readers and, in fact, all young readers benefit from increased scaffolding to support comprehension development, including demonstrations, pictures, diagrams, charts, collaboration with other students, instruction to deepen students' breadth and depth of conceptual knowledge, and connections that capitalize on students' interests and motivations. Finally, families and communities can read and discuss appropriately challenging themed books of interest as found in the Three for the Road program to add to children's background knowledge and develop their abilities to think and talk about a variety of texts.

Field and Classroom Applications

- Make a poster showing steps students can take to produce a text summary.
- Select a popular children's story. Parse the story into its story structure parts: setting, characters, problem, goal, events, and resolution. Make a story map like the one shown in this chapter.
- Summarize the *Report of the National Reading Panel* (2000) describing their findings on text comprehension. Make a poster displaying these major findings.

- In small groups, examine several narrative and expository texts. With your peers, discuss how to activate or build students' background knowledge before reading these texts.
- Organize into literature circle groups. Examine a set of children's books to read as a group. Use reciprocal teaching strategies to discuss one chapter of the book during class.

Recommended Resources

Print

Beck, I., & McKeown, M. (2006). *Improving comprehension with questioning the author: A fresh and expanded view of a powerful approach.* New York: Scholastic.

Dewitz, P., Leahy, S. B., Jones, J., & Sullivan, P. M. (2010). *The essential guide to selecting and using core reading programs.* Newark, DE: International Reading Association.

Essley, R. (2010). *Visual tools for differentiating content area instruction*. New York: Scholastic.

International Reading Association. (2010). *Standards for the assessment of reading and writing revised*. Newark, DE: International Reading Association/ National Council of Teachers of English.

Kelley, M. J., & Clausen-Grace, N. (2007). *Comprehension shouldn't be silent: From strategy instruction to student independence*. Newark, DE: International Reading Association.

Malloy, J. A., Marinak, B. A., & Gambrell, L. B. (Eds.). (2010). *Essential readings on motivation*. Newark, DE: International Reading Association.

Ogle, D. (2011). *Partnering for content literacy: PRC2 in action*. Boston: Pearson/Allyn & Bacon.

Web Resources

www.backflip.com/login.ihtml
Backflip helps students discover how to take information from a web site and organize this information on your own home page.

www.literacy.uconn.edu/compre.htm
The Literacy Web has myriad resources for teaching reading comprehension provided by the University of Connecticut.

www.readingcomprehensionconnection.com/reading_lesson.php
Reading Comprehension Connection provides tips for assisting English learners.

http://www.rhlschool.com/reading.htm
RHL School provides free comprehension worksheets.

The Power of Classroom Practice
www.myeducationlab.com

Go to Topic 6, Comprehension, in the MyEducationLab (www.myeducationlab.com) for your course, where you can:

- Find learning outcomes for Comprehension along with the national standards that connect to these outcomes.
- Complete Assignments and Activities that can help you more deeply understand the chapter content.
- Apply and practice your understanding of the core teaching skills identified in the chapter with the Building Teaching Skills and Dispositions learning units. (optional)
- Examine challenging situations and cases presented in the IRIS Center Resources. (optional)
- Access video clips of CCSSO National Teachers of the Year award winners responding to the question "Why Do I Teach?" in the Teacher Talk section. (optional)
- Check your comprehension on the content covered in the chapter by going to the Study Plan in the Book Resources for your text. Here you will be able to take a chapter quiz, receive feedback on your answers, and then access Review, Practice, and Enrichment activities to enhance your understanding of chapter content. (optional)

Go to the Topic A+RISE in the MyEducationLab (www.myeducationlab.com) for your course. A+RISE® Standards2Strategy™ is an innovative and interactive online resource that offers new teachers in grades K–12 just in time, research-based instructional strategies that:

- Meet the linguistic needs of ELLs as they learn content.
- Differentiate instruction for all grades and abilities.
- Offer reading and writing techniques, cooperative learning, use of linguistic and nonlinguistic representations, scaffolding, teacher modeling, higher order thinking, and alternative classroom ELL assessment.
- Provide support to help teachers be effective through the integration of listening, speaking, reading, and writing along with the content curriculum.
- Improve student achievement.
- Are aligned to Common Core Elementary Language Arts standards (for the literacy strategies) and to English language proficiency standards in WIDA, Texas, California, and Florida.

STANDARDS
for Reading Professionals and Guiding Principles for Educators

IRA Standards for Reading Professionals

Standard 1: Foundational Knowledge

Element 1.1

Candidates understand major theories and empirical research that describe the cognitive, linguistic, motivational, and sociocultural foundations of reading and writing development, processes, and components, including word recognition, language comprehension, strategic knowledge, and reading–writing connections.

Element 1.2

Candidates understand the historically shared knowledge of the profession and changes over time in the perceptions of reading and writing development, processes, and components.

Common Core Standards

Teachers should be familiar with the following standards.

Reading: K–5

Key Ideas and Details

1. Read closely to determine what the text says explicitly and to make logical inferences from it; cite specific textual evidence when writing or speaking to support conclusions drawn from the text.

2. Determine central ideas or themes of a text and analyze their development; summarize the key supporting details and ideas.

3. Analyze how and why individuals, events, and ideas develop and interact over the course of a text.

Craft and Structure

4. Interpret words and phrases as they are used in a text, including determining technical, connotative, and figurative meanings, and analyze how specific word choices shape meaning or tone.

5. Analyze the structure of texts, including how specific sentences, paragraphs, and larger portions of the text (e.g., a section, chapter, scene, or stanza) relate to each other and the whole.

Integration of Knowledge and Ideas

7. Integrate and evaluate content presented in diverse media and formats, including visually and quantitatively, as well as in words.

8. Delineate and evaluate the argument and specific claims in a text, including the validity of the reasoning as well as the relevance and sufficiency of the evidence.

9. Analyze how two or more texts address similar themes or topics in order to build knowledge or to compare the approaches the authors take.

Range of Reading and Level of Text Complexity

10. Read and comprehend complex literary and informational texts independently and proficiently.

Reading: Grades 6–12

Key Ideas and Details

1. Read closely to determine what the text says explicitly and to make logical inferences from it; cite specific textual evidence when writing or speaking to support conclusions drawn from the text.

2. Determine central ideas or themes of a text and analyze their development; summarize the key supporting details and ideas.

3. Analyze how and why individuals, events, and ideas develop and interact over the course of a text.

Craft and Structure

4. Interpret words and phrases as they are used in a text, including determining technical, connotative, and figurative meanings, and analyze how specific word choices shape meaning or tone.

5. Analyze the structure of texts, including how specific sentences, paragraphs, and larger portions of the text (e.g., a section, chapter, scene, or stanza) relate to each other and the whole.

6. Assess how point of view or purpose shapes the content and style of a text.

Integration of Knowledge and Ideas

7. Integrate and evaluate content presented in diverse formats and media, including visually and quantitatively, as well as in words.

8. Delineate and evaluate the argument and specific claims in a text, including the validity of the reasoning as well as the relevance and sufficiency of the evidence.

9. Analyze how two or more texts address similar themes or topics in order to build knowledge or to compare the approaches the authors take.

Range of Reading and Level of Text Complexity

10. Read and comprehend complex literary and informational texts independently and proficiently.

Response to Intervention

6. Expertise

• Success for culturally and linguistically diverse students depends on teachers and support personnel who are well prepared to teach in a variety of settings. Deep knowledge of cultural and linguistic differences is especially critical for the prevention of language and literacy problems in diverse student populations.

Assessing Reading Comprehension

IRA Standards for Reading Professionals

Standard 3: Assessment and Evaluation

Element 3.1

Candidates understand types of assessments and their purposes, strengths, and limitations.

Element 3.2

Candidates select, develop, administer, and interpret assessments, both traditional print and electronic, for specific purposes.

Element 3.3

Candidates use assessment information to plan and evaluate instruction

Common Core Standards

Teachers must be able to assess students' ability to do the following.

Reading: K–5

Key Ideas and Details

1. (See previous)

2. (See previous)

3. (See previous)

Craft and Structure

4. (See previous)

5. (See previous)

6. Assess how point of view or purpose shapes the content and style of a text.

Integration of Knowledge and Ideas

7. (See previous)

8. (See previous)

9. (See previous)

Range of Reading and Level of Text Complexity

10. (See previous)

Reading: Grades 6–12

Key Ideas and Details

1. (See previous)

2. (See previous)

3. (See previous)

Craft and Structure

4. (See previous)

5. (See previous)

6. (See previous)

Integration of Knowledge and Ideas

7. (See previous)

8. (See previous)

9. (See previous)

Range of Reading and Level of Text Complexity

10. (See previous)

Response to Intervention

3. Assessment

An RTI approach demands assessment that can inform language and literacy instruction meaningfully.

• Assessment should reflect the multidimensional nature of language and literacy learning and the diversity among students being assessed. The utility of an assessment is dependent on the extent to which it provides valid information on the essential aspects of language and literacy that can be used to plan appropriate instruction.

• Assessments, tools, and techniques should provide useful and timely information about desired language and literacy goals. They should reflect authentic language and literacy activities as opposed to contrived texts or tasks generated specifically for assessment purposes. The quality of assessment information should not be sacrificed for the efficiency of an assessment procedure.

- Multiple purposes for assessment should be clearly identified and appropriate tools and techniques employed. . . . Particular care should be taken in selecting assessments for ELLs and for students who speak an English dialect that differs from mainstream dialects.

- Efficient assessment systems involve a layered approach in which screening techniques are used both to identify which students require further (diagnostic) assessment and to provide aggregate data about the nature of student achievement overall.

What Are the Most Effective Ways to Teach Reading Comprehension?

IRA Standards for Reading Professionals

Standard 2: Curriculum and Instruction

Element 2.1

Candidates use foundational knowledge to design or implement an integrated, comprehensive, and balanced curriculum.

Element 2.2

Candidates use appropriate and varied instructional approaches, including those that develop word recognition, language comprehension, strategic knowledge, and reading–writing connections.

Element 2.3

Candidates use a wide range of texts (e.g., narrative, expository, and poetry) from traditional print, digital, and online resources.

Standard 4: Diversity

Element 4.1

Candidates recognize, understand, and value the forms of diversity that exist in society and their importance in learning to read and write.

Element 4.2

Candidates use a literacy curriculum and engage in instructional practices that positively impact students' knowledge, beliefs, and engagement with the features of diversity.

Element 4.3

Candidates develop and implement strategies to advocate for equity.

Standard 5: Literate Environment

Element 5.1

Candidates design the physical environment to optimize students' use of traditional print, digital, and online resources in reading and writing instruction.

Element 5.2

Candidates design a social environment that is low risk and includes choice, motivation, and scaffolded support to optimize students' opportunities for learning to read and write.

Element 5.3

Candidates use routines to support reading and writing instruction (e.g., time allocation, transitions from one activity to another, discussions, and peer feedback).

Common Core Standards

Reading: K–5

Key Ideas and Details

1. (See previous)

2. (See previous)

3. (See previous)

Craft and Structure

4. (See previous)

5. (See previous)

6. (See previous)

Integration of Knowledge and Ideas

7. (See previous)

8. (See previous)

9. (See previous)

Range of Reading and Level of Text Complexity

10. (See previous)

Reading: Grades 6–12

Key Ideas and Details

1. (See previous)

2. (See previous)

3. (See previous)

Craft and Structure

4. (See previous)

5. (See previous)

6. (See previous)

Integration of Knowledge and Ideas

7. (See previous)

8. (See previous)

9. (See previous)

Range of Reading and Level of Text Complexity

10. (See previous)

Response to Intervention

1. Instruction

- Whatever approach is taken to RTI, it should ensure optimal instruction for every student at all levels of schooling. It should prevent serious language and literacy problems through increasingly differentiated and intensified assessment and instruction and reduce the disproportionate number of minority youth and ELLs identified as learning disabled.
- Instruction and assessment conducted by the classroom teacher are central to the success of RTI and must address the needs of all students, including those from diverse cultural and linguistic backgrounds.
- The success of RTI depends on the classroom teacher's use of research-based practices.
- Research on instructional practices must provide not only information about what works, but also what works with whom, by whom, in what contexts, and on which outcomes.

- When core language and literacy instruction is not effective for a particular student, it should be modified to address more closely the needs and abilities of that student.

2. Responsive Teaching and Differentiation

- RTI is centrally about optimizing language and literacy instruction for particular students. This means that differentiated instruction, based on instructionally relevant assessment, is essential.

5. Systemic and Comprehensive Approaches

- RTI needs to be integrated within the context of a coherent and consistent language and literacy curriculum that guides comprehensive instruction for all students.

Meeting Diverse Needsfor Tiers 1 and 2 in Comprehension Instruction

IRA Standards for Reading Professionals

Standard 5: Literate Environment

Elements 5.1, 5.2, 5.3 (See previous)

Common Core Standards

Reading: K–5

Key Ideas and Details

1. (See previous)

2. (See previous)

3. (See previous)

Craft and Structure

4. (See previous)

5. (See previous)

6. (See previous)

Integration of Knowledge and Ideas

7. (See previous)

8. (See previous)

9. (See previous)

Range of Reading and Level of Text Complexity

10. (See previous)

Reading: Grades 6–12

Key Ideas and Details

1. (See previous)

2. (See previous)

3. (See previous)

Craft and Structure

4. (See previous)

5. (See previous)

6. (See previous)

Integration of Knowledge and Ideas

7. (See previous)

8. (See previous)

9. (See previous)

Range of Reading and Level of Text Complexity

10. (See previous)

Response to Intervention

2. Responsive Teaching and Differentiation

- RTI is centrally about optimizing language and literacy instruction for particular students.
- Instruction and materials selection must derive from specific student–teacher interactions and not be constrained by packaged programs. Students have different language and literacy needs, so they may not respond similarly to instruction—even when research-based practices are used.

5. Systemic and Comprehensive Approaches

- Approaches to RTI must be sensitive to developmental differences in language and literacy among students at different ages and grades. Although many prevailing approaches to RTI focus on the early elementary grades, it is essential for teachers and support personnel at middle and secondary levels to provide their students with the language and literacy instruction they need to succeed in school and beyond.

Motivation and Engagement Strategies for Teaching Reading Comprehension

IRA Standards for Reading Professionals

Standard 5: Literate Environment

Element 5.2 (See previous)

Response to Intervention

1. Instruction

- Instruction and assessment conducted by the classroom teacher are central to the success of RTI and must address the needs of all students, including those from diverse cultural and linguistic backgrounds.

- The success of RTI depends on the classroom teacher's use of research-based practices.
- Research on instructional practices must provide not only information about what works, but also what works with whom, by whom, in what contexts, and on which outcomes.

Internet Reciprocal Teaching

IRA Standards for Reading Professionals

Standard 5: Literate Environment

Element 5.1 (See previous)

Common Core Standards

Reading: K–5

Integration of Knowledge and Ideas

7. (See previous)

Reading: Grades 6–12

Integration of Knowledge and Ideas

7. (See previous)

Response to Intervention

1. Instruction

- Whatever approach is taken to RTI, it should ensure optimal instruction for every student at all levels of schooling. It should prevent serious language and literacy problems through increasingly differentiated and intensified assessment and instruction

and reduce the disproportionate number of minority youth and ELLs identified as learning disabled.

- Research on instructional practices must provide not only information about what works, but also what works with whom, by whom, in what contexts, and on which outcomes.

IRA Standards for Reading Professionals

Standard 4: Diversity   **Elements 4.1, 4.2, 4.3** (See previous)

Response to Intervention

4. Collaboration

- Involving parents and students and engaging them in a collaborative manner is critical to successful implementation. Initiating and strengthening collaborations among school, home, and communities, particularly in urban and rural areas, provides the basis for support and reinforcement of students' learning.

8

Writing

Teacher Knowledge	Classroom Assessment	Evidence-Based Teaching Practices	Response to Intervention (RTI)
What Teachers Need to Know About Teaching Writing	Classroom Writing Assessment	Evidence-Based Writing Instruction	Using Tier 2 Writing Interventions

Chapter Questions

■ What are the stages of writing development? How are the writing development stages for English learners similar or different from English-only students?

■ What are the core writing skills to be learned at each level, and how are they assessed in the classroom?

■ If you were to assemble a "menu" of evidence-based strategies for teaching the writing process, what would it include?

■ How can quick writes be used effectively in Tier 2 instruction as part of your Response to Intervention program?

■ Why is *motivation to write* different from *motivation to read*, and how does that difference manifest itself in the classroom?

■ How might you use online wiki writing programs as part of your content literacy instruction to improve student learning?

■ If you were to use traveling tales backpacks in your writing program to involve parents in their children's writing development, what kinds of home-based activities would you include?

Key Terms

Nation's Report Card on Writing

Recursive writing

Prephonemic stage

Early phonemic stage

Letter-naming stage

Transitional stage

National core writing standards

Performance-based assessment (PBA)

Authentic assessment

Rubrics

Six-trait model

Writing process instruction

Free writing

Author's chair

Interactive writing

Writing workshop

Mini-lesson

Writing center

Quick write

POW + TREE

Generous reading

Self-efficacy

Write-talks

Reading and analyzing nonfiction strategy (RAN)

Wiki writing

e-Reading and e-responding

Camp Imagination

Traveling tales backpack

Motivation and Engagement	Technology and New Literacies	Family and Community Connections
Motivating and Engaging Students to Write	Technology and New Literacies That Promote Writing	How Family and Community Connections Can Foster Writing

Vignette: It Begins

Three-year-old Laura sits quietly on the living room couch next to her parents as they visit with a neighbor. In her hands are four unlined index cards and an old, tooth-marked pencil. After several minutes, she slips down from the couch and timidly approaches their visitor clutching one index card behind her back. Impulsively she thrusts the card into the waiting hand of the visitor. He studies the marks she has made on the card. "Wow, Laura!" he exclaims. "You are writing!" Laura's smile stretches from ear to ear. "I really wrote, didn't I?" ■

Since the earliest days of humanity, people have had a strong desire to share their thoughts in writing. The written word is a potential time machine by which one's ideas and experiences can be shared virtually forever. We see written "time machines" in the drawings of cave dwellers many millennia ago, in the Egyptian hiero-glyphs of 3100 B.C.E., in the Declaration of Independence, or in an e-mail record submitted as evidence in a court of law. In all cases, writing is pointless without a reader to receive the message. Thus, writing and reading are complementary and essential processes of communication.

Writing surely must have been in-vented *before* reading. Perhaps it began when one of our forebears decided to record his thoughts about something important on a stone wall for another person to see. Perhaps the message had to do with a food source or a danger in the environment. The creator of the message had to somehow *encode* it into print—that is, generate a written symbol that represented the idea. The intended recipient of the message coming along later would then need to be able to *decode* it, or translate the written symbols into language or thought.

For over three decades in the United States, National Assessment of Educational Progress (NAEP) assessments have been conducted about every 4 years in reading, mathematics, science, writing, and other subjects. NAEP is a congressionally autho-rized project of the National Center for Education Statistics (NCES) within the Insti-tute of Education Sciences of the U.S. Department of Education. Using a 300-point standardized scale score to describe student performance levels, the Nation's Re-port Card provides the public a continuing and nationally representative measure of achievement in various subjects over time. You can receive a free copy of the Nation's Report Card on writing online at http://nationsreportcard.gov/writing_2007.

In 2007 the latest **Nation's Report Card on Writing** was issued by NAEP (Sala-hu-Din, Persky, & Miller, 2008), and the results were not impressive. In short, there has been modest improvement in writing achievement through grade 12 over the past decade. For instance, little better than one-third of all eighth-grade students tested scored at the Proficient level (scale scores between 175 and 230), described as representing "solid academic performance. Students reaching this level have demonstrated competency over challenging subject matter" (p. 6). Because "Proficient" essentially indicates students performing at or above grade level this statistic causes us concern. In contrast, more than half of eighth-graders scored at the so-called Basic level (scale scores of 115–174), which is described as only "partial mastery of prerequisite knowledge and skills that are fundamental for proficient work at a given grade" (p. 6).

NAEP (Salahu-Din, Persky, & Miller, 2008) also breaks writing performance data into subcategories, comparing scores by racial/ethnic group, by family income, and by gender. In sum, there continue to be vast gaps in writing development within these classifications. Females outperform males by a huge margin (scale score 166 vs. 146). Children from poverty circumstances (i.e., those qualified to receive free or reduced-price lunches) scored well below children from more affluent families (139 vs. 164). The White/Black and White/Hispanic gaps also continue to be formidable (164 vs. 141 and 164 vs. 142, respectively). Taken together we conclude that writing development in the United States has been relatively stagnant over the past decades and there is certainly room for us to improve teaching and learning in this area.

Teacher Knowledge

What Teachers Need to Know About Teaching Writing

As it happens, learning to write helps children become better readers and comprehenders of all types of text (Akhaven, 2008; Tierney & Shanahan, 1996). A number of years ago, the authors of this text separately decided to leave college teaching and return to public schools as first-grade teachers. It was the first time either of us had established writing as a key part of our reading programs. Of course, we had included writing in our previous curricula but not the full writing process as described by early leaders in the field such as Donald Graves (1983) and Lucy Calkins (1986). In a word, this addition to our instructional programs was powerful. Our students learned to write with excitement and passion, and their reading development was greatly accelerated (Reutzel & Cooter, 1990). So if you are wondering why we include a chapter on writing in a reading methods textbook, research and our own firsthand experience have convinced us that writing and reading are reciprocal processes that simply *must* be taught together (Córdova & Matthiesen, 2010; Shanahan, 2006).

How Is Reading Related to Writing?

Reading and writing are often thought of as mirror images of each other (Reutzel & Cooter, 2011). Walter Loban (1964) once said that the relationship between reading and writing is "so striking to be beyond question" (p. 212). It happens that reading and writing share a number of traits or underlying processes (Tierney & Shanahan, 1996), but they also have some unique traits as well (Culham, 2010). As Shanahan (2006) notes, they have somewhat different cognitive "footprints." Let's take a brief look at ways reading and writing are close cousins.

In the *Handbook of Writing Research*, Shanahan (2006) explains that "reading and writing are dependent upon shared cognitive abilities (e.g., visual, phonological,

● ● ●

IRA Standards for Reading Professionals: Standard 1, Elements 1.1, 1.3; Standard 6, Element 6.2

Common Core Standards: Writing: K–5, Text Types and Purposes (items 1–3), Production and Distribution of Writing (items 4–6), Research to Build and Present Knowledge (items 7–9), Range of Writing (item 10); Writing: Grades 6–12, Text Types and Purposes (items 1–3), Production and Distribution of Writing (items 4–6), Research to Build and Present Knowledge (items 7–9), Range of Writing (item 10)

Response to Intervention: Expertise

and semantic systems or short- and long-term memory), and anything that improves these abilities may have implications for both reading and writing development" (p. 174). Shanahan's review of the research concludes that readers and writers rely on four common knowledge bases:

1. *Content knowledge.* Writing has to be about *something.*

2. *Metaknowledge.* Knowing about the functions of reading and writing, that readers and writers interact, and that monitoring one's own meaning-making while writing or reading is critical. New learning often happens through examining and reexamining information from a variety of perspectives, and reading and writing provide alternate perspectives (Shanahan, 2006). A person's culture, by the way, can have an impact—positive or negative—on how well the functions of reading and writing are understood. For example, a second-language learner from an Asian country may not have the same view of how writing is understood in the United States compared to a native-born North American citizen.

3. *Knowledge of specific written language components.* Aspects of language such as phonemic (speech sounds) and orthographic (spelling) knowledge underlie reading and writing.

4. *Procedural knowledge.* Understanding how to access, use, and generate information during reading and writing (Hampton & Resnick, 2009a; Mason, Herman, & Au, 1991) includes an awareness of strategies intentionally used in reading and writing, such as predicting, questioning, and summarizing.

Figure 8.1

Laura's Scribbles

How Writing Develops

Young children discover early in life that writing is the sharing of ideas. In our opening vignette, Laura demonstrated her growing understanding that writing can be a tool for recording thoughts on paper to share with others. She came to this understanding without formal spelling and writing instruction. After carefully observing others in her environment, Laura risked acting like a skilled writer and tried out her hypothesis about how printed language functions.

Many of us have seen children attempting to solve the printed language puzzle through drawing and scribbling. One may be tempted to dismiss these early attempts at writing as cute, but certainly not *real* writing (see Figure 8.1). This judgment may be as misguided as concluding that a flower in its early stages of development is not truly a flower because it does not resemble a full-blown bloom.

Through careful study over a period of decades, researchers have discovered that young children pass through certain developmental stages in their writing and spelling similar to those discussed with respect to oral language and reading development. An understanding of these stages helps teachers recognize the roots of writing and spelling development and enables them to nurture scribbling and drawing into the flower of writing.

Scribbling and Drawing Stage. When young children first take a pencil or crayon in hand, they use this instrument to explore the vast empty space on a blank sheet of paper. In its earliest stages, children's writing is often referred to by adult observers as *scribbling* (Bear, Invernizzi, Templeton, & Johnston, 2000).

These random marks are the wellsprings of writing discovery. As shown in Figure 8.1, Laura's scribbles appear to be the result of acting on the paper just to see what happens, perhaps without any particular intent. Her scribbles do not demonstrate much of what adults normally consider to be conventional or even purposeful writing. In Figure 8.2, Laura's scribbles begin to reveal an exploration of alternative forms when compared to her previous markings. Circles, curved lines, and letter-like forms begin to appear as part of Laura's writing exploration.

Some time later, Laura's scribbles begin to look more and more like adult cursive writing. Note in Figure 8.3 that the marks have become linear, moving from left to right. When questioned, Laura could tell what she meant by each of the scribbles reproduced in Figure 8.3. Unlike her marks in Figure 8.1, Laura's later scribbling represented her meaning in a more conventional way. Laura revealed that these later scribbles were a "Christmas wish list." Often, letter-like writing or shapes, as shown in Laura's Christmas list, are used repeatedly in early writing attempts. Clay (1987) calls the tendency to reuse and repeat certain scribblings and drawings **recursive writing**. The purpose for recursive writing seems to be the need for comfort and familiarity as children prepare to move into the next levels of writing development.

Figure 8.2

Laura's Scribbles as Exploration

Figure 8.3

Laura's Scribble Cursive Writing: Christmas List

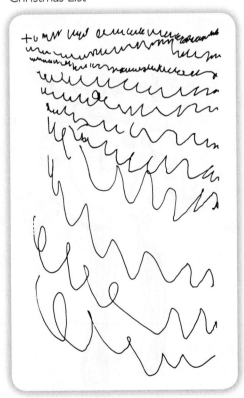

Weeks later, Laura produced the writing found in Figure 8.4. Note in this example that she uses drawings to carry part of her intended message. In addition, directly above the head of Laura's drawing of a young girl, one can detect the emergence of letter-like forms etched in broken detail. When queried about the intent of these letter-like forms, Laura responded, "That says 'Laura!'" Evidently, Laura had discovered at this point in her development as a writer that drawings can supplement a message and that writing is different from drawing.

In another example, 4-year-old Toby produced the writing found in Figure 8.5. Toby used human forms to represent members of his family in a thank-you letter. One sees letter-like symbols randomly scattered about the page. Near the center, Toby signed his name. By looking carefully, one can see the upside-down letter *b* and what looks like a letter *y*, which Toby chose to represent his name. Thus, during this initial stage of writing development, Laura and Toby used scribbling, drawing, and disconnected letter-like forms to explore and record their meanings on paper. These children had discovered that writing is a way to communicate meaning, and that although drawing and writing are complementary processes, they are not the same.

Prephonemic Stage. The next stage of writing and spelling development among young children is often called the **prephonemic stage** (Temple, Nathan, Burris, & Temple, 1993). At this stage, children begin to use real letters—usually capitals—to represent meaning. However, their letters do not represent their phonemic or sound values; rather, they are used as placeholders for meaning, representing anything from

Figure 8.4

Laura's Self Portrait

Figure 8.5

Toby's Thank You Letter

a syllable to an entire thought. Chaundra, a kindergartener, produced the writing in Figure 8.6. Note Chaundra's use of letters to represent meaning. Only by asking the child to explain the meaning can one readily discern that her letters function as meaning placeholders and not as representations of phonemic values.

Clay (1975) points out that children in the prephonemic stage of writing development will usually produce a string of letters and proudly display their work to a parent while asking, "What does this say?" or "What did I write?" In many families today, children do this with magnetic letters on refrigerator doors: They meticulously arrange a string of letters and then ask what they have written.

Early Phonemic Stage.   During the next stage of writing development, called the **early phonemic stage** (Temple et al., 1993), children begin to use letters—usually capitalized consonants—to represent words. Children at this stage of writing development have discovered that letters represent sound values. They write words represented by one or two consonant letters—usually the beginning or ending sounds of the word. In Figure 8.7, Samantha uses only consonants to represent the word *house* in her message.

Temple and colleagues (1993) suspect that the tendency for children in the early phonemic stage to represent a word with only one or two letters is the result of an inability to "hold words still in their minds" while they examine them for phonemes and match these to known letters (p. 101). Although this may be true, it is also possible that children at this stage are continuing to learn certain letters of the alphabet.

Figure 8.6

Chaundra's Prephonemic Writing

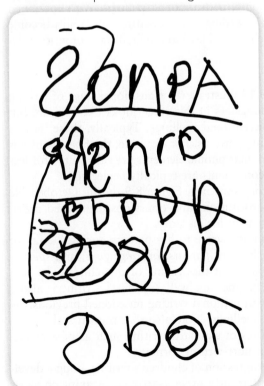

Figure 8.7

Samantha's Early Phonemic Writing: A House

Figure 8.8

Chris's Letter-Naming Stage Writing: Rainbow

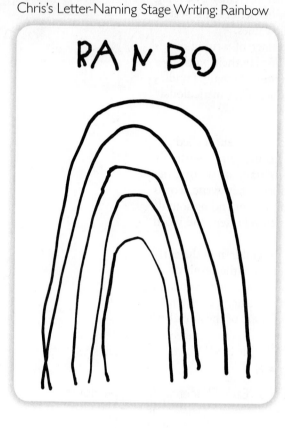

It may also be true that writers in this stage of development have not developed the ability to segment more than the initial or final sounds in a word. Certainly any of these possibilities would lead to the incomplete representation of words as found in the early phonemic stage of writing development. This is an area needing much more investigation (Teale, 1987; Templeton, 1995).

Letter-Naming Stage. The **letter-naming stage** of writing development is a small but important jump from the early phonemic stage. This stage is characterized by the use of more than one or two consonants with at least one vowel to represent the spellings of words. Chris, a kindergartener, produced an example of the letter-naming stage of writing in response to his teacher's urging him to write about the rainbow he had seen the day before (see Figure 8.8).

Although Chris continues to use capital letters exclusively, vowels have begun to appear in his writing. He has clearly discovered that words are made up of phonemes, both vowels and consonants, that these phonemes occur in an auditory sequence, and that these phonemes are properly represented in printed form from left to right. Although Chris does not yet read independently, he has made important discoveries about print that have nurtured his acquisition of reading, which will in turn inform his acquisition of conventional spellings. With continued experiences in reading, Chris's writing will rapidly become more closely aligned with standard spelling and lead to the final stage of writing development, the transitional stage.

Transitional Stage. Figures 8.9 and 8.10 illustrate the **transitional stage** of writing and spelling. Writing produced by youngsters in this stage looks like English, but words are a mix of phonetic and conventional spellings. Typically, these writers neglect or overgeneralize certain spelling patterns. For example, the final silent *e* is sometimes omitted by these writers, familiar phonic elements are substituted for less familiar phonic elements, and double consonants are typically neglected.

Devin, a first-grader, wrote the story shown in Figure 8.9 during October. He demonstrates not only some of the substitutions and omissions mentioned previously, but also a top-to-bottom arrangement for his story.

Figure 8.10 shows a note that Candice wrote to her parents during the fall of her second-grade year. Notice the spellings of *parents, hurting, guys,* and *special.* Some of the spellings are unconventional, but the writing of this child looks very much like English and communicates the message well. Candice's writing is also a good example of the characteristics of transitional writing mentioned previously—the mix of standard and nonstandard spellings. Note also that transitional writers have discovered the use of other features of standard writing such as possessives, punctuation, and the standard letter- or note-writing format.

These examples demonstrate the progression of children's writing along a developmental continuum, originating with their early attempts to make meaning on paper

Figure 8.9

Devin's Halloween Story

through scribbling and drawing to later refinements including the use of conventional spelling, grammar, and mechanics.

One note of caution should be sounded at this point: Although we may discuss oral language, writing, and reading development in terms of stages through which children pass, teachers should not use this information to try to hasten development or expect that children will—or even should—pass through each stage of development in a prescribed order. Rather, teachers should use this information as a basis for understanding and supporting children's language learning by providing an environment rich in print and print use, gentle guidance, and enthusiastic encouragement as children struggle to solve the writing puzzle. Just as children learned to speak within a nurturing home environment filled with supportive oral language users, they also develop into readers and writers within print-rich school environments filled with the support and encouragement of other competent readers and writers. Figure 8.11 integrates information about oral language, reading, and writing development to show that these modes of language learning are developmentally similar.

The Writing Development of English Learners. Rubin and Carlan (2005) have conducted important research that helps teachers use the writing samples of English learners (ELs) to better understand children's literacy development. The

Figure 8.10

Candice's Note to Her Parents

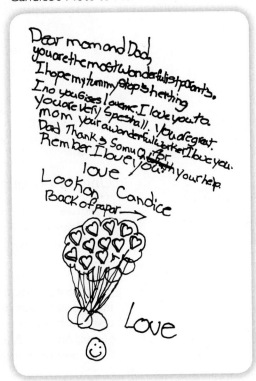

Figure 8.11

Development Across the Language Modes of Oral Language, Reading, and Writing

Oral Language Acquisition	Reading Development Stages	Writing Development Stages
Sounds, cooing, babbling	Picture-governed attempts: Story not formed	Scribbling and drawing
Holophrases and telegraphic speech	Picture-governed attempts: Story formed	Prephonemic
Vocabulary growth and negation language structures	Picture-governed attempts: Written language like—print not watched	Early phonemic
Vocabulary growth and interrogative structures	Print-governed attempts: Print watched	Letter-naming
Vocabulary growth, analogical substitutions, and passive language structures	Print-governed attempts: Strategies imbalanced	Transitional
Adult-like language structures, continuing vocabulary growth, and the ability to articulate all the sounds of the language	Print-governed attempts: Independent reading	Conventional

parallels to the stages just described are indeed remarkable. In Table 8.1 we share a summary of their findings comparing the stages of writing development of English speakers, Spanish-only speakers, and bilingual children.

Unique Writing Patterns Used by Authors

Narrative texts (fiction) are organized in a story grammar scheme using such common elements as setting, theme, characterization, plot, and resolution. Expository text (nonfiction), however, is quite different: Its structure tends to be much more compact, detailed, and explanatory (Heilman, Blair, & Rupley, 2001). Five common expository text structures have been described (Meyer & Freedle, 1984; Williams, 2005): description, collection, causation, problem/solution, and comparison. When preparing to teach units in the content areas, teachers need to establish which expository text structures are used and organize for writing instruction accordingly (Montelongo, Herter, Ansaldo, & Hatter, 2010). The following list provides short descriptions of the five expository text patterns along with examples taken from content textbooks.

Table 8.1

Comparison of Stages of Writing Development for English-Speaking, Spanish-Speaking, and Bilingual Children

Monolingual English Speakers' Stages of Writing Development	Monolingual Spanish Speakers' Stages of Writing Development	Bilingual Spanish–English Speakers' Stages of Writing Development
Precommunicative stage Know the difference between writing and drawing. Write with scribbles, mock letters, and real letters unconnected to sounds.	Levels 1 & 2 Know the difference between writing and drawing. Write with scribbles, mock letters, and real letters unconnected to sounds.	Generally the same as monolingual English and Spanish, except some children will write the same letters and symbols in both languages but read them differently in English and in Spanish.
Semiphonetic stage Letters are written to represent some of the sounds in words.	Level 3 Each syllable in a word is usually represented by a vowel.	Generally similar to monolingual English, except some children will write the same words in both languages but read them differently in English and Spanish.
Phonetic stage Letters are written to represent most sounds in words.	Level 4 Letters are written to represent most sounds in words.	Generally similar to monolingual English and Spanish. Some errors are made because of different letter–sound relationships in the two languages.
Transitional stage Letters are written according to common spelling patterns and include silent letters.	No corresponding level.	Similar to English monolingual stage with some errors caused by different letter–sound relationships in the two languages. Vocabulary and sentence structure become more complex.
Conventional stage Writing is generally correct.	Level 5 Writing is generally correct.	Writing is generally correct. Vocabulary and sentence structure become more complex.

From Rubin, R., & Carlan, V. (2005, May). Using Writing to Understand Bilingual Children's Literacy Development. *The Reading Teacher, 58*(8), pp. 728–739. Reprinted with permission of the International Reading Association.

- *Description.* Explains something about a topic or presents a characteristic or setting for a topic.

> *Decimals* are another way to write fractions when the denominators are 10, 100, and so on.
>
> (from *Merrill Mathematics* [Grade 5], 1985, p. 247)

- *Collection.* A number of descriptions (specifics, characteristics, or settings) presented together.

> **Water Habitats**
>
> Freshwater habitats are found in ponds, bogs, swamps, lakes, and rivers. Each freshwater habitat has special kinds of plants and animals that live there. Some plants and animals live in waters that are very cold. Others live in waters that are warm. Some plants and animals adapt to waters that flow fast. Others adapt to still water.
>
> (from *Merrill Science* [Grade 3], 1989, p. 226)

- *Causation.* Elements grouped according to time sequence with a cause–effect relationship specified.

> **America Enters the War**
>
> On Sunday, December 7, 1941, World War II came to the United States. At 7:55 A.M. Japanese warplanes swooped through the clouds above Pearl Harbor. Pearl Harbor was

the American naval base in the Hawaiian Islands. A deadly load of bombs was dropped on the American ships and airfield. It was a day, Roosevelt said, that would "live in infamy." *Infamy* (IN fuh mee) means "remembered for being evil."

The United States had been attacked. That meant war.

(from *The United States: Its History and Neighbors* [Grade 5], Harcourt Brace Jovanovich, 1985, p. 493)

- *Problem/Solution.* Includes a relationship (between a problem and possible causes) and a set of solution possibilities, one of which can break the link between the problem and its cause.

Agreement by Compromise (Events That Led to the Civil War)

For a while there was an equal number of Southern and Northern states. That meant that there were just as many Senators in Congress from slave states as from free states. Neither had more votes in the Senate, so they usually reached agreement on new laws by compromise.

(from *The United States and the Other Americas* [Grade 5], Macmillan, 1980, p. 190)

- *Comparison.* Organizes factors on the basis of differences and similarities. Comparison does not contain elements of sequence or causality.

Segregation

Segregation laws said that blacks had to live separate, or apart, from whites. Like whites, during segregation blacks had their own parks, hospitals, and swimming pools. Theaters, buses, and trains were segregated.

Many people said that the segregation laws were unfair. But in 1896, the Supreme Court ruled segregation legal if the separate facilities for blacks were equal to those for whites. "Separate but equal" became the law in many parts of the country.

But separate was not equal. . . . One of the most serious problems was education. Black parents felt that their students were not receiving an equal education in segregated schools. Sometimes the segregated schools had teachers who were not as well educated as teachers in the white schools. Textbooks were often very old and out-of-date, if they had any books at all. But in many of the white schools the books were the newest ones. Without a good education, the blacks argued, their students would not be able to get good jobs as adults.

Finally in 1954, the Supreme Court changed the law.

(Adapted from *The American People* [Grade 6], American Book Company, 1982, p. 364)

● ● ●

IRA Standards for Reading Professionals: Standard 3, Elements 3.1, 3.2, 3.3

Common Core Standards: Writing: K–12, Text Types and Purposes (items 1–3), Production and Distribution of Writing (items 4, 5), Research to Build and Present Knowledge (items 7–9)

Response to Intervention: Assessment

Classroom Assessment

Classroom Writing Assessment

The staring point for writing assessment is to answer the question *Which writing skills should be learned and assessed at each grade level?* The answer to this question lies in evidence-based end-of-year benchmark skills, national core writing standards, and/or writing standards used by your state. In the first part of Pillar Two we identify many of the skills to be assessed.

Once we know *what* is to be assessed, the next question is *How can I quickly and efficiently assess students' use of writing skills at each level of development?* There are generally two perspectives for analyzing student compositions (Moskal, 2003): analytic and holistic. Because they are quick, efficient, and can be constructed using research-based standards, teachers often use rubrics for assessing different aspects or traits of writing (Hampton, Murphy, & Lowry, 2009; Shermis, Burstein, & Leacock, 2006). In this section we include an overview of writing rubrics and how they are tied to evidence-based writing standards.

What Are the Writing Skills to Be Learned at Each Grade Level (K–6)?

Burns, Griffin, and Snow (1999), in their book *Starting Out Right,* summarize skills to be learned in writing for grades K through 3 according to evidence-based research. These should be viewed as "end-of-year benchmark skills," or targets for every child to attain by the end of the school year in order to be on track in his or her development.

Kindergarten

- Writes uppercase and lowercase letters
- Writes own name
- Uses invented spellings to express meaning
- Uses invented spellings to write teacher-dictated words
- Is becoming aware of the differences between kid writing and conventional writing

First Grade

- Spells three- and four-letter short vowel words conventionally
- Writes texts for others to read
- Writes independently using a mix of invented and conventional spellings
- Uses basic or terminal punctuation (periods, question marks, exclamation points) and capitalization
- Produces a variety of types of compositions and texts (e.g., stories, information texts, poems, notes, recipes, journal entries)

Second Grade

- Correctly spells previously studied words and spelling patterns in own writing
- Represents the complete sound of the word when spelling independently (invented spellings)
- Writes using formal language patterns rather than oral language patterns at appropriate places in own writing
- Makes reasonable judgments about what to include in own writing
- Can productively discuss ways to improve own writing and that of others
- Is able to use, with assistance, conferencing, revision, and editing processes to improve the quality of own writing
- Writes informative, well-structured reports with assistance
- Attends to spelling, mechanics, and presentation for final products
- Produces a variety of types of compositions

Third Grade

- Begins to incorporate literary words, language patterns, figures of speech, and elaborate descriptions in own writing
- Correctly spells previously studied words and spelling patterns in own writing
- Combines information from multiple sources in writing reports
- Productively discusses ways to clarify own writing and that of others
- Uses conferencing, revision, and editing processes to improve the quality of own writing
- Independently reviews work for spelling, mechanics, and presentation
- Produces a variety of written work in various formats including multimedia forms

Adapted with permission from *Starting Out Right: A Guide to Promoting Children's Reading Success,* 1999, by the National Academy of Sciences, courtesy of the National Academies Press, Washington, DC.

State Writing Standards

Teachers in grades 4 through 6 must also have a clear understanding of the writing skills expected of normally developing students. In the United States, under No Child Left Behind and subsequent legislation, the various states have established standards for gauging reading and writing development. In Figure 8.12 we share an excerpt from the grade-level goals and accompanying performance objectives for grades 4 through 6 developed by the state of California. Because they are founded on evidence-based reading research, the California standards essentially mirror those developed by the other states. The full California standards may be downloaded from the Internet on their website at www.cde.ca.gov/standards.

National Core Writing Standards

One of the challenges we face in writing assessment is the lack of a common "roadmap" for measuring student development. Ongoing efforts to unify evidence-based standards in reading and writing are beginning to bear fruit. In 2010 the Council of Chief State School Officers (CCSSO) and the National Governors Association (NGA) jointly released *The Common Core State Standards for English Language Arts and Literacy in History/Social Studies, Science, and Technical Subjects*. This document resulted from a broad-based effort to create **national core writing standards** for K through 12 based on comparisons of the different state standards "in order to help ensure that all students are college and career ready in literacy no later than the end of high school" (p. 3). In Table 8.2 (pp. 331–334) we share the common core state standards for grades K through 5. All other standards may be downloaded from www.corestandards.org. Our best advice is for teachers to consider both state and national core writing standards when constructing assessment tools.

How Do Teachers Assess Students' Writing Abilities?

With the passage of the federal No Child Left Behind legislation early in the twenty-first century came a soaring interest in educational assessment and "performance-based education," in which teachers design task-oriented instruction connected to the lives and learning needs of students using relevant tasks. **Performance-based assessment (PBA)**, sometimes known as **authentic assessment**, evaluates students' performance in completing a product that demonstrates their use of new skills and knowledge. PBA is in sharp contrast to more traditional methods of measurement such as paper-and-pencil tests. Some of the popular forms of PBA include journals, checklists, portfolios, projects, and rubrics.

What Are Rubrics?   Designed as tools to evaluate student performance on tasks that lead to completion of products, **rubrics** assess learning outcomes with clearly stated criteria for measuring student performances and skills. These criteria are typically narrative descriptions or checklists separated into levels of performance (high-level performance to lower-level performance) or degrees of proficiency with the targeted skills.

Figure 8.12

Writing Standards for Grades 4–6

STANDARD 1: WRITING STRATEGIES

*Coding System

First numeral = Grade level expectation
Second numeral = Standard
Third numeral = Skill number

Example: 5.2.3 = Fifth grade expectation, Standard 2 (Writing Applications), Skill #3 (Write research reports about important ideas, issues, or events . . .)

Standard 1: Grades 4–6

Grade 4: Students write clear, coherent sentences and paragraphs that develop a central idea. Their writing shows they consider the audience and purpose. Students progress through the stages of the writing process (e.g., prewriting, drafting, revising, editing successive versions).

Grade 5: Students write clear, coherent, and focused essays. The writing exhibits the students' awareness of the audience and purpose. Essays contain formal introductions, supporting evidence, and conclusions. Students progress through the stages of the writing process as needed.

Grade 6: Students write clear, coherent, and focused essays. The writing exhibits students' awareness of the audience and purpose. Essays contain formal introductions, supporting evidence, and conclusions. Students progress through the stages of the writing process as needed.

Performance Objectives: Grades 4–6

Organization and Focus

4.1.1 Select a focus, an organizational structure, and a point of view based upon purpose, audience, length, and format requirements.

4.1.2 Create multiple-paragraph compositions:
   a. Provide an introductory paragraph.
   b. Establish and support a central idea with a topic sentence at or near the beginning of the first paragraph.
   c. Include supporting paragraphs with simple facts, details, and explanations.
   d. Conclude with a paragraph that summarizes the points.
   e. Use correct indention.

4.1.3 Use traditional structures for conveying information (e.g., chronological order, cause and effect, similarity and difference, and posing and answering a question).

5.1.1 Create multiple-paragraph narrative compositions:
   a. Establish and develop a situation or plot.
   b. Describe the setting.
   c. Present an ending.

5.1.2 Create multiple-paragraph expository compositions:
   a. Establish a topic, important ideas, or events in sequence or chronological order.
   b. Provide details and transitional expressions that link one paragraph to another in a clear line of thought.
   c. Offer a concluding paragraph that summarizes important ideas and details.

6.1.1 Choose the form of writing (e.g., personal letter, letter to the editor, review, poem, report, narrative) that best suits the intended purpose.

6.1.2 Create multiple-paragraph expository compositions:
   a. Engage the interest of the reader and state a clear purpose.
   b. Develop the topic with supporting details and precise verbs, nouns, and adjectives to paint a visual image in the mind of the reader.
   c. Conclude with a detailed summary linked to the purpose of the composition.

6.1.3 Use a variety of effective and coherent organizational patterns, including comparison and contrast; organization by categories; and arrangement by spatial order, order of importance, or climactic order.

continued

Figure 8.12

Continued

Penmanship

4.1.4   Write fluidly and legibly in cursive or joined italic.

Research and Technology

4.1.5   Quote or paraphrase information sources, citing them appropriately.
4.1.6   Locate information in reference texts by using organizational features (e.g., prefaces, appendixes).
4.1.7   Use various reference materials (e.g., dictionary, thesaurus, card catalog, encyclopedia, online information) as an aid to writing.
4.1.8   Understand the organization of almanacs, newspapers, and periodicals and how to use those print materials.
4.1.9   Demonstrate basic keyboarding skills and familiarity with computer terminology (e.g., cursor, software, memory, disk drive, hard drive).
5.1.3   Use organizational features of printed text (e.g., citations, end notes, bibliographic references) to locate relevant information.
5.1.4   Create simple documents by using electronic media and employing organizational features (e.g., passwords, entry and pull-down menus, word searches, the thesaurus, spell checks).
5.1.5   Use a thesaurus to identify alternative word choices and meanings.
6.1.4   Use organizational features of electronic text (e.g., bulletin boards, databases, keyword searches, e-mail addresses) to locate information.
6.1.5   Compose documents with appropriate formatting by using word-processing skills and principles of design (e.g., margins, tabs, spacing, columns, page orientation).

Evaluation and Revision

4.1.10 Edit and revise selected drafts to improve coherence and progression by adding, deleting, consolidating, and rearranging text.
5.1.6   Edit and revise manuscripts to improve the meaning and focus of writing by adding, deleting, consolidating, clarifying, and rearranging words and sentences.
6.1.6   Revise writing to improve the organization and consistency of ideas within and between paragraphs.

STANDARD 2: WRITING APPLICATIONS: GENRES AND THEIR CHARACTERISTICS

Standard 2: Grades 4–6

Grade 4: Students write compositions that describe and explain familiar objects, events, and experiences. Student writing demonstrates a command of standard American English and the drafting, research, and organizational strategies outlined in Writing Standard 1.0.

Grade 5: Students write narrative, expository, persuasive, and descriptive texts of at least 500 to 700 words in each genre. Student writing demonstrates a command of standard American English and the research, organizational, and drafting strategies outlined in Writing Standard 1.0.

Grade 6: Students write narrative, expository, persuasive, and descriptive texts of at least 500 to 700 words in each genre. Student writing demonstrates a command of standard American English and the research, organizational, and drafting strategies outlined in Writing Standard 1.0.

Using the outline in Writing Standard 1.0, students:

Write Narratives

4.2.1   Write narratives:
   a. Relate ideas, observations, or recollections of an event or experience.
   b. Provide a context to enable the reader to imagine the world of the event or experience.
   c. Use concrete sensory details.
   d. Provide insight into why the selected event or experience is memorable.
5.2.1   Write narratives:
   a. Establish a plot, point of view, setting, and conflict.
   b. Show, rather than tell, the events of the story.

6.2.1 Write narratives:
  a. Establish and develop a plot and setting and present a point of view that is appropriate to the stories.
  b. Include sensory details and concrete language to develop plot and character.
  c. Use a range of narrative devices (e.g., dialogue, suspense).

Write Responses to Literature

4.2.2 Write responses to literature:
  a. Demonstrate an understanding of the literary work.
  b. Support judgments through references to both the text and prior knowledge.
5.2.2 Write responses to literature:
  a. Demonstrate an understanding of a literary work.
  b. Support judgments through references to the text and to prior knowledge.
  c. Develop interpretations that exhibit careful reading and understanding.
6.2.4 Write responses to literature:
  a. Develop an interpretation exhibiting careful reading, understanding, and insight.
  b. Organize the interpretation around several clear ideas, premises, or images.
  c. Develop and justify the interpretation through sustained use of examples and textual evidence.

Write Information/Research Reports

4.2.3 Write information reports:
  a. Frame a central question about an issue or situation.
  b. Include facts and details for focus.
  c. Draw from more than one source of information (e.g., speakers, books, newspapers, other media sources).
4.2.4 Write summaries that contain the main ideas of the reading selection and the most significant details.
5.2.3 Write research reports about important ideas, issues, or events by using the following guidelines:
  a. Frame questions that direct the investigation.
  b. Establish a controlling idea or topic.
  c. Develop the topic with simple facts, details, examples, and explanations.
6.2.3 Write research reports:
  a. Pose relevant questions with a scope narrow enough to be thoroughly covered.
  b. Support the main idea or ideas with facts, details, examples, and explanations from multiple authoritative sources (e.g., speakers, periodicals, online information searches).
  c. Include a bibliography.

Write Persuasive Letters or Compositions

5.2.4 Write persuasive letters or compositions:
  a. State a clear position in support of a proposal.
  b. Support a position with relevant evidence.
  c. Follow a simple organizational pattern.
  d. Address reader concerns.
6.2.2 Write expository compositions (e.g., description, explanation, comparison and contrast, problem and solution):
  a. State the thesis or purpose.
  b. Explain the situation.
  c. Follow an organizational pattern appropriate to the type of composition.
  d. Offer persuasive evidence to validate arguments and conclusions as needed.
6.2.5 Write persuasive compositions:
  a. State a clear position on a proposition or proposal.
  b. Support the position with organized and relevant evidence.
  c. Anticipate and address reader concerns and counterarguments.

continued

Figure 8.12

Continued

STANDARD 3: WRITTEN AND ORAL ENGLISH LANGUAGE CONVENTIONS

Standard 3: Grades 4–6

Grade 4–6: Students write and speak with a command of standard English conventions appropriate to this grade level.

Performance Objectives: Grades 4–6

Sentence Structure

4.3.1   Use simple and compound sentences in writing and speaking.
4.3.2   Combine short, related sentences with appositives, participial phrases, adjectives, adverbs, and prepositional phrases.
5.3.1   Identify and correctly use prepositional phrases, appositives, and independent and dependent clauses; use transitions and conjunctions to connect ideas.
6.3.1   Use simple, compound, and compound-complex sentences; use effective coordination and subordination of ideas to express complete thoughts.

Grammar

4.3.3   Identify and use regular and irregular verbs, adverbs, prepositions, and coordinating conjunctions in writing and speaking.
5.3.2   Identify and correctly use verbs that are often misused (e.g., lie/lay, sit/set, rise/raise), modifiers, and pronouns.
6.3.2   Identify and properly use indefinite pronouns and present perfect, past perfect, and future perfect verb tenses; ensure that verbs agree with compound subjects.

Punctuation

4.3.4   Use parentheses, commas in direct quotations, and apostrophes in the possessive case of nouns and in contractions.
4.3.5   Use underlining, quotation marks, or italics to identify titles of documents.
5.3.3   Use a colon to separate hours and minutes and to introduce a list; use quotation marks around the exact words of a speaker and titles of poems, songs, short stories, and so forth.
6.3.3   Use colons after the salutation in business letters, semicolons to connect independent clauses, and commas when linking two clauses with a conjunction in compound sentences.

Capitalization

4.3.6   Capitalize names of magazines, newspapers, works of art, musical compositions, organizations, and the first word in quotations when appropriate.
5.3.4   Use correct capitalization.
6.3.4   Use correct capitalization.

Spelling

4.3.7   Spell roots, inflections, suffixes and prefixes, and syllable constructions correctly.
5.3.5   Spell roots, suffixes, prefixes, contractions, and syllable constructions correctly.
6.3.5   Spell frequently misspelled words correctly.

Adapted from the California Department of Education English Language Arts Content Standards. www.cde.ca.gov/standards. Reprinted by permission.

Table 8.2

Common Core Writing Standards K–5

The following standards for K–5 offer a focus for instruction each year to help ensure that students gain adequate mastery of a range of skills and applications. Each year in their writing, students should demonstrate increasing sophistication in all aspects of language use, from vocabulary and syntax to the development and organization of ideas, and they should address increasingly demanding content and sources. *Students advancing through the grades are expected to meet each year's grade-specific standards and retain or further develop skills and understandings mastered in preceding grades.*

Kindergartners:	Grade 1 Students:	Grade 2 Students:
Text Types and Purposes		
1. Use a combination of drawing, dictating, and writing to compose opinion pieces in which they tell a reader the topic or the name of the book they are writing about and state an opinion or preference about the topic or book (e.g., *My favorite book is . . .*).	1. Write opinion pieces in which they introduce the topic or name the book they are writing about, state an opinion, supply a reason for the opinion, and provide some sense of closure.	1. Write opinion pieces in which they introduce the topic or book they are writing about, state an opinion, supply reasons that support the opinion, use linking words (e.g., *because, and, also*) to connect opinion and reasons, and provide a concluding statement or section.
2. Use a combination of drawing, dictating, and writing to compose informative/explanatory facts in which they name what they are writing about and supply some information about the topic.	2. Write informative/explanatory texts in which they name a topic, supply some facts about the topic, and provide some sense of closure.	2. Write informative/explanatory texts in which they introduce a topic, use facts and definitions to develop points, and provide a concluding statement or section.
3. Use a combination of drawing, dictating, and writing to narrate a single event or several loosely linked events, tell about the events in the order in which they occurred, and provide a reaction to what happened.	3. Write narratives in which they recount two or more appropriate sequenced events, include some details regarding what happened, use temporal words to signal event order, and provide some sense of closure.	3. Write narratives in which they recount a well-collaborated event or short sequence of events, include details to describe actions, thoughts, and feelings, use temporal words to signal event order, and provide a sense of closure.
Production and Distribution of Writing		
4. (Begins in grade 3)	4. (Begins in grade 3)	4. (Begins in grade 3)
5. With guidance and support from adults, respond to questions and suggestions from peers and add details to strengthen writing as needed.	5. With guidance and support from adults, focus on a topic, respond to questions and suggestions from peers, and add details to strengthen writing as needed.	5. With guidance and support from adults and peers, focus on a topic and strengthen writing as needed by revising and editing.
6. With guidance and support from adults, explore a variety of digital tools to produce and publish writing, including in collaboration with peers.	6. With guidance and support from adults, use a variety of digital tools to produce and publish writing, including in collaboration with peers.	6. With guidance and support from adults, use a variety of digital tools to produce and publish writing, including in collaboration with peers.
Research to Build and Present Knowledge		
7. Participate in shared research and writing projects (e.g., explore a number of books by a favorite author and express opinions about them).	7. Participate in shared research and writing projects (e.g., explore a number of "how-to" books on a given topic and use them to write a sequence of instructions).	7. Participate in shared research and writing projects (e.g., explore a number of books on a single topic to produce a report, record science observations).
8. With guidance and support from adults, recall information from experiences or gather information from provided sources to answer a question.	8. With guidance and support from adults, recall information from experiences or gather information from provided sources to answer a question.	8. Recall information from experiences or gather information from provided sources to answer a question.
9. (Begins in grade 4)	9. (Begins in grade 4)	9. (Begins in grade 4)
Range of Writing		
10. (Begins in grade 3)	10. (Begins in grade 3)	10. (Begins in grade 3)

continued

Table 8.2

Continued

Grade 3 Students:	Grade 4 Students:	Grade 5 Students:
Text Types and Purposes		

1. Write opinion pieces on topics or texts, supporting a point of view with reasons.
   a. Introduce the topic or text they are writing about, state an opinion, and create an organizational structure that lists reasons.
   b. Provide reasons that support the opinion.
   c. Use linking words and phrases (e.g., *because, therefore, since, for example*) to connect opinion and reasons.
   d. Provide a concluding statement or section.

1. Write opinion pieces on topics or texts, supporting a point of view with reasons and information.
   a. Introduce a topic or text clearly, state an opinion, and create an organizational structure in which related ideas are grouped to support the writer's purpose.
   b. Provide reasons that are supported by facts and details.
   c. Link opinion and reasons using words and phrases (e.g., *for instance, in order to, in addition*).
   d. Provide a concluding statement or section related to the opinion presented.

1. Write opinion pieces on topics or texts, supporting a point of view with reasons and information.
   a. Introduce a topic or text clearly, state an opinion, and create an organizational structure in which ideas are logically grouped to support the writer's purpose.
   b. Provide logically ordered reasons that are support by facts and details.
   c. Link opinion and reasons using words, phrases, and clauses (e.g., *consequently, specifically*).
   d. Provide a concluding statement or section related to the opinion presented.

---

2. Write informative/explanatory texts to examine a topic and convey ideas and information clearly.
   a. Introduce a topic and group related information together; include illustrations when useful to aiding comprehension.
   b. Develop the topic with facts, definitions, and details.
   c. Use linking words and phrases (e.g., *also, another, and, more, but*) to connect ideas within categories of information.
   d. Provide a concluding statement or section.

2. Write informative/explanatory texts to examine a topic and convey ideas and information clearly.
   a. Introduce a topic clearly and group related information in paragraphs and sections; include formatting (e.g., headings), illustrations, and multimedia when useful to aiding comprehension.
   b. Develop the topic with facts, definitions, concrete details, quotations, or other information and examples related to the topic.
   c. Link ideas within categories of information using words and phrases (e.g., *another, for example, also, because*).
   d. Use precise language and domain-specific vocabulary to inform about or explain the topic.
   e. Provide a concluding statement or section related to the information or explanation presented.

2. Write informative/explanatory texts to examine a topic and convey ideas and information clearly.
   a. Introduce a topic clearly, provide a general observation and focus, and group related information logically; include formatting (e.g., headings), illustrations, and multimedia when useful to aiding comprehension.
   b. Develop the topic with facts, definitions, concrete details, quotations, or other information and examples related to the topic.
   c. Link ideas within and across categories of information using words, phrases, and clauses (e.g., *in contrast, especially*)
   d. Use precise language and domain-specific vocabulary to inform about or explain the topic.
   e. Provide a concluding statement or section related to the information or explanation presented.

---

3. Write narratives to develop real or imagined experiences or events using effective technique, descriptive details, and clear event sequences.
   a. Establish a situation and introduce a narrator and/or characters; organize an event sequence that unfolds naturally.
   b. Use dialogue and descriptions of actions, thoughts, and feelings to develop experiences and events or show the response of characters to situations.

3. Write narratives to develop real or imagined experiences or events using effective technique, descriptive details, and clear event sequences.
   a. Orient the reader by establishing a situation and introducing a narrator and/or characters; organize an event sequence that unfolds naturally.
   b. Use dialogue and description to develop experiences and events or show the responses of characters to situations.

3. Write narratives to develop real or imagined experiences or events using effective technique, descriptive details, and clear event sequences.
   a. Orient the reader by establishing a situation and introducing a narrator and/or characters; organize an event sequence that unfolds naturally.
   b. Use narrative techniques, such as dialogue, descriptions, and pacing, to develop experiences and events or show the responses of characters to situations.

Grade 3 Students:	Grade 4 Students:	Grade 5 Students:
Text Types and Purposes (continued)		
c. Use temporal words and phrases to signal event order. d. Provide a sense of closure.	c. Use a variety of transitional words and phrases to manage the sequence of events. d. Use concrete words and phrases and sensory details to convey experiences and events precisely. e. Provide a conclusion that follows from the narrated experiences or events.	c. Use a variety of transitional words, phrases, and clauses to manage the sequence of events. d. Use concrete words and phrases and sensory details to convey experiences and events precisely. e. Provide a conclusion that follows from the narrated experiences or events.
Production and Distribution of Writing		
4. With guidance and support from adults, produce writing in which the development and organization are appropriate to task and purpose. (Grade-specific expectations for writing types are defined in standards 1–3 above.)	4. Produce clear and coherent writing in which the development and organization are appropriate to task, purpose, and audience. (Grade-specific expectations for writing types are defined in standards 1–3 above.)	4. Produce clear and coherent writing in which the development and organization are appropriate to task, purpose, and audience. (Grade-specific expectations for writing types are defined in standards 1–3 above.)
5. With guidance and support from peers and adults, develop and strengthen writing as needed by planning, revising, and editing. (Editing for conventions should demonstrate command of Language standards 1–3 up to and including grade 3.)	5. With guidance and support from peers and adults, develop and strengthen writing as needed by planning, revising, and editing. (Editing for conventions should demonstrate command of Language standards 1–3 up to and including grade 4.)	5. With guidance and support from peers and adults, develop and strengthen writing as needed by planning, revising, and editing, rewriting, or trying a new approach. (Editing for conventions should demonstrate command of Language standards 1–3 up to and including grade 5.)
6. With guidance and support from adults, use technology to produce and publish writing (using keyboarding skills) as well as to interact and collaborate with others.	6. With some guidance and support from adults, use technology, including the Internet, to produce and publish writing as well as to interact and collaborate with others; demonstrate sufficient command of keyboarding skills to type a minimum of one page in a single sitting.	6. With some guidance and support from adults, use technology, including the Internet, to produce and publish writing as well as to interact and collaborate with others; demonstrate sufficient command of keyboarding skills to type a minimum of two pages in a single sitting.
Research to Build and Present Knowledge		
7. Conduct short research projects that build knowledge about a topic.	7. Conduct short research projects that build knowledge through investigation of different aspects of a topic.	7. Conduct short research projects that use natural resources to build knowledge through investigation of different aspects of a topic.
8. Recall information from experiences or gather information from print and digital sources; take brief notes on sources and sort evidence into provided categories.	8. Recall relevant information from experiences or gather relevant information from print and digital sources; take notes and categorize information, and provide a list of sources.	8. Recall relevant information from experiences or gather relevant information from print and digital sources; summarize or paraphrase information in notes and finished work, and provide a list of sources.
9. (Begins in grade 4)	9. Draw evidence from literary or informational texts to support analysis, reflection, and research.	9. Draw evidence from literary or informational texts to support analysis, reflection, and research.

continued

Table 8.2

Continued

Grade 3 Students:	Grade 4 Students:	Grade 5 Students:
Research to Build and Present Knowledge (continued)		
	a. Apply *grade 4 Reading standards* to literature (e.g., "Describe in depth a character, setting, or event in a story or drama, drawing on specific details in the text [e.g., a character's thoughts, words, or actions]"). b. Apply *grade 4 Reading standards* to informational texts (e.g., "Explain how an author uses reasons and evidence to support particular points in a text").	a. Apply *grade 5 Reading standards* to literature (e.g., "Compare and contrast two or more characters, settings, or events in a story or a drama, drawing on specific details in the text [e.g., how characters interact]"). b. Apply *grade 5 Reading standards* to informational texts (e.g., "Explain how an author uses reasons and evidence to support particular points in a text, identifying which reasons and evidence support which point[s]").
Range of Writing		
10. Write routinely over extended time frames (time for research, reflection, and revision) and shorter time frames (a single sitting or a day or two) for a range of discipline-specific tasks, purposes, and audiences.	10. Write routinely over extended time frames (time for research, reflection, and revision) and shorter time frames (a single sitting or a day or two) for a range of discipline-specific tasks, purposes, and audiences.	10. Write routinely over extended time frames (time for research, reflection, and revision) and shorter time frames (a single sitting or a day or two) for a range of discipline-specific tasks, purposes, and audiences.

Moskal (2003) offers teachers some useful tips about writing rubrics for student evaluations. First, when developing scoring rubrics for writing, teachers should be certain that the assessment criteria are aligned with state and national standards. Many states have their own rubrics and timelines for writing assessment, and students should be given ample opportunities to practice the kinds of writing on which they will be evaluated. For example, the state of Florida has a very helpful website for teachers providing this information (see the "Sunshine State Standards" online at www.firn.edu/doe/menu/sss.htm).

Second, rubric criteria should be (a) expressed in terms of observable behaviors, (b) written in specific, straightforward, and meaningful language, and (c) designed to show clear distinctions between scoring levels. Third, rubric criteria should be explained to students prior to the writing experience in language that is easy for them to understand. When conducting a writing assessment, teachers should also ensure that students have access to appropriate writing tools (e.g., dictionaries, thesaurus, ample writing materials, computers) that support the completion of assessment activities. Fourth, the rubric criteria should be fair and free from bias.

Holistic Scoring Rubrics. Some rubrics use only a single scale to evaluate the larger writing process (Moskal, 2003). With such holistic scoring rubrics, teachers evaluate a piece of writing for its overall quality (i.e., all of the traits that make up the writing task are evaluated in combination—as a whole). Teachers are encouraged not to become overly concerned with any one aspect of writing but to look at the composition as one entity. Many states offer holistic scoring rubrics for teachers to use in preparing their students for high-stakes testing (i.e., testing linked to the No Child Left Behind federal legislation). Figure 8.13 features the rubric offered to Florida teachers for holistic scoring.

Figure 8.13

Example of a Holistic Scoring Rubric

6 Points

The writing is focused, purposeful, and reflects insight into the writing situation. The paper conveys a sense of completeness and wholeness with adherence to the main idea, and its organizational pattern provides for a logical progression of ideas. The support is substantial, specific, relevant, concrete, and/or illustrative. The paper demonstrates a commitment to and an involvement with the subject, clarity in presentation of ideas, and may use creative writing strategies appropriate to the purpose of the paper. The writing demonstrates a mature command of language (word choice) with freshness of expression. Sentence structure is varied, and sentences are complete except when fragments are used purposefully. Few, if any, convention errors occur in mechanics, usage, and punctuation.

5 Points

The writing focuses on the topic, and its organizational pattern provides for a progression of ideas, although some lapses may occur. The paper conveys a sense of completeness or wholeness. The support is ample. The writing demonstrates a mature command of language, including precision in word choice. There is variation in sentence structure, and, with rare exceptions, sentences are complete except when fragments are used purposefully. The paper generally follows the conventions of mechanics, usage, and spelling.

4 Points

The writing is generally focused on the topic but may include extraneous or loosely related material. An organizational pattern is apparent, although some lapses may occur. The paper exhibits some sense of completeness or wholeness. The support, including word choice, is adequate, although development may be uneven. There is little variation in sentence structure, and most sentences are complete. The paper generally follows the conventions of mechanics, usage, and spelling.

3 Points

The writing is generally focused on the topic but may include extraneous or loosely related material. An organizational pattern has been attempted, but the paper may lack a sense of completeness or wholeness. Some support is included, but development is

erratic. Word choice is adequate but may be limited, predictable, or occasionally vague. There is little, if any, variation in sentence structure. Knowledge of the conventions of mechanics and usage is usually demonstrated, and commonly used words are usually spelled correctly.

2 Points

The writing is related to the topic but includes extraneous or loosely related material. Little evidence of an organizational pattern may be demonstrated, and the paper may lack a sense of completeness or wholeness. Development of support is inadequate or illogical. Word choice is limited, inappropriate, or vague. There is little, if any, variation in sentence structure, and gross errors in sentence structure may occur. Errors in basic conventions of mechanics and usage may occur, and commonly used words may be misspelled.

1 Point

The writing may only minimally address the topic. The paper is a fragmentary or incoherent listing of related ideas or sentences or both. Little, if any, development of support or an organizational pattern or both is apparent. Limited or inappropriate word choice may obscure meaning. Gross errors in sentence structure and usage may impede communication. Frequent and blatant errors may occur in the basic conventions of mechanics and usage, and commonly used words may be misspelled.

Unscorable

The paper is unscorable because

- the response is not related to what the prompt requested the student to do.
- the response is simply a rewording of the prompt.
- the response is a copy of a published work.
- the student refused to write.
- the response is illegible.
- the response is incomprehensible (words are arranged in such a way that no meaning is conveyed).
- the response contains an insufficient amount of writing to determine if the student was attempting to address the prompt.
- the writing folder is blank.

From Florida Writing Assessment Program FLORIDA WRITES! www.firn.edu/doe/sas/fw/fwaprubr.htm. Example of a holistic scoring rubric appears by permission of the Florida Department of Education, Assessment and School Performance Office, Tallahassee, Florida 32399-0400.

Analytic Scoring Rubrics. Dividing writing performance into distinct components or traits, analytic scoring rubrics evaluate each component using a separate scale. As an example, we share in Figure 8.14 a four-level analytic rubric that is available free to teachers on the website readwritethink.org, a joint project of the International Reading Association and the National Council of Teachers of English. This high-quality website features rubrics, complete lesson plans, and other tools for teachers.

The Six-Trait Writing Model

In 1983, the Beaverton, Oregon, school district sought a means of assessing student writing that could lead to more effective writing instruction. They examined research conducted by Paul Diederich (1974), featured in his book *Measuring Growth in*

Figure 8.14

Compare and Contrast Rubric

Compare and Contrast Rubric				
Category	**4**	**3**	**2**	**1**
Purpose and Supporting Details	The paper compares and contrasts items clearly. The paper points to specific examples to illustrate the comparison. The paper includes only the information relevant to the comparison.	The paper compares and contrasts items clearly, but the supporting information is general. The paper includes only the information relevant to the comparison.	The paper compares and contrasts items clearly, but the supporting information is incomplete. The paper may include information that is not relevant to the comparison.	The paper compares or contrasts, but does not include both. There is no supporting information or support is incomplete.
Organization and Structure	The paper breaks the information into whole-to-whole, similarities-to-differences, or point-by-point structure. It follows a consistent order when discussing the comparison.	The paper breaks the information into whole-to-whole, similarities-to-differences, or point-by-point structure but does not follow a consistent order when discussing the comparison.	The paper breaks the information into whole-to-whole, similarities-to-differences, or point-by-point structure, but some information is in the wrong section. Some details are not in a logical or expected order, and this distracts the reader.	Many details are not in a logical or expected order. There is little sense that the writing is organized.
Transitions	The paper moves smoothly from one idea to the next. The paper used comparison and contrast transition words to show relationships between ideas. The paper uses a variety of sentence structure and transitions.	The paper moves smoothly from one idea to the next, but there is little variety. The paper uses comparison and contrast transition words to show relationships between ideas.	Some transitions work well; but connections between other ideas are fuzzy.	The transitions between ideas are unclear or nonexistent.
Grammar and Spelling (Conventions)	Writer makes no errors in grammar or spelling that distract the reader from the content.	Writer makes 1–2 errors in grammar or spelling that distract the reader from the content.	Writer makes 3–4 errors in grammar or spelling that distract the reader from the content.	Writer makes more than 4 errors in grammar or spelling that distract the reader from the content.

From www.ReadWriteThink.org. Reprinted with permission of the International Reading Association.

English. Diederich had assembled a group of writers, editors, attorneys, business executives, and teachers of English, natural science, and social science, presenting them with student essays to read and rank order into three groups: effective, somewhat effective, and problematic. The group was also asked to discuss why they ranked the papers as they did. Interestingly, Diederich found that the various members of the group described virtually the same qualities in the writing samples, including ideas and content, organizational structure, voice, and mechanics.

Beaverton teachers decided to repeat Diederich's study with a group of 17 teachers and a writing consultant. They read, rank ordered, and took notes on hundreds of student papers and found that they largely agreed with Diederich's conclusions. The Beaverton teachers' notes were eventually condensed into a six-trait scoring guide. The Oregon Department of Education (ODE) adopted this **six-trait model** for its statewide writing assessment. Oregon currently uses a 6-point scale for assessing student development on each writing trait. In the next section, we describe the six traits and ODE scoring guidelines, also adopted by many school districts in North America and beyond.

Describing the Six Traits of Writing.

1. *Ideas and content.* The writer's main ideas, purpose for writing, and supporting details. How well does the writer communicate and support his or her ideas through the provision of examples, facts, anecdotes, and details appropriate to the target audience? ODE criterion: *The ideas are clear, focused, complete, and well developed with specific details.*

2. *Organization.* The structure of a written composition, including the writer's ability to hold the central meaning throughout the document. How well does the writer organize information in a clear sequence and make connections and transitions among ideas, sentences, and paragraphs? ODE criterion: *The paper moves naturally from one idea to the next, with a strong beginning and ending.*

3. *Voice.* The writer's unique quality of expression, which is closely allied to style—formal, casual, academic, or anecdotal. How well does the author express himself or herself? ODE criterion: *The writing style is lively and interesting and is appropriate to the audience and topic.*

4. *Word choice.* The writer's use of words that are appropriate to the topic and audience, as well as her or his ability to convey the intended message and emotion. How well does the author choose between a word and just the right word, which as Mark Twain once said is like the difference between the *lightning* and the *lightning bug?* ODE criterion: *Words are carefully selected to convey precise meaning, images, and tone.*

5. *Sentence fluency.* The writer's understanding and application of the underlying structures of language. How well does the writing create a natural flow of language when read aloud? ODE criterion: *Sentences are smooth, varied, and carefully constructed.*

6. *Conventions.* The writer's knowledge of spelling, grammar, punctuation, capitalization, and penmanship. How well does the author understand the mechanics of writing? ODE criterion: *Correct spelling, grammar, usage, punctuation, capitalization, and paragraphing are used throughout the paper.*

Rubrics for Evaluation of the Six Traits.
Over the years, six-trait scoring has been revised and marketed by various entities, each having a unique twist on the popular

Figure 8.15

Scoring Rubric for the Six Traits

Score	Evaluation	Description
6	Exemplary	The paper showed outstanding performance and exceptional control in this trait of writing.
5	Strong	The paper showed many strengths, and the writer seemed to be perfecting control of the writing.
4	Proficient	The paper showed more strengths than weaknesses, and the writer seemed to be gaining control of the writing.
3	Developing	The paper needs further development in this trait because the writer seemed only partially in control of the writing.
2	Emerging	The paper needs quite a bit more development, but the writer is addressing this writing trait.
1	Beginning	The paper needs significant development and represents a very beginning effort.

● ● ●

IRA Standards for Reading Professionals:
Standard 2, Elements 2.1, 2.2, 2.3; Standard 4, Element 4.1; Standard 5, Elements 5.1, 5.2, 5.3

Common Core Standards: Writing: K–5, Text Types and Purposes (items 1–3), Production and Distribution of Writing (items 4–6), Research to Build and Present Knowledge (items 7–9), Range of Writing (item 10); Writing: Grades 6–12, Text Types and Purposes (items 1–3), Production and Distribution of Writing (items 4–6), Research to Build and Present Knowledge (items 7–9), Range of Writing (item 10)

Response to Intervention:
Instruction; Systemic and Comprehensive Approaches

Figure 8.16

An Alternate Three-Level Scoring Rubric for the Six Traits

Score	Evaluation	Description
3	Proficient/Exemplary	Outstanding performance and exceptional control in this trait of writing.
2	Developing	Some evidence of the trait, but further development is needed.
1	Emergent	Represents little or no evidence of this trait.

model. Some evaluate each trait using a 3-point, 5-point, or 6-point scale. Figure 8.15 shows a 6-point rubric derived from the scale used by the Oregon Department of Education (n.d.).

Scoring six traits on six levels can be time-consuming for busy classroom teachers, so we have crafted an alternative three-level scoring model for your consideration (see Figure 8.16).

Evidence-Based Teaching Practices

Evidence-Based Writing Instruction

Writing instruction has changed significantly over past decades. Teachers once assigned students writing tasks such as preparing essays, reports, or research papers, expecting students to submit one draft of their work and then move on to the next focus of study. Based on this "one-draft mentality" (Calkins, 1986), students learned that writing was a one-phase process that resulted in either success or failure. In more recent years, researcher-practitioners like Donald Graves (1983) and his protégé Lucy Calkins (1994) have helped teachers and students understand that writing is a *process* rather than a one-shot, "quick-and-dirty" project. Children are taught to understand and use the phases of authorship.

Understanding the Writing Process

Writing process instruction (also known as *process writing*) teaches the kinds of thinking processes skilled writers use in producing different forms of text. By taking on the author's mindset, children are better able to learn from models of good writing how skillful writers paint pictures with words, how they choose words that convey just the right meaning, and craft sentences that grab the attention of readers. Through writing process instruction, children become wordsmiths and begin to enjoy the works of other authors on new and higher levels.

Professional writers do not move rigidly from one stage of writing to the next. It can be very instructive to examine the various stages through which writers progress in producing text, which have been identified as prewriting, drafting, revising, editing, and publishing. Students can benefit from learning these stages through our modeling, mini-lessons, and practice sessions.

Prewriting Stage.   *Prewriting* is the getting-ready-to-write stage (Tompkins, 2004). Writing begins with an idea or message the writer wants to express. Many teachers help students begin the writing process by asking them to brainstorm a list of topics they might be interested in writing about at some point in the future. These should be topics that generate a certain amount of emotion in the student, as it is this emotional engagement that helps drive the entire writing process through to completion.

Click on A+RISE—WIDA ELP Standard Strategies in the MyEducationLab (www.myeducationlab.com) for your course. Next, select the Strategy Card Index tab, scroll to Writing for grades K–5, and select the Process Writing strategy.

Donald Graves in his classic book, *Writing: Teachers and Children at Work* (1983), suggests that teachers model each of the stages in the writing process to help students see adult examples. For the first step in prewriting, called *brainstorming,* the teacher might list at the overhead projector or whiteboard several topics that he or she is interested in writing about—sailing, collecting antiques, attending wrestling matches, or traveling to South Pacific islands. It is important that teachers explain to the class *why* each topic is appealing to them. A brainstorming session sometimes helps children who are having difficulty discovering topics of interest. The key to success is helping students find topics that generate emotion, which, as we have noted, helps provide energy for the writing process.

After students have selected an interesting topic, they gather information by conducting research. This information gathering may simply involve recalling a special event, thinking about a favorite place, or trying to imagine what life might have been like before television. Other purposes for writing might require students to gather information at the library, surf the Internet for the latest news on a subject, interview family members or people in the community, or send e-mail to local, state, or federal agencies.

Click on A+RISE—Literacy Strategies in the MyEducationLab (www.myeducationlab.com) for your course. Next, select the Strategy Card Index tab, scroll to Writing for grades K–5, and select the Prewriting Techniques strategy.

Once the student writer has settled on a topic and collected useful support information, he or she is ready to begin organizing ideas for presentation—in short, to develop a plan for writing of some kind. This plan's form is relatively unimportant, but the writer should have some kind of organizational scheme for the composition. This step helps make the piece clear, concise, and thorough. Two formats depicting the story theme "My Birthday Trip to Universal Studios," written by an intermediate student named Jina, are presented as examples in Figures 8.17 and 8.18.

Figure 8.17

Semantic Web

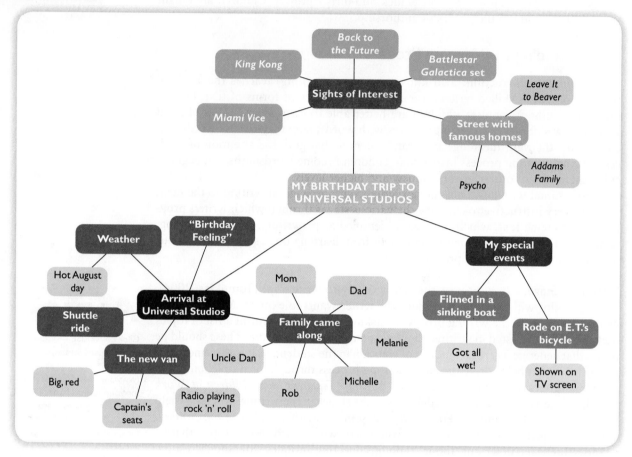

Sometimes children have a difficult time getting started with their composition, or even coming up with an idea compelling enough to commit to paper. In this situation, it is usually helpful to engage in **free writing,** during which students simply sit for a sustained period of time and write down anything at all that comes to mind. What often emerges is a rather rambling narrative with many idea fragments. Lucy Calkins (1986, 1994) suggests that children begin free writes by simply listing things in their immediate environment until they come to an idea they wish to write about. After students have an organized set of ideas about which to write and have constructed alternative leads, they are ready for the drafting stage.

Drafting Stage. The drafting stage represents an author's first attempt to put ideas in writing. Teachers should emphasize that the most important part of drafting is simply getting thoughts down on paper, not mechanical correctness. A first draft is often referred to as "sloppy copy." Such fine points as verb tense, subject–verb agreement, or spelling correctness are *not* important at this stage. Rather, the expression of *ideas* is the paramount consideration. The following useful tips can help students as they draft:

- Write as though you were telling a story to an interested friend.
- Use your own "voice" instead of trying to sound like your favorite author.

Click on A+RISE—WIDA ELP Standard Strategies in the MyEducationLab (www.myeducationlab.com) for your course. Next, select the Strategy Card Index tab, scroll to Writing for grades K–5, and select the Drafting Techniques strategy.

Figure 8.18

Structured Overview

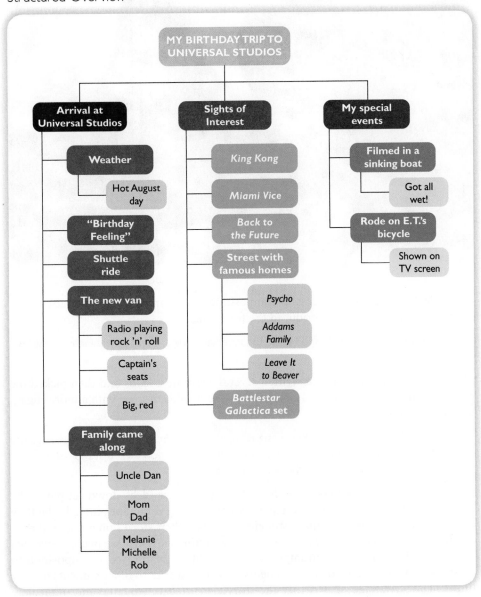

- Use words that create a picture in the reader's mind. Your words should be descriptive and clear.
- Be sure to describe sights, sounds, smells, and other sensory images that are important parts of the story you want to tell.
- Say what you want to say directly. (More is not necessarily better. Sometimes less is more if words are chosen well.)

During the drafting process, the writer can create several opening sentences or alternative leads for his or her piece. Having an interesting beginning, one that grabs

Corbis Royalty Free

the reader, helps create a successful composition. For example, Jina's first attempt to begin her story might have produced the following:

> On my birthday my family and I went to Universal Studios. It was a very fun day that I will never forget.

On the other hand, if Jina had written several alternative leads and then picked the most exciting one to begin her story, perhaps she would come up with a more engaging introduction:

> Imagine a birthday party with King Kong, E.T., and the stars from "Miami Vice" as your guests! That's exactly what happened to me on my 13th birthday. If you think that's something, hold on to your seat while I tell you the rest of my story.

Struggling students may have difficulty getting their ideas down on paper the first time they attempt to draft. Frequently handwriting difficulties impede the flow of ideas. One solution is to allow students to dictate their stories on audio and then transcribe the material onto paper later. This solution helps keep struggling students from becoming frustrated and improves their ability to transcribe a composition to paper. Another option is to allow students to dictate stories to older students or peer tutors. The advantage here is that the storyteller can get valuable and immediate feedback from the peer tutor, aiding in the clarity of the composition.

Revising and Editing. Once the draft has been completed, the author is ready to begin the stages of revising and editing. *Revising,* or "re-visioning" (taking a second look), involves improving the first draft by including new ideas—or perhaps rearranging current ideas. *Editing* is the process of rereading the manuscript to find errors and omissions. This phase of the writing process is often a joint effort between the author and peer editors—often classmates—who offer constructive criticism.

The revision process can take several forms. Perhaps the most traditional method is the student–teacher writing conference, in which the student meets with the teacher after she has read the composition. The teacher asks questions and offers suggestions

A+RISE

Click on A+RISE—WIDA ELP Standard Strategies in the MyEducationLab (www.myeducationlab.com) for your course. Next, select the Strategy Card Index tab, scroll to Writing for grades K–5, and select the Revising Techniques ELL strategy.

Figure 8.19

Writing Evaluation Form

Writing Evaluation Form

Student Name _____   Date _____

Title of Composition _____

Overall Evaluation of the Composition:
——→

Underdeveloped   Partially Ready   Advanced   Excellent

Areas Needing Further Development

_____ Character development   _____ Conflict resolution   _____ Grammar
_____ Setting   _____ Story closure   _____ Punctuation
_____ Conflict description   _____ Spelling   _____ Capitalization

---

for revisions. Some teachers like to use a form for recording their comments (see Figure 8.19).

Because many students prefer to get suggestions from their peers before the final publishing stage, another option for improving compositions is peer editing. Students help each other in a collaborative and risk-free environment. Though some students are able to work one-on-one with their peers successfully, peer editing is often more effective in small groups known as *teacherless writing teams* or *peer editing conferences*. Three to four students work together to produce their best work. At each stage of the writing process, students share their writing with the team, and team members question the author and offer suggestions for improvement.

During the editing process, students check compositions for misspelled words, usage errors, poor sentence construction, missing topic sentences, awkward language, and coherence. Many teachers encourage students to use word banks (key word lists on the subject), a thesaurus, and a dictionary or the spelling and grammar checking features on word processing programs. Although some advocate consulting reference tools during the drafting stage, Calkins (1986, 1994) recommends reserving them for these final stages of the writing process.

During the editing stage, writers use proofreaders' marks. These notations clarify an author's additions, deletions, or rearrangements of information on manuscripts. Figure 8.20 features several examples of proofreaders' marks teachers might consider demonstrating to young writers.

Many schools now provide students with personal computers (PCs) for writing projects. Although these devices make the editing process both quick and relatively painless, students must first learn keyboarding skills. Selected computer applications for assisting writing development are discussed in greater detail later in this chapter.

Publishing. A natural desire for most authors, young or seasoned, is to share their compositions with an audience. For

Click on A+RISE—WIDA ELP Standard Strategies in the MyEducationLab (www.myeducationlab.com) for your course. Next, select the Strategy Card Index tab, scroll to Writing for grades K–5, and select the Publishing Ideas strategy.

Figure 8.20

Proofreaders' Marks

Text with Proofreader Markings	Explanation
injured Jamie carried the ∧ puppy home.	∧ is for inserting missing words
Let's go ⌐to Mark's house⌐over⌐	∩ is for moving text
Let's go to Mark's house ~~over~~.	ℓ is for marking out text

children, publishing can take many exciting forms. One publishing experience common in elementary classrooms is called the **author's chair.** Each day at a designated time, young authors who have completed compositions can sign up to share their work in the author's chair. When the appointed time arrives, students take turns reading their creations to the class, answering questions about their stories and reaping generous applause. Other forms of publishing include letter writing to pen pals, school officials, favorite authors, and media stars or making stories into classroom books, newspapers, and yearbooks. The key to success in publishing is that students feel their writing projects have an audience.

How Do Interactive Writing Procedures Help Learners Acquire New Writing Skills?

Interactive writing (Gipe, 2006) can be a powerful way to organize writing instruction and, at the same time, improve reading development for young learners. In recent research (Jones, Reutzel, & Fargo, 2010) interactive writing and writing workshop (discussed later) were discovered to be equally effective in promoting the attainment of early reading skills such as phonological awareness, alphabet knowledge, and word reading. The idea is for the teacher to demonstrate new ideas about writing for learners in their zones of proximal development—ideas that bridge the reading and writing processes and help students grow in each language area. We begin with a very flexible method of writing instruction known as Writing Aloud, Writing To, followed by activities that fit nicely into this paradigm. Later, we describe other activities that make writing connections with books and other texts for students, followed by bookmaking ideas.

Writing Aloud, Writing To: A Way of Structuring Your Teaching.   In read-aloud activities, teachers share books orally with students and model such reading essentials as comprehension strategies and decoding skills. Writing Aloud, Writing To (Cooter, 2002; Gunning, 2006) is an adaptation of Routman's (1995) technique for getting students' attention and demonstrating various aspects of the writing process. Writing Aloud, Writing To has been used with great success in the Dallas Reading Plan, a massive teacher-education project in Texas that resulted in significant improvement in student writing and reading achievement levels. The Writing To part of the method comes from the notion of writing to, with, and by: In a balanced program of writing instruction, teachers should engage daily in writing *to* students (demonstrations and mini-lessons), writing *with* students (guided practice sessions in which students implement new writing skills with the help of the teacher or a more skilled peer), and writing *by* students (independent writing sessions in which they practice their newly acquired skills).

The materials you will need depend greatly on the kinds of writing strategies you plan to model. In general, we like to use an overhead projector, transparencies, and erasable markers or a large tablet on an easel for writing demonstrations with groups. If the demonstration involves a computer, it is usually best to conduct Writing Aloud, Writing To sessions in small groups unless you have access to a computer projection system.

As with materials, the strategies you will employ will be based on the writing/reading connections you choose to emphasize. Routman (1995) and Cooter (2002) do, however, provide us with some useful tips for Writing Aloud, Writing To.

- The teacher thinks aloud while writing in front of the students.
- Students watch the teacher as he writes and sometimes read aloud with the teacher as he says explicitly what he is doing. This may include the writer's think-

ing processes, format that has been chosen and why, layout of the piece, spacing, handwriting, spelling, punctuation, and discussion of vocabulary.

- Teachers help students relate the spoken word to the written word at all times.
- The teacher often asks questions that relate to the conventions of writing or features of text.

A graphic was prepared for the Dallas Reading Academy (Cooter, 2002) that summarizes key elements of Writing Aloud, Writing To based on the work of Regie Routman (1995). It is shown in Figure 8.21.

Morning Message.   A morning message is brief, no more than two to six sentences at students' ability level for attending to and producing print (Payne & Schulman, 1998). Topics for the morning message are based on recent or upcoming school or class events and ideas or experiences individual students want to share. Typically, the teacher writes the first sentence of the morning message. It might read, "Good morning, first grade! Today is ____" or "Wow! Yesterday was really special because ____." Leads such as this get students reading and thinking to start the day.

Next, read the first sentence of the morning message aloud to students. Then, while pointing, have students read it with you. Ask students if they have anything they would like to write to fill in the next part of the morning message. As children offer suggestions, ask them questions like "What will we write first?" or "How many

Figure 8.21

Writing Aloud, Writing To

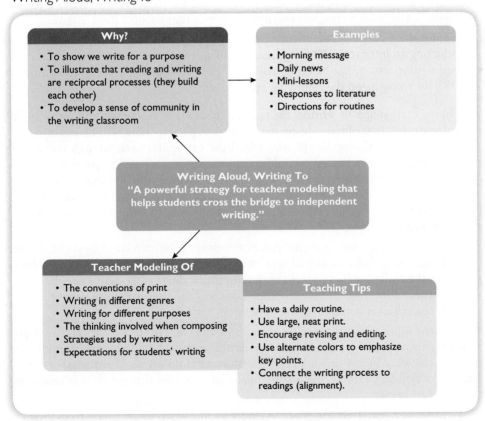

sounds do we hear in the first word? Let's clap and count the sounds." Sharing the pen with students, write two to six sentences to complete the morning message.

In kindergarten and early first grade, some teachers prepare pictures to be used in place of words to keep the writing of the morning message moving along more rapidly. But by grades 2 or 3, most students will be able to write their messages quite rapidly. Keep the editing pen handy so that you can fix mistakes in spelling, punctuation, and capitalization as you talk about them. Morning message provides a nice means of sharing the responsibilities for writing between students and teacher and is an ideal segue into shared writing.

Shared Writing.   A shared writing session focuses on the teacher writing *with* children—what is sometimes called "sharing the pen" (McCarrier, Pinnell, & Fountas, 1999). Teachers can employ shared writing for several purposes.

- Connect reading and writing by using literature as a take-off point for writing reproductions, innovations, and new texts
- Help students develop increasingly sophisticated writing skills
- Demonstrate saying words slowly and connecting sounds in words to letters and letter combinations
- Expand students' repertoire of writing genres and forms
- Help children learn how the spelling process works

The subject and form of shared writing may vary greatly depending on the developmental levels of the students and the context of experiences in the classroom. Typically in the early years, the teacher helps students write simple sentences. As students learn more about the writing process and different types of writing forms and genres, the teacher structures writing activities that become more complex.

Conducting an Interactive Writing Lesson.   There is no one correct way to teach a shared writing lesson, but based on the writings of McCarrier, Pinnell, and Fountas (1999), we recommend the following approaches:

1. In the early stages of writing, the teacher should help students compose a simple message drawn from literature or from the group's experiences. For example, in *The Very Hungry Caterpillar* (Carle, 1986) the caterpillar eats through one apple on Monday. If the teacher asked children to innovate on what the caterpillar ate on Monday, a child might offer the following: "On Monday, he ate through one tomato." As the teacher asks students to replace text with new words, as in the preceding example, the entire message is reread from the beginning to help students remember how composing proceeds.

2. Teacher and students share the pen as a message is written word by word. When new words are added to a line of text, the children reread the line up to the added word. In the earliest stages of writing development, the teacher may write the word for students. With time and development, the teacher shares the pen, inviting children to contribute a letter, several letters, or an entire word.

3. Where appropriate, the teacher encourages the child to stretch the word and say it slowly to predict the letters by analyzing the sounds. Children may attempt any letter in the word in any order. Working within the child's zone of proximal development á la Vygotsky (1962), the teacher fills in those letters that the child is unable to analyze on his own.

4. The teacher can construct a word wall, as recommended by Cunningham (2000), which might be used as a writing resource for students. Words can be listed on the wall as "Words We Know and Can Write," "Words We Almost Know," and "Words We Need to Analyze and Write with Help."

5. As teachers and children write interactively, the teacher helps children learn directionality, punctuation, spaces, features of print, and capitalization. In this fashion, children learn the mechanics and the authoring processes necessary to produce high-quality writing products.

Shared writing sessions typically last from 5 to 15 minutes, depending on the nature of the text to be produced. The goal of the interactive writing is neat, legible, and sensible text.

The Writing Workshop

Writing workshop is an organizational structure for teaching composition skills that can be modified as needed. As noted earlier, this way of orchestrating instruction can help children learn early reading skills (Jones et al., 2010). Instruction can be organized into five phases: teacher sharing time, mini-lesson, state of the class, workshop activities, and student sharing time. Figure 8.22 depicts our organizational scheme for the writing workshop.

Figure 8.22

The Writing Workshop

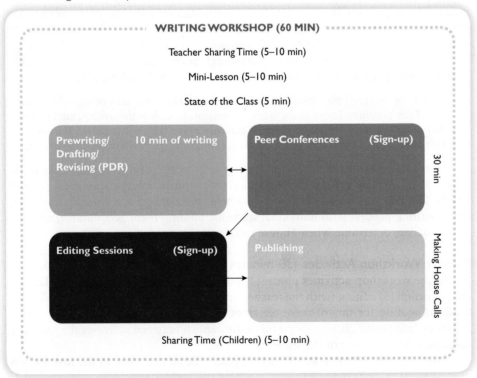

Phase 1: Teacher Sharing Time (5 to 10 minutes). The purpose of teacher sharing time is to present students with language and experiences through writing that stimulate the natural energies of thinking (Holdaway, 1984). The substance of these teacher-led presentations is usually an assortment of brain-enticing poems, songs, stories, and exposition written by the teacher. The goal is to inspire students to strike out on new adventures in writing. This brief phase should serve as a stimulating introduction to the rest of the writing period.

Phase 2: Mini-Lesson (5 to 10 minutes). The **mini-lesson** (Calkins, 1986, 1994) is a brief time for teaching skills. Class discussions about activities such as selecting good ideas to write about, gathering reference materials, conducting interviews, organizing information, and publishing are all viable topics. Some common mini-lesson ideas suggested by Atwell (1987) include the following:

illustrations	narrative leads
essay writing	spelling
form	writing good fiction
mythology (Greek and Roman)	the dictionary
resumé writing	genre
writing conferences with yourself	job applications
correspondence	punctuation
focus	style
writing short stories	

Teachers usually share examples from their own writing or those volunteered by students during mini-lessons. The main focus of the mini-lesson at all grade levels is helping students write with quality at their stage of development.

Phase 3: State of the Class (5 minutes). In the state-of-the-class phase of the writing workshop, the teacher simply lists each student's name on the left side of a chart and students fill in the blanks for each day, indicating what they will be doing (e.g., drafting, peer conferencing, editing, publishing). Sometimes writing instructors, like Atwell, prefer to complete the state-of-the-class chart in the whole-class setting:

> I think the [state-of-the-class] conference is worth three minutes of the whole class's time. I can't begin to know all the ways my students find ideas for writing, but I do know that eavesdropping is right up there. When they make their plans public, writers naturally teach each other about new options for topic and genre. (Atwell, 1987, p. 90)

By recording students' plans for writing and saving them over the weeks of the school year, teachers can see almost at a glance who is failing to progress (Atwell, 1987). This phase of the writing workshop helps teachers set deadlines for key stages of the writing process with individual students, holding them accountable, and also helps teachers determine when "house calls" may be needed.

Phase 4: Workshop Activities (30 minutes). Four activities operate concurrently during the workshop activities phase: (1) prewriting, drafting, and revising; (2) peer conferencing; (3) editing (with the teacher or peers); and (4) preparing for publishing. Students sign up for one of these activities each day and work accordingly during the workshop period. It may be useful to distinguish between activities the teacher is engaged in versus those of the students.

For the teacher, several activities take place during this time. In the first 10 minutes or so of the writing workshop, teachers themselves engage in sustained silent writing (SSW). In working on a written product of their choice, teachers provide children with models of positive writing behavior as well as writing samples for teacher sharing time. After SSW, the teacher is ready to move on to making individual "house calls" and working with students in private editing sessions.

Students largely move at their own pace during writing workshop activities and select from the four tasks identified. If they choose to prewrite, draft, or revise, students might select topics for narratives, gather resources and references, conduct interviews, create outlines for organizing their documents, and eventually produce drafts.

Once students finish their first drafts, they are ready to sign up for a peer conference. During peer conferencing, small groups of students, usually three or four, read each other's first drafts and make recommendations for revisions. Peer conferences are sometimes known as "teacherless writing groups" because the teacher is not involved during this analysis phase unless invited by the group for consulting purposes.

Teachers have told us that some students learning the writing workshop system want to peer conference almost all the time. This can be somewhat problematic because even though we want to encourage peer collaboration students need to focus most of their time on writing (i.e., drafting, revising, editing). One solution is to establish guidelines differentiating peer conferences from what might be termed "1-minute conferences." A student who needs a quick opinion about a composition can usually arrange a 1-minute conference with a peer. Students should not require more than three 1-minute conferences during a writing workshop session.

Group etiquette rules for student interactions should be established early in the school year to ensure maximum productivity and to minimize conflicts. Role-playing is one way to form group-developed rules. Students should be able to come up with a list of their own group etiquette rules that are applicable for all group experiences.

A word regarding classroom noise levels seems warranted. Whenever teachers begin to experiment with modes of instruction that allow students to work on their own or in small groups, the noise level will invariably go up. This may be distressing at first for some teachers, but this issue can be addressed. If the class becomes unruly, then appropriate steps must be taken to maintain class control. More often than not, however, the increase in classroom noise should be viewed as the sound of learning and creative interaction. Silvia Ashton-Warner (1963) refers to this kind of classroom hubbub as "peaceful noise."

> Once the peer conference group meets and considers each student's manuscript, members make suggestions for improvement. Of course, authors are free to accept or reject their peers' suggestions. Manuscript revisions follow the peer conference, paving the way for an editing session with the teacher. (p. 86)

Editing sessions are special times for students to meet with the teacher to discuss their writing projects and receive independent skill instruction or coaching. To take part in an editing session, a student signs up the day before the conference and submit a copy of his or her writing project. This allows teachers time to read the composition and prepare notes for the student. Teachers should avoid writing directly on the composition. Instead, remarks should be made on a separate sheet of paper or a stick-on note to prevent defacing the project. When examining some narrative compositions, it may be a good idea to refer to a story grammar outline to make sure all important elements have been included. Semantic and syntactic considerations should also be discussed.

After the editing session, students frequently need to edit or revise further before publishing. It may be desirable for the student and teacher to have an additional editing session to go over modifications before publishing. A visit to the publishing center to put the writing project into final form is the last stop.

One final point: Publishing does not necessarily happen with every writing project. Sometimes a student will say to the teacher, "I'm running out of interest for this story. May I work on another one?" Most writers occasionally run out of gas during a project and start a new one. Some may have several projects in process. It is not the number of publications a student produces during a given period that is important, but the process itself. Although it is desirable that students reach closure on a regular basis with writing projects, it does not have to happen every time.

Phase 5: Sharing Time (5 to 10 minutes). The writing workshop concludes with student sharing time or publishing. Students proceed to sharing time only with the approval of the teacher after an editing session.

Even students who may be publishing their writing project outside of class (e.g., putting their book in the school library or submitting their work to a children's magazine) should take part in sharing time. This allows other students to see and enjoy the finished products. The most common format for sharing time is the author's chair experience, in which students sit before the group and share their composition.

The Writing Center

The **writing center** is an integral part of the writing workshop approach in the K–3 classroom. Because of the nature of the multiple activities occurring in the writing center, it should be located away from the quiet areas designated for silent sustained writing.

Figure 8.23

Writing Center

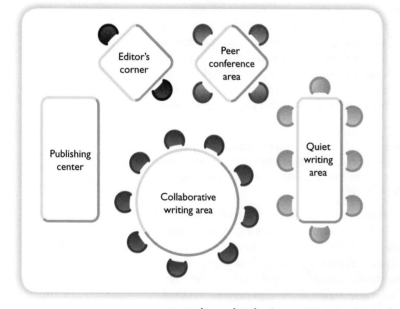

The writing center (see Figure 8.23) often includes three smaller integrated areas:

- Work area for collaborative writing projects, conferences, and editing
- Quiet area for silent sustained writing away from collaborative areas
- Publishing area with necessary supplies

As noted, a space for collaborative writing is designated for children to interact with teachers and peers about their group writing projects—or for individual authors to get ideas or feedback. A conference area with table and chairs or just a quiet carpeted corner can function as a location for conducting peer–student or teacher–student conferences about developing writing projects. An editing area can be located at a desk or table near the conference area. An older student, the teacher, or an adult volunteer can function as an editor for student-authored works in the classroom. An editor's visor, printer's apron, various writing and marking media, and a poster displaying editorial marks can be located here for the editor's use. The publishing area should be stocked with pencils, pens, markers, staplers, and paper of various colors and sizes for covers.

Materials also should be available for students to bind or publish their final writing products in a variety of ways. The location for each of the many supplies in this area can be indicated by a printed label or an outline of the object; doing so makes it easier for students to help in keeping the publishing area neat and tidy. Student works published in this area may take the form of big books, shape books, micro-books, accordion books, letters, notes, lists, posters, bulletin boards, and murals.

The First 6 Weeks of Writing Instruction

From the first day of school, you must show students that you consider them to be competent writers (albeit at their own stage of development). In this section, we offer some general guidelines for structuring writing instruction for the first 6 weeks of school.

Week 1. Writing and reading are reciprocal processes and should be started at the same time. In order to get a sense of momentum established right away, do the following.

• Introduce writing mini-lessons working with the whole group. Mini-lessons could focus on selecting appropriate topics, using graphic organizers, crafting opening sentences (leads), and learning the conventions of writing.

• Make in-class writing assignments to help you begin the assessment process.

• Introduce students to the writing center, the variety of tools available, and their purposes and correct uses.

• Introduce students to the notion of using a "writer's notebook" for gathering brainstorming ideas, completed graphic organizers, "sloppy copy" first drafts, and so forth. This can take the form of a pocket folder, a file folder kept in an easily accessible storage unit, or a tabbed three-ring binder.

Weeks 2 and 3

• Have students begin making entries in their writer's notebooks.

• Explain how student writing folders are to be used to store work.

• Introduce the rudiments of letter writing and have students use that format to write a letter to a friend or family member.

Weeks 4 Through 6

• Conduct mini-lessons in small- and large-group settings, focusing primarily on revising and editing fundamentals.

• Post and discuss numerous writing models for each stage of the writing process that meet curriculum or state assessment requirements for best-quality work. Students need to see examples of competent work to understand the expectations.

• Conference with two to three students per day about their progress using work samples in their writing folders.

• Conduct small- and whole-group guided writing sessions.

• Introduce writing backpacks as homework assignments that involve parents.

• If adult volunteers are available, begin to assign them to struggling writers to assist in specific areas of need. You must first train the volunteers on writing activities they can deliver and then match them to students having that particular need.

Click on A+RISE—WIDA ELP Standard Strategies in the MyEducationLab (www.myeducationlab.com) for your course. Next, select the Strategy Card Index tab, scroll to Writing for grades K–5, and select the Graphic Organizers strategy.

Using Tier 2 Writing Interventions

Written expression remains a primary means of communication in modern society and is used to assess knowledge across academic content areas (Mason, Benedek-Wood, & Valasa, 2009). Thus, students' academic achievement often depends on the ability to write well (Mason, Benedek-Wood, & Valasa, 2009). As we saw earlier, results from the National Assessment of Educational Progress 2007 writing test were unimpressive; 74 percent and 65 percent of students in 8th and 12th grades, respectively, did not meet the proficiency skill level in writing (Salahu-Din et al., 2008). This is a clear indication that many if not most students will, from time to time, require Tier 2 classroom interventions to help continue their growth as writers.

In this part of the chapter we begin by sharing two strategies for assisting struggling writers that may be used in small-group settings for Tier 2 instruction: quick write and POW + TREE. Then we turn our attention to English learners (ELs) and their special needs through a strategy called *generous reading and writing*.

Quick Writes and POW + TREE

A **quick write** uses writing as a vehicle to activate students' prior knowledge on a particular topic (Fisher & Frey, 2008) and can promote various types of thinking such as (1) reflecting on prior knowledge, (2) recalling specific information, (3) summarizing content, or (4) expressing thoughts, opinions, reactions, or questions (Mason et al., 2009). Quick writes can be used at the beginning, middle, or end of a lesson to draw out student thinking about specific topics and incorporate writing to make learning connections across subject areas.

Quick writes usually begin with the teacher posing a question to which students respond by writing for 10 minutes about their thoughts. As with many writing activities, struggling writers often write too little and with little development of a thesis or argument. Mason and colleagues (2009) illustrate this problem with an example of a student who responded cryptically to a question about free downloads on the Internet and authors' rights: "When people download music from the Internet it should be free. People put that music on the Internet for free so why do other people that visit that page have to pay?" (p. 305).

Quick writes can be developed and extended to written summaries using two proven organizing tools (Graham & Perin, 2007): POW and TREE. POW is an acronym for a three-step planning strategy (Pick my idea, Organize my notes and ideas, Write and say more). TREE is another mnemonic for helping students expand and organize their thinking and writing (Topic sentence, Reasons [three or more], Examine, Ending). Used together as **POW + TREE** students are helped to become more fluent and reflective writers (Mason et al., 2009). In Figure 8.24 we share the POW + TREE mnemonic for classroom use. As with the introduction of all new tools and strategies, teachers should provide direct instruction and a gradual release of responsibility to students with POW + TREE: introduce and explain, teacher modeling and think aloud, guided practice, and independent practice.

Understanding English Learners Through Generous Reading

Lucy Spence (2010) shares a writing sample from an English learner (EL) named "Delia" (a pseudonym) from her research on an approach to assessment known as generous reading:

> I believe that people Have to help
> the world be a batter places. Lot
> of animals are dieing of the water
> because the water is polluted and animals
> drink the water and they die (p. 634)

Generous reading is an informal way of looking beyond grammar and spelling miscues to "hear" a student's message. In the instance just noted, using a generous reading perspective will allow teachers to readily see that Delia has great concern for pollution and the welfare of animals. Generous reading helps us to take into consideration the multiple cultures, home language, history, and social settings that EL students draw on as they write (Coady & Escamilla, 2005).

It was learned in landmark research conducted by Edelsky (1986) that ELs construct theories about writing as they apply and transfer grammar rules, use complex syntax and stylistic devices, and make modifications based on audience awareness. Edelsky's findings call into question formally held beliefs that "poor children who speak non-standard varieties of one or more languages are language-deficient or semi lingual" (p. 59).

Because generous reading can be time-consuming for busy teachers—an average of about 20 minutes per student artifact (depending on length and complexity, of course), Spence (2010) suggests using generous reading with only a few (three to five) EL students per week. Be sure to keep ongoing records of students' progress and use these insights to plan your next steps in writing instruction. The most promising aspect of generous reading is the potential to help teachers expand their understanding of EL writing over time.

Figure 8.24

POW + TREE Mnemonic

POW

P ick my idea

O rganize my ideas

W rite and say more

TREE

T opic sentence—"What do I believe?"
The topic sentence, like the trunk of a tree, supports a belief.

R easons—3 or more
Why do I believe this?
Will my readers believe this?
Do I have a counterargument?
Does it change my belief?

E xplain reasons
Say more about each reason.
Reasons and explanations, like the roots of a tree, provide the base for a belief.

E nding—wrap it up right!
Like the earth wraps around the tree, making it secure, an ending secures a belief.

From Mason, L. H., Benedek-Wood, E., & Valasa, L. (2009, December). Teaching Low-Achieving Students to Self-Regulate Persuasive Quick Write Responses. *Journal of Adolescent & Adult Literacy, 53*(4), pp. 303–312. Reprinted with permission of the International Reading Association.

Motivating and Engaging Students to Write

Motivation to write is a very different animal from *motivation to read*. Readers can be motivated to read in order to know more about a topic of interest and link new information to that which they already know. Readers are consumers. Writers, on the other hand, are producers of text rather than consumers. They must persist in the writing task frequently without feedback from another person and do not always feel entirely competent at the undertaking (Hidi & Boscolo, 2006).

One of our jobs as teachers is to help young writers have a sense of **self-efficacy**—a positive belief about one's ability to perform a task at a developmentally appropriate level.

● ● ●

IRA Standards for Reading Professionals: Standard 5, Element 5.2

Response to Intervention: Instruction

How we structure writing experiences and offer feedback determines the kind of self-efficacy learners will possess in our classroom. Following are some strategies we feel help teachers accomplish the twin goals of effective teaching and building student self-efficacy.

Write-Talks

Book talks are a popular activity for helping students learn about new books and motivating recreational reading. The idea is that students prepare a short introductory talk about a favorite book for the class. They explain a little about the nature of the book, then read aloud an excerpt that leaves readers wondering what will come next. When we do book talks we usually end by saying something like, "And if you want to know what happens, I guess you'll just have to read the book!"

Teacher Amy Wilson (2008) asked herself one day why she was not doing something similar to book talks to engender a love of writing and created **write-talks.** She developed several research-based steps for conducting write-talks and found the activity quite successful in motivating young writers.

> *Step 1: Ask your students to identify and discuss adults they admire.* Identified individuals can be invited to give write-talks in your classroom about real aspects of their lives. Parents tend to be the most common people students think of, but others (e.g., scout leaders, musicians, grandparents, athletes) are also possible candidates.

> *Step 2: Invite adults to give write-talks in your classroom.* One of the authors remembers well a third-grade student in his class who suggested her grandfather who grew up in the Cajun culture in southern Louisiana. He first read aloud some of his memories from childhood prepared for the event and then later shared one of his favorite books, *Cajun Night Before Christmas* (Trosclair, 2000). The students were absolutely enthralled by his write-talk and oral reading. This led to students writing about their own experiences which they compared and contrasted to our visitor's, as well as creative rewrites of favorite Christmas and other stories.

> *Step 3: Ask students to prepare a list of questions for the guest writer before, during, and after the write-talk.*

> *Step 4: Use examples from your write-talk guests to examine aspects of writing that are relevant to your curriculum.*

A lesson plan using write-talks can be downloaded online at www.readwritethink.org under the title "Write-Talks: Students Discovering Real Writers, Real Audiences, Real Purposes."

Reading and Analyzing Nonfiction (RAN) Strategy

Tony Stead (2001, 2006), an Australian teacher, points out that some 85 percent of all reading that we do as adults is nonfiction or informative in nature, but most of what we deal with in K–3 classrooms is personal narrative or fiction. We believe that all learners are motivated by an increased diet of nonfiction reading and writing activities. Not only that, children truly enjoy expository texts. Reading informational writing can help children do the following:

- Increase their concept knowledge and vocabulary
- Learn important research skills with a variety of tools
- Develop cooperative learning abilities

- Distinguish the writing patterns and styles used by authors in constructing informational texts

Stead (2006) explains that good learning with expository/informational texts has students talking, listening, seeing, exploring, questioning, observing, and sharing. In the **reading and analyzing nonfiction strategy (RAN)**, Stead has produced innovations on the popular K-W-L strategy (Ogle, 1986) to promote small-group interactive learning. Featured in Figure 8.25 is an example of our interpretation of Stead's RAN model completed by a group of students beginning a study of arachnids (spiders).

With the RAN strategy learners begin by working as a team to list what they *think* they know about the subject. This creates an implicit understanding in the learner's mind that some of what they think they know may not be true and that it is okay to have some knowledge that is not accurate.

The second part of RAN involves students in looking for information about the subject—researching. Stead (2006) explains that information resources must be preselected by the teacher to ensure that students do not become frustrated in trying to locate information or lose precious time reading unrelated or unreliable sources. After the team's research is completed, they compile what they have learned in the

Figure 8.25

Reading and Analyzing Nonfiction (RAN) Team Learning Form: Arachnids Example

What We *Think* We Know About This Topic	Information We Have *Confirmed*	New Information and Facts We Have Learned	Some *Misconceptions* We Have Learned About This Topic	We *Now* Wonder....
They're scary	Songs about spiders* we found on the Internet:	The scientific name for spiders is arachnids.	Some people think spiders have hair, so they must be mammals. Spiders are not mammals, they are insects.	What is the biggest spider in North America, since we live there?
We think there is a song about an Eensy Weensy spider	Eensy Weensy Spider Spider Dance Busy Spider Four Little Spiders	There are 37,000 species of arachnids.	Some think spiders kill people, but no one has died from a spider bite in 20 years.	What is the strongest kind of silk made by spiders?
My cousin says to stay away from them 'cause they'll hurt you	Most spiders carry venom to stun or kill creatures they want to eat, not to hurt humans.	Some spiders eat insects we don't like such as flies and mosquitoes. Others eat frogs, fish, lizards, and snakes.	All spiders eat bugs—not true. Some eat animals.	Can you make clothes out of spider silk?
They kill people every now and then	Of all spiders only about 25 are thought to have venom that can hurt humans. Not all spiders are poisonous.		Some people think there are spiders that are as big as a cat, or even bigger. This is not true since the biggest spider is the size of a dinner plate.	Do any spiders live under water?
All spiders are poisonous	Two venomous spiders in the U.S. are the black widow and brown recluse—but they have not been proven to kill people in more than 20 years.			Where did the name "arachnid" come from?
The biggest spider is as big as a cat	The biggest spider is the Goliath bird eater tarantula. It is found in the rainforests of northeastern South America, and can be as big as a dinner plate. It can grab birds from their nests! The smallest spider is from Borneo and is the size of a pinhead.			

Adapted from *National Geographic News. Spider Sense: Fast Facts on Extreme Arachnids.* (n.d.). Retrieved March 31, 2007, from http://news.nationalgeographic.com/news/2004/06/0623_040623_spiderfacts.html.

*Titles from Music & Rhyme Station: Spider songs and rhymes. (n.d.). Retrieved March 31, 2007, from www.preschoolexpress .com/music_station03/music_station_oct03.shtml. Full text and tunes listed.

columns labeled "Information We Have Confirmed" and "New Information and Facts We Have Learned." In doing this, students give evidence that they recognize the validity of some of their previous knowledge and can articulate their new knowledge. In the next column of the summary form, students list misconceptions about the topic they have debunked as a result of their research.

The final column of the RAN Team Learning Form is directed toward what the learners still wonder about. For the topic of spiders, learners may wonder how they can tell which spiders are poisonous or which spiders can be found in their home town. If they are learning about zebras, they might wonder if the stripes are as different as fingerprints in humans. This "wondering" column is driven by students' research and frequently results in higher levels of learning and comprehension.

RAN can be quite useful as a prewriting tool. To help students use RAN to move into the drafting stage of writing, teachers must provide direct and explicit modeling examples.

Figure 8.26

Structure for Written Retellings

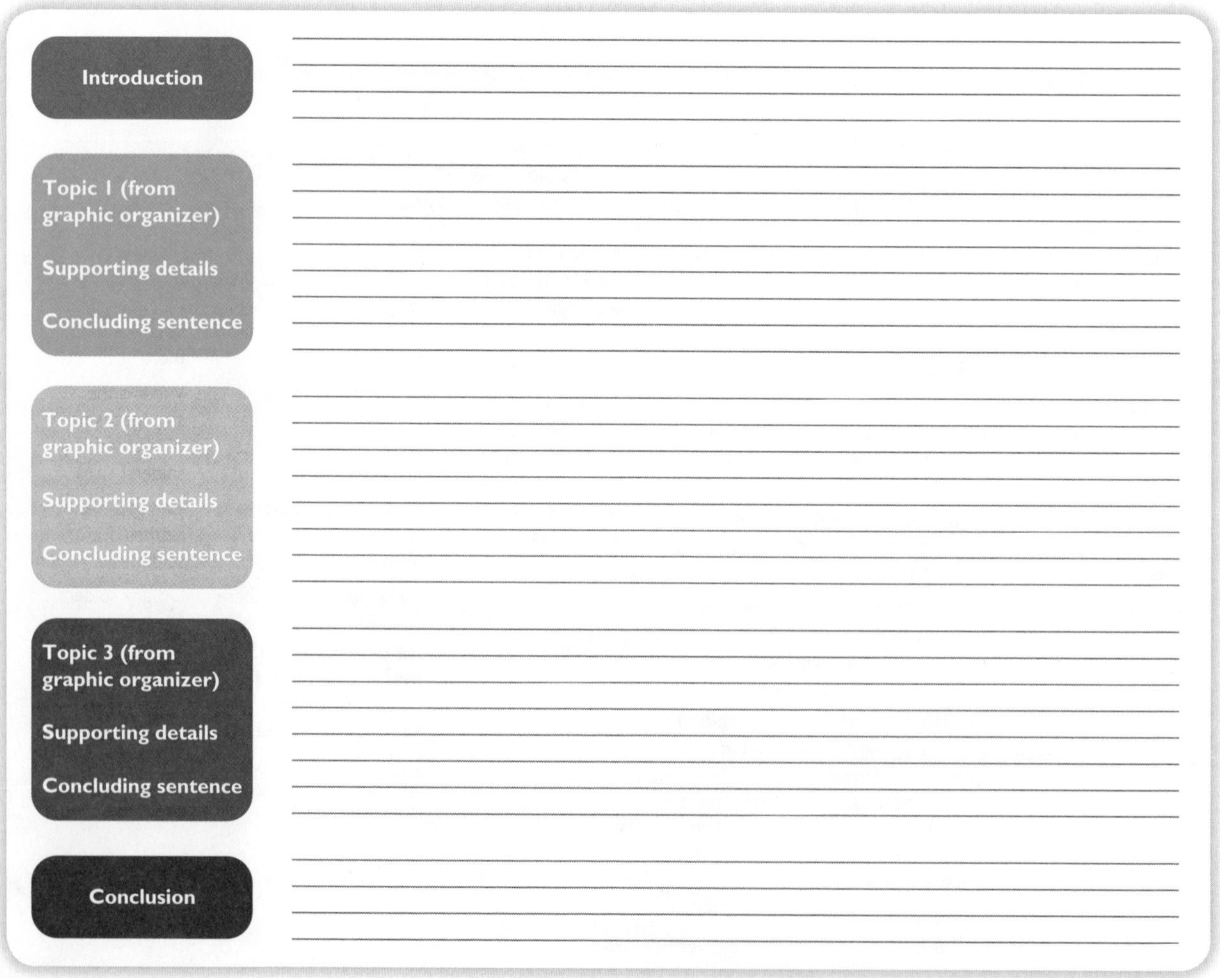

From Cooter, K. S. (2007). *Tinkertoy writing (revised): A systemic approach for grades K–5.* Unpublished manuscript.

For teacher "think-aloud" modeling, it may be helpful to use a graphic organizer like the one recommended in the Memphis Striving Readers Project called "Structure for Written Retellings" or SWR (Cooter, 2006), as shown in Figure 8.26. A completed version of the SWR is shown in Figure 8.27, in which the teacher has

Figure 8.27

Example of a Completed Structure for Written Retellings on Arachnids

Introduction

Spiders are very interesting creatures, and are even scary to some people. The scientific name for spiders is "arachnids," and they are insects. There are 37,000 kinds of spiders. There are even songs about spiders we learn in school. In this report we will learn facts and misconceptions about this special living thing we learned in our book and on the Internet.

Topic 1 (from graphic organizer)

Supporting details

Concluding sentence

One misconception is that all spiders are poisonous. Some spiders are poisonous, or "venomous," but not all spiders have venom. Spiders use venom to stun or kill creatures they want to eat. Of over 37,000 kinds of spiders, only about 25 have venom that can hurt humans. Two spiders in the U.S. with venom that can hurt humans are the black widow and the brown recluse, but no one has been proven killed in over two decades (20 years).

Topic 2 (from graphic organizer)

Supporting details

Concluding sentence

Another misconception is that some spiders can be larger than a cat. Spiders come in many sizes. The largest is the Goliath birdeater tarantula. It is found in the rain forests of northeastern South America, and can be as big as a dinner plate. It can grab birds from their nests! The smallest spider is from Borneo and is the size of a pinhead. So, there are no spiders larger than a cat, but they can be very large and also very small.

Topic 3 (from graphic organizer)

Supporting details

Concluding sentence

One thing we learned is that different arachnids eat different things. Many spiders eat insects, but not all do. There are spiders who dine on birds, frogs, fish, lizards, and snakes. So it is not true that all spiders eat bugs!

Topic 4 (from graphic organizer)

Supporting details

Concluding sentence

There are other things about arachnids, or spiders, that we still do not know. What is the largest spider in North America? Is it as big as the Goliath birdeater tarantula? We hope not. Also, is the silk spiders make all the same kind? How strong is their silk? Could you make clothes out of spider silk? We wonder where the name "arachnid" came from. And what about water spiders? Do any of them actually live under water? We still have a lot to learn about arachnids.

Conclusion

Spiders, or arachnids, are very interesting insects. They come in many sizes, live on different things, and some are poisonous. We want to know more about this special creature.

demonstrated how information gathered using RAN could be transposed onto the Structure for Written Retellings (SWR) graphic organizer to create a first draft of a summary paper. (*Note:* In modeling, teachers should use alternative examples of previously learned material cast in the RAN format because it is the *process,* not the content, that is being emphasized.)

Technology and New Literacies

Technology and New Literacies That Promote Writing

●●●

IRA Standards for Reading Professionals: Standard 5, Element 5.1

Common Core Standards: Writing: K–12, Production and Distribution of Writing (item 6)

Response to Intervention: Instruction

Writing is one of the most prevalent skills needed in a digital age. From e-mails and text messaging to wiki writing to blogging, learners have myriad opportunities to practice their drafting, editing, and publishing skills in ways never imagined just a few decades ago (Sylvester & Greenidge, 2009; Zawilinski, 2009). Here are some ideas we have used successfully in federally funded research projects in schools with some of the country's most economically disadvantaged children (Reutzel & Cooter, 2011).

Wiki Writing

The term *wiki* refers to a jointly authored document that is searchable and contains links to other parts of the document and/or to related information on the Internet. Unlike *blogs,* which limit readers to offering comments about the content of an electronic document, wikis allow visitors to the online site to change the content. The online encyclopedia Wikipedia (www.wikipedia.org) is a popular wiki example.

Wiki writing (Morgan & Smith, 2008) in the classroom has students researching topics and creating online multimedia reports using wiki technology to encourage collaboration between students and the teacher. The first order of business for the teacher is to set up a classroom wiki site on one of the online resources available. PBWiki (pbwiki.com) and the Edublogs affiliate Wikispaces (www.wikispaces.com) are examples of sites often used by classroom teachers to set up their own wiki writing projects. Students will then need explicit instruction and modeling as to how wikis work, explaining terms like *usernames* and *passwords* and showing ways they can create their own composition pages for reports within the classroom wiki site. You will also need to teach students basic wiki text skills using revising and editing tools as well as other online resources (grammar, thesaurus).

Once they understand the schedule and due dates, students begin conducting research in the school library and online. Collaboration is an important aspect of wiki writing (Morgan & Smith, 2008), so students might be assigned to teams with the responsibility of making regular comments and recommendations on team members' work. Virtual sticky notes and footnotes are wiki tools usually available for this purpose.

Morgan and Smith (2008) suggest ideas for using wiki writing. First, remember that wikis are almost "bulletproof." Any mistake can be easily fixed and original

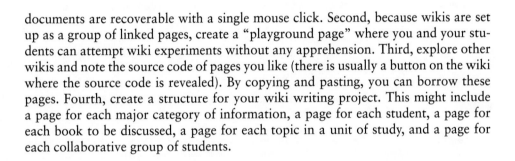

documents are recoverable with a single mouse click. Second, because wikis are set up as a group of linked pages, create a "playground page" where you and your students can attempt wiki experiments without any apprehension. Third, explore other wikis and note the source code of pages you like (there is usually a button on the wiki where the source code is revealed). By copying and pasting, you can borrow these pages. Fourth, create a structure for your wiki writing project. This might include a page for each major category of information, a page for each student, a page for each book to be discussed, a page for each topic in a unit of study, and a page for each collaborative group of students.

e-Reading and e-Responding

A study by Lotta Larson (2009) presented research on students who, instead of reading traditional texts and writing in student response journals, read e-books on laptop computers and responded to readings in electronic response journals. **e-Reading and e-responding** were shown to improve student engagement and increase writing to such an extent in the fifth-grade classroom studied that the teacher, Mrs. Stitt, decided to move her literacy circles online.

Laptop or other personal computers are needed, along with e-books you have selected. Larson lists some sources for free online e-books (see Table 8.3). Students will choose one e-book title from the selection to read. Also present a handout for prompt writing such as Figure 8.28, which was used by students in Mrs. Stitt's fifth grade and can be easily adapted for your own use.

In the Larson (2009) study, Mrs. Stitt's fifth-grade students had the choice of reading the e-book version of one of two books. In this case, there were 15 reading and responding sessions in which students participated. While reading, students share their reactions, questions, and thoughts about the e-book in an electronic response journal. After reading the e-book, students log onto an online message board to discuss and respond to the reading. Because the e-books, e-journals, and online message boards are acquired through the laptop, the transition to each activity is relatively seamless.

Table 8.3

Online Resources for e-Books and e-Responding

Free e-Books	www.getfreebooks.com This is a free e-books site where you can access legal, downloadable e-books for free.
	Public library websites Checkout your local library website for opportunities to "check out" e-books. (Library card is often required.)
e-Books for purchase	www.ebooks.com This site offers a large selection of children's and young adults e-books in multiple formats.
	www.fictionwise.com Fictionwise.com has a comprehensive collection of fiction and nonfiction books in a variety of popular e-book formats.
Online literature response	moodle.org Moodle is a free course management system that can by used for asynchronous message board discussions.
	www.epals.com ePals.com offers schools and districts safe e-mail solutions, blogging, and opportunities for collaborative projects.
	www.pbwiki.com Using the Peanut Butter Wiki site, students can create a wiki to discuss books online.

Form Larson, L. C. (2009). Reader Response Meets New Literacies: Empowering Readers in Online Learning Communities. *The Reading Teacher, 62*(8), pp. 638–648. Reprinted with permission of the International Reading Association.

As with all new learning, it is important for the teacher to explicitly explain, model, and allow for student practice on each of the tasks to be performed. If possible, explanations and modeling are best done with the whole class using a laptop, projector, and screen. Some of the most obvious and critical elements to explain include log-in procedures, how to respond to prompts, and vocabulary (e.g., *thread, prompt, post*). It is a good idea to offer a reminder that this is a learning activity and that students are expected to stay on task and use appropriate language. In a typical session, students read and respond in their e-journals before reading and responding to other responses from classmates.

Larson (2009) explains that students were shown how to construct five kinds of research-based prompts to deepen the quality of threaded discussions and, we believe, promote higher-order comprehension: experiential prompts, aesthetic prompts, cognitive prompts, interpretative prompts, and clarification prompts.

- *Experiential prompts.* Focus on what the reader brings to the experience (i.e., prior knowledge and experiences). These threads might begin with the question, "Have you ever . . ."

- *Aesthetic prompts.* Inspire, as Larson (2009, p. 643) reports, "heartfelt, and sometimes heated, discussions among group members." They promote emotional reactions to the text such as empathy or character identification.

- *Cognitive prompts.* Encourage students to make predictions, solve problems, make inferences, and other higher-order responses.

Figure 8.28

Instructional Handout for Prompt Writing

Name: _____   Group: _____

1. Think about the part that you read today in your book.

   What did you like?
   What questions do you have?
   What did this chapter make you feel or think about?
   What would you have done if you were in a similar situation?

2. Write two quality prompts (new threads) that can be used to start a good discussion in your group. Your prompts should relate to the book.

3. You will post your BEST prompt on the Message Board. Your prompt must be approved by Mrs. Stitt BEFORE you post.

   Prompt 1: _____

   _____

   _____

   Prompt 2: _____

   _____

   _____

Check your work:

☐ My prompt relates to the book.

☐ My prompts are open-ended and cannot be answered with a simple "yes" or "no."

☐ My prompts make my group members think about what they have read.

From Larson, L. C. (2009). Reader Response Meets New Literacies: Empowering Readers in Online Learning Communities. *The Reading Teacher, 62*(8), pp. 638–648. Reprinted with permission of the International Reading Association.

- *Interpretative prompts.* Involve higher-level reasoning and analysis. Readers are often encouraged to think about moral values, meaning, or message, making judgments. You can expect students to offer rich replies and express personal thoughts and viewpoints.

- *Clarification prompts.* Request more information to find an answer to a specific question related to the text. Entries often offer myriad perspectives. These prompts help students make sense of what they are learning. As noted, see Figure 8.28 for an instructional handout to help students construct prompts. We feel this strategy would be equally useful with nonfiction and fiction texts.

IRA Standards for Reading Professionals: Standard 4, Elements 4.1, 4.2, 4.3

Common Core Standards: Writing: K–12, Production and Distribution of Writing (item 4)

Response to Intervention: Collaboration

Family and Community Connections

How Family and Community Connections Can Foster Writing

Family and community involvement is indeed a pillar of comprehensive literacy education. In this section we explore two options for strengthening these connections that have seen success in increasing student learning. The first, Camp Imagination, is a terrific summer program you may be able to get started at your school. The second, Traveling Tales Backpacks, is a strategy we have used extensively in our own classroom practices as a means for getting parents directly involved in the writing development of their children.

Camp Imagination

Educators are always concerned about the "summer slump" when students' reading and writing skills tend to regress during the summer break. Many argue that a lengthy summer vacation does not make good educational sense and is simply an anachronism unique to American education, a leftover of agrarian times when children were needed to help in family farming. Many European schools, for instance, break for about one month during summer, thus lengthening the school year and significantly lessening the summer slump impact. Since the latter part of the twentieth century, scores of school districts, churches, and social agencies have experimented with summer programs aimed at helping some of the more at-risk students keep their literacy skills developing.

Camp Imagination (Jurand, 2009) is a summer tutoring program in Kansas for elementary students that has enjoyed great success. In this model students from a number of schools in the same school district are bussed to a single school for tutoring. Sessions meet for 3 hours each morning over 3½ weeks. Tutoring is separated into two instructional groups: primary (kindergarten and grade 1) and intermediate (grades 2 through 4), with low teacher–student ratios (we feel about eight to ten students per teacher would be optimal).

The curriculum of Camp Imagination has a central thrust of incorporating visualization in the writing process. Jurand (2009) explains that students participate in four field experiences: *Fishing at the neighborhood pond, Hiking on the prairie, Visiting a local nature center,* and *Touring the city fire department.* Field experiences provide motivation for students to write through real-world events that give students purpose and audience. Students record immediate responses to the field experiences in their art/writing journals. Classes brainstorm ideas through discussion around digital photographs taken during the outings. Once a topic is decided, the students create artistic illustrations using a variety of media including markers, crayons, pencils, clay, and watercolors. These products are always referred to respectfully as their "art work." This picture-writing is used as part of the prewriting process serving to incorporate visualization in the writing process.

Although each day of the summer tutoring program looks a bit different, elements are all related to a writing workshop framework similar to our previous discussion. Mini-lessons focus on topics such as choosing words, learning and practicing writing conventions, selecting writing topics, and using art to stimulate understanding of details. Students write descriptive narratives, personal memoirs, and informational technical pieces. Teachers also integrate quality literature as touchstone literary pieces in the mini-lessons.

Camp concludes after 3½ weeks of field experiences and writing. In the closing activity, students choose their favorite experience and continue to expand the piece using the complete writing process. All final products are evaluated using six-trait analysis (described earlier).

Traveling Tales Backpack

We have used the **traveling tales backpack** (Reutzel & Fawson, 1990; Reutzel & Fawson, 1998; Yellin & Blake, 1994) strategy to involve parents and children in collaborative writing projects. A traveling tales backpack (see Figure 8.29) is filled with writing media and guidelines for parents to work with their children at home in producing a self-selected writing project.

The backpack is sent home with the student for two nights. To maximize involvement and success, parents are contacted by phone or note before the backpack is sent home. Parents and children can choose a variety of ways to respond to their favorite book: They can write shape stories, pocketbooks, accordion books, or cards. Included in the traveling tales backpack is a letter to parents with guidelines on how to engage their child in the writing process.

After completing the writing project together, parent and child are invited to share their work with the class in the author's chair at school. After sharing, the written product is placed on display for students to read and enjoy.

Figure 8.29

Traveling Tales Backpack

Summary

Writing instruction is an essential part of a comprehensive literacy program. Among numerous benefits, writing shares the same cognitive processes as reading (Shanahan, 2006), helps children crystallize their understanding of important reading skills such as phonics and other word recognition skills (Juel & Minden-Cupp, 2004), and has great power in helping students deepen procedural knowledge about how to access, use, and generate information (Mason et al., 1991).

In this chapter we saw how writing develops, progressing from scribbles and drawing in the early stages to transitional and fluent written communications. Comprehensive writing instruction ensures that students learn logical stages of the writing process and involves the construction of both narrative writing and expository passages in various forms. Thus, students learn the logic of writing conventions used by myriad writers—they become "insiders" in the world of authoring texts. Over time, student writers begin to read in order to learn how their author-peers maneuver the English language to tell a story or expound on ideas to guide the construction of their own compositions.

Part of our journey through this chapter involved an exploration of the specific writing skills to be learned at each level and how to assess student knowledge in a real-world classroom. Tools added to our assessment toolboxes included the use of story grammars, rubrics, and the six-trait scoring assessment paradigm. These tools help us to monitor student progress, differentiate instruction by forming small groups according to student needs, and plan "next steps" in instruction.

Once we have gathered initial assessment data on student knowledge in writing the teacher is ready to begin instruction. We learned about the basic stages of the writing process that may be used to author everything from poetry to biographies. We also saw how critical the teacher's role is in modeling the writing process, and in establishing collaborative writing activities such as Writing Aloud, Writing To as well as shared writing, interactive writing lessons, and the writing workshop.

Differentiating instruction is critical if we are to meet the needs of every learner. Appropriate uses of technology for reaching English learners (ELs) and students with special needs were explored including generous reading, classroom wiki writing, and e-responding. We also saw how Ogle's (1986) popular K-W-L strategy can be modified to better motivate students' written academic summaries through Stead's (2001, 2006) reading and analyzing nonfiction strategy (RAN).

Families have an important role to play in student learning, as we saw in this chapter on writing. A powerful strategy we have used ourselves, traveling tales backpacks (Reutzel & Fawson, 1998; Yellin & Blake, 1994), was described in some detail. We also took a look at a summer program called Camp Imagination where students are taught to use imagery and art as part of the writing process. Using these and the other evidence-based ideas presented in this chapter can help you create a community of writers in your own classroom!

Field and Classroom Applications

- This activity is intended for those who are practicing teachers or teacher education students working closely with a teacher in a practicum experience. We call this activity "The Investigator." Assume the role of an investigator to discover and describe instructional resources for writing that are available to teachers at your school. Complete a summary chart for your investigator's notebook (it can take any form) showing specific materials of any type (books, nonprint materials, computer-related items, etc.) available to supplement your writing curriculum. You should search for the following resources that may be available at your school:
  - Resources available in your school library
  - Resources for accommodating struggling readers and writers
  - Graphic organizer resources
  - Computer resources (hardware and software, as well as on the Internet)
  - Resources to help students with their written retellings about new subject-related information.
  Using your notebook, write a brief news article (two to three double-spaced pages) reporting on what you find. Be sure to include a statement of needs that your principal should consider to help you do your job as a core content teacher. *Note:* Be sure to attach your summary chart with your news article as backup support.

- This is an activity for teacher education students or practicing teachers we call "Sage on the Stage." It may be done as a small-group activity or individually. Assume the role of a master teacher who is now touring the country conducting 3-day seminars for elementary or middle school teachers (you decide). Your task is to develop "real-world classroom examples" to illustrate proven assessment or writing instruction strategies.
  a. Select four writing assessment and/or teaching strategies from this chapter for your workshop.
  b. Develop model examples you can share with the teachers attending your seminar. Be sure to identify key textbook readings and any supplemental materials you might use.
  c. Create a list of resources for writing instruction based on what is available at your school (if you are already a teacher) or with a partner school (if you are a teacher education student). This will help you produce an authentic presentation with actual school resources.
  d. Develop a lesson plan or handout showing how you would implement these strategies specifically. State clearly which writing assessment or teaching strategy you would use and the procedure. Remember, this will be new information for teachers in your seminar, so they will need for you to be *very* specific.

Recommended Resources

Print Resources

Common Core Standards Initiative. (2010). *The common core state standards for English language arts & literacy in history/social studies, science, and technical subjects.* Washington, DC: The Council of Chief State School Officers and the National Governors Association.

Culham, R. (2010). *Traits of writing.* New York: Scholastic.

Hampton, S., & Resnick, L. B. (2009). *Reading and writing with understanding.* Newark, DE: International Reading Association.

Salahu-Din, D., Persky, H., & Miller, J. (2008). *The nation's report card: Writing 2007* (NCES 2008-468). Washington, DC: National Center for Education Statistics, Institute of Education Sciences, U.S. Department of Education.

Sloan, M. S. (2008). *Teaching young writers to elaborate.* New York: Scholastic.

Web Resources

www.readwritethink.org

Read Write Think is a special website for teachers co-sponsored by the International Reading Association and the National Council of Teachers of English. Provides free lesson plans and other instructional aids for teaching reading and the other language arts.

http://en.wikipedia.org/wiki/Main_Page

Wikipedia is a free encyclopedia that anyone can edit or provide information on myriad topics.

http://news.nationalgeographic.com/kids/Kids News

National Geographic features different people, animals, and places each month with facts, games, activities, and related links.

http://interactive2.usgs.gov/learningweb/students

The U.S. Geological Survey provides scientific information intended to help educate the public about natural resources, natural hazards, geospatial data, and issues that affect our quality of life. Discover selected online resources, including lessons, data, maps, and more, to support teaching, learning, education (K–12), and university-level inquiry and research.

www.smithsonianeducation.org

Smithsonian Education has education resources and information, lesson plans, field trips, and fun interactive activities for educators, families, and students.

http://pbskids.org

Watch PBS Kids shows and play research-based educational games and activities.

www.ozprojects.edna.edu.au/sibling/home

The OzProjects website provides access to a host of resources to support students' involvement in online projects. There is a Teachers' Group section for educators new to online projects where you can view ideas for projects and/or create an account (no charge) and enroll in projects which have been created by the OzProjects team. You can also request an OzProjects space to create your own online project. After requesting and developing your own project in OzClassrooms you can invite others to join your project if you wish.

www.starfall.com

Starfall began as a free public service to motivate children to read with phonics. Their systematic phonics approach and phonemic awareness practice is targeted for preschool, kindergarten, first grade, second grade, special education, homeschool, and English language development (ELD, ELL, ESL).

www.funbrain.com

Funbrain provides online educational games for kids of all ages (math, grammar, science, spelling, history).

The Power of Classroom Practice

www.myeducationlab.com

Go to Topic 7, Writing, in the MyEducationLab (www.myeducationlab.com) for your course, where you can:

- Find learning outcomes for Writing along with the national standards that connect to these outcomes.
- Complete Assignments and Activities that can help you more deeply understand the chapter content.
- Apply and practice your understanding of the core teaching skills identified in the chapter with the Building Teaching Skills and Dispositions learning units. (optional)
- Examine challenging situations and cases presented in the IRIS Center Resources. (optional)
- Access video clips of CCSSO National Teachers of the Year award winners responding to the question "Why Do I Teach?" in the Teacher Talk section. (optional)
- Check your comprehension on the content covered in the chapter by going to the Study Plan in the Book Resources for your text. Here you will be able to take a chapter quiz, receive feedback on your answers, and then access Review, Practice, and Enrichment activities to enhance your understanding of chapter content. (optional)

Go to the Topic A+RISE in the MyEducationLab (www.myeducationlab.com) for your course. A+RISE® Standards2Strategy™ is an innovative and interactive online resource that offers new teachers in grades K–12 just in time, research-based instructional strategies that:

- Meet the linguistic needs of ELLs as they learn content.
- Differentiate instruction for all grades and abilities.
- Offer reading and writing techniques, cooperative learning, use of linguistic and nonlinguistic representations, scaffolding, teacher modeling, higher order thinking, and alternative classroom ELL assessment.
- Provide support to help teachers be effective through the integration of listening, speaking, reading, and writing along with the content curriculum.
- Improve student achievement.
- Are aligned to Common Core Elementary Language Arts standards (for the literacy strategies) and to English language proficiency standards in WIDA, Texas, California, and Florida.

STANDARDS
for Reading Professionals and Guiding Principles for Educators

IRA Standards for Reading Professionals

Standard 1: Foundational Knowledge

Element 1.1

Candidates understand major theories and empirical research that describe the cognitive, linguistic, motivational, and sociocultural foundations of reading and writing development, processes, and components, including word recognition, language comprehension, strategic knowledge, and reading–writing connections.

Element 1.3

Candidates understand the role of professional judgment and practical knowledge for improving all students' reading development and achievement.

Standard 6: Professional Learning and Leadership

Element 6.2

Candidates display positive dispositions related to their own reading and writing and the teaching of reading and writing, and pursue the development of individual professional knowledge and behaviors.

Common Core Standards

Teachers should be familiar with the following standards.

Writing: K–5

Text Types and Purposes

1. Write arguments to support claims in an analysis of substantive topics or texts, using valid reasoning and relevant and sufficient evidence.

2. Write informative/explanatory texts to examine and convey complex ideas and information clearly and accurately through the effective selection, organization, and analysis of content.

3. Write narratives to develop real or imagined experiences or events using effective technique, well-chosen details, and well-structured event sequences.

Production and Distribution of Writing

4. Produce clear and coherent writing in which the development, organization, and style are appropriate to task, purpose, and audience.

5. Develop and strengthen writing as needed by planning, revising, editing, rewriting, or trying a new approach.

6. Use technology, including the Internet, to produce and publish writing and to interact and collaborate with others.

Research to Build and Present Knowledge

7. Conduct short as well as more sustained research projects based on focused questions, demonstrating understanding of the subject under investigation.

8. Gather relevant information from multiple print and digital sources, assess the credibility and accuracy of each source, and integrate the information while avoiding plagiarism.

9. Draw evidence from literary or informational texts to support analysis, reflection, and research.

Range of Writing

10. Write routinely over extended time frames (time for research, reflection, and revision) and shorter time frames (a single sitting or a day or two) for a range of tasks, purposes, and audiences.

Writing: Grades 6–12

The grades 6–12 standards on the following pages define what students should understand and be able to do by the end of each grade. They correspond to the College and Career Readiness (CCR) anchor standards below by number. The CCR and grade-specific standards are necessary complements—the former providing broad standards, the latter providing additional specificity—that together define the skills and understandings that all students must demonstrate.

Text Types and Purposes

1. Write arguments to support claims in an analysis of substantive topics or texts, using valid reasoning and relevant and sufficient evidence.

2. Write informative/explanatory texts to examine and convey complex ideas and information clearly and accurately through the effective selection, organization, and analysis of content.

3. Write narratives to develop real or imagined experiences or events using effective technique, well-chosen details, and well-structured event sequences.

Production and Distribution of Writing

4. Produce clear and coherent writing in which the development, organization, and style are appropriate to task, purpose, and audience.

5. Develop and strengthen writing as needed by planning, revising, editing, rewriting, or trying a new approach.

6. Use technology, including the Internet, to produce and publish writing and to interact and collaborate with others.

Research to Build and Present Knowledge

7. Conduct short as well as more sustained research projects based on focused questions, demonstrating understanding of the subject under investigation.

8. Gather relevant information from multiple print and digital sources, assess the credibility and accuracy of each source, and integrate the information while avoiding plagiarism.

9. Draw evidence from literary or informational texts to support analysis, reflection, and research.

Range of Writing

10. Write routinely over extended time frames (time for research, reflection, and revision) and shorter time frames (a single sitting or a day or two) for a range of tasks, purposes, and audiences.

Response to Intervention

6. Expertise

- Important dimensions of teachers' expertise include their knowledge and understanding of language and literacy development, their ability to use powerful assessment tools and techniques, and their ability to translate information about student performance into instructionally relevant instructional techniques.

- Success for culturally and linguistically diverse students depends on teachers and support personnel who are well prepared to teach in a variety of settings. Deep knowledge of cultural and linguistic differences is especially critical for the prevention of language and literacy problems in diverse student populations.

Classroom Writing Assessment

IRA Standards for Reading Professionals

Standard 3: Assessment and Evaluation

Element 3.1

Candidates understand types of assessments and their purposes, strengths, and limitations.

Element 3.2

Candidates select, develop, administer, and interpret assessments, both traditional print and electronic, for specific purposes.

Element 3.3

Candidates use assessment information to plan and evaluate instruction.

Common Core Standards

Teachers must be able to assess students' ability to do the following.

Writing: K–12

Text Types and Purposes

1. Write arguments to support claims in an analysis of substantive topics or texts, using valid reasoning and relevant and sufficient evidence.

2. Write informative/explanatory texts to examine and convey complex ideas and information clearly and accurately through the effective selection, organization, and analysis of content.

3. Write narratives to develop real or imagined experiences or events using effective technique, well-chosen details, and well-structured event sequences.

Production and Distribution of Writing

4. Produce clear and coherent writing in which the development, organization, and style are appropriate to task, purpose, and audience.

5. Develop and strengthen writing as needed by planning, revising, editing, rewriting, or trying a new approach.

Research to Build and Present Knowledge

7. Conduct short as well as more sustained research projects based on focused questions, demonstrating understanding of the subject under investigation.

8. Gather relevant information from multiple print and digital sources, assess the credibility and accuracy of each source, and integrate the information while avoiding plagiarism.

9. Draw evidence from literary or informational texts to support analysis, reflection, and research.

Response to Intervention

3. Assessment

- Assessments, tools, and techniques should provide useful and timely information about desired language and literacy goals. They should reflect authentic language and literacy activities as opposed to contrived texts or tasks generated specifically for assessment purposes. The quality of assessment information should not be sacrificed for the efficiency of an assessment procedure.
- Multiple purposes for assessment should be clearly identified and appropriate tools and techniques employed. . . . Particular care should be taken in selecting assessments for ELLs and for students who speak an English dialect that differs from mainstream dialects.

- Efficient assessment systems involve a layered approach in which screening techniques are used both to identify which students require further (diagnostic) assessment and to provide aggregate data about the nature of student achievement overall. Initial (screening) assessments should not be used as the sole mechanism for determining the appropriateness of targeted interventions. Ongoing progress monitoring must include an evaluation of the instruction itself and requires observation of the student in the classroom.
- Classroom teachers and reading/literacy specialists should play a central role in conducting language and literacy assessments and in using assessment results to plan instruction and monitor student performance.

Evidence-Based Writing Instruction

IRA Standards for Reading Professionals

Standard 2: Curriculum and Instruction

Element 2.1

Candidates use foundational knowledge to design or implement an integrated, comprehensive, and balanced curriculum.

Element 2.2

Candidates use appropriate and varied instructional approaches, including those that develop word recognition, language comprehension, strategic knowledge, and reading–writing connections.

Element 2.3

Candidates use a wide range of texts (e.g., narrative, expository, and poetry) from traditional print, digital, and online resources.

Standard 4: Diversity

Element 4.1

Candidates recognize, understand, and value the forms of diversity that exist in society and their importance in learning to read and write.

Standard 5: Literate Environment

Element 5.1

Candidates design the physical environment to optimize students' use of traditional print, digital, and online resources in reading and writing instruction.

Element 5.2

Candidates design a social environment that is low risk and includes choice, motivation, and scaffolded support to optimize students' opportunities for learning to read and write.

Element 5.3

Candidates use routines to support reading and writing instruction (e.g., time allocation, transitions from one activity to another, discussions, and peer feedback).

Common Core Standards

Writing: K–5

Text Types and Purposes

1. (See previous)

2. (See previous)

3. (See previous)

Production and Distribution of Writing

4. (See previous)

5. (See previous)

6. (See previous)

Research to Build and Present Knowledge

7. (See previous)

8. (See previous)

9. (See previous)

Range of Writing

10. (See previous)

Writing: Grades 6–12

Text Types and Purposes

1. (See previous)

2. (See previous)

3. (See previous)

Production and Distribution of Writing

4. (See previous)

5. (See previous)

6. (See previous)

Research to Build and Present Knowledge

7. (See previous)

8. (See previous)

9. (See previous)

Range of Writing

10. (See previous)

Response to Intervention

1. Instruction

- The success of RTI depends on the classroom teacher's use of research-based practices.
- Research on instructional practices must provide not only information about what works, but also what works with whom, by whom, in what contexts, and on which outcomes. The effectiveness of a particular practice needs to have been demonstrated with the types of students who will receive the instruction, taking into account, for example, whether the students live in rural or urban settings or come from diverse cultural and linguistic backgrounds.
- RTI is centrally about optimizing language and literacy instruction for particular students. This means that differentiated instruction, based on instructionally relevant assessment, is essential.
- Instruction and materials selection must derive from specific student–teacher interactions and not be constrained by pack-

aged programs. No single approach to instruction or intervention can address the broad and varied goals and needs of all students, especially those from different cultural and linguistic backgrounds.

5. Systemic and Comprehensive Approaches

- RTI needs to be integrated within the context of a coherent and consistent language and literacy curriculum that guides comprehensive instruction for all students.
- Specific approaches to RTI need to be appropriate for the particular school or district culture and take into account leadership, expertise, the diversity of the student population, and the available resources.
- Approaches to RTI must be sensitive to developmental differences in language and literacy among students at different ages and grades.

Using Tier 2 Writing Interventions

IRA Standards for Reading Professionals

Standard 5: Literate Environment

Elements 5.1, 5.2, 5.3 (See previous)

Common Core Standards

Writing: K–5

Text Types and Purposes

1. (See previous)

2. (See previous)

3. (See previous)

Production and Distribution of Writing

4. (See previous)

5. (See previous)

6. (See previous)

Research to Build and Present Knowledge

7. (See previous)

8. (See previous)

9. (See previous)

Range of Writing

10. (See previous)

Writing: Grades 6–12

Text Types and Purposes

1. (See previous)

2. (See previous)

3. (See previous)

Production and Distribution of Writing

4. (See previous)

5. (See previous)

6. (See previous)

Research to Build and Present Knowledge

7. (See previous)

8. (See previous)

9. (See previous)

Range of Writing

10. (See previous)

2. Responsive Teaching and Differentiation

- Instruction and materials selection must derive from specific student–teacher interactions and not be constrained by packaged programs.

5. Systemic and Comprehensive Approaches

- RTI needs to be integrated within the context of a coherent and consistent language and literacy curriculum that guides comprehensive instruction for all students.

Motivating and Engaging Students to Write

IRA Standards for Reading Professionals

Standard 5: Literate Environment

Element 5.2 (See previous)

Response to Intervention

1. Instruction

- Instruction and assessment conducted by the classroom teacher are central to the success of RTI and must address the needs of all students, including those from diverse cultural and linguistic backgrounds.

- The success of RTI depends on the classroom teacher's use of research-based practices.
- Research on instructional practices must provide not only information about what works, but also what works with whom, by whom, in what contexts, and on which outcomes.

Technology and New Literacies That Promote Writing

IRA Standards for Reading Professionals

Standard 5: Literate Environment

Element 5.1 (See previous)

Common Core Standards

Writing: K–12
Production and Distribution of Writing

6. Use technology, including the Internet, to produce and publish writing and to interact and collaborate with others.

Response to Intervention

1. Instruction

- Whatever approach is taken to RTI, it should ensure optimal instruction for every student at all levels of schooling. It should prevent serious language and literacy problems through increasingly differentiated and intensified assessment and instruction and reduce the disproportionate number of minority youth and ELLs identified as learning disabled.

- Research on instructional practices must provide not only information about what works, but also what works with whom, by whom, in what contexts, and on which outcomes.

IRA Standards for Reading Professionals

Standard 4: Diversity

Element 4.1 (See previous)

Element 4.2

Candidates use a literacy curriculum and engage in instructional practices that positively impact students' knowledge, beliefs, and engagement with the features of diversity.

Element 4.3

Candidates develop and implement strategies to advocate for equity.

Common Core Standards

Writing: K–12

Production and Distribution of Writing

4. (See previous)

Response to Intervention

4. Collaboration

- Involving parents and students and engaging them in a collaborative manner is critical to successful implementation. Initiating and strengthening collaborations among school, home, and communities, particularly in urban and rural areas, provides the basis for support and reinforcement of students' learning.

Part Three

The Reading Teacher's Toolbox

9

Evidence-Based Programs, Interventions,
and Standards for Reading Instruction

10

Assessment

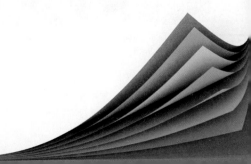

Evidence-Based 9
Programs, Interventions, and Standards for Reading Instruction

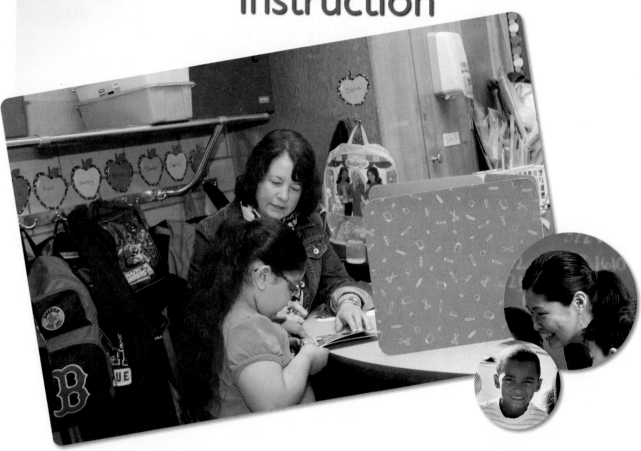

Teacher Knowledge	**Classroom Assessment**	**Evidence-Based Teaching Practices**	**Response to Intervention (RTI)**
Standards and Programs for Reading Instruction	Assessing the Effectiveness of Core Reading Programs	Evidence-Based Reading Instruction Programs	Supplementary Reading Intervention Programs

Chapter Questions

■ How can awareness of "standards" help teachers provide effective reading instruction, especially for the most transient students?

■ What are various instruments that can be used to assess the quality of a core reading program?

■ What are evidence-based supplemental reading programs for helping struggling readers succeed?

■ Which reading programs have been shown to be effective with English learners (ELs)?

■ How can teachers encourage students to engage in core and supplemental reading programs with greater interest and motivation?

■ Describe some reading programs and standards that relate to the use of new technologies to teach children to read.

■ How can teachers help parents and interested stakeholders including EL parents better understand reading standards and how to help their children succeed?

Key Terms

Standards

Standards-based movement

Common Core Standards

Core reading program (CRP)

Scope and sequence chart

Decodable readers

Criterion-referenced test (CRT)

Classwide peer tutoring (CWPT)

Reading Recovery

Early Intervention in Reading (EIR)

Motivation and Engagement	Technology and New Literacies	Family and Community Connections
Programs and Standards Focused on Motivation and Engagement	Programs and Standards Focused on Technology and New Literacies	How Can Teachers Help Parents and Communities Better Understand Reading Programs and Standards?

Vignette: Which Reading Program Is Best?

It's Friday morning, 8:00 A.M. You are attending a meeting of the newly established Core Reading Program Adoption Committee for your school district. The committee's task is to choose a new reading program. Just one month into your first year as a teacher, you and your teammates must review a plethora of core reading programs, supplemental materials for reading instruction, and sundry other kits and manipulatives. The 40-by-40-foot conference room is absolutely packed with the latest offerings from major- and minor-league publishers, and properly coiffed sales representatives are waiting in the hallway like obedient soldiers to retrieve any needed information at a moment's notice. Great food and beverages are provided.

The state's reading standards have been made available for your convenience as you match required skills to appropriate materials.

It all sounds straightforward, but where do you begin? Some of your colleagues feel strongly that a program that best matches the state standards should be selected. Others think that materials that supposedly help teachers teach to the state test are imperative. Still others like the programs with lots of "free stuff," like classroom libraries and technology support. As a new teacher, this latter option is especially appealing; you don't have much to work with beyond the relatively few supplies and materials you inherited from your predecessor. However, you admit that the other arguments may make better sense. After all, you will be judged by how well your students perform on the state standards and test.

But you also know that you are there to represent those who have no voice—the students. What should you do? ▪

Many published and nationally marketed programs for reading instruction are available to teachers and schools. Although many publishers claim to offer comprehensive curriculums, in our view, no reading instructional program has ever been designed—or ever will be designed—that can meet the needs of all learners. Therefore, it is important for teachers to know their learners' current developmental levels, the essentials of reading instruction, state and federal reading **standards,** and the currently available reading instruction programs and materials that can be used to meet the needs of their students.

Our focus, as we discuss reading instruction standards and reading instruction programs, are the "Big Five" instructional strands drawn from the report of the National Reading Panel (2000): phonemic awareness, phonics, vocabulary, comprehension, and fluency. In this chapter, we examine core reading programs of instruction that all claim to address these five reading instruction essentials. We begin by acquainting you with a description of the standards-based movement in the United States and how it has impacted the development of core reading programs.

Teacher Knowledge

Standards and Programs for Reading Instruction

In the opening vignette, our new teacher was caught between the horns of a difficult dilemma: how to balance her need to provide children access to high-quality books and motivating reading experiences with the twin demands for evidence- and standards-based teaching by state and national governments. Add to this quandary high-stakes testing mandated by state and national governments to hold schools and educators accountable for the efficacy of the reading instruction provided to students. In the past decade, standards-based curricula and assessments have been prescribed as a treatment for the poor performance and accountability of many public schools (Rothstein & Jacobsen, 2009; Watt, 2005; Zuzovsky & Libman, 2006). Billions of dollars have been spent on developing new core reading instruction programs that are ostensibly evidence based as well as on state or national high-stakes tests, in part so that federal and state agencies can rank and sort schools in terms of student achievement (Baines & Stanley, 2006; Rothstein & Jacobsen, 2009). Current political conditions in the nation as of this writing seem to point to no reduction or change in this direction.

Overview of the Standards-Based Movement

According to Watt (2005), the **standards-based movement** in the United States began as an outgrowth of a public debate over the rather tepid national and international academic performance of schoolchildren on measures of reading, not to mention similarly tepid performance in other academic areas such as mathematics and science. Concern for the effectiveness and competitiveness of U.S. education was heightened following the release of a number of national studies in the 1980s, most especially the report of the National Commission on Excellence in Education in 1983 entitled *A Nation at Risk*. In general, these reports sparked calls for the reform of public education by either decentralizing authority to local communities or, conversely, by giving more authority to state and federal agencies.

In 1989, then-President George H. W. Bush convened the Charlottesville Education Summit, attended by (then-governor) Bill Clinton and the nation's other 49 governors. The goal was to identify ways to make the U.S. more internationally competitive by 2000. Watt (2005, pp. 3–4) described the outcome:

> They reached agreement to establish a process for setting national education goals, seeking greater flexibility and accountability in using federal resources to meet the goals, undertaking a state-by-state effort to restructure the education system, and reporting annually on progress in achieving the goals (Vinovskis, 1999). . . . The six National Education Goals became the foundation for America 2000 and later Goals 2000, and provided the impetus for defining national standards based in academic disciplines.
>
> A multiplicity of trends in U.S. education had concurred [sic] by this time leading conservatives and liberals to forge a consensus about focusing on what students should know and be able to do. Policy-makers set nationally recognized groups in key disciplines [with] the task of developing national standards consisting of content,

●●●

IRA Standards for Reading Professionals: Standard 1, Elements 1.1, 1.2, 1.3

Common Core Standards: Reading: K–12, Key Ideas and Details (items 1–3), Craft and Structure (items 4–6), Integration of Knowledge and Ideas (items 7–9), Range of Reading and Level of Text Complexity (item 10); Writing: K–12, Text Types and Purposes (items 1–3), Production and Distribution of Writing (items 4–6), Research to Build and Present Knowledge (items 7–9), Range of Writing (item 10); Speaking and Listening: K–12, Comprehension and Collaboration (items 1–3), Presentation of Knowledge and Ideas (items 4–6); Language: K–12, Conventions of Standard English (items 1, 2), Knowledge of Language (item 3), Vocabulary Acquisition and Use (items 4–6)

Response to Intervention: Expertise

performance, and opportunity-to-learn standards. **Content standards** refer to broad descriptions of knowledge and skills that students should achieve in particular subject areas. **Performance standards** are examples and definitions of knowledge and skills in which students need to demonstrate proficiency. **Opportunity-to-learn standards,** which address conditions necessary at each level of the education system to provide all students with opportunities to master content standards and meet performance standards, provide criteria covering six elements. These elements refer to the quality and availability of curricula, materials and technology, the capability of teachers to meet learning needs, the availability of professional development, the alignment of the curriculum to content standards, the adequacy of school facilities for learning, and the application of non-discriminatory policies.

It seems fair to conclude that when George W. Bush was elected president in 2000 he used the outcomes generated by the Charlottesville Education Summit to form the basis of the No Child Left Behind (NCLB) legislation passed in 2001. Approved by Congress with near-unanimous support, NCLB in effect federalized the standards-based movement and required all states to conform or risk losing federal tax dollars. NCLB also caused the producers of reading programs, tests, and support materials to conform to mandated "evidence-based" standards.

Pressure to adopt and use standards for improving educational performance has not slackened with the election of President Barack Obama in 2008 and the appointment of Arne Duncan as U.S. Secretary of Education. "Race to the Top" (2010) is a federal initiative that challenges U.S. schools to close not only the national achievement gap between and among students but also the international student achievement gap between the United States and other countries around the globe. As part of this race to the top, states and school districts were asked to adopt a series of standards referred to as **Common Core Standards** (2010) to prepare students to succeed in college and the workplace as well as to compete in a global economy.

To institutionalize demands that reading instruction programs, assessments, and supplemental interventions meet rigorous standards of evidence for effectiveness, the U.S. government created the What Works Clearinghouse (see the URL at the end of this chapter) as a part of the Institute of Education Sciences (IES), a branch of the U.S. Department of Education. Reading instruction programs and assessments that do not meet rigorous standards of evidence for efficacy should not be adopted or adopted only with major reservations by state or local education agencies for instruction and assessment. Regardless of where one stands on the philosophy of the standards-based and evidence-based movements and their implementation, it is nevertheless a matter of current law with considerable public support that dramatically influences the types and quality of reading instruction materials and assessments receiving official sanction from state and federal governments.

Where Can I Find My State's Reading Standards and Approved Reading Assessments?

Even though the federal government has taken increasing interest in the economic and political power of schooling, the responsibility for providing educational opportunity rests with individual states as delegated by the Tenth Amendment of the U.S. Constitution. Because each state has a constitutional mandate to provide educational opportunities for their citizens, you should seek out the specific reading standards articulated by your own state department of education and the state-mandated tests for measuring their acquisition by students. This information is typically available to teachers online.

What Are Core Reading Programs?

Core reading programs (CRPs), in one form or another, have played an integral role in U.S. reading instruction for centuries and are likely to continue to do so well into the future (DeWitz, Leahy, Jones, & Sullivan, 2010; Giordano, 2001; Hoffman, 2001; McCallum, 1988; Reutzel, 1991). According to DeWitz, Leahy, Jones, and Sullivan (2010), historically core reading instruction programs have been termed *basals* because they served as the "base" for reading instruction. For our purposes, we will use the more contemporary "core reading program" rather than "basal" program. DeWitz, Leahy, Jones, and Sullivan (2010) describe a core reading program as a collection of student reading selections, skill activities, teachers' manuals, and supplemental reading instruction materials applied in elementary and middle school classrooms according to a basic structure: "Stories are introduced, knowledge and vocabulary are developed, stories are read and discussed, and students' responses to text are made. Skills are taught sometimes before the story, sometimes afterward" (p. 33). Simmons and Kame'enui (2003) explain that core reading programs are the primary instructional tool that teachers use to teach children to read and to ensure that they reach reading levels that meet or exceed grade-level standards. Research indicates that 80 percent of U.S. schoolchildren receive their reading instruction in whole or part from a core reading program (Education Market Research, 2007).

Anatomy of a Core Reading Program

Core reading programs are typically composed of a common set of instructional materials.

- A student text containing stories, information selections, and poetry
- A teacher's edition (TE) with ready-made lessons, teacher prompts, and the students' text in miniature
- Student activity pages usually in blackline copy
- A teacher's edition of the student activity pages
- Supplemental practice activities (usually in the form of blackline masters that can be duplicated)
- Enrichment activities (also usually blackline masters)
- Big books
- Leveled readers
- Phonic or decodable readers
- End-of-unit and end-of-book tests

Other supplemental core reading program materials can usually be acquired at additional cost: picture cards, picture-with-letter cards, letter cards, word cards for display on word walls, pocket charts, classroom trade book libraries, more big books, and technology resources such as CDs, DVDs, and publisher websites. In addition, many core reading programs provide a computer-based system for record keeping, management of the reading skills taught and mastered, and additional or alternative assessments. Because so many teachers employ core reading programs, we will describe the basic components and provide examples of current core reading programs available in U.S. schools.

The Core Reading Program Teacher's Edition (TE).   For new teachers and veterans alike, perhaps the most important part of the core reading program is the teacher's edition (TE) because it contains instructional guidance and support (see Figure 9.1). For many new teachers, the core reading program TE is the most significant resource available for initial professional development.

Within the pages of the teacher's edition, one usually finds three important features: (1) the scope and sequence chart of the skills to be taught in the core reading program, (2) a reduced version or facsimile of the students' text, and (3) recommended lesson plans and other teacher supports (see Figures 9.2 and 9.3).

A **scope and sequence chart** describes in great detail the range of skills and or concepts to be taught in a core reading program as well as the sequence in which these are to be presented during the school year. Current scholars argue that the number of skills taught within most core reading programs is entirely too large and the nature of the skills taught are often unrelated to the scientific evidence base. More confusingly, even within the same core reading program the same skill may be called by more than one name or term (Block & Duffy, 2008; Dewitz, Jones, & Leahy, 2009; Dewitz et al., 2010).

The entire student core reading anthology or text, shown as a reduced facsimile, is included for convenience of the teacher in the TE. Lesson plans in the core reading program are also included to save the classroom teacher preparation time; how-

Figure 9.1

Example of a Teacher's Edition Cover from the Macmillan/McGraw-Hill Core Reading Program

From *Macmillan/McGraw-Hill: Treasures* (2007). (Teacher's ed., Grade 1, Unit 1). Copyright 2007 by the McGraw-Hill Companies, Inc. Reprinted by permission.

Figure 9.2

A Scope and Sequence Chart Showing the Range of Skills to Be Taught in a Core Reading Program

From *SRA Open Court Reading: Keep Trying* (2005). (Teacher's edition, Level 1, Unit 7, Appendix, p. 48). Copyright 2005 by the McGraw-Hill Companies, Inc. Reprinted by permission.

Figure 9.3

Example of the Internal Pages from a Core Reading Program Teacher's Edition

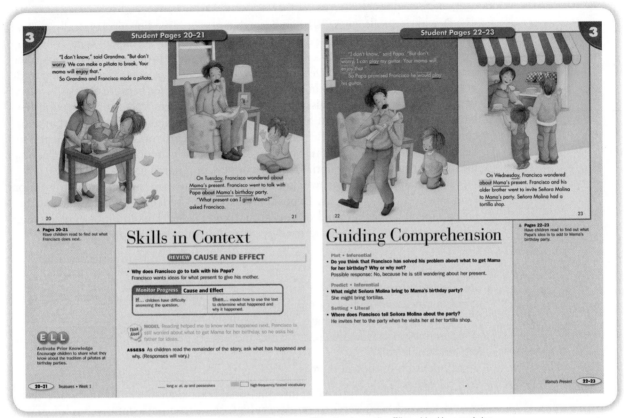

ever, few teachers follow these lessons with absolute fidelity in practice (Dewitz et al., 2010). Currently published core reading programs typically continue to design reading lessons around a modified sequence of the now somewhat dated DRTA, or directed reading thinking activity (Stauffer, 1969).

We believe it is important to understand that the teacher's edition is a resource to be used discriminately—not a script to be followed rigidly. Teachers and administrators should not allow the core reading program TE to dictate every aspect of reading instruction. Rather, teachers should be encouraged to decide on appropriate TE use with a particular group of children based on student data and needs.

The Students' Core Reading Text or Anthology.   The students' core reading text is an anthology of original contemporary and classic stories, poems, news clips, and expository text selections. Some selections have been created expressly for inclusion in the core reading text. Other selections have been adapted from contemporary and classic children's literature or trade books. High-quality artwork generally accompanies the selections. Interspersed throughout the student core reading text, one may also find poems, jokes, riddles, puzzles, informational essays, and special skill or concept lessons. Some core reading program student texts contain questions children should be able to answer after reading the selections. Intermediate-grade core reading texts often contain a glossary of words that students can refer to when decoding new words or to determine the meanings of unfamiliar or new words found in the text.

Dewitz and colleagues (2010) indicate that new core reading texts typically contain a short introductory reading passage followed by the main reading passage follow-up that is either a poem or nonfiction. Current core reading program student texts often include authentic literature selections that were published originally in individual trade books prior to their inclusion in the core anthology. However, because of costs involved in the reproduction and permission for use of original artwork, core reading publishers have sometimes cut the beautiful artwork that supports and sustains the text in many children's books (Reutzel & Larsen, 1995). The lack of artwork may be detrimental for beginning readers who often rely heavily on pictures for support to construct ongoing meaning throughout their initial readings of new or unfamiliar texts.

It is encouraging that newer core reading texts increasingly include information or nonfiction text selections. Expository texts help students increase their vocabularies as well as background or conceptual knowledge. Duke (2000) explains that information texts can be recognized by several distinctive features:

- A function to communicate information about the social or natural world
- Factual content
- Technical vocabulary
- Classificatory or definitional material
- Graphic elements like maps, graphs, and diagrams
- Varying text structures (e.g., cause and effect, problem and solution, compare and contrast)
- Repetition of topical themes

Duke (2000) found a scarcity of informational texts available in 20 first-grade classrooms selected from very low and very high socioeconomic status school districts. To compound this scarcity, there was relatively little informational material available in school libraries and on classroom walls and other display surfaces in the schools. As a result, young students in low socioeconomic classrooms read information texts only 3.6 minutes per day on average.

Moss and Newton (2001) investigated the amount of information text available in second-, fourth-, and sixth-grade core reading series, finding that only 16 to 20 percent of selections could be classified as information texts. The preponderance of selections were largely narrative or fictional (66 percent). In a more current analysis of selection types found in current programs, Dewitz and colleagues (2010, p. 65) identified an average of 29.4 percent of core reading selections as expository or information across four major core reading programs. Thus, one shortcoming of current programs is a relative lack of balance between fiction and nonfiction, depriving students of informational texts necessary for increasing student word knowledge and vocabulary. It is critical that teachers ensure that all students are exposed to a balanced diet of informational text, even if that means supplementing heavily the core reading program with additional nonfiction. At least one-half of the reading curriculum, if not more, should involve the reading of informational texts.

Beginning Reading Texts

Beginning core reading selections are designed to control word difficulty and decoding problems as well as text levels. Although teachers often feel the need to supple-

ment these texts with high-quality literature for read-alouds, these controlled texts serve two purposes: (1) providing students guided practice with decoding elements previously taught by the teacher and (2) offering sufficient reading challenge so as to not overwhelm young students' emerging reading skills.

Controlling Word Difficulty and Frequency.   Control over word difficulty in beginning reading texts presumably allows for the systematic introduction of a predetermined number of unfamiliar words in each story (Dewitz et al., 2010; Hiebert & Sailors, 2009; Hoffman, 2001). Control of word difficulty is typically achieved by using simpler words or words with fewer syllables in place of longer words and by shortening sentences. Core reading program publishers have, for many years, controlled the language of beginning reading texts by using simple one-syllable words. Town and Holbrook (1857), in the *Progressive Reading* series, were perhaps the earliest educators to explain the use of controlled texts in beginning reading materials:

> The authors, satisfied that the most simple language is best adapted to the class of pupils for whom this Reader is designed, have adhered, as strictly as possible, to the one-syllable system. They have departed from it only when necessary to avoid any stiffness of style, or weakness of expression, which might arise from too closely following it in every instance.

Compare the following 1865 and 2002 core reading program beginning texts.

1865

John stands by his father.
"I will be a good boy, father."

2002

We will load the boat.
We will load soap on the boat.
The boat will float.
We will load coats on the boat.*

*Reprinted with permission from The McGraw-Hill Companies from D. Fertig, *Load the Boat*, pp. 3–5, 2002.

Controlling the difficulty of words encountered in core reading stories supposedly renders text less difficult to read. However, research conducted decades ago by P. D. Pearson (1974) challenged the idea that shorter sentences are easier to read. Pearson found that short, choppy sentences are actually more difficult to read because explicit connecting or sequencing words such as *because, and, so, then, before,* and *after* are deleted from the text and consequently must be inferred by the reader in order to comprehend the text. Thus, short choppy sentences and simple words may render the word recognition tasks easier for beginning readers but may increase the difficulty of comprehending the text. Fortunately, most beginning reading selections are so simplistic that there is little for beginning readers to comprehend in undemanding text that is quite easy to understand.

Controlling Decoding Problems. In most currently published core reading programs students are provided supplemental reading books known as **decodable readers** (Dewitz et al., 2010; Foorman, Francis, Fletcher, Schatschneider, & Mehta, 1998; Hiebert & Sailors, 2009). Decodable texts are designed to provide extended teacher-guided practice in applying knowledge of particular phonic elements, such as short *a*, by controlling the phonic structure of the words used in these books (e.g., *Nan* and *Dan*).

Decodable readers are sold as an integral part of the newer core reading programs (Dewitz et al., 2010). An example of a decodable reader is shown in the following excerpt.

> **Liz** *(Short for Lizard)* *
> Liz can zip in.
> Liz can zip out.
> Liz can zigzag up.
> Liz can zigzag down.
> Liz can zap a bug.
> Zap! Liz has a bug for a snack.

Although decodable readers can be useful for guiding students to apply their phonics instruction in the act of reading a text, it should go without saying that students seldom encounter such contrived texts outside of school settings. As a consequence, controlling vocabulary by using decodable readers continues to draw criticism from some scholars and teachers on the grounds that these are senseless or "inconsiderate" texts that tend to cause students to perceive reading as primarily a decoding task rather than an act of constructing meaning (Allington, 1997; Armbruster, 1984; Hiebert & Martin, 2001; Hiebert & Sailors, 2009). The lack of real content or a discernable storyline in these decodable texts—particularly if they are overused—is suspected of causing children to quickly lose interest in reading.

Controlling Text Levels. Leveled texts are also sold as an integral part of today's core reading programs. Most current reading programs provide as many as four leveled books for each week's unit of reading instruction. The leveled books usually represent on-level, above-level, and below-level books as well as books for ELs.

Leveled books have been examined using any number of text indexes to determine gradients of difficulty, complexity, or challenge. Some publishers continue to level texts for difficulty by using obsolete readability formulas that measure numbers

*From Lee, J. (2002). *SRA Open Court*, Level 1, Practice Book 24, Phonics Readers, pp. 3–8. Copyright The McGraw-Hill Companies. Reprinted by permission.

of words in a sentence or numbers of syllables in words, such as the Dale-Chall, Fry, or Raygor readability formulas from the 1940s, 50s, and 60s. Some current core reading program publishers have determined the difficulty of leveled texts by using an approach developed by Fountas and Pinnell (1999; Pinnell & Fountas, 2002) called *A–Z leveling*. The A–Z approach for determining the difficulty or challenge level of beginning reading books is characterized by counting numbers of lines of on the page, consistent placement of pictures on the page, the repetition of syntactic units ranging from a phrase to a group of sentences (e.g., "Run, run, as fast as you can. You can't catch me, I'm the Gingerbread Man"), or other qualitative criteria.

Many current core reading program publishers have turned to the use of complex computer text difficulty analysis programs such as Lexiles, produced by Metametrics Corporation. Lexile procedures are well beyond the abilities of most classroom educators to apply in leveling books for instructional purposes. However, scientists have published online a significant number of titles of books already leveled using the Lexile approach (see www.lexile.com). Lexile levels generally run from 0 to over 2000 in increments of 50 points. For the elementary school, texts for grades 1 through 8 generally run from 200 to over 1200 Lexile points. Online conversion charts (see Web Resources at end of this chapter) are available for comparing the different types of book leveling processes described here and for helping teachers to interpret the levels assigned by these different text leveling approaches (see Figure 9.4). The leveled books provided by current core reading programs are intended to give teachers additional opportunities to guide the reading practice of students in appropriately challenging texts.

Workbooks and Worksheets

In many classrooms, the most used parts of the core reading program are the workbooks and worksheet activities (Osborn, 1985). In fact, if any part of a reading lesson has been neglected by teachers in core reading programs, it is seldom the workbook pages or worksheets (Durkin, 1984; Mason, 1983). Although this situation may have moderated in recent years, workbook pages and worksheets nevertheless remain an integral part of today's core reading programs (Dewitz et al., 2010). It appears that some publishers,

Figure 9.4

Conversion Guide for Leveled Texts

Developmental Category	Grade Level	Letter Level	Numeric Level	Lexile Level
Emergent	K	A	1	
		B	2	
		C	3,4	
Emergent/ Early	K/1	D	5,6	
		E	7,8	200–400
Early	1	F	9,10	
		G	11,12	
		H	13,14	
		I	15,16	
Early/Fluent	2	J	18	
		K	20	
		L	24	300–600
		M	28	
Fluent	3	N	30	
		O	34	500–800
		P	38	
	4	Q	40	
		R	40	600–900
	5	S	44	
		T	44	700–1000
		U	50	
	6	V	60	700–1000
		W	60	800–1050
		X	60	
Advanced Fluent	7	Y	70	850–1100
	8	Z	80	900–1150
	8+	Z+	90	1000–1200

Retrieved on June 22, 2010, from www.benchmarkeducation.com/teacher-resources/general/reading-level-guide.html. Conversion Guide for Leveled Texts developed by Benchmark Education Company. Reprinted by permission.

Figure 9.5

Core Reading Program Skill Practice/Workbook

From *SRA: Imagine It!* (2008). Skills Practice 2, Annotated Teacher's Edition. Copyright 2008 by the McGraw-Hill Companies, Inc. Reprinted by permission.

as evidenced by their continued inclusion of workbook pages or skill sheets as part and parcel of core reading programs (see Figure 9.5), continue to see seatwork as an important part of the school literacy program (Allington & Cunningham, 2006).

Workbook pages and worksheets are not intended to supplant time for structured, well-planned, and explicit reading instruction and teacher-guided practice of reading skills. Rather, workbooks and worksheets are designed for students to independently practice skills, strategies, and literary understandings previously explicitly taught and gradually released to the student by the teacher during guided practice. Also, workbooks and worksheets are often used as a type of formative or progress-monitoring "paper-and-pencil" assessment. In addition, many teachers also use workbooks and worksheets to manage, direct, or focus student activity in independent learning centers when the teacher is actively working with small groups of children in teacher-guided small-group reading instruction. Used in these ways, workbooks and worksheets play at least three distinct roles in classrooms—independent practice, progress-monitoring assessment, and classroom management to facilitate teacher-directed small-group reading instruction.

Past research has indicated that primary-grade students spend up to 70 percent of the time allocated for reading instruction—or 49 minutes per day—in independent practice or completion of worksheets, whereas less than 10 percent of total reading instructional time—or about 7 to 8 minutes per day—is devoted to silent reading. Other studies (Knapp, 1991) indicate that many teachers assign or provide time for only small amounts of real reading and writing—in some cases less than 5 minutes per day.

Jachym, Allington, and Broikou (1989) and Allington and Cunningham (2006) report that seatwork (independent completion of worksheets) is displacing many of the more important aspects of reading instruction, such as the acquisition of good books and time spent in actual reading. Based on these findings, it seems obvious that workbooks have been misused and overused. However, when teachers judiciously select workbook pages and worksheets to support and reinforce concepts and skills provided during teacher-guided instruction, students benefit from valuable independent practice and feedback on their progress in relation to specific reading skills, strategies, and literary understandings. Dole, Osborn, and Lehr (1990, pp. 8–15) provide six guidelines for assessing the worth of workbook and worksheet-type reading tasks in the Workbooks subtext for the Core Reading Programs: Adoption Guidelines project.

Standards and Guidelines for Analyzing Workbook Tasks

1. When analyzing the content of workbook tasks, look for tasks that
   - Are integrated with the lessons in the teacher's manual and with the student textbook

- Relate to the most important (and workbook-appropriate) instruction in the lessons
- Are based on the reading selections
- Use vocabulary that is from current or previous lessons
- Increase in difficulty as grade level increases

2. When analyzing the content of workbook task design, look for tasks for which
   - The student must read all of the possible choices before selecting an answer
   - Student responses can be judged correct or incorrect
   - Student responses indicate to the teacher what the student knows
   - Students can successfully complete part two of the task without successfully completing part one

3. When analyzing the practice and review tasks, look for tasks that provide
   - Sufficient practice
   - Independent practice
   - Extra practice
   - Systematic review

4. When analyzing instructional language, look for tasks that
   - Use language consistent with the rest of the program
   - Are accompanied by brief explanations of purpose or explanatory titles that students understand
   - Have clear and easy-to-follow instruction, with attention to consistency, sentence length, and directional steps

5. When evaluating reading and writing responses, look for tasks that
   - Provide opportunities for students to respond in their own words
   - Provide opportunities for students to apply several comprehension strategies or decoding skills in one task

6. When evaluating the considerateness to students, look for
   - Repeated use of task formats
   - Consistent responses
   - Occasional tasks that are fun
   - Few or no nonfunctional tasks

Reprinted by permission.

Workbooks and worksheets can be a valuable resource for teachers and students when applied correctly. On the other hand, when misused or overused, workbooks and worksheets can be a debilitating deterrent to students' reading growth and motivation.

Assessment

Although workbooks and worksheets can be used for informal progress-monitoring assessment of reading skill, strategy development, and literary understandings among students, most current core reading programs provide end-of-unit or end-of-book tests for summative evaluation of this learning (Dewitz et al., 2010). Core program assessments are generally **criterion-referenced tests (CRTs)** because the items included are directly related to the specific skills, strategies, or concepts taught in the core reading program's unit, level, or student text. As the stakes are raised higher and higher in terms of standardized assessment measures, many programs are correlating

Figure 9.6

Core Reading Program Teacher's Editions Show How Program Elements Correspond with Nationally Published Standardized Tests

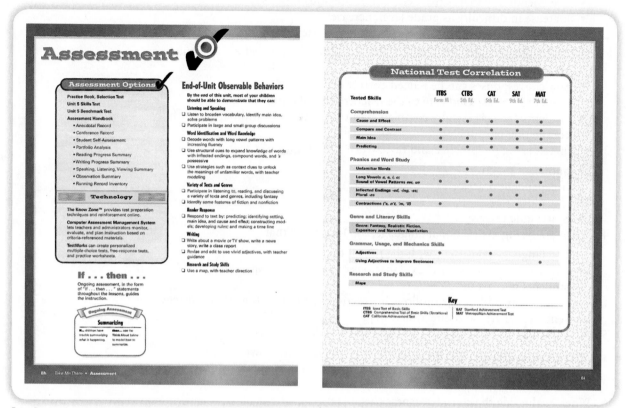

From *Reading Street Teacher Edition Grade 1 Vol. 5.* Copyright © 2007 Pearson Education, Inc., or its affiliates. Used by permission. All rights reserved.

skills, strategies, and literary understandings with nationally published standardized tests (see Figure 9.6).

Just as workbooks and worksheets can be abused, so can core reading program assessments (Paris & Hoffman, 2004). With the advent of Response to Intervention (RTI) models incorporated into regular education classroom practices, teachers are now asked to progress monitor students more frequently and with greater intent (Fuchs, Fuchs, & Vaughn, 2008). In many ways, we run the risk in this high-stakes testing environment of killing the cow by weighing too often and not feeding it enough!

Core reading program assessments should provide classroom teachers with efficient but reliable and valid information about the quantity and quality of children's literacy learning to inform, shape, and direct future instructional choices and selection of instructional interventions. Assessment results should not be used to label children or embarrass teachers. Two poignant examples of the misuse of test data are found in the books *First Grade Takes a Test* (Cohen, 1980) and *Testing Miss Malarkey* (Finchler, 2000). No single test score should ever form the basis for making life-changing decisions about children's learning or their teachers' competence. Administrators and teachers must be extremely cautious in the use and interpretation of single test scores.

Student Data Management Systems

A student data management system allows teachers to keep accurate records regarding each child's progress and response to instruction. Maintaining sufficient, accurate data on student responses to classroom instruction is an important part of the larger concept of student and teacher accountability. Most current core reading programs provide computer-based or electronic data management systems for keeping records on children's progress through the skills outlined in the scope and sequence chart of the program. Most often, the assessment of core reading skills still involves paper-and-pencil testing or worksheet administration. However, in recent years some core reading programs are providing teachers and students access to program assessments either on a CD or online. The scores obtained on these exercises are entered into a master list or record available electronically, tracking student progress throughout the elementary years.

However, surveys indicate that relatively few teachers, only 34 percent, use the assessments provided by the core reading program to track student progress (Paris, Paris, & Carpenter, 2002). This is unfortunate because current programs provide a full range of accessible assessments to progress monitor student response to instruction, including tests for screening or placement, benchmark measures, thematic reviews, weekly lesson testing, and diagnostic assessments in phonemic awareness, phonics, fluency, vocabulary, comprehension skills, strategies, and concepts (Dewitz et al., 2010).

Although increasingly elegant with the addition of CD-ROM technology and online availability, student data management systems should go well beyond keeping track of assessment scores. Carefully analyzing these scores and the individual responses to assessment items can help teacher gain insights into both students successes as well as their failures to understand and apply instructed skills, strategies, and concepts (Taylor, 2008).

Core Reading Programs: Summary

In summary, core reading programs are typically composed of three commonly provided elements—a teacher's edition, student text or anthology, and workbook/worksheets—as well as a host of supplementary kits, charts, cards, tests, CDs, online technology, picture cards, big books, additional practice exercises, and assessment/record-keeping systems (Dewitz et al., 2009, 2010).

Although core reading programs offer teachers a rich and easily accessible resource for providing systematic, sequenced, and structured reading instruction throughout the elementary and middle grades, teachers must nonetheless be careful to use these resources with judgment and skill. Recent analyses of core reading programs have shown them to be deficient in terms of the range, coherence, quantity, and quality of skill instruction and access to varied text types, narrative, poetic, and expository (Block & Duffy, 2008; Dewitz et al., 2009, 2010). Teachers may need to supplement core programs with access to trade books, additional guided practice, and explicit instruction. To be effective, teachers will need to regularly progress monitor students' responses to classroom reading instruction, as well as students' behaviors, interests, and motivation. When core reading programs are used judiciously as a resource by knowledgeable classroom teachers, they provide a valuable resource for schools, administrators, teachers, and students in teaching and learning to read.

Production of Core Reading Programs

Core Reading Programs (CRPs) are often controlled and owned by large, diversified corporations that do not focus exclusively on publishing for educational settings.

Instead, the publishers of CRPs are subsidiary corporations of larger and highly diversified corporate entities. CRPs are currently produced by a relative few big publishing houses that often offer more than one CRP for use in schools:

- Houghton Mifflin/Harcourt
- Macmillan/McGraw-Hill
- Scott Foresman

A chief editor typically oversees the production of a core reading program with the assistance of a senior authoring team, a group of individuals in the field of reading who are known and respected as experts. One unfortunate outcome of today's CRP production process is the diminishing role of the senior authoring team. Many CRP authors lament the fact that they have little to say about the literature or the lessons in current CRPs (Dewitz et al., 2010). In fact, it is inaccurate to call these reading experts program authors. It would be more accurate to call them program reviewers because they only give input on the literature selections and lessons that have been produced by in-house or out-of-house CRP development teams.

Core reading programs are often recognized and known by the name of the publishing houses that produce them although this is not always the case. Over the past 20 years, the number of core program publishers that have survived the intense competition, demanding and sometimes invasive state and federal standards, and the vicissitudes of economic change has dwindled from over 20 to a half dozen or fewer.

Minor revisions of core reading programs occur every few years; major revision cycles take place every 5 or 6 years. Major revisions are usually slated for completion during the same years that Texas, California, and Florida adopt new core reading programs statewide. Consequently, the "Texas, California, and Florida" effect is known to exert considerable influence on the content and quality of new core programs (Dewitz et al., 2010, pp. 43–45). In reading circles, one often hears the axiom, "As Texas, California, and Florida go, so goes the nation."

Organization of Core Reading Programs

Core reading programs are designed to take teachers and students through a series of reading selections, lessons, and activities toward increasingly sophisticated reading skills and understandings. Each core reading program typically provides several student texts or anthologies of reading selections for each grade level. For example, the teacher's edition of the *Scott Foresman Reading Street* (2007) core reading program describes the program's organization by grade level and theme, as shown in Figure 9.7.

Current CRP teacher's editions usually include all or most of the following important features:

- Philosophical statements
- A skills overview for each unit
- Classroom routines
- Suggestions for accommodating ELs and special-needs students
- Assessments tied to national and state standards and tests
- Technology supports including student data management systems
- Themes
- Projects
- Assessments
- A glossary
- A bibliography
- A scope and sequence chart

Figure 9.7

Organization of a Core Reading Program for K–6

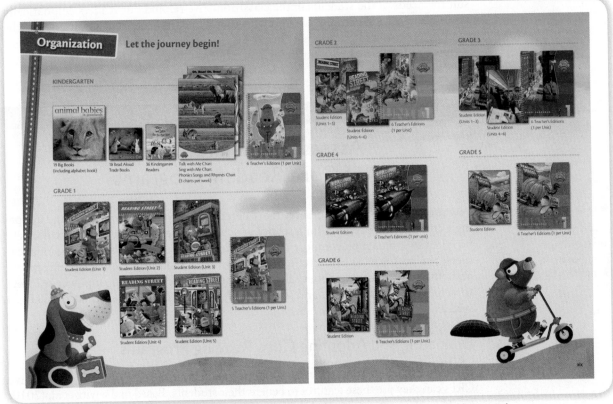

The scope and sequence chart is a year-by-year curricular plan, usually in chart form found in the CRP teacher's edition, which includes the instructional objectives and skills associated with a specific CRP. Objectives and skills are arranged in the scope and sequence chart by categories and grade levels. It is in the scope and sequence chart that teachers learn about the objectives of the CRP and the sequence of lessons designed to accomplish the objectives.

Most contemporary CRPs are organized into themed units, with several selections organized around a selected theme or topic; still others are organized into arbitrarily divided units of instruction. Most CRPs still follow a modified version of the directed reading thinking activity (DRTA) format developed by Russell Stauffer in 1969. This format can be represented in nine discrete parts or steps of a reading lesson.

1. Activating prior knowledge and building background
2. Delivering skill lessons in phonics, spelling, vocabulary, and comprehension
3. Previewing and predicting
4. Setting the purpose
5. Guiding the reading
6. Confirming predictions
7. Responding to comprehension discussion questions
8. Providing skill instruction and practice in oral language, writing, grammar, phonics, handwriting, comprehension, and fluency
9. Ideas and projects for enrichment

Reading lessons are arranged for teachers into a daily planner or day-by-day, weeklong format. It is intended that teachers will not use all of the resources in the CRP teacher's edition, but rather will select those resources on a daily basis that best suit the needs of the students in the classroom. We remind our readers emphatically that CRP teachers' editions are resources to augment the teacher's knowledge of the reading process and the needs of his or her students. CRP teachers' editions are not scripts to be followed without judgment, skill, and teacher decision making.

Classroom Assessment

Assessing the Effectiveness of Core Reading Programs

●●●

IRA Standards for Reading Professionals:
Standard 3, Elements 3.1, 3.2, 3.3

Few professional decisions deserve more careful attention than evaluating and adopting a core reading program for a school or school district. Because teachers will likely be asked to evaluate one or more core reading programs during their professional careers, teachers need to understand how to evaluate and select these CRPs effectively and efficiently. Learning about CRP adoption processes will also empower teachers to help reform, restructure, and strengthen future revisions and editions of CRPs as well as the adoption processes.

Evaluating and Adopting Core Reading Programs

Only after teachers are sufficiently well informed about the characteristics of effective CRPs can they use these features to benefit their students. Based on Dewitz et al. (2010, pp. 186–187), we recommend the following guidelines for CRP adoption processes:

- Create a CRP adoption committee.
- Set goals.
  - Review board policies, state laws, and district guidelines for CRP adoption processes, especially conflict of interest and ethics guidelines.
  - Study state and district objectives for grade-level reading instruction.
- Learn about evidence-based reading instruction and preferred instructional practices derived from research findings.
  - Examine relevant research reports and syntheses to learn what research says about specific elements and practices related to effective reading instruction.
  - Visit schools that are evidencing outstanding reading instructional outcomes to review practices and CRPs used in these settings.
  - Solicit input from outside reading experts at universities and research institutes or from state and federal offices of education.
- Select or develop a CRP evaluation instrument to be used by committee members during the adoption process.
  - Understand available CRP screening and evaluation tools.
  - Field test one or more of these tools with past CRP committee members who have experience in the process.
  - See free online resources such as *A Consumer's Guide to Evaluating a Core Reading Program* at http://reading.uoregon.edu/curricula/con_guide.php and the *Essential Guide to Selecting and Using Core Reading Programs* at

www.reading.org/General/Publications/Books/SupplementalContent/bk707_supplement.aspx.

- Carefully review and discuss the process with the CRP adoption committee members.
  - Who will make the final decision?
  - How will that person or group defend this decision to other stakeholders?
- Contact CRP publishers to review CRPs.
  - Identify the major CRPs of interest to review.
  - Arrange a central location for CRP materials to be stored and reviewed.
  - Schedule CRP publisher presentations to the adoption committee.
- Read and evaluate CRPs using the selected evaluation tool.
- Pilot CRPs with a few selected schools or classrooms within the district or school.
  - Decide who will pilot the CRP and how the data will be collected and analyzed.
  - Determine the duration of the CRP pilot.
  - Arrange with CRP publishers to provide the necessary materials for the CRP pilot.
- Negotiate contract prices for the CRPs with and without various supplementary materials.
  - Work out cost and amount of CRP publisher-provided inservice for teachers and curriculum leaders to learn about how to use the program if adopted.
- Review CRP evaluation data and make final recommendations.
  - Develop a communication plan to announce recommendations.
  - Prepare presentations for the school board, parent organizations, and teachers' union.
  - Write up purchase orders for individual schools or districts.
  - Create a staff professional development plan for implementing the newly adopted CRP.

Because many reading teachers are concerned with curriculum changes that reflect a decided move toward evidence-based reading instructional practices in CRPs, we strongly recommend that classroom professionals obtain Dewitz, Leahy, Jones, and Sullivan's (2010) materials, worksheets, and procedures for evaluating and adopting core reading programs (see website at end of chapter). These authors provide guides for grade-level program evaluation and selection, parent and community input forms, as well as classroom reading instruction observation guides for assessing the effectiveness of teachers using various CRPs during scheduled pilot projects prior to making a CRP selection. It would also be helpful for the CRP adoption committee to receive copies of *The Essential Guide to Selecting and Using Core Reading Programs* by Dewitz, Leahy, Jones, and Sullivan (2010) and published by the International Reading Association to study prior to beginning the process of adopting a new CRP in a school or school district.

A Consumer's Guide to Evaluating a Core Reading Program

Another instrument for evaluating CRPs was developed by Simmons and Kame'enui (2003) called *A Consumer's Guide to Evaluating a Core Reading Program* (see Figure 9.8). It focuses primarily on grades K through 3 and offers guidelines for evaluating the "Big Five" essentials of reading instruction identified by the National Reading Panel (2000): phonemic awareness, phonics, vocabulary, comprehension, and fluency.

Figure 9.8 Excerpts from *A Consumer's Guide to Evaluating a Core Reading Program*

Phonemic Awareness is the ability to hear and manipulate the sound structure of language. It is a strong predictor of reading success. Phonemic awareness is an auditory skill and consists of multiple components.

High-Priority Items—Phonemic Awareness Instruction

Rating	Criterion	Evidence		
		Initial Instruction	Week _____	Week _____
⦿⦿⦿	1. Allocates appropriate amount of daily time to blending, segmenting, and manipulating tasks until proficient. **(w)** [NRP, p. 2–41]			
⦿⦿⦿	2. Incorporates letters into phonemic awareness activities. **(w)** [NRP, p. 2–41]			

First-Grade Phonemic Awareness Instruction—High Priority
Tally the number of elements with each rating.   ⦿_____ ⦿_____ ⦿_____

High-Priority Items—Phonics Instruction

Rating	Criterion	Evidence		
		Initial Instruction	Week _____	Week _____
⦿⦿⦿	1. Progresses systematically from simple word types (e.g., consonant-vowel-consonant) and word lengths (e.g., number of phonemes) and word complexity (e.g., phonemes in the word, position of blends, stop sounds) to more complex words. **(ss)** [NRP, p. 2–132]			
⦿⦿⦿	2. Models instruction at each of the fundamental stages (e.g., letter–sound correspondences, blending, reading whole words). **(w)** and **(ss)**			

continued

High-Priority Items—Phonics Instruction

Rating	Criterion	Evidence		
		Initial Instruction	Week ___	Week ___
○ ● ●	3. Provides teacher-guided practice in controlled word lists and connected text in which students can apply their newly learned skills successfully. (**w**)			
○ ● ●	4. Includes repeated opportunities to read words in contexts in which students can apply their knowledge of letter–sound correspondences. (**w**) and (**ss**) [NRP, p. 3–28]			
○ ● ●	5. Uses decodable text based on specific phonics lessons in the early part of the first grade as an intervening step between explicit skill acquisition and the students' ability to read quality trade books. Decodable texts should contain the phonics elements and sight words that students have been taught. (**w**) and (**ss**)			

First-Grade Phonics and Instruction—High Priority
Tally the number of elements with each rating.

● ——— ● ● ——— ●

High-Priority Items—Connected Text and Fluency Instruction

Rating	Criterion	Evidence		
		Initial Instruction	Week ___	Week ___
○ ● ●	1. Introduces passage reading soon after students can read a sufficient number of words accurately. (**w**)			

Figure 9.8 Continued

High-Priority Items—Connected Text and Fluency Instruction

Rating	Criterion	Evidence		
		Initial Instruction	Week ___	Week ___
⬤⬤⬤	2. Contains regular words comprising letter sounds and word types that have been taught. **(w)** and **(ss)**			
⬤⬤⬤	3. Contains only high-frequency irregular words that have been previously taught. **(ss)**			
⬤⬤⬤	4. Uses initial stories/passages composed of a high percentage of regular words (minimum of 75–80% decodable words). **(w)**			
⬤⬤⬤	5. Builds toward a 60-word-per-minute fluency goal by end of grade. **(ss)** [NRP, p. 3–4]			
⬤⬤⬤	6. Includes sufficient independent practice materials of appropriate difficulty for students to develop fluency. **(w)** and **(ss)** [NRP, p. 3–28]			

First-Grade Connected Text and Fluency Instruction—High Priority
Tally the number of elements with each rating.   ⬤ ___   ⬤ ___   ⬤ ___

High-Priority Items—Vocabulary Instruction

Rating	Criterion	Evidence		
		Initial Instruction	Week ___	Week ___
⬤⬤	1. Provides direct instruction of specific concepts and vocabulary. **(w)**			

High-Priority Items—Vocabulary Instruction

Rating	Criterion	Evidence		
		Initial Instruction	Week ___	Week ___
⚪🔘⚫	2. Provides repeated and multiple exposures to critical vocabulary. **(w)** and **(st)**			
⚪🔘⚫	3. Integrates words into sentences and asks students to tell the meaning of the word in the sentence and to use it in a variety of contexts. **(w)**			

First-Grade Vocabulary Instruction—High Priority
Tally the number of elements with each rating. ⚫ _____ 🔘 _____ ⚪ _____

High-Priority Items—Reading Comprehension Instruction

Rating	Criterion	Evidence		
		Initial Instruction	Week ___	Week ___
⚪🔘⚫	1. Guides students through sample text in which teachers think out loud as they identify the components of story structure. **(w)** [NRP, p. 4–122]			
⚪🔘⚫	2. Provides plentiful opportunities to listen to and explore narrative and expository text forms and to engage in interactive discussion of the messages and meanings of the text. **(ss)** [NRP, p. 4–109]			
⚪🔘⚫	3. Explicitly teaches critical comprehension strategy (e.g., main idea, literal, inferential, retell, prediction). **(w)** and **(ss)**			

First-Grade Reading Comprehension Instruction—Discretionary
Tally the number of elements with each rating. ⚫ _____ 🔘 _____ ⚪ _____

continued

Figure 9.8 Continued

Summary of First-Grade Ratings

High-Priority Items

Phonemic Awareness Instruction (2)	● ● ○ __ __ __
Phonics Instruction (5)	● ● ○ __ __ __
Irregular Words Instruction (2)	● ● ○ __ __ __
Connected Text and Fluency Instruction (6)	● ● ○ __ __ __
Vocabulary Development (3)	● ● ○ __ __ __
Reading Comprehension Instruction (3)	● ● ○ __ __ __

First-Grade High-Priority Totals	● ● ○ __ __ __

Discretionary Items

Phonemic Awareness Instruction (5)	● ● ○ __ __ __
Phonics Instruction (4)	● ● ○ __ __ __
Irregular Words Instruction (2)	● ● ○ __ __ __
Connected Text and Fluency Instruction (2)	● ● ○ __ __ __
Vocabulary Development (3)	● ● ○ __ __ __
Reading Comprehension Instruction (3)	● ● ○ __ __ __

First-Grade Discretionary Totals	● ● ○ __ __ __

First-Grade Design Features

● ● ○	1. Aligns and coordinates the words used in phonics/word recognition activities with those used in fluency building.
● ● ○	2. Provides ample practice on high-priority skills.
● ● ○	3. Provides explicit and systematic instruction.
● ● ○	4. Includes systematic and cumulative review of high-priority skills.
● ● ○	5. Demonstrates and builds relationships between fundamental skills leading to higher-order skills.

Additional Comments

From Simmons, D. C., & Kame'enui, E.J. (2003). *A Consumer's Guide to Evaluating a Core Reading Program, Grades K–3: A Critical Elements Analysis.* Eugene: University of Oregon. Reprinted by permission.

Recent Evaluations of Core Reading Programs

A number of evaluations of prominent core reading programs and supplemental reading programs have been conducted in recent years by various state departments of education (SDE). Florida, Oregon, Maryland, Indiana, Ohio, Kentucky, California, Utah, and Texas are just a few of the states conducting such reviews in connection with Reading First funding. Kentucky and Ohio provide two good examples available on the Internet. To see Ohio's core reading program evaluation instrument online refer to the URL at the end of this chapter.

In many cases, the SDEs have opted to use Simmons and Kame'enui's (2003) *A Consumer's Guide to Evaluating a Core Reading Program* to aid them in this process. One such evaluation on CRP effectiveness was the *Oregon Reading First Center (ORFC): Review of Comprehensive Programs* (ORFC Curriculum Review Panel, 2004). Despite only considering reading programs for grades K to 3 on measures of phonemic awareness, phonics, and fluency while ignoring reading comprehension and vocabulary development, the report is useful for examining the relative strengths of the evaluated programs in the three areas considered.

In Table 9.1 we offer a summary of the reading programs reviewed and their relative rating in each of the three areas considered. Our rankings summary from the ORFC reflects the mean score on "high priority" skills for all grade levels reviewed. Also, please note that we are only including the ORFC findings for what we considered to be CRPs. We will examine their findings for two other supplemental reading programs (Reading Mastery and Success for All) later in this chapter.

As noted, Dewitz, Leahy, Jones, and Sullivan (2010) conducted a lengthy evaluation of CRPs and also published a major research report focused specifically on reading comprehension instruction provided in major CRPs adopted across the United States. They found that many CRPs strongly endorsed by the Oregon Reading First Center using *A Consumer's Guide to Evaluating a Core Reading Program* (Simmons & Kame'enui, 2003) were deficient in reading comprehension instruction. This

Table 9.1

The Oregon Reading First Center (ORFC) Review of Reading Programs in the Areas of Phonemic Awareness, Phonics, and Fluency

Core Program	Ranking: Phonemic Awareness Instruction	Ranking: Phonics Instruction	Ranking: Fluency	Overall Ranking
Houghton Mifflin	1	1	2	1
Open Court (McGraw-Hill)	4	4	1	2
Harcourt	2	2	3	2
Scott Foresman	5	3	4	4
Macmillan (McGraw-Hill)	3	5	5	5
Wright Group	6	6	6	6
Rigby	7	7	7	6

Data from http://reading.uoregon.edu.

should not be too surprising because simply adopting a CRP using *A Consumer's Guide to Evaluating a Core Reading Program* does not evaluate the vocabulary or comprehension instruction. More seriously, McGill-Franzen, Zmach, Solic, and Zeig (2006) found that students in CRPs recommended by the Oregon Reading First project were less likely to pass state reading assessments than were students in schools or districts using other CRPs not recommended. Based on these findings, a failure to evaluate CRP's instruction across the five essential elements of effective reading instruction results in a deficient review of CRP quality during the adoption process that may negatively impact the quality of the instruction ultimately provided.

Evidence-Based Teaching Practices

Evidence-Based Reading Instruction Programs

● ● ●

IRA Standards for Reading Professionals: Standard 2, Elements 2.1, 2.2, 2.3

Response to Intervention: Instruction; Systemic and Comprehensive Approaches

To determine which programs to review in this section, we turned to the What Works Clearinghouse (WWC) reading program review found online (see the URL at the end of this chapter). We will review the evidence presented for major, bestselling CRPs generally available for adoption by U.S. and Canadian schools and school districts. Afterward, we will present information about effective programs for classroom instruction that are not among the most widely used or adopted CRPs in schools and school districts.

Houghton Mifflin: *Invitations to Literacy*

A CRP developed by the Houghton Mifflin Company *Invitations to Literacy* is a K to 8 core instruction program available nationally and internationally. The philosophy guiding program development is that literacy instruction should stimulate, teach, and extend students' communication and thinking skills so that they can become effective readers, writers, and lifelong learners. *Invitations to Literacy* (2008) is organized around thematic units. The CRP includes hands-on activities that allow students to collaborate or share information on a theme-related project with other classrooms around the world (for example, participating in a collaborative poem-writing exercise) and virtual field trips to Internet sites that have content, activities, and projects related to the theme.

The What Works Clearinghouse review made the following summary evaluation: "The WWC identified 4 studies of *Houghton Mifflin: Invitations to Literacy* that were published or released between 1993 and 2008. . . . No studies of *Houghton Mifflin: Invitations to Literacy* that fall within the scope of the Beginning Reading protocol meet WWC evidence standards. The lack of studies meeting WWC evidence standards means that, at this time, the WWC is unable to draw any conclusions based on research about the effectiveness or ineffectiveness of *Houghton Mifflin: Invitations to Literacy*" (What Works Clearinghouse, 2008a).

SRA/McGraw-Hill: *Open Court Reading*

Open Court Reading is a core reading program for grades K through 6 published by SRA/McGraw-Hill. It is designed to explicitly teach decoding, comprehension, inquiry and investigation, and writing in systematic progression. At the beginning of each unit of instruction in a section entitled "Preparing to Read," lessons focus on phonemic awareness, sounds and letters, phonics, fluency, and word knowledge. In the second part of each unit, called "Reading and Responding," reading for understanding is emphasized by engaging students in reading literature and providing instruction in comprehension, inquiry, and practical reading skills and strategies. In the final part of each unit of instruction, labeled "Language Arts," instruction focuses on developing students' communication skills by working on spelling, vocabulary, and the writing process, as well as English language conventions such as grammar, speaking, and penmanship while also providing basic computer skills for composition.

The What Works Clearinghouse (WWC) reviewed *Open Court Reading* in the following summary evaluation: "The WWC identified 30 studies of *Open Court Reading* that were published or released between 1985 and 2007. No studies of *Open Court Reading* that fall within the scope of the Beginning Reading review meet WWC evidence standards. The lack of studies meeting WWC evidence standards means that, at this time, the WWC is unable to draw any conclusions based on research about the effectiveness or ineffectiveness of *Open Court Reading*. It is noteworthy, that this CRP is among the most well researched programs (30 studies published) even though the quality of the research did not meet the WWC's stringent standards for rigorous design and reporting" (What Works Clearinghouse, 2008b).

Macmillan/McGraw-Hill: *Treasures Reading*

Treasures Reading is a K through 6 comprehensive reading language arts program published by Macmillan/McGraw-Hill, containing authentic literature and high-quality information texts at a variety of grade levels. CD-based and online games, activities, and interactive whiteboard resources are available with this new CRP. Units of instruction are organized thematically and offer teachers a weeklong lesson plan divided into daily elements of instruction, text reading, and other instructional activities. Leveled readers, both narrative and expository, practice books, intervention anthologies, teacher-guided lessons, picture cards, information cards, home–school connections for the computer, as well as a host of differentiated practice activity sheets available in paper copy, CD, and online are provided. The program offers teacher management systems support and help for English learners (ELs). High-quality literature coupled with explicit instruction and ample practice ensures that students grow as lifelong readers and writers. Assessments are provided as well as decodable books for phonics practice.

The What Works Clearinghouse has not reviewed the *Treasures Reading* CRP because the 2009 edition is new as of this writing. Thus no evidence is available to draw any conclusions based on research about the effectiveness or ineffectiveness of *Treasures Reading*.

Houghton-Mifflin Harcourt: *Story Town*

Story Town is a K through 6 comprehensive reading language arts program published by Harcourt. This CRP contains authentic literature and high-quality information texts at a variety of grade levels. Similar to other CRP offerings, this program provides teachers CD-based and online games, activities, and interactive whiteboard resources. Units of instruction are organized thematically and offer teachers a weeklong lesson plan divided into daily elements of instruction, text reading, and other instructional activities. Leveled readers, both narrative and expository, practice books, intervention anthologies, teacher-guided lessons, picture cards, information cards, home–school connections for the computer, as well as a host of differentiated practice activity sheets available in paper copy, CD, and online. The *Story Town* program offers teachers online management systems support and other special supports for English learners (ELs). High quality literature coupled with explicit instruction and ample practice opportunities ensure that students grow as life-long readers and writers. Theme, unit, and benchmark assessments are provided to support this program as well as decodable books for phonics practice.

The What Works Clearinghouse has not reviewed the *Story Town Reading* CRP because the 2009 edition is new as of this writing. Thus no research evidence has been made available as of this date to draw any conclusions based on research about the effectiveness or ineffectiveness of *Story Town Reading*.

Success for All

Success for All (SFA) is a whole-school reform model that includes a reading, writing, and oral language development program for students in prekindergarten through eighth grade. Classroom reading instruction is delivered in daily 90-minute blocks to students grouped by reading ability. Immediate intervention with tutors who are certified teachers is given each day to those students who are having difficulty reading at the same level as their classmates.

Originally developed for struggling readers, the goal of the SFA program is to have all children reading on grade level by third grade, with no retentions and referrals to special education for reading problems. Robert Slavin, Director of the Center for Research and Effective Schooling for Disadvantaged Students at Johns Hopkins University, and his colleagues developed the SFA program. The SFA program is grounded on three premises:

1. The primary-grade classroom is the best place to work on ensuring children's school success.
2. Additional instruction should be provided to students as soon as they are identified as needing it.
3. Educators need to think creatively about the use of school resources, personnel, and instructional time.

SFA focuses on quality reading instruction in grades K to 3 as well as providing supplementary support in the form of individual tutoring sessions. Students are placed into heterogeneous classroom groupings for most of the day, but in the 90-minute reading instructional block, children are regrouped into "ability" groups of 15 to 20 students across the grade levels 1 through 3. Regrouping according to reading levels allows direct whole-group instruction and is intended to eliminate the overreliance on seatwork and worksheets found in many classrooms.

For students who are not responsive to whole-class instruction in their reading groups, supplementary individual tutoring for 20 minutes per day is provided in the SFA program. Tutoring sessions focus on the same strategies and skills taught in the whole-class sessions and, whenever possible, the classroom teacher is freed up by the use of classroom aides to provide the tutoring sessions. SFA also recommends that children attend half-day preschool and full-day kindergarten to accelerate progress in learning to read successfully. Multiple evaluations have shown that SFA is an effective program for reducing referrals to special education and grade-level retentions. However, studies indicate that SFA has not achieved its stated goal of helping every child read on grade level by the end of third grade (Slavin, Madden, Dolan,

Annie Fuller

& Wasik, 1996; Slavin, Madden, Karweit, Dolan, & Wasik, 1992; Slavin, Madden, Karweit, Livermon, & Dolan, 1990).

In the *Oregon Reading First Center (ORFC): Review of Comprehensive Programs* (ORFC Curriculum Review Panel, 2004), SFA was fairly weak in the areas of phonemic awareness (6th), phonics (7th), and fluency (6th) when compared to eight other leading core programs. One study of SFA meets the What Works Clearinghouse (WWC) evidence standards and six studies meet WWC evidence standards with reservations. Altogether, the studies included nearly 4,000 students attending more than 70 elementary schools across the United States. The seven studies focused on students in grades K through 3 who received the SFA intervention for varying amounts of time.

Based on these seven studies, the WWC considers the extent of evidence for SFA to be medium to large for alphabetics, comprehension, and general reading achievement. No studies that meet WWC evidence standards with or without reservations addressed fluency. Success for All was found to have positive effects on alphabetics, mixed effects for comprehension, and potentially positive effects on general reading achievement.

Classwide Peer Tutoring

Classwide peer tutoring (CWPT) is a peer-assisted instructional strategy designed to be integrated with most core reading programs. This approach provides students with increased opportunities to practice reading skills by asking questions and receiving immediate feedback from a peer tutor. Pairs of students take turns tutoring each other to provide needed practice in reading concepts and skills initially taught by the teacher. The teacher must create age-appropriate peer teaching materials for the peer tutors; these materials take into account tutees' language skills and disabilities. CWPT can be used for content area subjects in addition to the teaching of reading.

A single study of CWPT met the What Works Clearinghouse evidence standards. The study included more than 200 students from six urban elementary schools in

Kansas. The WWC considers the extent of evidence for CWPT to be small in general reading achievement. No studies that met WWC evidence standards with or without reservations addressed alphabetics, fluency, or comprehension. Thus, in summary, CWPT was found by the WWC to have potentially positive effects on general reading achievement.

Little Books

Little Books are book sets designed for interactive or dialogic oral book reading between parents and children or teachers and students. Little Books focus on thematic topics familiar to children. They are written with significant numbers of high-frequency words and use simple phrases and sentences. Little Books also have strong links between illustrations and text.

One study of Little Books met the What Works Clearinghouse evidence standards. The study included 325 kindergarten students from 12 rural and urban schools in Newfoundland, Canada. Three variations on using Little Books (at home only, at school only, and both at home and school) were compared to a condition that did not use Little Books.

The WWC considers the extent of evidence for Little Books to be small for general reading achievement. No studies of Little Books that met WWC standards with or without reservations addressed outcomes in the domains of alphabetics, fluency, and comprehension. Little Books was found by WWC-sponsored researchers reviewing this CRP to have potentially positive effects on general reading achievement.

Response to Intervention (RTI)

Supplementary Reading Intervention Programs

IRA Standards for Reading Professionals: Standard 4, Elements 4.1, 4.2

Response to Intervention: Responsive Teaching and Differentiation

In 1998, Pikulski reviewed the effectiveness of several national reading programs designed to prevent reading failure and assist students who struggle with learning to read. Later, similar reviews of the effectiveness of supplemental intervention programs were published by other researchers, committees, and state departments of education (e.g., Maryland Evaluation Committee, 2006; ORFC Curriculum Review Panel, 2004; St. John & Loescher, 2001) to help us better understand their relative merits. Most recently, supplemental reading instruction programs have been thoroughly reviewed and the results have been published on the What Works Clearinghouse website of the U.S. Department of Education Institute of Education Sciences. The programs discussed in this section are among those rated as showing at least small or moderate effects for raising students' reading achievement when implemented as small-group or one-to-one interventions with struggling or diverse-needs learners.

Reading Recovery

Reading Recovery, developed by clinical child psychologist Marie Clay, is an early intervention program designed to reduce reading failure in the first grade for the lowest performing 20 percent of students. The aim of the program is to help low-achieving children catch up to the level of their age-related peers. Reading Recovery

(RR) was imported to the United States by faculty at the Ohio State University (Allington, 1992). Reading Recovery teachers enroll in a yearlong course of graduate studies with regular follow-up professional development seminars to keep training current and approved (Lyons & Beaver, 1995). Teachers of RR must receive training from an approved RR teacher trainer at one of several approved sites throughout the nation.

The average RR student is recovered from below-grade-level performance in an average of 12 to 14 weeks. After recovery, children show normal development after release from the program. Students in New Zealand and in the United States demonstrate the substantial positive effects this invention has on young children's reading and writing development (Clay, 1990a; DeFord, Lyons, & Pinnell, 1991; Pinnell, DeFord, & Lyons, 1994).

Children selected for the RR program receive one-to-one, intensive daily reading instruction for 30 minutes. During this instructional period, teachers and children engage in five major activities in a sequenced and structured format.

Click on A+RISE—Literacy Strategies in the MyEducationLab (www.myeducationlab.com) for your course. Next, select the Strategy Card Index tab, scroll to Reading for Emergent and Beginning Readers, and select the Modified Reading Recovery Lesson strategy.

1. The first activity is the rereading of at least two familiar books ("familiar rereads") students have read previously with the assistance and guidance of the RR teacher, who also takes a daily "running record" of each student's oral reading.

2. During a running record, the teacher notes which words are read accurately or inaccurately and analyzes the inaccuracies for the cue system the student uses or neglects to use to inform upcoming instructional emphasis and planning.

3. The teacher and student work with letters and words. A typical activity is word-making using plastic magnetic letters on a cookie sheet. The teacher might show the word *ran* and ask the child to blend the sounds to pronounce the word. Then the teacher might remove the *r*, substitute *f*, and ask the child to blend the new sound to get the word *fan*.

4. Next, the child dictates a sentence or two; this is called a *story* in RR terminology. The teacher helps the child write the "story" by stretching words with the child, encouraging him or her to write the letter for each sound to form each word. After each word is written, the teacher asks the student to reread the words until the entire sentence is written. After reading the entire sentence, the teacher cuts the sentence into words strips and asks the student to reorder the word strips into the sentence.

5. The final activity in an RR lesson is the introduction of a new story. The teacher has preread the story and noted challenges and obstacles the child might face in his or her reading. The teacher walks the student through the pictures, introducing new vocabulary, sounding out "tricky" words with the student (often using a small whiteboard and marker), and discussing any unfamiliar concepts or language. Then the child reads the book with careful guidance, support, and feedback from the teacher.

Some educators have suggested that RR may be too expensive to realistically implement on a wide scale in the United States, where the reading failure rate exceeds 20 percent. However, with over 80 percent of children in RR moving to discontinuance and grade-level performance in less than a semester of intensive instruction and continuing to make acceptable progress, it seems that RR is substantially more cost-effective than are many of the commonly tried remedial options, including special education, for addressing the needs of low-performing children (Dyer, 1992).

In their 2007 review of the Reading Recovery program, the What Works Clearinghouse rated RR as highly effective in assisting struggling readers in improving general reading achievement. Reading Recovery received their highest or next-to-highest ratings for alphabetics (phonics and word attack skills), reading fluency, and comprehension growth as well.

Early Intervention in Reading

Early Intervention in Reading (EIR) is a program designed to provide extra instruction to groups of students at risk of failing to learn to read. The EIR program uses picture books to stress instruction in phonemic awareness, phonics, and contextual analysis, along with repeated reading and writing. In grades K to 2 the program is based on whole-class instruction, with supplemental small-group instruction provided to struggling readers. In grades 3 to 4, the program consists of small-group instruction for 20 minutes, 4 days a week. Teachers are trained for 9 months using workshops and an Internet-based professional development program.

One study of EIR meets What Works Clearinghouse evidence standards. That study included 12 teachers and 59 students in first grade from one Midwestern state. Based on this one study, the WWC considers the extent of evidence for EIR to be small for alphabetics and comprehension. No studies that meet WWC evidence standards examined the effectiveness of EIR in the fluency or general reading achievement domains. EIR was found to have potentially positive effects on alphabetics and comprehension.

Reading Mastery

Reading Mastery is a supplemental reading program best suited to students having severe reading problems, for whom traditional programs and methods have failed. It may also be useful as a supplemental reading program for students at high risk of reading failure and for English language learners (Gunn, Biglan, Smolkowski, & Ary, 2000; Gunn, Smolkowski, Biglan, & Black, 2002). The What Works Clearinghouse describes the program as follows:

> Reading Mastery is a direct instruction program designed to provide explicit, systematic instruction in English language reading. Reading Mastery is available in two versions, Reading Mastery Classic levels I and II (for use in grades K–3) and Reading Mastery Plus, an integrated reading-language program for grades K–6. The program begins by teaching phonemic awareness and sound-letter correspondence and moves into word and passage reading, vocabulary development, comprehension, and building oral reading fluency. Later lessons continue to emphasize accurate and fluent decoding while teaching students the skills necessary to read and comprehend and to learn from expository text. Lessons are designed to be fast-paced and interactive. Students are grouped by similar reading level, based on program placement tests. The program includes placement assessments and a continuous monitoring system.

Reading Mastery was originally developed by Siegfried Engelmann under the title Distar Reading for use in Project Follow Through as part of the direct instruction teaching model. It is marketed by SRA/McGraw-Hill.

In the *Oregon Reading First Center (ORFC): Review of Comprehensive Programs* (ORFC Curriculum Review Panel, 2004), Reading Mastery ranked highest in high-priority standards of all nine programs reviewed in the areas of phonemic awareness, phonics, and fluency. There is no extant impartial evidence we can find as to Reading Mastery's benefits to vocabulary learning or comprehension development. The What Works Clearinghouse rated Reading Mastery as having "potentially positive effects," though this evaluation is based on only one recorded study with English learners.

Reading Expeditions: *Language, Literacy, & Vocabulary!*

The National Geographic Society, a nonprofit organization famous for high-quality publications, has introduced a new informational text series called *Language, Literacy, & Vocabulary!* (LLV). The Reading Expeditions component of *Language, Literacy, & Vocabulary!* for students in grades 3 through 8 uses a powerful "sheltered-instruction approach" that combines essential science and social studies content with nonfiction reading skills and strategies. This affordable program features the following:

- 48 high-interest, age-appropriate science and social studies titles
- Key vocabulary repeated and applied in different contexts
- Content broken down into manageable units
- Limited text loads; simple text layouts and sentence patterns
- Academic vocabulary with on-page definitions
- Comprehension strategies and fluency practice
- Research and writing opportunities
- Rich instructional support and tools based on latest research
- Differentiated instruction for various stages of English language proficiency and reading development
- Alignment with national and state standards

McNabb (2006) summarized a recent study of the effectiveness of *Language, Literacy, & Vocabulary!* as follows:

> The study was conducted in urban Illinois public schools with 259 students in 4 schools, 90 students in the treatment groups and 169 students in the control groups. . . . A thorough analysis of the data collected indicates that the students in treatment groups made statistically significant gains in their content area literacy development compared with students who did not use the *Language, Literacy, & Vocabulary!* curriculum. In each curriculum group, the mean improvement from pretest to posttest was substantially higher for the students in the treatment groups.

Language, Literacy, & Vocabulary! has been adopted as a key supplemental program in the Memphis research study of the federal Striving Readers project because of its infusion of scientifically based reading research (SBRR) in an appealing informational text format.

Scott Foresman: *Early Reading Intervention*

The *Scott Foresman Early Reading Intervention* is designed to provide at-risk kindergarten and first-grade students with an intervention to improve reading achievement. A teacher or teacher aide delivers 126 30-minute daily lessons to small groups of two to five students. The components of the intervention include four teacher guides and resource packages that accompany each teacher guide.

Early Reading Intervention is organized in a carefully planned sequence of skills and the explicit instruction and systematic review are intended to ensure student success. The first 15 minutes of the lesson focus on phonological awareness and alphabetic understanding and the next 15 minutes center on writing and spelling. An

Assessment Handbook that accompanies the *Early Reading Intervention* includes a placement test, progress monitoring, and exit tests.

A 5-year longitudinal research study of the *Scott Foresman Early Reading Intervention* examined 441 kindergarten children from seven Title I schools in the Pacific Northwest. Results indicated that students who participated in the *Scott Foresman Early Reading Intervention* exceeded established DIBELS subtest benchmarks at least 2 months earlier and showed greater achievement than the students in other comparative interventions. The content and instructional design of the *Scott Foresman Early Reading Intervention* is aligned with current scientifically based reading research. Scientific research supports the use of this intervention to prevent reading difficulties in kindergarten and first grade students based on a review of this program by researchers at the Florida Center for Reading Research (n.d.).

How Can Core Reading Programs Be Adapted to Assist the Struggling Reader?

Struggling readers benefit by reading the same text more than once. Called *repeated readings,* the teacher typically introduces the story as a shared book or story experience, after which students attempt to read the book alone or with a friend (Routman, 1988). If the story has rhyme or a regular pattern, it may be sung or chanted. Repeated readings of stories help children achieve a sense of accomplishment, improve comprehension, and build fluency.

Many times, at-risk readers are very reluctant to become risk takers. Teachers simply must find ways of breaking the ice for them and create classroom safety nets. Supported, or "buddy," reading allows students to read aloud core reading program stories, either taking turns or in unison. By rereading these supported selections, students' fluency and comprehension improve. Another variation is for teacher–student combinations to read together. Similar to the procedure known as *neurological impress* (Hollingsworth, 1978), the student and teacher read aloud in unison at a comfortable rate. For first readings, the teacher usually assumes the lead in terms of volume and pace. In subsequent repeated readings during NIM, the student is encouraged to assume the lead.

What Effective Programs Are Available for Helping Students with Diverse Cultural or Language Needs Succeed?

The Bilingual Cooperative Integrated Reading and Composition (BCIRC) program, an adaptation of the Cooperative Integrated Reading and Composition (CIRC) program, was designed to help Spanish-speaking students succeed in reading Spanish and then making a successful transition to English reading. The Cooperative Integrated Reading and Composition (CIRC) is a comprehensive reading and writing program for students in grades 2 through 8. It includes story-related activities, direct instruction in reading comprehension, and integrated reading and language arts activities. Pairs of students (grouped either by or across ability levels) read to each other, predict how stories will end, summarize stories, write responses, and practice spelling, decoding, and vocabulary. Within cooperative teams of four, students work to understand the main idea of a story and work through the writing process. The CIRC process includes teacher instruction, team practice, peer assessment, and team/partner recognition. The Spanish version of the program, Bilingual Cooperative Integrated Reading and Composition (BCIRC), was designed for grades 2 to 5. In this adaptation of CIRC, students complete tasks that focus on reading, writing, and language activities in Spanish and English, while working in small cooperative learning groups. One study of BCIRC met the What Works Clearinghouse evidence standards with reservations. The BCIRC study included 222 students in second and third grades from seven schools in El Paso, Texas. BCIRC was found to have potentially positive effects on reading achievement and English language development.

Students who do not possess first-language literacy should be taught to read and write in their native language if possible to support and validate them as worthwhile individuals. In addition, reading instruction in children's first language helps them capitalize on what they already know about their primary language and culture to build concepts that can facilitate the acquisition of English (August & Shanahan, 2006; Freeman & Freeman, 1992; Krashen & Biber, 1988). In any case, teachers must be sensitive to these students' special needs, which include needs for safety and security, to belong and be accepted, and to have self-esteem (Peregoy & Boyle, 1993).

Teachers should help English as a second language (ESL) or English learners (EL) feel at ease when they arrive in the classroom by assigning them a "personal buddy" who, if possible, speaks the language of the newcomer. This buddy is assigned to help the new student through the school day, routines, and so on. Another approach is to avoid changes in the classroom schedule by following a regular and predictable routine each day, which provides a sense of security. To create a sense of belonging, assign the student to a home group for an extended period of time. A home group offers a small social unit of concern focused on helping the newcomer adapt to everyday life. Finally, self-esteem is enhanced when an individual's worth is affirmed. Opportunities for the newcomer to share her or his language and culture during daily events in the classroom provide a useful way to integrate her or him into the ongoing classroom culture.

To help ESL or EL students succeed in classrooms where core reading programs are the focus of instruction, Law and Eckes (1990, p. 92) recommend the following:

- Supplement the core reading program as much as possible with language experience stories.
- Encourage extensive reading. Gather core reading program student texts or anthologies from as many different levels as possible. Also acquire easier textbooks in content areas as well as trade books to provide a wide range of reading topics.
- Expose children to the many different types of reading available in the "real" world (magazines, *TV Guide*, newspapers, product labels, signs, etc.).

Click on A+RISE— Literacy Strategies in the MyEducationLab (www. myeducationlab.com) for your course. Next, select the Strategy Card Index tab, scroll to English Language Learners, and select the Using Questions to Teach English Language Learners strategy.

Motivation and Engagement

Programs and Standards Focused on Motivation and Engagement

For many years, researchers have found that reading comprehension is positively affected when students are interested in the reading materials (Asher, 1980; Corno &

IRA Standards for Reading Professionals: Standard 5, Element 5.2

Randi, 1997). This is so much the case that interest in reading materials has been shown also to compensate for a student's lack of comprehension strategies specifically and reading ability generally (Sweet, 1997).

The Student Reading Interest Survey (SRIS)

The Student Reading Interest Survey (SRIS) provides teachers with an efficient and effective tool to gain insights into student interests (see Figure 9.9). To administer the SRIS to primary-age students you will need the following materials:

- One laminated copy of the questions found in the Student Reading Interest Survey
- One paper copy for recording individual student responses
- One paper copy for recording categories of class responses

Once the necessary materials are obtained, schedule a time during the day to meet with students individually to administer the SRIS. Using a laminated copy of the SRIS, seat the child comfortably next to you at a table in a quiet corner of the classroom. (This survey may also be given by an aide or volunteer so long as he or she has been trained to completely record answers.) Ask children each question and record the answers given. After each response, be sure to tell each child that if he or she remembers anything else to tell you to feel welcome to share it at a later time.

After the entire class has been surveyed, compile the individual responses into a class survey response profile. Record abbreviated answers to each question for each

Figure 9.9

Student Reading Interest Survey

In-School Interests

What is the title of your favorite book that you have read?
Do you have a favorite book title that someone has read to you?
What kinds of books do you like to read on your own?
Do you have favorite books, magazines, or comic books at home?
Do you ever read the newspaper at home? If so, what parts of the newspaper do you read?
What is your favorite school subject (other than recess and lunch)?
Have you ever done a special research project? What was the topic?

Out-of-School Interests

What do you do for fun on weekends or after school?
Do you have a hobby? If so, what?
What is your favorite TV show?
What is your favorite movie?
Do you play sports? If so, what?
Do you like animals or have a pet?
Do you have favorite video or computer games?
If you search the Internet, what do you generally look for as you search?
Have you ever collected something like coins, stamps, and so on? If you have, what?

From Reutzel and Cooter, *Strategies for Reading Assessment and Instruction*, 4th ed. © 2011 by Pearson Education, Inc. Reproduced by permission of Pearson Education, Inc.

student in the class response profile. Look over the responses to each question by all of the children for categories of interests to be observed in your teaching and reading materials acquisition plan.

During the year, particularly if children's writing skills are well developed, distribute the SRIS to the entire group of children. Ask them to write their answers to the SRIS questions on their own copy and turn them in. Make any changes you discover throughout the year on the class profile sheet. This updated information about your students' reading interests will help you adjust your selection of topics and reading materials as the year progresses to increase your students' motivation and engagement in reading.

DeWitz and colleagues (2010) report interest ratings of selections found in CRPs at the third- and fifth-grade levels. On a scale of 1 to 5, the selections found in Macmillan/McGraw-Hill's core reading program had an interest rating of 3.20 across all categories of reading selections and materials provided, whereas Harcourt had an overall interest rating of 3.04 and Houghton Mifflin Reading showed an interest rating of 3.18. Using these ratings, one can easily see that most of the reading selections provided are moderately interesting to a cross section of third- and fifth-grade students nationally, with no major differences in interest rating between these three nationally used core reading programs.

Accelerated Reader

One program that boasts the ability to increase students' reading motivation is the Accelerated Reader (AR) program, a computer-based independent reading practice program in which students read texts, answer questions, and receive points as an incentive for reading. AR involves two major components, the Accelerated Reader software and Accelerated Reader Best Classroom Practices (formerly called Reading Renaissance). Accelerated Reader software is a computerized supplementary reading practice and motivation program. Accelerated Reader relies nearly exclusively on independent reading practice as a way of managing student performance by providing students and teachers feedback from quizzes based on books the students read and awarding incentive points to motivate continued reading. Accelerated Reader Best Classroom Practices are a set of recommended principles on guided independent reading (or teachers' direction of students' interactions with text) that ensure Accelerated Reader is implemented with accountability.

Two studies of Accelerated Reader meet What Works Clearinghouse evidence standards. One of the studies evaluated 572 students from grades K to 3 attending 11 schools in a southern school district in the United States. The second study included 32 students in grade 3 attending one school in the Pacific Northwest. Based on these two studies, the WWC considers the extent of evidence for Accelerated Reader to be medium to large for comprehension and small for reading fluency and general reading achievement. No studies that meet WWC evidence standards with or without reservations examined the effectiveness of Accelerated Reader in the alphabetic and decoding domain. Accelerated Reader was found by the WWC review to have no discernible effects on reading fluency, mixed effects on comprehension, and potentially positive effects on general reading achievement.

Mallette, Henk, and Melnick (2004) studied the effectiveness of claims made that the use of the AR program motivates children of all reading levels. Little empirical research has examined this claim for validity. Mallette and colleagues' (2004) findings indicated that AR positively influenced academic reading attitudes but not recreational reading attitudes. Conversely, AR was found to negatively influence two types of self-perceptions in low-achieving male readers. Consequently, the use of AR may not be equally motivating for all types of readers as claimed and should be used cautiously for the purpose of motivating readers, especially with low-achieving boys.

Technology and New Literacies

Programs and Standards Focused on Technology and New Literacies

● ● ●

IRA Standards for Reading Professionals: Standard 2, Element 2.3; Standard 5, Element 5.1

Common Core Standards: Reading: K–5, Integration of Knowledge and Ideas (item 7); Writing: K–5, Production and Distribution of Writing (item 6)

The National Reading Panel (2000) found that technology could be used to effectively teach children to read. Since that time, technology standards have been published by the International Society for Technology in Education, which teachers should know and use to guide their reading and other academic instruction (see URL at end of chapter). Core reading programs marketed at the national level are increasingly making use of new literacies and technology. One such program that has been shown to be effective is the SuccessMaker reading program, which is a set of computer-based courses used to supplement regular classroom reading instruction in grades K through 8. With adaptive lessons tailored to a student's reading level, SuccessMaker aims to improve understanding in areas such as phonological awareness, phonics, fluency, vocabulary, comprehension, and concepts of print.

"Foundations" courses aim to help students develop and maintain reading skills. "Exploreware" courses provide opportunities for exploration, open-ended instruction, and development of analytical skills. The computer analyzes students' skills development and assigns specific segments of the program, introducing new skills as they become appropriate. As the student progresses through the program, performance is measured by the probability of the student answering the next exercise correctly, which determines the next steps of the lesson.

Three studies of SuccessMaker meet the What Works Clearinghouse evidence standards with some reservations. The three studies included 450 students, ranging in age from 9 to 16 years, who attended elementary, middle, and middle-high schools in Alabama, Illinois, and Virginia. Based on these three studies, the WWC considers the extent of evidence for SuccessMaker to be small for alphabetics, reading fluency, and general literacy achievement, and medium to large for comprehension. SuccessMaker was found to have no discernible effects on students' acquisition of alphabetic (decoding) and reading fluency, but showed potentially positive effects on comprehension and general literacy achievement. There are many other core and supplementary reading programs that make use of computer and other new literacy technologies available for purchase that do not at this time have evidence of effectiveness available. Teachers would be well advised to check the What Works Clearinghouse or the Florida Reading Research Center websites for updated information on computer and new literacy technologies core and supplemental reading program effectiveness. See Web Tools You Can Use in the Classroom for access to these sites.

WEB TOOLS YOU CAN USE IN THE CLASSROOM

Online Reading Programs and Resources

SuccessMaker combines a powerful, standards-aligned reading with a learner-friendly interface that students will want to use. SuccessMaker uses a balanced, integrated approach to reading instruction that meets the What Works Clearinghouse research standard for effectiveness. It offers a strong instructional focus on developing phonological awareness, phonics, reading fluency, vocabulary, and comprehension skills through a lesson-based format that allows students to practice and apply these skills.

- When you go to SuccessMaker at www.pearsonschool.com/index.cfm?locator=PSZk99, you can hear from those who have used the program. You can also try out the demo yourself.

- Become familiar with the International Society for Technology in Education (ISTE) standards at www.iste.org and learn how these standards can inform your reading instruction. This site also offers other sources of guidance for using technology in the classroom.

- Visit What Works Clearinghouse at www.ies.ed.gov/ncee/wwc to read about evidence based reading programs that work in the classroom.

- To read about research on effective reading programs that is being conducted and distributed, visit the Florida Reading Research Center at www.fcrr.org and read about current projects and related information.

Family and Community Connections

How Can Teachers Help Parents and Communities Better Understand Reading Programs and Standards?

Many parents and interested stakeholders are aware of the standards-based movement in education as a result of its politicization and publicity surrounding state testing and federal legislation. However, most people who are not educators, and probably some who are, find standards-based education to be confusing at best. Fortunately, there are free resources available that you can use to explain reading standards to parents and others. There are also many free online resources for interested parents who want to be more effective in helping their children succeed in learning to read and in working with their local school and their children's teachers to help their children succeed.

The following splendid free resources can help you get started assisting parents with their children's reading success:

● ● ●

IRA Standards for Reading Professionals: Standard 4, Elements 4.1, 4.2, 4.3

Response to Intervention: Collaboration

- *Big Dreams: A Family Book About Reading.* Available free online from the National Institute for Literacy at www.nifl.gov/partnershipforreading/publications/pdf/big_dreams.pdf or order by telephone at 1-800-228-8813.
- *Put Reading First: Helping Your Child Learn to Read—A Parent Guide* (available in Spanish). Available free online from the National Institute for Literacy at www.nifl.gov/partnershipforreading/publications/Parent_br.pdf or order by telephone at 1-800-228-8813.
- *A Child Becomes a Reader.* Available free online from the National Institute for Literacy at www.nifl.gov/partnershipforreading/publications/reading_pre.pdf or order by telephone at 1-800-228-8813.
- *Reading Tips for Parents.* Available free online from the U.S. Department of Education at www2.ed.gov/parents/read/resources/readingtips/index.html.
- *Reading is Fundamental for Parents.* Available free online from Reading Is Fundamental at www.rif.org/parents.
- *Early Beginnings: Early Literacy Knowledge and Instruction.* Available free online from the National Institute for Literacy at www.nifl.gov/publications/pdf/NELPEarlyBeginnings09.pdf or order by telephone at 1-800-228-8813.

Summary

For reading instruction to be effective, teachers must first be aware of the development and sequence of reading skills to be learned. Thus, we began this important chapter with a discussion of the evidence-based skills and related curriculum standards for reading instruction. Reading curriculum standards help us understand the progression of reading development in five essential areas of instruction: phonemic awareness, phonics, vocabulary, comprehension, and fluency.

In the past several decades or so, standards-based curriculums and assessments have been prescribed as a cure for the poor performance and lack of accountability of many public schools (Watt, 2005; Zuzovsky & Libman, 2006). Literally billions of dollars have been spent on programs and state tests, in part so that federal and state agencies can rank schools in terms of student achievement. Indeed, the No Child Left Behind (NCLB) legislation and more recently the reauthorization of the Elementary Secondary Education Act (ESEA) have grown directly out of the standards-based movement. An understanding of the most essential skills adopted by state and other governmental agencies help teachers plan for classroom assessments and subsequent instruction tied to evidence-based research.

Core reading programs, also known as *basal programs,* are a collection of student texts and workbooks, teachers' manuals, and supplemental materials for teaching reading and sometimes writing instruction. Core reading programs are used primarily in the elementary and middle school grades as a foundation for consistent, basic instruction. We learned about valuable resources in selecting core reading programs titled *A Consumer's Guide to Evaluating a Core Reading Program* and *The Essential Guide to Selecting and Using Core Reading Programs,* which offer evidence as to the effectiveness of different reading instruction programs. In the end, core reading programs provide teachers with one of many tools for meeting the reading needs of every child.

When core programs are not effective for some learners, there are supplemental reading programs for struggling readers teachers can consider. An online tool to help teachers select effective supplementary programs and other resources is the What Works Clearinghouse (see URLs at the end of this chapter).

At this point in time, there are few reading programs for English learners (ELs) that have been shown effective through rigorous scientific research. However, in this chapter we did learn about some promising practices that may be used to supplement instruction for this growing population. In general, the most logical approach is for teachers to supplement their instruction with strategies proven to be effective with English-only students as identified throughout this book in the areas of phonemic awareness, phonics, reading vocabulary, comprehension, and fluency (August & Shanahan, 2006).

It is important that we help parents understand reading standards and find practical ways to help their children become literate. Parents are the first and often the best teachers. We learned about free research-supported tools we can use to educate parents about reading standards and home supports, including *Put*

Reading First: Helping Your Child Learn to Read—A Parent Guide and *Early Beginnings: Early Literacy Knowledge and Instruction*. These booklets are a good place to start and with the others provided can help every child become a successful reader.

Field and Classroom Applications

- Go to your local school district or university curriculum materials library. Select a leading core reading program (CRP). Locate the following items in the teacher's edition: (a) the scope and sequence chart, (b) the parts of a directed reading lesson, (c) the skill lessons, (d) the workbooks, and (e) the book tests or assessment materials. Use *A Consumer's Guide to Evaluating a Core Reading Program, Grades K–3: A Critical Elements Analysis* by Simmons and Kame'enui (2003) or *The Essential Guide to Selecting and Using Core Reading Programs* by Dewitz and colleagues (2010) to evaluate the program. Report the results to your class.
- Select a leveled book. Go through the parts of a Reading Recovery lesson and write a plan about how you would introduce this as a new book to a struggling reader.

- Interview a teacher in the field about the strengths and weaknesses of his or her current core reading program (CRP). Find out how and what parts of the CRP this teacher uses or does not use. Find out how he or she supplements reading instruction with other materials to meet the needs of all students.
- Visit a classroom in a local elementary school where Success for All is used. Observe the teacher's reading instruction. Which parts of the SFA program did the teacher use? Which parts did the teacher omit? Write an essay about your observations.
- Prepare a published core reading program lesson to be taught in the schools. Secure permission to teach this lesson in a local grade-level appropriate classroom. Write a reflective essay about your experience detailing successes, failures, and necessary changes.

Recommended Resources

Print Resources

Dewitz, P., Leahy, S. B., Jones, J., & Sullivan, P. M. (2010). *The essential guide to selecting and using core reading programs*. Newark, DE: International Reading Association.

Hiebert, E. H., & Sailors, M. (2009). *Finding the right texts: What works for beginning and struggling readers*. New York: Guilford Press.

Simmons, D. C., & Kame'enui, E. J. (2003). *A consumer's guide to evaluating a core reading program, Grades K–3: A critical elements analysis*. Eugene: University of Oregon.

Web Resources

http://reading.uoregon.edu/curricula/con_guide.php
A Consumer's Guide to Evaluating a Core Reading Program

www.reading.org/General/Publications/Books/SupplementalContent/bk707_supplement.aspx
Essential Guide to Selecting and Using Core Reading Programs

www.whatworks.ed.gov
What Works Clearinghouse

www.ngschoolpub.org
Language, Literacy, & Vocabulary!

www.lexile.com
Lexile Reading Levels

www.readingfirstohio.org/assets/pdf/Eval_Guide_for_Supplemental_&_Intervention.pdf
Ohio's core reading program evaluation instrument

www.ngschoolpub.org
National Geographic School Publications

www.fcrr.org
Florida Reading Research Center

www.iste.org/Content/NavigationMenu/NETS/
ForTeachers/2008Standards/NETS_for_
Teachers_2008.htm
International Society for Technology in Education
Standards

www.tesol.org
Teachers of English to Speakers of Other Languages
(TESOL)

www.benchmarkeducation.com/teacher-resources/general/
reading-level-guide.html
Conversion guide for leveled texts

The Power of Classroom Practice
www.myeducationlab.com

Go to Topic 11, Struggling Readers; Topic 12, English
Language Learners; and Topic 13, Media/Digital
Literacy, in the MyEducationLab (www.myeducationlab.
com) for your course, where you can:

- Find learning outcomes for Struggling Readers,
  English Language Learners, and Media/Digital
  Literacy along with the national standards that
  connect to these outcomes.
- Complete Assignments and Activities that can help
  you more deeply understand the chapter content.
- Apply and practice your understanding of the core
  teaching skills identified in the chapter with the
  Building Teaching Skills and Dispositions learning
  units. (optional)
- Examine challenging situations and cases presented in
  the IRIS Center Resources. (optional)
- Access video clips of CCSSO National Teachers of the
  Year award winners responding to the question "Why
  Do I Teach?" in the Teacher Talk section. (optional)
- Check your comprehension on the content covered
  in the chapter by going to the Study Plan in the Book
  Resources for your text. Here you will be able to take
  a chapter quiz, receive feedback on your answers, and
  then access Review, Practice, and Enrichment activities
  to enhance your understanding of chapter content.
  (optional)

Go to the Topic A+RISE in the MyEducationLab
(www.myeducationlab.com) for your course. A+RISE®
Standards2Strategy™ is an innovative and interactive
online resource that offers new teachers in grades K–12
just in time, research-based instructional strategies that:

- Meet the linguistic needs of ELLs as they learn
  content.
- Differentiate instruction for all grades and abilities.
- Offer reading and writing techniques, cooperative
  learning, use of linguistic and nonlinguistic repre-
  sentations, scaffolding, teacher modeling, higher
  order thinking, and alternative classroom ELL
  assessment.
- Provide support to help teachers be effective through
  the integration of listening, speaking, reading, and
  writing along with the content curriculum.
- Improve student achievement.
- Are aligned to Common Core Elementary Language
  Arts standards (for the literacy strategies) and to
  English language proficiency standards in WIDA,
  Texas, California, and Florida.

STANDARDS
for Reading Professionals and Guiding Principles for Educators

IRA Standards for Reading Professionals

Standard 1: Foundational Knowledge

Candidates understand the theoretical and evidence-based foundations of reading and writing processes and instruction.

Element 1.1

Candidates understand major theories and empirical research that describe the cognitive, linguistic, motivational, and sociocultural foundations of reading and writing development, processes, and components, including word recognition, language comprehension, strategic knowledge, and reading–writing connections.

Element 1.2

Candidates understand the historically shared knowledge of the profession and changes over time in the perceptions of reading and writing development, processes, and components.

Element 1.3

Candidates understand the role of professional judgment and practical knowledge for improving all students' reading development and achievement.

Candidates use instructional approaches, materials, and an integrated, comprehensive, balanced curriculum to support student learning in reading and writing.

Common Core Standards

Reading: K–12

Key Ideas and Details

1. Read closely to determine what the text says explicitly and to make logical inferences from it; cite specific textual evidence when writing or speaking to support conclusions drawn from the text.

2. Determine central ideas or themes of a text and analyze their development; summarize the key supporting details and ideas.

3. Analyze how and why individuals, events, and ideas develop and interact over the course of a text.

Craft and Structure

4. Interpret words and phrases as they are used in a text, including determining technical, connotative, and figurative meanings, and analyze how specific word choices shape meaning or tone.

5. Analyze the structure of texts, including how specific sentences, paragraphs, and larger portions of the text (e.g., a section, chapter, scene, or stanza) relate to each other and the whole.

6. Assess how point of view or purpose shapes the content and style of a text.

Integration of Knowledge and Ideas

7. Integrate and evaluate content presented in diverse media and formats, including visually and quantitatively, as well as in words.

8. Delineate and evaluate the argument and specific claims in a text, including the validity of the reasoning as well as the relevance and sufficiency of the evidence.

9. Analyze how two or more texts address similar themes or topics in order to build knowledge or to compare the approaches the authors take.

Range of Reading and Level of Text Complexity

10. Read and comprehend complex literary and informational texts independently and proficiently.

Writing: K–12

Text Types and Purposes

1. Write arguments to support claims in an analysis of substantive topics or texts, using valid reasoning and relevant and sufficient evidence.

2. Write informative/explanatory texts to examine and convey complex ideas and information clearly and accurately through the effective selection, organization, and analysis of content.

3. Write narratives to develop real or imagined experiences or events using effective technique, well-chosen details, and well-structured event sequences.

Production and Distribution of Writing

4. Produce clear and coherent writing in which the development, organization, and style are appropriate to task, purpose, and audience.

5. Develop and strengthen writing as needed by planning, revising, editing, rewriting, or trying a new approach.

6. Use technology, including the Internet, to produce and publish writing and to interact and collaborate with others.

Research to Build and Present Knowledge

7. Conduct short as well as more sustained research projects based on focused questions, demonstrating understanding of the subject under investigation.

8. Gather relevant information from multiple print and digital sources, assess the credibility and accuracy of each source, and integrate the information while avoiding plagiarism.

9. Draw evidence from literary or informational texts to support analysis, reflection, and research.

Range of Writing

10. Write routinely over extended time frames (time for research, reflection, and revision) and shorter time frames (a single sitting or a day or two) for a range of tasks, purposes, and audiences.

Speaking and Listening: K–12

Comprehension and Collaboration

1. Prepare for and participate effectively in a range of conversations and collaborations with diverse partners, building on others' ideas and expressing their own clearly and persuasively.

2. Integrate and evaluate information presented in diverse media and formats, including visually, quantitatively, and orally.

3. Evaluate a speaker's point of view, reasoning, and use of evidence and rhetoric.

Presentation of Knowledge and Ideas

4. Present information, findings, and supporting evidence such that listeners can follow the line of reasoning and the organization, development, and style are appropriate to task, purpose, and audience.

5. Make strategic use of digital media and visual displays of data to express information and enhance understanding of presentations.

6. Adapt speech to a variety of contexts and communicative tasks, demonstrating command of formal English when indicated or appropriate.

Language: K–12

Conventions of Standard English

1. Demonstrate command of the conventions of standard English grammar and usage when writing or speaking.

2. Demonstrate command of the conventions of standard English capitalization, punctuation, and spelling when writing.

Knowledge of Language

3. Apply knowledge of language to understand how language functions in different contexts, to make effective choices for meaning or style, and to comprehend more fully when reading or listening.

Vocabulary Acquisition and Use

4. Determine or clarify the meaning of unknown and multiple-meaning words and phrases by using context clues, analyzing meaningful word parts, and consulting general and specialized reference materials, as appropriate.

5. Demonstrate understanding of word relationships and nuances in word meanings.

6. Acquire and use accurately a range of general academic and domain-specific words and phrases sufficient for reading, writing, speaking, and listening at the college and career readiness level; demonstrate independence in gathering vocabulary knowledge when encountering an unknown term important to comprehension or expression.

Response to Intervention

6. Expertise

All students have the right to receive instruction from well-prepared teachers who keep up to date and supplemental instruction from professionals specifically prepared to teach language and literacy (IRA, 2000).

- Teacher expertise is central to instructional improvement, particularly for students who encounter difficulty in acquiring language and literacy. RTI may involve a range of professionals; however, the greater the literacy difficulty, the greater the need for expertise in literacy teaching and learning.
- Important dimensions of teachers' expertise include their knowledge and understanding of language and literacy development, their ability to use powerful assessment tools and techniques, and their ability to translate information about student performance into instructionally relevant instructional techniques.

- The exemplary core instruction that is so essential to the success of RTI is dependent on highly knowledgeable and skilled classroom teachers (IRA, 2003).
- Professionals who provide supplemental instruction or intervention must have a high level of expertise in all aspects of language and literacy instruction and assessment and be capable of intensifying or accelerating language and literacy learning.
- Success for culturally and linguistically diverse students depends on teachers and support personnel who are well prepared to teach in a variety of settings. Deep knowledge of cultural and linguistic differences is especially critical for the prevention of language and literacy problems in diverse student populations.
- Expertise in the areas of language and literacy requires a comprehensive approach to professional preparation that involves preservice, induction, and inservice education. It also requires opportunities for extended practice under the guidance of knowledgeable and experienced mentors.

IRA Standards for Reading Professionals

Standard 3: Assessment and Evaluation

Candidates use a variety of assessment tools and practices to plan and evaluate effective reading and writing instruction.

Element 3.1

Candidates understand types of assessments and their purposes, strengths, and limitations.

Element 3.2

Candidates select, develop, administer, and interpret assessments, both traditional print and electronic, for specific purposes.

Element 3.3

Candidates use assessment information to plan and evaluate instruction.

Evidence-Based Reading Instruction Programs

IRA Standards for Reading Professionals

Standard 2: Curriculum and Instruction

Candidates use instructional approaches, materials, and an integrated, comprehensive, balanced curriculum to support student learning in reading and writing.

Element 2.1

Candidates use foundational knowledge to design or implement an integrated, comprehensive, and balanced curriculum.

Element 2.2

Candidates use appropriate and varied instructional approaches, including those that develop word recognition, language comprehension, strategic knowledge, and reading–writing connections.

Element 2.3

Candidates use a wide range of texts (e.g., narrative, expository, and poetry) from traditional print, digital, and online resources.

Response to Intervention

1. Instruction

- A successful RTI process begins with the highest quality core instruction in the classroom—that is, instruction that encompasses all areas of language and literacy as part of a coherent curriculum that is developmentally appropriate for preK–12 students and does not underestimate their potential for learning. This core instruction may or may not involve commercial programs, and it must in all cases be provided by an informed, competent classroom teacher.
- The success of RTI depends on the classroom teacher's use of research-based practices. As defined by IRA (2002), *research based* means "that a particular program or collection of instructional practices has a record of success. That is, there is reliable, trustworthy, and valid evidence to suggest that when the program is used with a particular group of children, the children can be expected to make adequate gains in reading achievement."
- Research evidence frequently represents the effectiveness of an instructional practice on average, which suggests that some students benefited and others did not. This means that instruction must be provided by a teacher who understands the intent of the research-based practice being used and has the professional expertise and responsibility to plan instruction and adapt programs and materials as needed (see also principle 6, Expertise).
- When core language and literacy instruction is not effective for a particular student, it should be modified to address more closely the needs and abilities of that student. Classroom teachers, at times in collaboration with other experts, must exercise their best professional judgment in providing responsive teaching and differentiation (see also principle 2).

5. Systemic and Comprehensive Approaches

RTI must be part of a comprehensive, systemic approach to language and literacy assessment and instruction that supports all preK–12 students and teachers.

- RTI needs to be integrated within the context of a coherent and consistent language and literacy curriculum that guides comprehensive instruction for all students. Core instruction—indeed, all instruction—must be continuously improved to increase its efficacy and mitigate the need for specialized interventions.
- Specific approaches to RTI need to be appropriate for the particular school or district culture and take into account leadership, expertise, the diversity of the student population, and the available resources. Schools and districts should adopt an approach that best matches their needs and resources while still accomplishing the overall goals of RTI.
- A systemic approach to language and literacy learning within an RTI framework requires the active participation and genuine collaboration of many professionals, including classroom teachers, reading specialists, literacy coaches, special educators, and school psychologists. Given the critical role that language development plays in literacy learning, professionals with specialized language-related expertise such as speech-language pathologists

- and teachers of ELLs may be particularly helpful in addressing students' language difficulties.
- Approaches to RTI must be sensitive to developmental differences in language and literacy among students at different ages and grades. Although many prevailing approaches to RTI focus on the early elementary grades, it is essential for teachers and support personnel at middle and secondary levels to provide their students with the language and literacy instruction they need to succeed in school and beyond.

- Administrators must ensure adequate resources and appropriate scheduling to allow all professionals to collaborate.
- Ongoing and job-embedded professional development is necessary for all educators involved in the RTI process. Professional development should be context specific and provided by professional developers with appropriate preparation and skill to support school and district personnel. Professional expertise is essential to improving students' language and literacy learning in general as well as within the context of RTI (see also principle 6).

Supplementary Reading Intervention Programs

IRA Standards for Reading Professionals

Standard 4: Diversity

Candidates create and engage their students in literacy practices that develop awareness, understanding, respect, and a valuing of differences in our society.

Element 4.1

Candidates recognize, understand, and value the forms of diversity that exist in society and their importance in learning to read and write.

Element 4.2

Candidates use a literacy curriculum and engage in instructional practices that positively impact students' knowledge, beliefs, and engagement with the features of diversity.

Response to Intervention

2. Responsive Teaching and Differentiation

The RTI process emphasizes increasingly differentiated and intensified instruction or intervention in language and literacy.

- RTI is centrally about optimizing language and literacy instruction for particular students. This means that differentiated instruction, based on instructionally relevant assessment, is essential. Evidence shows that small-group and individualized instruction are effective in reducing the number of students who are at risk of becoming classified as learning disabled.
- Instruction and materials selection must derive from specific student–teacher interactions and not be constrained by pack-

aged programs. Students have different language and literacy needs, so they may not respond similarly to instruction—even when research-based practices are used. No single approach to instruction or intervention can address the broad and varied goals and needs of all students, especially those from different cultural and linguistic backgrounds.
- The boundaries between differentiation and intervention are permeable and not clearcut. Instruction or intervention must be flexible enough to respond to evidence from student performance and teaching interactions. It should not be constrained by institutional procedures that emphasize uniformity.

Programs and Standards Focused on Motivation and Engagement

IRA Standards for Reading Professionals

Standard 5: Literate Environment

Candidates create a literate environment that fosters reading and writing by integrating foundational knowledge, instructional practices, approaches and methods, curriculum materials, and the appropriate use of assessments.

Element 5.2

Candidates design a social environment that is low risk and includes choice, motivation, and scaffolded support to optimize students' opportunities for learning to read and write.

IRA Standards for Reading Professionals

Standard 2: Curriculum and Instruction

Candidates use instructional approaches, materials, and an integrated, comprehensive, balanced curriculum to support student learning in reading and writing.

Element 2.3

Candidates use a wide range of texts (e.g., narrative, expository, and poetry) from traditional print, digital, and online resources.

Standard 5: Literate Environment

Candidates create a literate environment that fosters reading and writing by integrating foundational knowledge, instructional prac-

tices, approaches and methods, curriculum materials, and the appropriate use of assessments.

Element 5.1

Candidates design the physical environment to optimize students' use of traditional print, digital, and online resources in reading and writing instruction.

Common Core Standards

Reading: K–5

Integration of Knowledge and Ideas

7. Integrate and evaluate content presented in diverse media and formats, including visually and quantitatively, as well as in words.

Writing: K–5

Production and Distribution of Writing

6. Use technology, including the Internet, to produce and publish writing and to interact and collaborate with others.

How Can Teachers Help Parents and Communities Better Understand Reading Programs and Standards?

IRA Standards for Reading Professionals

Standard 4: Diversity

Elements 4.1, 4.2 (See previous)

Element 4.3

Candidates develop and implement strategies to advocate for equity.

Response to Intervention

4. Collaboration

RTI requires a dynamic, positive, and productive collaboration among professionals with relevant expertise in language and literacy. Success also depends on strong and respectful partnerships among professionals, parents, and students.

- Collaboration should be focused on the available evidence about the needs of students struggling in language and literacy. School-level decision-making teams (e.g., intervention teams, problem-solving teams, RTI teams) should include members with relevant expertise in language and literacy, including second-language learning.
- Collaboration should increase, not reduce, the coherence of the instruction experienced by struggling readers. There must be

congruence between core language and literacy instruction and interventions. This requires a shared vision and common goals for language and literacy instruction and assessment, adequate time for communication and coordinated planning among general education and specialist teachers, and integrated professional development.
- Involving parents and students and engaging them in a collaborative manner is critical to successful implementation. Initiating and strengthening collaborations among school, home, and communities, particularly in urban and rural areas, provides the basis for support and reinforcement of students' learning.

10

Assessment

Chapter Questions

- What are the principles of effective classroom reading assessment?

- Why is it important to use screening assessments during the first days of school?

- What commercial reading tests are available for classroom use?

- What are outcome assessments?

- What are diagnostic assessments and how are they different from other assessments?

- What are student profiling and classroom profiling? How is profiling used to form needs-based reading groups?

- What is meant by "IF–THEN Thinking"?

Key Terms

Assessment

High-stakes tests

Reliability

Validity

Outcome assessments

Screening assessments

Diagnostic assessments

Progress-monitoring assessments

Kid watching

Expository text frames

Content area reading inventory (CARI)

Informal reading inventory (IRI)

Curriculum-based measurement (CBM)

Profiling

IF–THEN thinking

| Diagnostic Assessments | Getting Organized: Profiling Your Class | IF–THEN Thinking |

Vignette: Great Teaching Begins with Assessment!

When I was in my second year of teaching, I moved to a new school in order to teach third grade—my dream job. The other three third-grade teachers at Mt. Juliet Elementary School were smart and welcoming as we began planning for our new year. One problem, they explained, was that we would have almost 120 students and little, if any, assessment information about our students' reading abilities and needs. One teacher asked, "Bob, since you're still fresh from college, what did they teach you about beginning-of-the-year reading assessment?"

I broke into a cold sweat as I wracked my brain for some semblance of an intelligent thought. Then I remembered something. "One thing I have used is an informal reading inventory. It's a

published reading test that teachers can use to determine students' overall reading level, how well they comprehend what they read, and how well they deal with phonics and other word attack skills."

"Have you got one with you?" asked Ms. Holden, a veteran teacher whom everyone seemed to admire.

"Yes," I responded, "and I had a chance to use it with quite a few of my fourth-grade children last year and during summer school."

That did it. Before I knew it, my colleagues had elected me to screen *all* third graders at Mt. Juliet Elementary using my trusty informal reading inventory and chart their strengths and needs so that we could plan small-group instruction. (They agreed, as their part of the bargain, to take my students into their classes mornings of the first week of school so that I could test each child one at a time.)

In the end, the plan worked as a starting point for our reading instruction. The data from my initial screening helped us group children according to their reading needs *across* all of our classrooms. This experience was an epiphany for me. I saw firsthand the power assessment gives us to provide every child, from the first days of school, the reading instruction he or she needs.—RBC ■

Reading assessment is the tool that informs your teaching. **Assessment** may be broadly defined as "the ongoing, systematic collection of information on all students" (Mariotti & Homan, 2010, p. 1). In many ways, what we are about is trying to find out what is going on inside students' heads while they are reading (White, 2008). In Chapter 1 we identified classroom reading assessment as one of the "pillars" of effective reading programs. Elsewhere in the text we explain how key assessment strategies are used to plan instruction in such areas as oral language development, phonics, reading comprehension, fluency, and so forth. These assessment strategies help teachers know which reading skills each child already has and which he or she has yet to develop.

Assessment happens in effective classrooms *before, during,* and *after* instruction has taken place. It is essential for making sure every student receives appropriate educational experiences and then verifying that learning has taken place. With the array of data teachers can assemble through classroom reading assessment, they are able to analyze and plan "just-in-time" instruction that meets the needs of every student.

One thing you may notice in this chapter is an absence of the "pillar" sections as seen in previous chapters. That is because this chapter focuses strictly on the second pillar—assessment. So in this chapter we supplement what you have learned about classroom reading assessment by considering the guiding principles of effective reading assessment, thinking about schoolwide assessment concerns, learning important assessment terminology teachers should know, and investigating national issues surrounding reading assessment. We also provide more wide-ranging assessment strategies not discussed in earlier chapters that are quite useful. Let's begin at the beginning with a brief summary of the governing principles and fundamental purposes of reading assessment.

Principles and Purposes of Reading Assessment

The following principles of classroom assessment (Reutzel & Cooter, 2011) are intended to help teachers decide which strategies should be adopted to improve their classroom instruction. They are based on our own classroom experiences, current research in the field, and expert opinions expressed to us by successful classroom teachers.

●●●
IRA Standards for Reading Professionals: Standard 1, Elements 1.2, 1.3; Standard 3, Elements 3.1, 3.2, 3.3

Common Core Standards: All

Response to Intervention: Expertise; Assessment

Principles of Reading Assessment

Principle 1: Assessment Informs Instruction.   When considering whether to perform any sort of reading assessment, the teacher should ask, "Will this procedure help me make important instructional decisions regarding my students' reading needs?" The procedure should yield rich insights as to materials and ways of offering instruction (skills to be learned next, grouping based on student needs, etc.) that can positively affect students' reading growth. The assessment–teaching process, which is shown in Figure 10.1, begins with an understanding of required state standards, common core standards under development for the nation, and a careful survey of what is known about students using available information (home surveys, cumulative records, informal assessments, student self-assessments, and the like).

Next, the teacher forms hypotheses about where each student is in his or her reading development (Mariotti & Homan, 2010). The task is to select assessment procedures that will help the teacher better understand student abilities and confirm or reject earlier hypotheses. Armed with information

Figure 10.1

Assessment–Teaching Process

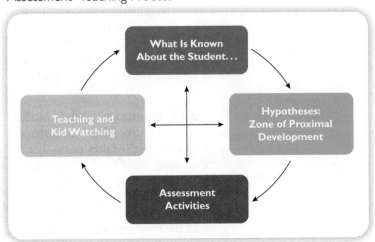

obtained from these processes, the teacher's lessons are aimed at helping the student improve in reading proficiency.

Principle 2: Assessment Procedures Should Help Teachers Discover What Children *Can* Do, Not Just What They Cannot Do. Rather than spending precious classroom time trying to identify the myriad skills students *do not* possess, many teachers focus on determining the skills they *do* possess and then decide what students are ready for next in reading development (i.e., building on students' strengths to help them develop new skills). Once teachers understand student strengths in reading, it becomes much easier to decide which learning experiences should be offered to help them develop further.

David Mager/Pearson Learning Photo Studio

Principle 3: Every Assessment Procedure Should Have a Specific Purpose. Sometimes we can fall into the habit of giving reading tests just because they are our "standard operating procedure" rather than selecting assessment activities as an integral part of providing high-quality instruction. For instance, it is common practice in many schools for students identified by their teacher as having reading problems to be given a "battery" of tests (i.e., a preselected set of tests) to discover what the problem seems to be. This one-size-fits-all approach fails to take into account what is already known about the student's reading ability and the specific *purpose* of the assessment experience (e.g., for diagnosis, for provision of data for progress reports, for information to be given to parents). We need to enter into student assessment with a clear purpose (see later section titled "Four Purposes of Reading Assessment").

Principle 4: Classroom Assessment Should Be Linked to Core Standards. Passage of the No Child Left Behind Act and other state and federal legislation in reading generated a pervasive emphasis on classroom assessment. Core standards established by the individual states and professional organizations, such as the International Reading Association (IRA), the National Council of Teachers of English (NCTE), and the Common Core Standards Initiative (2010), describe evidence-based reading skills that are typically mastered by the end of each school year. These benchmark skills (as they are often referred to) should be monitored on a regular basis.

Principle 5: Assessment Should Not Supplant Instruction. Reading instruction in many schools mirrors their state's mandated curriculum and reading tests—sometimes referred to as **high-stakes tests**—because whether or not a child is retained can be decided using these tests. In this situation, it is clear that reading tests are driving instruction—rather than being used as an assessment of the student's needs. Thus, it is important that we make sure that the state tests are measuring appropriate core reading skills at each grade level as determined through evidence-based research. If some of the core reading skills at your grade level are not being addressed by mandated tests, then teachers *must* use the kind of supplemental assessments offered throughout this book if every child is to have their reading needs met.

Principle 6: Effective Classroom Assessment Makes Use of Both Valid and Reliable Instruments.   Although master teachers are comfortable using many informal assessment processes to gather information about students' reading progress, instruments that possess validity and reliability evidence are sometimes necessary. These assessment tools give teachers consistent and trustworthy feedback for adapting or modifying their teaching to meet individual needs.

Reliability evidence demonstrates whether student performance will be measured in a stable and consistent manner (Jennings, Caldwell, & Lerner, 2006). In other words, a reliable test is one that provides the same results for the same children with repeated testing no matter who administers the test. Reliability is reported numerically with a coefficient (a perfect reliability score for a test would be 1.0). Salvia, Ysseldyke, and Bolt (2009) explain that if a test is used for screening it should have a reliability of .80 or better. If a test is to be used for decisions about individual students, such as placement in Title I or special education, the test's reliability should be .90 or higher.

Measures of **validity** indicate the degree to which tests measure what their developers claim they measure (Jennings et al., 2006). If a test measures reading, then it should measure the complete reading act, or at least the area of reading specified by the test-makers (e.g., phonics, reading comprehension), not some other skill, ability, or construct.

Validity and reliability considerations are likewise important when selecting assessments we plan to use with English learners (ELs). One of the problems with many tests, however, is that the students by whom reliability and validity norms are established may come from English-only populations (or nearly so). Thus, poor test scores in reading and writing for some EL children may reflect more on their lack of English proficiency that on literacy skill attainment.

Four Purposes of Reading Assessment

Because reading assessment removes children from precious instructional time in the classroom, we should be mindful of the four purposes of reading assessment. These purposes, by the way, are embedded in the federal Reading First and No Child Left Behind legislation and are built on principles of valid and reliable measurement (see principle 6 previously). These purposes are depicted metaphorically in Figure 10.2 as a chalice.

Figure 10.2

Purposes of Reading Assessment

   1. *Outcome assessment.* At the open end or broadest part of the chalice, because it involves the whole class, is **outcome assessment.** Outcomes are the results of our reading program in terms of student test scores and other hard data. The main purpose of outcome assessment is to survey the reading achievement of the class as a whole. It provides a snapshot of the reading program's effectiveness when compared to established end-of-year reading benchmarks (standards) for each grade level.

   2. *Screening assessments.* In order for differentiated instruction to occur, the focus of assessment shifts to individual students. **Screening assessments** provide initial information about students' reading development. These assessments, which should be quick but also provide reliable and valid data, should help teachers place students into preliminary instructional groups based on their general reading abilities and needs. They provide an especially critical "first look" at students who may be at risk and in need of special instructional services.

3. *Diagnostic assessments.* Invariably, teachers notice that some students are having unusual difficulty with targeted reading skills and strategies even after comprehensive instruction has been offered over time (i.e., via Tier 1 instruction). This is sometimes an indicator that Tier 2 instruction may be needed as part of Response to Intervention (RTI) to supplement your core program. **Diagnostic assessments** can provide in-depth information about each student's particular strengths and needs for Tier 2 instruction. These assessments are a bit more involved and take longer to administer. Sometimes a reading specialist, an educational psychologist, a certified diagnostician, or a bilingual specialist may be needed to administer a diagnostic test because of the time investment involved or because special training is needed. Students requiring Tier 3 interventions for reading via special education, Title I programs, or other options for supplemental instruction often undergo diagnostic testing for initial placement or for retention in these programs.

4. *Progress-monitoring assessments.* Encircling the chalice in Figure 10.2 are **progress-monitoring assessments.** These are an essential part of every reading teacher's daily plan, which is why they surround all other assessments (and students) represented in the chalice. Progress-monitoring assessments provide ongoing and timely feedback as to how well individual students are responding to teaching. This allows the teacher to continually reevaluate her or his instruction and make adjustments as needed.

The following framework shows which purposes of assessment are appropriate at each level of RTI.

- *Tier 1: Core Classroom Instruction* (i.e., developmental and differentiated instruction)
  - Screening assessments. Use at the beginning of the school year for initial needs assessments and throughout the year prior to beginning new units of study.
  - Progress-monitoring assessments. Use during instruction to monitor student understanding and emerging competencies or to determine whether reteaching certain parts of direct instruction is needed (e.g., modeling, guided practice, independent practice).
  - Outcome assessments. Use at the conclusion of direct instruction to determine whether learning objectives have been met or whether reteaching is indicated.
- *Tier 2: Supplemental Intervention*
  - Diagnostic assessment. Use to determine in greater depth specific skills, strategies, and knowledge the learner may need, as well as any special learning needs that should be accommodated.
  - Progress-monitoring assessments. Use during instruction to monitor student learning and whether reteaching certain parts of direct instruction is needed (e.g., modeling, guided practice, independent practice).
  - Outcome assessments. Use at the conclusion of supplemental instruction to determine whether (1) learning objectives have been met (2) reteaching is indicated, or (3) additional intensity of instruction should be considered (i.e., Tier 3).
- *Tier 3: Intensive Intervention*
  - At this level the same three assessment types and purposes as in Tier 2 are indicated.

Where Do We Begin? A Classroom Teacher's Perspective

In the remainder of this chapter we take a closer look at reading assessment, adding special reading assessment strategies to those presented in earlier chapters. It seems logical to us that we should start with the kinds of assessments you might use every day. Screening assessments for the first days and weeks of school and progress-monitoring assessments used daily to check the effectiveness of your teaching are the daily bread-and-butter tasks by which you will validate and judge teaching and learning effectiveness. Because these assessments—screening and progress monitoring—may be used more or less interchangeably, we group them together in the upcoming sections. How will you know which assessment tool is best for screening or progress monitoring? Not to worry. Early in the next section we provide you with a handy chart in Figure 10.3 that helps you decide.

Screening and Progress-Monitoring Assessments

It is essential to give screening assessments during the first days of school and for students who come to you after the school year has begun. These assessments are easy to administer and yield extremely useful information. You may actually decide to apply many of these same tools for progress monitoring.

Screening Assessments

The first day of school is always magical. It is a day filled with hope, expectation, and, for some, even fear. Your young charges walk slowly into your classroom—some tall and gangly, some short, some smiling, some moving very cautiously. It is the day when you begin to establish classroom management routines and get to know each student a little. It is also the day they begin to form opinions about you.

The first week of school should include a basketweave of assessment activities that are quick and efficient while yielding a lot of important information about your pupils' reading abilities. They should also be pleasant and nonthreatening, because some of your students will have had repeated experience with failure and you don't want to lose them.

Screening Assessments for English Learners

Many school districts are seeing a major influx of English learners (ELs). For teachers not having English as a second language (ESL) training, the law requires that an ESL teacher provide screening services. ELs, unlike students enrolled in special education programs, do not have Individual Education Plans (IEPs). So be prepared to meet with your ESL consulting teacher to help plan appropriate differentiated reading/writing instruction to meet the needs of your EL children.

Progress Monitoring in the Reading Classroom

Progress monitoring is an essential part of teaching. As you learn more about your students, you plan instruction that you believe will best meet their needs. In essence, you try to find the zone of proximal development for each reading skill area for each student—not a simple task. Thus, as you offer targeted instruction in small groups, you constantly reassess each student's growth to see if learning is occurring and then tailor your instruction based on what you discover.

So how do you decide which of the tests or strategies that follow in this section should be used, either for screening or progress monitoring? In Figure 10.3 we offer a kind of "IF–THEN" chart to help you choose. IF–THEN Thinking works like this: *IF you have a particular need that is represented by one of the assessments listed along the left-hand column, THEN you determine the particular test or assessment strategy that is appropriate for screening or progress monitoring by checking the appropriate row to the right.* Following Figure 10.3 is a detailed description of many of these strategies (others may be found in Chapters 2 through 8). Let's get started!

Kid Watching

For many teachers, the most basic assessment strategy is systematic observation of children engaged in the reading act, or **kid watching.** New Zealand educator Marie Clay, in her classic book *The Early Detection of Reading Difficulties* (1985), explains her philosophy concerning observations:

> I am looking for movement in appropriate directions. . . . For if I do not watch what [the student] is doing, and if I do not capture what is happening in records of some kind, Johnny, who never gets under my feet and who never comes really into a situation where I can truly see what he is doing, may, in fact, for six months or even a year, practice behaviours that will handicap him in reading. (p. 49)

Observation and systematic data collection during observation are critical tools at the teacher's disposal for the early assessment of students and their abilities. However, you need to know what to watch for. One semester a young student teacher was busily making anecdotal notes on a clipboard as she watched second graders working away. The students were engaged in activities such as reading, planning writing projects, working at a computer station, listening to books on tape while following along in small books, and several other reading–learning tasks. When the student teacher was asked by the visiting college supervisor what she was working on, she said, "I'm trying to figure out where the children are in their reading development." The supervisor responded, "That's great! How do you know what to watch for?" The student teacher appeared bewildered, so the supervisor said, "If you have time later, I'd like to share with you information about reading milestones. They are observable learning stages that can be noted as part of your assessment profiling system." The student teacher quickly accepted the offer and welcomed the information enthusiastically.

To be an effective "kid watcher," you must gain an understanding of end-of-year benchmark reading skills (Cooter, 2003), or the reading milestones through which children grow. Knowing which of these skills students have and have not acquired will help you construct a classroom profile and plan whole-class, small-group, and individualized instruction. Having a copy of end-of-year benchmark or core reading standards (Common Core Standards Initiative, 2010) will help you add validity to your kid watching. (*Note:* State standards are provided online on the webpage for each state's department of education.)

Assessing Reading Interests and Self-Perception

On the most basic level, we need to know what kinds of books and materials will be of interest to our students. This helps us choose (or avoid) certain topics of interest

Figure 10.3

Selected Screening and Progress-Monitoring Assessment Strategies

	Appropriate for SCREENING? (First days/weeks)	Appropriate for PROGRESS MONITORING?
CATEGORY: Interests and Self-Perception		
Comprehensive Reading Inventory	YES	NO
Burke Interview	YES	YES
Self-Rating Scale–Subject Areas	YES	YES
Background Knowledge	YES	YES
Family Survey	YES	NO
Kid-Watching	NO	YES
Screening Checklists	YES	YES
Concepts About Print	YES	YES (for emergent readers only)
CATEGORY: Phonemic Awareness (PA) and Alphabet Knowledge (AK)		
PA- Recognizing Rhyming Words	YES (in small groups)	YES
PA- Oddity Task	YES (in small groups)	YES
PA- Same–Different Word Pairs	YES (in small groups)	YES
PA- Syllables and Counting Syllables	YES (in small groups)	YES
PA- Auditory Sound Blending	YES (in small groups)	YES
PA- Segmenting Sounds	YES (in small groups)	YES
AK- Alphabet Identification	YES (in small groups)	YES
AK- Letter Production	YES (in small groups)	YES
CATEGORY: Decoding and Word Attack		
Running Records	YES (first three weeks)	YES
CATEGORY: Vocabulary		
Oral Reading Assessment	NO	YES
Vocabulary Flash Cards	YES	YES
CATEGORY: Comprehension		
Questioning (Bloom)	YES	YES (use mainly higher levels)
Retelling–Story Grammars (Oral)	YES (in small groups)	YES
Retelling–Using Graphic Organizers	YES (in small groups)	YES
Retelling–Written Summaries	NO	YES
Expository Text Frames	YES (in small groups)	YES
Cloze	YES	YES
Maze	YES	YES
Content Area Reading Inventory (CARI)	YES (in small groups)	YES
CATEGORY: Fluency		
Multidimensional Fluency Scale (MFS)	YES (in small groups)	YES
Rubric for evaluation	NO	YES
CATEGORY: Commercial Tools		
Informal reading inventories	YES (in first three weeks)	YES (quarterly)
Curriculum-based measurements (CBM)	YES (in first month)	YES (quarterly)

for small-group instruction, as interest can have a powerful effect on student reading performance (Guthrie, Hoa, Wigfield, Tonks, & Perencevich, 2006). We also want to be sure to ask the obvious question: *Are you a good reader? Why?*

In this section, we share some essential tools to screen students for interest and self-perception.

Attitude/Interest Inventories.   Getting to know students is critical if the teacher is to have insights into their background knowledge and oral language abilities. It is also useful in selecting reading materials that will be of interest to students. An interest inventory that is administered either one-to-one or in small groups is a great tool for getting to know students. However, there are many inventories from which you can choose, and all interest inventories are not created equal. Furthermore, not all questions on the inventory can tell you what is helpful in choosing appropriate reading materials for instruction.

In Chapter 7 dealing with reading comprehension, we offered interest inventories that we find to be helpful. So you may want to revisit these in the Classroom Assessment section of that chapter. Following is another kind of instrument that helps you determine students' sense of self-efficacy, their belief about their own reading abilities.

The Burke Reading Interview.   The Burke Reading Interview (Burke, 1987) provides some initial insights into how students see themselves as readers and the reading task in general. The following questions have been adapted from the Burke procedure:

1. When you are reading and come to a word you don't know, what do you do? What else can you do?
2. Which of your friends is a good reader? What makes him or her a good reader?
3. Do you think your teacher ever comes to a word she doesn't know when reading? What do you think she does when that happens?
4. If you knew that one of your friends was having problems with his or her reading, what could you tell your friend that would help?
5. How would a teacher help your friend with reading problems?
6. How do you think you learned to read?
7. Are you a good reader?
8. What would you like to be able to do better as a reader?

Self-Rating Scales for Subject Area Reading

No one knows better than the reader how he or she is doing in reading. A teacher carrying out an assessment agenda should never overlook the obvious: Ask kids how they're doing. Although this is best achieved in a one-to-one discussion setting, large class sizes frequently make it a prohibitive practice. A good alternative to one-to-one interviews for older elementary children is a student self-rating scale, in which students complete a questionnaire tailored to obtain specific information about the reader from the reader's point of view. One example is illustrated in Figure 10.4 for a teacher interested in reading and study strategies used with social studies readings. Whichever reading skills are to be surveyed, remember to keep self-rating scales focused and brief.

Assessing Background Knowledge

Children's background knowledge and experiences are among the most important contributors (or inhibitors) of comprehension. Researchers have determined that students

Figure 10.4

Self-Rating Scale: Reading Social Studies

Reading Social Studies

Name _____   Date _____

1. The first three things I usually do when I begin reading a chapter in social studies are (number 1, 2, 3):

   _____ Look at the pictures.

   _____ Read the chapter through one time silently.

   _____ Look at the new terms and definitions.

   _____ Read the questions at the end of the chapter.

   _____ Read the first paragraph or introduction.

   _____ Skip around and read the most interesting parts.

   _____ Skim the chapter.

   _____ Preview the chapter.

2. What is hardest for me about social studies is . . .

3. The easiest thing about social studies is . . .

4. The thing(s) I like best about reading social studies is(are) . . .

---

who possess a great deal of background information about a subject tend to recall greater amounts of information more accurately from reading than do students with little or no background knowledge (Mills, 2009; Pressley, 2000). It is also known that well-developed background information can sometimes inhibit the comprehension of new information if it conflicts with prior knowledge or assumptions about a specific topic. Thus, knowing how much knowledge a reader has about a concept or topic can help teachers better prepare students to read and comprehend successfully.

It is also critical that we assess the background knowledge of English learners (ELs) and not just make assumptions that may be stereotypes. Background knowledge and experiences as well as the cultures of ELs can vary widely. Relatedly, remember that students with similar cultural origins can be quite different due to rural versus urban backgrounds.

One way that teachers can assess background knowledge and experience is to use a procedure developed by Langer (1984) for assessing the amount and content of students' background knowledge about selected topics, themes, concepts, and events. Use the following procedure (Reutzel & Cooter, 2011):

- Select a story for students to read.
- Construct a list of specific vocabulary terms or story concepts related to the topic, message, theme, or events to be experienced in reading the story. For example, you might have students read the story *Stone Fox* by John R. Gardiner, which is about a boy named Willy who saves his grandfather's farm from the tax collector.

- Construct a list of five to ten specific vocabulary terms or concepts related to the story, such as the following:
  broke
  taxes
  tax collector
  dogsled race
  samoyeds

- Ask students to respond to each of these terms in writing or through discussion. This is accomplished by using one of several stem statements (see Figure 10.5) such as, "What comes to mind when you think of paying bills and you hear the word *broke?*"

- Once students have responded to each of the terms, score responses to survey the class's knowledge (Figure 10.5). Assign the number of points that most closely represents the level of prior knowledge in the response to score each item. Divide the total score by the number of terms or concepts in the list to determine the average knowledge level of individual students.

- Compare these average scores against the Checklist of Levels of Prior Knowledge in Figure 10.5 for each student. By scanning the *X*'s in the checklist, you can get a sense of the entire class's overall level of prior knowledge. You can easily use information thus gathered to inform both the content and nature of your whole-group comprehension instruction.

Figure 10.5

Checklist of Levels of Prior Knowledge

Phrase 1	What comes to mind when . . . ?
Phrase 2	What made you think of . . . ?
Phrase 3	Have you any new ideas about . . . ?

Stimulus used to elicit student background knowledge _____

(Picture, word, or phrase etc.)

Much (3)	Some (2)	Little (1)
category labels	examples	personal associations
definitions	attributes	morphemes
analogies	defining characteristics	sound-alikes
relationships		personal experiences

Student name

Maria ____	____	X ____	
Jawan ____	X ____	____	____
____	____	____	____
____	____	____	____
____	____	____	____

Family Surveys of Reading Habits

We recently observed a friend of ours who has a heart condition going through his normal daily activities with a small radio-like device attached to his belt. When asked what this gadget was, he indicated that it was a heart monitor. He went on to say that the device constantly measured his heart rate for an entire day to provide the doctor with a reliable account of his normal heart rhythms in the real world of daily activity.

Traditional reading assessment has often failed to give teachers such a "real-world" look at students' reading ability by restricting the assessment to school settings. So the question posed here is "How do we acquire information about a student's reading habits and abilities away from the somewhat artificial environment of the school?" One way is to assess what is happening in the home using family surveys.

Family surveys are brief questionnaires (too long and they'll never be answered!) sent to adult family members periodically to maintain communication between the home and school. They also remind parents of the importance of reading in the home to support and encourage reading growth. When taken into consideration with other assessment evidence from the classroom, family surveys enable teachers to develop a more accurate profile of the child's reading ability. If possible, provide the family surveys in the native language of ELs' parents or have local translators help you make phone calls to the home so you can conduct the home survey orally. An example of a family survey is provided in Figure 10.6.

Figure 10.6

Family Survey

September 6, 20____

Dear Adult Family Member:

   As we begin the new school year, I would like to know a little more about your child's reading habits at home. This information will help me provide the best possible learning plan for your child this year. Please take a few minutes to answer the questions below and return in the self-addressed stamped envelope provided. Should you have any questions, feel free to phone me at XXX–XXXX.

Cordially,

Mrs. Shelley

1. My child likes to read the following at least once a week (check all that apply):

   Comic books _____   Sports page _____

   Magazines (example: *Highlights*) _____   Library books _____

   Cereal boxes _____   Cooking recipes _____

   T.V. Guide _____   Funny papers _____

   Others (please name):

2. Have you noticed your child having any reading problems? If so, please explain briefly.

3. What are some of your child's favorite books?

4. If you would like a conference to discuss your child's reading ability, please indicate which days and times (after school) would be most convenient.

Screening Checklists and Scales

Teachers often create their own screening checklists using the reading benchmarks for their grade level. Back in 1991, Lamme and Hysmith developed a popular scale that can help identify key developmental behaviors in emergent readers. It describes 11 levels often seen in the elementary school and can be used in tandem with the much more comprehensive reading benchmarks previously discussed. Following is an adaptation of that scale:

Level 11. The student can read fluently from books and other reading materials.

Level 10. The student seeks out new sources of information. He or she volunteers to share information from books with other children.

Level 9. The student has developed the ability to independently use context clues, sentence structure, structural analysis, and phonic analysis to read new passages.

Level 8. The student reads unfamiliar stories haltingly (not fluently), but requires little adult assistance.

Level 7. The student reads familiar stories fluently.

Level 6. The student reads word by word. He or she recognizes words in a new context.

Level 5. The student memorizes text and can pretend to "read" a story.

Level 4. The student participates in reading by doing such things as supplying words that rhyme and predictable text.

Level 3. The student talks about or describes pictures. He or she pretends to read (storytelling). He or she makes up words that go along with pictures.

Level 2. The student watches pictures as an adult reads a story.

Level 1. The student listens to a story but does not look at the pictures.

Many teachers find checklists including a Likert scale (a 5-point scale) can be useful in student portfolios because many reading behaviors become more fluent over time. One example, developed by Deborah Diffily, is shown in Figure 10.7.

Assessing Students' Reading of Nonfiction Texts

The key to effective expository text (i.e., nonfiction) instruction lies in the accurate identification of the types of nonfiction texts that students are able to read effectively, as well as the forms of expository writing that are difficult for them to comprehend. We have discovered that several rather common forms of reading assessment are easily adaptable to expository texts and can help teachers plan instruction. Offered in this section are some examples of each for your consideration.

Expository Text Frames. An assessment tool useful in identifying types of expository text patterns that may be troublesome for students is **expository text frames.** Based on the "story frames" concept (Fowler, 1982), expository text frames are completed by the student after reading an expository passage. Instruction can be focused much more precisely, based on student needs, as a result of this procedure.

To develop your own expository text frames for classroom assessment, you will need a reading selection from the adopted content textbook, a personal computer, and

Figure 10.7

Diffily's Classroom Observation Rating Scale

Student's Name _____   Date _____

Literacy Development Rating Scale

	Seldom				Often
Chooses books for personal enjoyment	1	2	3	4	5
Knows print/picture difference	1	2	3	4	5
Knows print is read from left to right	1	2	3	4	5
Asks to be read to	1	2	3	4	5
Asks that story be read again	1	2	3	4	5
Listens attentively during story time	1	2	3	4	5
Knows what a title is	1	2	3	4	5
Knows what an author is	1	2	3	4	5
Knows what an illustrator is	1	2	3	4	5
In retellings, repeats 2+ details	1	2	3	4	5
Tells beginning, middle, end	1	2	3	4	5
Can read logos	1	2	3	4	5
Uses text in functional ways	1	2	3	4	5
"Reads" familiar books to self/others	1	2	3	4	5
Can read personal words	1	2	3	4	5
Can read sight words from books	1	2	3	4	5
Willing to "write"	1	2	3	4	5
Willing to "read" personal story	1	2	3	4	5
Willing to dictate story to adult	1	2	3	4	5

Developed by Deborah Diffily, 1994. Reprinted with the permission of Deborah Diffily.

a printer or photocopier. Abbreviated examples of expository text frames for each of the primary expository text patterns are shown in Figures 10.8 through 10.12.

Before asking students to read the targeted selection, list the major vocabulary and concepts. Discuss what students already know about the topic and display it on the chalkboard or on chart paper. Next, have students read an expository selection similar to the one you will ask them to read in class. Once the passage has been read, model the process for completing expository text frames using examples. Finally, have students read the actual selection for the unit of study and complete the expository text frame(s) you have prepared for this passage.

Content Area Reading Inventory (CARI).   A **content area reading inventory (CARI)** (Readence, Bean, & Baldwin, 1992) is a teacher-created informal reading inventory that assesses whether students have learned sufficient reading and study strategies to succeed with content materials. Constructing a CARI can be quite time-consuming, but is well worth the effort.

Figure 10.8

Expository Text Frames: Description

Decimals are another way to write fractions when _____

_____

_____

_____

From Reutzel and Cooter, *Strategies for Reading Assessment and Instruction*, 3rd ed. © 2007 by Pearson Education, Inc.
Reproduced with permission of Pearson Education, Inc.

Figure 10.9

Expository Text Frames: Collection

Water Habitats

Freshwater habitats are found in _____, _____, _____, and rivers. Each freshwater habitat has special kinds of _____ and _____ that live there. Some plants and animals live in waters that are very _____. Others live in waters that are _____. Some plants and animals adapt to waters that flow_____.

From Reutzel and Cooter, *Strategies for Reading Assessment and Instruction*, 3rd ed. © 2007 by Pearson Education, Inc.
Reproduced with permission of Pearson Education, Inc.

Figure 10.10

Expository Text Frames: Causation

America Enters the War

On Sunday, December 7, 1941, World War II came to the United States. The entry of the United States into World War II was triggered by _____. Roosevelt said that it was a day that would "live in Infamy." *Infamy* (IN·fuh·mee) means remembered for being evil.

From Reutzel and Cooter, *Strategies for Reading Assessment and Instruction*, 3rd ed. © 2007 by Pearson Education, Inc.
Reproduced with permission of Pearson Education, Inc.

Figure 10.11

Expository Text Frames: Problem/Solution

Agreement by Compromise

Events that led to the Civil War

For a while there were an equal number of Southern and Northern states. That meant that there were just as many senators in Congress from slave states as from free states. Neither had more votes in the Senate, so they usually reached agreement on new laws by compromise. One way that the balance of power was maintained in Congress was _____

_____.

From Reutzel and Cooter, *Strategies for Reading Assessment and Instruction*, 3rd ed. © 2007 by Pearson Education, Inc.
Reproduced with permission of Pearson Education, Inc.

Figure 10.12

Expository Text Frames: Comparison

Segregation

Many people said that the segregation laws were unfair. But in 1896, the Supreme Court ruled segregation legal if _____
_____. "Separate but equal" became the law in many parts of the country. But separate was not equal. One of the most serious problems was education. Black parents felt

_____.

Sometimes the segregated schools had teachers who were not _____
_____ as teachers in the white schools. Textbooks were often
_____ if they had any books at all. But in many of

the white schools the books were _____.
Without a good education the blacks argued their children would not be able to get good jobs as adults.

From Reutzel and Cooter, *Strategies for Reading Assessment and Instruction*, 3rd ed. © 2007 by Pearson Education, Inc. Reproduced with permission of Pearson Education, Inc.

A CARI can be administered to groups of students and typically includes three major sections (Farr, Tulley, & Pritchard, 1989) that assess (1) student knowledge of and ability to use common textbook components (i.e., table of contents, glossary, index) and supplemental research aids (card catalog, reference books, periodicals); (2) student knowledge of important vocabulary and skills such as context clues; and (3) comprehension skills important to understanding expository texts.

For the last two sections of a CARI assessment, students are asked to read a selection from the adopted text. Readence and colleagues (1992) suggest contents of a CARI assessment and a scoring procedure, as shown in Figure 10.13.

To develop a CARI, use the following process:

Step 1: Choose a passage of at least three to four pages from the textbooks to be used. The passage selected should represent the typical writing style of the author.

Step 2: Construct about 20 questions related to the text. Readence and colleagues (1992) recommend eight to ten questions for Part I, four to six questions for Part II, and seven to nine questions for Part III. We recommend questions based on writing patterns used in the sample selection; they should reflect the facts, concepts, and generalizations in the selection.

Step 3: Explain to students that the CARI is not for grading purposes but is useful for planning teaching activities that will help them succeed. Be sure to walk students through the different sections of the CARI and model appropriate responses.

Step 4: Administer Part I first and then Parts II and III at separate times. It may take several sessions to work through a CARI. We recommend devoting only about 20 minutes per day to administering parts of a CARI so that other class needs are not ignored during the assessment phase.

From careful analysis of this assessment, teachers can plan special lessons to help students cope with difficult readings and internalize important information. Students can be grouped according to need for these lessons and practice strategies leading to success.

Figure 10.13

Suggestions for Content in a CARI

Part I: Textual Reading/Study Aids

1. Internal aids
2. Table of contents
3. Index
4. Glossary
5. Chapter introduction/summary
6. Information from pictures
7. Other aids included in the text
8. Supplemental research aids
9. Online card catalog searches
10. Periodicals
11. Encyclopedias
12. Other relevant resources that lead students to access additional information related to the content (e.g., online search engines like Google, video libraries, online university periodicals)

Part II: Vocabulary Knowledge

1. Knowledge and recall of relevant vocabulary
2. Use of context clues

Part III: Comprehension Skills and Strategies

1. Text-explicit (literal) information
2. Text-implicit (inferred) information
3. Knowledge of text structures and related strategies

Suggested Scoring Criteria

Percent Correct	Text Difficulty
86%–100%	Easy reading
64%–85%	Adequate for instruction
63% or below	Too difficult

Published Reading Tests for Screening and Progress-Monitoring Assessments

A number of products are available commercially to help teachers survey their students. Although these may be helpful, they can also be somewhat expensive. In this section, we present products that have been useful in our own classroom practices and meet with our general approval. We begin with the most valid of them all, informal reading inventories, or IRIs.

Informal Reading Inventory

The **informal reading inventory (IRI)** is an individually administered test (though some can be given to groups of children), often with graded word lists and story passages. The IRI is one of the best tools for observing and analyzing reading performance and for gathering information about how a student uses a wide range of reading strategies (Jennings et al., 2006). Emmett A. Betts is generally considered to be the first developer of the IRI; however, several other individuals contributed to its development as far back as the early 1900s (Johns & Lunn, 1983; Nilsson, 2008).

IRIs provide authentic assessments of the reading act (i.e., an IRI more closely resembles real reading than other reading tests). Students are better able to "put it all together" by reading whole stories or passages. Another advantage of IRIs is that they usually offer a systematic procedure for studying student miscues or reading errors.

IRIs are rather unusual when compared to other commercial reading tests. First, because they are "informal" many IRIs do not offer norms, reliability data, or validity information, though a few have begun offering validation information in recent years (see The Comprehensive Reading Inventory below). Second, IRIs provide a great deal of helpful information for teachers in making curricular decisions, especially for placing students into needs-based or guided reading groups (Fountas & Pinnell, 1996; McLaughlin, 2010). IRIs supply an estimate of each child's ability in graded or "leveled" reading materials, such as basal readers and books used for guided reading. IRIs usually offer student performance data in several key areas of reading: word identification via a running record, passage comprehension, and reading fluency.

IRIs tend to be somewhat different from each other. Beyond the usual graded word lists and reading passages, IRIs vary a great deal in the subtests offered (e.g., silent reading passages, phonics, interest inventories, concepts about print, phonemic awareness, auditory discrimination) and in the scoring criteria used to interpret reading miscues. Some argue (us included) that the best IRIs are constructed by classroom teachers themselves using reading materials from their own classrooms. Several examples of IRIs now used in many school systems follow:

- *The Comprehensive Reading Inventory: Measuring Reading Development in Regular and Special Education Classrooms.* The CRI (Cooter, Flynt, & Cooter, 2007) is a modern version of the traditional IRI concept, with both English and Spanish forms under one cover. The authors apply National Reading Panel (2000) and other more recent research on "alphabetics" (i.e., phonemic awareness, letter naming, phonics), vocabulary knowledge, comprehension processes, running records, fluency, and miscue analysis into an effective authentic reading assessment.

  Unlike most commercial IRIs on the market today, the CRI also includes validity and reliability data, a feature required by many states for tax-supported adoption by school districts. The authors include such research-based procedures as unaided/aided recall and story grammar comprehension evaluation, high-interest selections, appropriate length passages, both expository and narrative passages, and a time-efficient miscue grid system for quick analyses of running records.

- *Developmental Reading Assessment,* 2nd edition. The DRA2 (Beaver & Carter, 2010) is a popular informal reading inventory used in many schools offering graded reading passages for students to read, rubrics for evaluating students' oral reading, and a handy box in which to store student portfolios. The DRA2 features the following reliability analyses: (1) internal consistency reliability, (2) passage equivalency, (3) test–retest reliability, and (4) inter-rater and expert rater reliabilities.

- *The Critical Reading Inventory*, 2nd edition. The CRI-2 (Applegate, Quinn, & Applegate, 2008) adds two new aspects to the traditional formula: critical response questions and retelling rubrics. It also incorporates biographies and content area texts selected to closely match the classic definition of a story for comprehension assessment purposes (Nilsson, 2008).

• *The English–Español Reading Inventory.* This easy-to-use tool (Flynt & Cooter, 1999) offers complete informal reading inventories for prekindergarten through grade 12 students in both Spanish and English. The Spanish passages were carefully developed and field-tested with the aid of native Spanish-speaking teacher–researchers from the United States, Mexico, and Central and South America to avoid problems with dialect differences and to maximize their usefulness in United States classrooms.

Curriculum-Based Measurement

Curriculum-based measurement (CBM) is a tool for measuring student skill development in the areas of reading fluency, spelling, math, and written language (Coker & Ritchey, 2010). CBM uses "probes" developed from each school district's curriculum; thus, it measures what students are taught.

Curriculum-based measurement looks at three different areas that pertain to reading.

• Reading fluency measures how many words a student correctly reads in 1 minute. In practice, three reading probes are given and the middle or median score is reported.
• The spelling measure presents 10 words (at first grade) or 17 words (second through fifth grades). Spelling lists are scored for words spelled correctly.
• For the written expression task, students are presented with a story starter and given 3 minutes to write a story. Student work is scored for total words written, words spelled correctly, and correct writing sequences.

CBM procedures are usually used to screen for students who may be at risk for reading difficulty and to monitor student progress and response to interventions (i.e., Tier 1 and 2 RTI levels). Screenings are conducted three times each year in many school districts for all students: fall, winter, and spring. If a student receives additional support in reading, CBM might be administered several times weekly to evaluate the effects of the intervention. Similarly, CBM is often used for decision making when determining whether a student should receive special education services.

Outcome Assessments

Outcome assessments help us determine how effective our reading program and our teaching is in helping students attain grade-level standards or benchmarks. These kinds of tests are usually given to whole groups of students at once, but may be given individually when necessary. The following two measures are used nationally and are considered to be exemplars in this emerging area of reading assessment.

Dynamic Indicators of Basic Early Literacy Skills (DIBELS)

The Dynamic Indicators of Basic Early Literacy Skills, or DIBELS, are a set of four standardized, individually administered measures of early literacy development.

DIBELS was specifically designed to assess three of the "Big Five Ideas" of early literacy development: phonological awareness, alphabetic principle, and oral reading fluency (measured as a corrected reading rate) with connected text. Another test not directly linked to the Big Five Ideas in early literacy but used as a risk indicator is the Letter-Naming Fluency (LNF) measure. These short, efficient, and highly predictive measures are designed to be 1-minute, timed indicators used to regularly monitor the development of prereading and early reading skills.

Texas Primary Reading Inventory (TPRI)

The Texas Primary Reading Inventory, or TPRI, is an assessment tool that provides a picture of a student's reading progress in kindergarten, first, and second grades. Originally developed to help Texas teachers measure the state's "essential knowledge and skills" in reading, this instrument is suitable for outcome assessment as well as for screening and progress-monitoring assessment purposes. A quick screening section is designed to work together with a more detailed inventory section to help teachers identify strengths and problem areas as well as to monitor students' progress.

TPRI covers all five of the Big Five Ideas in early reading development: phonemic awareness, phonics (alphabetics), fluency, vocabulary, and comprehension strategies. The TPRI also provides an Interventions Activities Guide directly linked to student performance on the parts of the TPRI.

The TPRI is administered individually by the classroom teacher. In the screening section of the TPRI, three assessment measures are provided: (1) graphophonemic knowledge (phonics), (2) phonemic awareness, and (3) word reading. In the graphophonemic measure, students are assessed on their recognition of letters of the alphabet and their understanding of sound-to-symbol relationships. In the phonemic awareness measure, students are assessed on their ability to identify and manipulate individual sounds within spoken words so that letters can be linked to sounds. For the word reading measure of the screening portion of the TPRI, students are asked to identify a list of high-frequency words.

In the inventory section of the TPRI, students are assessed across seven measures: (1) book and print knowledge, (2) phonemic awareness, (3) listening comprehension, (4) graphophonemic knowledge, (5) reading accuracy, (6) reading fluency, and (7) reading comprehension. The TPRI, unlike the DIBELS, addresses the important role of concepts about print in the development of early reading.

The TPRI is based on longitudinal data on over 900 English-speaking students. More recently, the TPRI has also become available in Spanish, which, like DIBELS, has yet to be shown to be a valid and reliable indicator of reading development in this population. For a more extensive review of the TPRI, we recommend that you consult www.tpri.org.

Diagnostic Assessments

Diagnostic assessments provide in-depth information about students' particular strengths and needs and are typically used for struggling readers. Diagnostic assessments probe deeper than other assessments and take extra time to conduct. An educational psychologist, certified diagnostician, or a bilingual specialist is sometimes needed to administer certain tests due to time constraints or required special training. Students in special education or Title I programs for reading often require diagnostic testing.

Diagnosing Vocabulary Knowledge

When teachers notice students who seem to struggle with reading, it is logical for them to want to know the extent to which these students' vocabulary has developed. We recommend three tests for assessing a student's word knowledge or receptive vocabulary. One is intended for native English speakers, and the other two are for students who speak Spanish as their first language and are learning to speak and read in English.

- *Peabody Picture Vocabulary Test,* Third Edition. The PPVT-III (Dunn & Dunn, 1997) is a quickly administered test (11–12 minutes) that indicates the strength of a student's vocabulary knowledge compared to other students of the same age nationally. Results can help the teacher better understand the needs of students in terms of formal and informal vocabulary instruction.

- *Test de Vocabulario en Imágenes Peabody.* The TVIP (Dunn, Lugo, Padilla, & Dunn, 1986) is an adaptation of an early version of the previously described Peabody Picture Vocabulary Test for native Spanish speakers. It takes about 10 to 15 minutes to administer and measures Spanish vocabulary knowledge.

- *Woodcock-Muñoz Language Survey–Revised.* The WMLS (Woodcock, Muñoz-Sandoval, Ruef, & Alvarado, 2009) comes in English and Spanish forms. Teachers, particularly in urban centers, often have a large number of students who are English learners (ELs). The extent to which students have acquired a listening and speaking vocabulary in English is an important factor in reading instruction because reading is a language skill that depends on learners having a fairly strong English vocabulary. The WMLS is a widely used instrument throughout the United States (García, McKoon, & August, 2006a) that takes about 20 minutes to administer. It features two subtests: Oral Language and Reading/Writing.

Individual Diagnostic Reading Tests

Teachers sometimes believe it necessary to assess an individual student's reading ability using norm-referenced measures. This often happens when new students move into a school district without their permanent records, or when struggling readers are being considered for extra assistance programs such as Title 1 or special education services provided in inclusive classrooms.

The Woodcock Reading Mastery Tests–Revised (Woodcock, 1997; Woodcock, Mather, & Barnes, 1987) is a battery of six individually administered subtests intended to measure reading abilities from kindergarten through adult levels. Subtests cover visual–auditory learning, letter identification, word identification, word attack, word comprehension, and passage comprehension. Its design reveals a skills perspective of reading, dividing the assessment into two sections according to age and ability levels: readiness and reading achievement. The WRMT-R/NU reports norm-referenced data for both of its forms, as well as insights into remediation. Results may be calculated either manually or using the convenient scoring program developed for personal computers. The WRMT-R/NU is frequently used by teachers in special education and Title 1 reading programs.

Individually Administered Achievement Tests

It can be informative to know how well a student has developed over a wide range of academic subjects. Achievement tests are often given to whole groups of students at scheduled grade levels, but you may need this information right away to better understand a troubled reader's knowledge and abilities.

The Kaufman Test of Educational Achievement, Second Edition (Kaufman & Kaufman, 2010) is our preferred wide-range achievement test that can be individually administered as a diagnostic tool. Sometimes teachers require norm-referenced data to determine how a child is progressing compared to other children nationally, such as when teachers are working with a population of students who are performing at atypically high or low levels. That is, working with either

Thinkstock

struggling readers or gifted students over a long period of time may give teachers a distorted view of what "normal" achievement looks like. The KTEA-II, available in both English and Spanish forms, can provide useful insights in these situations.

The KTEA-II is a norm-referenced test yielding information in the areas of reading, mathematics, and spelling. Intended for students in grades 1 to 12, the KTEA-II is available in a brief form for quick assessments (when only standardized data are needed) and a comprehensive form, which provides both standardized data and insights into classroom remediation.

Getting Organized: Profiling Your Class

The assessment ideas presented in this chapter and in the Pillar 2 sections of previous chapters provide a means of measuring the development of various reading skills. But that is only one part of the reading teacher's job. Organizing and analyzing the assessment data—first for each child individually and then for the entire class—constitute an extremely important next step in instructional planning. Charting the reading skills students have learned and still need to acquire, both individually and as a class, is what we refer to as **profiling.**

Two Documents Needed for Profiling

Teachers need two profiling documents: a student profile document to record individual strengths and needs in some detail and a class profile document to help organize the entire class's data for the formation of needs-based reading groups. A profiling system should be driven either by the state's reading standards or the school district's scope and sequence skills list. These are usually provided in a curriculum guide to all teachers on assignment to a school.

Student Profiling Document. In Figure 10.14 you will see a partially completed student profiling document. Note that each skill has a blank space to note (1) the

Figure 10.14

A Partially Completed Student Profiling Form (Fall, 3rd Grade)

STUDENT PROFILE FORM—READING

Student: Molly H.

Teacher: Ms. K. Spencer

KEY: Reading Skill Development Rating

E = Emergent (not observed)
D = Developing (some evidence, but not fully competent)
P = Proficient (fully competent)

Date of Observation	Category	Benchmark Skill	Student Skill Level
October 14	Phonics	Uses phonic knowledge and structural analysis to decode words.	Proficient
December 5	Fluency	Reads aloud with fluency any text that is appropriately designed for grade level.	Developing (Molly read at 71 WCPM)
September 12	Comprehension	Summarizes major points from fiction and nonfiction texts.	Fiction—Proficient
August 15	Comprehension	Discusses similarities in characters and events across stories.	Proficient
	Comprehension	Discusses underlying theme or message when interpreting fiction.	

date the teacher observed the student performing the specified skill and (2) the degree (rating) to which the student was able to demonstrate the skill. For the latter, a 3-point rubric is provided: "E" for students who are just *emerging* with an awareness of the skill or who have not demonstrated any competency with the skill; "D" for students who are in the midst of *developing* competency in the skill; and "P" for students who have attained *proficiency* (i.e., mastery) of the skill. These designations are important because they help the teacher differentiate the needs of students in the class. The designations can also be useful for informing parents about how their child is developing as a reader.

Note that in the example provided in Figure 10.14, the child has skills at each level of development, as well as some with no designation at all. (This means that the child has not been tested for the skill.)

Class Profiling Document.   Accompanying the student profile is the class profile. (Always have both.) This document lists the same reading standards as the student profile, only in abbreviated form. Figure 10.15 features a partial classroom reading profile for third grade. Notice that the skills listed match those found in the individual student profile.

Figure 10.15

Partial Class Profiling Instrument

CLASS PROFILE (BLAST): THIRD-GRADE LITERACY MILESTONES

Teacher: _____   Date/Grading Period Completed: _____

> Instructions: Record the degree to which each milestone skill has been achieved by each student (**E** = Emergent, **D** = Developing Skill, **P** = Proficient) in each box corresponding to the student and skill in the grid.

Decoding and Word Recognition

3.D.1	Context clues, phonic knowledge, and structural analysis

Spelling and Writing

3.SW.1	Uses studied words and spelling patterns
3.SW.2	Uses the dictionary to check spelling
3.SW.3	Uses these aspects of the writing process:
	3.SW.3.1 Combines information/multiple sources
	3.SW.3.2 Revises and edits
	3.SW.3.3 Variety of written work
	3.SW.3.4 Graphic organizational tools
	3.SW.3.5 Descriptions and figurative language
	3.SW.3.6 Variety of formal sentence structures
3.SW.4.S.1	Orthographic patterns and rules (Spanish only)
3.SW.5.S.2	Spells words with three or more syllables using silent letters, dieresis marks, accents, verbs (Spanish only)

Oral Reading

3.OR.1 Reads aloud with fluency

Reading Fluency

3.F.1	Very few word-by-word interruptions
3.F.2	Reads mostly in larger meaningful phrases
3.F.3	Reads with expression
3.F.4	Attends consistently to punctuation
3.F.5	Rereads to clarify or problem-solve
3.F.6	Reads sixty (60) words per minute (minimum)

Language Comprehension and Response to Text

3.C.1	Comprehends both fiction and nonfiction on level

Figure 10.15

Continued

3.C.2	Reads chapter books independently											
3.C.3	Identifies problem words or phrases											
3.C.4	Summarizes fiction and nonfiction text											
3.C.5	Similarities: characters/events across stories											
3.C.6	Theme or message: interpreting fiction											
3.C.7	Nonfiction:											
	3.C.7.1 Cause/effect											
	3.C.7.2 Fact/opinion											
	3.C.7.3 Main idea/details											
3.C.8	Evaluation: Uses information/reasoning											
3.C.9	Word meaning from roots and affixes											
3.C.10	Dictionary: Determine meanings/usage											
3.C.11	Uses new vocabulary in own speech and writing											
3.C.12	Writing: Basic grammar/parts of speech											
3.C.13	Familiar w/read-aloud, independent reading, nonfiction											
3.C.14	Locates information using:											
	3.C.14.1 Tables of contents											
	3.C.14.2 Indexes											
	3.C.14.3 Internet search engines											
3.C.15	Connects literary texts with life experiences											

From Cooter, R. B., & Cooter, K. S. (1999). *BLAST!: Balanced Literacy Assessment System and Training.* Unpublished manuscript.

To demonstrate how individual student data can be collated into a class profile, we provide an example in Figure 10.16. This example is for decoding and word recognition, as well as spelling and writing skills assessment. It is easy to see how the teacher can begin forming reading groups based on student needs. For instance, the teacher not only might form a group of students who need to develop revising and editing skills, but also recognize that two groups are actually needed—one for those who are emerging in this ability (E-level students) and another for those who are a little further along, or developing (D-level students).

Figure 10.16

Needs-Based Groups

CLASS PROFILE (BLAST): THIRD-GRADE LITERACY MILESTONES

Teacher: _K. Spencer_ Date/Grading Period Completed: _12 - 14_

Instructions: Record the degree to which each milestone skill has been achieved by each student (**E** = Emergent, **D** = Developing Skill, **P** = Proficient) in each box corresponding to the student and skill in the grid.

	Dora	Paula	Ameenah	Jason	Rosa Maria	Harry	James	Dirk	Syporia	Alicia	Johnny	Anna
Decoding and Word Recognition												
3.D.1 Context clues, phonic knowledge, and structural analysis	P	P	P	D	D	P	P	D	P	D	P	P
Spelling and Writing												
3.SW.1 Uses studied words and spelling patterns	D	D	E	E	D	D	E	D	P	E	E	P
3.SW.2 Uses the dictionary to check spelling	D	D	D	D	D	D	P	D	D	D	E	P
3.SW.3 Uses these aspects of the writing process:												
3.SW.3.1 Combines information/multiple sources	E	E	E	E	E	E	E	E	E	E	E	E
3.SW.3.2 Revises and edits	D	D	D	E	E	E	E	D	D	E	E	P
3.SW.3.3 Variety of written work	E	D	P	E	D	P	E	D	E	E	E	P
3.SW.3.4 Graphic organizational tools	E	D	E	D	E	E	D	P	E	D	P	D
3.SW.3.5 Descriptions and figurative language	E	E	E	P	E	E	D	P	D	E	E	P
3.SW.3.6 Variety of formal sentence structures	D	D	D	D	E	D	D	D	E	D	D	P
3.SW.4.S.1 Orthographic patterns and rules (Spanish only)	D	P			D		D					
3.SW.5.S.2 Spells words with three or more syllables using silent letters, dieresis marks, accents, verbs (Spanish only)	P	P			P		D					

IF–THEN Thinking

An absolutely essential key to success in reading instruction is the teacher's ability to analyze reading assessment data and translate this information into a plan for instruction that meets students' learning needs. Earlier in this chapter, we referred to "IF–THEN" reasoning in analyzing reading data. **IF–THEN thinking** (Cooter, Flynt, & Cooter, 2007; Reutzel & Cooter, 2011) works similarly in relation to student and classroom assessment data:

If you have identified specific learning needs in reading for a student, **then** which reading skills and strategies are appropriate to offer the student next in your classroom instruction?

Said another way, the teacher must first collect a good bit of information through valid classroom assessments that begin to paint a picture of where the student is in his or her reading development. Once that picture begins to take shape and the teacher has an educated impression of what the student is able to do independently in reading and what the student needs to learn, she applies IF–THEN thinking:

If the student has this reading need (_____), **then** I should teach this reading skill (_____) using this teaching strategy (_____).

Cooter and colleagues (2007), in order to guide your instruction using IF–THEN thinking, have offered examples such as those provided in Tables 10.1 through 10.3 on the following pages. They describe a few common reading needs along with selected instructional strategies from a variety of sources.

Table 10.1

IF–THEN Chart for Phonemic Awareness

IF a Student Has This Learning Need ...	THEN Try Using a Strategy Like ...	Resources for These and Other Strategies
Initial Sounds	• Word families (same/different beginning sounds) • Songs and poetry • Word rubber-banding • Tongue twisters	**Selected Internet Resources** www.songsforteaching.com www.literacyconnections.com www.nifl.gov/partnershipforreading www.readingrockets.org
Phonemic Segmentation of Spoken Words	• Word rubber-banding • Add/take a sound from spoken words • Environmental print/logos • Songs, chants, raps, poetry	reading.uoregon.edu/pa/pa_features.php **Books** Blvevins, W. (1999). *Phonemic Awareness Songs and Rhymes* (Grades PreK–2). New York: Scholastic.
Blending Sounds into Spoken Words	• Add/take a sound • Word rubber-banding • Environmental print/logos • Songs, chants, raps, poetry • Odd word out	Opitz, M. (2000). *Rhymes and Reasons: Literature and Language Play for Phonological Awareness.* Portsmouth, NH: Heinemann.
Rhyming	• Songs, chants, raps, poetry • Alphabet books • Tongue twisters	Reutzel, D. R., & Cooter, R. B. (2011). *Strategies for Reading Assessment and Instruction* (5th ed.). Upper Saddle River, NJ: Merrill/Prentice Hall.

Table 10.2

IF–THEN Chart for Phonics and Other Word Attack Skills

IF a Student Has This Learning Need ...	THEN Try Using a Strategy Like ...	Resources for These and Other Strategies
Letter Sounds	• Explicit phonics instruction • Word boxes • Tongue twisters • Letter–sound cards • Making words • Nonsense words	**Selected Internet Resources** "Between the Lions" (PBS) http://pbskids.org/lions/games "BBC Schools" www.bbc.co.uk/schools/wordsandpictures/index.shtml www.adrianbruce.com/reading http://cwx.prenhall.com/bookbind/pubbooks/literacy-cluster http://toread.com
"C" Rule	• Explicit phonics instruction • Word boxes • Letter–sounds cards • Making words • Nonsense words	**Books** Rycik, M., & Rycik, J. (2007). *Phonics and Word Identification: Instruction and Intervention K–8.* Upper Saddle River, NJ: Merrill/Prentice Hall. Lucht, L. (2006). *The Wonder of Word Study: Lessons and Activities to Create Independent Readers, Writers, and Spellers.* Portsmouth, NH: Heinemann.
"G" Rule	• Explicit phonics instruction • Word boxes • Making words • Letter–sound cards	Cunningham, P. (2005). *Phonics They Use* (4th ed.). Boston: Allyn & Bacon/Longman. Reutzel, D. R., & Cooter, R. B. (2011). *Strategies for Reading Assessment and Instruction* (5th ed.). Upper Saddle River, NJ: Merrill/Prentice Hall.

Table 10.3

If–THEN Chart for Reading Fluency

IF a Student Has This Learning Need ...	THEN Try Using a Strategy Like ...	Resources for These and Other Strategies
Reading Rate	• Repeated readings • Choral reading • Buddy reading • Reading television captions	**Selected Internet Resources** http://pbskids.org/readingrainbow
Reading Accuracy/ Automaticity	• Oral recitation lesson • Assisted reading • Guided oral reading	**Books** Opitz, M., & Rasinski, T. (1998). *Good-Bye Round Robin: Effective Oral Reading Strategies.* Portsmouth, NH: Heinemann.
Quality/Prosody	• Repeated readings • Choral reading • Guided oral reading • Oral recitation lesson	Reutzel, D. R., & Cooter, R. B. (2011). *Strategies for Reading Assessment and Instruction* (5th ed.). Upper Saddle River, NJ: Merrill/Prentice Hall.

Summary

Assessment exists to inform and improve classroom teaching. When employed properly, assessments help teachers chart individual students' learning and proficiency with essential reading skills. Put another way, assessment helps teachers understand what each child *can* do in reading and what they are ready to learn next. Once teachers know where students are in their reading development they are able to plan appropriate "next steps" in instruction, select appropriate reading materials with which to teach, and plan small-group instruction according to the mutual needs of students.

Four purposes of reading assessment have been derived from two federal initiatives: No Child Left Behind and Reading First. *Outcome assessments* are intended to survey the reading achievement of the class as a whole and offer a kind of snapshot of the reading program's effectiveness. *Screening assessments* provide initial (beginning of the year or the beginning of a new part of the reading curriculum) or "first look" information about each student's ability. *Diagnostic assessments* give more in-depth information about students' individual strengths

and needs. *Progress-monitoring assessments* are an extremely valuable tool for teachers that provide ongoing and timely feedback as to how well individual students are responding to instruction currently in motion—real-time feedback.

A number of commercially published reading assessments commonly used in schools were presented. We grouped these according to the four purposes just summarized for your convenience.

Once student data has been gathered, the next phase of reading assessment requires interpretation of results. We described ways teachers can create student and classroom profiling documents to sort data and make decisions about small-group instruction. We also shared a way of selecting evidence-based teaching strategies that meet each students' needs, called "IF–THEN thinking." This is a classroom-proven method that is both quick and effective in selecting best teaching practices. In this way we can ensure that every child receives the reading instruction needed.

Field and Classroom Applications

- With a partner (or two), conduct a library search of professional journals (e.g., *Educational Leadership, Phi Delta Kappan*) and education periodicals (e.g., *Education Week*) and prepare a response to this question: *What are some of the issues regarding reading assessment?* Be sure to take a look at the literature relating to No Child Left Behind and Reading First legislation. Start with the year 2000 to get a good chronology of issues. Present a poster session of your findings to classmates.

- Develop a schedule for your classroom (name the grade level) that includes time for the daily assessment of at least four students. What typical assessment tools will you probably use during this time period? Identify at least four and justify your choices.
- Develop three evaluation checklist forms that could be used in your classroom or a grade level you specify for reading comprehension, word identification, and content reading strategies. Include a suggested rubric with a rationale for evaluating each student observation.

Recommended Resources

Print Resources

McAndrews, S. L. (2008). *Diagnostic literacy assessment and instructional strategies.* Newark, DE: International Reading Association.

Salvia, J., Ysseldyke, J., & Bolt, S. (2009). *Assessment in special and inclusive education.* Florence, KY: Wadsworth/Cengage Learning.

Web Resources

http://teams.lacoe.edu/reading/assessments/assessments
.html
   Assessment Tools (Los Angeles County Office of
   Education)

https://dibels.uoregon.edu
    DIBELS Home Page (University of Oregon)

www.readingrockets.org/article/14510
   Early Reading Assessment (Reading Rockets)

http://nces.ed.gov/nationsreportcard/reading
   Nation's Report Card in Reading (NAEP, USDOE)

http://www.sedl.org/reading/rad
   Reading Assessment Database (SEDL)

PEARSON

The Power of Classroom Practice
www.myeducationlab.com

Go to Topic 9, Assessment, in the MyEducationLab
(www.myeducationlab.com) for your course, where
you can:

- Find learning outcomes for Assessment along with the
  national standards that connect to these outcomes.
- Complete Assignments and Activities that can help
  you more deeply understand the chapter content.
- Apply and practice your understanding of the core
  teaching skills identified in the chapter with the
  Building Teaching Skills and Dispositions learning
  units. (optional)
- Examine challenging situations and cases presented in
  the IRIS Center Resources. (optional)
- Access video clips of CCSSO National Teachers of the
  Year award winners responding to the question "Why
  Do I Teach?" in the Teacher Talk section. (optional)
- Check your comprehension on the content covered
  in the chapter by going to the Study Plan in the Book
  Resources for your text. Here you will be able to take
  a chapter quiz, receive feedback on your answers, and
  then access Review, Practice, and Enrichment activities
  to enhance your understanding of chapter content.
  (optional)

Go to the Topic A+RISE in the MyEducationLab
(www.myeducationlab.com) for your course. A+RISE®
Standards2Strategy™ is an innovative and interactive
online resource that offers new teachers in grades K–12
just in time, research-based instructional strategies that:

- Meet the linguistic needs of ELLs as they learn
  content.
- Differentiate instruction for all grades and abilities.
- Offer reading and writing techniques, cooperative
  learning, use of linguistic and nonlinguistic repre-
  sentations, scaffolding, teacher modeling, higher
  order thinking, and alternative classroom ELL
  assessment.
- Provide support to help teachers be effective through
  the integration of listening, speaking, reading, and
  writing along with the content curriculum.
- Improve student achievement.
- Are aligned to Common Core Elementary Language
  Arts standards (for the literacy strategies) and to
  English language proficiency standards in WIDA,
  Texas, California, and Florida.

STANDARDS
for Reading Professionals and Guiding Principles for Educators

IRA Standards for Reading Professionals

Standard 1: Foundational Knowledge

Element 1.2

Candidates understand the historically shared knowledge of the profession and changes over time in the perceptions of reading and writing development, processes, and components.

Element 1.3

Candidates understand the role of professional judgment and practical knowledge for improving all students' reading development and achievement.

Standard 3: Assessment and Evaluation

Element 3.1

Candidates understand types of assessments and their purposes, strengths, and limitations.

Element 3.2

Candidates select, develop, administer, and interpret assessments, both traditional print and electronic, for specific purposes.

Element 3.3

Candidates use assessment information to plan and evaluate instruction.

Common Core Standards

Assessment of student abilities in reading and writing involves teacher knowledge of all Common Core Standards.

Response to Intervention

3. Assessment

An RTI approach demands assessment that can inform language and literacy instruction meaningfully.

- Assessment should reflect the multidimensional nature of language and literacy learning and the diversity among students being assessed. The utility of an assessment is dependent on the extent to which it provides valid information on the essential aspects of language and literacy that can be used to plan appropriate instruction.
- Assessments, tools, and techniques should provide useful and timely information about desired language and literacy goals. They should reflect authentic language and literacy activities as opposed to contrived texts or tasks generated specifically for assessment purposes. The quality of assessment information should not be sacrificed for the efficiency of an assessment procedure.
- Multiple purposes for assessment should be clearly identified and appropriate tools and techniques employed. Not all available tools and techniques are appropriate for all purposes, and different assessments—even in the same language or literacy domain—capture different skills and knowledge. Particular care should be taken in selecting assessments for ELLs and for students who speak an English dialect that differs from mainstream dialects.
- Efficient assessment systems involve a layered approach in which screening techniques are used both to identify which students require further (diagnostic) assessment and to provide aggregate data about the nature of student achievement overall. Initial (screening) assessments should not be used as the sole mechanism for determining the appropriateness of targeted interventions. Ongoing progress monitoring must include an evaluation of the instruction itself and requires observation of the student in the classroom.
- Classroom teachers and reading/literacy specialists should play a central role in conducting language and literacy assessments and in using assessment results to plan instruction and monitor student performance.

6. Expertise

- Important dimensions of teachers' expertise include their knowledge and understanding of language and literacy development, their ability to use powerful assessment tools and techniques, and their ability to translate information about student performance into instructionally relevant instructional techniques.
- Professionals who provide supplemental instruction or intervention must have a high level of expertise in all aspects of language and literacy instruction and assessment and be capable of intensifying or accelerating language and literacy learning.
- Success for culturally and linguistically diverse students depends on teachers and support personnel who are well prepared to teach in a variety of settings. Deep knowledge of cultural and linguistic differences is especially critical for the prevention of language and literacy problems in diverse student populations.

Part
Four

Bringing It All Together
in the Classroom

Effective Reading Instruction and Organization in Grades K–3

11

Teacher Knowledge	Classroom Assessment	Evidence-Based Teaching Practices	Response to Intervention (RTI)
What Do Teachers Need to Know and Do to Provide Effective K–3 Reading Instruction?	Assessing Students' Strengths and Needs in the K–3 Classroom: Arranging the Classroom to Support Assessment	Effective Reading and Writing Practices All Year Long	Meeting Diverse Needs of K–3 Learners

Chapter Questions

What are several characteristics of exemplary primary-grade teachers?

How can classrooms be arranged to support assessment of children throughout the school year?

What are several effective reading and writing practices for all year long?

How can teachers use differentiated small-group reading instruction to meet the requirements of a Response to Intervention (RTI) framework?

What are some ways of motivating students to read in primary-grade classrooms?

Describe several new technologies classroom teachers should know and use to teach primary-grade students to read and write.

What are some practices primary-grade teachers might employ to involve parents, caregivers, and community members in helping young children learn to read and write?

Key Terms

Classroom environment

Whole-class instructional area

Literacy centers

Word work center

Listening comprehension center

Paired reading fluency center

Content learning center

Flexible grouping

Daily lesson plans

Literacy curriculum

Interactive read-aloud

Language experience approach

Five-block reading/writing essentials model

Motivation and Engagement	Technology and New Literacies	Family and Community Connections
Motivation and Engagement in K–3 Classrooms	Technology and New Literacies in K–3 Classrooms	Making Family and Community Connections in the K–3 Years

Vignette: Looking in a Primary-Grade Classroom: Effective Reading Instruction at Work

I t is a warm, summerlike day at Mission Elementary School. We scurry down the covered walkways shielding us from direct sunlight to observe Ms. Rivera's second-grade class. As we enter Room 6, we are immediately struck with the "busy" noise we hear: Children are engaged in a variety of reading practice tasks in learning centers. We scan the room to locate Ms. Rivera. She is busily working with a small group of children.

"Please take out your whiteboards and markers," Ms. Rivera tells the students. "I think you can solve this problem, but we'll just have to wait and see. Here is the problem: Using the letters on our cookie sheet," she says, pointing to *a, e, i, c, h, l,* and *m*, "make the word *him.* You may work together. After you have done your very best, I want you to hold up your whiteboards so that I can see how each of you did."

Ms. Rivera leaves her small group deeply engaged in their problem to greet us. She tells us how she is working with this group of children to help them increase their ability to use phonics in reading and writing. Then pointing around the room, she shows us her other centers: a reading nook; an integrated curriculum center focused on science content where children are learning about how different kinds of weather affect rock; a listening center with small books, headphones, and a CD player; a comprehension strategy center where children are completing a categorization task using a graphic organizer of different kinds of soil for growing bean plants under the headings of clay, loam, and sand.

In this quick visit to Ms. Rivera's classroom, we find students busy having conversations about their work, reading, listening, and writing. We see them reading stories in the reading nook and engaged in learning new content knowledge and vocabulary. We see them using their acquired knowledge to carry out the many tasks that their teacher had organized and assigned. Ms. Rivera's room is an active place where children learn new and interesting things. Most important, they are learning that reading, writing, speaking, and listening are important tools for getting smarter. ■

Teacher Knowledge

What Do Teachers Need to Know and Do to Provide Effective K–3 Reading Instruction?

In the past decade or so, several major research reports have been published with the objective of describing and disseminating the knowledge, beliefs, and effective practices that exemplary K–3 teachers use to provide effective classroom literacy instruction (e.g., Block, Oakar, & Hurt, 2002; Pressley, Allington, Wharton-McDonald, Collins-Block, & Morrow, 2001; Rogg, 2001; Taylor, Pearson, Peterson, & Rodriguez, 2005). Taken together, these research reports reveal identifiable characteristics of teachers whose practices lead to exceptional reading achievement for their primary-grade students. These characteristics are listed in Figure 11.1.

What Teachers Need to Know to Provide Effective K–3 Reading Instruction

With the advent of each new school year, empty classroom walls and floors call out to the experienced and novice teacher alike, "Welcome back! What will we accomplish this year with this special, new group of learners?" And each new year, teachers are faced in late summer or early fall with the task of planning, organizing, and preparing the **classroom environment** soon to be occupied by lively, enthusiastic, and somewhat anxious young children. Planning the effective use of classroom space, literacy supplies, and teaching resources is one of the first challenges to be faced each year as teachers prepare for providing effective classroom literacy instruction.

First Steps: Preparing the Classroom Environment

The physical design and environment of each and every classroom exert a powerful influence on teaching and learning behaviors related to reading (Roskos & Neuman, 2001; Smith, Dickinson, Sangeorge, & Anastasopoulos, 2002). Research has demonstrated a clear relationship between the design of environments in classrooms, homes, and neighborhoods and the acquisition of reading and writing concepts, skills, and strategies (Morrow, Reutzel, & Casey, 2006; Roskos & Neuman, 2001).

Spending adequate time prior to the beginning of the school year in preparing the classroom for its eventual occupants—young children—will pay learning and management dividends all year. It is best if you can access literacy instructional materials, that is, the basal or the core reading program teacher's edition, district curriculum guide, and other relevant materials provided by the school at least 3 months prior to the beginning of the school year. Although you might not have this much lead time for planning, it is important that you begin thinking about designing the year's curriculum plan and daily lessons right away. It is also critical to get into your classroom at least 1 month prior to the beginning of the school year in order to prepare the environment, inventory classroom supplies, and acquire additional materials as necessary. Of course, each elementary school and school district will schedule different amounts of time for teachers' planning. You will need to check with your school principal or director to see what is possible.

Designing a Classroom Floor Plan

The major reason for carefully designing the physical environment of the classroom is to encourage children to learn from the environment and to interact productively with you and with each other. Designing a classroom floor plan will help you to effectively manage the environment while addressing the diverse learning needs of all the students in your care. Decisions about the classroom literacy environment generally focus on three major concerns: (1) how to structure the environment, (2) what to place into the environment, and (3) activities to be carried out in the environment.

IRA Standards for Reading Professionals: Standard 1, Elements 1.1, 1.2, 1.3

Common Core Standards: Reading: K–12, Key Ideas and Details (items 1–3), Craft and Structure (items 4–6), Integration of Knowledge and Ideas (item 7), Range of Reading and Level of Text Complexity (item 10); Writing: K–12, Text Types and Purposes (item 3), Production and Distribution of Writing (items 4–6), Research to Build and Present Knowledge (items 7, 9), Range of Writing (item 10); Speaking and Listening: K–12, Comprehension and Collaboration (items 1–3), Presentation of Knowledge and Ideas (items 4–6); Language: K–12, Conventions of Standard English (items 1, 2), Knowledge of Language (item 3), Vocabulary Acquisition and Use (items 4–6)

Response to Intervention: Expertise

Figure 11.1

Characteristics of Exemplary Primary-Grade Teachers

- *Instructional balance.* Teachers integrate explicit skills instruction seamlessly with authentic, connected text reading and writing practice and experiences.
- *Instructional density.* Teachers cover many more skills/concepts/strategies per hour of instruction. Every moment in the classroom is oriented toward the goal of promoting learning—even lining up for lunch or recess.
- *Instructional scaffolding.* Teachers provide sufficient support to help children independently perform literacy tasks.
- *Understanding and respect for developmental differences.* Teachers seek to determine each child's ZPD (zone of proximal development) through appropriate assessment prior to providing instruction and designing learning experiences.
- *Encouragement of self-regulation.* Teachers structure the classroom environment and learning activities so that students understand expectations, behaviors, and outcomes. Independence, cooperation, and task completion are emphasized.
- *Integration of reading and writing.* Teachers structure learning so that reading and writing are used in mutually supportive ways. Children learn to "read what they write" and "write what they read."
- *High expectations.* Teachers expect all children to learn and meet high standards of performance.
- *Good classroom management.* The classroom is well organized with clear procedural training about the purposes and expectations for each area of classroom space. Instructional routines and procedures are clearly defined, well understood, conspicuously displayed, and consistently applied.
- *Skills/concepts/strategies explicitly taught.* Teachers teach reading skills through explanation, demonstration, modeling, and gradual release of responsibility to students. Teachers believe that reading and writing are "taught," not "caught."
- *Access to and emphasis on books.* Teachers focus learning activities on a variety of real texts: poetry, songs, environmental print, stories, decodable books, pattern books, and information texts. Teachers also recognize the importance of providing access to a large quantity and variety of books of differing levels of challenge and using books as a primary means of scaffolding the acquisition of reading skills and strategies.
- *Volume of reading and writing.* Teachers structure classroom learning experiences so that every possible moment is focused on authentic reading and writing tasks rather than on completing "skill and drill" sheets.
- *Task difficulty matched to student competence.* Teachers make every effort to assess and monitor students to assure that the tasks assigned in reading and writing are of sufficient challenge to promote engagement and progress, but not to induce frustration and failure.
- *Connect literacy across the curriculum.* Teachers draw no stark boundaries between learning to read and write and reading and writing to learn. Teachers are as comfortable teaching content knowledge to children during reading and writing instruction as they are teaching reading and writing skills as tools for acquiring content knowledge.
- *Positive, personally reinforcing classroom environment.* Teachers create and maintain a classroom atmosphere of respect, support, and clear expectations. Children are taught to help, support, cooperate, and collaborate in the best interests of others as well as themselves.
- *Work is play in kindergarten.* Kindergarten teachers structure multiple play and exploration centers with literacy learning as the focus.
- *Multidimensional word recognition instruction.* Teachers teach children to use letter–sound information, word parts and patterns, and contextual information to identify unknown words.
- *Printed prompts prominently displayed.* Teachers recognize the human tendency to forget rules, routines, and procedures. Such critical information is conspicuously displayed in effective classrooms.
- *Teacher expectations.* Teachers hold high expectations for students to make substantial progress toward use of writing conventions (capitalization, spelling, handwriting, punctuation, form, and appearance) by year's end.
- *Daily allocated instruction and practice time.* Teachers engage children in a preponderance of reading and writing experiences and activities on a daily basis while allocating sufficient time daily for reading instruction and practice.

Our best advice is to begin simply. You will want to plan a whole-class instructional area along with a small-group instructional area and one or more literacy centers. As you feel able to manage a more complex classroom environment, you will most likely want to subdivide the classroom into additional multipurpose learning and instructional spaces.

Start by drawing a classroom floor plan. Measure the width and length of your classroom and plot it onto a piece of graph paper. Using graph paper helps you maintain a sense of scale. Think about where and how you want to conduct whole-class and small-group instruction as well as literacy center activities in the classroom space available. Carefully plan where you will locate literacy centers to reinforce reading instruction and provide students opportunities to practice reading skills, strategies, concepts, and processes.

Planning a Whole-Class Instructional Area

A **whole-class instructional area** is located near whiteboards, projector screens, or interactive computer whiteboards and well away from areas in the classroom designated for quiet activities. A large piece of well-padded carpet can be used to comfortably seat an entire class of young children in this area. Placing tables or desks around this carpeted area offers additional seating options for viewing materials to be presented by the teacher to the whole class. For management purposes, it is recommended that the carpet area be divided into individual spaces or squares so each child has an assigned place during "rug time."

Audiovisual projection and sound equipment such as a computer projector, document camera, or interactive whiteboard needs to be located in the whole-class instruction area. Other resources might include an easel for displaying enlarged print of stories, poems, riddles, songs, or group language experience charts; an electronic keyboard for music accompaniment; and a big book display easel for reading commercial or child-produced big books. Although not all schools will have all of these digital technology and display resources available, this certainly gives you a "wish list" for planning future classroom purchases to complete your reading instruction digital and print supplies teaching tool box. The whole-class instructional area should be clear of any visual obstructions that prevent children from viewing displayed information and may occupy up to 25 percent of the total available classroom floor space (see Figure 11.2).

When planning a whole-class instructional area, consider your answers to two important questions:

1. Where is the best place in my classroom for the whole group to see and interact with me when I am demonstrating or modeling a literacy skill, concept, process, or strategy?
2. How and where do I want my students to be seated during whole-group instruction—in their desks or at a table or on the rug or both?

Once you have come to decisions about the design of the whole-class instructional space, draw it on your classroom floor plan in as much detail as possible. It is important to consider details, as you will want to think about your needs as a teacher as you design this space. Think about several questions:

- Where should the dry erase whiteboard be positioned?
- Do you need a large chart paper tablet?
- Which should you use, a handheld chalkboard or dry erase board?

Figure 11.2

Whole-Class Learning and Sharing Area

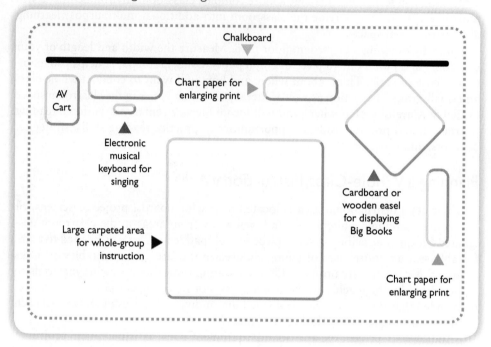

- Do you need a document camera connected to a computer projector?
- Do you have access to an interactive computer whiteboard?
- How will you share and display books, poems, song lyrics, and other text?
- Will you need a DVD or Blu-ray player, a computer, and monitor?
- Will you need access to a CD or MP3 player, or electronic keyboard or piano to teach?
- Do you need a pointer, highlight tape, markers, chalk, editing tape, or sticky notes?

Think through the types of instruction and modeling you will offer in this area and make a list of supplies you will likely need. Plan a place for storage of these materials as well as where these will be used or displayed.

Next, consider where and how you want to arrange your own workspace in the classroom. In some schools and classrooms, you may have a walled-off space or office directly adjacent to the classroom. However, in most schools the teacher's workplace is integrated into the regular classroom floor space. Our advice is that the teacher's work or office space should not be located in the classroom so as to be the dominant or central focus. We recommend that the teacher's desk be "sidelined" in a corner of the classroom (see Figure 11.3). Place your desk toward the wall: Doing so discourages you from spending time at your desk when children are in the classroom. Also, have your desk, bookshelf, files, computer, printer, and displays in a corner to protect these items from damage resulting from normal traffic flow.

With respect to workspace displays, we encourage teachers to prominently exhibit their college diplomas and teaching license in this area. Such a display speaks volumes about a teacher's professional preparation and qualifications. Be sure to

Figure 11.3

Teacher's Professional Space

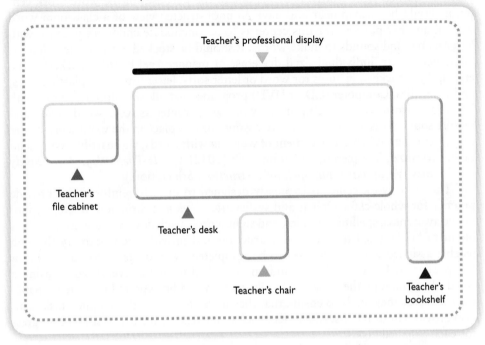

have a shelf where you can store and display professional books, journals, and reference materials. This, too, speaks to your professionalism. Having thought about your work or office space in the classroom, draw this workspace onto the classroom floor plan.

You are now ready to plan and design a small-group instruction area and the literacy centers you desire in your classroom.

Planning a Small-Group Instruction Area and Literacy Centers

When you plan a small-group instruction area and **literacy centers** in a classroom, there is much to contemplate. First, consider where to locate the small-group area. Next, determine how many literacy centers you can accommodte in your classroom floor space. You should also consider how many literacy centers you can reasonably manage. If you are an inexperienced teacher, have trouble with multitasking, or feel a need to have a more controlled classroom environment to start the year, you may not want more than two or three literacy centers to support your small-group instruction area.

For most teachers, the process of planning literacy centers starts by focusing on those that will provide students practice in the essential components of effective reading instruction. An excellent source of information for designing effective literacy centers is found in Morrow's (2002) book, *The Literacy Center: Contexts for Reading and Writing*. In what follows, we describe first literacy centers focused on essential components of reading instruction and then offer suggestions about additional literacy centers that might be desirable once the essential centers have been designed.

Essential Reading Instruction Center: Word Work. A **word work center** serves a variety of purposes. For example, it may focus children's attention on practicing partially learned sight words. If this is one of the purposes of the word work center, it should be located near and have an unobstructed view of a classroom word wall. If another purpose for this center is to accommodate children's practice with letter names and sounds to make words, it should be stocked with magnetic letters, laminated letters, individual-sized dry erase or magnetic gel boards, markers, erasers, zip-lock packets, pictures for word or letter sorts, letter trays with plastic letters, and letter tiles. Computer (CD or DVD) programs that allow children to work with letters and words can be set up in the word work center as well. Word, letter, and picture sound sorts and word and letter games have a place in the word work center too. (For a comprehensive treatment of working with words, we heartily recommend Bear, Invernizzi, Templeton, and Johnston's [2012] *Words Their Way: Word Study for Phonics, Vocabulary, and Spelling Instruction,* 5th edition.)

The word work center is expressly designed to directly reinforce and provide practice for whole-class explicit and systematic *previous* instruction in letters, phonemic awareness, spelling, phonics, and sight words. Each day's word work activities ought to be designed to reinforce instruction and provide accountability through teacher-assigned word work tasks to be completed by students in groups, pairs, or independently. For example, if children are asked to make several words using a word tile containing the *ick* word family, they should be expected to write on paper the *ick* words they made to ensure that they have engaged in the assigned task. This also provides informal assessment feedback to the teacher regarding student progress for each assigned task.

Essential Center: Listening Comprehension Center. The **listening comprehension center** is a spot in the classroom where students listen to books read aloud. A table, chairs, a CD or MP3 player, books on CD or in digital format for MP3 use, and six

to eight copies of each title are essential supplies for this center. If possible, the center should house multiple sets of headphones for listening. If this is not possible, we suggest that you find a way to mark the appropriate volume on the CD player, such as using fingernail polish to draw a line on the volume dial so that students can adjust the volume independently.

Directions for who is to distribute copies of books, how to insert the CD, and how to operate the CD player must be in place. It is also important that students be assigned several follow-up tasks to be completed after listening: You might have them sequence pictures to represent the order of the events in the story, write a summary, or orally retell the story to a partner. For very young readers, answers to comprehension questions can be yes or no or smiling or frowning faces. To encourage the development of listening comprehension, it is important that children should be held accountable for time spent in this center and that they listen and follow along in the book for a purpose. CD-ROM books can be easily used in listening comprehension centers. If a computer is the means of delivery in the listening comprehension center, no more than four children should be seated at a single unit to be able to effectively read along with the print.

Essential Center: Paired Reading Fluency Center.   A paired reading fluency center is used for a variety of reading tasks that can be pursued in pairs or with reading buddies. In terms of classroom space allocation, consider using the whole-class instructional area for the paired reading center, as these two activities typically do not occur simultaneously. You will need to provide a CD recorder, individual tapes, or access to computers for students' recording of their reading of assigned texts. Large pointers and frames for use with big books should also be supplied. You may want to consider providing stopwatches or cooking timers for students to assess their reading rate.

In this center, students may read sight word cards, phrases containing sight words, poetry, stories, and information texts. Children should read quietly aloud together or to one another. Students can be taught to use various choral reading techniques such as unison readings, echo readings, and mumble readings. Students should also be taught how to give one another feedback as to how they might improve their reading fluency.

To hold children accountable for their time spent in this center, you might have them read an assigned list of sight words or a repeatedly practiced text onto a computer audio file at prescribed intervals. You can then systematically check to see whether students are indeed practicing and benefiting from their time spent in this center. These benefits should increase accuracy and rate of sight word recognition and improve fluency and expression in oral reading.

We advise pairing students whose reading skills are slightly or moderately different because frustration often results when students are partnered with a peer whose reading skills are much different from their own. Some research has indicated that allowing students to choose their own partners produces better results and fewer squabbles between partners (Meisinger, Schwanenflugel, Bradley, Kuhn, & Stahl, 2002).

Essential Center: Vocabulary Center.   Vocabulary acquisition consists of three interrelated dimensions: (1) incidental vocabulary learning through exposure to new words in spoken and written language; (2) explicit vocabulary instruction on words that students need to learn to acquire a mature adult vocabulary or words they need to learn to become knowledgeable in a domain of study or knowledge; and (3) self-directed vocabulary learning, which involves cultivating an awareness and love of words through word play and through acquiring word learning strategies. The vocabulary center should directly focus on helping children review and deepen their knowledge of previously taught words and on helping them develop a love of and respect for words through word play.

As you plan a vocabulary learning center, consider acquiring several important sources for word learning, including dictionaries (especially picture dictionaries for younger children), a computer for searching word-learning sites, word study lists, a thesaurus, and a word history book, such as *Word Histories and Mysteries: From Abracadabra to Zeus,* by the editors of the American Heritage Dictionaries. You might also think about acquiring vocabulary games such as Taboo, Boggle, Apples to Apples, and so on. Other supplies might include a pocket chart for matching scrambled word meanings and words, "like-a-test" activities, a word wall of favorite new words and meanings, and the history of names such as the one found at www.behindthename.com. The center could feature a Jeopardy board for displaying new vocabulary words that students must define as a question to play the game. Teachers can produce their own Jeopardy games using the website www.jmu.edu/madison/teacher/jeopardy/jeopardy.htm and Microsoft PowerPoint. At the vocabulary center children should have opportunities to sort words into meanings, fill in vocabulary word maps, and interact with other children to review and deepen their knowledge of new and interesting word meanings.

Suggested Center: Literacy-Enriched Play Centers (Kindergarten). Play, according to Vygotsky (1978), involves the child in behavior that creates a new relationship between the field of meaning and the visual field—that is, between situations in thought and real situations (p. 104). Play is a child's *work*. Through it children learn how to engage in literacy tasks demanded in different situations in the real and imagined world and "try on" the language that people use in different places, situations, and vocations in life.

Grounded in the research of Neuman and Roskos (1992, 1997) as well as many other early childhood literacy educators (e.g., Morrow, 2002, 2005; Rogg, 2001), play centers are a significant part of effective preschool through kindergarten classrooms. Neuman and Roskos (1992, 1997) found that enriching play centers with a variety of situation-specific literacy tools (artifacts) and materials (props) increases children's use of literacy as part of their imaginative play. In other words, children incorporate more literate acts and behaviors into their imaginative play when literacy tools are present than when they are not. Also, embedding literacy learning in play centers encourages children to interact and collaborate with peers using language and literacy as a medium during play. Observations of young children at play have shown that in the presence of literacy tools appropriate to the social situation in the play center, children will engage in attempted and conventional reading and writing acts in collaboration with other children more often (Morrow, 1990; Neuman & Roskos, 1990, 1992, 1997).

Potential play centers considered to be appropriate in kindergarten classrooms include the following.

- *Offices.* Business offices, post offices, doctor's offices, newspaper offices
- *Businesses.* Labs, restaurants, bakeries, carpentry shops, art galleries, grocery stores, auto mechanics and repair shops
- *Travel.* Airports, airplanes, bus stations, buses, train stations, trains
- *Home.* Kitchens, home offices, schoolrooms, playrooms
- *Drama.* Plays, readers' theatre, puppetry, creative movement

For play centers to effectively press children into literacy behaviors, literacy tools and materials need to meet certain criteria and be appropriately arranged. Play centers also need to be organized so that literacy interactions between students are encouraged and supported. The play center is typically not a quiet place, but rather a very busy place where language and literacy acts are "tried on" for fun and fit. Design principles for organizing literacy tools and materials in the classroom and play centers are discussed in a later section of this chapter.

Suggested Center: Integrated or Content Curriculum Learning Centers. A **content learning center** focuses learning on concepts or processes found in a single curriculum subject such as mathematics, science, art, music, or social studies. An integrated learning center joins together several subjects and literacy into a single unit of exploration, discovery, and learning. Activities may initially focus on reading a particular book and following up with several projects, tasks, or assignments related to a particular topic. Or the center may initially involve children in several projects,

Annie Fuller

tasks, or applied learning assignments, and then progress to reading books to answer questions or add new insights and understandings.

For example, children may begin their work in this center by reading the book *Corn: From Farm to Table* by William Anton (1998). During the planning of a project or inquiry center focused on life cycles, you might begin by identifying resources available for learning about corn as a part of a life cycles science curriculum. Children could then look at different kinds of corn seeds under a magnifying glass or count how many corn kernels are in a row on a corncob, representing the numbers using Cuisenaire rods. Students might then make a popcorn snack using an air pop machine so they can see popcorn popping open. They might create a T-chart table or Venn diagram to compare corn with beans and peas in terms of features such as color, shape, taste, uses, and so on. For extended exploration, children could locate items at home that use corn or corn products and then write a brief report on their findings.

In these centers, the goal is to integrate literacy learning with another curricular area. In these centers, as in all others, it is critical to design accountability into the daily operation of the center. In the end, children might complete a series of brief assignments or tasks related to acquiring content knowledge or applying reading strategies.

Organizing Classroom Literacy Tools and Materials

Based on the literacy environmental research mentioned earlier, Reutzel and Morrow (2007) describe six criteria for selecting and arranging literacy tools and materials in K–3 classrooms: (1) appropriateness, (2) authenticity, (3) utility, (4) proximity, (5) uses, and (6) change.

We begin by considering the criterion of *appropriateness*. To determine the appropriateness of literacy tools or materials, ask yourself questions like the following:

- Are the literacy materials developmentally appropriate?
- Can students use these tools and materials safely?
- Can students use these tools and materials in purposeful ways?
- Can students use these tools and materials in socially meaningful ways in dialogic conversations?
- Will these literacy tools or materials help students explore and develop early literacy skills, concepts, and strategies? If so, how?

When selecting literacy tools and materials, you should also consider the criterion of *authenticity*. Ask yourself, *Are these tools used in school and out?* For example, if you put a recipe box, cards, and cookbook, menu, or newspaper food advertisements into a housekeeping play center, would these literacy tools and materials be found in almost any household?

When selecting literacy materials determine whether the literacy tools and materials fit the criterion of *utility*. In relation to this criterion ask: *Do these literacy tools serve useful literacy functions in society?* A partial listing of appropriate, authentic, and useful literacy tools and materials is found in Figure 11.4.

In terms of arrangement and organization, literacy tools should be considered for *proximity* to students and their activities. Children will not use literacy tools readily if they are stored in a location removed from the major area(s) of activity. Also, students must be able to easily access literacy tools and be able to return them to their proper place.

It is important that the teacher carefully suggest *possible uses* for the literacy tools and materials supplied. For example, you might explain that a message board in the classroom is used to post announcements, ask questions, or send personal communications. In a kitchen play center, a message board might be used to post a

Figure 11.4

Possible Literacy Props to Enrich Literacy Learning

Books, pamphlets, magazines	A tote bag for mail	Large plastic clips
Ledger sheets	Posters of children's books	Appointment book
Cookbooks	Small drawer trays	Signs (e.g., open/closed)
Labeled recipe boxes	Library book return cards	File folders
Personal stationery	A wide variety of children's	In/out trays
Grocery store ads/fliers	books	Business cards
Empty grocery containers	Telephone books	Self-adhesive notes and
Note cards	A sign-in/sign-out sheet	address labels
Pens, pencils, markers	ABC index cards	Bookmarks
Trays for holding items	Small plaques/decorative	Post office mailbox
Message pads	magnets	Computer/address labels
Envelopes of various sizes	Assorted forms	Calendars of various types
Racks for filing papers	Blank recipe cards	Posters/signs about mailing
Index cards	Emergency number decals	Stamps for marking books
Clipboards	Food coupons	Typewriter or computer
Stationery	Play money	keyboard
Stickers, stars, stamps, stamp	Small message board	Telephone
pads	Notepads of assorted sizes	Paper of assorted sizes

grocery list or telephone messages. In a science center, a message board might be used to list materials needed to conduct an experiment, to record the steps of the experiment, or to make a diagram for displaying the process or outcome of an experiment.

Finally, literacy tools and materials should be regularly *changed*—rotated or replaced. Like adults, young students grow weary of the same old thing. You should add to, delete from, and rotate literacy tools and materials on a regular basis in your K–3 classroom.

Making the Most of Classroom Display Areas to Support Literacy Learning

Immerse K–3 students in an environment of interesting and functional print. Display areas can be located almost anywhere in the classroom—on walls, windows, floors, doors, and ceilings. When possible, displays should be student-produced rather than teacher-produced. A message board for leaving notes is one means for teachers and students to communicate with each other. A sign-in board encourages even the very youngest children to write their names to begin the school day. Window writing using pens with water-soluble ink allow students to transcribe their stories, poems, jokes, riddles, and song lyrics onto the window glass. Windows are a fun and novel way to publish writing projects in classrooms or sign in at the beginning of the year. Many children are very intrigued by window-published writing projects.

Annie Fuller

A logo language wall or environmental print bulletin board can be devoted to print examples children bring from home. Logo language is both fun and instructionally useful because it helps even the youngest children know they can already read. Children bring labels from cans, cereal boxes, old packages, bumper stickers, and newspaper advertisements to display on a logo language or environmental print wall. This wall can be a resource for guided reading lessons and whole-group instruction throughout the year. (Be sure to remind students that they must label the contents of a can from home if they take the label off before it is used!)

Informational displays should be located in prominent places in the classroom for posting rules, calendars, lunch menus, TV guides, and posters. In addition, informational displays can be used to exhibit information about classroom routines, time schedules, hints on successful reading, the writing process, steps and media for publishing writing, lists of words the class knows, songs the class likes, favorite books, and so on.

Scheduling displays can be arranged for making appointments with peers and teachers for reading and writing conferences as well as editing sessions. Figure 11.5 shows an example of scheduling displays for these purposes.

Objects in the classroom may be labeled by even the youngest of students using "invented spellings" that they write on cards. For example, we have seen the following object labels written by young children in kindergarten classrooms: *seling* (ceiling), *klok* (clock), *weindos* (windows), *dr* (door), *fs* (fish), and *srk* (shark). During

Figure 11.5

Writing Peer Conference Sign-Up Board

Monday—Date _____

8:00 A.M.

Name of Author _____   Names of Peers _____

_____

8:15 A.M.

Name of Author _____   Names of Peers _____

_____

8:30 A.M.

Name of Author _____   Names of Peers _____

_____

Tuesday—Date _____

8:00 A.M.

Name of Author _____   Names of Peers _____

_____

8:15 A.M.

Name of Author _____   Names of Peers _____

_____

8:30 A.M.

Name of Author _____   Names of Peers _____

_____

language lessons, students can be alerted to look for these words in their reading and then alter these invented spellings. Many teachers find that within a matter of weeks, invented spellings used to label classroom objects will be revised to reflect conventional spellings (Calkins & Harwayne, 1987). Incidentally, we prefer to call these "temporary spellings" so that it is clear to children and parents that we will at some point learn the correct spellings. Other areas in the classroom can be used to display helpful reference information such as numbers, colors, alphabet letters, lunchtime menus, and classroom helpers. Remember that all classroom displays should be neat and clear to set the standard for published works in the classroom.

Planning and Organizing Storage Spaces

Devote selected areas in the classroom to storage of classroom and student materials. A writing storage area for children's emerging writing products is a must. Neatly file authors' folders, response journals, and learning logs in corrugated cardboard file boxes. You may wish to store students' writing drafts in three-ring binders on a bookshelf or in another accessible location. A small tablet for recording spelling words can be inserted into the pocket or sleeve of this writing draft binder. Be sure to put each child's name on his or her writing draft binder.

Annie Fuller

Each child needs a personal storage area in the classroom. We recommend vinyl tubs for this purpose. These tubs can house children's personal writing materials, pencil boxes, and belongings. They can also double as post office boxes. Each tub can have a name and a P.O. box number written on the front. These tubs can be stored in specially constructed shelves, along coat racks, on the tops of bookshelves, and on windowsills. Properly cleaned and covered with contact paper, two- to five-gallon ice cream buckets can be stacked along coat racks, cupboards, and windowsills for the same purposes without incurring the expense of purchasing tubs.

When you arrange staplers, paper punches, construction paper, and unlined paper for students' daily use, keep in mind easy accessibility and cleanup. The proper location of each item in the publishing area needs to be labeled to facilitate cleanup and maintenance. We strongly suggest that each item in this center be labeled with both a word and a picture for younger children's use. Also be sure to properly label sorting baskets or bins to facilitate easy cleanup of this area and improve its appearance. The publishing storage area should be located near other busy and potentially noisy areas in the classroom. Book storage areas, such as the classroom library, need to be properly located to facilitate retrieval, reshelving, and accessibility. You will learn more about how to design an effective classroom library in the next section of this chapter.

Word cards can be stored in labeled shoeboxes on the bookshelves in this area. Child-authored books are to be afforded the same respect as commercially produced books. A library card pocket and a checkout card should be placed in each child-authored book. These books should have a section in the classroom library where they can be read, reread, and checked out. Child-authored big books and charts can be given a prominent display area or stored along with other commercially published big books. Plastic pants hangers with clothespins, hooks, or specially designed pocket charts can be used to store or display big books and chart tablets effectively.

Storage for reference materials such as dictionaries, atlases, *The Guinness Book of World Records*, encyclopedias, almanacs, and spellers should be placed near the editing area in the classroom for access by students and editors. Writing media should be stored near where they are needed in the classroom. Plastic tubs or baskets, boxes,

Lisa Stirling/Digital Vision/Getty Images Royalty Free

cut-down milk containers, and the like can be used for both storage and sorting of writing materials. Crayons, markers, pencils, pens, erasers, and chalk can be stored in individual containers for storage. In this way, children can easily sort and clean up writing materials scattered during busy writing output times. Other containers should be made available for transporting small quantities of writing media from large-capacity storage bins to other classroom areas. These small transport containers can be taken to conference locations and collaborative project areas for use and returned and sorted for storage and cleanup.

Planning an Effective Classroom Library

A library is an important part of every classroom where many literacy tools and materials are often stored and displayed. Give careful thought to designing your classroom library. Reutzel and Fawson (2002) have written an accessible book titled *Your Classroom Library—Giving It More Teaching Power: Research-Based Strategies for Developing Better Readers and Writers* that details how to plan, organize, and use a classroom library to support an evidence-based, effective reading instructional program.

The classroom library is the place in the K–3 classroom where primary literacy tools and materials—books—and young children come together. Classroom libraries, like good restaurants, offer staple foods—a core book collection—along with exciting new recipes in the form of rotating books that come and go. Classroom libraries, like restaurants, also provide for dining in and for taking out, with take-home, check-out, book-trading, and book-ordering processes often already in place.

Classroom libraries should be more than mere haphazard collections of old or donated books, volumes purchased at sheltered workshops and garage sales, and items obtained from class book order points. Well-designed classroom libraries serve five important functions (Reutzel & Fawson, 2002): (1) to support instruction, (2) to facilitate learning about books, (3) to organize storage of classroom resources, (4) to provide resources for independent reading and curricular extensions, and (5) to offer a place for student talk and interaction about books.

1. *The classroom library supports reading instruction—in school and out.* Include in your classroom library books and other media materials to support student learning in all curricular areas. Materials related to the content areas of science, health, mathematics, history, economics, geography, music, art, drama, dance, language, grammar, spelling, literature, and computers should be provided. Build an adequate collection of fiction and nonfiction materials at a variety of reading levels to accommodate the many interests and reading skill levels of students desiring to check out books for take-home reading.

2. *The classroom library teaches children how to select appropriately challenging and interesting books.* The classroom library is a place where children can learn about a variety of literary genres as well as how to properly care for books. A book hospital with instructions on how to "operate" on torn pages, remove marks in the books, cover frayed edges, or fix broken bindings provides useful and relevant instruction for younger students.

3. *The classroom library provides an organized central storage location for classroom instructional resources.* Classroom libraries can provide additional space for organizing science equipment, CD and tape players, VHS tapes and DVDs, computers wired to the Internet, games, magazines, and other materials that support learning. In this respect, the classroom library mirrors the organization of media centers at the school and district levels.

4. *The classroom library is a resource—although not the only resource—for reading materials that support children's daily guided or independent reading.* The classroom library provides students readily accessible informational print materials, expository books, computer technology, and media for conducting research or completing thematic or research projects. It offers students the opportunity to browse and explore the world of print.

5. *The classroom library provides a setting for comfortably reading and talking about a book with a peer or the teacher.* The classroom library often provides an ideal location for the teacher to sit down next to a reader and have him or her read aloud. In this way, the teacher can conduct an informal assessment of each student's reading, maintaining a running record to monitor progress. This means that the classroom library should be organized to provide students furnishings, procedures, and opportunities to discuss and read aloud portions of the books they are reading independently.

Having a classroom library area is only the beginning. Making optimal use of the classroom library is the key to its effectiveness.

Grouping Students for Effective Reading Instruction

Grouping students for instruction is one of the ways teachers are able to address diverse learning needs and manage students' movement and activity when engaged in independent reading and literacy and learning center activities. Unlike instructional programs of the past that focused on grouping students by ability, today's delivery models make use of a wide variety of grouping plans. This practice is referred to as **flexible grouping.**

In flexible grouping, students are placed into temporary groups based on their level of independence as learners and their personal interests. Optiz (1998) says that flexible groups allow "students to work in differently mixed ability groups depending upon

Table 11.1

Understanding the Differences Between Ability Groups and Flexible Groups

Considerations for Grouping Decisions	Ability Groups	Flexible Groups
Assigning students to groups	Tests, informal reading inventories, and word list scores	Ability to read leveled books
Duration of groups	Static; long-term	Dynamic; change regularly
Instructional expectations	Dependent on level of students in the group (i.e., high, medium, or low achievers)	High expectations for all students regardless of achievement level
Forms of reading practice	Oral reading—barbershop or round robin reading	Guided oral and silent reading with feedback and discussion
Instructional materials	Core reading program; selections determined by teacher	Core reading program; trade and leveled books chosen by teacher
Mode of assessment	Criterion- or norm-referenced assessment	Observations, running records, informal checklists, progress-monitoring, assessments

the learning task at hand" (p. 10). There are several significant differences that separate ability groups from flexible groups as summarized in Table 11.1.

Flexible groups are established and reorganized on the basis of several well-articulated principles (Unsworth, 1984, p. 300):

- There are no permanent groups.
- Groups are periodically created, modified, or disbanded to meet new needs as they arise.
- At times there is only one group consisting of all pupils.
- Groups vary in size from two or three to nine or ten, depending on the group's purpose.
- Group membership is not fixed; it varies according to needs and purposes.
- Student commitment is enhanced when students know how the group's work relates to the overall program or task.
- Children are able to evaluate the progress of the group and the teacher's assessment of the group's work.
- There is a clear strategy for supervising the group's work.*

Flexible grouping strategies can also be used to accommodate student interests, learning styles, and social needs (Ford, 2005). For flexible grouping to function well in the classroom, the organization and purpose of tasks must be clearly understood; students must be well trained to handle the independence and collaboration inherent in the settings (i.e., independent literacy learning centers) for which flexible grouping is particularly well suited.

Planning the First Day of School in the K–3 Classroom

Planning for the first day of school is something that both excites and frightens teachers every year no matter how many years they have taught. Wong and Wong (1998) point out that one of the most critical parts of a successful first day is establishing

*Reprinted by permission of the International Reading Association.

Figure 11.6

Goals and Objectives to Begin the Year Successfully

- Send a letter home to parents *before* the year begins explaining how they can help their child succeed in early literacy instruction.
- Have classroom seating, learning centers, instructional spaces, materials, activities, and work planned and ready.
- Enthusiastically greet each child at the door, giving clear directions for what to do to find his or her place in the classroom.
- Prepare the classroom so that each child can find his or her place in the room (seating chart, nametags, labels) and be able to independently put away his or her things in an orderly manner.
- Introduce yourself to students.
- Get to know something about each child the first day.
- Discuss with students classroom rules and consequences.
- Establish a routine for getting the day started.
- Prepare a daily schedule and post it where students can see it.
- Encourage reading and writing from the first day—giving directions and receiving requests.
- Provide first-day literacy activities: interactive read-alouds, shared readings, and language experiences.

highly effective classroom management. Wang, Haertel, and Walberg (1994) examined 11,000 research reports to determine the factors that most influence student learning in school classrooms. They identified 28 factors, the most significant of which was classroom management. They concluded that a teacher who is "grossly inadequate in classroom management skills is probably not going to accomplish much" (Wong & Wong, 1998, p. 84).

What is classroom management? It is everything you do as a teacher to organize students, classroom resources, time, and classroom space so that effective instruction can take place. We have already discussed one issue that relates to effective classroom management: organizing classroom space and instructional tools and materials. To pull off a successful first day of school, you must carefully consider the goals and objectives that need to be accomplished in a K–3 classroom on that first day and in that first week of school. We would like to suggest the goals and objectives featured in Figure 11.6.

Preparing Parents and Students for Success: Making Initial Contact

Each year, at least 1 week before school begins, obtain a copy of your class list from the school principal. Along with this, request a list of parents' or caregivers' names and mailing addresses. Even better, if the school secretary can print mailing labels, request these. Compose one letter for parents and one for students. Letters should be welcoming, informative, and positive. You may also think about contacting someone in your local area to provide a translation of this letter for parents who speak and are literate in another language. We have worked with teachers who video the same message in the letter for parents who are not fully literate in one or more languages and then prepare a DVD to be played at home in which they can watch and hear the welcome message from the teacher. A sample letter (or video message) to a first-grade student's parent is shown in Figure 11.7.

A similar letter or video message to students can be included with your letter to parents. If at all possible, send students' letters in individually addressed envelopes. A sample letter to a kindergarten student is shown in Figure 11.8.

Figure 11.7

Sample Letter to a Parent

Dear Mr. and Mrs. _____,

Welcome to first grade! I want to tell you how excited I am to have _____ in my first grade class this year. First grade is an extraordinary year for all students during which they will learn to read and write. Because I know how much you care about your child's success in school, I'd like to offer some simple suggestions.

- Please ask your child every day what he or she has learned at school. Don't accept the response, "Nothin'." I can assure you that there will never be a day this year when children will learn nothing!
- Make time each day to read with your child. Reading at home helps children succeed at school.
- Get books in your home for your child to read. If you need some suggestions, ask me. I would be glad to give you a short list of good books.
- Point out print and discuss reading in your daily living—breakfast cereal boxes, grocery stores, post office, hospital, bus stops, and so on.
- Get some magnetic letters for your refrigerator door. Talk about letters and the sounds these letters represent at home. Spell out your child's name on the refrigerator door. Scramble the letters and have your child make his or her name. Play games with these letters to make words.
- Get your child a library card and make a weekly visit to the public or school library together.
- Provide your child with a variety of writing materials including pencils, crayons, markers, paper, thank-you notes, stationery, recipe cards, and so on. You can store these materials where you have some control of their use, but making them handy for your child will encourage him or her to write.
- Encourage your child to read. You have a strong influence on your child's attitude about reading. If reading is important to you, it is likely to be important to your child.

These are just a few things you can do to get your child off to a good start this year. Each week I will send home a report about what we will be learning in class in the week ahead as well as a summary of what we have learned during the past week. I will also include a couple of activities you can do with your child to (1) practice what he or she has learned this past week or (2) prepare him or her for what he or she will be learning the next week.

I look forward to working with you and your child this year. I pledge to you my very best efforts in making this year a successful and learning-filled one for _____.

Warmest regards,

_____

Figure 11.8

Sample Letter to a Kindergarten Student

Dear _____,

Hi! My name is _____. I will be your teacher this year in kindergarten. I am so excited that you will be in my class. I hope you are excited to come to school, too! We are going to have a wonderful time learning and playing together. I'll have a place ready for you to put your things when you arrive. I'll have a seat with your name on it and a nametag prepared for you. This way, we can get to know each other.

I look forward to meeting you on the first day of school. I'll be at the door to meet you and to help you get settled.

Your teacher,

_____

The First Day: First Impressions

Be sure to arrive early on the first day so you can be available to students and parents as they arrive. Greet each child with a smile at the door of the classroom. Ask his or her name and provide a nametag to wear that matches the one at his or her seat. Give each child simple directions for what to do after the initial greeting. We invited our first-graders to sign their names on the classroom windows using a water-soluble transparency marker. Alternatively, have a card or sign-in board where children can write their names or mark their names on a list to register their attendance.

Make sure that the room is completely ready for students. Have the classroom floor plan completed. Seating, storage, displays, and furnishings should all be arranged according to the floor plan. Whole-class and small-group teaching areas, literacy and learning centers, and storage spaces should be clearly marked with signs, posters, and labels. Students' storage areas, coat racks, seats, cubbies, and other areas should be labeled and ready. Wear a nametag similar to those you have prepared for students. Each child's seat or place at a table should have his or her nametag affixed. Arrange for something students can do at their seats as they arrive—a puzzle, a counting activity, or a reading activity.

Establish a Beginning Routine. Once the bell signals the beginning of the school day, you need to establish your opening routine. Taking attendance and lunch count are traditional activities at this time. An efficient way to take roll is to have an attendance board in your room: Each child takes a card with his or her name on it and places it into the appropriate name pocket, indicating the child is present. We also advise that, as students enter the room each day, they have at their seats a journal in which they can draw or write until instruction formally begins.

Another wall chart can be used for children to indicate whether they are eating school lunch. A simple chart can feature a picture of a lunch pail or bag (Brought My Own Lunch) on one side and a picture of a food tray (Eat School Hot Lunch) on the other side. Each child takes a clothespin with his or her name on it and places it on either side of the chart to indicate either school lunch or one brought from home.

We recommend having a "message of the day" on a classroom message board posted by the door. We also encourage a classroom environmental print wall where students can bring examples of environmental print for posting.

On the first day of school, tell, show, and select students to demonstrate your classroom routines. Post simple written directions near the classroom door to remind students about what they are to do after entering the classroom each day.

Establishing a Morning Routine. We recommend beginning the school day with a song illustrated and displayed on large chart paper. In our own first-grade classrooms, we sang "Good Morning, Says the Sun" to start our morning. Using a calendar chart, we reviewed the day, the days of the week, the month, and the season of the year. We also reviewed the weather for the day—sunny, partly cloudy, cloudy, foggy, rainy, or snowy. A school lunch chart shows the meal to be served that day. We display the daily schedule at the front of the room and review it each and every morning. We also make daily additions to and discuss our environmental print wall and our word wall.

Finally, as noted in the sample morning routine shown in Figure 11.9, we provide time daily for students to orally share something about themselves or their families. Although many teachers, parents, and administrators may question the value of "show-and-tell" (or as some call it, "bring-and-brag"), we find this time to be

Click on A+RISE— Literacy Strategies in the MyEducationLab (www. myeducationlab.com) for your course. Next, select the Strategy Card Index tab, scroll to the Emergent and Beginning Readers, and select the Morning Message strategy.

Figure 11.9

A Suggested Morning Routine

- Sing a song together.
- Review the calendar and weather chart.
- Review the school lunch menu.
- Review the daily schedule posted in the pocket chart.
- Review environmental print words and/or word wall words.
- Provide time for guided oral sharing.

especially valuable for getting to know our students and also for providing them with a comfortable setting in which they can expand their oral language. Typically we structure this time with established parameters about what to bring and share rather than allowing children to bring just anything. We send home a note to parents telling them what items would be appropriate and meaningful for show-and-tell. We model showing and telling on the first day of school as a means of introducing ourselves to students.

For the first month of school, we invite one child per day to bring a box labeled "All About Me," which students place three to five special items from home that reveal their interests, where they were born, their favorite food, and so on. "Show and Tell" can really give ELs a chance to share their culture. You may even want to encourage your ELs bring in a parent or grandparent to share interesting facts from the home country.

Making the Classroom Work: Rules and Consequences. Rules are expectations for appropriate student behavior in the classroom. Consequences are the responses to choices made about honoring the rules in the classroom. Classroom rules and consequences should be discussed on the first day of school. Teachers often solicit input from their students about rules that help everyone talk, listen, and get along with each other in order to learn. It is important that even the youngest children have an opportunity to express their needs and ideas related to classroom rules and consequences. It is wise to keep rules to a minimum for very young children. In practical terms, this means no more than five classroom rules.

Discuss with students the consequences for both keeping and breaking classroom rules. These can be listed on chart paper or poster board and displayed in a prominent location. Many teachers encourage their students to suggest rewards and potential consequences, but retain the final say in these matters. Our typical classroom rules and consequences are shown in Figure 11.10.

Figure 11.10

Classroom Rules and Consequences

- Raise your hand to ask to speak.
- Listen courteously when others are speaking.
- Keep hands, feet, and objects to yourself.
- Stop anything you are doing when you hear the signal to do so.
- Listen carefully to directions.

What Happens If You Choose to Break Our Classroom Rules

- 1st time—Verbal warning from the teacher
- 2nd time—Lose morning recess
- 3rd time—Lose morning and afternoon recesses
- 4th time—Call to parents
- 5th time—Go to principal and in-school discipline room

Reading from the Start: Getting Attention and Giving Directions. On the first day of school, we use written direction cue cards along with our oral directions. We tell students that we will not give oral directions after the first week of school; rather, we will use only the printed cue cards. We produce on laminated poster board a series of written cue cards that we place near a hotel register bell in the middle of the classroom. If we want students to line up, we ring the bell to get their attention. We then hold up a written cue card—for example, "Please line up quietly at the door." If we want students to come to the front of the room for whole-group instruction, we ring the bell and hold up a printed cue card that reads, "Please sit down quietly on the carpet." This process creates an immediate need for students to focus their attention on print. Giving directions in this way makes it clear from the outset of the school year that reading is necessary to function in the classroom environment.

Reading and Writing Activities on the First Day. Because we do not know a great deal on the first day about children's individual reading and writing development, activities should be done primarily with the whole class. Our past experiences have shown that some of the best activities on the first day (and every day thereafter) include interactive read-alouds, shared reading, language experience activities, and interactive writing. "What Happens When _____?" is a good first day theme. Read-alouds and other activities can focus on this theme or a variation thereof. Figure 11.11 features samples of first day kindergarten and first-grade literacy schedules.

Planning the First Week of K–3 Reading and Writing Instruction

Having survived the first day of school, we now turn our attention to planning the first full week of the new school year. The major goal of the first week is to get to know the children and their individual learning needs. This means that you will need to assess individual children while managing the whole class. This is not easy and requires careful thought and planning.

Figure 11.11

Kindergarten and First-Grade First Day Literacy Schedules

Half-Day Kindergarten (90 minutes literacy)

8:30–9:00 A.M.: Greet children and parents
9:00–9:10 A.M.: Morning routine (roll, lunch, weather, calendar)
9:10–9:20 A.M.: Sharing time
9:20–9:35 A.M.: Interactive read-aloud
9:35–10:05 A.M.: Shared reading of a big book
10:05–10:20 A.M.: Whole-class explicit lesson on letters and sight words
10:20–10:35 A.M.: Recess
10:35–10:45 A.M.: Science experiment: Magnets
10:45–11:00 A.M.: Shared writing/language experience chart
11:00–11:20 A.M.: Literacy-enriched dramatic play centers

First Grade (180 minutes literacy)

8:30–9:00 A.M.: Greet children and parents
9:00–9:10 A.M.: Morning routine (read morning message, roll, lunch, weather, calendar)
9:10–9:20 A.M.: Sharing time—oral language
9:20–9:35 A.M.: Interactive read-aloud: storybook
9:35–10:00 A.M.: Shared reading of enlarged text
10:00–10:30 A.M.: Whole-class science experiment to make a language experience chart after demonstrating experiment using balloons, water, and baking soda
10:30–10:45 A.M.: Recess
10:45–11:15 A.M.: Writing: language experience chart about science experiment
11:15–11:30 A.M.: Word work—whiteboard letter/sight word dictation
11:30–11:45 A.M.: Word wall Bingo—high-frequency sight words
11:45–11:55 A.M.: Phonemic awareness—blending and segmenting to make words
12:00–12:45 P.M.: Lunch
12:45–1:00 P.M.: Interactive read-aloud: Information book

Classroom Assessment

Assessing Students' Strengths and Needs in the K–3 Classroom: Arranging the Classroom to Support Assessment

● ● ●

IRA Standards for Reading Professionals: Standard 3, Elements 3.1, 3.2, 3.3

Response to Intervention: Assessment

Because a major goal at the beginning of a school year is to get to know students' individual learning needs in order to teach effectively, an assessment plan for this beginning period should be a major part of planning. Assessment of individual children is best carried out in a quiet area of the classroom. Gather the assessment tools (inventories, forms, books, and records) that you will use to assess students in a teacher assessment binder.

You will need to call each child away from independent or group work to the area of the classroom where you intend to conduct individual assessment. As you begin the assessment process, put the child at ease. Say that you want to learn about what he or she knows so that you can provide the best possible teaching during this next year.

You will also need to arrange meaningful independent seatwork and center work for the students you are not assessing. You might ask for parent volunteers to assist in the classroom during this first week to help with management, to read to students in small-group or whole-class sessions, and to interact with children in learning centers. It is important that you not plan to assess for more than 1 hour per day in kindergarten and 2 hours per day in first grade during the first week of the school year. We say this because consistent interaction with your students is of critical importance in establishing a sense of community in the classroom. Also, young children cannot sustain long periods of independent activity without teacher-guided interaction. The first week is also an ideal time to begin to train students in how to function in literacy and learning centers successfully and to practice how small groups will rotate through several learning centers each day using "dry runs."

Training Students to Effectively Use Literacy and Learning Centers

For learning centers to be effective, their use must be carefully explained and highly structured with clearly defined rules, directions, and tasks to be completed. Literacy and learning center work must result in the completion of assigned tasks so that students are held accountable for the time spent in centers. To train students in procedures and routines will require a few minutes each day, roughly 5 to 10 minutes over a period of about 4 to 6 weeks. During this daily 5 to 10 minutes of training time, students receive a series of procedural lessons on how to work effectively in the classroom and in the literacy learning centers placed in and around the classroom.

Week 1. During the first week of the school year, Reutzel and Morrow (2007) suggest ignoring learning centers and literacy materials placed in and around the room for students' eventual small-group and independent use.

Week 2. During the second week, mention to students that they will eventually be working in small groups and independently in the spaces designated around the classroom, but before they can do so, they will need to learn some skills and procedures. This heightens students' curiosity and motivation to learn the expectations and procedures to eventually enter and engage with these spaces and materials. Explain the purpose of each learning center: for listening, for paired reading, for alphabet and word work, for learning content, for writing, and so on. Tell students about one or two centers per day during the second week, but do not let students enter these spaces or use these materials yet.

Week 3.   During the third week, fully explain and model how students are to use one or two of the learning centers.

• On the first day of the third week you might model how students should go to the word work center in the classroom. Before going to this space, you might show them how they need to pick up their word work folders and quietly gather around the rules and the directions displayed for the day with other children in the word work center.

• On the second day of the third week, you might explain that you will appoint a team leader to lead the small group in a review of the rules and directions each day. You might model how this is to be accomplished through a quiet oral reading of the posted rules and the directions for working in the word work center that day. Be sure to model how the team leader is to ask if there are any questions and answer these when possible.

• On the third day of the third week, you might model how students are to take their places in the word work center and wait for the team leader to distribute any needed materials for completing the displayed task for the day. On this same day, you might discuss with students your expectation that assigned tasks will be completed in the time allotted either independently or with others, depending on the directions for the day. You might also demonstrate for students how they are to seat themselves for independent work in the word work center.

• On the fourth day of the third week of training, you might explicitly identify the consequences of failing to follow directions and obey the rules. You might direct children's attention to the posted consequences for failure to follow directions and behave appropriately in activity centers.

• On the last day of the third week of training, you might model the clean-up process for the selected learning centers. A bell or other signaling device can alert children that time for using the center has ended. You might model how students are to "freeze" quietly in place while the team leader gathers up materials and returns them to their proper storage places. A second bell or signal can tell children they have 15 to 30 seconds to tidy up their own materials and seating area. A final bell or signal can direct children to move to another reading center or return to their own seats in the classroom.

Training for using learning centers will likely require approximately 10 minutes per day for the entire third week of the school year. The process can be repeated at a slightly accelerated pace over the next 2 weeks with each of the remaining learning centers.

Role Playing the Use of Literacy and Learning Centers in the Classroom.   During the sixth and final week of training, teachers form small groups with team leaders for role playing the use of the learning centers and materials around the classroom. To begin the role play, students practice moving from their regular classroom seats

Figure 11.12

Center Rotation Management Schemes

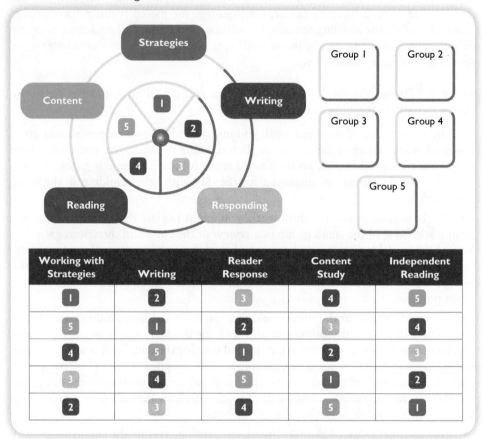

Working with Strategies	Writing	Reader Response	Content Study	Independent Reading
1	2	3	4	5
5	1	2	3	4
4	5	1	2	3
3	4	5	1	2
2	3	4	5	1

to their first assigned learning center. Movement from one learning center to another using planned rotations during the literacy time block is also practiced. We show two possible approaches for managing learning center group rotations in Figure 11.12.

Wise teachers realize that students must be able to role play these movements and behaviors to fully understand and internalize them. During role play, anyone who fails to follow directions *exactly* causes the entire group to stop and repractice the movement and expected behaviors. Remaining firm about meeting expectations as children role play their use of these spaces and materials will save many management problems later on.

Typically, 10 minutes per day for 1 week is sufficient to prepare children. During this 10-minute role play, students should (1) move from their seats into the designated learning centers, (2) read as a small group the posted rules and daily task directions, (3) settle into proper seating arrangements based on posted task directions, (4) distribute reading tasks and materials, and (5) practice cleaning up the center space and materials.

Of course, children become excited, anxious, and motivated to enter these learning centers as they engage in their role playing. We have found that displaying photographs of children properly engaged in various center activities is helpful in encouraging children to behave appropriately during center work. One teacher we know simply asks her students if they look like the children in the picture. If not, she asks what they should do about their behavior to align it with the learning activity as shown in the example picture.

Minimizing Transition Times and Maximizing Reading and Writing Practice and Instruction.   Training children for efficient movement between activities and into and out of various classroom literacy spaces is essential for minimizing transition times and maximizing literacy practice and instructional time. Here again, experience has taught us the value of using timers, stopwatches, and other devices to motivate children to accomplish transition tasks briskly and without dallying. Reducing transition times between activities and movements to other classroom spaces to only 1 minute allows the bulk of classroom time to be spent on reading and writing practice and instruction. We use three steps to achieve this worthwhile goal.

First, we use a consistent signal (ringing a hotel registration bell, turning off the lights, playing a familiar song on tape) to alert students to stop what they are doing, freeze, and listen for directions.

Second, we provide brief, well-sequenced, and repetitive oral directions coupled with written directions displayed on cue cards. Children must look, listen, and read to get the directions for what is to be done.

Third, we use our signal device once again to alert children to follow the oral and written directions to move to the next learning center.

A sample daily schedule for the first few weeks of school is shown in Figure 11.13, including time for providing daily procedural learning center lessons.

Figure 11.13

Kindergarten and First-Grade Daily Literacy Schedules

Half-Day Kindergarten (90+ Minutes of Literacy)
8:30–8:45 A.M.: Roll, lunch count, pledge
8:45–9:00 A.M.: Morning message and routine
9:00–9:10 A.M.: Oral language activities
9:10–9:25 A.M.: Interactive read aloud
9:25–9:45 A.M.: Shared reading of big book or enlarged print
9:45–9:55 A.M.: Sight word practice
9:55–10:10 A.M.: Letter name lesson
10:10–10:25 A.M.: Recess
10:25–10:55 A.M.: Content area knowledge building
10:55–11:25 A.M.: Small group literacy centers

Full-Day First Grade (180+ Minutes of Literacy)
8:30–8:45 A.M.: Roll, lunch count, pledge
8:45–9:00 A.M.: Morning message and routine
9:00–9:10 A.M.: Oral language activities
9:10–9:25 A.M.: Interactive read aloud
9:25–9:40 A.M.: Shared reading of big book or enlarged print
9:40–10:00 A.M.: Sight word practice
10:00–10:10 A.M.: Phonics
10:10–10:25 A.M.: Recess
10:25–10:55 A.M.: Core reading program instruction
10:55–11:25 A.M.: Fluency practice
11:25–11:45 A.M.: Vocabulary instruction
11:45–12:00 P.M.: Comprehension instruction
12:00–12:40 P.M.: Lunch
12:40–1:40 P.M.: Small group reading instruction

Preparing Written Lesson Plans to Build Teacher Capacity for Explicit Early Literacy Instruction

The first week is also a good time to start the best practice of writing **daily lesson plans.** It has been our experience that teachers who take the time to write and reflect on daily lesson plans provide higher quality instruction than those teachers who try to teach from a mere activity mentioned in a teacher's planning book or those who simply "fly by the seat their pants." To put it bluntly, the quality of outcomes in learning is directly related to the quality of the teacher's planning and delivery of instruction. To help you get a sense for the detail necessary in a daily lesson plan, a sample second-grade lesson plan for an oral guided reading of an information book is featured in Figure 11.14.

Written lesson plans look like a great deal of work, and they are. But to carefully think through each lesson while planning the materials, information, modeling, explanations, questions, and so on will result in greatly increased student learning. Written lesson plans also give you the satisfaction of knowing you did your best to plan, instruct, reflect on, and improve your teaching. Written lesson plans need to be developed daily for each learning center as well as for small-group and whole-class instruction. Careful planning is often the difference between a well-managed classroom and chaos.

After writing daily lesson plans, schedule a time for each literacy lesson and literacy learning center. This can be a simple listing of times when you will (1) teach a group literacy lesson, (2) assess individual children's literacy development, (3) rotate groups through literacy and learning centers, and (4) provide group and independent seatwork. We suggest following a general daily schedule for literacy instruction and assessment during the first week of school in K–3 classrooms, as was shown in Figure 11.13.

Designing a Yearlong Curriculum Plan

For most new teachers (and many experienced teachers as well), perhaps the most difficult schedule to create is the annual curriculum plan. The **literacy curriculum** is defined as a description of the reading and writing skills and strategies taught at a specific grade level. In planning your literacy curriculum, some of the best sources to begin with are (1) the state's curriculum standards, (2) the school district curriculum guide, and (3) the district's adopted basal or core reading program's scope and sequence chart. When designing your curriculum plan, it is important to remember that the teaching of a reading or writing skill to the level of student independence is not accomplished in one lesson but rather over multiple lessons throughout the year. Consequently, the curriculum plan also needs to include a schedule for reviewing previously taught lessons.

Because it would not be practical to describe the specifics of every state's standards, every basal reading program's scope and sequence, or every school district's curriculum guide, we instead use guidelines found in two prominent national reading research reports: *Starting Out Right: A Guide to Promoting Children's Reading Success* (Burns, Griffin, & Snow, 1999) and *Put Reading First: The Research Building Blocks for Teaching Children to Read, K–3* (Armbruster, Lehr, & Osborn, 2001). In Figure 11.15 (on page 487), we list the desired "evidence-based" grade-level accomplishments for K–3 students in reading. As you plan your curriculum, be sure to attend to each of these grade-level goals for student accomplishment.

Figure 11.14

Written Daily Lesson Plan—Second Grade

Title of Book   *Amazing Water*

Objective: Children will use several comprehension strategies to help them learn content knowledge from reading an information book.

Supplies Needed: *Amazing Water* big book, ice, water, different-shaped containers, hotplate, pan, mirror or piece of clear glass, word cards with pictures, graphic organizer

Step 1	Introduce the Book

Say: "This is an information book. An information book is different from a storybook. Let's talk for a moment about some of the differences. Information books give us facts, knowledge, and information about real things in our world like rocks, animals, or how to make chocolate! Storybooks are made up and are often not about real people or things in our world. Animals might talk, places might not really exist, and events might be imaginary."

Step 2	Activate Background Knowledge

Show students the different forms of water. Say: "Isn't water amazing?"

- Liquid—water in different-shaped containers
- Solid—ice cubes
- Gas—steam collected onto glass or mirror

Model by saying: "Before I read a book, I stop and think about what I know that connects to the book. If the book is about dogs, then I think about what I know about dogs. To become better readers, we need to stop and think about what we know about our book today. Now, stop and think about your own experiences with water. What do you think is amazing about water? If you have something to share, raise your hand and wait for your turn."

Step 3	Discuss the Author

Identify the author of the book. Point to his or her name on the book cover. Remind students that the author of a book is its writer.

Step 4	Table of Contents

Remind students that information books are different from storybooks. Information books have a table of contents at the beginning. The table of contents tells what is in the book and the order or sequence the author uses to organize the information he or she presents.

Step 5	Text Structure

Say: "Successful readers try to figure out how the author has put the book together. One of the ways authors put books together is to use a book web. Let's look at the board. I have on the board a book web for our book today, *Amazing Water*. Here, in the center of the book web, I have written the title of our book, *Amazing Water*. You also see that I have other picture/word cards on the board. Do you notice that the book web looks kind of like a spiderweb? That's why we call it a 'web.'

"The author of our book is going to tell us about water by describing each of the things we see in our book web. Having this web helps us see how the author wants us to read the book and how he wants us to remember the information. Let's look at what the author is going to tell us about water and how he wants us to remember it. At the end of the first web strand, we have a picture/word card that says *liquid*. So the author is going to tell us about water as a liquid. What else is the author going to tell us? Let's look at the other web strands: *solid, gas, weather,* and *forms of water*. Remember, the book web is to help us notice and think about how the author is going to tell us the information in the book."

Step 6	Predicting

"Notice that I have put picture/word cards along the chalkboard tray. Each of these picture/word cards fits underneath one of the five web strands around the title of our book. Let me show you what I mean." Pick up one picture/word card and think aloud about where and why this picture/word card goes here. Invite individual children to take each picture/word card and predict its place in the web.

Step 7	Question Generating

Say: "Before I read, I often think of some questions I'd like to answer as I read. Asking myself some questions helps me focus on important information and remember it. For example, I might want to ask, 'What makes water turn to ice?' Can you think of any questions you would like to ask before we read? Let's put a few up here."

continued

Figure 11.14
Continued

Step 8 Read

Read aloud with the children the big book *Amazing Water* in a shared reading.

Step 9 Elaborative Interrogation

Stop at statements shown below. Mark points in the big book for turning statements into questions using sticky notes showing a question mark before the following statements:

- Water is a liquid.
- Ice is a solid.
- Steam, or water vapor, is a gas.
- Lots of different kinds of weather are forms of water.

Model for children how to turn the statement "Water is a liquid" into a question: "Why is water a liquid?" Write question on chart paper or whiteboard. Invite students to turn the other statements into questions.

Step 10 Monitoring

Stop at points with a "Stop Sign" on a sticky note to monitor comprehension. Tell children: "Let's review what we have learned so far to see if you are getting it. If you are getting it or it *clicks*, then read on. If you aren't getting it or it *clunks*, then we need to use some 'fix up' strategies." (See Chapter 7.)

Pages to stop for monitoring:

Page 9
Page 13

Step 11 Making Inferences and Confirming

After reading, have students respond to the following questions:

- What new things did you learn about water from this book?
- What things do you feel you didn't understand?
- How could the author have made these ideas clearer? Give the author some advice.
- Who can tell me three different forms of water?
- Let's look at the questions we asked before we read the book. Can we answer any of these? Discuss.
- Let's look at our predictions in the *Amazing Water* book web. How did we do? Let's look closely.

Step 12 Summarizing

Say: "We are going to make a summary. A summary helps us organize what we know using a few big ideas. We are going to make a summary web of what we have learned about amazing water. I'm going to put up one sentence strip. It says, The Three Forms of Water. Can anyone tell me what the three forms of water are?" As students give the three forms of water, place three word cards—*liquid, solid,* and *gas*—around the sentence. Divide children into three groups. Give children word cards from the book containing terms like *rain, vapor, ice,* and others. Give each group three randomly selected word cards. Ask them to talk about each word and place it under the proper category of liquid, solid, or gas. Once they are finished, write one sentence to summarize the book: "Water is amazing because it can be a liquid, a solid, or a gas."

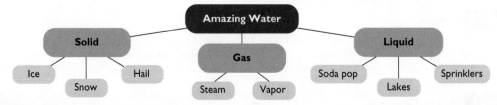

Step 13 Reflection

Think about where the lesson went well and where there were problems. Adjust the lesson plan to smooth out the problem spots.

Figure 11.15

Expected Literacy Accomplishments for K–2 Students

Kindergarten

Reading

- Engages in language activities and games to develop phonological and phonemic awareness—an awareness of word parts (phonemes, onsets, and rimes, etc., see Chapter 4)
- Understands basic book and print concepts
- Recognizes upper- and lowercase letters
- Makes connections between letters and sounds (alphabetic principle, see Chapter 4)
- Recognizes a few high-frequency words by sight
- Reads simple emergent or beginning reader books (memorized and finger-point reading)
- Notices when oral or book language doesn't make sense
- Makes predictions while listening to stories read aloud

Writing

- Writes upper- and lowercase letters
- Writes own name
- Uses invented spellings to express own meaning
- Uses invented spellings when writing teacher-dictated words
- Aware of the difference between "kid" writing and conventional writing

First Grade

Reading

- Makes transition from emergent (memorized and finger-point reading) to reading accurately what is recorded in the text
- Decodes regularly spelled one-syllable words and nonsense words
- Accurately reads and comprehends any text designed for first half of first grade
- Uses letter–sound knowledge (phonics) to sound out unfamiliar words
- Has a reading vocabulary of 300–500 sight words and easily sounded-out words
- Monitors own reading and self-corrects using language sense and context when reading fails to make sense
- Reads and comprehends story and information texts appropriate to the grade level
- Reads and comprehends simple written instructions
- Makes predictions and justifies predictions for stories
- Activates background knowledge and uses it to understand new information
- Can count the number of syllables and phonemes in one-syllable words
- Can blend and segment the phonemes of one-syllable words
- Can answer simple comprehension questions
- Engages voluntarily in a variety of reading and writing activities

Writing

- Spells three- and four-letter short vowel words conventionally
- Writes texts for others to read
- Writes independently using a mix of invented and conventional spellings
- Uses basic or terminal punctuation (period, question marks, exclamation marks) and capitalization
- Produces a variety of types of compositions and texts (stories, poems, notes, cards, recipes, journal entries, information texts, and so on)

Second Grade

Reading

- Reads and comprehends both fiction and nonfiction books at grade level
- Accurately decodes regular multisyllable words and nonsense words
- Uses letter–sound knowledge to decode unknown words
- Accurately decodes irregularly spelled words containing diphthongs, special vowel combinations, and common word endings
- Reads voluntarily for interest and own purposes
- Recalls facts and details
- Reads nonfiction to answer specific questions or for specific details
- Responds creatively to books through dramatizations, fantasy play, or oral presentations
- Discusses similarities in characters and events across texts
- Connects and compares information across texts
- Poses answers to how, what, why, and what-if questions

Writing

- Correctly spells previously studied words and spelling patterns in own writing
- Represents the complete sound of a word when spelling independently
- Writes using formal language patterns in place of oral language patterns at appropriate spots in own writing
- Makes reasonable judgments about what to include in own writing
- Productively discusses ways to clarify own writing and that of others
- With assistance, uses conferencing, revision, and editing processes to increase quality of own writing
- Given help, writes informative, well-structured reports
- Attends to spelling, mechanics, and presentation for final products
- Produces a variety of types of compositions

Based on grade level accomplishments found in Burns, M. S., Griffin, P., & Snow, C. E. (1999). *Starting Out Right: A Guide to Promoting Children's Reading Success.* Washington, DC: National Research Council.

The School Reading Coach: A Resource Not to Be Overlooked

Walpole and McKenna (2004; McKenna & Walpole, 2008) have written extensively about the role of a reading coach as a resource to classroom teachers. Just as football players benefit from feedback about their performance during a game, teachers can likewise improve the effectiveness of their reading instruction by having a skilled reading educator observe their practice and offer supportive suggestions for improvement. As a primary-grade classroom teacher, we encourage you to get to know your reading coach if your school is fortunate enough to have one. Reading coaches can help teachers locate and purchase materials for improving reading instruction; lead study groups of teachers in reading, discussing, and studying articles and books on effective reading instructional practices; carefully examine assessment data for making instructional decisions; and observe for and model effective instructional strategies in reading (Toll, 2005, 2008).

Newman and Cunningham (2009) found that when preschool and primary-grade teachers took advanced coursework on effective literacy instruction coupled with support from a reading coach, students' reading achievement was raised more than with coursework or coaching alone. Elish-Piper and L'Allier (2010) found that the more coaches spent time supporting classroom teachers as described above, the more students' achievement increased. In fact, reading coaches are very helpful when assisting the classroom teacher to assess students' reading progress and use these data to inform instruction. Get to know your reading coach and use this expertise to improve your teaching and the outcomes for your students.

Evidence-Based Teaching Practices

Effective Reading and Writing Practices All Year Long

● ● ●

IRA Standards for Reading Professionals: Standard 2, Elements 2.1, 2.2, 2.3

Response to Intervention: Instruction; Systemic and Comprehensive Approaches

Research consistently indicates that young children's reading and writing progress is most dramatically influenced by engaging them in substantial amounts of teacher-guided reading and writing practice (e.g., Morgan, Mraz, Padak, & Rasinski, 2009; National Early Literacy Panel, 2008; National Reading Panel, 2000; Shanahan & Lonigan, 2010; Stahl & McKenna, 2006). The power of effective, evidence-based reading and writing instruction is truly realized when teachers guide students to apply their knowledge of reading and writing skills, strategies, and concepts during the actual reading and writing of a variety of texts for a variety of purposes.

Interactive Reading Activities

There are any number of ways to organize activities and schedule instruction for each school day. However, it is important that students experience a variety of interactive settings in which they are taught the essential components of reading and writing coupled with large amounts of time allocated for reading and writing practice.

Groups for reading and writing interactions should be flexible to meet the needs of students and involve best practices associated with literacy instruction. In the next section, we discuss several effective ways to engage young children in teacher-guided reading and writing instruction and practice, including interactive read-alouds, shared reading, and the language experience approach.

Figure 11.16

Interactive Read-Aloud Guidelines

- Designate a legitimate time and place in the daily curriculum for reading aloud.
- Select quality books.
- Select literature that relates to other literature.
- Prepare by previewing the book.
- Group children to maximize opportunities to respond.
- Provide a brief introduction.
- Read with expression.
- Discuss literature in lively, invitational, thought-provoking ways.
- Encourage children's responses to the book.
- Allow time for discussion and interaction about the book.

Based on Hoffman, Roser, and Battle, 1993; Teale and Martinez, 1986.

Interactive Read-Aloud.   To begin our discussion of how to conduct effective classroom **interactive read-alouds,** we note that Teale and Martinez (1986) and Hoffman, Roser, and Battle (1993) have summarized read-aloud research and proposed guidelines for reading aloud to children. We have provided a few of these guidelines in Figure 11.16.

Most reading aloud to children in school takes place with the entire class (Anderson, 2007). Morrow (2009) reminds teachers to take advantage of the benefits associated with reading aloud to smaller groups of young children and one-to-one with individuals. Children whose reading development lags behind that of their peers can be helped a great deal by teachers, volunteers, or older peers who take time to read to them in small-group or one-to-one settings.

Shared Reading.   In 1979, Don Holdaway described the reading of bedtime stories as one of the earliest and most significant practices supporting the reading development of young children. Shared reading, or what is sometimes called the "shared book experience," is designed to be used with very young readers to model how readers look at, figure out, and operate on print. Shared reading experiences have been shown to be especially useful with young children in several scientific research studies (Eldredge, Reutzel, & Hollingsworth, 1996; Reutzel & Hollingsworth, 1993; Reutzel, Hollingsworth, & Eldredge, 1994).

Selecting a Book for a Shared Book Experience.   During shared reading, teachers typically use an enlarged text called a *big book* to demonstrate for students how to operate effectively on print (Barrett, 1982; Payne, 2005). When selecting big books for purchase, it is critical that teachers evaluate the size and legibility of the print from a distance of up to 15 feet away. Many publishers have simply enlarged the print found in traditionally sized books. The result can sometimes be print far too small to be effective with a group of children. The print in big books must be large enough so that the entire group of children can see it as easily as if they were sitting on your knee.

Shared reading books should have literary merit and engaging and meaningful content that sustains high interest. Illustrations in shared reading books and stories must augment and expand on the text (Payne, 2005). Pictures should tell or support the reading of the story in proper sequence. A well-planned selection of big books for shared reading experiences "hooks" children on the sounds and patterns of language while engaging their minds with meaningful content and knowledge and making clear the multiple purposes of reading. Big books chosen for shared reading ought to put reasonable demands on younger readers' capabilities. The number of unknown words in relation to known words in a new book selected for shared reading should not overwhelm students.

Big books selected for initial shared reading experiences should contain pictures that largely carry the storyline. Print in initial shared reading big books may amount to little more than a repeated line or two underneath the pictures, such as that found in the classic books *Brown Bear, Brown Bear, What Do You See?* or *Polar Bear, Polar Bear, What Do You Hear?* by Martin (1990, 1991). Print should occupy the same space on each page rather than move from place to place.

Shared reading experiences can and should be conducted with narrative (story texts) and information big books. There are many excellent new information big books to share with young children (Anderson, 2007).

Conducting a Shared Book Experience.   A shared book experience (see Figure 11.17) begins with the teacher introducing the book. The intent of the introduction is to heighten children's desire to read the story and help them draw on their own experiences to enjoy and interpret the story. The teacher may talk about the front and back of the book and may demonstrate certain features of the book, such as author and illustrator names, publisher, copyright, and title page. Next, the teacher may say, "Look at the pictures. What do you think the words will tell you?" After looking at the cover and reading the title aloud, children may want to relate personal anecdotes or make predictions about the relationship between the print and the pictures. The sensitive teacher will encourage and praise these contributions to the discussion and attempts to read the big book by the children.

Next, the teacher reads the story with "full dramatic punch, perhaps overdoing a little some of the best parts" (Barrett, 1982, p. 16). If the story possesses the characteristics outlined previously that make the text predictable, soon after the teacher begins reading, the children will begin chiming in on the repetitive and predictable parts. At key points, the teacher may pause during reading to encourage children to predict what is coming next in the book.

The shared reading book is reread on subsequent days by using hand and body movements, simple props related to the book, or rhythm instruments as excellent ways to increase student involvement and activity. Once a shared reading book has been reread twice, select something from the print in the book to examine in a "close reading." For example, in the big book *The Three Billy Goats Gruff: A Norwegian Folktale* (Appleby, 2001), the teacher may decide that students should begin to notice the sight word *the* in the text. To direct students' eyes, the teacher takes sticky notes from a pad and cuts several to the size necessary to cover or mask the word *the* in the text. As children and teacher engage in a "close reading" they note the masked words. The teacher unmasks the first *the* and asks students to look carefully at this word. What are the letters in the word? Invite a student to come up and copy the word from the

Figure 11.17

Conducting a Shared Book Experience

- Talk about the front and back of the book.
- Point out certain features of the cover and title page, such as the title, the author, and the illustrator.
- Invite students to look carefully at the book cover and ask, "What do you see?"
- Allow them to talk about what they see.
- Ask them, "What do you think the print will tell you about the picture?"
- Invite them to study the title carefully and read the title with you.
- Read the book with "full dramatic punch, perhaps overdoing a little some of the best parts" (Barrett, 1982, p. 16).
- As you read the story, invite children to join in on any repeated or predictable phrases or words they recognize.
- At key points during the shared reading, pause to encourage children to predict what is coming next in the story.
- After reading, invite children to share their responses to the book. Ask them to talk about their favorite parts, connect the book to their experiences, as well as discuss how well they were able to predict and participate.

book onto a large card. Each time the word *the* is encountered in the close read, it is unmasked and stressed aloud in the reading.

After the close reading, the teacher gives each child a *the* word card. The children are instructed to each pick up a pair of scissors from the basket and return to their seats. While at their seats they cut their cards into three letters and scramble the letters. Each child unscrambles the letters to form the word *the* on their desktops. Each child is given a new index card to write the word *the* to keep in his or her own word collection.

Interactive read-alouds and shared reading experiences ought to be the primary focus of reading instruction during the first 6 months of kindergarten and also during the first 4 to 6 weeks of first-grade reading instruction. Shared reading is gradually replaced in grade 2 with more work in small-group reading instruction.

Language Experience Approach.   As young children are initially challenged by the demands of transcription, many teachers turn to a long-practiced and very useful early writing instructional approach called *language experience*. The essence of the **language experience approach** is to use students' talk about personal or vicarious experiences as the basis for creating a piece of writing they can read. In this approach, children dictate text and the teacher writes, resulting in the creation of a group language experience chart. This means, of course, that the entire class has shared an experience such as a field trip, a new book read aloud, or the visit of an outside guest. The typical sequence of events associated with the creation of a group language experience chart follows:

Click on A+RISE—WIDA ELP Standard Strategies in the MyEducationLab (www.myeducationlab.com) for your course. Next, select the Strategy Card Index tab, scroll to Writing for grade K–5, and select the Language Experience Approach strategy.

1. Students participate in a common experience.
2. Teacher and students discuss the common experience.
3. Students dictate the chart while the teacher transcribes the dictation.
4. Teacher and students share in reading the chart.
5. The chart is used to learn about words and other important language concepts such as punctuation, left-to-right orientation, and sight words.

The selection of an interesting and stimulating experience or topic for students largely determines the success or failure of any language experience activity. Topics and experiences simply must capture the interest of children to provide the necessary motivation. The following examples show interesting ideas for supporting the creation of a group language experience chart:

- Our mother hamster had babies last night.
- Writing a new version of *The Napping House* (Wood, 1984).
- What mountain men did in the old days.
- What we want for our birthdays.
- Planning our Valentine's Day party.
- What did Martin Luther King, Jr., do?
- Sometimes I have scary dreams. Once . . .
- Once I got into trouble for . . .
- A classmate is ill; make a get-well card from the class.
- What we want to tell our parents for the open house tomorrow night.

Discuss the experience completely and engage students in conversation to support their discovery and use of new language. Help children assess what they have learned, encourage them to make personal connections, and motivate them to share with others their knowledge, experiences, and personal connections. Be careful not to dominate the discussion. Instead, ask many open-ended questions to promote discussion. Do not make the mistake of beginning dictation too early in the discussion to prevent a dull, even robotic recounting of the experience.

A Language Experience Example. Imagine reading aloud *The Polar Express* by Chris Van Allsburg (1985) a few weeks prior to Christmas in a first-grade classroom. After inviting children to discuss the book with you, ask, "If you had been chosen by Santa to receive the first gift of Christmas, what would you have chosen?" Call on individual children to give their ideas. After plenty of discussion, call on children to dictate aloud their best ideas for responding to this question. Record each child's dictation on the chart. With emergent readers, you may wish to record each child's dictation with different colored markers; the colors help children identify their own dictation more easily in the future. Later, you may write the children's names by their dictations. When the chart is complete, read the chart aloud to the children while pointing to each word. After reading the chart aloud, invite the children to read along a second time. Next, ask individual children to read their own responses aloud or invite volunteers to read aloud the responses of other children.

As the teacher, you may wish to read aloud a certain line from the chart and ask for a child to come up to the chart and point to the line you just read aloud. You may copy the lines of the chart on sentence strips and have children pick a sentence strip and match it to the line in the chart. Favorite words in the chart story can be copied onto word cards for matching activities as well. Thus, the text generated by the children for the chart story can be used in subsequent large- and small-group meetings to build the students' sight vocabulary of words in the chart, demonstrate word recognition strategies, and even help children learn about letter sounds for decoding purposes. The chart also can be copied onto a regular-sized sheet of paper and sent home with each child for individual reading practice.

Essentials of K–3 Classroom Reading Instruction: The Five-Block Model

Children develop a sense of security when the events of the school day revolve around a predictable sequence of anticipated activities. Although variety is the spice of life for children too, they find comfort in familiar instructional routines in a well-organized classroom (Holdaway, 1984). As a tip for beginning teachers or veterans who may experience problems with behavior management, we highly recommend the book *The First Days of School* (Wong & Wong, 2009) as a resource. It's great for helping teachers get the school year off to a good start with very basic routines and expectations. See the reference at the end of this chapter.

One approach that is increasingly used to organize the school day is the **five-block reading/writing essentials model.** Although this organizational framework was originally proposed for all K–12 students in the public schools of Chicago by Timothy Shanahan and his colleagues, we have implemented it successfully in the elementary school (K–6). We have found this organizational framework for reading and writing instruction to be both effective and manageable for many classroom teachers of elementary and middle school children.

The five-block reading/writing essentials model is a framework for scheduling and focusing daily reading and writing instruction so that all children receive daily instruction in the five essential components of reading: phonemic awareness, phonics, fluency, vocabulary, and comprehension strategies. In the five-block reading/writing essentials model, it is expected that the literacy instructional block will be scheduled for a minimum of 180 minutes (3 hours) per day in grades 1 and 2 and for 90 minutes (1.5 hours) in half-day kindergarten settings. It is best if this time is uninterrupted by outside intrusions.

The 180 minutes of allocated literacy instruction time in the five-block model is divided into four 30-minute contiguous blocks of instructional time followed by a 60-minute block of small-group differentiated reading instruction with the teacher and paired or independent reading and writing practice time. Kindergarten teachers should divide the amounts in half for each block. The five-block reading/writing essentials model is shown in Figure 11.18.

Timothy Shanahan (2004), a member of the National Reading Panel, reported that installing the five-block model of instructional time allocation for reading and writing instruction in the Chicago Public Schools led to significant improvements in K–12 student reading achievement scores in a single year. In addition to this endorsement of implementation efficacy, many Reading First schools across the nation have likewise implemented the five-block reading/writing essentials model. To give you, our reader, insight into how this model works in practice, we describe each of the five components in greater detail.

Figure 11.18

The Five-Block Reading/Writing Essentials Instruction Model

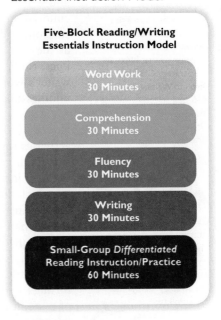

Word Work (30 Minutes). During this whole-group instructional time, teachers provide explicit instruction focused on recognizing and decoding words as well as on learning word structure and meanings. This time is devoted to the following activities:

1. Teaching younger students to recognize the alphabet letters (uppercase and lowercase)
2. Training students to hear sounds in spoken words (phonological and phonemic awareness)
3. Helping students learn to recognize and spell a body of high-frequency sight words
4. Instructing students in decoding and spelling simple CV, CVC, CVVC, CVCe words
5. Informing students about prefixes, suffixes, word tense, and singular and plural forms
6. Providing vocabulary instruction

In kindergarten and first grade, instruction during word work time is focused primarily on learning and writing the alphabet letters, recognizing and spelling sight words, and decoding and spelling simple two- or three-letter words. In second and third grade, the focus shifts from word recognition and spelling to understanding the structure and meanings of words. In the intermediate and middle school years, the primary focus of word work is concentrated on acquiring a vast store of word meanings and increasing reading vocabularies.

Writing (30 Minutes). During this whole-group instructional time, teachers focus student attention on the core elements of the elementary school writing curriculum,

Click on A+RISE—WIDA ELP Standard Strategies in the MyEducationLab (www.myeducationlab.com) for your course. Next, select the Strategy Card Index tab, scroll to Writing for Grade K–5, and select the Graphic Organizer strategy.

Click on A+RISE— Literacy Strategies in the MyEducationLab (www. myeducationlab.com) for your course. Next, select the Strategy Card Index tab, scroll to Fluency, and select the Repeated Reading strategy.

Click on A+RISE— Literacy Strategies in the MyEducationLab (www. myeducationlab.com) for your course. Next, select the Strategy Card Index tab, scroll to Comprehension with Nonfictional Texts, and select the Reciprocal Teaching strategy.

on a variety of writing products, and on the various phases of the writing process within the context of a writer's workshop. With respect to the core elements of the writing curriculum, teachers explain and model word choice, organization, word and sentence fluency, ideas, conventions, voice, and presentation. Teachers also help children understand the various forms of writing such as narration, exposition, persuasion, and poetry. In addition, students are engaged in a variety of writing tasks as they produce letters, reports, recipes, poems, bumper stickers, newspaper headlines, riddles, and so on. All of this occurs within the supportive framework of the writer's workshop (Calkins, 1994), which provides students with teacher-modeled mini-lessons, drafting, conferencing, revising, editing, and publishing.

Fluency (30 Minutes).   This 30-minute period is divided into two separate sets of activities for teacher and students: explicit fluency instruction with the whole class and small-group or paired fluency practice. During the first 8 to 10 minutes of this block of instruction, the teacher explains and models various aspects of reading fluency including accuracy, rate, and expression.

During the remaining 20 to 22 minutes, the teacher engages students in whole-class, small-group, and oral repeated reading practice to build automaticity. With very young children in kindergarten and first grade, fluency practice may focus on accurately and quickly recognizing and writing alphabet letters, high-frequency sight words, and reading easily decodable words (CV, CVC). This practice can occur through engagement with a variety of fluency practice activities. Choral readings of texts in unison or in echo voices help students get a sense of how to read with fluency.

Encouraging students to reread a passage helps them read more fluently, thus enabling greater comprehension. One very effective strategy is to engage students in the performance of readers' theatre productions. A range of readers' theatre scripts can be obtained on the Internet at www.aaronshep.com/rt/RTE.html, http://scriptsforschools .com, and www.geocities.com/Athens/Thebes/9893/readerstheater.htm.

Students who have achieved grade-level automaticity in decoding print can benefit from wide oral and silent individually monitored reading (Reutzel, 2006; Stahl, 2004). Wide reading means that oral or silent reading ranges across a prescribed set of genre types for a given period of time, say a 9-week quarter (fairy tales, biographies, information books, stories, etc.), and each student's silent reading is monitored periodically using oral reading—often randomly—by the teacher. For the teacher, the bulk of this time is devoted to meeting individually with five to eight students for 2 minutes each to hold individual fluency assessment conferences. Students sign up for a fluency assessment conference with the teacher. Students read a teacher-selected grade- or instructional-level text for 1 minute while the teacher tracks errors, rate, and expression. Information yielded by these assessment conferences is used to set student fluency goals and inform later fluency instruction.

Comprehension Strategy (30 Minutes).   During this whole-group instructional time, teachers provide explicit comprehension strategy instruction for all students, even for those in kindergarten and first grade. In these early grades, comprehension strategy instruction may take place through listening rather than reading. But for those students in second grade on up, daily attention to explicit comprehension strategy instruction is a critical part of a comprehensive, balanced reading program.

Teachers explain (1) which comprehension strategy is to be learned, (2) why it is important to learn, and (3) when and where the strategy can be applied with effectiveness. Next the teacher models how to use the strategy in connection with reading and discussing a text. Very often, this modeling includes a teacher think-aloud to help students get a toehold on the workings of the mind when engaging with text. During a think-aloud, the teacher shares her thoughts about the application of a comprehension strategy, which can include answering questions, generating questions to be answered, understanding narrative structure, using graphic organizers, monitoring one's own comprehension processes, summarizing, making inferences, visualizing imagery, predicting, and connecting text to one's background experiences. Once the teacher has modeled a comprehension strategy, she carefully scaffolds the release of responsibility for using this strategy to the individual student (Pearson & Gallagher, 1983). She accomplishes this by sharing parts of the task with students. For example, in responding to a question, the teacher may give the answer and ask students to offer support for it based on their knowledge or what is contained in the text. The teacher may then reverse these roles by having students answer a question while she offers supportive information. Following this, the teacher may have students work in small groups or pairs, sharing the task of answering questions as they assume roles such as question answerer and answer justifier.

Finally, students practice answering and justifying their answers to questions independently. Daily comprehension strategy instruction should focus on using strategies to understand text—not on learning the strategy per se.

Allocating sufficient time to the essential elements of reading and writing instruction is of paramount importance. Time on task and academic learning time have long been shown to directly influence children's reading and writing achievement. However, allocating more time without an appropriate instructional focus will yield little. The Five-Block Reading/Writing Essentials Model helps teachers focus on important elements of reading and writing instruction while allocating sufficient amounts of time for that instruction.

Meeting Diverse Needs of K–3 Learners

Research by Mathes, Denton, Fletcher, Anthony, Francis, and Schatschneider (2005) has shown that small-group differentiated reading instruction has significant positive effects on struggling young readers' achievement in reading. The approach to instruction taken during small-group differentiated reading instruction, such as guided reading as compared with a scripted reading program, does not seem to make much of a difference. What does seem to matter is that students with similar instructional needs are grouped together into clusters of five to six students for targeted and intensive reading instruction focused on reading appropriately challenging but supportive texts while applying their knowledge of the essentials of reading— phonemic awareness, phonics, fluency, vocabulary, and comprehension strategies. It is also important that teachers monitor students' progress regularly and periodically change group membership. As noted, time spent is focused on teaching students the essentials of reading instruction. More recently these characteristics of instruction, assessment, and grouping for instruction have been associated with a Response to Intervention (RTI) framework for providing targeted reading instruction to students with differing needs, including ELs, who have been found to learn equally well from

IRA Standards for Reading Professionals: Standard 4, Elements 4.1, 4.2

Response to Intervention: Responsive Teaching and Differentiation high-quality, evidence-based reading instruction (August & Shanahan, 2006; Lipson & Wixon, 2010).

Differentiated reading instruction small groups typically meet daily for 20 minutes. This allows the teacher to have at least three small groups for differentiated reading instruction. If more than three groups are necessary to meet diverse student needs, the teacher might meet only every other day with the more advanced students' small group.

In order to support small-group differentiated reading instruction, teachers need to provide for collaborative and independent practice of reading and writing skills, strategies, and concepts by other students in the classroom who are not involved in small-group instruction. To accomplish this many teachers have students engage in one of three different activities: (1) independent seatwork, (2) reading with a partner or independently at their seats, or (3) working through a series of literacy or learning centers distributed around the classroom. Any of these three can be effectively used to promote student reading growth, but because of their complexity in implementation, we describe the use of literacy or learning centers.

To begin, you may want to create only one literacy center for a single small group (five to six children) to visit daily for about 20 minutes. Other students—those not in small-group differentiated reading instruction or not involved in this single literacy center—remain in their seats, either working on carefully selected seatwork activities or reading with a buddy such as a cross-age peer tutor or in paired reading with another student in the classroom. Cross-age peer tutoring that involves trained older students reading with younger, less experienced students and providing them feedback, as well as paired reading of peers within the classroom, have long proven their worth in helping to provide effective reading practice (Labbo & Teale, 1990; Osborn, Lehr, & Hiebert, 2003; Topping, 2006).

Motivation and Engagement

Motivation and Engagement in K–3 Classrooms

●●●

IRA Standards for Reading Professionals:
Standard 5, Element 5.2

Pressley, Dolezal, Raphael, Mohan, Roehrig, and Bogner (2003) provide an extensive listing of elements that promote academic motivation in primary-grade classrooms. In Figure 11.19 we have selected and displayed a few of the more important motivational elements provided by these authors related specifically to reading and reading instruction. On the flip side, there are elements in a primary classroom that actually undermine student motivation to read and participate actively in reading instruction. We include a few of these elements as well in Figure 11.19.

Primary-grade teachers who motivate students to read and participate actively in reading instruction begin with the design of the classroom environment and the psychological and social atmosphere established in the classroom and then consider the nature, content, and quality of the instruction provided as well as the effective management of student behaviors in the classroom. Teachers who are well prepared to teach, display enthusiasm for reading and reading instruction, manage the classroom and students well, and engage students in dialogue about books and reading will motivate students to read books and participate actively in classroom conversations about books.

Figure 11.19

Elements of Reading Motivation in Primary-Grade Classrooms

Elements That Motivate Students to Read

- Classrooms are filled with interesting books of differing genres and varying levels of difficulty.
- Teachers read aloud or give books talks about interesting books—what Gambrell (1996) has called "blessing the book."
- Teachers hold high expectations for students.
- Teachers hold students accountable for time spent reading.
- Teachers give students choice in relation to books they read.
- Teachers give rewards for reading that do not relate to reading, such as stickers, candy, or pizza.
- Teachers provide clear directions and instruction in precise, easy-to-follow steps and procedures.
- Teachers give students time and opportunities to talk with them or with peers about books.
- Teachers stress through example and reminders the importance of reading different types of books and doing so regularly.

Elements That Undermine Motivation to Read

- Teachers display few examples of student writing or work related to their reading in the classroom.
- Teachers communicate that reading is boring or not a skill that students will find exciting, useful, or enjoyable.
- Teachers give rewards for reading when students already love to read.
- Teachers do not monitor for student understanding during oral, guided, or independent reading.
- Teachers assume students are familiar with the content of reading and do not check for, activate, or build relevant student background knowledge.
- The pace of the reading instruction is targeted at the "low and slow" and loses the majority of student attention.
- Teachers do not model the thinking processes or the steps needed to implement a variety of reading strategies and concepts.

Technology and New Literacies

Technology and New Literacies in K–3 Classrooms

The use of digital technologies in classrooms is no longer a luxury but rather a necessity for teaching the generation of students in today's primary-grade classrooms (Malloy, Castek, & Leu, 2010). The use of the Internet is fast becoming central to the way in which youngsters experience their world. This fact is fundamentally shifting what is means to become literate in the twenty-first century (Roberts, Foehr, & Rideout, 2005).

Primary-grade teachers need to provide opportunities for their students to read materials presented on screen and online. See Web Tools You Can Use in the Classroom for a listing of some possibilities.

Today, children can even use cell phones to look up word meanings by dialing CHA CHA and asking for a word's meaning. Writing on computers and keyboarding will no longer be considered an option because students' abilities to write will only be assessed using computers in most states in the nation. Children who are unfamiliar with writing in technology-mediated environments will likely score poorly

●●●
IRA Standards for Reading Professionals: Standard 2, Element 2.3; Standard 5, Element 5.1

Common Core Standards: Reading: K–5, Integration of Knowledge and Ideas (item 7); Writing: K–5, Production and Distribution of Writing

WEB TOOLS YOU CAN USE IN THE CLASSROOM

K–3 Reading Instruction

Students not only need to be able to read traditional print books, but also practice reading the books with computer-guided reading practice programs such as any of the following:

- You can access two programs for K–3 readers: The Headsprout reading online program at www.headsprout.com or the Starfall online reading program at www.starfall.com.

- To provide P–3 children effective, technology-based reading and writing practice, we recommend Scholastic's Wiggleworks program at http://teacher.scholastic.com/products/wiggleworks.

- Taking students on Internet virtual field trips can extend the reading of information texts in the primary grades in exciting ways. Take a virtual field trip to the San Diego Zoo by going to www.sandiegozoo.org/zoo/animal_zones or enjoy viewing and learning about exhibits at the Art Institute of Chicago at www.artic.edu/aic/collections/exhibitions.

- Children can even meet a famous author whose books they have been reading and learn about how he or she writes at Scholastic's free writing with writers website at http://teacher.scholastic.com/writewit.

- Students can use the Web to look up word meanings at http://kids.yahoo.com/reference/dictionary/english.

on computer-based writing assessments. Consequently, teaching younger students how to operate word processing programs like Clicker 5 (2006) or Write: Outloud 6 (2005) or even Microsoft Word for drafting, revising, and publishing their writing projects is a necessity in primary-grade classrooms. Desktop publishing programs are also a way to invite younger students to engage in writing in technology-mediated environments. Easy Books Deluxe, Kidworks Deluxe, and Storybook Weaver Deluxe are a few examples of desktop publishing programs that can be purchased and used in primary grade classrooms (Lovell & Phillips, 2009).

Students will need to become familiar with presentation software programs, such as PowerPoint, to publish and share their writing projects in a digitally mediated classroom environment. Student publications could be set up as a timed slideshow in the classroom on a computer projector for the traditional "Back to School Night." Illustrating stories and writing projects can be easily done by helping students learn about Google Images in which images of almost anything imaginable can be accessed to complement students' story or expository writing projects.

Teaching today's primary-grade students using technology is natural for this generation of learners, and primary-grade classroom teachers need to focus time and resources on helping young students develop reading and writing behaviors in online print materials. In fact, a recent study demonstrated that reading instruction with interactive whiteboard technologies (IWT), in which students used lap-sized response boards that connected to a teacher's classroom-sized interactive whiteboard, resulted in learning equality for mainstream students and ELs (Lopez, 2010). Perhaps one day, children's beginning reading books known in the past as "primers" will be read by future generations not in traditional paper print books but using electronic readers.

Family and Community Connections

Making Family and Community Connections in the K–3 Years

Evidence continues to mount showing the indispensable nature of the partnership between parents and schools. In schools that serve disadvantaged children, where teachers are teaching and children are learning to read against the odds, strong school–family partnerships are cited as chief ingredients in the success formula (Morrow, Mendelsohn, & Kuhn, 2010; Taylor, Pearson, Clark, & Walpole, 2000). It is never too late to start a school–family community partnership. The first step is to just start! Begin by identifying participants during parent–teacher conferences, but don't stop with children's parents or caregivers. You may also find partners in local businesses, government agencies, and senior citizen centers who can provide tutoring, learning center supervision, and oral reading to or with young children.

Once a group of participants has been identified, determine the time and location of meetings. If you want to include all parents and other potential participants, it is important that you plan to provide child care, transportation, and other incentives (Vopat, 1994, 1998). We have found that providing a meal as a part of evening parent-and-community involvement meetings is a real hit, as are read-alouds and free take-home books. Parents, volunteers, tutors, businesses, and agencies need to be willing to sign a commitment document indicating that they are in the project for the duration. In many cases, it is a good idea to offer parent-and-community involvement workshops or seminars in multilingual formats to encourage broad participation.

Seminars or workshops are best based on involving parents and other participants in the ongoing aspects of the school's reading instruction program: thematic units, writing workshops, reading aloud books, and so on. Parents and other community partners want to experience the curriculum and learn ways to help children succeed in learning to read (Paratore, Krol-Sinclair, Brooke, & Schick, 2010). Although agendas should be planned for workshops or seminars, it is important that these be flexible so that participants can help in building or fleshing out projects based on their interests and desires. Starting a study group in which participants read and discuss important documents, books, and materials together can be most helpful. Also, be sure to include at least one quality read-aloud book to be shared with participants for each seminar, session, or workshop (Ladson-Billings, 2010). Vopat (1998) discusses using a "Roving Parent or Community Partner Journal," which is sent between home and school and in which teachers and parents or other community partners can communicate questions or issues of common concern.

Communicate your learning goals and curriculum clearly to parents, partners, and students. Neither the curriculum nor expected outcomes should be considered "classified" information. Projects that target how parents and other partners can help children learn the curriculum and achieve expected outcomes are usually well received. If the means you are using to communicate with parents and partners isn't working, don't give up. Try another method, such as phone calls, newsletters, telephone trees, and so on. It has also been useful to provide a place on regular grade reports for parents to write a response, question, or concern back to you, the teacher. Family histories also have been shown to be an effective way to get parents, community partners, and students involved in an initial activity that focuses on identity and roots. These need to be shared in subsequent parent-and-community

IRA Standards for Reading Professionals: Standard 4, Elements 4.1, 4.2, 4.3

Response to Intervention: Collaboration

involvement workshops and seminars as a regular part of the meeting. Remember that most barriers to parent-and-community partner involvement are found within schools and school practices—not within parents or the community.

Project FLAME (Shanahan, Mulhern, & Rodriquez-Brown, 1995) has provided one of a very few examples of how to involve ELs' parents in the learning to read process. In the FLAME project, EL parents are provided English classes in the school at times convenient to their schedules to increase their own ability to support their students' learning of English and learning to read in English. EL parents, like other parents, benefit from information about increasing access to books in the home in both the primary language and in English. They need opportunities to learn about selecting appropriate reading materials for their children, applying strategies for parent–child interactive book reading, teaching alphabet letter names and sounds, and having fun with language games, poems, and songs. It is equally important that EL parents feel at ease in the school setting. For this reason, it would be important to communicate with parents in a warm, inviting setting, such as a dinner at the school with some small workshop break-out groups, in which they can learn how to contact and interact with the school administration and teachers in effective ways. Many schools now have persons on staff or otherwise available to provide translation services that bridge linguistic and cultural differences between the home and the school.

Start today. Start small or large or somewhere in between, but get started! Think of one thing you can do to connect your classroom and school with families and communities, whether it is your first year of teaching or your thirtieth. And don't forget to listen to parents and partners; they have much to share because of how much they care (Edwards, 2010).

Summary

In this chapter, we describe the characteristics of exemplary K–3 teachers from research. The best teachers provide instructional balance, density, and scaffolding; understand young children's reading development; encourage student self-regulation during reading instruction and practice; integrate reading and writing into other curriculum areas; hold high expectations for students to learn; engage in good classroom management; explicitly teach reading skills, concepts, and strategies; provide access to a variety of print materials; engage students in authentic reading and writing practice; allocate sufficient instructional time to increase student achievement; display useful procedural and conceptual information in the classroom; provide positive, specific feedback to improve student performance; encourage literacy-enriched play in kindergarten; and offer multidimensional word recognition and word study instruction.

We then turned our attention to hallmarks of effective reading instruction in the primary grades, such as preparing a print-rich classroom environment. This process includes making a classroom floor plan and designing spaces within the classroom for whole- and small-group instruction and selected learning centers.

Essential and suggested learning centers were described in detail, including purposes, contents, organization, and procedures. Planning and organizing classroom storage spaces to support a variety of reading and writing functions were detailed with special focus given to organizing the classroom library. We also briefly discussed different ways of grouping students for reading instruction to meet their individual learning needs.

Next, we provided detailed information about how to get reading instruction off to a good start from the first day and the first week, and planning for effective instruction across the entire year. We discussed the importance of writing lesson plans to support explicit instruction of skills, concepts, and strategies during the school year. A sample explicit reading instruction lesson plan was provided followed by a listing of standards or accomplishments expected for students to achieve in grades K–3.

After this we described several excellent teaching practices that may be used to provide effective reading instruction and guided practice throughout the school year, including interactively reading aloud, shared reading experiences, and the language experience approach. Scheduling the daily reading instructional routine made use of a five-block reading/writing essentials models that included daily instructional attention to and practice in word work, fluency, comprehension/vocabulary, writing, and teacher-directed, small-group differentiated reading instruction and guided practice associated with Response to Intervention models of assessment and instruction. We discussed several aspects of primary-grade classrooms and instruction that serve to either motivate or undermine students' motivation to read. Next, we offered information about ways in which teachers can use digital technologies to enhance primary-grade reading instruction. Finally, developing and implementing a parent involvement program was offered as a way to connect school-based primary-grade reading instruction to families and communities.

Field and Classroom Applications

- Draw a classroom floor plan illustrating how you will arrange and utilize your classroom space during your first year of teaching. Give a supporting rationale for the design you choose. (Keep in mind the idea of beginning with simple classroom arrangements.)
- Prepare a letter to parents and students in which you introduce yourself and welcome them to your class. Discuss your letter with a parent you know. Ask him or her for feedback. How is your letter helpful? How might it be improved?
- Make a schedule of literacy activities you plan to use on the first day of school. Then develop individual lesson plans like those in this chapter for each of the activities you have scheduled.
- Develop a first-week plan of literacy activities. Then structure individual lesson plans like those in this chapter for each of the activities you have scheduled.
- Develop a yearlong plan to increase parental, family, and community involvement in your anticipated classroom. Go to the library and Internet to obtain copies of letters, training curricula, and communications ideas. Present your plan in the form of a trifold brochure to your classmates. Discuss and evaluate each other's work.

Recommended Resources

Print Resources

Campbell, R. (2001). *Read-alouds with young children*. Newark, DE: International Reading Association.

Diffily, D., & Sassman, C. (2004). *Teaching effective classroom routines: Establishing structure in the classroom to foster children's learning—from the first day of school and all through the year*. New York: Scholastic.

Dragan, P. B. (2001). *Literacy from day one*. Portsmouth, NH: Heinemann.

Drapeau, P. (2004). *Differentiated instruction: Making it work*. New York: Scholastic.

Gregory, G. H., & Chapman, C. (2002). *Differentiated instructional strategies: One size doesn't fit all*. Thousand Oaks, CA: Corwin Press.

Wong, H. K., & Wong, R. T. (1998). *The first days of school: How to be an effective teacher* (2nd ed.). Mountain View, CA: Harry K. Wong Publications.

Web Resources

www.behindthename.com
  Vocabulary literacy center for name learning

www.aaronshep.com/rt/RTE.html
http://scriptsforschools.com
www.geocities.com/Athens/Thebes/9893/readerstheater
  .htm
  Readers' theatre scripts

http://kids.yahoo.com/reference/dictionary/english
  Online children's dictionaries

www.headsprout.com
www.starfall.com
  Online reading programs

http://teacher.scholastic.com/products/wiggleworks
  Computer-based reading programs

www.sandiegozoo.org/zoo/animal_zones
www.artic.edu/aic/collections/exhibitions
  Virtual fieldtrips

http://teacher.scholastic.com/writewit
  Meet a famous author online

The Power of Classroom Practice

www.myeducationlab.com

Go to Topic 2, Emergent Literacy, and Topic 10, Organization and Management, in the MyEducationLab (www.myeducationlab.com) for your course, where you can:

- Find learning outcomes for Emergent Literacy and Organization and Management along with the national standards that connect to these outcomes.
- Complete Assignments and Activities that can help you more deeply understand the chapter content.
- Apply and practice your understanding of the core teaching skills identified in the chapter with the Building Teaching Skills and Dispositions learning units. (optional)
- Examine challenging situations and cases presented in the IRIS Center Resources. (optional)
- Access video clips of CCSSO National Teachers of the Year award winners responding to the question "Why Do I Teach?" in the Teacher Talk section. (optional)
- Check your comprehension on the content covered in the chapter by going to the Study Plan in the Book Resources for your text. Here you will be able to take a chapter quiz, receive feedback on your answers, and then access Review, Practice, and Enrichment activities to enhance your understanding of chapter content. (optional)

Go to the Topic A+RISE in the MyEducationLab (www.myeducationlab.com) for your course. A+RISE® Standards2Strategy™ is an innovative and interactive online resource that offers new teachers in grades K–12 just in time, research-based instructional strategies that:

- Meet the linguistic needs of ELLs as they learn content.
- Differentiate instruction for all grades and abilities.
- Offer reading and writing techniques, cooperative learning, use of linguistic and nonlinguistic representations, scaffolding, teacher modeling, higher order thinking, and alternative classroom ELL assessment.
- Provide support to help teachers be effective through the integration of listening, speaking, reading, and writing along with the content curriculum.
- Improve student achievement.
- Are aligned to Common Core Elementary Language Arts standards (for the literacy strategies) and to English language proficiency standards in WIDA, Texas, California, and Florida.

STANDARDS
for Reading Professionals and Guiding Principles for Educators

IRA Standards for Reading Professionals

Standard 1: Foundational Knowledge

Candidates understand the theoretical and evidence-based foundations of reading and writing processes and instruction.

Element 1.1

Candidates understand major theories and empirical research that describe the cognitive, linguistic, motivational, and socio-cultural foundations of reading and writing development, processes, and components, including word recognition, language comprehension, strategic knowledge, and reading–writing connections.

Element 1.2

Candidates understand the historically shared knowledge of the profession and changes over time in the perceptions of reading and writing development, processes, and components.

Element 1.3

Candidates understand the role of professional judgment and practical knowledge for improving all students' reading development and achievement.

Candidates use instructional approaches, materials, and an integrated, comprehensive, balanced curriculum to support student learning in reading and writing.

Common Core Standards

Reading: K–12
Key Ideas and Details

1. Read closely to determine what the text says explicitly and to make logical inferences from it; cite specific textual evidence when writing or speaking to support conclusions drawn from the text.

2. Determine central ideas or themes of a text and analyze their development; summarize the key supporting details and ideas.

3. Analyze how and why individuals, events, and ideas develop and interact over the course of a text.

Craft and Structure

4. Interpret words and phrases as they are used in a text, including determining technical, connotative, and figurative meanings, and analyze how specific word choices shape meaning or tone.

5. Analyze the structure of texts, including how specific sentences, paragraphs, and larger portions of the text (e.g., a section, chapter, scene, or stanza) relate to each other and the whole.

6. Assess how point of view or purpose shapes the content and style of a text

Integration of Knowledge and Ideas

7. Integrate and evaluate content presented in diverse media and formats, including visually and quantitatively, as well as in words.

Range of Reading and Level of Text Complexity

10. Read and comprehend complex literary and informational texts independently and proficiently.

Writing: K–12
Text Types and Purposes

3. Write narratives to develop real or imagined experiences or events using effective technique, well-chosen details, and well-structured event sequences.

Production and Distribution of Writing

4. Produce clear and coherent writing in which the development, organization, and style are appropriate to task, purpose, and audience.

5. Develop and strengthen writing as needed by planning, revising, editing, rewriting, or trying a new approach.

6. Use technology, including the Internet, to produce and publish writing and to interact and collaborate with others.

Research to Build and Present Knowledge

7. Conduct short as well as more sustained research projects based on focused questions, demonstrating understanding of the subject under investigation.

9. Draw evidence from literary or informational texts to support analysis, reflection, and research.

Range of Writing

10. Write routinely over extended time frames (time for research, reflection, and revision) and shorter time frames (a single sitting or a day or two) for a range of tasks, purposes, and audiences.

Speaking and Listening: K–12
Comprehension and Collaboration

1. Prepare for and participate effectively in a range of conversations and collaborations with diverse partners, building on others' ideas and expressing their own clearly and persuasively.

2. Integrate and evaluate information presented in diverse media and formats, including visually, quantitatively, and orally.

3. Evaluate speaker's point of view, reasoning, and use of evidence and rhetoric.

Presentation of Knowledge and Ideas

4. Present information, findings, and supporting evidence such that listeners can follow the line of reasoning and the organization, development, and style are appropriate to task, purpose, and audience.

5. Make strategic use of digital media and visual displays of data to express information and enhance understanding of presentations.

6. Adapt speech to a variety of contexts and communicative tasks, demonstrating command of formal English when indicated or appropriate.

Language: K–12

Conventions of Standard English

1. Demonstrate command of the conventions of standard English grammar and usage when writing or speaking.

2. Demonstrate command of the conventions of standard English capitalization, punctuation, and spelling when writing.

Knowledge of Language

3. Apply knowledge of language to understand how language functions in different contexts, to make effective choices for meaning or style, and to comprehend more fully when reading or listening.

Vocabulary Acquisition and Use

4. Determine or clarify the meaning of unknown and multiple-meaning words and phrases by using context clues, analyzing meaningful word parts, and consulting general and specialized reference materials, as appropriate.

5. Demonstrate understanding of word relationships and nuances in word meanings.

6. Acquire and use accurately a range of general academic and domain-specific words and phrases sufficient for reading, writing, speaking, and listening at the college and career readiness level; demonstrate independence in gathering vocabulary knowledge when encountering an unknown term important to comprehension or expression.

Response to Intervention

6. Expertise

All students have the right to receive instruction from well-prepared teachers who keep up to date and supplemental instruction from professionals specifically prepared to teach language and literacy (IRA, 2000).

- Teacher expertise is central to instructional improvement, particularly for students who encounter difficulty in acquiring language and literacy. RTI may involve a range of professionals; however, the greater the literacy difficulty, the greater the need for expertise in literacy teaching and learning.
- Important dimensions of teachers' expertise include their knowledge and understanding of language and literacy development, their ability to use powerful assessment tools and techniques, and their ability to translate information about student performance into instructionally relevant instructional techniques.
- The exemplary core instruction that is so essential to the success of RTI is dependent on highly knowledgeable and skilled classroom teachers (IRA, 2003).

- Professionals who provide supplemental instruction or intervention must have a high level of expertise in all aspects of language and literacy instruction and assessment and be capable of intensifying or accelerating language and literacy learning.
- Success for culturally and linguistically diverse students depends on teachers and support personnel who are well prepared to teach in a variety of settings. Deep knowledge of cultural and linguistic differences is especially critical for the prevention of language and literacy problems in diverse student populations.
- Expertise in the areas of language and literacy requires a comprehensive approach to professional preparation that involves preservice, induction, and inservice education. It also requires opportunities for extended practice under the guidance of knowledgeable and experienced mentors.

Assessing Students' Strengths and Needs in the K–3 Classroom

IRA Standards for Reading Professionals

Standard 3: Assessment and Evaluation

Candidates use a variety of assessment tools and practices to plan and evaluate effective reading and writing instruction.

Element 3.1

Candidates understand types of assessments and their purposes, strengths, and limitations.

Element 3.2

Candidates select, develop, administer, and interpret assessments, both traditional print and electronic, for specific purposes.

Element 3.3

Candidates use assessment information to plan and evaluate instruction.

3. Assessment

An RTI approach demands assessment that can inform language and literacy instruction meaningfully.

- Assessment should reflect the multidimensional nature of language and literacy learning and the diversity among students being assessed. The utility of an assessment is dependent on the extent to which it provides valid information on the essential aspects of language and literacy that can be used to plan appropriate instruction.
- Assessments, tools, and techniques should provide useful and timely information about desired language and literacy goals. They should reflect authentic language and literacy activities as opposed to contrived texts or tasks generated specifically for assessment purposes. The quality of assessment information should not be sacrificed for the efficiency of an assessment procedure.
- Multiple purposes for assessment should be clearly identified and appropriate tools and techniques employed. Not all available tools and techniques are appropriate for all purposes, and different assessments—even in the same language or literacy domain—capture different skills and knowledge. Particular care should be taken in selecting assessments for ELLs and for students who speak an English dialect that differs from mainstream dialects.
- Efficient assessment systems involve a layered approach in which screening techniques are used both to identify which students require further (diagnostic) assessment and to provide aggregate data about the nature of student achievement overall. Initial (screening) assessments should not be used as the sole mechanism for determining the appropriateness of targeted interventions. Ongoing progress monitoring must include an evaluation of the instruction itself and requires observation of the student in the classroom.
- Classroom teachers and reading/literacy specialists should play a central role in conducting language and literacy assessments and in using assessment results to plan instruction and monitor student performance.
- Assessment as a component of RTI should be consistent with the *Standards for the Assessment of Reading and Writing* developed jointly by the International Reading Association and the National Council of Teachers of English (2010).

Effective Reading and Writing Practices All Year Long

IRA Standards for Reading Professionals

Standard 2: Curriculum and Instruction

Candidates use instructional approaches, materials, and an integrated, comprehensive, balanced curriculum to support student learning in reading and writing.

Element 2.1

Candidates use foundational knowledge to design or implement an integrated, comprehensive, and balanced curriculum.

Element 2.2

Candidates use appropriate and varied instructional approaches, including those that develop word recognition, language comprehension, strategic knowledge, and reading–writing connections.

Element 2.3

Candidates use a wide range of texts (e.g., narrative, expository, and poetry) from traditional print, digital, and online resources.

Response to Intervention

1. Instruction

- A successful RTI process begins with the highest quality core instruction in the classroom—that is, instruction that encompasses all areas of language and literacy as part of a coherent curriculum that is developmentally appropriate for preK–12 students and does not underestimate their potential for learning. This core instruction may or may not involve commercial programs, and it must in all cases be provided by an informed, competent classroom teacher.
- The success of RTI depends on the classroom teacher's use of research-based practices. As defined by IRA (2002), *research based* means "that a particular program or collection of instructional practices has a record of success. That is, there is reliable, trustworthy, and valid evidence to suggest that when the program is used with a particular group of children, the children can be expected to make adequate gains in reading achievement."
- Research evidence frequently represents the effectiveness of an instructional practice on average, which suggests that some students benefited and others did not. This means that instruction must be provided by a teacher who understands the intent of the research-based practice being used and has the professional expertise and responsibility to plan instruction and adapt programs and materials as needed (see also principle 6, Expertise).
- When core language and literacy instruction is not effective for a particular student, it should be modified to address more closely the needs and abilities of that student. Classroom teachers, at times in collaboration with other experts, must exercise their best professional judgment in providing responsive teaching and differentiation (see also principle 2).

5. Systemic and Comprehensive Approaches

RTI must be part of a comprehensive, systemic approach to language and literacy assessment and instruction that supports all preK–12 students and teachers.

- RTI needs to be integrated within the context of a coherent and consistent language and literacy curriculum that guides comprehensive instruction for all students. Core instruction—indeed, all instruction—must be continuously improved to increase its efficacy and mitigate the need for specialized interventions.

- Specific approaches to RTI need to be appropriate for the particular school or district culture and take into account leadership, expertise, the diversity of the student population, and the available resources. Schools and districts should adopt an approach that best matches their needs and resources while still accomplishing the overall goals of RTI.

- A systemic approach to language and literacy learning within an RTI framework requires the active participation and genuine collaboration of many professionals, including classroom teachers, reading specialists, literacy coaches, special educators, and school psychologists. Given the critical role that language development plays in literacy learning, professionals with specialized language-related expertise such as speech-language pathologists and teachers of ELLs may be particularly helpful in addressing students' language difficulties.

- Approaches to RTI must be sensitive to developmental differences in language and literacy among students at different ages and grades. Although many prevailing approaches to RTI focus on the early elementary grades, it is essential for teachers and support personnel at middle and secondary levels to provide their students with the language and literacy instruction they need to succeed in school and beyond.

- Administrators must ensure adequate resources and appropriate scheduling to allow all professionals to collaborate.

- Ongoing and job-embedded professional development is necessary for all educators involved in the RTI process. Professional development should be context specific and provided by professional developers with appropriate preparation and skill to support school and district personnel. Professional expertise is essential to improving students' language and literacy learning in general as well as within the context of RTI (see also principle 6).

Meeting Diverse Needs of K–3 Learners

IRA Standards for Reading Professionals

Standard 4: Diversity

Candidates create and engage their students in literacy practices that develop awareness, understanding, respect, and a valuing of differences in our society.

Element 4.1

Candidates recognize, understand, and value the forms of diversity that exist in society and their importance in learning to read and write.

Element 4.2

Candidates use a literacy curriculum and engage in instructional practices that positively impact students' knowledge, beliefs, and engagement with the features of diversity.

Response to Intervention

2. Responsive Teaching and Differentiation

The RTI process emphasizes increasingly differentiated and intensified instruction or intervention in language and literacy.

- RTI is centrally about optimizing language and literacy instruction for particular students. This means that differentiated instruction, based on instructionally relevant assessment, is essential. Evidence shows that small-group and individualized instruction are effective in reducing the number of students who are at risk of becoming classified as learning disabled.

- Instruction and materials selection must derive from specific student–teacher interactions and not be constrained by pack-

aged programs. Students have different language and literacy needs, so they may not respond similarly to instruction—even when research-based practices are used. No single approach to instruction or intervention can address the broad and varied goals and needs of all students, especially those from different cultural and linguistic backgrounds.

- The boundaries between differentiation and intervention are permeable and not clearcut. Instruction or intervention must be flexible enough to respond to evidence from student performance and teaching interactions. It should not be constrained by institutional procedures that emphasize uniformity.

Motivation and Engagement in K–3 Classrooms

IRA Standards for Reading Professionals

Standard 5: Literate Environment

Candidates create a literate environment that fosters reading and writing by integrating foundational knowledge, instructional practices, approaches and methods, curriculum materials, and the appropriate use of assessments.

Element 5.2

Candidates design a social environment that is low risk and includes choice, motivation, and scaffolded support to optimize students' opportunities for learning to read and write.

Technology and New Literacies in K–3 Classrooms

IRA Standards for Reading Professionals

Standard 2: Curriculum and Instruction

Element 2.3 (See previous)

Standard 5: Literate Environment

Element 5.1

Candidates design the physical environment to optimize students' use of traditional print, digital, and online resources in reading and writing instruction.

Common Core Standards

Reading: K–5

Integration of Knowledge and Ideas

7. Integrate and evaluate content presented in diverse media and formats, including visually and quantitatively, as well as in words.

Writing: K–5

Production and Distribution of Writing

6. Use technology, including the Internet, to produce and publish writing and to interact and collaborate with others.

Making Family and Community Connections in the K–3 Years

IRA Standards for Reading Professionals

Standard 4: Diversity
Elements 4.1, 4.2 (See previous)

Element 4.3

Candidates develop and implement strategies to advocate for equity.

Response to Intervention

4. Collaboration

RTI requires a dynamic, positive, and productive collaboration among professionals with relevant expertise in language and literacy. Success also depends on strong and respectful partnerships among professionals, parents, and students.

- Collaboration should be focused on the available evidence about the needs of students struggling in language and literacy. School-level decision-making teams (e.g., intervention teams, problem-solving teams, RTI teams) should include members with relevant expertise in language and literacy, including second-language learning.
- Collaboration should increase, not reduce, the coherence of the instruction experienced by struggling readers. There must be congruence between core language and literacy instruction and interventions. This requires a shared vision and common goals for language and literacy instruction and assessment, adequate time for communication and coordinated planning among general education and specialist teachers, and integrated professional development.
- Involving parents and students and engaging them in a collaborative manner is critical to successful implementation. Initiating and strengthening collaborations among school, home, and communities, particularly in urban and rural areas, provides the basis for support and reinforcement of students' learning.

Effective

Academic Literacy Instruction in Grades 4–8

12

Chapter Questions

- What does research tell us about the special challenges of informational texts?

- How can teachers determine the most important information to be learned in expository texts selected for a unit of study?

- Describe effective teaching strategies that may be used before, during, and after students read expository texts.

- What are some viable options for addressing the needs of readers who struggle with expository texts?

- How can teachers make content learning sticky, motivational, and memorable for students?

- What are text-to-speech (TTS) technologies and how can they assist English learners (ELs) in understanding expository texts?

- Can you name and describe some of the new ways of involving parents with their children's homework assignments?

Key Terms

Academic literacy

Content area reading

Concept load

Expository text structures

Content analysis

Readability formula

Before, during, and after reading (B-D-A)

Fidelity of implementation

Implementation continuums

Previewing

Concept map

Fix-up strategies

Click or clunk

Written academic learning summaries (WALS)

Themed studies

Webbing

Segmented integration

Group-assisted reading

Dyad reading

Scaffolded think-aloud

Interactive homework

Homework hotlines

Homework voicemail

Parent lending library

Motivation and Engagement	Technology and New Literacies	Family and Community Connections
Motivating and Engaging Students in Grades 4–8 to Read	Technology and New Literacies That Promote Literacy in Grades 4–8	Family and Community Connections That Support Children Learning to Read Content Texts

Vignette: Holmes and His Protégés Solve the "Acid Mystery"

red Holmes* is teaching his eighth-graders about acids and bases in his science class. Not only does he want to teach these fundamental scientific concepts, he hopes to help his students apply what they are learning to better understand the acid rain phenomenon as specified in the school curriculum. Fred has a personal experience with acid rain: He learned from the state's agricultural extension agent last spring that his cherished magnolia tree met an early and unexpected death due to acid rain. So Fred has declared war on this repugnant phenomenon and wants his students to join the fight. But first, he must make sure they have a solid grounding in facts about acids in the environment.

Mr. Holmes began planning for the acids and bases unit by first constructing a content analysis of the important facts, concepts, and generalizations to be learned. After picking apart

the textbook chapter on this subject, as well as the supplemental readings he selected from other print and Internet sources, he constructed a simple graphic organizer showing the important information to be learned. From there he mapped out his entire unit over ten 50-minute class sessions using the lesson plan format adopted by the school district.

Holmes embedded key content literacy strategies in his acids and bases unit plan that would help all learners, including those reading 2 or more years below level, gain knowledge on high levels. In addition to a great deal of concept and vocabulary development, a fundamental strategy Holmes used throughout the unit was "three-level retelling" for better comprehension. First, students read and reread key information in groups of two or "buddy reading." This helped them gain reading fluency with the science texts while also providing multiple exposures to important information. After several readings, Holmes had students participate in a structured oral retelling exercise to help them realize what they had learned and discover other information they needed to review.

The second phase of science retelling had students working in small groups to retell using a graphic organizer. This step moved students from oral retelling to retelling-using-words-and-phrases. Fitting the newly learned information into a graphic organizer also helped his students see relationships between new concepts about acids and bases.

In the third and final retelling stage, Fred Holmes taught his young protégés how to use a graphic organizer to construct written summaries about what they were learning. As part of his modeling, Holmes shared with his students this graphic that portrays his thinking on

*Note: This vignette is closely based on the work of Mr. Fred Holmes, a science teacher in Memphis (TN). He has also served as a teacher-mentor on the federally funded Striving Readers project.

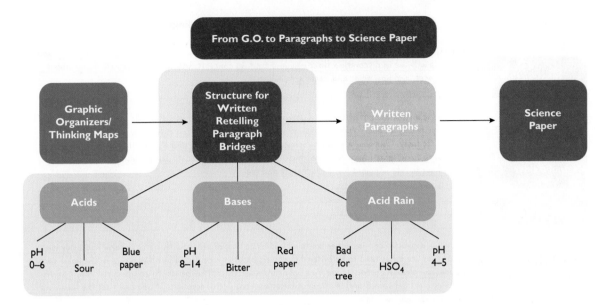

how to move information from a graphic organizer to paragraph form and then on again to a completed science paper summarizing what has been learned.

To make his modeling more concrete for his learners, Mr. Holmes presented a draft of what he called "Structure for Written Retelling Paragraph Bridges" based on the work of Kathleen S. Cooter. A completed paragraph bridge is shown on the next page. Armed with these new insights, Holmes's students were ready to begin trying their hands at moving information from their own graphic organizers into written summaries about acids and bases. When students completed this first study of acids and bases, they were prepared for the next stop on Mr. Holmes's unit: acid rain! ■

Changing Realities: Academic Literacy Instruction in the Transition Years

As students move into grade 3 and beyond, they transition from *learning to read* to *reading to learn.* Beyond the primary grades, and continuing on for the rest of their lives, the majority of reading our students will encounter will be informational and procedural texts (Ogle, 2011). As one teacher recently remarked to us,

> I have come to understand that, in a very real way, children do not truly begin learning to *read* until the upper elementary years and beyond. Before that time, they are mostly learning to *decode.* Now they learn how to use those skills to understand their world. *(Earlene Mills-House, Dallas Independent School District)*

Academic literacy, sometimes referred to as **content area reading** instruction, has to do with students applying their literacy skills in reading informational texts in order to acquire new knowledge in the subject areas of mathematics, science, social studies, and English language arts (Reutzel & Cooter, 2011). In other words, our goal is for children to become *scientifically literate, mathematically literate,* and so forth.

Masterful academic literacy teachers are able to establish effective and flexible classroom routines involving small- and large-group instruction, learning centers, and independent learning activities. From our own experiences, we can assure you that academic literacy instruction is as interesting as it is rewarding.

Structure for Written Retellings

Introduction	Have you ever tasted something sour? Well, if you have, then you tasted an acid. I want to invite you on a trip with me in discovering three new and exciting concepts. We will discover new things about acids, bases, and how acids and bases are similar.
Paragraph Bridge 1 Topic 1 (Bubble Map of Acids) **Supporting details** **Concluding sentence**	An acid is a substance that donates hydrogen ions when dissolved in water. Did you know that the soft drink Sprite was an acid? Another example of an acid is a lemon. You can tell an acid in other ways besides its taste. One way is if the substance has a pH between 0 and 6, then it is an acid. Also, if a substance turns blue litmus paper red then it is an acid. Lastly, acids can be dangerous; however, you don't have to take my word for it. Just taste and see!
Paragraph Bridge 2 Topic 2 (Bubble Map of Bases) **Supporting details** **Concluding sentence**	A base is a substance that either contains hydroxide ions or reacts with water to form hydroxide ions. Foods that are bases tend to be bitter. Moreover, bases can be found in other places in the home such as common cleaning products like Pine Sol or Windex. Bases can be identified using red litmus paper and has a pH between 8 and 14. Finally, bases are very useful especially if you can't see the hummingbird outside your window.
Paragraph Bridge 3 Topic 3 (Acids & Bases Double Bubble Map) **Supporting details** **Concluding sentence**	Acids and bases are different in so many ways, but they share a few things in common. For example, some people think that acids can be harmful, but strong bases can be just as harmful. Also, both acids and bases can conduct electricity. In contrast, they have different tastes. Acids are sour and bases are bitter. The pH of an acid is between 0 and 6, but the pH of a base is between 8 and 14. Lastly, acids and bases are important to know because whenever your stomach aches you might just need a base to calm your acidic stomach down.
Conclusion	In conclusion, acids and bases are interesting. They share many things in common, but they have may differences as well. While this journey may be over, our next adventure will be discovering the exciting and often dangerous changes caused by acid rain.

Keeping Our "Balance" in a World of High-Stakes Testing

Children in grades 4 through 8 range widely in their reading ability when it comes to informational or expository texts. At one end of the continuum you will discover students still struggling to conquer basic reading and writing skills, and at the other extreme are fluent readers champing at the bit for new challenges in books and online sources. A nonscientific but seemingly accurate way of figuring the range of reading ability in regular (i.e., non–special education) classrooms is plus or minus the grade level. So for a fifth-grade classroom figure plus or minus 5 years to compute the typical range of reading levels (K/1 through tenth-grade reading ability or higher). In our work with inner-city and other high-poverty schools, we have seen as many as 80 percent of students reading 2 or more years below grade level. Let's take a closer, more scientific look at reading levels in our schools.

In the latest national studies of reading and writing achievement (National Center for Education Statistics, 2010; Salahu-Din, Persky, & Miller, 2008), we see that test scores have essentially remained flat over the past decade at both fourth- and eighth-grade levels. These are the grade levels, of course, in which students need to have good academic literacy skills for reading and understanding informational texts. More important, only about one-third of students are able to read, and write about, informational texts at or above grade level.

There is little doubt that inadequate reading development contributes mightily to the high dropout rates in large urban school districts. Consequently, there is a great deal of pressure on intermediate and middle school teachers to show significant gains on high-stakes state tests. Research evidence reveals that this kind of pressure on teachers, by the way, fails to result in improved achievement (Nichols, Glass, & Berliner, 2006). Nevertheless, if we are not careful in this environment, we can lose our balance and focus our energies on test-taking strategies instead of helping student develop academic literacies.

Challenges of the Textbook Genre

Reading in grades 4 through 8 is a different ballgame for students than in the primary grades. Here the student is asked to read and understand nonfiction or expository texts in science, mathematics, and the social studies almost exclusively. We agree with others (e.g., Brent, 1994; Kornblith & Lasser, 2005) that textbooks are so different from any other type of book—including the nonfiction found in libraries and bookstores—that they should be classified as a distinct genre. Textbook reading can be an especially formidable hurdle for the struggling reader.

In this chapter, we look at ways we teachers help students succeed in reading and understanding subject area materials commonly found in the upper grades. We examine the unique ways in which textbooks and other information texts are written, and academic literacy strategies that help students succeed.

Teacher Knowledge

What Teachers Need to Know About Expository Writing and Reading

The Nature of Informational Texts

There are at least four different kinds of informational text commonly found in academic readings and textbooks: *argumentation, description, exposition,* and *narration.* The majority of these readings are expository in nature. Expository texts are written to convey information about a topic (Gregg & Sekeres, 2006). In academic instruction (i.e., mathematics, science, social studies, English/language arts) there needs to be good bit of emphasis on teaching academic vocabulary, comprehension strategies, improving reading fluency, and ways students can apply their writing skills to summarize what has been learned (Cooter & Cooter, in press).

Specialized Vocabulary and Concepts. A formidable task for every teacher is helping students learn previously unknown vocabulary. Vocabulary knowledge is built on previous background experiences (Heilman, Blair, & Rupley, 2001); linking the *known* to the *new.* Vocabulary in expository texts can be technical, specialized, and many times alien from students' experiences. Consider the kind of background building a teacher must construct for a science concept like *universe* or a math concept like *variable.* Teachers, therefore, must structure or scaffold instruction in order to somehow link what is already known to new vocabulary and concepts found in textbooks and other informational texts (Gregg & Sekeres, 2006). This can be especially challenging for teachers of English learners (ELs) and children with limited experience. We will look closer into that situation later in the chapter.

Students Need "Concrete" Learning Experiences.   The most effective way to teach students new vocabulary and concepts is through *concrete* or "hands-on" experiences (Fisher, Brozo, Frey, & Ivey, 2011). For example, if one wanted to teach students from rural Wyoming about life in New York City, the most effective way would be to take them there for a visit. Similarly, the very best way one could teach students about space travel would be to put them through astronaut training and then fire them into space on a mission. Obviously, neither of these experiences is feasible, so we must seek the best concrete experiences within our reach as teachers.

Going back many years, educators (e.g., Dale, 1969; Estes & Vaughan, 1978) have suggested hierarchies for choosing classroom activities ranging from concrete to abstract experiences. Such hierarchies help teachers select learning activities of a more concrete nature and review past practices for curriculum redesign purposes. We have developed a composite version of these hierarchies, which we present in Figure 12.1. Notice that as one ascends to the top of the classroom experiences pyramid, activities become more concrete and thus easier for students to assimilate.

Increased Concept Load.   Concept load (also called *concept density*) has to do with the number of new ideas and the amount of technical vocabulary introduced by an author in a passage (Singer & Donlan, 1989). Expository readings found in textbooks and in online instructional materials are often much more difficult to understand than narrative or story readings because of greater concept load (Harris & Sipay, 1990). In story reading, elements such as setting, plot, and characters are laced with information quite familiar to most readers. Expository text writers, however, usually present new and abstract information unfamiliar to the reader, which requires the building of new schemas or memory structures in the brain. Authors who introduce several new concepts in a single sentence or paragraph, called *high concept load,* create a situation that is extremely difficult for many readers.

Consider the following passage about the history of Mesopotamia and one of their early heroes. Words that carry rather deep meaning and require a good bit of vocabulary, background, and concept knowledge are underlined to emphasize concept load.

GILGAMESH

In early <u>Sumerian</u> history, <u>priests</u> were also the kings of the <u>city-states</u>. Gilgamesh was one of the most <u>heroic priest-kings</u> of this time. He was the priest-king of Uruk which was located on the <u>Euphrates River</u> <u>approximately</u> fifty miles northwest of <u>Ur.</u> The oldest written story in the world <u>delineates</u> Gilgamesh's <u>legendary</u> <u>deeds</u>. In the story, Gilgamesh is <u>characterized</u> as being both human and <u>divine</u>. Gilgamesh and his <u>companion</u>, Enkidu, <u>journey</u> the world <u>performing</u> heroic <u>acts</u>.

High concept load reading materials often create a major obstacle for readers lacking sufficient background experiences. One way to supplement conceptually dense textbooks is to select several smaller books that concentrate on just a few

Figure 12.1

Pyramid of Classroom Experiences

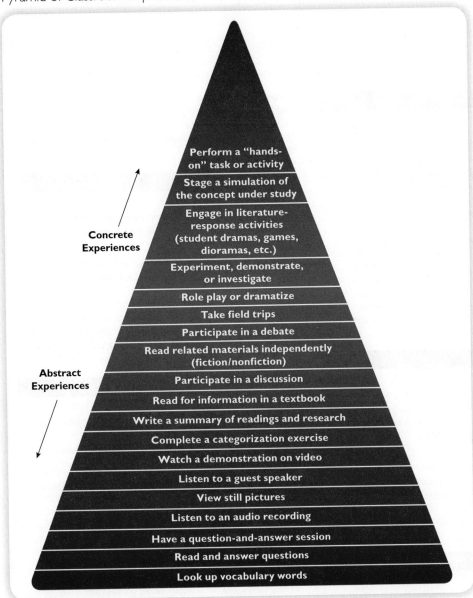

topics at a time and then cover them in some depth using concrete experiences. An excellent example is the *Reading Expeditions* series of books on topics in science and social studies by National Geographic. These are also written on four different reading levels to accommodate struggling readers.

Unique Writing Patterns. Narrative texts comprise such elements as setting, theme, characterization, and plot. Expository texts, however, are quite different: their structure tends to be much more compact, detailed, and explanatory (Heilman et al., 2001). Five common writing patterns, or **expository text structures**, have been described by Cook and Mayer (1988): *generalization, enumeration, sequence,* *classification*, and *comparison/contrast*. Meyer and Freedle (1984) add a sixth: *cause and effect*. A description of each of these structures is provided in Figure 12.2 based on the work of Cook and Mayer (1988, p. 449) and Meyer and Freedle (1984).

Figure 12.2

Writing Patterns Found in Expository Text

Generalization

Description
Passage always has a main idea. Most of the other sentences in the passage try to provide evidence for the main idea by either clarifying or extending. Some sentences explain the main idea by using examples or illustrations; these tend to *clarify* the main idea. Other sentences explain the main idea in more detail; these *extend* the main idea.

Example
Irritability is defined as an organism's capacity to respond to conditions outside itself, or an organism's response to a stimulus from the environment. The stimulus may be light, temperature, water, sound, the presence of a chemical substance, or a threat to life. The organism's response is the way it reacts to stimulus. For example, a plant may have a growth response. This happens when a root pushes toward water or a stem grows unevenly and bends toward light.

Enumeration

Description
Facts listed one after another. There are two general kinds of enumeration passages: specified, which lists facts by numbering them, and unspecified, which lists facts in paragraph form, with each fact stated in one or more sentences.

Example
There are four general properties of solids: (1) *Tenacity* is a measure of a solid's resistance to being pulled apart. (2) *Hardness* is a measure of a substance's ability to scratch another substance. (3) *Malleability* refers to a solid's ability to be hammered or rolled into thin sheets. (4) *Ductility* is the ability to be drawn out in the form of wires.

Sequence

Description
Describes a continuous and connected series of events or the steps in a process. Examples of sequences include changes as the result of growth, a biological process, steps in an experiment, or the evolution of some event.

Example
Hearing occurs in five separate stages. First, sound waves are captured by the external portion of the ear. The outer ear's function is to focus or concentrate these sound waves. During the second stage, the sound waves travel down the auditory canal (a tube embedded in the bones of the skull) and strike the tympanic membrane or eardrum. The third stage occurs when the vibrations of the eardrum begin a series of similar vibrations in several small

bones. These vibrations are transmitted to the inner ear, called the cochlea, during the fourth stage. At this point, the vibrations are turned into neural impulses that are sent to the brain. The fifth and final stage of the hearing process is the brain's interpretation of the sound patterns.

Classification

Description
Groups or segregates material into classes or categories. Develops a classification system to be used in the future to classify items.

Example
Experimental variables can be grouped into one of two categories: manipulated and controlled. A manipulated variable that can be acted on directly. The flow of steam into a room is an example of a manipulated variable, as it can be controlled directly. In contrast, a controlled variable cannot be acted on directly. The temperature of a room is an example of a controlled variable because it must be achieved through manipulating another variable. In this case, it must be achieved through manipulating the flow of steam.

Comparison/Contrast

Description
Primary objective is to examine the relationship between two or more things. Comparison can analyze both similarities and differences, whereas contrast focuses only on differences.

Example
There are two different hypotheses for the origin of the earth. The nebular hypothesis maintains that our planet began in an aggregation of interstellar gas and dust. This theory is gaining more and more acceptance. In contrast, the comet-produced hypothesis states that the earth began as a piece of the sun that was ripped out by a comet. The first hypothesis assumes the earth began as small elements that combined into larger ones. The latter hypothesis asserts the earth was essentially already formed when it began taking on its present-day characteristics.

Cause/Effect

Description
The relationship between two things when one thing makes something else happen. Elements are usually grouped according to a time sequence, resulting in a cause–effect relationship.

Example
The North Pole has 24 hours of daylight on the first day of the summer because the sun never drops below the horizon on that day.

When preparing to teach units in the content areas, teachers need to establish which expository text structures are used and organize for instruction accordingly (Hall, 2004). According to Montelongo and colleagues (Montelongo, Jiménez, Hernández, & Hosking, 2006):

> Research has shown that reading comprehension and the recall of information are dependent on a student's ability to recognize organizational text structures (Cook & Mayer, 1988). The recognition of an organizational pattern enables the student to form a mental representation of the information and to see the logical relationships advanced by the author. Good readers use textbook structure to abstract main ideas and to help them remember propositions from their readings. (p. 29)

Suggestions for teaching textbook structure to students are included later in this chapter. Let's take a look now at what good readers do as they encounter expository texts.

What Good Readers of Expository Texts Do

In 2007 the National Institute for Literacy issued a summary of research entitled *What Content-Area Teachers Should Know About Adolescent Literacy*. In this report the authors talk about what good readers do as they read expository texts. In Table 12.1 we summarize their findings in the areas of decoding text, morphology (the study of word structure), reading fluency, vocabulary, text comprehension, writing, and motivation. Our task as teachers is to help all of our students attain these behaviors and abilities.

Table 12.1

What Good Readers of Expository Texts Do

Literacy Area	What Good Readers of Expository and Academic Texts Do
Decoding	• Have a good understanding of sounds in spoken words (phonemic awareness) and how these sounds are manipulated to form words. These connections are made at the syllable level. • Use strong phonics skills to quickly identify and pronounce unknown words.
Morphology	• Use their knowledge of words parts (root words, affixes) to recognize complex words.
Fluency	• Recognize words automatically and are better able to understand text when reading aloud or silently. • Are more confident about the content and meaning of what they have read. • Tend to complete work faster and with higher quality than less fluent readers.
Vocabulary	• Have a wide-ranging knowledge of oral and print vocabulary. • Can use their robust vocabulary knowledge as a tool to decipher the meanings of unknown words.
Text Comprehension	• Are purposeful, strategic, and critical readers. • Are able to understand the content presented in various types of print and digital text with minimal or no assistance.
Writing	• Can write across various genres and academic disciplines. • Employ different strategies according to the demands of a writing assignment. • Use *self-regulation strategies* to help them plan, organize, and revise their work independently. These strategies include goal-setting, self-instruction, and self-monitoring.
Motivation	• Perceive that they have control over their reading and writing tasks even when assignments are highly structured. • Direct their reading and writing performance toward goals they want to achieve. • Are always engaged readers and writers. They are motivated, and once engaged in a reading or writing task, take pleasure in it and are motivated to continue (persistence). Accomplishing tasks increases motivation for future tasks.

Classroom Assessment

Assessing Academic Literacy Instruction in Grades 4–8

In thinking about assessment relative to academic literacy instruction teachers need to both analyze the unique reading demands of the texts you plan to assign and also discover the particular reading and writing abilities of your students. By analyzing text demands you will have a better idea about any instructional adaptations you may need to make in order for all students to learn new information. Analyzing each student's reading abilities and needs further assists you in planning effective instruction. In this section we examine strategies for accomplishing both of these assessment goals.

Analyzing Texts: Performing a Content Analysis

One of the best ways to begin planning for content area instruction using expository texts is to perform a **content analysis.** This is an essential process for establishing instructional objectives and structuring learning activities for your students (Martorella, 2008). The purpose of a content analysis is to identify the important facts, concepts, and generalizations presented in a given unit of study. By carefully analyzing information to be presented and determining which skills are to be learned by students, the teacher arrives at important decisions about *what* to teach (not all information is essential knowledge), how to teach it, how to provide guided and independent practice, and how to assess students' knowledge and skills. Content analysis, then, can be the springboard for creating a strong unit of study.

Facts are individual bits of information that are known to be true. In a science unit dealing with our solar system, some of the facts presented might have to do with atmosphere, satellites, and Saturn. In a history unit pertaining to the life and accomplishments of Dr. Martin Luther King, Jr., the teacher might focus on facts related to the March on Washington, sit-ins, the sanitation workers' strike in Memphis, and Civil Rights legislation.

Concepts are categories into which we group all facts or phenomena known through our experiences (Martorella, 2000). In the previous example of a unit about the solar system, satellites and Saturn could be grouped into the single concept *objects orbiting the sun.* Concepts are usually stated in a simple word, phrase, or sentence expressive of the characteristics shared by facts or phenomena.

A *generalization* is a principle or conclusion that applies to the entire class or sample being examined (Harris & Hodges, 1995). In the classroom, generalization is often teacher-generated, written in the language of students, and usually expressed in complete sentences. Generalizations organize and summarize a large amount of information, sometimes an entire unit, as in the following examples:

> There are many reasons why Harry Truman, perhaps an unlikely president, chose public life.

> Our solar system is made up of many satellites.

Once facts, concepts, and generalizations have been identified by the teacher as the focus of study, he or she organizes them into some form of graphic representation—a traditional outline, a semantic web, a structured overview, or some other graphic organizer. Arranging information in this way allows the teacher to make decisions about instructional content and delivery.

Teachers sometimes discover that the textbook adopted by their district or school contains information that is not relevant to the major concepts around which they plan to structure their lesson. They may find that some material may actually confuse students' understanding and skill development. In this event, the teacher needs to determine whether the information in question helps students build important background knowledge. Remember: Not all skills and knowledge are of equal importance for adult citizens to know (e.g., Is it really critical that students memorize the names of *all* the wives of Henry VIII?). If some information described in the textbook or your curriculum guide is obscure or serves no real purpose, it should not be included in your lesson plans.

Figures 12.3 and 12.4 feature examples of partially finished content analysis graphic representations by two middle school teachers. Notice that they are essentially schema maps.

Analyzing Texts: Readability Considerations

Another concern of teachers preparing content material for instruction is text difficulty or *readability*. Text difficulty is most often measured using a **readability formula**. The purpose of a readability formula is to determine the grade-level equivalent—or

Figure 12.3

Partial Content Analysis for a Unit on *Matter*

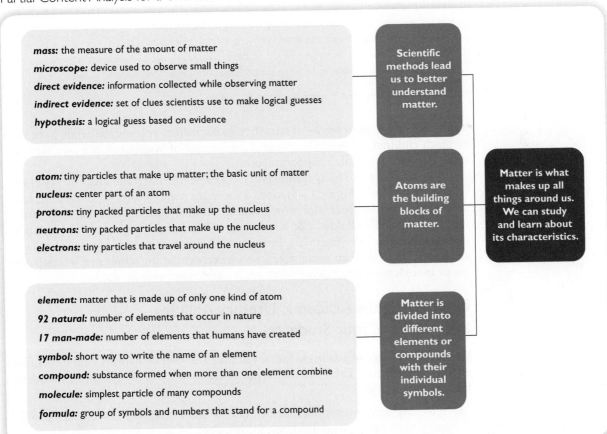

Courtesy of David Harlan, Fifth-Grade Teacher, Sage Creek Elementary School, Springfield, Utah.

Figure 12.4

Partial Content Analysis of Events Leading to the Civil War

Generalization

Differences between states in the North and South led to the Civil War.

Concept

The northern economy was based on industry; the southern economy was based on agriculture.

Facts

Samuel Slater built many factories in the North.

In these factories, Slater discovered that machines could be used instead of people to make things more quickly and cheaply.

Soon, things made in northern factories were being sold to people living in southern states.

Farmers discovered that cotton could be processed more quickly and easily with the cotton gin than by hand.

Many southern farmers grew cotton and sold it to people living in northern states.

Many immigrants became factory workers; many slaves were forced to work in cotton fields.

Concept

Both the North and the South fought for control of the government.

Facts

The North wanted laws favoring business and industry; the South wanted laws favoring farming and slavery.

Northerners wanted any new states entering the Union to be free states.

Southerners wanted any new states entering the Union to be slave states.

In 1820, when Missouri asked to become a state, there were 11 free and 11 slave states in the Union.

Northerners wanted Missouri to be a free state; Southerners wanted Missouri to be a slave state.

Courtesy of Laurie McNeal, Fifth-Grade Unit, Brigham Young University.

approximate difficulty level—of narrative or expository reading materials to be used to teach children. Sentence length and complexity of vocabulary are two elements often measured in readability formulas.

A number of readability formulas are available for classroom use. The Fry (1977) readability formula (Figure 12.5), one of the more popular formulas available, bases its estimates on sentence and word length. Another formula that many regard as more user friendly (Baldwin & Kaufman, 1979) is the Raygor (1977) readability graph (Figure 12.6 on page 522). Instead of having to count the number of syllables contained in a 100-word passage, teachers merely count the number of words having six or more letters. Readability software programs are also available.

Discovering the Academic Literacy Abilities and Needs of Your Students

Knowing the range of academic literacy abilities of your students is vital to planning effective instruction. There are four types of classroom assessment used in academic literacy instruction:

1. *Screening assessments* (intended to take a quick snapshot of your class to discover students' general academic knowledge)
2. *Progress monitoring* (checking for understanding and learning while a unit of study is under way)

Figure 12.5

The Fry Readability Formula

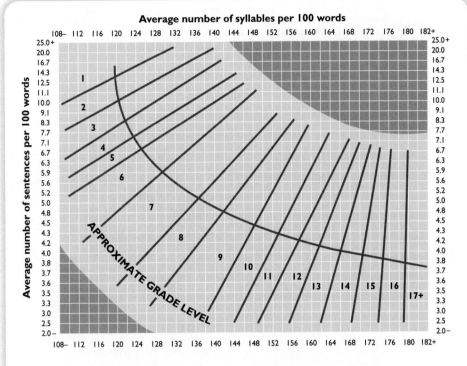

Expanded Directions for Working the Readability Graph

1. Randomly select three sample passages and count out exactly 100 words each, beginning with the beginning of a sentence. Do count proper nouns, initializations, and numerals.

2. Count the number of sentences in the 100 words, estimating length of the fraction of the last sentence to the nearest one-tenth.

3. Count the total number of syllables in the 100-word passage. If you don't have a hand counter available, an easy way is to simply put a mark above every syllable over one in each word, then when you get to the end of the passage, count the number of marks and add 100. Small calculators can also be used as counters by pushing numeral 1, then pushing the + sign for each word or syllable when counting.

4. Enter graph with *average* sentence length and *average* number of syllables; plot dot where the two lines intersect. Area where the dot is plotted will give you the approximate grade level.

5. If a great deal of variability is found in syllable count or sentence count, putting more samples into the average is desirable.

6. A word is defined as a group of symbols with a space on either side; thus, *Joe, IRA, 1945,* and *&* are each one word.

7. A syllable is defined as a phonic symbol. Generally, there are as many syllables as vowel sounds. For example, *stopped* is one syllable and *wanted* is two syllables. When counting syllables for numerals and initializations, count one syllable for each symbol. For example, *1945* is four syllables, *IRA* is three syllables, and *&* is one syllable.

From Fry, Edward. (1977). "Fry's Readability Graph: Clarifications, Validity, and Extension to Level 17." *Journal of Reading, 21,* pp. 242–252.

3. *Outcome assessments* (end-of-unit measures to find out if your students learned what you intended them to learn)

4. *Diagnostic assessments* (used for measuring Response to Intervention instruction for students needing extra help)

Figure 12.6

The Raygor Readability Formula

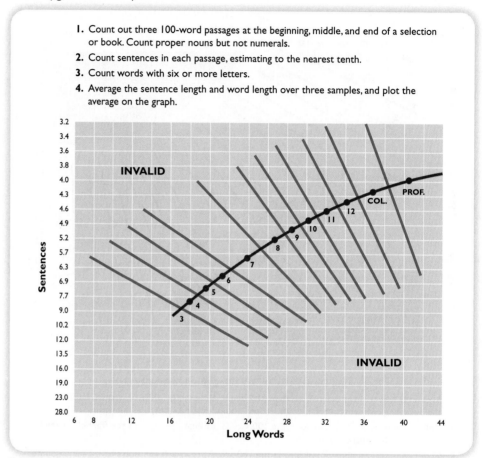

1. Count out three 100-word passages at the beginning, middle, and end of a selection or book. Count proper nouns but not numerals.
2. Count sentences in each passage, estimating to the nearest tenth.
3. Count words with six or more letters.
4. Average the sentence length and word length over three samples, and plot the average on the graph.

From A. L. Raygor. (1977). "The Raygor Readability Estimate: A Quick and Easy Way to Determine Difficulty." In P. D. Pearson (Ed.), *Reading: Theory, Research, and Practice. Twenty-Sixth Yearbook of the National Reading Experience* (pp. 259–263). Clemson, SC: National Reading Conference. Reprinted by permission.

In this section we explore your options for three of these types of assessment: screening, progress-monitoring, and outcome assessments together because the strategies we suggest may be used for any of these purposes separately or in combination.

We learned earlier in this chapter how to construct a content analysis in order to determine the facts, concepts, and generalizations you choose to teach in an academic unit of study (social studies, science, etc.). The content analysis you construct for each new unit of study is a valuable tool in constructing your own screening, progress-monitoring, and outcome assessments customized to your unit of study, so be sure and have that at your fingertips for this is your starting point in creating screening assessments.

Screening, progress-monitoring, and outcome assessments in academic literacy are typically administered to the whole class at once. They are constructed to measure students' knowledge and ability in three key areas: *vocabulary knowledge, comprehension abilities* (once a passage has been read), and *fluency* (in this case, reading speed and accuracy). Use the following instructions for creating these assessments.

Academic Vocabulary Assessments.   Which academic words should you use for your student assessments? Academic vocabulary and concepts can be identified from your content analysis in the facts and concepts section. You may also use key words found in bold type in the readings to be assigned. Earlier in the text we offered two key strategies, *word maps* and *vocabulary definitions,* that are especially useful tools in academic literacy assessment. Following are two additional assessments recommended by Stahl and Bravo (2010) stemming from their review of evidence-based research.

The Vocabulary Knowledge Scale (VKS).   VKS is a self-report assessment that has been shown to be effective with English learners as well as native speakers of English. It may be administered as a screening assessment, progress-monitoring tool, and/or as an outcome assessment. The VKS combines students' self-reported knowledge with a constructed response so as to have students demonstrate their knowledge of each academic word or concept. Students begin by identifying their level of knowledge about each teacher-selected word. The VKS format and scoring guide fall into these five categories:

1. I don't remember having seen this word before.
   (1 point)
2. I have seen this word before, but I don't think I know what it means.
   (2 points)
3. I have seen this word before, and I think it means _____.
   (Synonym or translation; 3 points)
4. I know this word. It means _____.
   (Synonym or translation; 4 points)
5. I can use this word in a sentence: _____.
   (If you do this section, please also do category 4; 5 points).

Stahl and Bravo (2010) offer guidelines for scoring:

> Any incorrect response in category 3 yields a score of 2 points for the total item even if the student attempted category 4 and category 5 unsuccessfully. If the sentence in category 5 demonstrates the correct meaning but the word is not used appropriately in the sentence context, a score of 3 is given. A score of 4 is given if the wrong grammatical form of the target word is used in the correct context. A score of 5 reflects semantically and grammatically correct use of the *target* word. (p. 571)

The VKS has been used successfully, by the way, to assess academic vocabulary knowledge in elementary classrooms at the earliest levels (though the assessment may need to be given orally for emergent readers). The VKS principles can be administered using a larger number of words in one session. An example is offered in Figure 12.7 using selected terms from a unit of study on the Holocaust.

Vocabulary Recognition Task.   The vocabulary recognition task (VRT) is a teacher-constructed yes–no task used to estimate vocabulary recognition in a content area (Stahl, 2008). The VRT has teachers select a group of words that students will be held accountable for in a content unit. As with the VKS, it combines self-report with student demonstrations of their background knowledge. In Figure 12.8 we see a sample VRT by Stahl and Bravo (2010) based on vocabulary associated with a unit on insects. In this progress-monitoring example students circled the words that they were able to read and that were related to the topic.

Figure 12.7

Vocabulary Knowledge Scale (VKS): The Holocaust

Term	How well I know this term . . .
Memoirs	1. I don't remember having seen this word before. 2. I have seen this word before, but I don't think I know what it means. 3. I have seen this word before, and I think it means _____. 4. I know this word. It means _____. 5. I can use this word in a sentence: _____.
Holocaust	1. I don't remember having seen this word before. 2. I have seen this word before, but I don't think I know what it means. 3. I have seen this word before, and I think it means _____. 4. I know this word. It means _____. 5. I can use this word in a sentence: _____.
Auschwitz	1. I don't remember having seen this word before. 2. I have seen this word before, but I don't think I know what it means. 3. I have seen this word before, and I think it means _____. 4. I know this word. It means _____. 5. I can use this word in a sentence: _____.
Anti-Semitism	1. I don't remember having seen this word before. 2. I have seen this word before, but I don't think I know what it means. 3. I have seen this word before, and I think it means _____. 4. I know this word. It means _____. 5. I can use this word in a sentence: _____.
Final Solution	1. I don't remember having seen this word before. 2. I have seen this word before, but I don't think I know what it means. 3. I have seen this word before, and I think it means _____. 4. I know this word. It means _____. 5. I can use this word in a sentence: _____.

As a posttest or outcome assessment, students complete the VRT and categorize the selected words under provided headings on a concept web (see Figure 12.9). In this example, a student scored a "hit" (H) when the word was circled correctly (noted with a check mark) or a "false alarm" (FA) if an unrelated word was incorrectly circled. The proportion of words truly known, P(K), was determined with the following formula:

$$P(K) = P(H) - P(FA) / 1 - P(FA)$$

In this example, webs received two scores: (1) total number of words correctly sorted by category, and (2) percentage of words correctly selected that were correctly sorted by category. Researchers Anderson and Freebody (1983) determined that a yes–no task is a reliable and valid measure of vocabulary assessment and is a better measure of student knowledge than a multiple-choice task, particularly for younger students.

Comprehension Assessments. In addition to comprehension assessment strategies we showcased earlier in the text, we add three more easy-to-implement assessments found to be effective academic literacy education.

Figure 12.8

Vocabulary Recognition Task: Progress-Monitoring Assessment

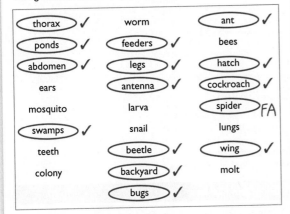

VRT—Insects
(Pretest and Posttest)

We *have been** learning about insects. Below you see a list of words. Put a circle around the words you are able to read and are sure have something to do with insects. Do not guess, because wrong answers will lower your score.

(thorax) ✓	worm	(ant) ✓
(ponds) ✓	(feeders) ✓	bees
(abdomen) ✓	(legs) ✓	(hatch) ✓
ears	(antenna) ✓	(cockroach) ✓
mosquito	larva	(spider) FA
(swamps) ✓	snail	lungs
teeth	(beetle) ✓	(wing) ✓
colony	(backyard) ✓	molt
	(bugs) ✓	

Correctly chosen targets or hits (H) ____14____

Incorrectly chosen foils or false alarms (FA) ____1____

Known (K) word scores may be calculated using one of the following three options.

　Classroom score calculation option A
　(H – FA = K)
　14 – 1 = 13

　Classroom score calculation option B
　(Percentage of correct choices = K)

　14 + 6 = 20　20/25 = 80%

　Proportion (P) known calculation option C
　(P [H] – P[FA] / 1 – P[FA] = P [K])

$$\frac{14/18 - 1/7}{1 - 1/7} = \frac{.778 - .143}{1 - .143} = \frac{.635}{.857} = .741$$

*For pretest, change the wording to *will be*.

From Stahl, K. A. D., & Bravo, M. A. (2010). Contemporary Classroom Vocabulary Assessment for Content Areas. *The Reading Teacher, 63*(7), pp. 566–578. Reprinted with permission of the International Reading Association.

Figure 12.9

VRT Concept Web (Posttest/Outcome Assessment)

VRT Web
(Posttest Only)

Types of Insects	Places Insects Live
beetle bugs ant cockroach spider	ponds swamps backyard

Insects' Body Parts	Other Insect Words
thorax abdomen feelers legs antenna wing	hatch

Words Correct ____14/18____

Percentage of correctly categorized hits ____100%____

From Stahl, K. A. D., & Bravo, M. A. (2010). Contemporary Classroom Vocabulary Assessment for Content Areas. *The Reading Teacher, 63*(7), pp. 566–578. Reprinted with permission of the International Reading Association.

Academic Knowledge Quick-Screening (AKQS). Used at one of the research sites in the federal Striving Readers research project (Cooter & Cooter, in press), the AKQS is a five-item question-and-answer test used as a screening assessment of students' knowledge about an upcoming unit of study. The five items are constructed from an adaptation of Marzano's (2007) question stems, which seem largely built on the seminal work of Bloom (1956). These are generic questions at each of Marzano's comprehension levels with blanks to be filled in by the teacher using key concepts derived from a content analysis of the unit of study. At least four of your questions should use "higher-order thinking" questions (i.e., applying, analyzing, generating, integrating, evaluating). In Figure 12.10 we share the academic knowledge quick-screening template.

Vocabulary Assessment Magazine (VAM).   Though this strategy has "vocabulary" in its title, it is really a mixture of both vocabulary and content knowledge. The VAM was originally created to measure students' science knowledge, comprehension

Figure 12.10

Academic Knowledge Quick-Screening (Planning Template)

Directions for the teacher: To construct an AKQS for a new unit of study, create five questions on key topics you want all students to learn using the question stems below. At least four of your questions should use "higher-order thinking" question stems (i.e., applying, analyzing, generating, integrating, evaluating).

Knowing Level

Who did ___?
When was ___?
What is ___?
Identify the ___ in the ___.
Describe ___.
Which ___ best defines ___?
Which ___ is characteristic of ___?
Which ___ is an example of ___?

Organizing Level

Categorize ___ according to ___.
Classify ___ according to ___.
How is ___ alike or different from ___?
What is most (or least) important about ___?
In your own words, tell ___.

Applying Level

Give some instance which ___.
How is ___ related to ___?
How is ___ an example of ___?
How would you use this information?
What do you need to solve this problem?
What are possible solutions to ___?

Analyzing Level

What are the attributes of ___?
What evidence can you list for ___?
What are the components, parts or features of ___?
What patterns or relationships do you see in ___?
Outline, web, or diagram ___.

What are the main ideas ___?
What can be concluded about ___?

Generating Level

How many ways can you think of to ___?
What would happen if ___?
Predict what would be true if ___.
How can you explain ___?
Elaborate about ___.
What would you predict/infer from ___?
What solutions would you suggest for ___?
If you were ___, how would you have ___?

Integrating Level

Devise a plan ___.
Summarize ___.
How many ways can you think of to ___?
Conclude what the result would be if ___.
What generalizations can you make?
If you could pull this all together in 3–4 sentences, what would you say?

Evaluating Level

What do you think about ___? Why?
Which ___ is most significant and why?
What are your sources? How do you know they are credible?
Did you detect any biases?
Judge what would be the best way to ___.
What criteria did you use?
What is your point of view about this?
Are there other points of view about this?
How effective was ___?

strategy use, and reading comprehension of science texts (Stahl & Bravo, 2010).

There are two parts to the VAM: brief reading passages coupled with open-ended literacy questions pertaining to the passage and subject knowledge items. The open-ended questions linked to the expository passage you plan to use for instruction ask students to apply comprehension strategies (e.g., making predictions, posing questions, making inferences, summarizing) and text feature (use of illustrations) knowledge (Stahl & Bravo, 2010). The second part of the assessment is made up largely of knowledge items about the subject under study. In the example seen in Figure 12.11, students studying a unit on plants were asked to draw and label two different types of roots and write a sentence describing their drawings. Drawing and labeling are literacy practices important in scientific studies; hence the use of this mode of assessment in the VAM is to measure students' science knowledge in this example.

Oral Retellings of Expository Texts. McGee (1982) found good readers in the elementary grades are aware of expository text structures. One of the most effective ways to find out if a child understands expository text is to use oral retellings (Duke & Bennett-Armistead, 2003; Moss, 2004). An oral retelling is a verbal recounting of a text that has been read either silently or orally. Asking children to retell an expository text involves describing the contents of the text including the main or superordinate ideas, the minor or subordinate details, and the underlying organization of the ideas in the text (compare/contrast, cause-effect, description, enumeration, etc.). Oral expository text retellings assess content comprehension and text structure knowledge in holistic, sequenced, and organized ways. In Chapter 7 we provided details on how teachers may use oral retellings with expository texts.

Fluency Assessments.   In Chapter 5 we offered two strategies that are excellent in academic literacy assessment: the one-minute reading sample and the multidimensional fluency scale. The one-minute reading sample is quick and easy to administer and interpret; this should be your primary tool for screening and ongoing assessments. The latter provides greater depth of analysis for assessing students you feel may be struggling.

Figure 12.11

Vocabulary Assessment Magazine (VAM)

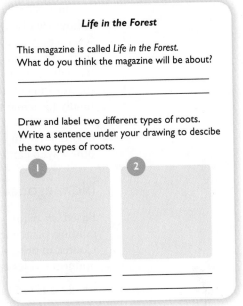

From Stahl, K. A. D., & Bravo, M. A. (2010). Contemporary Classroom Vocabulary Assessment for Content Areas. *The Reading Teacher, 63*(7), pp. 566–478. Reprinted with permission of the International Reading Association.

Evidence-Based Teaching Practices

Evidence-Based Instruction Practices for Organizing to Teach Content *and* Reading

The very nature of academic literacy instruction is that it is one part reading instruction (i.e., how to read informational texts effectively) and one part content learning. That is why in the last section we talked about how to assess your students' reading abilities as well as conduct assessments on the texts to be used, whether in print or digital forms. As we organize instructional units using informational texts, we need to keep these twin dimensions in mind. Otherwise, we risk leaving students behind.

In the last section, we discussed how teachers perform a content analysis. This is how we discover the text demands of the material we plan to use (i.e., readability level, concept load). Now we are ready to learn about ways to organize units of instruction that promote literacy in the subject area to be studied. In this section, we will learn (1) an organizational framework for planning your units, (2) advanced innovations on the organizational framework that have shown to be effective, and finally (3) some suggestions about how you might work effectively with an instructional coach who may be available in your school. We begin first with a few "nonnegotiables" in academic literacy instruction based on our own research and that of others who came before us.

Nonnegotiables of Academic Literacy Instruction

Based on many years of research and classroom practice, there seem to be certain guiding principles or *nonnegotiables* of academic literacy instruction (Cooter & Cooter, in press; Corpus & Giddings, 2010). We think you will see the spirit of these nonnegotiables embedded throughout this section.

• *Less is more.* Students are better able to absorb new skills strategies for understanding informal texts if they are few in number. It is best to carefully select a relative few evidence-based skills and strategies to teach your students and then practice them until they become automatic—a part of them. As a Dallas literacy coach, Adelise Harris, once remarked, "We can't just *sprinkle* students with strategies, we must *marinate* them until they are soaked to the bone and own the strategy!"

• *Use high-quality texts.* If we want to keep our students engaged and on task, we must choose expository texts that are interesting and speak to this generation (Blasingame, 2007). All too often the adopted textbooks are boring and high on concept load. With the advent of the Internet and other quality resources, we must supplement our program liberally with rich and enticing texts.

• *Offer students choice.* A problem we often see in content instruction is the one-size-fits-all mode of instruction (i.e., exclusively whole-group instruction). Human beings are motivated by choice, even when there are only two or three options. Choices in texts to be read, group activities, and required products (i.e., research papers, poster sessions, online presentations, readers' theatre scripts) cause students to be motivated and engaged.

• *Offer students voice.* We learn through talking about new ideas. Throughout this book we have highlighted the idea of joint productive activities (JPA) as small-group cooperative learning activities (see CREDE online for a summary of dialogic learning activities on the website noted at the end of the chapter). Whether you use JPAs or not, create opportunities for your students to come together for highly structured discussions about new ideas.

• *Students are apprentices.* It is our jobs as teachers to find out what students know (and need to learn next)—what Vygotsky (1986) calls their *zone of proximal development*—and then lead them to greater levels of knowledge and ability. This assumes certain roles for teachers (as coaches) and students (as apprentices). Earlier in the book we have represented this philosophy in words and graphics. The apprenticeship model (Corpus & Giddings, 2010) is summarized in Figure 12.12.

Figure 12.12

Apprenticeship Model

Introduction	Modeling	Guided Practice	Independent Practice	Summative Assessment
Teacher: Explains what we are learning and why	**Teacher:** Demonstrates multiple times the new skill/strategy	**Teacher:** Offers multiple opportunities for students to practice the new skill/strategy with ever-lessening assistance	**Teacher:** Sets the parameters for a task wherein students demonstrate competence	**Teacher:** Determines whether competence has been reached (mastery), or if the learning cycle should be repeated
Student: Attends to the presentation and responds	**Student:** Active observer who questions for understanding	**Student:** Takes on ever-increasing responsibility for completing the task	**Student:** Performs the assigned task with no assistance	

- *Marry well, divorce less.* Once you decide on a way of organizing academic literacy instruction in your classroom (hopefully, you will start with the framework that follows), stay with it for more than a year so that you will become proficient. Much too often we assemble great strategies and materials but then throw it aside if we do not get the results we hoped for the first time; that is, we get a "divorce" from the program we assembled before we know it well ourselves in favor of something new and untried (Cooter, 2004). Implementing what you design well takes time, practice, and experience. Remember, you are a learner, too!

The B-D-A Organizational Framework

Over the past two decades we have been honored to serve with a number of school districts as chief designers and lead researchers on federally funded literacy projects. From this work we have learned firsthand what seems to work best in academic literacy with some of the most economically disadvantaged students and the teachers who serve them.

Before, during, and after reading, or **B-D-A**, is a construct for organizing instruction that has a proven track record. In short, teachers plan for what students do *before* they read a new informational text, what they are doing *during* their reading of a text, and what they do *after* they read informational texts to crystallize their learning. B-D-A maximizes student learning potential. Of course, this model has implications at each stage for teachers as well (i.e., what should *we* be doing B-D-A students read texts).

In this section we now share with you evidence-based practices shown to be effective in our research in the federally funded Memphis Striving Readers Project from 2006 to 2011 (Cooter & Cooter, in press) with schools serving some of the most severely limited children living in poverty predicaments. Information about all eight of the Striving Readers research projects can be found online at the website included at the end of this chapter.

Strategies for vocabulary learning, reading comprehension, and reading fluency are presented using the before, during, and after reading framework. Because some of the strategies we present were already described in earlier chapters, we only mention these and add some additional tips for their use. For new strategies not previously mentioned, we provide full descriptions.

Before Reading Strategies: Vocabulary Learning. In Chapter 6 on vocabulary we learned about academic word walls, or AW[2] (Cooter, 2009). This is a mainstay tool for academic vocabulary development and should be used from the first day or so of a new content unit. But let's introduce a nuance to AW[2] by considering one of our nonnegotiable beliefs: *marry well, divorce less.* This is the idea that we get better at using a teaching tool like AW[2] by gaining experience with it over time until we have mastered the strategy ourselves.

Practicing a teaching strategy properly and consistently is known as **fidelity of implementation.** Instructional coaches and teachers often use tools like rubrics or implementation continuums to help teachers self-assess how well they are applying new teaching strategies in their classroom. **Implementation continuums** (Cooter, Mathews, Thompson, & Cooter, 2004) are clear and concise structures that help teachers across a school or school district develop a common understanding of evidence-based teaching practices. They may take the form of rubrics that present agreed-on benchmark teaching practices and materials. Teachers apply implementation continuums to monitor their teaching practices and work toward consistency according to a standard. Principals also use implementation continuums to gauge the extent to which a selected practice is employed in daily instruction throughout a school. Implementation continuums typically move from descriptions of traditional practices to stages of execution more in line with the evidence-based practice.

In Table 12.2 we present a teacher self-evaluation continuum for AW[2] (Reutzel & Cooter, 2011) developed as part of the Memphis Striving Readers project to help teachers figure out how well they are implementing the strategy. We urge you to use this tool as you first begin using AW[2] to plan your lessons and then revisit it from time to time for a personal status check on your fidelity of implementation.

A+RISE

Click on A+RISE—Literacy Strategies in the MyEducationLab (www.myeducationlab.com) for your course. Next, select the Strategy Card Index tab, scroll to Vocabulary for grades 6–12, and select the Concept Illustrations strategy.

Before Reading Strategies: Comprehension. Student-apprentices in academic literacy often find textbooks and other expository texts to be intimidating at times. We have found that they benefit from and enjoy a structure they can follow to preview what they are about to learn *before* actually reading the text. **Previewing** helps students to survey a new text before reading and begin making associations with their prior learning. THIEVES (Manz, 2002) is an acronym for the steps students can take in previewing new expository texts in a systematic way for science, social studies, and English language arts texts.

The idea is to encourage students to become THIEVES—that is, "steal" important information from the new text before they read it. THIEVES identifies elements of the text (textbook chapter, supplemental book, online website, etc.) that should be reviewed in advance of actual reading. This helps students access prior knowledge and set purposes for reading. Figure 12.13 (on page 532) displays a template of the survey elements identified by THIEVES that you can copy and use with your students along with key questions for each step.

Table 12.2

Teacher Self-Evaluation Continuum for AW[2]

Exemplary A	Above Average B	Acceptable C	Early Implementation D	Traditional Instruction E
Teacher explicitly describes the AW[2] vocabulary activity, provides a purpose, and explains why it is helpful.	Teacher explicitly describes the AW[2] vocabulary activity and provides a purpose for learning it.	Teacher introduces AW[2] activity and explains its purpose.	Teacher gives directions for activities that provide some meaningful interaction with new academic words (e.g., using words in a crossword puzzle, writing sentences using new words).	Teacher identifies or distributes a list of new academic vocabulary to be learned.
New words are introduced, explained, and connected to students' prior learning (e.g., using graphic organizers like semantic maps).	Teacher models the strategy, sometimes using a "think aloud" strategy to clarify.	Teacher models/ demonstrates the strategy in a step-by-step manner.	Teacher provides some modeling of vocabulary activities, but engages students in dialogue while also modeling.	Teacher assigns independent activities (e.g., looking up dictionary definitions, fill-in-the-blank activities, matching, other worksheets).
Involves students in word selection (i.e., new words to be learned).	After modeling the AW[2] strategy, the teacher engages students in discussion to determine whether more modeling is required.	Teacher reads aloud texts containing new academic words.	Teacher reviews new vocabulary as needed according to observations	Homework is assigned (e.g., worksheets, activities from textbook) for vocabulary learning.
Teacher models the strategy using a "think aloud" strategy to clarify.		Teacher explains expectations for students for each AW[2] activity.	A summative assessment is given at the end of the academic unit of study to check for new academic vocabulary knowledge.	An end-of-unit test is given to check for new academic vocabulary knowledge.
Teacher and students have meaningful dialogues about all new words to be learned.		Teacher invites student input and questions in order to check their understanding at each phase of the activity.		
Students compile list of new academic vocabulary for future use.		Teacher observes students while they are working to assess learning.		
Students create their own tests or other products using new academic vocabulary to demonstrate their understanding.		Teacher reassesses students' understanding and reteaches as reviews as needed.		
Teacher disaggregates formative and summative assessment data to inform instruction and determine which students may need additional instruction.				

From Reutzel and Cooter, *Strategies for Reading Assessment and Instruction: Helping Every Child Succeed.* © 2011 by Pearson Education, Inc. Reproduced with permission of Pearson Education, Inc.

Before **Reading Strategies: Fluency.**   In Chapter 5 we offered a plethora of fluency activities you will be able to use in your classes. Students, as we mentioned in our nonnegotiables earlier, enjoy choice. So using a variety of those strategies will help you keep things *spicy*.

One before-reading fluency routine was developed by David Paige (in press) while serving as a middle school teacher. In Paige's whole-class choral reading routine

Figure 12.13

THIEVES: A Previewing Text Strategy

What I am doing?	*What did I steal?*	*What additional questions do I have?*
Previewing the Text	**Getting Ready to Read**	**Generating Questions** who, what, when, where, why, how
T–Title • What is it? • What do I already know about this topic? • What does it have to do with the preceding chapter? • Does it express a point of view? • What do I think we will be reading about?		
H–Headings • What does this heading let me know I will be reading about? • What is the topic of the paragraph beneath it? • How can I turn this heading into a question that is likely to be answered in the actual content?		
I–Introduction • Is there an opening, perhaps italicized? • Does the first paragraph introduce the chapter? • What does the introduction let me know I will be reading about? • Do I know anything about this already?		
E–Every first sentence in a paragraph • What else did I learn about the topic? • What predictions can I make about what I am about to learn?		
V–Visuals and vocabulary • Are there photographs, drawings, maps, charts, graphs? • What can I learn from them? • How do the captions help me better understand the meaning? • Is there a list of key vocabulary terms and definitions? • Are there important words in boldface type throughout the chapter? • Do I know what they mean? Can I tell the meaning from the sentences in which they are embedded?		
E–End-of-chapter questions • What do the questions ask? • What information do they earmark as important? • What information do I learn from the question? • Let me keep in mind the questions I am to answer so that I may annotate my text where pertinent information is located.		
S–Summary • What new information is there? or • What summary can I make from the preview?		

Adapted from Manz, S. (2002). A Strategy for Previewing Textbooks: Teaching Readers to Become THIEVES. *The Reading Teacher, 55*(5), 434–435.

students practice reading a summary of an upcoming textbook chapter a week or more ahead of instruction to "prep" students. This whole-class (or small-group) choral activity acquaints them with new vocabulary found in the textbook chapter and the author's style while improving their rapid identification of new words. Texts may be taken directly from the textbook, for instance, the summary at the end of the upcoming textbook chapter or other text, but may need to be slightly modified. Figure 12.14 is Paige's before-reading fluency routine in a simple weekly plan. After the first day it usually only takes about 5 to 10 minutes of class time, but yields great results.

Figure 12.14

Before-Reading Fluency Routine

Monday

Before Reading

Step 1: Introducing New Words

Before modeling the text, select specific words that the students may not be familiar with or may have difficulty pronouncing. Pay particular attention to unfamiliar content words and concepts. Your content analysis will help you decide on these words.

Next, the teacher models the selected words (read aloud for the class) while students are looking at the word. Students repeat the target word after the teacher pronounces it.

Step 2: Modeling the Text

While students are following along silently with their text, the teacher models reading the text aloud. Use appropriate expressive reading and reading rate, and pay attention to commas, periods, and phrases.

During Reading (Still Monday)

Step 3: First Reading

Students now read the text aloud in unison. To begin the class reading together, the teacher uses a "3-2-1" countdown. Teacher must read aloud in a loud voice while "traveling" the room during the reading making a mental note of difficult words and phrases to review after reading.

After Reading (Still Monday)

Step 4: Review Problem Words and Phrases

The teacher models words and phrases that were difficult for the class and asks the class for questions regarding any text that was confusing or difficult.

Step 5: Do a Second Reading (Monday only)

The final activity for your first day is to do a final reading of the text with your class.

Tuesday and Wednesday

Step 6: Rereadings

Students read the text once each day as in Step 3. As students become familiar with the text, it is important to transfer responsibility for reading to them. To do this, the teacher simply reduces vocal volume (as with the neurological impress method) each reading. Explain to students that they must listen to each other in order to "stay together" during the reading.

Thursday and Friday:

Step 7: "Let's change it up!"

On the final two days of fluency practice the teacher or, better yet, the students choose another choral reading activity to use with the text. This could include echo reading, antiphonal reading, or unison reading.

Tips for Implentation

David Paige (in press) offers the following recommendations to enhance the process.

Audio recording. Record the class on Monday while they are doing the first reading using a tape or digital recorder. Play the recording back for the students at the end of the second reading. Record the class on Friday and compare (play) the two readings for the class.

Motivation. Student motivation is key. This should be presented as a fun way to help everyone in class become a better reader. Challenge the class to reach for a perfect performance on Friday. Readings on Monday through Thursday can be thought of as "rehearsal readings."

Class monitoring. The teacher must "walk the room" during readings to keep students on task. Encourage students who may not be reading to join in! Whatever you do, however, embarrass no one.

Adapted from Paige, D. "That Sounded Good! Rethinking Whole-Class Choral Reading," *The Reading Teacher.*

Figure 12.15

Semantic Feature Analysis: Automobiles

	2-Doors	**Hybrid**	**SUV**	**Gas Guzzler**	**High Gas Mileage**
Suburban	–	–	+	+	–
Prius	+	+	–	–	+
Escort	+	–	–	–	+
Range Rover	–	–	+	+	–

During **Reading Strategies: Vocabulary.**   A number of different strategies can be used to promote vocabulary learning.

Semantic Feature Analysis.   SFA (Anders & Bos, 1986) is a strategy that features a grid to help students understand how vocabulary and concepts are related to one another. Students using SFA are helped to see connections from known vocabulary to the new and master important concepts. This strategy helps students think critically about words and concepts possessing similar relationships and characteristics. SFA is quite flexible and may be used before, during, and after students read their unit materials. Following are the recommended steps for implementing semantic feature analysis in the example shown in Figure 12.15 (Cooter & Cooter, in press):

1. A class of vocabulary words is selected by the teacher (e.g., automobiles).
2. Examples of the word class are provided by students and listed (one in each box) in the left-hand row of the SFA grid (e.g., Suburban, Prius, Escort, Escalade).
3. Features of the word class are provided by students and listed across the top (one in each box after skipping the first box) of each column (e.g., two-doors, high gas mileage, gas guzzler, SUV, compact).
4. Using either a + or a – students determine which class examples possess which features.

Modeling the strategy throughout, teachers should employ instructional conversations to clarify and extend student knowledge.

Concept Maps.   A **concept map** is a graphic organizer showing the relationships between concepts. A concept map usually consists of cells (circles or other shapes) that contains a concept or vocabulary term, with connecting lines that explain the relationship between the cells. Arrows describe the direction of the relationship and can be read like a sentence by the concept map's author. Remember, when students work together to create concept maps they engage in a good bit of dialogue, and this deepens learning and helps increase students' vocabulary learning (Cooter & Cooter, in press).

There are four kinds of concept maps that are distinguished by their different formats for representing information: *spider, hierarchy, flowchart,* and *systems* concept maps. As the following descriptions show, each can work well with subject area studies.

1. The spider concept map is organized by placing the central theme or unifying factor in the center of the map, with outwardly radiating subthemes surrounding the central theme.
2. The hierarchy concept map presents information in a descending order of importance, with the most important information placed on the top.

3. The flowchart concept map organizes information in a linear or nondimensional format.
4. The systems concept map organizes information in a format that is similar to a flowchart, with the addition of inputs and outputs.

An example of each type of concept map is presented in Figure 12.16. To introduce concept maps to your students, you might use the following plan adapted from directions created by the Department of Chemistry and Biochemistry at the University of Delaware. This is another example of dialogic teaching involving a good bit of student interaction.

- *Brainstorming phase.* From memory, identify words or phrases that you *think* are in any way associated with the topic of study. Make a list of these items and print them neatly on small sticky notes, one per note. This is a brainstorming process, so write down everything that anyone in your group thinks of at this point. Your objective here is to generate the largest possible list you can. Before your group completes this step, you may have a *lot* of ideas.

- *Organizing phase.* Spread out your sticky notes on a flat surface so everyone can see them. Create groups and subgroups of related words and phrases. Try to group items to emphasize hierarchies or how things are related. Feel free to rearrange items and introduce new items. Note that some concepts will fall into multiple groupings. This will become important later.

- *Layout phase.* On a large sheet of paper, try to come up with an arrangement (layout) that best represents your collective understanding of the interrelationships and connections among groupings. Feel free to rearrange things at any time during this phase. Use a consistent hierarchy in which the most important concepts are in the center or at the top. Within subgroupings, place closely related items near to each other. Do not expect your layout to be like that of other groups.

- *Linking phase.* Use a version of one of the concept map formats (i.e., spider, hierarchical, flowchart, systems) with lines and/or arrows that best represent relationships between connected items.

- *Finalizing and sharing your concept map.* After your group has agreed on an arrangement of items that shows your understanding, convert the concept map into a permanent form that others can view and discuss.

Be creative in your use of colors, shapes, border thickness, and so on to communicate your group's understanding. Give your concept map a title. If you want to construct your final concept map on a computer, try using PowerPoint. In reviewing your concept map, consider the following attributes:

- *Accuracy and thoroughness.* Are the concepts and relationships correct? Are important concepts missing?
- *Organization.* Is the concept map laid out in such a way that higher-order relationships are apparent and easy to follow? Does your concept map have a title?
- *Appearance.* Is the assignment done with care, showing attention to details such as spelling and penmanship? Is it neat and orderly or is it chaotic and messy?

Figure 12.16

Concept Map Formats

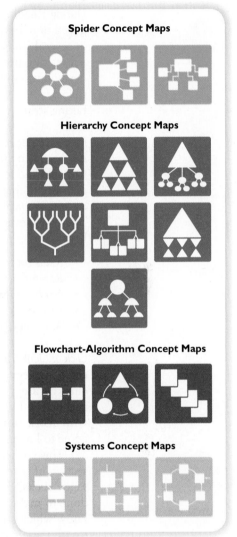

Click on A+RISE—WIDA ELP Standard Strategies in the MyEducationLab (www.myeducationlab.com) for your course. Next, select the Strategy Card Index tab, scroll to Comprehension, and select the Spider Web Diagram strategy.

- *Creativity.* Are there unusual elements that aid communication or stimulate interest without being distracting or over the top?

During Reading Strategies: Comprehension.   When your students are actively engaged in reading expository texts while in the *during* phase, we want to assist them in several ways. First, we want to help them know what to do when comprehension is breaking down. We call these **fix-up strategies.** Second, we want to monitor their developing comprehension. One potent way to accomplish this second goal is to help them learn to write academic summaries. Finally, students benefit from learning note-taking strategies. Let's take a closer look at these three areas.

Fix-Up Strategies.   Teaching students to actively monitor their own comprehension has been shown to significantly improve reading comprehension (Boulware-Gooden, Carreker, & Joshi, 2007). The act of monitoring one's unfolding comprehension of text and taking steps to "fix" comprehension when it is not occurring is referred to as *metacognition* or, sometimes, as *metacomprehension* (Reutzel & Cooter, 2011). There are several basic fix-up strategies good readers employ when reading comprehension in expository texts begins to break down.

- *Read on* for clarification.
- *Reread* the sentence.
- *Go back* and reread the paragraph.
- *Seek* information from the glossary or reference materials available online.
- *Ask* someone near you who may be able to help, such as a classmate.

Click or Clunk Strategy.   Another idea you can introduce to your students is the **click or clunk** strategy (Carr, 1985), which was briefly introduced in Chapter 7. The click or clunk strategy was designed to help students recognize when and where their comprehension breaks down during reading. When coupling the click or clunk strategy with instruction on the comprehension "fix-up" strategies noted above, students can come to know what to do to detect and correct comprehension breakdowns.

This strategy urges readers to reflect at the end of each sentence, paragraph, or section of reading by stopping and asking themselves whether the meaning or message "clicks" for them—or goes "clunk." If it clunks, what is wrong? What can be done to make sense of it? Once a breakdown has been detected, it is important to know which strategies to select in repairing broken comprehension, as well as when to use these strategies. A classroom "fix-up" poster displaying the key strategies is most helpful to students.

To demonstrate the use of a "fix-up" poster, model for students using a think-aloud process to help them develop a sense for when to select certain repair strategies for failing comprehension. Read part of a text aloud and, as you proceed, reveal to students your thinking, the hypotheses you have formed for the text, and anything that strikes you as difficult or unclear. By doing so, you demonstrate for students the processes that successful readers use to comprehend a text. Next, remind them of the click or clunk strategy. Gradually release the responsibility for modeling metacognitive strategies to the children during follow-up lessons on metacognitive monitoring. Display the repair strategies in a prominent place in your classroom. Be sure to draw your students' attention to these strategies throughout the year.

Written Academic Learning Summaries (WALS).   In Chapter 7 we learned about three levels of retelling as a way of gauging how well students are learning from expository texts: oral retelling, retelling using graphic organizers, and written retellings. Written retellings are by far the most sophisticated retellings learners can do to demonstrate their understanding of expository texts. In recent research with students living in high-poverty circumstances (Cooter & Cooter, 2008; Cooter & Cooter, in press), a structure was found to be effective for teaching these students how to write summaries called **written academic learning summaries (WALS).**

Written academic learning summaries (WALS) is an evidence-based activity that helps students write about what they are learning in core subject area texts (mathematics, science, social studies, English/language arts). Benefits to students include deeper and more permanent learning of important information, enhanced reading comprehension in informational texts, increased vocabulary learning, and better preparation of students for higher-level coursework in middle and high school. WALS specifically helps students bridge from new vocabulary they have acquired to a graphic organizer that features a structure for written retellings (Cooter, 2002), which helps students connect concepts and see relationships, and finally to create a written summary of three to five paragraphs. Figure 12.17 shows the process used in the WALS strategy.

For implementing WALS, students, in addition to your usual academic texts, will need to have writing materials and easy access to your academic word wall or equivalent where new academic terms are displayed and used in interactive activities.

Robert and Kathleen Cooter (2008) developed an explicit step-by-step framework to implement WALS for the first time, as shown in Table 12.3. The structure for written summaries (Cooter, 2002) and an example of a completed summary for teacher modeling are shown in Figures 12.18 and 12.19 (on pages 539 and 540), respectively.

Note-Taking Strategies. There are many different systems for teaching students how to take notes as they listen (Cooter & Flynt, 1996; Lapp, Flood, & Farnan, 2004). However, common threads of most note-taking systems include recommendations about how notes should initially be recorded during a unit of instruction, the need for subsequent reorganization and expansion of the notes, and a strong recommendation for frequent review. Before discussing each of the components of effective note taking, we would first like to suggest a couple of general guidelines derived from the work of Cooter and Flynt (1996).

1. Students should be asked to obtain a single notebook specifically for learning note-taking skills. Dedicating a notebook for this purpose will help them keep the notes organized and will make it easier for you to collect and examine the notes.
2. If notetaking is important to you, then some type of credit should be given to students who do a good job of recording and organizing their notes.
3. Adapt the amount and style of lecturing to your students' ability level. If you have an advanced class, more sophisticated lectures might be warranted. On the other hand, if your class has little experience with note taking and effective listening techniques, you might want to begin slowly and use a lot of visuals or perhaps a listening outline to assist students in determining and writing important information.

Figure 12.17

The Written Academic Learning Summaries (WALS) Process

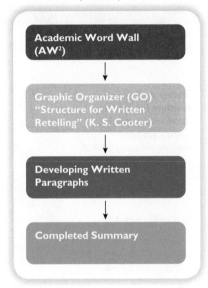

Click on A+RISE—WIDA ELP Standard Strategies in the MyEducationLab (www.myeducationlab.com) for your course. Next, select the Strategy Card Index tab, scroll to Writing for grades 6–12, and select the Content Flipbook strategy.

Table 12.3

Steps for Implementing WALS

Teaching Steps	Things You Should Do with Your Students
Introducing written academic learning summary (WALS)	1. Explain the purpose of the strategy and why it is helpful in writing a good summary of what they have learned. Describe (with enthusiasm) what you hope they will learn and why you feel it is important. 2. Check for understanding and reteach as needed.
Teacher modeling of the structure for written summaries to create a written academic learning summary (WALS)	3. Modeling is to be teacher-led with little or no student feedback—they are observing you as you "think out loud" how you go about moving information from a thinking map to the structure for written retellings, then expanding the key words and phrases into sentences. Using language students can understand, explain the steps explicitly. Read aloud sections you are creating and how you know when each section is satisfactory or when sections need further editing and revising. 4. Begin by modeling how you might create a three-paragraph summary. After this is done, show how you could expand it to a five-paragraph summary using two additional topics and their supporting details. 5. Check for understanding and reteach as needed.
Guided practice 1 Small-group activity (i.e., joint productive activity) with teacher monitoring and feedback	6. Explicitly restate the key steps of the structure for written summaries to create a written academic learning summary (WALS) that you will want students to do in a small-group activity (or in pairs), also known as a joint productive activity (JPA). 7. Have students working in small groups or pairs take a thinking map they have created (or one you provide) to create a written summary using the MCLA format. Instructional conversation—include conversation about students' experiences so far using the structure for written summaries to create a written academic learning summary (WALS) and your feedback (see Figure 12.17). 8. Assessment: check for understanding using key questions (write these out ahead of time). *Hint:* bloom's taxonomy of questioning is always a good source.
Guided practice 2 Individual practice with teacher or peer feedback	9. Now, design an activity whereby students on their own attempt using the structure for written summaries to create a written academic learning summary (WALS). Students should then share their written summary with the teacher or a "peer editing group" for feedback. 10. The teacher should now lead an instructional conversation about what has been learned or understood about the process and ways they can make their written summaries better. 11. Assessment: check for understanding using key questions (write these out ahead of time), and decide if you will need to reteach all or some of the students how to use the process.
Student independent use of the strategy and assessment Student works alone with limited support	12. Design and implement an independent activity (students working on their own) using the strategy for using thinking maps to create a written summary. Assessment: check for understanding using key questions (write these out ahead of time). 13. Decide if you will need to reteach all or some of the students how to use the structure for written summaries to create a written academic learning summary (WALS).

Traditional note-taking systems such as the Cornell system (Pauk, 2000) and Palmatier's note-taking system for learning (1973) share several features that we recommend for use in training students on how to listen and take notes on lecture information.

1. *Students should divide their notebook paper into two columns.* The left column should be about 2 or 3 inches wide, or one-third of the paper width. The remaining two-thirds of the page is used for recording the notes.

2. *Students should write information in a modified outline form on the right side of the page.* Students should indent subtopics and minor ideas using letters and numbers and should be encouraged to use abbreviations to minimize time spent in writing down information. Heavily emphasized points should be marked with asterisks or stars.

Figure 12.18

Structure for Written Summaries

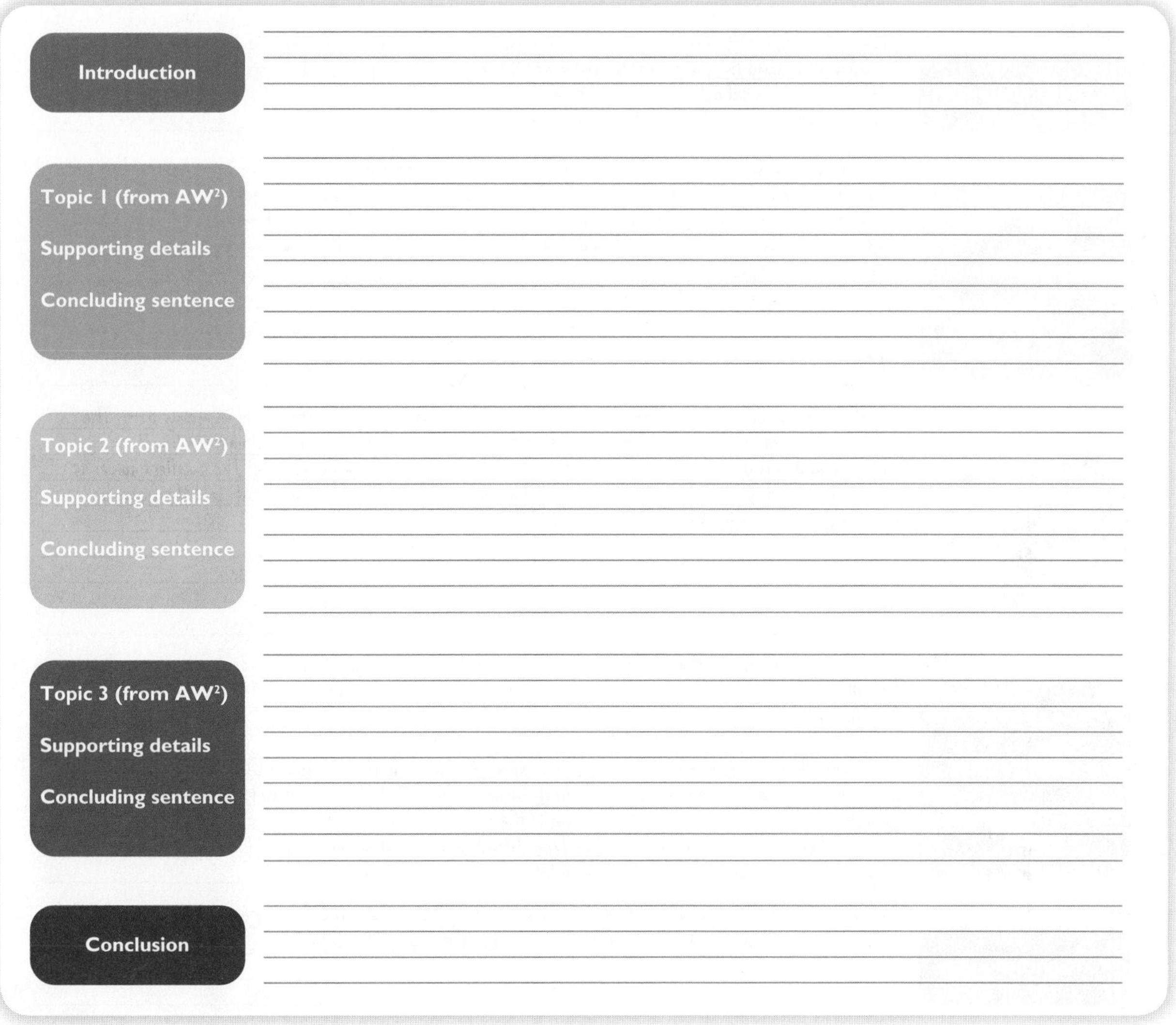

Introduction	
Topic 1 (from AW²) **Supporting details** **Concluding sentence**	
Topic 2 (from AW²) **Supporting details** **Concluding sentence**	
Topic 3 (from AW²) **Supporting details** **Concluding sentence**	
Conclusion	

From Cooter, K. S. (2002). *A Structure for Written Retellings.* Unpublished manuscript.

3. *Students should organize and expand their notes as soon as possible.* Early in the school year, considerate teachers provide in-class time for this task. At this time the students literally rewrite their notes on similarly lined paper. The purpose is for the students to write all abbreviations, expand phrases, and make sure that the information is sequentially organized. This is obviously a form of practice.

4. *Students should fill in the left margin for aid in study and review.* As they reread their notes, students identify topics, key terms, and questions that might assist them in remembering the lecture information recorded on the right side of the paper.

5. *Students use their notes for study and review.* Students can now cover up the right-hand side of the paper and use the memory triggers they have recorded on the left-hand side for review. As they move down the left-hand side of the page,

Figure 12.19

Completed Written Retelling for Modeling on *Arachnids*

Introduction

Spiders are very interesting creatures, and are even scary to some people. The scientific name for spiders is "arachnids," and they are insects. There are 37,000 kinds of spiders. There are even songs about spiders we learn in school. In this report we will learn facts and misconceptions about this special living thing we learned in our book and on the Internet.

Topic 1 (from AW²)

Supporting details

Concluding sentence

One misconception is that all spiders are poisonous. Some spiders are poisonous, or "venomous," but not all spiders have venom. Spiders use venom to stun or kill creatures they want to eat. Of over 37,000 kinds of spiders, only about 25 have venom that can hurt humans. Two spiders in the U.S. with venom that can hurt humans are the black widow and the brown recluse, but no one has been proven killed in over two decades (20 years).

Topic 2 (from AW²)

Supporting details

Concluding sentence

Another misconception is that some spiders can be larger than a cat. Spiders come in many sizes. The largest is the Goliath birdeater tarantula. It is found in the rain forests of northeastern South America, and can be as big as a dinner plate. It can grab birds from their nests! The smallest spider is from Borneo and is the size of a pinhead. So, there are no spiders larger than a cat, but they can be very large and also very small.

Topic 3 (from AW²)

Supporting details

Concluding sentence

One thing we learned is that different arachnids eat different things. Many spiders eat insects, but not all do. There are spiders who dine on birds, frogs, fish, lizards, and snakes. So it is not true that all spiders eat bugs!

There are other things about arachnids, or spiders, that we still do not know. What is the largest spider in North America? Is it as big as the Goliath birdeater tarantula? We hope not. Also, is the silk spiders make all the same kind? How strong is their silk? Could you make clothes out of spider silk? We wonder where the name "arachnid" came from? And what about water spiders? Do any of them actually live under water? We still have a lot to learn about arachnids.

Conclusion

Spiders, or arachnids, are very interesting insects. They come in many sizes, live on different things, and some are poisonous. We want to know more about this special creature.

From Reutzel and Cooter, *Strategies for Reading Assessment and Instruction*, 4th ed. © 2011 by Pearson Education, Inc. Reproduced with permission of Pearson Education, Inc.

students use the headings, key terms, and questions as a means of assessing their ability to remember and paraphrase what they have recorded.

Comprehension Windows Strategy. CWS (Bass & Woo, 2008, p. 571) was designed as an informational text strategy using an easy-to-create instructional prop to enhance students' comprehension during reading and writing. CWS helps students build content knowledge, organize facts, structure critical thinking, and use proper documentation and citations. This strategy is appropriate for small collaborative groups or individual work. To implement CWS, you will need the usual materials used in academic content studies and you will need to construct a CWS "prop." A prototype

Figure 12.20

Comprehension Window Strategy (CWS) Prop Prototype

[Back]

References: Include—author/date of publication/name of source/publisher

1.

2.

3.

4.

Fold line (folds like a tent; use file folder type of material)

TOPIC

× F O L D ×

Cut up to Xs

Heading 1	**Heading 2**	**Heading 3**
(Place sticky notes with new information under appropriate CWS flap—students can organize each heading later.)		

From Bass, L., & Woo, D. G. (2008). Comprehension Window Strategy: A Comprehension Strategy and Prop for Reading and Writing Informational Text. *The Reading Teacher, 61*(7), pp. 571–575. Reprinted with permission of the International Reading Association.

created by Bass and Woo (2008) is shown in Figure 12.20. You will also need file folders, scissors, pens, and sticky notes for headings.

Bass and Woo (2008, p. 573) offer the following guidelines for using the comprehension windows strategy (CWS).

Teacher Preparation

- Begin with a letter-size (recycled) file folder (school secretary, parents, and local businesses are good sources)
- Cut along fold to create two equal halves (each folder will make two CWS props)
- Fold each piece in half lengthwise creating a tent
- Provide ample information sticky notes for every student

Procedure

- Label each CWS flap with the appropriate headings using sticky notes (e.g., *Important People, Events Before, What Happened?*)
- Label back section as *References*
- As students gather information, they write a complete reference citation for each source on the back section of the tent, numbering the references (alphabetical order can be done later)
- On each sticky note, students record one idea and its corresponding reference number
- Sticky notes are positioned under the appropriate CWS flaps to help students sort and categorize information.

Once information has been gathered, students are ready to engage in writing process activities (prewriting, drafting, revising, editing, publishing). This can be done individually or in small groups. Students begin by organizing information using the information sticky notes from each CWS flap one flap at a time. Information sticky notes can be placed and organized on a flat surface as a preliminary stage leading to a final product. Some possible final products include poster sessions, PowerPoint presentations, reenactments, or author's chair (to share compositions).

Click on A+RISE—Literacy Strategies in the MyEducationLab (www.myeducationlab.com) for your course. Next, select the Strategy Card Index tab, scroll to Fluency for grades 6–12, and select the Radio Readers strategy.

During Reading Strategies: Fluency.   Choral reading helps students learn to effortlessly read technical texts, strengthens vocabulary knowledge, and improves comprehension. In Chapter 5 on fluency, we provided information on ways of implementing three types of choral reading: unison, echo, and antiphonal. In this chapter we also offered Paige's procedure for introducing choral reading as part of your content instruction. Now we take the final step to help you implement choral reading well, with good fidelity of implementation. In Table 12.4 we offer an implementation continuum (Cooter & Cooter, in press) used by literacy coaches and teacher to perfect the application of choral reading.

Click on A+RISE—WIDA ELP Standard Strategies in the MyEducationLab (www.myeducationlab.com) for your course. Next, select the Strategy Card Index tab, scroll to Vocabulary for grades 6–12, and select the Mad Three Minutes strategy.

After Reading Strategies: Vocabulary.   Once students have completed their initial expository readings in a unit of study, we want to be sure that new knowledge crystallizes in their long-term memories. The mainstay of vocabulary learning that provides multiple exposures and thought is the academic word wall discussed in Chapter 6. Use of academic word walls continues to play an important part in your after reading regime. Now we add another strategy to your teaching tool kit.

The Frayer Model (Frayer, Frederick, & Klausmeir, 1969) is a classic strategy that helps students understand new vocabulary and concepts in relation to what is already known. This model is especially useful for nonfiction terms or academic vocabulary because it presents essential and nonessential information related to the term, as well as examples and nonexamples. Frayer is a splendid after reading strategy because it causes students to think about new vocabulary and analyze how it relates to their prior knowledge and experiences.

Table 12.4

Implementation Continuum for Whole-Class/Group Choral Reading

Exemplary A	Above Average B	Acceptable C	Early Implementation D	Traditional Instruction E
Teacher conducts a preassessment to gain some understanding of the range of students' reading abilities with on-level textbook readings (e.g., timed reading, cloze passages, maze passages). Data is used to decide whether supplemental readings may be needed for some students (i.e., differentiating instruction).	Teacher conducts a preassessment to gain some understanding of the range of students' reading abilities with on-level textbook readings.	Teacher introduces and explains the purpose of choral reading.	Teacher introduces one of the choral reading activities (unison, echo, or antiphonal).	Uses "round robin" or "popcorn reading" for oral reading practice.
Puts the text selection in context and explains the purpose of choral reading.	Models the reading and attends to punctuation, uses appropriate prosody (voice intonation), volume, and reading speed.	New or unfamiliar academic words from the text are pronounced.	Teacher and students practice reading a passage from their textbook together.	When students read aloud, they do so without previewing the text or having it modeled.
New academic and other challenging words from the text are pronounced.	Teacher uses a "countdown" queuing system (e.g., 3-2-1) so that students begin together.	Models the choral reading strategy with a reasonably loud voice.	Teacher has 5-minute choral reading practice one to three times per week using the current unit of study.	Teacher remains in one place during oral reading practice.
Models the reading and attends to punctuation, uses appropriate prosody (voice intonation), volume, and reading speed. Students are given an opportunity for further vocabulary decoding or pronunciation.	Teacher travels about the room during the reading to attend to reading other difficulties, and makes mental notes for reteaching or clarifying.	Teacher uses a "countdown" queuing system (e.g., 3-2-1) so that students begin together. Teacher travels about the room during the reading.		
Teacher uses a "countdown" queuing system (e.g., 3-2-1) so that students begin together. Teacher travels about the room during the reading to attend to reading miscues or other difficulties, and makes mental notes for re-teaching or clarifying. Teacher reviews difficult words and phrases after each subsequent reading.	Teacher reviews difficult words and phrases after one of the readings.	Teacher uses the same passage from the textbook for each CR session during the week.		
On the second and third day of CR teacher uses the same passage from the textbook as before. Each day, the teacher's voice becomes less loud/dominant as students become familiar with the passage.	Teacher has 5-minute choral reading practice each day using the same text selection.	Teacher has 5-minute choral reading practice for at least 4 days during the week using the same text selection.		
Teacher uses the same passage as before, but may now employ either antiphonal reading or echo reading.	The passage selected is at least 1–3 weeks ahead of the teacher's curriculum.	The passage selected is at least 1–3 weeks ahead of the teacher's curriculum.		
The passage selected is at least 1–3 weeks ahead of the teacher's curriculum.				

Figure 12.21

Frayer Model

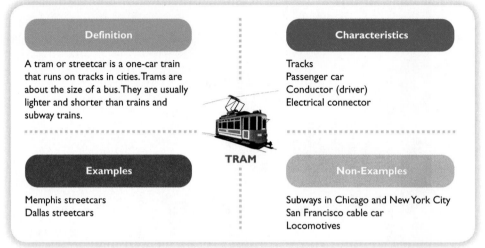

Adapted from Frayer, D., Frederick, W. C., & Klausmeir, H. J. (1969). *A Schema for Testing the Level of Concept Mastery* (Working Paper No. 16). Madison: University of Wisconsin, Wisconsin Research and Development Center for Cognitive Learning.

To implement this strategy you will need a blank Frayer Model form on a computer, image projector, or overhead projector for demonstration purposes. Students will need paper and pencils for note taking. The teacher presents or helps students determine essential and nonessential information about a concept, find examples and nonexamples of the concept, and recognize coordinate and subordinate relationships to the concept. This classification procedure can be done as a group, in dyads, or individually. Shown in Figure 12.21 is an example of a completed Frayer Model.

After Reading Strategies: Comprehension.   Earlier we investigated written academic learning summaries (WALS) as a method for helping students display their new knowledge. In after reading stages we continue to work with students using WALS to expand their written summaries and cement learning.

Now let's add a gaming aspect to comprehension development with something called "six degrees of separation." The goal of the Six Degrees of Separation game (Cooter & Cooter, in press) is for students to create a web in which they connect one term to another term in six or fewer steps. The two terms to be connected are decided by the teacher. The notion of six degrees of separation (also referred to as the "human web") refers to the idea that, if a person is one step away from each person they know and two steps away from each person who is known by one of the people they know, then everyone is at most six steps away from any other person on Earth. Michael Gurevich conducted seminal work in his empirical study of the structure of social networks in his 1961 Massachusetts Institute of Technology doctor of philosophy dissertation titled *Ithiel de Sola Pool*.

The following is an actual activity used in Memphis, Tennessee, in a research project in which the Six Degrees of Separation game (Cooter & Cooter, in press) was first developed. This example is from a middle school social studies class in which the teacher is explaining the game (see Figures 12.22 through 12.25).

We are learning about how cultures in the United States have differences, but are also connected. I would like for each of you in your teams to first draw a concept map that begins with Memphis, Tennessee, at its center, and then somehow find a connection to Missoula, Montana. I have included at each table the steps you can use to construct your concept map. At each of your tables I have also given you copies of a book titled *Missoula, Montana: Communities and Their Locations* to help you learn more about this American city.

When your team finishes your concept map and everyone agrees it is ready, you will then post your concept map on the wall for our "Gallery Walk."

To win this game, we must all agree as a class that your team had the fewest complex connections (for example culture, industry, geography) which get them from A to B, not simple ones (nonexamples are street names, people names, simple geography like "trees").

Each person in our class has a yellow sticky note and will place it on the six degrees map they vote for as the winner—you cannot vote for your own.

Figure 12.22

Six Degrees of Separation Game: Early Brainstorming Phase—Connecting the Terms *Texas* and *Sharks*

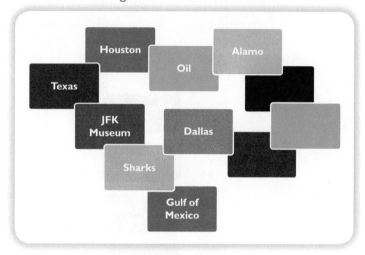

Let me show you an example of a completed six degrees map with complex connections and an example of a poor one. See if you can see why the first one is a good example and why the second one is a poor example. I would like to know your thinking, so jot down your thoughts on a piece of paper for our discussion. Remember, the task was to connect *Texas* and *shark*.

Figure 12.23

Organization Phase: A Simple "Spider" Concept Map—Six Steps or Less Path from *Texas* to *Sharks* Noted in Red

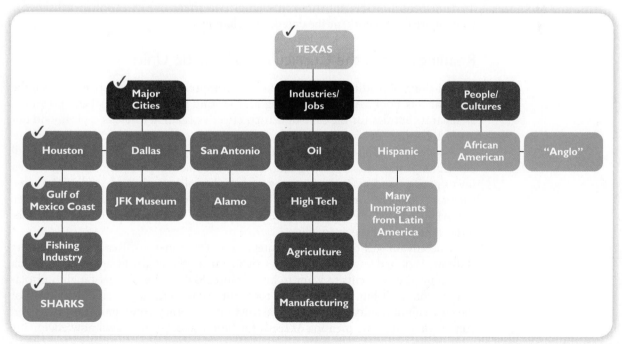

Figure 12.24

Final Concept Map: A Quality Example Connecting *Texas* and *Sharks* in Five Steps

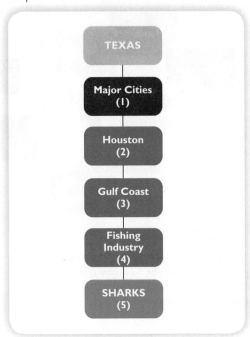

Figure 12.25

Hierarchical Concept Map: A Poor Example Connecting *Texas* and *Sharks* in Three Steps—Did Not Use Complex Terms

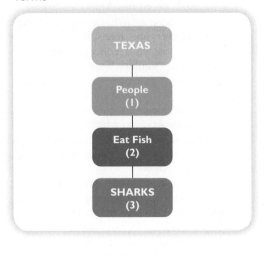

After **Reading Strategies: Fluency.**   Two very popular fluency strategies we discussed earlier in Chapter 5 were *readers' theatre* and *radio reading*. Because a teacher's time is at a premium and constructing script examples for your students of radio plays and readers' theatre can be quite time-consuming, we offer some great online websites for content area instruction at the end of this chapter.

Reading Across the Curriculum: Thematic Units

The teaching of reading and writing using a comprehensive perspective has been the focus of this book. Although reading and writing have sometimes been presented as separate entities for the sake of clarity, effective reading teachers typically do not apply these literacy skills separately. Rather, they are integrated across the curriculum so that boundaries between reading and writing virtually cease to exist. In full curriculum integration, reading and writing become integral parts of subject area investigations and vice versa by way of interdisciplinary **themed studies.** A theme such as "Changes" or "Exploration" can become an exciting classroom experience involving social studies, the sciences, mathematics, literature, art, music, and other important areas of the curriculum.

The advantages of curriculum integration are numerous. Reading and writing skills are acquired and refined within a rich context of real-world significance, which in turn inspires students to want to know more. Skills are no longer taught in isolation as rote drill but are learned as tools for communicating ideas. Integration of the curriculum results in a blend of instruction in literacy communication skills and content as well as the planting of seeds for future searches for new knowledge.

Guidelines for Conducting Themed Studies.   Themed studies involve total curriculum integration. A brief summary of the essential components of themed studies—as identified from the work of Paradis (1984) and Gamberg and colleagues (Gamberg, Kwak, Hutchings, & Altheim, 1988)—follows.

• *Selecting a theme.* Themes that meet the criteria previously described should be chosen.

• *Identifying resources.* The teacher should identify and collect resources before beginning the unit. Examples include nonfiction books, other pertinent print media (e.g., documents, travel brochures, and government publications), hands-on materials that pertain to the topic, nonprint media (videotapes, films, radio recordings), relevant basal stories or literacy selections, and computer-related material. Resources also include community members and the opportunities afforded by field trips.

• *Brainstorming.* Themed studies involve brainstorming on the part of both teacher and students. Teachers brainstorm as part of the planning process to antici-
pate ways that curriculums can be integrated into the unit and to assist in the selection of materials. Paradis (1984) offers a brainstorming web (Figure 12.26) to assist teachers in this process. Students are also encouraged to brainstorm as a way of becoming involved initially with the topic. Brainstorming helps students focus their thinking, articulate their interests and background knowledge, and develop an appreciation for the ideas of their peers. It also encourages collaboration—a highly prized skill in both school and the workplace.

Figure 12.26

Teacher Brainstorming Web for Themed Studies

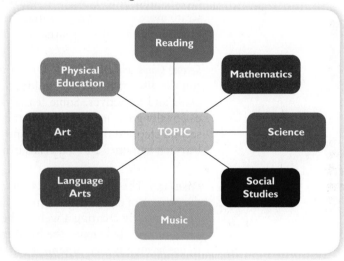

• *Demonstrating learning.* Students complete projects and tasks that demonstrate their newly acquired knowledge. Projects like those cited for themed units generally apply here. In addition, students may complete other products such as displays, speeches, demonstration fairs, and guided tours.

Teachers building themed studies search for ways to incorporate reading and other basic literacy skills into content subjects because they know that these processes help students deepen their knowledge of the wider world. The dynamic created in these cross-curricular units is quite powerful and spawns many positive outcomes in the classroom, including heightened interest in the subject matter and a sense of empowerment (Cox & Zarillo, 1993; Wepner & Feeley, 1993).

After many years of helping school districts around the United States build thematic units, we have discovered several practices that speed the process of curricular integration. The most efficient way to begin is by first constructing a themed literature unit using the process described in this chapter; this achieves full integration of the language arts within the context of great literature. Themed literature units also contain all the essential elements of a comprehensive reading program, such as daily reading and writing, the teaching of nonnegotiable skills, literature response, cooperative groups, opportunities to practice fluency, and student self-evaluation. Once teachers build themed literature units as the curriculum core it becomes a relatively simple matter to infuse the content areas. Finally, we have learned that once teachers go through the process of building thematic units, they better understand all the essential elements and can re-create the process in the future in their own way—keeping some elements and deleting others—to create a balanced learning system that meets the needs of their students.

Planning thematic units involves five major phases that can be applied equally well in grades 4 through 8. These phases are theme selection, setting goals and objectives, webbing, choosing major activities and materials, and unit scaffolding.

Theme Selection. In many ways, the success of thematic units depends on the concept chosen to be the theme. It must be broad enough to accomplish linkage between the various content subjects, address local and state requirements listed in curriculum guides (Pappas, Kiefer, & Levstik, 1990), include quality nonfiction and fiction, and still be interesting to youngsters. Topics like "Our State's History" or "Nutrition" can be far too confining for the kinds of engaging learning experiences we hope to craft. There are a large number of possible topics, which might give teachers a good starting point; these include "Legends," "Survival," "Heroes," "Changes," "Seasons," and "Journeys." If the theme selected is broad enough, teachers will discover creative and enticing ways to weave various content subjects into the unit. To demonstrate more clearly ways thematic units can be constructed, we build on the themed literature unit called "Journeys."

Setting Goals and Objectives. Once the theme has been selected, teachers should consult the district curriculum guide and other available resources to determine possible goals and objectives. Some teachers prefer to do this step first because themes occasionally grow logically out of the required curriculum. Whether done as a first or second step, establishing goals and objectives must come early so that appropriate learning activities and materials can be chosen.

Webbing. The next step in planning thematic units is **webbing,** which is essentially the process of creating a schematic or schema map of the linkage between each aspect of the unit. By creating a web of the major aspects of the proposed unit, the teacher can gain a global view—the big picture. Webs can also be revised and adapted later to use as an advance organizer for students at the beginning of the thematic unit. In Figure 12.27, we see an initial (not fully developed) thematic unit web for the "Journeys" theme. The theme now spans three additional content areas: social studies, science, and mathematics. Major activities have also been suggested, which is the next topic we explore.

We have found that planning daily activities is greatly facilitated by webbing each content component separately. Teachers should include in the web such information as key reference books, computer software, important questions to be answered, special activities, and demonstrations they may wish to perform. In Figure 12.28 (on page 550), we share a web used in the science portion of the "Journeys" theme.

Choosing Major Activities and Materials. One of the joys of thematic units is that they infuse the curriculum with great ideas, activities, and materials that energize learners. What a great alternative this is for teachers ready for modest yet powerful change! Activities chosen for thematic units provide students with opportunities to apply literacy skills in a wider-world context. Sometimes students complete these activi-

Figure 12.27

Initial Thematic Unit Web: Journeys

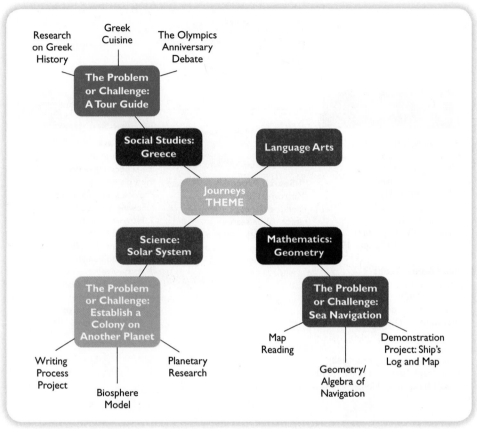

ties independently, other times as part of a problem-solving team. Occasions for personal exploration and reflection are also seen as valuable aspects of thematic unit activities.

Many and diverse materials are required to create an engaging and relevant thematic unit. Both fiction and nonfiction materials are needed to plan rich and interesting activities. The core materials are books, lots of books of every kind. Pappas and colleagues (1990) got it just right when they said, "as with chocolate, you never have enough books!" Other essential tools are reference materials, fiction books that awaken imaginations, and nonfiction books to read aloud. Teachers will also need to locate what are known by historians as "primary source materials"—original sources of information.

Unit Scaffolding. The final stage of planning is unit scaffolding. At this point, the teacher determines just how long the unit should run and makes final decisions about which activities to include. Typically, thematic units last 1 to 2 weeks in grades 4 through 6 (Wiseman, 1992) and up to 4 or 5 weeks in the middle school. The teacher should resist the temptation to run units for months at a time; this usually becomes too much of a good thing and turns high student interest into boredom.

Figure 12.28

Science Web for Journeys Theme

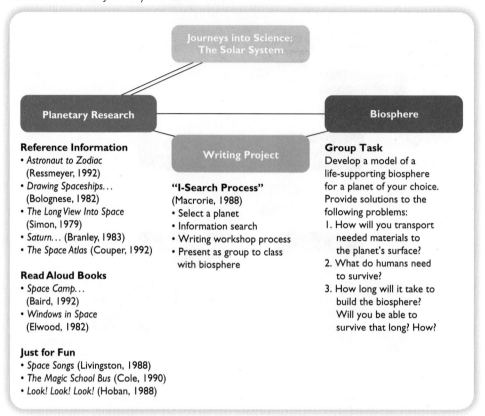

Core Subject Matter Themes. Within each core subject matter, teachers need to create themes that will resonate with their students—help them understand the real world applications of each core subject.

Social Studies. In the social studies component, the problem/challenge activity is for students working in groups of four to assume the role of travel agents charged with the responsibility of developing a "tour guide" for clients traveling to Greece. Required parts of the tourist guide involve information about ancient Greece, Greek cuisine, and the founding of the Olympics in ancient Greece. Students in each group present what they have learned to the class, or other classes, in the form of an enlarged travel brochure.

Science. The problem/challenge activity for science has student groups assume the role of astronauts aboard a space shuttle. Their mission is to travel to a planet of their choosing and establish a colony. This activity involves scientific research into such concepts as what humans need to sustain life, surface conditions on the selected planet, useful natural resources on the planet (if any), and information about the building of life-supporting human environments (biospheres). To present their findings, students in each group will draft a report in the form of a book using the writing process and construct a model of the biosphere they propose to build on the planet surface.

Mathematics.   The problem/challenge activity in mathematics is for students to assume the role of sea voyagers who must navigate their ship to Greece from the United States. Students can complete this project independently or with a partner. Skills involved include basics in map reading, geometry as related to navigation, translation of miles per hour to knots, and journal writing. The product is a ship's log, which details daily destinations, map coordinates, travel times, and (if desired) some brief information about what students see at each port.

Theme Integration.   One of the decisions teachers must make is whether the unit is to be fully integrated and presented as a seamless curriculum. Some teachers in grades 4 through 6 in nondepartmentalized situations may operate a unit for a few days or a week. For example, in a "Journeys" unit, the teacher may focus almost exclusively on the social studies problem/challenge. When the social studies portion is concluded, the class may move on to the science problem/challenge, focusing on that aspect for entire days at a time. The mathematics problem/challenge may come next. The value of seamless integration is that students use critical thinking and problem-solving skills in much the same way as adults in the working world. They also use literacy skills throughout the day. A third advantage is that students move from one problem/challenge to another every few days, thus maintaining a higher level of interest. Unfortunately, seamless integration cannot be achieved very easily in departmentalized middle schools—self-contained classrooms are generally necessary.

Another option for organizing thematic units that can be used in departmentalized situations is **segmented integration,** in which the core subject area teacher develops each content area portion concurrently. A sample daily schedule depicting how this integration might occur in a departmentalized middle school setting is shown in Figure 12.29. Segmented integration permits teachers in fully departmentalized schools to develop thematic units collaboratively as faculty teams. Sometimes all teachers in a departmentalized team will choose to take part in the thematic unit; on other occasions, one or two teachers may work independently on a unit to satisfy district or state mandates.

Figure 12.29

Segmented Integration for Journeys Theme

8:30–9:30	**Language Arts:** Themed Literature Unit on Journeys
9:30–10:45	**Social Studies:** Greece/Tour Guide
10:55–11:30	Computer Lab
11:30–12:30	**Science:** Solar System/Biosphere Model
12:30–1:00	Lunch
1:00–2:15	**Specials:** Library, P.E.
2:30–3:25	**Mathematics:** Sea Navigation

Tier 2 Instructional Plans for Grades 4–8

Problems for struggling readers can become acute during the upper elementary and middle school years. If not addressed, these problems often worsen and compound, resulting in student frustration, discouragement, and declining achievement. Students not reading on or near grade level by the end of grade 3 typically do not close the performance gap. Indeed, the gap can widen and contribute to the dropout crisis in grades 9 and 10. Thus, it is critical that struggling readers benefit from a proactive

Response to Intervention (RTI) Tier 2 instructional plan in grades 4 to 8 aimed at improving both fundamental reading abilities and academic literacy.

In this section we review some widely used commercial programs useful in helping struggling readers in grades 4 through 8 close the achievement gap. Next, we suggest some basic strategies that may be used for all learners to help them succeed in content reading materials. Finally, we share recent thinking on ways to help English learners (ELs) succeed in understanding informational texts.

Commercial Programs for Low-Performing Readers

We believe the long-term solution to reading problems lies in improving teacher expertise and providing sufficient learning materials, appropriate and safe classroom environments, and proper support from family and community members. In the end, it really does take a village to properly raise a child.

Nevertheless, there are several commercial reading programs available that may be helpful as supplemental tools in helping struggling readers accelerate their general reading development. We include in our descriptions below the latest research evidence as to the effectiveness of each program according to the What Works Clearinghouse (http://ies.ed.gov/ncee/wwc), an agency of the U.S. Department of Education, and other research-based resources.

Reading is FAME.   This four-course reading program (Omaha, NE: Boys Town) for adolescents reading 2 or more years below grade-level expectancy was developed at the world famous Father Flanagan's Boys Town in Omaha, Nebraska. Students enrolled in FAME courses are grouped according to their reading needs and receive small-group instruction for 40 to 50 minutes daily. Professional training and support from the Boys Town Reading Center is required for teachers who will deliver the program to students. Each of the four courses is offered using direct instruction, word activities, computer activities, and pre- and posttesting along with other assessments and evaluations. Though used in many urban school districts with multiple testimonials available, we were unable to locate any empirical research evidence as to the effectiveness of this program. For more information, see their website, which is noted at the end of this chapter.

Read 180.   This computer-assisted program (New York: Scholastic) is designed for students in grades 3 through 12 whose reading is below proficiency. It involves a daily 90-minute session that couples computer-based activities and small-group instruction. From our own experiences in the Dallas and Memphis school districts, we know firsthand that Read 180 can be quite expensive and difficult to implement with good fidelity. A review of research issued by the What Works Clearinghouse (WWC) in July of 2010 stated:

> No studies of *READ 180*® that fall within the scope of the Students with Learning Disabilities review protocol meet What Works Clearinghouse (WWC) evidence standards. The lack of studies meeting WWC evidence standards means that, at this time, the WWC is unable to draw any conclusions based on research about the effectiveness or ineffectiveness of *READ 180*® on students with learning disabilities. (p. 1)

From 1996 through 2011 extensive evidence-based research as part of the federally funded Striving Readers project has been investigating the efficacy of Read 180. We anticipate results from these studies will provide definitive evidence as to this program's costs and benefits to learners.

Reading Mastery.   Designed to provide systematic instruction in reading to K–6 students, Reading Mastery (SRA/McGraw-Hill) is often used as an intervention program for struggling readers, as a supplement to a school's core reading program, or as a stand-alone reading program. It is available in three versions: Reading Mastery Classic (for use in grades pre-K–3), Reading Mastery Plus (for grades K–6), and Reading Mastery Signature Edition (for use in grades K–5). During the implementation of Reading Mastery, students are grouped with other students having similar needs based on program placement tests.

A report of evidence-based research issued by What Works Clearinghouse in August of 2010 stated:

> One study of *Reading Mastery* . . . meets What Works Clearinghouse (WWC) evidence standards, and one study meets WWC evidence standards with reservations. The studies included 361 students in grades 4 and 5, who attended schools in the Midwestern and northwestern United States. Based on two studies, the WWC considers the extent of evidence for *Reading Mastery* on adolescent learners to be small for the reading fluency and comprehension domains. No studies that meet WWC evidence standards with or without reservations examined the effectiveness of *Reading Mastery* on adolescent learners in the alphabetics or general literacy achievement domains. (p. 1)

In sum, there is little research evidence as to the effectiveness of Reading Mastery. Of the research that exists, WWC concludes that this program has "potentially positive" effects on improving reading fluency and "no discernable effects" on improving comprehension.

Accelerated Reader.   Described as a guided reading intervention, Accelerated Reader (Renaissance Learning) uses reading practice and computerized quizzes to supplement K–12 reading instruction. According to a report issued in August 2010, What Works Clearinghouse

> reviewed 318 studies on *Accelerated Reader*™. One study, a randomized controlled trial, meets WWC evidence standards, and a second study, a quasi-experimental design, meets WWC evidence standards with reservations. The two studies include 2,877 students from grades 4–8 in Oregon and Texas. Based on these studies, the WWC found the *Accelerated Reader*™ to have no discernible effects on reading fluency or comprehension for adolescent learners. (p. 1)

Comprehension "Strategy Families"

One issue for struggling readers is how they use (or fail to use) comprehension strategies as they read informational texts. As we noted in Chapter 7, research indicates that teaching children how to use combinations of comprehension strategies as they read, or multiple comprehension strategies (McKeown, Beck & Blake, 2009), yields particularly strong results for improving children's reading achievement. Dana (1989) has grouped several effective reading comprehension strategies for struggling readers that can be used with relative ease and in minimal time. Also, these strategies have similar or complementary functions in aiding comprehension. The first strategy family explained below, SIP (summarize, image, predict), helps students focus on content. The second strategy, EEEZ (take it easy, explain, explore, expand), is a set of elaborative strategies that can be used as a postreading experience to "help anchor the content in memory" (Dana, 1989, p. 32). The acronyms for these strategies remind students of important steps they are to follow.

SIP. The SIP set of strategies is reportedly consistent with Anderson's (1970) findings that students benefit from learning activities that require attention to content and active engagement in processing.

> *S* reminds students to *summarize* the content of each page or naturally divided section of the text. This summarization of text invites students to reflect on and interact with content.

> *I* represents the notion of *imaging*. This is a reminder that students should form an internal visual display of the content while reading, which provides a second imprint of the text's content.

> *P* reminds students to *predict* while reading. As each page or naturally divided section is read, students should pause to predict what they might learn next. While reading the section predicted, students verify, revise, or modify predictions according to what they learned. This process of predicting and verifying can carry students through entire selections and help hold their interest.

EEEZ. The EEEZ strategy gets students to elaborate mentally on new content to facilitate long-term retention. In her introduction to this strategy, Dana (1989) explains:

> After reading, it is recommended that students review what they have read in light of the purpose that was set for the reading assignment. Students are told that after reading they should "take it easy" (EEEZ) and make an attempt to explain (E) the content in a manner commensurate with the purpose set for reading. They might have to answer questions, generate questions, define a concept, or provide a summary. (p. 33)

> Two additional strategies are represented by the EEEZ acronym:

> *E: Explore* the same content material as it has been described by other authors of different texts. These comparisons often help clarify important ideas.

> *E: Expand* the subject matter by reading other texts that go beyond the content covered by the original text.

After expanding, students should respond to the original purpose for reading the assignment and embellish their responses with additional content discovered during the EEEZ process.

Improving Fluency

All students, and especially struggling readers, should spend significant amounts of time—20 to 30 minutes per day—in the act of reading if they are to grow and progress. Krashen's (1992) research demonstrates that 20 minutes of daily sustained reading in materials of high interest and appropriate difficulty can help students grow by as much as 6 months per year in overall reading fluency. Daily sustained reading builds vocabulary knowledge and sharpens students' reading skills. Group-assisted reading can help build reading fluency with middle schoolers.

Group-Assisted Reading. As a method to help struggling readers improve reading fluency and comprehension, **group-assisted reading** (Eldredge, 1990; McLaughlin, 2010) can be quite effective. In practice, group-assisted reading involves a pair or group of students reading text material in unison, emphasizing correct phrasing, intonation, and pitch. Teachers read each book many times with students until students can read it fluently with expression. In a variation of group-assisted reading called **dyad reading,** the teacher's role is assumed by a peer "lead reader." Both group-assisted and dyad reading groups have been shown to be more effective with at-risk readers than more traditional methods (Eldredge, 1990; Eldredge & Quinn, 1988).

Writing Workshops. It is crucial that a writing workshop be established as part of the comprehensive reading program. Although not empirically tested, we believe a writing dyad system (students writing together in pairs) would be helpful to students having learning problems. Reading and writing are reciprocal processes: When students gain abilities in one, the other grows stronger as well. For example, as students are taught word-spelling strategies as part of writing development, their phonics and decoding skills are strengthened. When using author studies as part of teaching writing styles, student interest in books and reading likewise increases. Thus, writing is a mainstay in any literacy program for students having reading difficulties.

Helping English Learners Do Well with Expository Texts

English language learners can be particularly challenged by expository texts. This section describes research-proven methods for helping ELs interact with informational text.

Modifying Linguistic Variables. Limited knowledge of a second language can prevent learners from making full use of semantic, syntactic, and other clues in content reading materials. Kang (1994) suggests the following tactics to help ELs with content demands:

- Reduce the vocabulary load.
- Preteach key vocabulary concepts before students read an assigned passage.
- Use prereading questions; highlight text, notes, or questions in the margins; and create graphic organizers to help students attend to important information.
- Use postreading discussion groups to expose ELs to more complex language input.

Modifying Knowledge Variables. A second variable affecting an EL's ability to learn from reading content area texts is background knowledge. In some cases, a text may presuppose culture-specific background knowledge that is not part of these students' experiences. Likewise, some ELs may focus their reading too heavily on the print (decoding), thus failing to activate their prior knowledge to assist in understanding content area text. In either of these scenarios, Kang (1994) and Corpus and Giddings (2010) suggest strategies for before, during, and after reading that can help ELs succeed in reading content area texts.

Before Reading
- Use semantic mapping.
- Conduct structured overviews.
- Discuss contradictions, opposing examples, exceptions, categories, and comparisons related to concepts in the native language.

During Reading
- Supply pattern guides.
- Use marginal glosses.

After Reading
- Conduct semantic feature analysis.
- Structure small-group discussion.

Vocabulary Bookmarks

We like very much a simple and easy idea suggested by Maureen McLaughlin (2010) for helping ELs and native English speakers improve their academic vocabulary knowledge. Vocabulary bookmarks motivate students to monitor their understanding and learn new words (McLaughlin, 2010, p. 106). In essence, students choose words from their assigned readings they feel the whole class should discuss. Three bits of information are written by students on the bookmark provided by the teacher: (1) the word, (2) what the student thinks is the meaning of the word, and (3) the page number where the word was found. Each student presents their word to the whole class (or in a small group), reads the word in context from the text, and then shares what they feel the word means. This is followed by a group discussion of the word to come to consensus on its meaning. We think it would be a good idea to then have all students add each identified word to their own word banks for future use in writing. In Figure 12.30 we share a vocabulary bookmark for your classroom use.

Figure 12.30

Vocabulary Bookmark

My name _____

Book/Source _____

Page No. _____   Paragraph _____

This is a word I think we need to talk about: _____

I think it must mean: _____

_____

_____

_____

Motivation and Engagement

Motivating and Engaging Students in Grades 4–8 to Read

Students in grades 4–8 are bombarded with all sorts of stimuli and distractions in their lives. From television to cell phones to Facebook, media provide huge stimulation that motivates them to persist in their involvement. English learners often have these distractions coupled to the task of learning to communicate in a new language. These factors can make the education enterprise for teachers even more challenging. Our question becomes how to get our students motivated and engaged in this milieu?

In Malcolm Gladwell's (2002) popular book, *The Tipping Point: How Little Things Can Make a Big Difference,* he talks about the history of success of such television programs for children as *Blue's Clues* and *Sesame Street.* He concludes that repetition works if children learn something new with each repetition and that problems have to be complex enough to challenge and engage learners but easy enough to conquer. Corpus and Giddings (2010) conclude that when we want children to learn new information, we must make it *sticky* and memorable by presenting it in ways that are both practical and personal. This makes sense to us, so we set out to find new ideas in the literature about how to orchestrate this kind of learning in academic literacy situations.

Scaffolded Think-Alouds

One of the ways teachers can help ELs and students who may be struggling in academic literacy is by carefully structuring or *scaffolding* each phase of the learning experience. This helps us to maintain a learning challenge yet make the learning task manageable, which then helps keep students engaged. Another way of keeping students motivated and engaged is by linking new information to personal experiences by using discussion. The **scaffolded think-aloud** (McLaughlin, 2010) combines all of these features. You can use the following structure that we have adapted from the work of McLaughlin (2010) to construct scaffolded think-aloud activities for content literacy instruction.

- *Step 1: Explain.* Begin by selecting a passage from your academic unit to read aloud to your students. The passage should be challenging enough so that students will have to think strategically to understand the new ideas. Explain that we use think-alouds as teachers to model for students how we make connections in an informational text to what we already know and understand how we think strategically. Then introduce the passage (i.e., title and topic).

- *Step 2: Demonstrate.* Before reading the text, think aloud about how you make connections to this text. Use such statements as "This title makes me think . . ." or "I read something about this on the Internet . . ." or "I remember seeing something like this when I traveled to . . ." This demonstrates how you make connections to prior knowledge. As you read the passage, think aloud to demonstrate comprehension strategies you use to monitor your own understanding, apply "fix-up" strategies, and visualize what you are learning.

- *Step 3: Guided practice.* After demonstrating think-alouds several times for your students, have them practice with a partner. Match English learners with native English speakers as partners.

- *Step 4: Practice.* After students become comfortable with think-alouds, have them demonstrate it with a partner using a text they are interested in themselves.

- *Step 5: Reflect.* Ask students to write about how thinking aloud helps them to better understand new information in content texts and provide examples.

Singing Across the Curriculum

William Bintz (2010) has adapted a favorite idea of elementary teachers to academic literacy instruction known as "singing across the curriculum." The idea is simple: have students take familiar tunes and rewrite the lyrics so that they summarize new information learned from academic texts. The following two samples are provided by Bintz (p. 685):

The Cloud Song (sung to the tune of "London Bridge Is Falling Down")

Cirrus clouds are way up high
Highest clouds, in the sky,
Cirrus clouds are way up high
Clouds, thin and wispy.
Cirrus clouds are made of ice
Seen before, rain or snow,
Cirrus clouds are made of ice
Clouds, thin and wispy.
Nice weather brings cumulus

Perfect day, puffy clouds,
Nice weather brings cumulus
Clouds, fluffy, puffy.
Sunny days bring cumulus
See the shapes, in the clouds,
Sunny days bring cumulus
Clouds, fluffy, puffy.
When nimbus clouds are in the sky
Take cover quick, watch that wind,
When nimbus clouds are in the sky
A storm is nearby!
Nimbus clouds bring storms right in
Heavy rain, lots of wind.
Nimbus clouds bring storms right in
Cu-mu-lo-nim-bus!
Stratus clouds are way down low
Layers of gray, rain and snow,
Stratus clouds are way down low
Clouds, gray and low.

Magnets (sung to the tune of "Row, Row, Row Your Boat")

Pull, pull, pull some things,
Pull with all your might.
Use magnetite from a rock
And it will work just right
Mag, mag, magnetite
Contains a lot of iron.
It's from Magnesia and is magnetic
At least that's what we're told.
Say, say, say those words,
In front of Mom and Dad.
Wow! They'll think your teacher is
The best you ever had!

From Bintz, W. P. (2010, May). "Singing Across the Curriculum," *The Reading Teacher,* 63(8), 683–686. Reprinted with permission of the International Reading Association.

In the next section, we turn our attention to technology and new literacies that are, by their nature, quite motivational.

Technology and New Literacies That Promote Literacy in Grades 4–8

Information and communication technologies provide engaging ways for teaching and learning in content classes (Dalton & Grisham, in press). Following are two ideas to add to your growing list of activities from our book.

Voice Blogging for English Learners (and Others)

Research by Sun (2009) has found that voice blogging can be a powerful vehicle for improving learning and language ability with English learners (ELs). Our interpretation of the concept is that students (1) write summaries in English about what they are learning, (2) record an oral reading of their summary into a classroom online site with voice recording ability or on a digital recorder of their own that others may listen to, (3) listen to other students' voice blog recordings to compare, and (4) revise their original scripts and voice blogs as needed. One of the available services for voice blogs is Google Voice Blog (see web link at the end of this chapter), although our sense is that most teachers would find it just as effective for students to use a cassette or digital recorder for this purpose. Table 12.5 is based on Sun's (2009) blogging stages (with which students may need some assistance).

eVoc Strategies

An "eVoc strategy" (Dalton & Grisham, in press) is a technology-based method used by teachers to develop students' vocabulary learning and *evoke* interest in words. Such strategies rely on digital tools and resources as part of the instructional mix, as in the following two examples.

- *WordSift.* A free "word cloud" tool available on the Internet (www.wordsift .com), WordSift can be used to create a word cloud based on text that is cut and pasted into the application. WordSift offers important learning supports. Words can be selected in order to show a collection of related Google images, a word map from its Visual Thesaurus, or a listing of sentences using the word in different contexts. WordSift also sorts words by difficulty and identifies academic words. WordSift supports several different languages, which can be very helpful, a feature particularly helpful to English learners (Adesope, Lavin, Thompson, & Ungerleider, 2010).

- *Text-to-speech tool and audio books.* Sometimes the high readability of some texts on the Internet (i.e., long and complex sentences and paragraphs) can be a

Table 12.5

Voice Blogging for English Learners (and Others)

Blogging Stages	Strategies
Conceptualizing	1. Planning what to say and how to say it 2. Developing an appropriate voice blog topic 3. Listening to others' blogs for ideas and asking advice from peers 4. Consulting a dictionary/thesaurus or searching the Internet 5. Note taking on ideas
Brainstorming	1. Outlining main and supporting ideas 2. Translating from my first language to English 3. Writing a script before recording and asking for feedback from peers
Articulation	1. Rehearsing before recording; on my own first, then read to a partner 2. Recording my voice blog into a digital recorder (or to a classroom online site)
Monitoring	1. Listening to my recorded blog, re-recording, or uploading it 2. Monitor other blog entries in terms of content, organization, and language usage
Evaluating	1. Reevaluating my blog content, organization, and language usage after listening to other blogs 2. Redoing my blog as needed/if needed

Adapted from Sun, Y. (2009). Voice blog: An exploratory study of language learning. *Language Learning & Technology, 13*(2), 88–103.

WEB TOOLS YOU CAN USE IN THE CLASSROOM

Free Text-to-Speech (TTS) Programs

There are free TTS tools available that can be saved onto a computer's tool bar for easy access. Both of the ones listed below are great for converting expository and narrative texts from assigned readings into audio recordings with which students can follow along for improved text comprehension, vocabulary building, and fluency.

- Natural Readers, www.naturalreaders.com, is a free, downloadable text-to-speech (TTS) software package that features natural sounding voices. It is easy to use and converts any written text into spoken words. For example, you can convert text from such programs as MS Word, web page text, PDF files, and e-mail. Natural Readers also converts written texts into audio files such as for iPods, MP3 players, or WAV for your CD player.

- Like Natural Readers, Balabolka, www.cross-plus-a.com/balabolka.htm, is a text-to-speech (TTS) program. Balabolka uses various versions of Microsoft Speech API (SAPI) that allows users to modify voice parameters (e.g., rate and pitch). You can also apply a special substitution list to change the spellings of words. On-screen text can be saved as a WAV, MP3, OGG, or WMA file. The program can read the clipboard content; view the text from DOC, EPUB, FB2, HTML, ODT, PDF, and RTF files; customize font and background color; control reading from the system tray or by the global hot keys.

problem for our students. One solution is to permit students to listen to texts with a text-to-speech (TTS) tool or if available, audio narration (Dalton & Grisham, in press). This gives students access to age-appropriate content and grade-level curriculum. For struggling readers and English learners, TTS can help improve reading speed and comprehension as well as reduce stress. See Web Tools You Can Use in the Classroom for a list of TTS Tools.

Family and Community Connections

Family and Community Connections That Support Children Learning to Read Content Texts

Deborah Diffily (2004), in her book titled *Teachers and Families Working Together*, provides one of the most extensive summaries of ideas on how to connect families and communities to student learning. In this section we summarize and expand on some of her proven strategies we feel are particularly applicable to students in grades 4 through 8.

Interactive Homework

Interactive homework (Epstein, 2001; Nagel, 2008) is a tool whereby parents work with their child to complete an assigned homework task. Much like the joint productive activity (JPA) idea we have discussed elsewhere, interactive homework inspires

Figure 12.31

Interactive Homework Assignment: Global Warming

Dear Parents,

Please read with your child the attached article on global warming titled "Signs from Earth" by Tim Appenzeller and Dennis R. Dimick from *National Geographic Magazine*. After you have read the article, talk about possible answers and then write your responses to the following questions in the space provided (or on another sheet of paper):

1. Why do these authors feel global warming is real? How much of the warming do these authors feel is our fault? Write down at least two facts the authors give as their "proof" of global warming.

2. Why do you think some people feel that global warming is not really happening? Write down at least two reasons you have heard people say is "proof" that global warming is either NOT true, or why human beings have nothing to do with global warming.

Parents, please be sure your child brings with him/her the written answers to these homework questions tomorrow for our classroom discussion. Both you and your child are asked to sign and date the homework answers.

If you would like to learn more about global warming, you may find a copy of this article online at http://magma.nationalgeographic.com/ngm/0409/feature1. You may also want to watch the Academy Award winning film "An Inconvenient Truth" which is now available on DVD.

Thank you for your assistance!

Ms. Brown

Parent's Signature/Date _____

Student's Signature/Date _____

a conversation about ideas between the parent and child and connects the primary caregiver to the classroom. Figure 12.31 shows one example of an interactive homework assignment related to science on the theme of global warming.

Homework Hotline and Homework Voicemail

Diffily (2004) explains that telephone calls are often used by teachers to connect with families, but often this tool is used only when there is a problem. Many school districts offer **homework hotlines** for parents and students to provide help for completion of homework assignments. These hotlines are typically staffed by volunteer teachers on a rotation basis and should be promoted where they are available.

Another kind of telephone connection tool used by some teachers to connect with families is the **homework voicemail.** In this instance, teachers use the telephone voicemail system provided to teachers by many school systems (as an answering machine) to record daily homework assignments. In this way parents are able to check each day to find out what their child's homework assignments are so as to ensure follow-through at home. This is an easy way for teachers to provide whole-class assignments to parents with just one short recording.

Websites

Many families have access to the Internet either on home, on their jobs, or through the public library (Diffily, 2004). It is becoming more commonplace for teachers to have their own website as part of the school's website or through their own resources. One tool provided free to teachers as a community service is www.schoolnotes.com. Here teachers can create notes for homework assignments and post them online in just seconds. They also provide many other free resources for elementary and middle school teachers and their students.

Parent Lending Library

Many parents do not have access to appropriate books on school subjects for their children or books that help "coach" parents on effective learn-at-home strategies they can use. A **parent lending library** (Diffily, 2004) can be housed in a special parent resource room or in the school's library for easy access anytime during the school day.

Summary

We have just concluded a very rich chapter detailing how students in grade 4 through 8 can be helped to apply reading skills to learn more about the world around them. Research informs us that there are indeed special reading challenges associated with expository or informational texts. In the field of content area reading instruction, teachers must help students learn how to apply reading and writing skills in mathematics, science, social studies, and the English/language arts texts. This reading terrain is complicated by the distinctive expository text writing patterns used by nonfiction authors. There are marked increases in concept density (i.e., more ideas in smaller chunks of text), unique readability considerations, and significant higher-level comprehension demands.

In preparing to teach, we learned that it is wise to begin with a content analysis. Here teachers assess the important knowledge and vocabulary to be learned: the facts, concepts, and generalizations. This provides the kind of preteaching knowledge needed to organize ideas and plan scaffolded instruction. At this stage of preparation teachers also seek out supplemental texts and materials to ensure understanding by learners who read on a variety of reading levels.

We learned about successful strategies for delivering instruction. The key is to consider what activities to offer students before, during, and after they read informational texts. Also discussed was a proven interdisciplinary strategy, themed studies, which integrates the content areas (e.g., science, mathematics, literature, and social studies) with reading and writing instruction. The advantages of this kind of curriculum integration are numerous. Reading and writing abilities are acquired and refined within a rich context of real-world significance, which in turn inspires students to want to know more.

In this chapter we saw how struggling readers can be helped to succeed in content area reading. There are commercial programs available that help struggling readers improve basic reading abilities such as Scholastic's Read 180. We can also help struggling readers by teaching them to use comprehension skills in unison, or "strategy families," by helping them improve reading fluency, and by providing group-assisted reading (dyads and buddy reading). We likewise saw how English learners (ELs) can be helped to succeed in reading content texts by modifying linguistic and knowledge variables. In this way we put research to work in our classrooms and ensure reading success for all learners.

A number of other research-proven strategies were presented that help motivate students to stay with and conquer content texts. Included were ways to increase the "stickiness factor" so that new information becomes more memorable and accessible in future learning. New technologies are another motivational realm we discussed for making content learning even more potent for English learners (ELs) and struggling students.

Finally, we discovered innovative ways for involving parents in the education process. Teachers can stay connected to parents through interactive homework assignments and by using volunteer homework hotlines and teacher-created homework voicemails. Many teachers are creating their own Internet websites that are connected to their school's website, others are using free online tools like schoolnotes.com. We also discussed the creation of parent lending libraries to help parents have access to books for reading at home, as well as adult-oriented books that help provide "coaching" on effective strategies they can use to help their child read to learn.

Field and Classroom Applications

- Select a chapter from a social studies book on a level of your choice. Applying the descriptors for expository text patterns discussed in this chapter, identify the patterns of development (e.g., description, comparison) used in the chapter. How often does each pattern occur in the chapter? Are any patterns missing? If so, what might you do to compensate for these omissions? Is it possible that omission of some patterns could lead to learning difficulties for some children? If so, why?
- A thorough content analysis is the foundation for successful teaching in the content areas. To practice and refine this ability, try the following:
  - Form a group with two or three of your colleagues.
  - Select several lengthy magazine articles having to do with various topics relevant to core subjects (social studies, math, science). You may want to extract your articles from such magazines as *Air & Space* or *National Geographic*.
  - After group members read their article, each should develop a content analysis to present to the rest of the group. By comparing analyses, it will

be possible to detect whether important bits of information have been neglected and if superfluous information has been included.

- Search the Internet to compile a list of useful sites for the teaching of content area vocabulary and concepts for two topics of your choice. Construct an annotated bibliography of these sites to share with your classmates or colleagues.
- Develop a themed literature unit using one of the following themes: "Courage," "Relationships," "Discovering New Worlds," "Changes," or "Animals." Include a web of the unit, a list of books chosen from popular children's literature, possible reading strategies to be taught in teacher-directed sessions, and ideas for literature response activities.
- Develop an outline of Tier 2 strategies you will use in your Response to Intervention (RTI) plan for content area reading. Be sure to include vocabulary, comprehension, and fluency strands. Share with at least two experienced teachers for their input on refining your plan.

Recommended Resources

Print Resources

Cooter, R. B., Flynt, E. S., & Cooter, K. S. (2007). *The comprehensive reading inventory.* Upper Saddle River, NJ: Prentice Hall.

Corpus, D., & Giddings, A. (2010). *Planning & managing effective reading instruction across the content areas.* New York: Scholastic.

Fisher, D., Brozo, W. G., Frey, N., & Ivey, G. (2011). *50 instructional routines to develop content literacy.* Boston: Pearson.

National Institute for Literacy. (2007). *What content-area teachers should know about adolescent literacy.* Jessup, MD: Author. Available at http://literacyacademy.edublogs.org/ under "Links."

Web Resources

www.boystownusa.org/educators/reading-is-fame
  Boys Town Reading

http://crede.berkeley.edu
  Dialogic learning guidelines (CREDE)

http://googlevoiceblog.blogspot.com
  Google Voice Blog

www.ngschoolpub.org
  Reading Expeditions

www.schoolnotes.com
  School Notes

www.wordsift.com
  WordSift

www2.ed.gov/programs/strivingreaders/index.html
  Striving Readers Projects

Professional Organizations

www.nctm.org
  National Council of Teachers of Mathematics

www.socialstudies.org
  National Council for the Social Studies

www.nsta.org
  National Science Teachers Association

www.reading.org
  International Reading Association

www.ncte.org
National Council of Teachers of English

Radio Plays and Readers' Theatre Websites

http://teachingheart.net/readerstheater.htm
Garden of Praise

www.myteacherpages.com/webpages/JGriffin/readers.cfm
Joann Griffin (Channelview ISD)

www.educationworld.com/a_curr/reading/ReadersTheater/ReadersTheater005.shtml
Education World

www.readwritethink.org
International Reading Association Teacher Resources

Text-to-Speech (TTS) Tools

www.naturalreaders.com
Natural Readers

www.cross-plus-a.com/balabolka.htm
Balabolka

The Power of Classroom Practice

www.myeducationlab.com

Go to Topic 8, Reading and Writing in the Content Areas, in the MyEducationLab (www.myeducationlab.com) for your course, where you can:

- Find learning outcomes for Reading and Writing in the Content Areas along with the national standards that connect to these outcomes.
- Complete Assignments and Activities that can help you more deeply understand the chapter content.
- Apply and practice your understanding of the core teaching skills identified in the chapter with the Building Teaching Skills and Dispositions learning units. (optional)
- Examine challenging situations and cases presented in the IRIS Center Resources. (optional)
- Access video clips of CCSSO National Teachers of the Year award winners responding to the question "Why Do I Teach?" in the Teacher Talk section. (optional)
- Check your comprehension on the content covered in the chapter by going to the Study Plan in the Book Resources for your text. Here you will be able to take a chapter quiz, receive feedback on your answers, and then access Review, Practice, and Enrichment activities to enhance your understanding of chapter content. (optional)

Go to the Topic A+RISE in the MyEducationLab (www.myeducationlab.com) for your course. A+RISE® Standards2Strategy™ is an innovative and interactive online resource that offers new teachers in grades K–12 just in time, research-based instructional strategies that:

- Meet the linguistic needs of ELLs as they learn content.
- Differentiate instruction for all grades and abilities.
- Offer reading and writing techniques, cooperative learning, use of linguistic and nonlinguistic representations, scaffolding, teacher modeling, higher order thinking, and alternative classroom ELL assessment.
- Provide support to help teachers be effective through the integration of listening, speaking, reading, and writing along with the content curriculum.
- Improve student achievement.
- Are aligned to Common Core Elementary Language Arts standards (for the literacy strategies) and to English language proficiency standards in WIDA, Texas, California, and Florida.

References

Chapter 1

Afflerbach, P. (2007). *Understanding and using reading assessment: K–12*. Newark, DE: International Reading Association.

American Federation of Teachers. (1999). *Teaching reading is rocket science. What expert teachers of reading should know and be able to do*. Washington, DC: Author.

Anderson, R. C., Hiebert, E. F., Scott, J. A., & Wilkinson, I. A. G. (1985). *Becoming a nation of readers: The report of the commission on reading*. Washington, DC: The National Institute of Education.

Armbruster, B. B., Lehr, F., & Osborn, J. (2001). *Put reading first: The research building blocks for teaching children to read*. Washington, DC: U.S. Department of Education.

Au, K. H. (2010). Culturally responsive instruction: What is it, and how do we incorporate it in the classroom? *Reading Today, 27*(3), 30–31.

August, D., & Shanahan, T. (2006). *Developing literacy in second-language learners: Report of the National Literacy Panel on language-minority children and youth*. Mahwah, NJ: Lawrence Erlbaum.

Bridwell, N. (1965). *Clifford the big red dog*. New York: Scholastic.

Burkins, J. M. (2009). *Practical literacy coaching: A collection of tools to support your work*. Newark, DE: International Reading Association.

Burns, M. S., Griffin, P., & Snow, C. E. (Eds.). (1999). *Starting out right: A guide to promoting children's reading success*. Washington, DC: National Academy Press.

Carlisle, J. F., Phelps, G., Rowan, B., & Johnson, D. J. (2006). *Development of a test of teachers' knowledge about early reading*. Technical Report 1: Assessment of pedagogical content knowledge of reading. Ann Arbor: University of Michigan.

Coleman, J. S. (1966). *Equality of educational opportunity (EEOS)*. Washington, DC: U.S. Department of Health, Education, and Welfare.

Compton-Lilly, C. (2009). What can new literacy studies offer to the teaching of struggling readers? *The Reading Teacher, 63*(1), 88–90.

Cooter, R. B. (2004). *Perspectives on rescuing urban literacy education: Spies, saboteurs, and saints*. Mahwah, NJ: Lawrence Erlbaum.

Darling-Hammond, L. (2006). *Powerful teacher education: Lessons from exemplary programs*. San Francisco, CA: Jossey-Bass.

Darling-Hammond, L., Wise, A. E., & Klein, S. A. (1999). *License to teach: Building a profession for 21st century schools*. San Francisco, CA: Jossey-Bass.

Dickinson, D. K., & Tabors, P. O. (Eds.). (2001). *Young children learning at home and school: Beginning literacy with language*. Baltimore: Paul H. Brookes.

Duffy, G. G. (2004). *Explaining reading: A resource for teaching concepts, skills, and strategies*. New York: Guilford Press.

Durkin, D. (1966). *Children who read early: Two longitudinal studies*. New York: Teachers College Press.

Education Trust. (2008). *Achievement in America*. Retrieved February 10, 2010, from http://old.inclusion-ny.org/uploaded/summitPresentation.ppt

Evertson, C. M., & Weinstein, C. S. (2006). *Handbook of classroom management: Research, practice, and contemporary issues*. Mahwah, NJ: Lawrence Erlbaum.

Ferguson, R. F. (1991). Paying for public education: New evidence on how and why money matters. *Harvard Journal of Legislation, 282*, 465–498.

Fielding, L., Kerr, N., & Rosier, P. (1998). *The 90% reading goal*. Kennewick, WA: National Reading Foundation.

Flippo, R. F. (2003). *Assessing readers: Qualitative diagnosis and instruction*. Portsmouth, NH: Heinemann.

Fuchs, D., Fuchs, L. S., & Vaughn, S. (2008). *Response to intervention: A framework for reading educators*. Newark, DE: International Reading Association.

Gambrell, L. B., & Marinak, B. A. (2009). *The sixth pillar of effective reading practice: Reading motivation*. Paper presented at the Annual Meeting of the Association of Literacy Educators and Researchers (ALER), Charlotte, North Carolina.

Gamse, B. C., Jacob, R. T., Horst, M., Boulay, B., & Unlu, F. (2008). *Reading First impact study final report* (NCEE 2009-4038). Washington, DC: National Center for Education Evaluation and Regional Assistance, Institute of Education Sciences, U.S. Department of Education. Available at http://ies.ed.gov/ncee/pubs/20094038.asp

Greenwald, R., Hedges, L., & Laine, R. (1996). The effect of school resources on student achievement. *Review of Educational Research, 66*, 361–396.

Harris, A. J., & Hodges, R. E. (Eds.). (1981). *A dictionary of reading and related terms*. Newark, DE: International Reading Association.

Haselkorn, D., & Harris, L. (2001). *The essential profession: American education at the crossroads*. Belmont, MA: Recruiting New Teachers.

Hobbs, R. (2005). Literacy for the information age. In J. Flood, S. B. Heath, & D. Lapp (Eds.), *Handbook of research on teaching literacy through the communicative and visual arts* (pp. 7–14). Mahwah, NJ: Lawrence Erlbaum.

Hoffman, J. V., Sailors, M., Duffy, G., & Beretvas, S. N. (2004). The effective classroom literacy environment: Examining the validity of the TEX-IN3 Observation System. *Journal of Literacy Research, 36*(3), 303–334.

Jordan, G. E., Snow, C. E., & Porche, M. V. (2000). Project EASE: The effect of a family literacy project on kindergarten students' early literacy skills. *Reading Research Quarterly, 35*, 524–546.

Kintsch, W. (2004). The construction-integration model of text comprehension and its implications for instruction. In R. B. Ruddell & N. J. Unrau (Eds.), *Theoretical models and processes* of reading (5th ed., pp. 94–120). Newark, DE: International Reading Association.

Kozol, J. (1991). *Savage inequalities.* New York: Harper Perennial.

Leu, D. J. (2002). The new literacies: Research on reading instruction with the Internet. In A. E. Farstrup & S. Samuels (Eds.), *What research has to say about reading instruction* (pp. 310–336). Newark, DE: International Reading Association.

Lipson, M. Y., & Wixson, K. K. (2009). *Assessment and instruction of reading and writing difficulties: An interactive approach* (4th ed.). Boston: Allyn & Bacon.

Malloy, J. A., Castek, J. M., & Leu, D. J. (2010). Silent reading and online reading comprehension. In E. H. Hiebert & D. R. Reutzel (Eds.), *Revisiting silent reading: New directions for teachers and researchers* (pp. 221–240). Newark, DE: International Reading Association.

Martin, B. (1990). *Brown bear, brown bear, what do you see?* New York: Henry Holt.

McCardle, P., & Chhabra, V. (2004). *The voice of evidence in reading research.* Baltimore: Paul H. Brookes.

McKenna, M. C., Labbo, L. D., Kieffer, R. D., & Reinking, D. (2006). *International handbook of literacy and technology, Vol. II.* Mahwah, NJ: Lawrence Erlbaum.

McKenna, M. C., & Stahl, K. A. D. (2009). *Assessment for reading instruction* (2nd ed.). New York: Guilford Press.

Messaris, P. (2005). Introduction. In J. Flood, S. B. Heath, & D. Lapp (Eds.), *Handbook of research on teaching literacy through the communicative and visual arts* (pp. 3–6). Mahwah, NJ: Lawrence Erlbaum.

Mokhtari, K., Kymes, A., & Edwards, P. (2008). Assessing the new literacies of online reading comprehension: An informative interview with W. Ian O'Byrne, Lisa Zawilinski, J. Greg McVerry, and Donald J. Leu at the University of Connecticut. *The Reading Teacher, 62*(4), 354–357.

Moore, J. (2004). Mentoring teacher change: Even Cinderella had a coach. In R. B. Cooter (Ed.), *Perspectives on rescuing urban literacy education: Spies, saboteurs, and saints* (pp. 83–94). Mahwah, NJ: Lawrence Erlbaum.

Morgan, B., & Smith, R. D. (2008). A Wiki for classroom writing. *The Reading Teacher, 62*(1), 80–82.

Morrow, L. M., Reutzel, D. R., & Casey, H. (2006). Organization and management of language arts teaching: Classroom environments, grouping practices, and exemplary instruction. In C. Evertson (Ed.), *Handbook of classroom management* (pp. 559–582). Mahwah, NJ: Lawrence Erlbaum.

Mosenthal, J., Lipson, M., Torncello, S., Russ, B., & Mekkelsen, J. (2004). Contexts and practices of six schools successful in obtaining reading achievement. *Elementary School Journal, 104*(5), 343–367.

National assessment of educational progress report, 1994: Reading. Washington, DC: National Center for Educational Statistics and the U.S. Department of Education.

National Commission on Teaching and America's Future (NCTAF). (2006). *NCTAF emphasizes need for 21st century teaching and learning: Meeting summary.* St. Paul, MN: Author.

National Commission on Teaching and America's Future. (1996). *What matters most: Teachers for America's future.* Woodbridge, VA: Author.

National Early Literacy Panel. (2008). *Developing early literacy: Report of the National Early Literacy Panel.* Jessup, MD: National Institute for Literacy.

National Reading Panel (NRP). (2000). *Report of the National Reading Panel: Teaching children to read.* Washington, DC: National Institute of Child Health and Human Development.

National Research Council. (2001). *Scientific research in education.* Report of the Committee on Scientific Principles for Education Research. Washington, DC: National Academy Press.

National Right to Read Foundation. (2001). Retrieved February 15, 2010, from www.nrrf.org 20-01.htm

Neuman, S. B. (1999). Books make a difference: A study of access to literacy. *Reading Research Quarterly, 34,* 286–311.

Neuman, S. B., & Celano, D. (2001). Access to print in low-income and middle-income communities: An ecological study of four neighborhoods. *Reading Research Quarterly, 36*(1), 8–26.

Neuman, S. B., & Celano, D. (2006). The knowledge gap: Implications of leveling the playing field for low-income and middle-income children. *Reading Research Quarterly, 42*(2), 176–201.

Neuman, S. B., & Cunningham, L. (2009). The impact of professional development and coaching on early language and literacy instructional practices. *American Educational Research Journal, 46*(2), 532–566.

No Child Left Behind Act. (2001). Retrieved February 15, 2010, from www2.ed.gov/nclb/landing.jhtml

Obama, B. H. (2005). *Literacy and education in a 21st century economy.* Retrieved from November 23, 2010, from http://obamaspeeches.com/024-Literacy-and-Education-in-a-21st-Century-Economy-Obama-Speech.htm

Opitz, M. F. (1998). *Flexible grouping in reading: Practical ways to help all students become better readers.* New York: Scholastic.

Paratore, J. R. (2003). Building on family literacies: Examining the past and planning the future. In A. DeBruin-Parecki & B. Krol-Sinclair (Eds.), *Family literacy: From theory to practice* (pp. 8–27). Newark, DE: International Reading Association.

Pressley, M., Allington, R. L., Wharton-McDonald, R., Collins-Block, C., and Morrow, L. M. (2001). *Learning to read: Lessons from exemplary first-grade classrooms.* New York: Guilford Press.

Reutzel, D. R., & Cooter, R. B. (2011). *Strategies for reading assessment and instruction: Helping every child succeed* (4th ed.). Boston: Pearson/Allyn & Bacon.

Reutzel, D. R., Morrow, L. M., & Casey, H. (2009). Meeting the needs of diverse learners: Effective management of language arts instruction. In L. M. Morrow, R. Rueda, & D. Lapp (Eds.), *Handbook of research on literacy and diversity* (pp. 254–273). New York: Guilford Press.

Risko, V. J., Roller, C. M., Cummins, C., Bean, R. M., Block, C. C., Anders, P. L., & Flood, J. (2008). A critical analysis of research on reading teacher education. *Reading Research Quarterly, 43*(3), 252–288.

Rodriquez-Brown, F., Fen Li, R., & Alborn, J. A. (1999). Hispanic parents' awareness and use of literacy-rich environments at home and in the community. *Education and Urban Society, 32,* 41–57.

Rodriquez-Brown, F., & Meehan, M. A. (1998). Family literacy and adult education: Project FLAME. In M. C. Smith (Ed.), *Literacy for the 21st century: Research, policy, practices and the National Adult Literacy Survey* (pp. 175–193). Westport, CT: Greenwood.

Rowan, B., Correnti, R., & Miller, R. J. (2002). What large-scale survey research tells us about teacher effects on students achievement: Insights from the *Prospectus* study of elementary schools. *Teachers College Record, 104*(8), 1525–1567.

Sadder, M., & Nidus, G. (2009). *The literacy coach's game plan: Making teacher collaboration, student learning, and school improvement a reality.* Newark, DE: International Reading Association.

Sanders, W. (1998). Value-added assessments. *The School Administrator, 11*(55), 24–27.

Sanders, W. L., & Horn, S. P. (1994). The Tennessee value-added assessment system (TVAAS): Mixed-model methodology in educational assessment. *Journal of Personnel Evaluation in Education, 8*(3), 299–311.

Sanders, W. L., & Rivers, J. C. (1996). Cumulative and residual effects of teachers on future student academic achievement. Knoxville: University of Tennessee Value-Added Research and Assessment Center.

Scheerens, J., & Bosker, R. (1997). *The foundations of educational effectiveness.* New York: Pergamon.

Shanahan, T. (2006). Relations among oral language, reading, and writing development. In C. MacArthur, S. Graham, & J. Fitzgerald (Eds.), *Handbook of writing research* (pp. 171–183). New York: Guilford Press.

Shanahan, T., Mulhern, M., & Rodriquez-Brown, F. (1995). Project FLAME: Lessons learned from a family literacy program for minority families. *The Reading Teacher, 48,* 40–47.

Smith, F. (1985). *Reading without nonsense* (2nd ed.). New York: Teachers College Press.

Snow, C. E., Burns, M. N., & Griffin, P. (1998). *Preventing reading difficulties in young children.* Washington, DC: National Academy Press.

Snow, C. E., Griffin, P., & Burns, M. S. (2005). *Knowledge to support the teaching of reading: Preparing teachers for a changing world.* San Francisco, CA: Jossey-Bass.

Stanovich, P. J., & Stanovich, K. E. (2003). *Using research and reason in education: How teachers can use scientifically-based research to make curricular and instructional decisions.* Washington, DC: National Institute for Literacy.

Strickland, D. S., Snow, C., Griffin, P., Burns, M. S., & McNamara, P. (2002). *Preparing our teachers: Opportunities for better reading instruction.* Washington, DC: John Henry Press.

Sweet, R. W. (2004). The big picture: Where we are nationally on the reading front and how we got here. In P. McCardle and V. Chhabra (Eds.), *The voice of evidence in reading research* (pp. 13–46). Baltimore: Paul H. Brookes.

Taylor, B. M., Pearson, P. D., Clark, K. E., & Walpole, S. (1999). *Beating the odds in teaching all children to read* (Ciera Report No. 2-006). Ann Arbor, MI: Center for the Improvement of Early Reading Achievement.

Taylor, J. B. (2006). *My stroke of insight: A brain scientist's personal journey.* New York: Viking.

Tierney, R. J., & Shanahan, T. (1991). Research on the reading-writing relationship: Interactions, transactions, and outcomes. In R. Barr, M. L. Kamil, P. Mosenthal, & P. D. Pearson (Eds.), *Handbook of reading research* (Vol. II). New York: Longman.

Toll, C. A. (2007). *Lenses on literacy coaching: Conceptualizations, functions, and outcomes.* Norwood, MA: Christopher-Gordon.

Tracey, D. H., & Morrow, L. M. (2006). *Lenses on reading: An introduction to theories and models.* New York: Guilford Press.

Turner, J., & Paris, S. (1995). How literacy tasks influence children's motivation for literacy. *The Reading Teacher, 48*(8), 662–673.

U.S. Department of Education. (1983). *A Nation at Risk.* Retrieved November 23, 2010, from www2.ed.gov/pubs/NatAtRisk/risk.html

U.S. Department of Education. (1994). *Goals 2000: Educate America Act.* Retrieved February 15, 2010, from www2.ed.gov/legislation/GOALS2000/TheAct/index.html

U.S. Department of Education. (1998). *The Reading Excellence Act.* Retrieved November 23, 2010, from www.fp.gov/fp/attachments/publications/acronym.doc

U.S. Department of Education. (2009). *American Recovery and Reinvestment Act (ARRA).* Retrieved from www.ed.gov/blog/2010/02/arra-saving-education-jobs-and-promoting-reform

Wepner, S. B., Valmont, W. J., & Thurlow, R. (2000). *Linking literacy and technology: A guide for K–8 classrooms.* Newark, DE: International Reading Association.

Wigfield, A. (1997). Motivations, beliefs, and self-efficacy in literacy development. In J. T. Guthrie & A. Wigfield (Eds.), *Reading engagement: Motivating readers through integrated instruction.* Newark, DE: International Reading Association.

Wolfersberger, M., Reutzel, D. R., Sudweeks, R., & Fawson, P. F. (2004). Developing and validating the Classroom Literacy Environmental Profile (CLEP): A tool for examining the "print richness" of elementary classrooms. *Journal of Literacy Research, 36*(2), 211–272.

Chapter 2

Allington, R. L., & Cunningham, P. (1996). *Schools that work.* New York: HarperCollins College Publishers.

Alvermann, D. E., Smith, L. C., & Readence, J. E. (1985). Prior knowledge activation and the comprehension of compatible and incompatible text. *Reading Research Quarterly, 20*(4), 420–436.

Anderson, R., Pearson, P., & Bolt, B. (1984). *A schema-theoretic view of basic processes in reading comprehension.* Technical Report No. 306. Retrieved from ERIC database.

Armbruster, B. B., Lehr, F., & Osborn, J. (2001). *Put reading first: The research building blocks for teaching children to read.* Washington, DC: U.S. Department of Education.

Arya, P., Wilson, G., & Martens, P. (2009, November). "We-e-el-l" or "We'll": Children negotiating orthographic features of A Letter to Amy. *The Reading Teacher, 63*(3), 224–233.

Athans, S. K., & Devine, D. (2010). *Fun-tastic activities for differentiating comprehension instruction, grades 2–6.* Newark, DE: International Reading Association.

Au, T. K., Depretto, M., & Song, Y. K. (1994). Input vs. constraints: Early word acquisition in Korean and English. *Journal of Memory and Language, 33,* 567–582

August, D., Branum-Martin, L., Cardenas-Hagan, E., & Francis, D. J. (2009). The impact of an instructional intervention on the science and language learning of middle grade English language learners. *Journal of Research on Educational Effectiveness, 2*(4), 345–376.

August, D., Carlo, M., Dressler, C., & Snow, C. (2005). The critical role of vocabulary development for English language learners. *Learning Disabilities Research and Practice, 20*(1), 50–57.

August, D., & Pease-Alvarez, L. (1996). *Attributes of effective programs and classrooms serving English language learners.* Santa Cruz, CA: National Center for Research on Cultural Diversity and Second Language Learning.

August, D., & Shanahan, T. (2006). *Developing literacy in second-language learners: Report of the National Literacy Panel on language-minority children and youth.* Mahwah: NJ: Lawrence Erlbaum.

August, D., Snow, C., Carlo, M., Proctor, C. P., Rolla de San Francisco, A., Duursma, E., & Szuber, A. (2006). Literacy development in elementary school second-language learners. *Topics in Language Disorders, 26*(4), 351–364.

Bakhtin, M. (1982). *The dialogic imagination: Four essays.* Austin: University of Texas Press.

Biemiller, A. (2006). Vocabulary development and instruction: A prerequisite for school learning. In D. K. Dickinson & S. B. Neuman (Eds.), *Handbook of early literacy* (Vol. 2, pp. 41–51). New York: Guilford Press.

Bierman, K. L., Domitrovich, C. E., Nix, R. L., Gest, S. D., Welsh, J. A., Greenberg, M. T., et al. (2008). Promoting academic and social-emotional school readiness: The Head Start *REDI* program. *Child Development, 79*(6), 1802–1817.

Bransford, J. C., & Johnson, M. K. (1972). Contextual prerequisites for understanding: Some investigations of comprehension and recall. *Journal of Verbal Learning and Verbal Behavior, 11,* 717–726.

Bruner, J. (1978). The role of dialog in language acquisition. In A. Sinclair, R. J. Jarvella, & W. M. Levelt (Eds.), *The child's conception of language* (pp. 241–256). New York: Springer-Verlag.

Burns, M. S., Griffin, P., & Snow, C. E. (Eds.). (1999). *Starting out right: A guide to promoting children's reading success.* Committee on the Prevention of Reading Difficulties in Young Children, Commission on Behavioral and Social Sciences and Education, National Research Council. Washington, DC: National Academy Press.

Carlisle, J. F. (2004). Morphological processes that influence learning to read. In C. A. Stone, E. R. Silliman, B. J. Ehren, & K. Apel (Eds.), *Handbook of language and literacy: Development and disorders* (pp. 318–339). New York: Guilford Press.

Chapman, L. J., & Hoffman, M. (1977). *Developing fluent reading.* Milton Keynes, England: Open University Press.

Chomsky, N. (1974). *Aspects of the theory of syntax* (2nd ed.). Cambridge, MA: MIT Press.

Chomsky, N. (1979). Human language and other semiotic systems. *Semiotica, 25,* 31–44.

Clark, E. (1993). *The lexicon in acquisition.* Cambridge, UK: Cambridge University Press.

Collins-Block, C., & Pressley, M. (2002). *Comprehension instruction: Research-based best practices.* New York: Guilford Press.

Cooter, K. S. (2006). When mama can't read: Counteracting intergenerational illiteracy. *The Reading Teacher, 59*(7), 698–702.

Cooter, K. S., & Cooter, R. B. (in press). *Urban literacy instruction: Teaching city kids to read.* Boston: Pearson.

Cox, C. (2002). *Teaching language arts* (4th ed.). Boston: Allyn & Bacon.

CREDE. (2010). *The CREDE five standards for effective pedagogy and learning: Instructional conversation.* Berkeley, CA: The Center for Research on Education, Diversity & Excellence (CREDE). Retrieved from http://crede.berkeley.edu/research/crede/instruc_conv.html

Cunningham, A. E., Perry, K. E., Stanovich, K. E., & Stanovich, P. J. (2004). Disciplinary knowledge of K–3 teachers and their knowledge calibration in the domain of early literacy. *Annals of Dyslexia, 54*(1), 139–167.

Dickinson, D. K., McCabe, A., & Sprague, K. (2003). Teacher Rating of Oral Language and Literacy (TROLL): Individualizing early literacy instruction with a standards-based rating tool. *The Reading Teacher, 56*(6), 554–564.

Dickinson, D. K., & Tabors, P. O. (2001). *Beginning literacy with language.* Baltimore: Paul H. Brookes.

Dockrell, J., Sylva, K., Huxford, L., & Roberts, F. (2009). Oral language skills in the early years. Retrieved from www.ican.org.uk/early%20talk/resources/~/media/ICAN%20website/4%20Early%20Talk/Research/OralLangSkillsintheEYCh4July09PDF.ashx

D'Odorico, L. (1984). Nonsegmental features in prelinguistic communications: An analysis of some types of infant cry and noncry vocalizations. *Journal of Child Language, 11,* 17–27.

Dooley, C. (2010). Young children's approaches to books: The emergence of comprehension. *The Reading Teacher, 64*(2), 120–130.

Draganski, B., Gaser, C., Kempermann, G., Kuhn, H. G., Winkler, J., Christian Buchel, C., & May, A. (2006). Temporal and spatial dynamics of brain structure changes during extensive learning. *The Journal of Neuroscience, 26*(23), 6314–6317.

Dunn, L. M., Smith, J. O., Dunn, L. M., & Horton, K. B. (2002). *Peabody Language Development Kits (Revised).* Boston: Pearson/PsychCorp.

Dutro, S., & Moran, C. (2003). Rethinking English language instruction: An architectural approach. In G. G. Garcia (Ed.), *English learning: Reaching the highest level of English literacy* (pp. 227–258). Newark, DE: International Reading Association.

Dyson, A. H. (1983). The role of oral language in early writing processes. *Research in the Teaching of English, 17*(1), 1–25.

Farrar, E. B. (1985). *Accelerating the oral language of children of low socio-economic status.* Belle Glade, FL: Unpublished Dissertation. (ERIC Document Reproduction Service No. ED 262 913)

Fields, M. V., & Spangler, K. L. (2000). *Let's begin reading right: A developmental approach to emergent literacy.* Upper Saddle River, NJ: Merrill.

Fillmore, L. W., & Snow, C. E. (2000). *What teachers need to know about language.* Special report from ERIC Clearing House on Languages and Linguistics. Available at www.cal.org/ericcll/teachers/teachers.pdf

Friedman, T. (2005). *The world is flat: A brief history of the twenty-first century.* New York: Farrar, Straus, & Giroux.

Gentile, L. M. (2003). *The oracy instructional guide: Linking research and theory to assessment and instruction.* Carlsbad, CA: Dominie Press.

Gersten, R., & Baker, S. (2000). *Effective instruction for English-language learners: What we know about effective instructional practices for English language learners.* Eugene: University of Oregon, Eugene Research Institute.

Glazer, S. M. (1989). Oral language and literacy development. In D. S. Strickland & L. M. Morrow (Eds.), *Emerging literacy: Young children learn to read and write* (pp. 16–26). Newark, DE: International Reading Association.

Gleason, J. B. (1989). *The development of language* (2nd ed.). Upper Saddle River, NJ: Merrill/Prentice Hall.

Goetz, E. T., Reynolds, R. E., Schallert, D. L., & Radin, D. I. (1983). Reading in perspective: What real cops and pretend burglars look for in a story. *Journal of Educational Psychology, 75*(4), 500–510.

Goodman, K. S. (1986). *What's whole in whole language?* Ontario, Canada: Scholastic.

Gopnik, A., Meltzoff, A. N., & Kuhl, P. K. (1999). *The scientist in the crib: Minds, brains, and how children learn.* New York: William Morrow.

Greenhalgh, K. S., & Strong, C. J. (2001). Literate language features in spoken narratives of children with typical language and children with language impairments. *Language, Speech, & Hearing Services in Schools, 32*(2), 114–126.

Hall, R. (1984). *Sniglets.* New York: Collier Books.

Halliday, M. A. K. (1975). *Learning how to mean: Explorations in the development of language.* London: Edward Arnold.

Harste, J. C., Woodward, V. A., & Burke, C. L. (1984). *Language stories and literacy lessons.* Portsmouth, NH: Heinemann.

Hart, B., & Risley, T. R. (1995). *Meaningful differences in the everyday experience of young American children.* Baltimore: Paul H. Brookes.

Hart, B., & Risley, T. R. (2002). *The social world of children: Learning to talk.* Baltimore: Paul H. Brookes.

Hoff-Ginsberg, E. (1991). Mother–child conversation in different social classes and communicative settings. *Child Development, 62*(4), 782–796.

Hoff-Ginsberg, E. (2006). How contexts support and shape language development. *Developmental Review, 26*(1), 55–88.

Huebner, C. E. (2000). Promoting toddlers' language development: A randomized trial of a community-based intervention. *Journal of Applied Developmental Psychology, 21,* 513–535.

Huebner, C. E. (2001). *Hear-and-say reading with toddlers.* Bainbridge Island, WA: Bainbridge Island Rotary (instructional video). To order, contact: Hear and Say Reading Program, Rotary Club of Bainbridge Island, PO Box 11286, Bainbridge Island, WA 98110.

Huebner, C. E., & Meltzoff, A. N. (2005). Intervention to change parent–child reading style: A comparison of instructional methods. *Applied Developmental Psychology, 26,* 296–313.

Johnson, D. D. (2001). *Vocabulary in the elementary and middle school.* Boston: Allyn & Bacon.

Kaderavek, J. N., & Justice, L. M. (2005). The effect of book genre in repeated readings of mothers and their children with language impairment: A pilot investigation. *Child Language Teaching and Therapy, 21*(1), 75–92.

Kearsley, R. (1973). The newborn's response to auditory stimulation: A demonstration of orienting and defensive behavior. *Child Development, 44,* 582–590.

Kessen, W., Levine, J., & Wendrich, K. (1979). The imitation of pitch in infants. *Infant Behavior and Development, 2,* 93–100.

Kintsch, W., & Kintsch, E. (2005). Comprehension. In S. G. Paris & S. A. Stahl (Eds.), *Children's reading comprehension and assessment* (pp. 71–92). Mahwah, NJ: Lawrence Erlbaum.

Krashen, S. D. (1985). *The input hypothesis: Issues and implication.* New York: Longman.

Kynard, C. (2008). "The Blues Playingest Dog You Ever Heard Of": (Re)positioning literacy through African American blues rhetoric. *Reading Research Quarterly, 43*(4), 356–373.

Lenneberg, E. H. (1964). *New directions in the study of language.* Cambridge, MA: MIT Press.

Lightbrown, P. M., & Spada, N. (1999). *How languages are learned* (Rev. ed.). New York: Oxford University Press.

Loban, W. (1976). *Teaching language and literature: Grades seven–twelve* (NCTE Research Report No. 18). Urbana, IL: National Council of Teachers of English.

Long, M. H. (1991). Focus on form: Design features in language teaching methodology. In K. de Bot, D. Coste, R. Ginsberg, & C. Kramsch (Eds.), *Foreign language research in cross-cultural perspective* (pp. 39–52). Amsterdam: John Benjamins.

Marzano, R. J. (1998). *A theory-based meta-analysis of research on instruction* (Contract No. RJ96006101). Aurora, CO: Office of Educational Research and Improvement, Department of Education, Midcontinent Regional Educational Laboratory.

McKissack, P. C. (1986). *Flossie and the fox.* New York: Dial Books for Young Readers.

McGee, L. M., & Ukrainetz, T. A. (2009). Using scaffolding to teach phonemic awareness in preschool and kindergarten. *The Reading Teacher, 62*(7), 599–603.

Menyuk, P. (1988). *Language development knowledge and use.* Glenview, IL: Scott Foresman/Little, Brown College Division.

Missal, K. N., & McConnell, S. R. (2004). *Technical report: Psychometric characteristics of individual growth and development indicators: Picture naming, rhyming, and alliteration.* Minneapolis: University of Minnesota.

Moats, L. C. (1994). The missing foundation in teacher education: Knowledge of the structure of spoken and written language. *Annuals of Dyslexia, 44,* 81–102.

Moats, L. C. (2000). *Speech to print: Language essentials for teachers.* Baltimore: Paul H. Brookes.

Moffett, J. (1983). *Teaching the universe of discourse.* Boston: Houghton Mifflin.

Mohr, K. A. J. (2003). Children's choices: A comparison of book preferences between Hispanic and non-Hispanic first-graders. *Reading Psychology: An International Quarterly, 24*(2), 163–176.

Moran, C. (1996). *Content area instruction for students acquiring English: Power of two languages.* New York: MacMillan/McGraw-Hill.

Morrow, L. M. (2001). *Literacy development in the early years: Helping children read and write* (4th ed.). Boston: Allyn & Bacon.

Morrow, L. M. (2005). *Literacy development in the early years: Helping children read and write* (5th ed.). Boston: Allyn & Bacon.

Morrow, L. M., & Gambrell, L. B. (2001). Literature-based instruction in the early years. In S. B. Neuman & D. K. Dickinson (Eds.), *Handbook of early literacy research* (pp. 348–360). New York: Guilford Press.

Murray, A. D. (1990). Fine-tuning of utterance length to preverbal infants: Effects on later language development. *Journal of Child Language, 17,* 511–525.

Nash, B., & Nash, G. (1980). *Pundles.* New York: Stone Song Press.

Nash, B., & Nash, G. (1983). *Pundles II.* New York: GD/Perigee Book.

National Center for Education Statistics. (2010). *The Nation's Report Card: Grade 12 reading and mathematics 2009 national and pilot state results* (NCES 2011-455).

National Early Literacy Panel. (2008). *Developing early literacy: Report of the National Early Literacy Panel.* Washington, DC: National Institute for Literacy.

National Institute for Literacy. (2010). *Early beginnings: Early literacy knowledge and instruction.* Jessup, MD: Author.

National Reading Panel (NRP). (2000). *Report of the National Reading Panel: Teaching children to read.* Washington, DC: National Institute of Child Health and Human Development.

National Research Council. (1998). *Preventing reading difficulties in young children.* Washington, DC: National Academy Press.

Norton, D. E., & Norton, S. (2003). *Through the eyes of a child: An introduction to children's literature* (6th ed.). Upper Saddle River, NJ: Merrill/Prentice Hall.

Oakley, G., & Jay, J. (2008). "Making time" for reading: Factors that influence the success of multimedia reading in the home. *The Reading Teacher, 62*(3), 246–255.

Pancsofar, N., & Vernon-Feagans, L. (2006). Mother and father language input to young children: Contributions to later language development. *Journal of Applied Developmental Psychology, 27*(6), 571–587.

Pankake, J., & Pankake, M. (1988). *A prairie home companion folk song book.* New York: Viking.

Paul, R. (2001). *Language disorders from infancy through adolescence* (2nd ed.). St. Louis, MO: Mosby.

Payne, R. K. (1998). *A framework for understanding poverty.* Highlands, TX: RFT Publishing.

Pearman, C. J. (2008). Independent reading of CD-ROM storybooks: Measuring comprehension with oral retellings. *The Reading Teacher, 61*(8), 594–602.

Pearson, P. D., Hansen, J., & Gordon, C. (1979). The effect of background knowledge on children's comprehension of implicit and explicit information. *Journal of Reading Behavior, 11*(3), 201–209.

Peterson, P., Carta, J., & Greenwood, C. (2005). Teaching milieu language skills to parents in multiple risk families. *Journal of Early Intervention, 27,* 94–109.

Piaget, J. (1955). *The language and thought of the child.* New York: World.

Piaget, J. (1959). *The language and thought of the child* (3rd ed.). London: Routledge & Kegan.

Pinnell, G. S. (1998). The language foundation of Reading Recovery. Keynote address to the 3rd International Reading Recovery Institute, Cairns, Australia.

Pinnell, G. S., & Jaggar, A. M. (2003). Oral language: Speaking and listening in elementary classrooms. In J. Flood, D. Lapp, J. R. Squire, & J. M. Jensen (Eds.), *Handbook of research on teaching the English language arts* (2nd ed., pp. 881–913). New York: McMillan.

Piper, T. (1998). *Language and learning: The home and school years* (2nd ed.). Upper Saddle River, NJ: Merrill/Prentice Hall.

Polacco, P. (1992). *Chicken Sunday.* New York: Penguin.

Rance-Roney, J. (2010). Jump-starting language and schema for English-language learners: Teacher-composed digital jumpstarts for academic reading. *Journal of Adolescent & Adult Literacy, 53*(5), 386–395.

Remaly, B. K. (1990). *Strategies for increasing the expressive vocabulary of kindergarten children.* Fort Lauderdale, FL: Nova University. (ERIC Document Reproduction Service No. ED 332 234)

Reutzel, D. R., & Cooter, R. B. (2011). *Strategies for reading assessment and instruction: Helping every child succeed* (4th ed.). Boston: Allyn & Bacon/Pearson.

Reutzel, D. R., & Hollingsworth, P. M. (1991). Investigating the development of topic-related attitude: Effect on children's reading and remembering text. *Journal of Educational Research, 84*(5), 334–344.

Roskos, K. A., Tabors, P. O., & Lenhart, L. A. (2009). Joining oral language and early literacy. In K. A. Roskos, P. O. Tabors, & L. A. Lenhart (Eds.), *Oral language and early literacy in preschool* (pp. 1–6). Newark, DE: International Reading Association.

Rumelhart, D. E. (1980). Schemata: The building blocks of cognition. In R. J. Spiro (Ed.), *Theoretical issues in reading comprehension* (pp. 33–58). Hillsdale, NJ: Lawrence Erlbaum Associates.

Saaristo-Helin, K. (2009). Measuring phonological development: A follow-up study of five children acquiring Finnish. *Language and Speech, 52*(1), 55–77.

Sanford, A. J., & Garrod, S. C. (1981). *Understanding written language.* New York: Wiley.

Scarborough, H. S. (2001). Connecting early language and literacy to later reading (dis)abilities: Evidence, theory, and practice. In S. B. Neuman & D. K. Dickinson (Eds.), *Handbook of early literacy research* (Vol. 1, pp. 97–110). New York: Guilford.

Scarborough, H. S., & Dobrich, W. (1994). On the efficacy of reading to preschoolers. *Developmental Review, 14,* 245–302.

Seefeldt, C., & Barbour, N. (1986). *Early childhood education: An introduction.* Upper Saddle River, NJ: Merrill/Prentice Hall.

Shanahan, T. (2006). Relations among oral language, reading, and writing development. In C. A. MacArthur, S. Graham, & J. Fitzgerald (Eds.), *Handbook of writing research* (pp. 171–185). NY: Guilford.

Smith, F. (1977). The uses of language. *Language Arts, 54*(6), 638–644.

Smith, F. (1988). *Understanding reading* (4th ed.). Hillsdale, NJ: Lawrence Erlbaum Associates.

Smith, P. G. (2001). *Talking classrooms: Shaping children's learning through oral language instruction.* Newark, DE: International Reading Association.

Snow, C. E., Burns, M. N., & Griffin, P. (1998). *Preventing reading difficulties in young children.* Washington, DC: National Academy Press.

Snow, C. E., Griffin, P., & Burns, M. S. (2005). *Knowledge to support the teaching of reading: Preparing teachers for a changing world.* San Francisco: Jossey-Bass.

Snow, C. E., Scarborough, H. S., & Burns, M. S. (1999). What speech-language pathologists need to know about early reading. *Topics in Language Disorders, 20*(1), 48–58.

Stern, D. N., & Wasserman, G. A. (1979). *Maternal language to infants.* Paper presented at a meeting of the Society for Research in Child Development, Ann Arbor, MI.

Straub, S. B. (2003). Read to me: A family literacy program for young mothers and their babies. In A. DeBruin-Parecki & B. Krol-Sinclair (Eds.), *Family literacy: From theory to practice* (pp. 184–201). Newark, DE: International Reading Association.

Straub, S. B., & DeBruin-Parecki, A. (2003). *Read to me: A unique high school program linking teenage mothers, their babies, and books.* Paper presented at the 47th Annual Convention of the International Reading Association, San Francisco, CA.

Tharpe, R. G., & Gallimore, R. (1988). *Rousing minds to life.* Cambridge, MA: Cambridge University Press.

Tompkins, G. E. (1998). *Language arts: Content and teaching strategies* (4th ed.). Upper Saddle River, NJ: Merrill Prentice Hall.

Tompkins, G. E. (2010). *Literacy for the 21st Century: A balanced approach* (5th ed.). Boston: Pearson.

Tompkins, G. E. (2011). *Literacy in the early grades: A successful start for preK–4 readers and writers* (3rd ed.). Boston: Pearson.

Trelease, J. (1995). *The new read-aloud handbook* (4th ed.). New York: Penguin.

Vukelich, C., & Christie, J. (2009). How children learn to read and write. In C. Vukelich & J. Christie (Eds.), *Building a foundation for preschool literacy* (pp. 1–15). Newark, DE: International Reading Association.

Vygotsky, L. S. (1978). *Mind in society.* Cambridge, MA: Harvard University Press.

Vygotsky, L. S. (1986). *Thought and language.* Boston: MIT Press.

Vygotsky, L. S. (1990). *Mind in society.* Boston: Harvard University Press.

Warren, S. F. (2001). The future of early communication and language intervention. *Topics in Early Childhood Special Education, 20*(1), 33–38.

Watson, R. (2001). Literacy and oral language: Implications for early literacy acquisition. In S. B. Neuman & D. K. Dickinson (Eds.), *Handbook of early literacy research* (pp. 43–53). New York: Guilford.

Westburg, L. (2010). Thoughts about the NELP report from Laura Westburg. National Center for Family Literacy. Retrieved September 9, 2010, from www.famlit.org/node/930

Whitehurst, G. J., Arnold, D. S., & Epstein, J. N. (1994). A picture book reading intervention in day care and home for children from low income families. *Developmental Psychology, 30*, 679–689.

Whitehurst, G. J., Falco, F. L., & Lonigan, C. J. (1988). Accelerating language development through picture book reading. *Developmental Psychology, 24*, 552–559.

Wiig, E. H., Becker-Redding, U., & Semel, E. M. (1983). A cross-cultural comparison of language abilities of 7- to 8- and 12-to-13-year-old children with learning disabilities. *Journal of Learning Disabilities, 16*(10), 576–585.

Williams, C., Phillips-Birdsong, C., Hufnagel, K., Hungler, D., & Lundstrom, R. P. (2009). Word study instruction in the K–2 classroom. *The Reading Teacher, 62*(7), 570–578.

Chapter 3

Adams, M. J. (1990). *Beginning to read: Thinking and learning about print.* Cambridge, MA: MIT Press.

Adams, M. J. (2001). Alphabetic anxiety and explicit, systematic phonics instruction: A cognitive science perspective. In S. B. Neuman & D. K. Dickinson (Eds.), *Handbook of early literacy research* (pp. 66–80). New York: Guilford Press.

Adams, M. J. (2006). The promise of automatic speech recognition for fostering literacy growth in children and adults. In M. C. McKenna, L. D. Labbo, R. D. Kieffer, & D. Reinking (Eds.), *International handbook of literacy and technology, vol. II* (pp. 109–128). Mahwah, NJ: Lawrence Erlbaum.

Adams, M. J., Foorman, B. R., Lundberg, I., & Beeler, T. (1998). *Phonemic awareness in young children: A classroom curriculum.* Baltimore, MD: Paul H. Brookes.

Allington, R. L. (2002). *Big brother and the national reading curriculum: How ideology trumped evidence.* Portsmouth, NH: Heinemann.

Allington, R. L. (2006). Fluency: Still waiting after all these years. In S. J. Samuels & A. E. Farstrup (Eds.), *What research has to say about fluency instruction* (pp. 94–105). Newark, DE: International Reading Association.

American Federation of Teachers. (1999). *Teaching reading is rocket science. What expert teachers of reading should know and be able to do.* Washington, DC: Author.

Armbruster, B. B., Lehr, F., & Osborn, J. (2001). *Put reading first: The research building blocks for teaching children to read.* Washington, DC: U.S. Department of Education.

August, D., & Shanahan, T. (2006). *Developing literacy in second-language learners: Report of the National Literacy Panel on language-minority children and youth.* Mahwah, NJ: Lawrence Erlbaum.

Baghban, M. (1984). *Our daughter learns to read and write: A case study from birth to three.* Newark, DE: International Reading Association.

Barrett, F. L. (1982). *A teacher's guide to shared reading.* Richmond Hill, Ontario, Canada: Scholastic-TAB.

Bear, D. R., Templeton, S., Invernizzi, M., & Johnston, F. (2008). *Words their way: Word study for phonics, vocabulary, and spelling instruction* (4th ed.). Upper Saddle River, NJ: Merrill/Prentice Hall.

Bissex, G. L. (1980). *Gnys at wrk: A child learns to write and read.* Cambridge, MA: Harvard University Press.

Blevins, W. (1997). *Phonemic awareness activities for early reading success.* New York: Scholastic.

Blevins, W. (1998). *Phonics from A to Z: A practical guide.* New York: Scholastic Professional.

Block, C. C., Oakar, M., & Hurt, N. (2002). The expertise of literacy teachers: A continuum from preschool to grade 5. *Reading Research Quarterly, 37*(2), 178–206.

Brooks, G., Cole, P., Davies, P., Davis, B., Frater, G., Harman, J., et al. (2002). *Keeping up with the children.* London: Basic Skills.

Burns, M. S., Griffin, P., & Snow, C. E. (Eds.). (1999). *Starting out right: A guide to promoting children's reading success.* Washington, DC: National Academy Press.

Bus, A. G., de Jong, M. T., & Verhallen, M. (2006). CD-ROM talking books: A way to enhance early literacy. In M. C. McKenna, L. D. Labbo, R. D. Kieffer, & D. Reinking (Eds.), *International handbook of literacy and technology, vol. II* (pp. 129–142). Mahwah, NJ: Lawrence Erlbaum.

Cepeda, N. J., Coburn, N., Rohrer, D., Wixted, J. T., Mozer, M. C., & Pashler, H. (2009). Optimizing distributed practice: Theoretical analysis and practical implications. *Experimental Psychology, 56*(4), 236–246.

Cepeda, N. J., Pashler, H., Vul, E., Wixted, J. T., & Rohrer, D. (2006). Distributed practice in verbal recall tasks: A review and quantitative synthesis. *Psychological Bulletin, 132*(3), 354–380.

Cepeda, N. J., Vul, E., Rohrer, D., Wixted, J. T., & Pashler, H. (2007). Spacing effects in learning: A temporal ridgeline of optimal retention. *Psychological Science, 19*(11), 1095–1102.

Clay, M. (1966). *Emergent reading behavior.* Unpublished doctoral dissertation, University of Auckland.

Clay, M. M. (1972). *Sand and stones.* Exeter, NH: Heinemann.

Clay, M. M. (1975). *What did I write? Beginning writing behaviour.* Portsmouth, NH: Heinemann.

Clay, M. M. (1979). *Reading: The patterning of complex behaviour.* Exeter, NH: Heinemann.

Clay, M. M. (1991). *Becoming literate: The construction of inner control.* Portsmouth, NH: Heinemann.

Clay, M. M. (1993). *An observation survey of early literacy achievement.* Portsmouth, NH: Heinemann.

Clay, M. M. (2000a). *Concepts about print: What have children learned about the way we print language?* Portsmouth, NH: Heinemann.

Clay, M. M. (2000b). *No shoes* and *Follow me, moon.* Portsmouth, NH: Heinemann.

Clay, M. M. (2002). *An observation survey of early literacy achievement* (2nd ed.). Portsmouth, NH: Heinemann.

Cummins, J. (1981). The role of primary language development in promoting educational success for language minority students. In California State Department of Education (Ed.), *Schooling and language minority students: A theoretical framework* (pp. 3–49). Los Angeles: Evaluation, Dissemination and Assessment Center, California State University.

daCruz-Payne, C. (2005). *Shared reading for today's classroom.* New York: Scholastic.

Day, K. C., & Day, H. D. (1979). Development of kindergarten children's understanding of concepts about print and oral language. In M. L. Kamil & A. H. Moe (Eds.), *Reading research: Studies and applications (Twenty-eighth yearbook of the National Reading Conference)* (pp. 19–22). Clemson, SC: National Reading Conference.

DeBruin-Parecki, A., & Krol-Sinclair, B. (2003). *Family literacy: From theory to practice.* Newark, DE: International Reading Association.

Denny, T. P., & Weintraub, S. (1966). First graders' responses to three questions about reading. *Elementary School Journal, 66,* 441–448.

Denton, C. A., Ciancio, D. J., & Fletcher, J. M. (2006). Validity, reliability, and utility of the Observation Survey of Early Literacy Achievement. *Reading Research Quarterly, 41*(1), 8–34.

Downing, J. (1970). The development of linguistic concepts in children's thinking. *Research in the Teaching of English, 4,* 5–19.

Downing, J. (1971–1972). Children developing concepts of spoken and written language. *Journal of Reading Behavior, 4,* 1–19.

Downing, J., & Oliver, P. (1973). The child's concept of a word. *Reading Research Quarterly, 9,* 568–582.

Duffy, G. G. (2004). *Explaining reading: A resource for teaching concepts, skills, and strategies.* New York: Guilford Press.

Duke, N. K. (2000). 3.6 minutes per day: The scarcity of informational texts in first grade. *Reading Research Quarterly, 35*(2), 202–224.

Durkin, D. (1966). *Children who read early: Two longitudinal studies.* New York: Teachers College Press.

Early Childhood–Head Start Taskforce. (2002). *Teaching our youngest: A guide for preschool teachers and child care and family providers.* Washington, DC: U.S. Departments of Education and Health and Human Services.

Edmunds, K. M., & Bauserman, K. L. (2006). What teachers can learn about reading motivation through conversations with children. *The Reading Teacher, 59*(5), 414–424.

Ehri, L. C., & Sweet, J. (1991). Fingerpoint-reading of memorized text: What enables beginners to process the print? *Reading Research Quarterly, 26,* 442–462.

Enz, B. J. (2003). The ABCs of family literacy. In A. De-Bruin-Parecki & B. Krol-Sinclair (Eds.), *Family literacy: From theory to practice* (pp. 50–67). Newark, DE: International Reading Association.

Fielding, L., Kerr, N., & Rosier, P. (1998). *The 90% reading goal.* Kennewick, WA: National Reading Foundation.

Fitzgerald, J., Armendum, S. J., & Gutherie, K. M. (2008). Young Latino students' English-reading growth in all English classrooms. *Journal of Literacy Research, 40*(1), 59–94.

Fry, E. (2004). Phonics: A large phoneme-grapheme frequency count revisited. *Journal of Literacy Research, 36*(1), 85–98.

Garan, E. M. (2002). *Resisting reading mandates: How to triumph with the truth.* Portsmouth, NH: Heinemann.

Goodman, K. S. (1986). *What's whole in whole language?* Ontario, Canada: Scholastic.

Goswami, U. (2000). Phonological and lexical processes. In M. L. Kamil, P. B. Mosenthal, P. D. Pearson, & R. Barr (Eds.), *Handbook of reading research* (Vol. 3, pp. 251–268). Mahwah, NJ: Lawrence Erlbaum.

Goswami, U. (2001). Early phonological development and the acquisition of literacy. In S. B. Neuman & D. K. Dickinson (Eds.), *Handbook of early literacy research* (pp. 111–125). New York: Guilford Press.

Griffith, P. L., & Olson, M. W. (1992). Phonemic awareness helps beginning readers break the code. *The Reading Teacher, 45,* 516–523.

Guthrie, J. T., & Humenick, N. M. (2004). Motivating students to read: Evidence for classroom practices that increase reading motivation and achievement. In P. McCardle & V. Chhabra (Eds.), *The voice of evidence in reading research* (pp. 329–354). Baltimore: Brookes Publishing.

Halliday, M. A. K. (1975). *Learning how to mean: Explorations in the development of language.* London: Edward Arnold.

Hansen, J. (1987). *When writers read.* Portsmouth, NH: Heinemann.

Heath, S. B. (1983). *Ways with words.* Cambridge, UK: Cambridge University Press.

Hiebert, E. H., Pearson, P. D., Taylor, B. M., Richardson, V., & Paris, S. G. (1998). *Every child a reader: Applying reading research in the classroom.* Ann Arbor, MI: Center for the Improvement of Early Reading Achievement.

Johns, J. L. (1980). First graders' concepts about print. *Reading Research Quarterly, 15,* 529–549.

Jordan, G. E., Snow, C. E., & Porche, M. V. (2000). Project EASE: The effect of a family literacy project on kindergarten students' early literacy skills. *Reading Research Quarterly, 35,* 524–546.

Juel, C. (1988). Learning to read and write: A longitudinal study of the fifty-four children from first through fourth grade. *Journal of Educational Psychology, 80*(4), 437–447.

Justice, L. M., Pence, K., Bowles, R. B., & Wiggins, A. (2006). An investigation of four hypotheses concerning the order by which 4-year-old children learn the alphabet letters. *Early Childhood Research Quarterly, 21*(3), 374–389.

Krauss, R. (1945). *The carrot seed.* New York: Scholastic.

Krech, B. (2000). *Fresh & fun: Teaching with kids' names (Grades K–2).* New York: Scholastic.

Kuby, P., & Aldridge, J. (1994). Direct vs. indirect environmental print instruction and early reading ability in kindergarten children. *Reading Psychology 18*(2), 91–104.

Lancaster, L. (2001). Staring at the page: The function of gaze in a young child's interpretation of symbolic forms. *Journal of Childhood Literacy, 1*(2), 131–152.

Lobel, A. (1981). *On market street.* New York: Scholastic.

Lomax, R. G., & McGee, L. M. (1987). Young children's concepts about print and reading: Toward a model of word reading acquisition. *Reading Research Quarterly, 22*(2), 237–256.

Mathes, P. G., Denton, C. A., Fletcher, J. M., Anthony, J. L., Francis, D. J., & Schatschneider, C. (2005). The effects of theoretically different instruction and student characteristics on the skills of struggling readers. *Reading Research Quarterly, 40*(2), 148–183.

McGee, L. M., & Richgels, D. J. (2003). *Designing early literacy programs: Strategies for at-risk preschool and kindergarten children.* New York: Guilford.

McQueen, L. (1985). *The little red hen.* New York: Scholastic.

Meltzer, N. S., & Himse, R. (1969). The boundaries of written words as seen by first graders. *Journal of Reading Behavior, 1,* 3–13.

Miesels, S. J., & Piker, R. A. (2001). An analysis of early literacy assessments used for instruction. (Ciera Report No. 2-013). Ann Arbor, MI: Center for the Improvement of Early Reading Achievement.

Mohr, K. A. J. (2003). Children's choices: A comparison of book preferences between Hispanic and non-Hispanic first-graders.

Reading Psychology: An International Quarterly, 24(2), 163–176.

Morris, D., Bloodgood, J. M., Lomax, R. G., & Perney, J. (2003). Developmental steps in learning to read: A longitudinal study in kindergarten and first grade. *Reading Research Quarterly, 38*(3), 302–328.

Morrow, L. M., Tracey, D. H., Woo, D. G., & Pressley, M. (1999). Characteristics of exemplary first-grade literacy instruction. *The Reading Teacher, 52*(5), 462–476.

National Association for the Education of Young Children (NAEYC). (2009). *Developmentally appropriate practice in early childhood programs* (3rd ed.). Washington, DC: Author.

National Early Literacy Panel. (2008). *Developing early literacy: Report of the National Early Literacy Panel.* Jessup, MD: National Institute for Literacy.

National Reading Panel. (2000). *Report of the National Reading Panel: Teaching children to read.* Washington, DC: National Institute of Child Health and Human Development.

Neuman, S. B. (1999). Books make a difference: A study of access to literacy. *Reading Research Quarterly, 34,* 286–311.

Neuman, S. B. (2001). The role of knowledge in early literacy. *Reading Research Quarterly, 36*(4), 468–475.

Neuman, S. B., & Celano, D. (2001). Access to print in low-income and middle-income communities: An ecological study of four neighborhoods. *Reading Research Quarterly, 36*(1), 8–26.

Neuman, S. B., & Roskos, K. (1993). Access to print for children of poverty: Differential effects of adult mediation and literacy-enriched play settings on environmental and functional print tasks. *American Educational Research Journal, 30*(1), 95–122.

O'Connor, R. E., Harty, K. R., & Fulmer, D. (2005). Tiers of intervention in kindergarten through third grade. *Journal of Learning Disabilities, 38,* 532–538.

Orellana, M. F., & Hernandez, A. (1999). Talking the walk: Children reading urban environmental print. *The Reading Teacher, 52*(6), 612–619.

Paratore, J. R. (2003). Building on family literacies: Examining the past and planning the future. In A. DeBruin-Parecki & B. Krol-Sinclair (Eds.), *Family literacy: From theory to practice* (pp. 8–27). Newark, DE: International Reading Association.

Pashler, H. (2006). *Optimizing resistance to forgetting.* Paper presented at the 2006 Institute of Education Sciences 2006 Research Conference, Washington, DC.

Piasta, S. B., & Wagner, R. K. (2010). Developing early literacy skills: A meta-analysis of alphabet learning and instruction. *Reading Research Quarterly, 45*(1), 8–38.

Pressley, M. (2002). *Reading instruction that works: The case for balanced teaching* (2nd ed.). New York: Guilford Press.

Pressley, M., Allington, R. L., Wharton-McDonald, R., Collins-Block, C., & Morrow, L. M. (2001). *Learning to read: Lessons from exemplary first-grade classrooms.* New York: Guilford Press.

Pressley, M., Dolezal, S. E., Raphael, L. M, Mohan, L., Roehrig, A. D., & Bogner, K. (2003). *Motivating primary-grade students.* New York: Guilford Press.

Proudfoot, G. (1992). Pssst! There is literacy at the laundromat. *English Quarterly, 24*(1), 10–11.

Ramey, S. L., & Ramey, C. T. (2006). Early educational interventions: Principles of effective and sustained benefits from targeted early educational programs. In D. K. Dickenson & S. B. Neuman (Eds.), *Handbook of early literacy research* (Vol. 2, pp. 445–459). New York: Guilford Press.

Rasinski, T. V. (2003). *The fluent reader: Oral reading strategies for building word recognition, fluency, and comprehension.* New York: Scholastic.

Reid, J. F. (1966). Learning to think about reading. *Educational Research, 9,* 56–62.

Reutzel, D. R. (2006). Hey teacher, when you say fluency, what do you mean?: Developing fluency and meta-fluency in elementary classrooms. In T. V. Rasinski, C. Blachowicz, & K. Lems (Eds.), *Fluency instruction: Research-based best practices* (pp. 62–85). New York: Guilford Press.

Reutzel, D. R., & Cooter, R. B. (2011). *Strategies for reading assessment and instruction: Helping every child succeed* (4th ed.). Boston: Pearson/Allyn & Bacon.

Reutzel, D. R., & Mitchell, J. P. (2005). High-stakes accountability themed issue: How did we get here from there? *The Reading Teacher, 58*(4), 2–4.

Reutzel, D. R., Oda, L. K., & Moore, B. H. (1989). Developing print awareness: The effect of three instructional approaches on kindergartners: Print awareness, reading readiness, and word reading. *Journal of Reading Behavior, 21*(3), 197–217.

Reutzel, D. R., Young, J. R., Fawson, P.C., Morrison, T. G., & Wilcox, B. (2003). Reading environmental print: The role of concepts of print in discriminating young readers' responses. *Reading Psychology 24*(2), 123–162.

Roswell, F. G., & Chall, J. S. (1963). *Auditory blending test.* New York: Essay Press.

Schmidt, K. (1985). *The gingerbread man.* New York: Scholastic.

Shanahan, T. (2003a). *A framework for improving reading achievement.* Paper presented at the National Conference on Family Literacy and the California Family Literacy Conference, Long Beach, California, March 16, 2003.

Shanahan, T. (2003b). Research-based reading instruction: Myths about the National Reading Panel report. *The Reading Teacher, 56*(7), 646–655.

Shanahan, T. (2004). Critiques of the National Reading Panel report: Their implications for research, policy, and practice. In P. McCardle & V. Chhabra (Eds.), *The voice of evidence in reading research* (pp. 235–266). Baltimore: Paul H. Brookes.

Shanahan, T., Mulhern, M., & Rodriquez-Brown, F. (1995). Project FLAME: Lessons learned from a family literacy program for minority families. *The Reading Teacher, 48,* 40–47.

Shaywitz, S. E., & Shaywitz, B. A. (2004). Neurobiologic basis for reading and reading disability. In P. McCardle & V. Chhabra (Eds.), *The voice of evidence in reading research* (pp. 417–444). Baltimore: Paul H. Brookes.

Slaughter, J. J. (1993). *Beyond storybooks: Young children and the shared book experience.* Newark, DE: International Reading Association.

Smith, F. (1977). The uses of language. *Language Arts, 54*(6), 638–644.

Smith, F. (1985). *Reading without nonsense* (2nd ed.). New York: Teachers College Press.

Smith, N. B. (2002). *American reading instruction—special edition.* Newark, DE: International Reading Association.

Smolkin, L. B., & Donovan, C. A. (2001). The contexts of comprehension: The information book read aloud, comprehension acquisition, and comprehension instruction in a first-grade classroom. *Elementary School Journal, 102*(2), 97–122.

Snow, C. E., Burns, M. N., & Griffin, P. (1998). *Preventing reading difficulties in young children.* Washington, DC: National Academy Press.

Stage, S., Sheppard, J., Davidson, M. M., & Browning, M. M. (2001). Prediction of first-graders' growth in oral reading fluency using kindergarten letter fluency. *Journal of School Psychology, 39*(3), 225–237.

Stahl, K. (2004). Proof, practice, and promise: Comprehension strategy instruction in the primary grades. *The Reading Teacher, 57*(7), 598–609.

Taylor, B. M., Pearson, P. D., Peterson, D. S., & Rodriguez, M. C. (2005). The CIERA school change framework: An evidence-based approach to professional development and school reading improvement. *Reading Research Quarterly, 40*(1), 40–69.

Taylor, N. E. (1986). Developing beginning literacy concepts: Content and context. In D. B. Yaden, Jr., & S. Templeton (Eds.), *Metalinguistic awareness and beginning literacy* (pp. 173–184). Portsmouth, NH: Heinemann.

Teale, W. H. (1986). Home background and young children's literacy development. In W. H. Teale and E. Sulzby (Eds.), *Emergent literacy* (pp. 173–206). Norwood, NJ: Ablex.

Treiman, R., Levin, I., & Kessler, B. (2007). Learning of letter names follows similar principles across languages: Evidence from Hebrew. *Journal of Experimental Child Psychology, 96*(2), 87–106.

Tunnell, M. O., & Jacobs, J. S. (1989). Using "real" books: Research findings on literature based reading instruction. *The Reading Teacher, 42*, 470–477.

Turner, J., & Paris, S. (1995). How literacy tasks influence children's motivation for literacy. *The Reading Teacher, 48*(8), 662–673.

Vopat, J. (1994). *The parent project: A workshop approach to parent involvement.* York, ME: Stenhouse.

Vukelich, C. (1994). Effects of play interventions on young children's reading of environmental print. *Early Childhood Research Quarterly, 9*(2), 153–170.

West, L. S., & Egley, E. H. (1998). Children get more than a hamburger: Using labels and logos to enhance literacy. *Dimensions of Early Childhood, 26*(3–4), 43–46.

Wonder-McDowell, C., Reutzel, D. R., & Smith, J. A. (in press). Does instructional alignment matter?: Effects on struggling second-grade students' reading achievement. *Elementary School Journal.*

Yaden, D. B., Jr., & Templeton, S. (Eds.). (1986). *Reading research in metalinguistic awareness: A classification of findings according to focus and methodology.* Portsmouth, NH: Heinemann.

Yeh, S. (2003). An evaluation of two approaches for teaching phonemic awareness to children in Head Start. *Early Childhood Research Quarterly, 18*(1), 511–529.

Yopp, H. K. (1988). The validity and reliability of phonemic awareness tests. *Reading Research Quarterly, 23*, 159–177.

Yopp, H. K. (1992). Developing phonemic awareness in young children. *The Reading Teacher, 45*(9), 696–703.

Yopp, H. K., & Troyer, S. (1992). *Training phonemic awareness in young children.* Unpublished manuscript.

Chapter 4

Adams, M. J. (1990). *Beginning to read: Thinking and learning about print—a summary.* Urbana, IL: Center for the Study of Reading.

August, D., & Shanahan, T. (2006). *Developing literacy in second-language learners: A report of the National Literacy Panel on language-minority children and youth.* Mahwah, NJ: Lawrence Erlbaum.

Barracca, D., & Barracca, S. (1990). *Taxi dog.* New York: Dial Books.

Barton, D., Miller, R., & Macken, M. A. (1980). Do children treat clusters as one unit or two? *Papers and Reports on Child Language Development, 18*, 137.

Betts, E. A. (1946). *Foundation of reading instruction.* New York: American Book.

Blachman, B. A. (1984). Relationship of rapid naming ability and language analysis skills to kindergarten and first-grade reading achievement. *Journal of Educational Psychology, 76*, 610–622.

Blevins, W. (1997). *Phonics from A to Z: A practical guide.* New York: Scholastic Professional.

Burns, M. S., Griffin, P., & Snow, C. E. (Eds.). (1999). *Starting out right: A guide to promoting children's reading success.* Committee on the Prevention of Reading Difficulties in Young Children, Commission on Behavioral and Social Sciences and Education, National Research Council. Washington, DC: National Academy Press.

Byrne, B., & Fielding-Barnsley, R. (1990). Acquiring the alphabetic principle: A case for teaching recognition of phoneme identity. *Journal of Educational Psychology, 82*(4), 805–812.

Cepeda, N. J., Coburn, N., Rohrer, D., Wixted, J. T., Mozer, M. C., & Pashler, H. (2009). Optimizing distributed practice: Theoretical analysis and practical implications. *Experimental Psychology, 56*(4), 236–246.

Cepeda, N. J., Pashler, H., Vul, E., Wixted, J. T., & Rohrer, D. (2006). Distributed practice in verbal recall tasks: A review and quantitative synthesis. *Psychological Bulletin, 132*(3), 354–380.

Cepeda, N. J., Vul, E., Rohrer, D., Wixted, J. T., & Pashler, H. (2007). Spacing effects in learning: A temporal ridgeline of optimal retention. *Psychological Science, 19*(11), 1095–1102.

Clay, M. M. (1972). *Reading: The patterning of complex behaviour.* Exeter, NH: Heinemann.

Clay, M. M. (1985). *The early detection of reading difficulties* (3rd ed.). Portsmouth, NH: Heinemann.

Clay, M. M. (1993). *An observation survey of early literacy achievement.* Portsmouth, NH: Heinemann.

Clay, M. M. (2003). *Reading recovery.* Retrieved March 24, 2010, from http://readingrecovery.org.

Cooter, R. B., Mathews, B., Thompson, S., & Cooter, K. S. (2004). Searching for lessons of mass instruction? Try reading strategy continuums. *The Reading Teacher, 58*(4), 388–393.

Cunningham, P. M. (1980). Teaching *were, with, what,* and other "four-letter" words. *The Reading Teaching, 34*, 160–163.

Cunningham, P. M. (1995). *Phonics they use* (2nd ed.). New York: HarperCollins.

Cunningham, P. M. (2008). *Phonics they use: Words for reading and writing* (5th ed.). Boston: Pearson/Allyn & Bacon.

Durkin, D. (1989). *Teaching them to read* (5th ed.). Boston: Allyn & Bacon.

Durrell, D. D. (1940). *Improvement of basic reading abilities.* New York: World Book.

Fawson, P. C., Ludlow, B., Reutzel, D. R., Sudweeks, R., & Smith, J. A. (2006). Examining the reliability of running records: Attaining generalizable results. *Journal of Educational Research, 100*(2), 113–126.

Flynt, E. S., & Cooter, R. B. (2004). *The Flynt/Cooter reading inventory for the classroom* (5th ed.). Upper Saddle River, NJ: Merrill/Prentice Hall.

Fry, E. B., Kress, J. E., & Fountoukidis, D. L. (2006). *The reading teacher's book of lists* (5th ed.). San Francisco: Jossey-Bass.

Fuchs, D., Fuchs, L. S., & Vaughn, S. (2008). *Response to intervention: A framework for reading educators.* Newark, DE: International Reading Association.

Gambrell, L. B. (2007). Technology and the engaged literacy learner. In M. C. McKenna, L. D. Labbo, R. D. Keiffer, & D. Reinking (Eds.), *International handbook of literacy and technology* (Vol. II, pp. 289–294). Mahwah, NJ: Lawrence Erlbaum.

Harris, C. (2009). Meet the new school board: Board games are back—And they're exactly what your curriculum needs. *School Library Journal, 55*(5), 24–26.

Honig, B., Diamond, L., & Gutlohn, L. (2000). *Teaching reading: Sourcebook for kindergarten through eighth grade.* Novato, CA: Arena Press.

Horn, E. (1919). Principles of method in teaching spelling as derived from scientific investigation. In G. M. Whipple (Ed.), *Fourth report of the Committee on Economy of Time in Education,* Eighteenth Yearbook of the National Society for the Study of Education. Bloomington, IL: Public School Publishing.

Hughes, J. (2010). *Connecting to the 21st-century student: Educators must work to understand and motivate a new kind of digital learner.* Retrieved March 19, 2010, from www.edutopia.org/ikid-digital-learner.

Hull, M. A. (1989). *Phonics for the teacher of reading.* Upper Saddle River, NJ: Merrill/Prentice Hall.

International Dyslexia Association. (2006). What is dyslexia? Retrieved March 24, 2010, from www.interdys.org/FAQ.htm.

Jackson, J. (2009). Game-based teaching: What educators can learn from videogames. *Teaching Education, 20*(3), 291–304.

Lass, B., & Davis, B. (1985). *The remedial reading handbook.* Upper Saddle River, NJ: Prentice Hall.

Moustafa, M. (1997). *Beyond traditional phonics: Research discoveries and reading instruction.* Portsmouth, NH: Heinemann.

Murray, B. A., Brabham, E. G., Villaume, S. K., & Veal, M. (2008). The Cluella study: Optimal segmentation and voicing for oral blending. *Journal of Literacy Research, 4*(4), 395–421.

National Reading Panel (NRP). (2000). *Report of the National Reading Panel: Teaching children to read.* Washington, DC: National Institute of Child Health and Human Development.

Owston, R., Wideman, H., Ronda, N., & Brown, C. (2009). Computer game development as a literacy activity. *Computers & Education, 53*(3), 977–989.

Pashler, H. (2006). *Optimizing resistance to forgetting.* Paper presented at the 2006 Institute of Education Sciences 2006 Research Conference, Washington, DC.

Piasta, S. B., & Wagner, R. K. (2010). Developing early literacy skills: A meta-analysis of alphabet learning and instruction. *Reading Research Quarterly, 45*(1), 8–38.

Rasinski, T. V., & Padak, N. (1996). Five lessons to increase reading fluency. In L. R. Putnam (Ed.), *How to become a better reading teacher: Strategies for assessment and intervention* (pp. 255–266). Columbus, OH: Merrill/Prentice Hall.

Reutzel, D. R., & Cooter, R. B. (2011). *Strategies for reading assessment and instruction: Helping every child succeed* (4th ed.). Boston: Pearson/Allyn & Bacon.

Snow, C. E., Burns, M. N., & Griffin, P. (1998). *Preventing reading difficulties in young children.* Washington, DC: National Academy Press.

Stanovich, E., & West, R. F. (1989). Exposure to print and orthographic processing. *Reading Research Quarterly, 24*(4), 402–433.

Thorndike, E. L., & Lorge, I. *Thorndike-Lorge magazine count.* (1944). New York: Columbia University.

Treiman, R. (1985). Onsets and rimes as units of spoken syllables: Evidence from children. *Journal of Experimental Child Psychology, 39,* 161–181.

Vellutino F. R., & Scanlon D. M. (2002). The Interactive Strategies approach to reading intervention. *Contemporary Educational Psychology, 27,* 573–635.

Walpole, S., & McKenna, M. C. (2004). *The literacy coach's handbook: A guide to research-based practice.* New York: Guilford Press.

Wiener, R. B., & Cohen, J. H. (1997). *Literacy portfolios: Using assessment to guide instruction.* Upper Saddle River, NJ: Merrill/Prentice Hall.

Woodcock, R. W. (1997). *Woodcock Reading Mastery Tests–Revised (WRMT–R).* Circle Pines, MN: American Guidance Service.

Woodcock, R., Mather, N., & Barnes, E. K. (1987). *Woodcock reading mastery tests–revised.* Circle Pines, MN: American Guidance Service.

Zeno, S. M., Ivens, S. H., Millard, R. T., & Duvvuri, R. (1995). *The educator's word guide.* New York: Touchstone Applied Science.

Chapter 5

Adams, M. J. (2005). Charlesbridge Reading Fluency Program. Retrieved April 29, 2010, from www.charlesbridge.com/school/pdf/fluency.

Allington, R. L. (1977). If they don't read much, how they ever gonna get good? *Journal of Reading, 21,* 57–61.

Allington, R. L. (1983). Fluency: The neglected goal of reading. *The Reading Teacher, 36,* 556–561.

Allington, R. L. (1984). Oral reading. In R. Barr, M. L. Kamil, & P. Mosenthal (Eds.), *Handbook of reading research* (Vol. 1, pp. 829–864). New York: Longman.

Allington, R. L. (2001). *What really matters for struggling readers: Designing research-based programs.* New York: Addison-Wesley Longman.

Allington, R. L. (2002). *Big brother and the national reading curriculum: How ideology trumped evidence.* Portsmouth, NH: Heinemann.

Anderson, R. C., Wilkinson, I. A. G., & Mason, J. M. (1991). A microanalysis of the small-group, guided reading lesson: Effects of an emphasis on global story meaning. *Reading Research Quarterly, 26*(4), 417–441.

August, D., & Shanahan, T. (2006). *Developing literacy in second-language learners: A report of the National Literacy Panel on language-minority children and youth.* Mahwah, NJ: Lawrence Erlbaum.

Brown, K. J. (1999). What kind of text—for whom and when? Textual scaffolding for beginning readers. *The Reading Teacher, 53*(4), 292–307.

Bryan, G., Fawson, P. C., & Reutzel, D. R. (2003). Sustained silent reading: Exploring the value of literature discussion with three non-engaged readers. *Reading Research and Instruction, 43*(1), 47–73.

Cooter, R. B., & Griffith, R. (1989). Thematic units for middle school: An honorable seduction. *Journal of Reading, 32*(8), 676–681.

Dowhower, S. (1987). Effects of repeated readings on second-grade transitional readers' fluency and comprehension. *Reading Research Quarterly, 22,* 389–406.

Dowhower, S. (1991). Speaking of prosody: Fluency's unattended bedfellow. *Theory into Practice, 30*(3), 158–164.

Eldredge, J. L., Reutzel, D. R., & Hollingsworth, P. M. (1996, Summer). Comparing the effectiveness of two oral reading practices: Round-robin reading and the shared book experience. *Journal of Literacy Research, 28*(2), 201–225.

Fitzgerald, J., Amendum, S. J., & Guthrie, K. M. (2008). Young Latino students' English-reading growth in all-English classrooms. *Journal of Literacy Research, 40*(3), 59–94.

Gambrell, L. B., Wilson, R. M., & Gnatt, W. N. (1981). Classroom observations of task-attending behaviors of good and poor readers. *Journal of Educational Research, 74,* 400–404.

Good, R. H., & Kamiski, R. A. (Eds.). (2002). *Dynamic indicators of basic early literacy skills* (6th ed.). Eugene, OR: Institute for the Development of Educational Achievement. Retrieved from http://dibelsuoregon.edu

Greene, F. (1979). Radio reading. In C. Pennock (Ed.), *Reading comprehension at four linguistic levels* (pp. 104–107). Newark, DE: International Reading Association.

Griffith, L. W., & Rasinski, T. V. (2004). A focus on fluency: How one teacher incorporated fluency with her reading curriculum. *The Reading Teacher 58*(2), 126–137.

Hasbrouck, J., & Tindal, G. (2006). Oral reading fluency norms: A valuable assessment tool for reading teachers. *The Reading Teacher, 59*(7), 636–645.

Heckleman, R. G. (1966). Using the neurological impress remedial reading technique. *Academic Therapy, 1,* 235–239, 250.

Heckleman, R. G. (1969). A neurological impress method of remedial reading instruction. *Academic Therapy, 4,* 277–282.

Henk, W. A. (1983). Adapting the NIM to improve comprehension. *Academic Therapy, 19,* 97–101.

Hennings, K. (1974). Drama reading: An on-going classroom activity at the elementary school level. *Elementary English, 51,* 48–51.

Hiebert, E. H., & Fisher, P. (2006). Fluency from the first: What works with first graders. In T. V. Rasinski, C. Blachowicz, & K. Lems (Eds.), *Fluency instruction: Research-based best practices* (pp. 279–294). New York: Guilford Press.

Hiebert, E. H., & Reutzel, D. R. (2010). *Silent reading revisited: New directions for teachers and researchers.* Newark, DE: International Reading Association.

Hintze, J. M., & Christ, T. J. (2004). An examination of variability as a function of passage variance in CBM progress monitoring. *School Psychology Review, 33*(2), 204–217.

Hoffman, J. V. (2003). Foreword. In T. V. Rasinski, *The fluent reader: Oral reading strategies for building word recognition, fluency, and comprehension* (pp. 5–6). New York: Scholastic.

Hollingsworth, P. M. (1970). An experiment with the impress method of teaching reading. *The Reading Teacher, 24,* 112–114.

Hollingsworth, P. M. (1978). An experimental approach to the impress method of teaching reading. *The Reading Teacher, 31,* 624–626.

Hudson, R. F., Lane, H. B., & Pullen, P. C. (2005). Reading fluency assessment and instruction: What, why, and how? *The Reading Teacher, 58*(8), 702–714.

Huey, E. B. (1908). *The psychology and pedagogy of reading.* New York: Macmillan.

Jenkins, J. R., Fuchs, L. S., Van den Broek, P., Espin, C., & Deno, S. L. (2003). Accuracy and fluency in list and context reading of skilled and RD groups: Absolute and relative performance levels. *Learning Disabilities Research and Practice, 18*(4), 237–245.

Juel, C. (1991). Cross-age tutoring between student athletes and at-risk children. *Reading Teacher, 45*(3), 178–186.

Kame'enui, E. J., & Simmons, D. C. (2001). The DNA of reading fluency. *Scientific Studies of Reading, 5*(3), 203–210.

Kelley, M., & Clausen-Grace, N. (2006). R^5: The sustained silent reading makeover that transformed readers. *The Reading Teacher, 60*(2), 148–156.

Kelley, M., & Clausen-Grace, N. (2010). R^5: A sustained silent reading makeover that works. In E. H. Hiebert & D. R. Reutzel (Eds.), *Silent reading revisited: New directions for teachers and researchers* (pp. 168–180). Newark, DE: International Reading Association.

Klenk, L., & Kibby, M. W. (2000). Remediating reading difficulties: Appraising the past, reconciling the present, constructing the future. In M. L. Kamil, P. B. Mosenthal, P. D. Pearson, and R. Barr (Eds.), *Handbook of reading research* (Vol. 3., pp. 667–690). Mahwah, NJ: Lawrence Erlbaum.

Koskinen, P., Wilson, R., & Jensema, C. (1985). Closed captioned television: A new tool for reading instruction. *Reading World, 24*(1), 1–7.

Krashen, S. (2002). More smoke and mirrors: A critique of the National Reading Panel report on fluency. In R. L. Allington (Ed.), *Big brother and the national reading curriculum: How ideology trumped evidence* (pp. 112–124). Portsmouth, NH: Heinemann Educational Books.

Kuhn, M. (2005). Helping students become accurate, expressive readers: Fluency instruction for small groups. *The Reading Teacher, 58*(4), 338–345.

Kuhn, M. R., & Schwanenflugel, P. J. (2006). Fluency oriented reading instruction: A merging of theory and practice. In K. A. Stahl & M. C. McKenna (Eds.), *Reading research at work: Foundations of effective practice* (pp. 205–216). New York: Guilford Press.

Kuhn, M. R., & Stahl, S. A. (2000). *Fluency: A review of developmental and remedial practices.* Center for the Improvement of Early Reading Achievement—Report #2-008, Ann Arbor: University of Michigan.

Kuhn, M. R., & Woo, D. G. (2008). Fluency oriented reading: Two whole-class approaches. In M. R. Kuhn & P. J. Schwanenflugel (Eds.), *Fluency in the classroom* (pp. 17–35). New York: Guilford Press.

LaBerge, D., & Samuels, S. J. (1974). Toward a theory of automatic information processing in reading. *Cognitive Psychology, 6,* 293–323.

Manning, M., Lewis, M., & Lewis, M. (2010). Revisiting silent sustained reading: An update of the research. In E. H. Hiebert & D. R. Reutzel (Eds.), *Silent reading revisited: New directions for teachers and researchers* (pp. 112–128). Newark, DE: International Reading Association.

Martin, B., & Archambault, J. (1987). *Knots on a counting rope.* New York: Holt, Rinehart and Winston.

Menon, S., & Hiebert, E. H. (2005). A comparison of first graders' reading with little books or literature based basal anthologies. *Reading Research Quarterly, 40*(1), 12–36.

National Reading Panel (NRP). (2000). *Report of the National Reading Panel: Teaching children to read.* Washington, DC: National Institute of Child Health and Human Development.

Neuman, S., & Koskinen, P. (1992). Captioned television as comprehensible input: Effects of incidental word learning from context for language minority students. *Reading Research Quarterly, 27*(3), 94–106.

Opitz, M. F., & Rasinski, T. V. (2008). *Good-bye round robin: 25 effective oral reading strategies* (2nd ed.). Portsmouth, NH: Heinemann.

Paris, S. G., Carpenter, R. D., Paris, A. H., & Hamilton, E. E. (2005). Spurious and genuine correlates of children's reading comprehension. In S. G. Paris & S. A. Stahl (Eds.), *Children's reading comprehension and assessment* (pp. 131–160). Mahwah, NJ: Lawrence Erlbaum.

Pikulski, J. J., & Chard, D. J. (2005). Fluency: Bridge between decoding and reading comprehension. *The Reading Teacher, 58*(6), 510–519.

Pressley, M. (2000). What should comprehension instruction be the instruction of? In M. L. Kamil, P. B. Mosenthal, P. D. Pearson, & R. Barr (Eds.), *Handbook of reading research* (Vol. 3, pp. 545–561). Mahwah, NJ: Erlbaum.

Pressley, M. (2006). *Reading instruction that works: The case for balanced teaching* (3rd ed.). New York: Guilford Press.

Rasinski, T. (1989). Fluency for everyone: Incorporating fluency instruction in the classroom. *The Reading Teacher, 42*(9), 690–693.

Rasinski, T. (2000). Speed does matter. *The Reading Teacher, 54*(2), 146–151.

Raskinski, T. V. (2003). *The fluent reader: Oral reading strategies for building word recognition, fluency, and comprehension.* New York: Scholastic.

Rasinski, T. V. (2006a). A brief history of reading fluency. In S. J. Samuels & A. E. Farstrup (Eds.), *What research has to say about fluency instruction* (pp. 4–23). Newark, DE: International Reading Association.

Rasinski, T. V. (2006b). Reading fluency instruction: Moving beyond accuracy, automaticity, and prosody. *The Reading Teacher, 59*(7), 704–707.

Rasinski, T. V., Blachowicz, C., & Lems, K. (2006). *Fluency instruction: Research-based best practices.* New York: Guilford Press.

Rasinski, T. V., & Padak, N. (1996). Five lessons to increase reading fluency. In L. R. Putnam (Ed.), *How to become a better reading teacher: Strategies for assessment and intervention* (pp. 255–266) Columbus, OH: Merrill/Prentice Hall.

Rasinski, T. V., Reutzel, D. R., Chard, D., & Linan-Thompson, S. (2010). Reading fluency. In P. Afflerbach, M. L. Kamil, E. Moje, & P. D. Pearson (Eds.), *Handbook of reading research* (Vol. IV). Philadelphia, PA: Routledge.

Reutzel, D. R. (2006). Hey teacher, when you say fluency, what do you mean? Developing fluency and meta-fluency in elementary classrooms. In T. V. Rasinski, C. Blachowicz, & K. Lems (Eds.), *Fluency instruction: Research-based best practices* (pp. 62–85). New York: Guilford Press.

Reutzel, D. R., & Cooter, R. B. (2011). *Strategies for reading assessment and instruction: Helping every child succeed* (4th ed.). Boston: Pearson/Allyn & Bacon.

Reutzel, D. R., Fawson, P. C., & Smith, J. A. (2008). Reconsidering silent sustained reading: An exploratory study of scaffolded silent reading (ScSR). *Journal of Educational Research, 102*(1), 37–50.

Reutzel, D. R., & Hollingsworth, P. M. (1993). Effects of fluency training on second graders' reading comprehension. *Journal of Educational Research, 86*(6), 325–331.

Reutzel, D. R., Jones, C. D., Fawson, P. C., & Smith, J. A. (2008). Scaffolded silent reading (ScSR): An alternative to guided oral repeated reading that works! *The Reading Teacher, 62*(3), 194–207.

Reutzel, D. R., Jones, C. D., & Newman, T. H. (2010). Scaffolded silent reading (ScSR): Improving the conditions of silent reading practice in classrooms. In E. H. Hiebert & D. R. Reutzel (Eds.), *Silent reading revisited: New directions for teachers and researchers* (pp. 129–150). Newark, DE: International Reading Association.

Richards, M. (2000). Be a good detective: Solve the case of oral reading fluency. *The Reading Teacher, 53*(7), 534–539.

Robinson, B. (1972). *The best Christmas pageant ever.* New York: HarperCollins.

Samuels, S. J. (1979). The method of repeated reading. *The Reading Teacher, 32,* 403–408.

Samuels, S. J. (2006). Toward a model of reading fluency. In S. J. Samuels & A. E. Farstrup (Eds.), *What research has to say about fluency instruction* (pp. 24–46). Newark, DE: International Reading Association.

Samuels, S. J. (2007). The DIBELS tests: Is speed of barking at print what we mean by fluency? *Reading Research Quarterly, 42*(1), 563–566.

Samuels, S. J., & Farstrup, A. E. (2006). *What research has to say about fluency instruction.* Newark, DE: International Reading Association.

Searfoss, L. W. (1975). Radio reading. *The Reading Teacher, 29,* 295–296.

Sloyer, S. (1982). *Reader's theater: Story dramatization in the classroom.* Urbana, IL: National Council of Teachers of English.

Smith, N. B. (2002). *American reading instruction* (special ed.). Newark, DE: International Reading Association.

Stahl, S. (2004). What do we know about fluency? In P. McCardle & V. Chhabra (Eds.), *The voice of evidence in reading research* (pp. 187–211). Baltimore: Paul H. Brookes.

Stahl, S. A., Bradley, B., Smith, C. H., Kuhn, M. R., Schwanenflugel, P., Meisinger, E., et al. (2003). *Teaching children to become fluent and automatic readers.* Paper presented at the annual meeting of the American Educational Research Association, Chicago.

Stahl, S. A., & Heubach, K. (2006). Fluency-oriented reading instruction. In K. A. Dougherty Stahl & M. C. McKenna (Eds.), *Reading research at work: Foundations of effective practice* (pp. 177–204). New York: Guilford Press.

Stahl, S. A., Heubach, K., & Cramond, B. (1997). *Fluency-oriented reading instruction.* Athens, GA/Washington, DC: National Reading Research Center and U.S. Department of Education, Office of Educational Research and Improvement, Educational Resources Information Center.

Stayter, F. Z., & Allington, R. L. (1991). Fluency and the understanding of texts. *Theory into Practice, 30*(3), 143–148.

Viorst, J. (1987). *Alexander and the terrible, horrible, no good, very bad day.* New York: Aladdin.

Vygotsky, L. S. (1978). *Mind in society.* Cambridge, MA: Harvard University Press.

Wolf, M., & Katzir-Cohen, T. (2001). Reading fluency and its intervention. *Scientific Studies of Reading, 5*(3), 211–229.

Wood, K. D. (1983). A variation on an old theme: 4-way oral reading. *The Reading Teacher, 37*(1), 38–41.

Worthy, J., & Broaddus, K. (2002). Fluency beyond the primary grades: From group performance to silent, independent reading. *The Reading Teacher, 55*(4), 334–343.

Wright, G., Sherman, R., & Jones, T. B. (2010). *Developmental considerations in transferring oral reading skills to silent reading.* In E. H. Hiebert & D. R. Reutzel (Eds.), *Silent reading revisited: New directions for teachers and researchers* (pp. 57–66). Newark, DE: International Reading Association.

Zutell, J., & Rasinski, T. (1991). Training teachers to attend to their students' oral reading fluency. *Theory into Practice, 30*(3), 211–217.

Chapter 6

Adams, M. J. (1990). *Beginning to read: Thinking and learning about print.* Cambridge, MA: MIT Press.

Arter, L. M., & Nilsen, A. P. (2009). Using *Lemony Snicket* to bring smiles to your vocabulary lessons. *The Reading Teacher, 63*(3), 235–238.

Ashton-Warner, S. (1963). *Teacher.* New York: Touchstone Press.

Au, K. H. (1993). *Literacy instruction in multicultural settings.* Fort Worth, TX: Harcourt Brace.

Bear, D., Invernizzi, M., Templeton, S., & Johnston, F. (2007). *Words their way: Word study for phonics, vocabulary, and spelling instruction.* Boston: Pearson.

Beck, I. L., McKeown, M. G., & Kucan, L. (2002). *Bringing words to life: Robust vocabulary instruction.* New York: Guilford Press.

Berne, J. I., & Blachowicz, C. Z. (2008). What reading teachers say about vocabulary instruction: Voices from the classroom. *The Reading Teacher, 62*(4), 314–323.

Biemiller, A. (2006). Vocabulary development and instruction: A prerequisite for school learning. In D. K. Dickinson & S. B. Neuman (Eds.), *Handbook of early literacy* (Vol. 2) pp. 41–51. New York: Guilford Press.

Blewitt, P., Rump, K. M., Shealy, S. E., & Cook, S. A. (2009). Shared book reading: When and how questions affect young children's word learning. *Journal of Educational Psychology, 101*(2), 294–304.

Burns, M. S., Griffin, P., & Snow, C. E. (Eds.). (1999). *Starting out right: A guide to promoting children's reading success.* Committee on the Prevention of Reading Difficulties in Young Children, Commission on Behavioral and Social Sciences and Education, National Research Council. Washington, DC: National Academy Press.

Clark, E. (1993). *The lexicon in acquisition.* Cambridge, UK: Cambridge University Press.

Cobuild Staff. (2002). *Collins Cobuild new student's dictionary* (2nd ed.). Scarborough, Ontario: HarperCollins Canada.

Cooter, K. S. (2003). *Preparing middle school students for the TAKS in writing: A professional development seminar.* Dallas, TX: Seminar series presented for selected middle schools in the Dallas Independent School District. Unpublished manuscript.

Cooter, R. B. (2010). *Rousing minds to life: Ways to kindle vocabulary learning in young learners.* Truman State University Language and Literacy Conference, Kirksville, MO.

Cooter, R. B., & Cooter, K. S. (2010). *Improving content literacy in urban, high poverty middle schools: An inter-professional staff development model.* Research paper presentation at the Association of Literacy Educators and Researchers, Omaha, NE.

Cooter, R. B., Jr., Mills-House, E., Marrin, P., Mathews, B., & Campbell, S. (1999). Family and community involvement: The bedrock of reading success. *The Reading Teacher, 52*(8), 891–896.

Coxhead, A. (2000). A new academic word list. *TESOL Quarterly, 34*(2), 213–238.

Coyne, M. D., McCoach, D. B., Loftus, S., Zipoli, R., & Kapp, S. (2009). Direct vocabulary instruction in kindergarten: Teaching for breadth versus depth. *Elementary School Journal, 110*(1), 1–18.

Cunningham, A. E., & Stanovich, K. E. (1998). What reading does for the mind. *American Educator, 22,* 8–15.

Cunningham, P. M. (2000). *Phonics they use: Words for reading and writing* (3rd ed.). Boston, MA: Allyn and Bacon.

Dade County Schools. (2011). *Having a word wall vs. doing a word wall.* Miami, FL: Regional Center II. Retrieved June 6, 2010, from www.region2.dadeschools.net

Delacre, L. (1996). *Golden tales: Myths, legends and folktales from Latin America.* New York: Scholastic.

Delpit, L. D. (1988). The silenced dialogue: Power and pedagogy in educating other people's children. *Harvard Educational Review, 58*(3), 280–298.

Dickinson, D. K., & Tabors, P. O. (Eds.). (2001). *Young children learning at home and school: Beginning literacy with language.* Baltimore, MD: Paul H. Brookes.

Dunn, L., & Dunn, L. M. (1997). *Peabody picture vocabulary test—third edition* (PPVT-III). Circle Pines, MN: American Guidance Service.

Dunn, L., Lugo, D. E., Padilla, E. R., & Dunn, L. M. (1986). *Test de vocabulario en imágenes Peabody* (TVIP). Circle Pines, MN: American Guidance Service.

Flexner, S. B. (2003). *Random House Webster's unabridged dictionary.* New York: Random House.

Frayer, D., Frederick, W. C., & Klausmeir, H. J. (1969). *A schema for testing the level of concept mastery* (Working Paper No. 16). Madison: University of Wisconsin, Wisconsin Research and Development Center for Cognitive Learning.

Graves, M. F., Brunetti, G. J., & Slater, W. H. (1982). The reading vocabularies of primary grade children of varying geographic and social backgrounds. In J. A. Harris & L. A. Harris (Eds.), *New inquiries in reading research and instruction* (pp. 99–104). Rochester, NY: National Reading Conference.

Graves, M. F., & Slater, W. H. (1987). *Development of reading vocabularies in rural disadvantaged students, intercity disadvantaged students and middle class suburban students.* Paper presented at AERA conference, Washington, DC.

Hoover, H. D., Dunbar, S. B., & Frisbie, D. A. (2005). *Iowa Tests of Basic Skills (ITBS): Forms A, B, and C.* Rolling Meadows, IL: Riverside.

Johnson, D., & Pearson, P. D. (1984). *Teaching reading vocabulary.* New York: Holt, Rinehart and Winston.

Johnson, D. D. (2001). *Vocabulary in the elementary and middle school.* Boston: Allyn & Bacon.

Krashen, S. (1993). *The power of reading: Insights from the research.* Englewood, CO: Libraries Unlimited.

Lane, H. B., & Allen, S. (2010). The vocabulary-rich classroom: Modeling sophisticated word use to promote word consciousness and vocabulary growth. *The Reading Teacher, 63*(5), 362–370.

L'Engle, M. (1962). *A wrinkle in time.* New York: Dell.

Lervag, A., & Aukrust, V. G. (2010). Vocabulary knowledge is a critical determinant of the difference in reading comprehension growth between first and second language learners. *Journal of Child Psychology and Psychiatry, 51*(5), 612–620.

McKee, D. (1990). *Elmer.* London: Red Fox.

McKenna, M. C., & Stahl, S. A. (2003). *Assessment for reading instruction.* New York: Guilford Press.

McKeown, M. G., & Beck, I. L. (1988). Learning vocabulary: Different ways for different goals. *Remedial and Special Education, 9*(1), 42–52.

Murphy, M. E. (Ed.). (2004). *Longman dictionary of American English* (3rd ed.). Harlow, Essex, UK: Longman.

Nagy, W. E., Herman, P. A., & Anderson, R. C. (1985). Learning words from context. *Reading Research Quarterly, 20,* 233–253.

Nash, R. (1999). *NTC's dictionary of Spanish cognates thematically organized.* New York: McGraw-Hill.

National Reading Panel (NRP). (2000). *Report of the National Reading Panel: Teaching children to read.* Washington, DC: National Institute of Child Health and Human Development.

National Research Council. (1998). *Preventing reading difficulties in young children.* Washington, DC: National Academy Press.

Partnership for Reading (2001). *Put reading first: The research building blocks for teaching children to read.* Washington. DC: The Partnership for Reading. Report available online at www .nifl.gov/partnershipforreading

Paulsen, G. (1987). *Hatchet.* New York: Simon & Schuster.

Pearson, P., Hiebert, E. H., & Kamil, M. L. (2007, April/May/June). Vocabulary assessment: What we know and what we need to learn. *Reading Research Quarterly, 42*(2), 282–296.

Provensen, A., & Provensen, M. (1983). *The glorious flight: Across the channel with Louis Bleriot.* New York: Viking Penguin.

Putman, S. M., & Kingsley, T. (2009). The atoms family: Using podcasts to enhance the development of science vocabulary. *The Reading Teacher, 63*(2), 100–108.

Put reading first: The research building blocks for teaching children to read. (2001). Washington, DC: The Partnership for Reading. Available online at www.nifl.gov/partnershipforreading

Rance-Roney, J. (2010). Jump-starting language and schema for English-language learners: Teacher-composed digital jumpstarts for academic reading. *Journal of Adolescent & Adult Literacy, 53*(5), 386–395.

Rasinski, T. (1998, September). *Reading to learn: Vocabulary development strategies.* Paper presented at the Fall Session of the Dallas Reading Plan Grades 4–6 Professional Development Series, Dallas, TX.

Rasinski, T. V. (2010). *The fluent reader.* New York: Scholastic.

Reutzel, D. R., & Cooter, R. B. (2011). *Strategies for reading assessment and instruction: Helping every child succeed* (4th ed.). Boston: Pearson/Allyn & Bacon.

Reutzel, D. R., & Cooter, R. B. (2007). *Strategies for reading assessment and instruction: Helping every child succeed* (3rd ed.). Upper Saddle River, NJ: Merrill/Prentice Hall.

Reutzel, D. R., & Fawson, P. C. (1990). Traveling tales: Connecting parents and children in writing. *The Reading Teacher, 44,* 222–227.

Rowling, J. K. (2009). *Harry Potter and the deathly hallows.* New York: Arthur A. Levine Books/Scholastic.

Rupley, W. H., Logan, J. W., & Nichols, W. D. (1998/1999). Vocabulary instruction in a balanced reading program. *The Reading Teacher, 52*(4), 336–346.

Rupley, W. H., Blair, T. R., & Nichols, W. D. (2009). Effective reading instruction for struggling readers: The role of direct/explicit teaching. *Reading & Writing Quarterly, 25*(2–3), 125–138.

Sanacore, J., & Palumbo, A. (2009). Understanding the fourth-grade slump: Our point of view. *Educational Forum, 73*(1), 67–74.

Schwartz, R. M., & Raphael, T. E. (1985). Concept of definition: A key to improving students' vocabulary. *The Reading Teacher, 39*(2), 198–205.

Sinatra, R. C., Stahl-Gemake, J., & Berg, W. (1984). Improving reading comprehension of disabled readers through semantic mapping. *Reading Teacher, 38*(1), 22–29.

Smith, F. (1987). *Insult to intelligence.* New York: Arbor House.

Snicket, L. (2000). *The ersatz elevator: Book the sixth.* New York: HarperCollins.

Snicket, L. (2001). *The hostile hospital: Book the eighth.* New York: HarperCollins.

Stahl, S. A. (1986). Three principles of effective vocabulary instruction. *Journal of Reading, 29*(7), 662–668.

Stahl, S. A., Hare, V. C., Sinatra, R., & Gregory, J. F. (1991). Defining the role of prior knowledge and vocabulary in reading comprehension: The retiring of number 41. *Journal of Reading Behavior, 23*(4), 487–507.

Stahl, S., & Nagy, W. (2006). *Teaching word meanings.* Mahwah, NJ: Lawrence Erlbaum.

Taylor, D. B., Mraz, M., Nichols, W. D., Rickelman, R. J., & Wood, K. D. (2009). Using explicit instruction to promote vocabulary learning for struggling readers. *Reading & Writing Quarterly, 25*(2–3), 205–220.

Townsend, D. (2009). Building academic vocabulary in after-school settings: games for growth with middle school english-language learners. *Journal of Adolescent & Adult Literacy, 53*(3), 242–251.

Trelease, J. (2009). *The read aloud handbook* (6th ed.). New York: Penguin.

Webb, S. A. (2009). The effects of pre-learning vocabulary on reading comprehension and writing. *Canadian Modern Language Review, 65*(3), 441–470.

Wheatley, E. A., Muller, D. H., & Miller, R. B. (1993). Computer-assisted vocabulary instruction. *Journal of Reading, 37*(2), 92–102.

Williams, K. (1997). *Expressive vocabulary test.* Circle Pines, MN: American Guidance Service.

Winters, R. (2009). Interactive frames for vocabulary growth and word consciousness. *The Reading Teacher, 62*(8), 685–690.

Wood, A. (1990). *Weird parents.* New York: Dial Books for Young Readers.

Woodcock, R. W., McGrew, K. S., & Mather, N. (2001). *Woodcock-Johnson tests of achievement* (WJ III). Rolling Meadows, IL: Riverside.

Woodcock, R. W., & Muñoz-Sandoval, A. F. (1993). *Woodcock-Muñoz language survey (WMLS)*, English and Spanish forms. Chicago: Riverside.

Yopp, R. H., & Yopp, H. K. (2000). *Literature-based reading activities* (3rd ed.). Boston: Allyn & Bacon.

Chapter 7

Allington, R. L. (2006). Fluency: Still waiting after all these years. In S. J. Samuels & A. E. Farstrup (Eds.), *What research has to say about fluency instruction* (pp. 94–105). Newark, DE: International Reading Association.

Anderson, R., & Pearson, P. (1984). *A schema-theoretic view of basic processes in reading comprehension.* Technical Report No. 306. Retrieved from ERIC database.

Barrett, T. (1972). Taxonomy of reading comprehension. *Reading 360 Monograph.* Boston: Ginn.

Beck, I. L. (1986). Using research on reading. *Educational Leadership, 43*(7), 13–15.

Beck, I. L., & McKeown, M. G. (2001). Text talk: Capturing the benefits of read-aloud experiences for young children. *Reading Teacher, 55*(1), 10–20.

Beck, I., & McKeown, M. (2006). *Improving comprehension with questioning the author: A fresh and expanded view of a powerful approach.* New York: Scholastic.

Biddulph, F., & Biddulph, J. (1992). *How do spiders live?* Bothell, WA: The Wright Group.

Bleich, D. (1978). *Subjective criticism*. Baltimore: Johns Hopkins University Press.

Bloom, B. (1956). *Taxonomy of educational objectives*. New York: David McKay.

Brown, A. L., Day, J. D., & Jones, R. S. (1983). The development of plans for summarizing texts. *Child Development, 54,* 968–979.

Brown, H., & Cambourne, B. (1987). *Read and retell*. Portsmouth, NH: Heinemann.

Brozo, W. (2010). The role of content literacy in an effective RTI program. *The Reading Teacher, 64*(2), 147–150.

Carr, E. (1985). The vocabulary overview guide: A metacognitive strategy to improve vocabulary comprehension and retention. *Journal of Reading, 28*(8), 684–689.

Christensen, K. R. (2010). Syntactic reconstruction and reanalysis, semantic dead ends, and prefrontal cortex. *Brain & Cognition, 73*(1), 41–50.

Clyne, M., & Griffiths, R. (2005). *Sand*. Parsippany, NJ: Pearson Education.

Coleman, E. (1996). *White socks only*. Morton Grove, IL: Albert Whitman.

Collins, A. M., & Quillian, M. R. (1969). Retrieval time from semantic memory. *Journal of Verbal Learning and Verbal Behavior, 8,* 240–247.

Collins, A., & Smith, E. (1980). *Teaching the process of reading comprehension* (Tech. Rep. No. 182). Urbana-Champaign: University of Illinois at Urbana-Champaign, Center for the Study of Reading.

Cooter, R. B. (2004). The pillars of urban literacy instruction: Prerequisites for change. In R. B. Cooter (Ed.), *Perspectives on rescuing urban literacy education: Spies, saboteurs, and saints*. Mahwah, NJ: Lawrence Erlbaum.

Cooter, R. B., Flynt, E. S., & Cooter, K. S. (2007). *The comprehensive reading inventory: Measuring reading development in regular and special education classrooms*. Boston: Pearson Education.

Cutting, B., & Cutting, J. (2002). *Is it a fish?* Sunshine Science Series. Bothell, WA: Wright Group/McGraw-Hill Publishing.

Dewitz, P., Jones, J., & Leahy, S. (2009, April/May/June). Comprehension strategy instruction in core reading programs. *Reading Research Quarterly, 44*(2), 102–126.

Dickinson, D. K., & Smith, M. W. (1994). Long-term effects of preschool teachers' book readings on low-income children's vocabulary and story comprehension. *Reading Research Quarterly, 29,* 104–122.

Donovan, C. A., & Smolkin, L. B. (2002). Considering genre, context, and visual features in the selection of trade books for science instruction. *The Reading Teacher, 55*(6), 502–520.

Duffy, G. G. (2003). *Explaining reading: A resource for teaching concepts, skills, and strategies*. New York: Guilford Press.

Duke, N. K., & Bennett-Armistead, V. S. (2003). *Reading and writing informational text in the primary grades: Research-based practices*. New York: Scholastic.

Durkin, D. (1978). What classroom observations reveal about reading comprehension instruction. *Reading Research Quarterly, 14*(4), 482–533.

Dymock, S., & Nicholson, T. (2010). High five! Strategies to enhance comprehension of expository text. *The Reading Teacher, 24*(3), 166–178.

El-Dinary, P. B. (2002). Challenges implementing transactional strategies instruction for reading comprehension. In C. Collins-Block & M. Pressley (Eds.), *Comprehension instruction: Research-based best practices* (pp. 201–218). New York: Guilford Press.

Gambrell, L. B., & Almasi, J. F. (1996). *Lively discussions: Fostering engaged reading*. Newark, DE: International Reading Association.

Gambrell, L. B., Pfeiffer, W., & Wilson, R. (1985). The effects of retelling upon reading comprehension and recall of text information. *Journal of Educational Research, 78,* 216–220.

Hare, V. C, & Borchordt, K. M. (1984). Direct instruction of summarization skills. *Reading Research Quarterly, 20*(1), 62–78.

Institute of Education Sciences (IES). (2010, April). *WWC intervention report: Dialogic reading*. Washington, DC: What Works Clearinghouse.

Kelley, M. J., & Clausen-Grace, N. (2007). *Comprehension shouldn't be silent: From strategy instruction to student independence*. Newark, DE: International Reading Association.

Kelly, M., & Clausen-Grace, N. (2010). Using a text feature walk to guide students through expository text. *The Reading Teacher, 64*(3).

Kintsch, W. (2004). The construction-integration model of text comprehension and its implications for instruction. In R. B. Ruddell & N. J. Unrau (Eds.), *Theoretical models and processes of reading* (5th ed., pp. 94–120). Newark, DE: International Reading Association.

Krauss, R. (1945). *The carrot seed*. New York: Scholastic.

Lapp, D., Fisher, D., & Johnson, K. (2010). Text mapping plus: Improving comprehension through supported retellings. *Journal of Adolescent & Adult Literacy, 53*(5), 423–426.

Leu, D. J., Coiro, J., Castek, J., Hartman, D., Henry, L. A., & Reinking, D. (2008). Research on instruction and assessment in the new literacies of online reading comprehension. In C. Collins-Block, S. Parris, & P. Afflerbach (Eds.), *Comprehension instruction: Research-based best practices*. New York: Guilford Press.

Lindsay, P. H., & Norman, D. A. (1977). *Human information processing: An introduction to psychology*. New York: Academic Press.

Manyak, P. C., & Bauer, E. B. (2008). Explicit code and comprehension instruction for English learners. *The Reading Teacher, 61*(5), 432–434.

Marcell, B., DeCleene, J., & Juettner, M. (2010). Caution! Hard hat area! Comprehension under construction: Cementing a foundation of comprehension strategy usage that carries over to independent practice. *The Reading Teacher, 63*(8), 687–691.

McGee, L. M. (1982). Awareness of text structure: Effects on children's recall of expository text. *Reading Research Quarterly, 17*(4), 581–590.

McKeown, M. G., Beck, I. L., & Blake, R. K. (2009, July/August/September). Rethinking reading comprehension instruction: A comparison of instruction for strategies and content approaches. *Reading Research Quarterly, 44*(3), 218–253.

McKeown, M. G., Beck, I. L., & Worthy, M. J. (1993). Grappling with text ideas: Questioning the author. *The Reading Teacher, 46*(7), 560–565.

McMahon, S. I., & Raphael, T. E. (1997). *The book club connection: Literacy learning and classroom talk*. New York: Teachers College Press.

Meyers, P. A. (2006). The princess storyteller, Clara clarifier, Quincy questioner, and the wizard: Reciprocal teaching adapted for kindergarten students. *The Reading Teacher, 59*(4), 314–325.

Mills, K. A. (2009). Floating on a sea of talk: Reading comprehension through speaking and listening. *The Reading Teacher, 63*(4), 325–329.

Morrow, L. M. (1985). Retelling stories: A strategy for improving children's comprehension, concept of story structure, and oral language complexity. *Elementary School Journal, 85,* 647–661.

Morrow, L. M. (2005). *Literacy development in the early years: Helping children read and write* (5th ed.). Boston: Allyn & Bacon.

Moss, B. (1997). A qualitative assessment of first graders' retelling of expository text. *Reading Research and Instruction, 37*(1), 1–13.

National Reading Panel (NRP). (2000). *Report of the National Reading Panel: Teaching children to read.* Washington, DC: National Institute of Child Health and Human Development.

Noyce, R. M., & Christie, J. F. (1989). *Integrating reading and writing instruction.* Boston: Allyn & Bacon.

Oczkus, L. (2003). *Reciprocal teaching at work: Strategies for improving reading comprehension.* Newark, DE: International Reading Association.

Palincsar, A. M. (2003). Collaborative approaches to comprehension instruction. In C. E. Snow & A. P. Sweet (Eds.), *Rethinking reading comprehension* (pp. 99–114). New York: Guilford Press.

Palincsar, A. S. (1986). Reciprocal teaching. In *Teaching reading as thinking.* Oak Brook, IL: North Central Regional Educational Laboratory.

Palincsar, A. S., & Brown, A. L. (1984). Reciprocal teaching of comprehension-fostering and comprehension-monitoring activities. *Cognition and Instruction, 1,* 117–175.

Paris, S. G., & Stahl, S. A. (2005). *Children's reading comprehension and assessment.* Mahwah, NJ: Lawrence Erlbaum.

Paris, S. G., Wasik, B., & Turner, J. C. (1991). The development of strategic readers. In R. Barr, M. L. Kamil, P. Mosenthal, & P. D. Pearson (Eds.), *Handbook of reading research, Vol. II* (pp. 641–668). New York: Longman.

Parsons, L. (1990). *Response journals.* Portsmouth, NH: Heinemann.

Pereira-Laird, J. A., & Deane, F. P. (1997). Development and validation of a self-report measure of reading strategy use. *Reading Psychology, 18*(3), 185–235.

Peterson, R., & Eeds, M. (1990). *Grand conversations: Literature groups in action.* New York: Scholastic.

Potter, B. (1986). *The tale of Peter Rabbit.* New York: Scholastic.

Pressley, M. (2000). What should comprehension instruction be the instruction of? In M. L. Kamil, P. B. Mosenthal, P. D. Pearson, & R. Barr (Eds.), *Handbook of reading research* (Vol. 3, pp. 545–561). Mahwah, NJ: Erlbaum.

Pressley, M. (2002). Comprehension strategies instruction: A turn-of-the-century status report. In C. Collins-Block & M. Pressley (Eds.), *Comprehension instruction: Research-based best practices* (pp. 11–27). New York: Guilford Press.

Pressley, M. (2006). *Reading instruction that works: The case for balanced teaching* (3rd ed.). New York: Guilford Press.

Pressley, M., Gaskin, I. W., Wile, D., Cunicelli, E. A., & Sheridan, J. (1991). Teaching literacy strategies across the curriculum: A case study at Benchmark School. In J. Zutell & S. McCormick (Eds.), *Learner factors/teacher factors: Issues in literacy research and instruction: Fortieth yearbook of the National Reading Conference* (pp. 219–228). Chicago: National Reading Conference.

RAND Reading Study Group. (2002). *Reading for understanding: Toward an R&D program in reading comprehension.* Santa Monica, CA: RAND.

Raphael, T. E. (1982). Question-answering strategies for children. *The Reading Teacher, 36,* 186–191.

Raphael, T. E. (1986). Teaching question answer relationships, revisited. *The Reading Teacher, 39*(6), 516–523.

Raphael, T. E., & Au, K. H. (2005). QAR: Enhancing comprehension and test-taking across grade and content areas. *The Reading Teacher, 59*(3), 206–221.

Raphael, T., & Pearson, P. D. (1985). Increasing students' awareness of sources of information for answering questions. *American Educational Research Journal, 22*(2), 217–235.

Reinking, D., & Castek, J. (2007, November). *Developing Internet comprehension to adolescents who are at risk to become dropouts: A three-year IES research grant.* Paper presented at the National Reading Conference. Austin, TX.

Reutzel, D. R., & Cooter, R. B. (2000). *Teaching children to read: Putting the pieces together* (3rd ed.). Upper Saddle River, NJ: Merrill/Prentice Hall.

Reutzel, D. R., & Cooter, R. B. (2011). *Strategies for reading assessment and instruction: Helping every child succeed* (4th ed.). Boston: Pearson/Allyn & Bacon.

Reutzel, D. R., & Fawson, P. C. (1989). Using a literature webbing strategy lesson with predictable books. *The Reading Teacher, 43*(3), 208–215.

Reutzel, D. R., & Fawson, P. C. (1991). Literature webbing predictable books: A prediction strategy that helps below-average, first-grade readers. *Reading Research and Instruction, 30*(4), 20–30.

Reutzel, D. R., Smith, J. A., & Fawson, P. C. (2005). An evaluation of two approaches for teaching reading comprehension strategies in the primary years using science information texts. *Early Childhood Research Quarterly, 20,* 276–305.

Richgels, D. J., & Wold, L. S. (1998). Literacy on the road: Backpacking partnerships between school and home. *The Reading Teacher, 52*(1), 18–29.

Rinehart, S. D., Stahl, S. A., & Erickson, L. G. (1986). Some effects of summarization training on reading and studying. *Reading Research Quarterly, 21*(4), 422–438.

Ring, S. (2003). *Bridges.* Boston, MA: Newbridge.

Rosenblatt, L. M. (1978). *The reader, the text, and the poem.* Carbondale, IL: Southern Illinois University Press.

Rosenblatt, L. M. (1989). Writing and reading: The transactional theory. In J. M. Mason (Ed.), *Reading and writing connections* (pp. 153–175). Boston: Allyn & Bacon.

Rosenblatt, L. M. (2004). The transactional theory of reading and writing. In R. B. Ruddell & N. J. Unrau (Eds.), *Theoretical models and processes of reading* (5th ed., pp. 1363–1398). NWP Publications.

Rosenshine, B., & Meister, C. (1994). Reciprocal teaching: A review of nineteen experimental studies. *Review of Educational Research, 64,* 479–530.

Rumelhart, D. E. (1981). Schemata: The building blocks of cognition. In J. T. Guthrie (Ed.), *Comprehension and teaching: Research reviews* (pp. 3–26). Newark, DE: International Reading Association.

Seidenberg, P. L. (1989). Relating text-processing research to reading and writing instruction for learning disabled students. *Learning Disabilities Focus, 5*(1), 4–12.

Shanahan, T., & Beck, I. L. (2006). Effective literacy teaching for English-language learners. In D. August & T. Shanahan (Eds.),

Developing literacy in second-language learners: Report of the National Literacy Panel on language-minority children and youth (pp. 415–488). Mahwah, NJ: Lawrence Erlbaum.

Shonkoff, J. P., & Phillips, D. A. (2000). *From neurons to neighborhoods: The science of early childhood development.* Washington, DC: John Henry Press.

Shore, R. (1997). *Rethinking the brain: New insights into early development.* New York: Families and Work Institute.

Shulman, L. (2001). *Ways of measuring: Then and now.* Northborough, MA: Sundance Publishers.

Stahl, K. A. D. (2009). Assessing the comprehension of young children. In S. E. Israel and G. G. Duffy (Eds.), *Handbook of research on reading comprehension* (pp. 428–448). New York: Routledge.

Taba, H. (1975). *Teacher's handbook for elementary social studies.* Reading, MA: Addison-Wesley.

Tompkins, G. E. (2006). *Literacy for the 21st century: A balanced approach.* Upper Saddle River, NJ: Merrill/Prentice Hall.

Turner, J., & Paris, S. (1995). How literacy tasks influence children's motivation for literacy. *The Reading Teacher, 48*(8), 662–673.

van Dijk, T. A. (1999). *Context models in discourse processing.* Mahwah, NJ: Lawrence Erlbaum.

Vlach, S., & Burcie, J. (2010). Narratives of the struggling reader. *The Reading Teacher, 63*(6), 522–525.

Wang, S., & Morris, R. G. M. (2010). Hippocampal-neocortical interactions in memory formation, consolidation, and reconsolidation. *Annual Review of Psychology, 61*(1), 49–79.

Whaley, J. F. (1981). Readers' expectations for story structures. *Reading Research Quarterly, 17,* 90–114.

Williams, J. P. (2005). Instruction in reading comprehension for primary-grade students: A focus on text structure. *Journal of Special Education, 39*(1), 6–18.

Zarillo, J. (1989). Teachers' interpretations of literature-based reading. *The Reading Teacher, 43*(1), 22–29.

Zwann, R. A. (1999). Embodied cognition, perceptual symbols, and situated cognition. *Discourse Processes, 28*(1), 81–88.

Chapter 8

Akhavan, N. (2008). *The content-rich reading & writing workshop.* New York: Scholastic.

American people, The (Grade 6). (1982). New York: American.

Ashton-Warner, S. (1963). *Teacher.* New York: Touchstone Press.

Atwell, N. (1987). *In the middle: Writing, reading, and learning with adolescents.* Portsmouth, NH: Heinemann.

Bear, D. R., Invernizzi, M., Templeton, S., & Johnston, F. (2000). *Words their way: Word study for phonics, vocabulary, and spelling instruction* (2nd ed.). Upper Saddle River, NJ: Merrill/Prentice Hall.

Burns, M. S., Griffin, P., & Snow, C. E. (Eds.). (1999). *Starting out right: A guide to promoting children's reading success.* Committee on the Prevention of Reading Difficulties in Young Children, Commission on Behavioral and Social Sciences and Education, National Research Council. Washington, DC: National Academy Press.

Calkins, L. (1986). *The art of teaching writing.* Portsmouth, NH: Heinemann.

Calkins, L. (1994). *The art of teaching writing.* Westport, CT: Heinemann.

Carle, E. (1986). *The very hungry caterpillar.* New York: Scholastic.

Clay, M. M. (1975). *What did I write? Beginning writing behaviour.* Portsmouth, NH: Heinemann.

Clay, M. M. (1987). *Writing begins at home: Preparing children for writing before they go to school.* Portsmouth, NH: Heinemann.

Coady, M., & Escamilla, K. (2005). Audible voices, visible tongues: Exploring social realities in Spanish-speaking students' writing. *Language Arts, 82*(6), 462–471.

Common Core Standards Initiative. (2010). *The common core state standards for English language arts & literacy in history/social studies, science, and technical subjects.* Washington, DC: The Council of Chief State School Officers and the National Governors Association.

Cooter, K. S. (2006). *Tinkertoy writing: A systematic approach for grades K–5.* Unpublished manuscript.

Cooter, R. B. (2002). *Systemic reform efforts in a large urban school district: Implementing balanced literacy instruction.* Keynote address presented at the Balanced Reading Special Interest Group session, 47th Annual Conference of the International Reading Association, San Francisco, CA.

Córdova, R. A., & Matthiesen, A. L. (2010, March). Reading, writing, and mapping our worlds into being: Shared teacher inquiries into whose literacies count. *The Reading Teacher, 63*(6), 452–463.

Culham, R. (2010). *Traits of writing.* New York: Scholastic.

Cunningham, P. M. (2000). *Phonics they use: Words for reading and writing* (3rd ed.). Boston: Allyn & Bacon.

Diederich, P. B. (1974). *Measuring growth in English.* Urbana, IL: National Council of Teachers of English.

Edelsky, C. (1986). *Writing in a bilingual program: Había una vez.* Norwood, NJ: Ablex.

Engel, T., & Streich, R. (2006, April). Yes, there is room for soup in the curriculum: Achieving accountability in a collaboratively planned writing program. *The Reading Teacher, 59*(7), 660–679.

Evers, A. J., Lang, L. F., & Smith, S. V. (2009, March). An ABC literacy journey: Anchoring in texts, bridging language, and creating stories. *The Reading Teacher, 62*(6), 461–470.

Fisher, D., & Frey, N. (2008). *Improving adolescent literacy: Content area strategies at work* (2nd ed.). Upper Saddle River, NJ: Pearson/Prentice Hall.

Gammill, D. M. (2006, May). Learning the write way. *The Reading Teacher, 59*(8), 754–762.

Gibson, S. A. (2008, December). An effective framework for primary-grade guided writing instruction. *The Reading Teacher, 62*(4), 324–334.

Gipe, J. P. (2006). *Multiple paths to literacy: Assessment and differentiated instruction for diverse learners, K–12.* Upper Saddle River, NJ: Merrill/Prentice Hall.

Glasswell, K., & Kamberelis, G. (2007, April/May/June). Drawing and redrawing the map of writing studies. *Reading Research Quarterly, 42*(2), 304–323.

Graham, S., & Perin, D. (2007). A meta-analysis of writing instruction for adolescent students. *Journal of Educational Psychology, 99*(3), 445–476.

Graves, D. H. (1983). *Writing: Teachers and children at work.* Portsmouth, NH: Heinemann.

Gunning, T. G. (2006). *Assessing and correcting reading and writing difficulties* (3rd ed.). Boston: Allyn & Bacon.

Hampton, S., Murphy, S., & Lowry, M. (2009). *Using rubrics to improve student writing.* Newark, DE: International Reading Association.

Hampton, S., & Resnick, L. B. (2009a). Effective writing. In *Reading and writing with understanding* (pp. 55–72). Newark, DE: National Center on Education and the Economy and University of Pittsburgh.

Hampton, S., & Resnick, L. B. (2009b). *Reading and writing with understanding*. Newark, DE: International Reading Association.

Heilman, A. W., Blair, T. R., & Rupley, W. H. (2001). *Principles and practices of teaching reading* (10th ed.). Upper Saddle River, NJ: Merrill/Prentice Hall.

Hidi, S., & Boscolo, P. (2006). Motivation and writing. In C. A. MacAuthur, S. Graham, & J. Fitzgerald (Eds.), *Handbook of writing research* (pp. 144–157). New York: Guilford.

Holdaway, D. (1984). *Stability and change in literacy learning*. Portsmouth, NH: Heinemann.

Hsu, C. (2009, October). Writing partnerships. *The Reading Teacher, 63*(2), 153–158.

Jones, C. D., Reutzel, D. R., & Fargo, J. D. (2010). Comparing two methods of writing instruction: Effects on kindergarten students' reading skills. *The Journal of Educational Research, 103*(5), 327–341.

Juel, C., & Minden-Cupp, C. (2004). Learning to read words: Linguistic units and instructional strategies. In R. B. Ruddell & N. J. Unrau (Eds.), *Theoretical models and processes of reading* (5th ed., pp. 313–364). Newark, DE: International Reading Association.

Jurand, E. K. (2009). Camp Imagination: A summer writing tutoring program for students at risk. In J. C. Richards, & C. A. Lassonde (Eds.), *Literacy Tutoring That Works* (pp. 172–181). Newark, DE: International Reading Association.

Kara-Soteriou, J., Zawilinski, L., & Henry, L. A. (2007, April). Children's books and technology in the classroom: A dynamic combo for supporting the writing workshop. *The Reading Teacher, 60*(7), 698–707.

Larson, L. C. (2009). Reader response meets new literacies: Empowering readers in online learning communities. *The Reading Teacher, 62*(8), 638–648.

Loban, W. D. (1964). *Language ability: Grades seven, eight, and nine*. Berkeley, CA: University of California. [ERIC Ed 001275.]

Mallozzi, C. A., & Malloy, J. A. (2007). Reading and writing connections. *Reading Research Quarterly, 42*(1), 161–166.

Mason, L. H., Benedek-Wood, E., & Valasa, L. (2009, December). Teaching low-achieving students to self-regulate persuasive quick write responses. *Journal of Adolescent & Adult Literacy, 53*(4), 303–312.

Mason, J., Herman, P. A., & Au, K. H. (1991). Reading: Children's developing knowledge of words. In J. Flood, J. M. Jensen, D. Lapp, & J. R. Squire (Eds.), *Handbook of research on teaching the language arts*. New York: Macmillan.

McCarrier, A., Pinnell, G. S., & Fountas, I. C. (1999). *Interactive writing: How language and literacy come together, K–2*. Portsmouth, NH: Heinemann.

Merrill Mathematics (Grade 5). (1985). Upper Saddle River, NJ: Merrill/Prentice Hall.

Merrill Science (Grade 3). (1989). Upper Saddle River, NJ: Merrill/Prentice Hall.

Meyer, B. J. F., & Freedle, R. O. (1984). Effects of discourse type on recall. *American Educational Research Journal, 21*(1), 121–143.

Montelongo, J., Herter, R. J., Ansaldo, R., & Hatter, N. (2010, May). A lesson cycle for teaching expository reading and writing. *Journal of Adolescent & Adult Literacy, 53*(8), 656–666.

Morgan, B., & Smith, R. D. (2008). A wiki for classroom writing. *The Reading Teacher, 62*(1), 80–82.

Moskal, B. M. (2003). *Developing classroom performance assessments and scoring rubrics: Part II*. College Park, MD: ERIC Clearinghouse on Assessment and Evaluation. [ED 481715.]

National Institute for Literacy. (2007). *What content-area teachers should know about adolescent literacy*. Jessup, MD: Author.

Ogle, D. M. (1986). K-W-L: A teaching model that develops active reading of expository text. *The Reading Teacher, 39*(6), 564–570.

Payne, C. D., & Schulman, M. B. (1998). *Getting the most out of morning message and other shared writing lessons*. New York: Scholastic.

Reutzel, D. R., & Cooter, R. B., Jr. (1990). Whole language: Comparative effects on first-grade reading achievement. *Journal of Educational Research, 83*, 252–257.

Reutzel, D. R., & Cooter, R. B. (2011). *Strategies for reading assessment and instruction: Helping every child succeed* (4th ed.). Boston: Allyn & Bacon.

Reutzel, D. R., & Fawson, P. C. (1990). Traveling tales: Connecting parents and children in writing. *The Reading Teacher, 44*, 222–227.

Reutzel, D. R., & Fawson, P. C. (1998). Global literacy connections: Stepping into the future. *Think, 8*(2), 32–34.

Routman, R. (1995). *Invitations*. Portsmouth, NH: Heinemann.

Rubin, R., & Carlan, V. (2005, May). Using writing to understand bilingual children's literacy development. *The Reading Teacher, 58*(8), 728–739.

Salahu-Din, D., Persky, H., & Miller, J. (2008). *The nation's report card: Writing 2007* (NCES 2008-468). Washington, DC: National Center for Education Statistics, Institute of Education Sciences, U.S. Department of Education.

Shanahan, T. (2006). Relations among oral language, reading, and writing development. In C. A. MacArthur, S. Graham, & J. Fitzgerald (Eds.), *Handbook of writing research* (pp. 171–186). New York: Guilford Press.

Shermis, M. D., Burstein, J., & Leacock, C. (2006). Applications of computers in assessment and analysis of writing. In C. A. MacArthur, S. Graham, & J. Fitzgerald (Eds.), *Handbook of writing research*. New York: Guilford.

Sloan, M. S. (2008). *Teaching young writers to elaborate*. New York: Scholastic.

Spence, L. K. (2010, May). Generous reading: Seeing students through their writing. *The Reading Teacher, 63*(8), 634–642.

Stead, T. (2001). *Is that a fact? Teaching nonfiction writing K–3*. Portland, ME: Stenhouse.

Stead, T. (2006). *The use of non-fiction informational text in developing comprehension*. Presentation at the Texas State Reading Association Annual Conference, November 11, 2006.

Sylvester, R., & Greenidge, W. (2009, December). Digital storytelling: Extending the potential for struggling writers. *The Reading Teacher, 63*(4), 284–295.

Teale, W. H. (1987). Emergent literacy: Reading and writing development in early childhood. In J. E. Readence, R. S. Baldwin, J. P. Konopak, & H. Newton (Eds.), *Research in literacy: Merging perspectives* (pp. 45–74). Rochester, NY: National Reading Conference.

Temple, C., Nathan, R., Burris, N., & Temple, F. (1993). *The beginnings of writing* (3rd ed.). Boston: Allyn & Bacon.

Templeton, S. (1995). *Children's literacy: Contexts for meaningful learning*. Princeton, NJ: Houghton Mifflin.

Tierney, R. J., & Shanahan, T. (1996). Research on the reading–writing relationship: Interactions, transactions, and outcomes. In R. Barr, M. L. Kamil, P. Mosenthal, & P. D. Pearson (Eds.), *Handbook of reading research* (Vol. 2, pp. 246–280). Mahwah, NJ: Erlbaum.

Tompkins, G. E. (2004). *Teaching writing: Balancing process and product* (4th ed.). Upper Saddle River, NJ: Pearson/Merrill/Prentice Hall.

Trosclair. (2000). *Cajun night before Christmas.* Gretna, LA: Pelican.

United States and the other Americas, The (Grade 5). (1980). Upper Saddle River, NJ: Merrill/Prentice Hall.

United States: Its history and neighbors, The (Grade 5). (1985). San Diego. CA: Harcourt Brace.

Vygotsky, L. S. (1962). *Thought and language.* Cambridge, MA: MIT Press.

Wall, H. (2008, October). Interactive writing beyond the primary grades. *The Reading Teacher, 62*(2), 149–152.

Williams, J. P. (2005). Instruction in reading comprehension for primary-grade students: A focus on text structure. *Journal of Special Education, 39*(1), 6–18.

Wilson, A. (2008, March). Motivating young writers through write-talks: Real writers, real audiences, real purposes. *The Reading Teacher, 61*(6), 485–487.

Yellin, D., & Blake, M. E. (1994). *Integrating language arts: A holistic approach.* New York: Harper-Collins.

Zawilinski, L. (2009, May). HOT Blogging: A framework for blogging to promote higher order thinking. *The Reading Teacher, 62*(8), 650–661.

Chapter 9

Allington, R. L. (1992). How to get information on several proven programs for accelerating the progress of low-achieving children. *The Reading Teacher, 46*(3), 246–248.

Allington, R. L. (1997, August–September). Overselling phonics. *Reading Today, 14*, 15.

Allington, R. L., & Cunningham, P. M. (2006). *Schools that work: Where all children read and write.* Boston: Allyn and Bacon.

Armbruster, B. B. (1984). The problem of "inconsiderate text." In G. G. Duffy, L. R. Roehler, & J. Mason (Eds.), *Comprehension instruction: Perspective and suggestions.* New York: Longman.

Asher, S. R. (1980). Topic interest and children's reading comprehension. In R. J. Spiro, B. C. Bruce, & W. F. Brewer (Eds.), *Theoretical issues in reading comprehension* (pp. 525–534). Hillsdale, NJ: Erlbaum.

August, D., & Shanahan, T. (2006). *Developing literacy in second-language learners: A report of the National Literacy Panel on language-minority children and youth.* Mahwah, NJ: Lawrence Erlbaum Associates.

Baines, L. A., & Stanley, G. K. (2006). The iatrogenic consequences of standards-based education. *The Clearing House, 79*(3), 119–123.

Block, C. C., & Duffy, G. G. (2008). Research on teaching comprehension: Where we've been and where we're going. In C. C. Block & S. R. Parris (Eds.), *Comprehension instruction: Research-based best practices* (pp. 19–37). New York: Guilford Press.

Clay, M. M. (1990a). The Reading Recovery Programme, 1984–88: Coverage, outcomes and Education Board district figures. *New Zealand Journal of Educational Studies, 25*, 61–70.

Clay, M. M. (1990b). What is and what might be in evaluation (Research currents). *Language Arts, 67*(3), 288–298.

Cohen, M. (1980). *First grade takes a test.* New York: Dell Books.

Common Core State Standards Initiative. (2010). Retrieved June 22, 2010, from www.corestandards.org.

Corno, L., & Randi, J. (1997). Motivation, volition, and collaborative innovation in classroom literacy. In J. T. Guthrie & A. Wigfield (Eds.), *Reading engagement: Motivating readers through integrated instruction* (pp. 51–67). Newark, DE: International Reading Association.

DeFord, D. E., Lyons, C. A., & Pinnell, G. S. (1991). *Bridges to literacy: Learning from Reading Recovery.* Portsmouth, NH: Heinemann.

Dewitz, P., Jones, J., & Leahy, S. (2009). Comprehension strategy instruction in core reading programs. *Reading Research Quarterly, 44*(2), 102–106.

Dewitz, P., Leahy, S. B., Jones, J., & Sullivan, P. M. (2010). *The essential guide to selecting and using core reading programs.* Newark, DE: International Reading Association.

Dole, J. A., Osborn, J., & Lehr, F. (1990). *A guide to selecting basal reader programs.* Urbana-Champaign, IL: Center for the Study of Reading.

Duke, N. K. (2000). 3.6 minutes per day: The scarcity of informational texts in first grade. *Reading Research Quarterly, 35*(2), 202–224.

Durkin, D. (1984). Is there a match between what elementary teachers do and what basal reader manuals recommend? *The Reading Teacher, 37*, 734–745.

Dyer, P. C. (1992). Reading Recovery: A cost effectiveness and educational-outcomes analysis. *ERS Spectrum, 10*, 10–19.

Education Market Research. (2007). *Elementary reading market: Teaching methods, textbooks/materials used and needed, and market size.* Rockaway Park, NY: Author.

Finchler, J. (2000). *Testing Miss Malarkey.* New York: Walker & Company.

Florida Center for Reading Research. (n.d.) *Scott Foresman Early Reading Intervention* [Review]. Retrieved June 16, 2010, from www.fcrr.org/FCRRReports/PDF/SF_ERI_Report.pdf

Foorman, B. R., Francis, D. J., Fletcher, J. M., Schatschneider, C., & Mehta, P. (1998). The role of instruction in learning to read: Preventing reading failure in at-risk children. *Journal of Educational Psychology, 90*(1), 37–55.

Fountas, I. C., & Pinnell, G. S. (1999). *Matching books to readers: Using leveled books in reading, K–3.* Portsmouth, NH: Heinemann.

Freeman, D. E., & Freeman, Y. S. (2000). *Teaching reading in multilingual classrooms.* Portsmouth, NH: Heinemann.

Freeman, Y. S., & Freeman, D. E. (1992). *Whole language for second language learners.* Portsmouth, NH: Heinemann.

Fuchs, D., Fuchs, L. S., & Vaughn, S. (2008). *Response to intervention: A framework for reading educators.* Newark, DE: International Reading Association.

Giordano, G. (2001). *Twentieth-century reading education: Understanding practices of today in terms of patterns of the past.* New York: JAI Press.

Gunn, B., Biglan, A., Smolkowski, K., & Ary, D. (2000). The efficacy of supplemental instruction in decoding skills for Hispanic and non-Hispanic students in early elementary school. *The Journal of Special Education, 34*(2), 90–103.

Gunn, B., Smolkowski, K., Biglan, A., & Black, C. (2002). Supplemental instruction in decoding skills for Hispanic and non-Hispanic students in early elementary school: A follow-up. *The Journal of Special Education, 36*(2), 69–79.

Hiebert, E. H., & Martin, L. A. (2001). The texts of beginning reading instruction. In S. B. Neuman & D. K. Dickinson (Eds.), *Handbook of early literacy* (pp. 361–376). New York: Guilford Press.

Hiebert, E. H., & Sailors, M. (2009). *Finding the right texts: What works for beginning and struggling readers*. New York: Guilford Press.

Hoffman, J. V. (2001). *Words on words in leveled texts for beginning readers*. Ann Arbor, MI: Center for the Improvement of Early Reading Achievement. Retrieved from www.ciera.org/library/presos/2001.

Hollingsworth, P. M. (1978). An experimental approach to the impress method of teaching reading. *The Reading Teacher, 31,* 624–626.

Invitations to Literacy, K–6. Boston, MA: Houghton Mifflin. Retrieved on November 9, 2010, from www.eduplace.com/rdg/itl

Jachym, N. K., Allington, R. L., & Broikou, K. A. (1989). Estimating the cost of seatwork. *The Reading Teacher, 43,* 30–37.

Knapp, M. S. (1991). *What is taught, and how, to the children of poverty: Interim report from a two year investigation.* Menlo Park, CA: SRI.

Krashen, S., & Biber, D. (1988). *On course.* Sacramento, CA: CABE.

Law, B., & Eckes, M. (1990). *The more than just surviving handbook: ESL for every classroom teacher.* Winnipeg, Canada: Peguis.

Lee, J. (2002). *Liz.* Columbus, OH: SRA/McGraw-Hill.

Lyons, C. A., & Beaver, J. (1995). Reducing retention and learning disability placement through reading recovery: An educationally sound, cost-effective choice. In R. L. Allington & S. A. Walmsley (Eds.), *No quick fix: Rethinking literacy programs in America's elementary schools* (pp. 116–136). New York: Teachers College Press.

Mallette, M. H., Henk, W. A., & Melnick, S. A. (2004). The influence of accelerated reader on the affective literacy orientations of intermediate grade students. *Journal of Literacy Research, 36*(1), 73–84.

Maryland Evaluation Committee. (2006). *Final report of the Maryland Evaluation Committee for selecting supplemental and intervention programs and materials.* Baltimore: Maryland State Department of Education.

Mason, J. (1983). An examination of reading instruction in third and fourth grades. *The Reading Teacher, 36*(9), 906–913.

McCallum, R. D. (1988). Don't throw the basals out with the bath water. *The Reading Teacher, 42,* 204–209.

McGill-Franzen, A., Zmach, C., Solic, K., & Zeig, J. L. (2006). The confluence of two policy mandates: Core reading programs and third-grade retention in Florida. *The Elementary School Journal, 107*(1), 67–91.

McNabb, M. (2006). *Evaluation study of Language, Literacy, & Vocabulary!* St. Charles, IL: Learning Gauge.

Moss, B., & Newton, E. (2001). An examination of the information text genre in basal readers. *Reading Psychology, 23*(1), 1–13.

National Commission on Excellence in Education. (1983). *A nation at risk.* Washington, DC: U.S. Department of Education.

National Reading Panel. (2000). *Report of the National Reading Panel: Teaching children to read.* Washington, DC: National Institute of Child Health and Human Development.

ORFC Curriculum Review Panel. (2004). *Oregon Reading First Center (ORFC): Review of comprehensive programs.* Eugene: University of Oregon.

Osborn, J. (1985). Workbooks: Counting, matching, and judging. In J. Osborn, P. T. Wilson, & R. C. Anderson (Eds.), *Reading education: Foundations for a literate America* (pp. 11–28). Lexington, MA: Lexington Books.

Paris, S. G., & Hoffman, J. V. (2004). Reading assessment in kindergarten through third grade: Findings from the Center for the Improvement of Early Reading Achievement. *The Elementary School Journal, 105*(2), 199–217.

Paris, S. G., Paris, A. H., & Carpenter, R. D. (2002). Effective practices for assessing young readers. In B. M. Taylor & P. D. Pearson (Eds.), *Teaching reading: Effective schools, accomplished teachers* (pp. 141–160). Mahwah, NJ: Erlbaum.

Pearson, P. D. (1974). The effects of grammatical complexity on children's comprehension, recall, and conception of certain semantic relations. *Reading Research Quarterly, 10*(2), 155–192.

Peregoy, S. F., & Boyle, O. F. (1993). *Reading, writing, and learning in ESL.* New York: Longman.

Pikulski, J. J. (1998). Preventing reading failure: A review of five effective programs. *The Reading Teacher, 48*(1), 30–39.

Pinnell, G. S., Deford, D. E., & Lyons, C. A. (1994). Comparing instructional models for the literacy education of high-risk first graders. *Reading Research Quarterly, 29*(1), 8–39.

Pinnell, G. S., & Fountas, I. C. (2002). *Leveled books for readers grades 3–6: A companion volume to guiding readers and writers.* Portsmouth, NH: Heinemann.

Race to the Top Grant Program. (2010). Retrieved June 22, 2010, from www2.ed.gov/programs/racetothetop/index.html.

Reutzel, D. R. (1991). Understanding and using basal readers effectively. In B. L. Hayes (Ed.), *Reading instruction and the effective teacher* (pp. 254–280). Boston: Allyn & Bacon.

Reutzel, D. R., & Larsen, N. S. (1995). Look what they've done to real children's books in the new basal readers. *Language Arts, 72*(7), 495–507.

Rothstein, R., & Jacobsen, R. (2009). Broad and balanced accountability. *Principal Leadership, 10*(1), 22–25.

Routman, R. (1988). *Transitions: From literature to literacy.* Portsmouth, NH: Heinemann.

Simmons, D. C., & Kame'enui, E. J. (2003). *A consumer's guide to evaluating a core reading program, Grades K–3: A critical elements analysis.* Eugene: University of Oregon.

Slavin, R. E., Madden, N. L., Dolan, L., & Wasik, B. A. (1996). *Every child, every school: Success for all.* Thousand Oaks, CA: Corwin.

Slavin, R. E., Madden, N. L., Karweit, N. L., Dolan, L., & Wasik, B. A. (1992). *Success for all: A relentless approach to prevention and early intervention in elementary schools.* Arlington, VA: Educational Research Services.

Slavin, R. E., Madden, N. A., Karweit, N. L., Livermon, B. J., & Dolan, L. (1990). Success for all: First-year outcomes of a comprehensive plan for reforming urban education. *American Educational Research Journal, 27,* 255–278.

Stauffer, R. G. (1969). *Directing reading maturity as a cognitive process.* New York: HarperCollins.

St. John, E. P., & Loescher, S. A. (2001). *Improving early reading: A resource guide for elementary schools.* Bloomington: Indiana Education Policy Center.

Sweet, A. (1997). Teacher perceptions of student motivation and their relation to literacy learning. In J. T. Guthrie & A. Wigfield (Eds.), *Reading engagement: Motivating readers through integrated instruction* (pp. 86–101). Newark, DE: International Reading Association.

Taylor, B. M. (2008). Tier 1: Effective classrooms reading instruction in the elementary grades. In D. Fuchs, L. S. Fuchs, & S. Vaughn (Eds.), *Response to intervention: A framework for reading educators* (pp. 5–25). Newark, DE: International Reading Association.

Town, S., & Holbrook, N. M. (1857). *Progressive primer.* Boston: Carter, Bazin & Company.

Vinovskis, M. A. (1999). *History and educational policymaking.* New Haven, CT: Yale University Press. (ERIC Document Reproduction Service No. ED 482261)

Watt, M. G. (2005). *Standards-based reforms in the United States of America: An overview.* (ERIC Document Reproduction Service No. ED490562)

What Works Clearinghouse. (2008a, December). *Houghton Mifflin: Invitations to Literacy* [Review]. Retrieved June 15, 2010, from http://ies.ed.gov/ncee/wwc/reports/beginning_reading/hm_invitations/index.asp

What Works Clearinghouse. (2008b, August). *Open Court Reading* [Review]. Retrieved June 15, 2010, from http://ies.ed.gov/ncee/wwc/reports/beginning_reading/open_court/index.asp

Zuzovsky, R., & Libman, Z. (2006). Standards of teaching and teaching tests: Is this the right way to go? *Studies in Educational Evaluation, 32*(1), 37–52.

Chapter 10

Appleby, E. (2001). *The three billy goats gruff: A Norwegian folktale.* New York: Scholastic.

Applegate, M. D., Quinn, K. B., & Applegate, A. J. (2008). *The critical reading inventory* (2nd ed.) (CRT-2). Upper Saddle River, NJ: Merrill/Prentice Hall/Pearson.

Barrett, F. L. (1982). *A teacher's guide to shared reading.* Ontario, Canada: Scholastic-TAB Publications.

Beaver, J., & Carter, M. (2010). *Developmental reading assessment* (2nd ed.) (DRA2). Boston: Pearson.

Burke, C. (1987). Burke reading interview. In Y. Goodman, D. Watson, & C. Burke (Eds.), *Reading miscue inventory: Alternative procedures.* New York: Owen.

Clay, M. (1985). *The early detection of reading difficulties.* Portsmouth, NH: Heineman.

Coker, J., & Ritchey, K. (2010). Curriculum-based measurement of writing in kindergarten and first grade: An investigation of production and qualitative scores. *Exceptional Children, 76*(2), 175–193.

Common Core Standards Initiative. (2010). *The common core state standards for English language arts & literacy in history/social studies, science, and technical subjects.* Washington, DC: The Council of Chief State School Officers and the National Governors Association.

Cooter, K. S. (2003). *Preparing middle school students for the TAKS in writing: A professional development seminar.* Dallas, TX: Seminar series presented for selected middle schools in the Dallas Independent School District. Unpublished manuscript.

Dunn, L., & Dunn, L. M. (1997). *Peabody picture vocabulary test—third edition* (PPVT-III). Circle Pines, MN: American Guidance Service.

Dunn, L., Lugo, D. E., Padilla, E. R., & Dunn, L. M. (1986). *Test de vocabulario en imágenes Peabody* (TVIP). Circle Pines, MN: American Guidance Service.

Flynt, E. S., & Cooter, R. B., Jr. (1999). *The Flynt/Cooter English–Español reading inventory.* Upper Saddle River, NJ: Merrill/Prentice Hall.

Fountas, I. C., & Pinnell, G. S. (1996). *Guided reading instruction: Good first teaching for all children.* Portsmouth, NH: Heinemann.

Fowler, G. L. (1982). Developing comprehension skills in primary students through the use of story frames. *The Reading Teacher, 36*(2), 176–179.

Guthrie, J. Y., Hoa, L. W., Wigfield, A., Tonks, S. M., & Perencevich, K. C. (2006). From spark to fire: Can situational reading interest lead to long-term reading motivation? *Reading Research and Instruction, 45*(2), 91–117.

Jennings, J. H., Caldwell, J., & Lerner, J. W. (2006). *Reading problems: Assessment and teaching strategies* (5th ed.). Boston: Pearson/Allyn & Bacon.

Johns, J. L., & Lunn, M. K. (1983). The informal reading inventory: 1910–1980. *Reading World, 23*(1), 8–18.

Kaufman, A. S., & Kaufman, N. L. (2010). *Kaufman test of educational achievement* (2nd ed.) (K-TEA II). Boston: Pearson.

Langer, J. A. (1984). Examining background knowledge and text comprehension. *Reading Research Quarterly, 19,* 468–481.

Mariotti, A. S., & Homan, S. P. (2010). *Linking reading assessment to instruction.* New York: Routledge.

McLaughlin, M. (2010). *Guided comprehension in the primary grades.* Newark, DE: International Reading Association.

Mills, K. A. (2009). Floating on a sea of talk: Reading comprehension through speaking and listening. *The Reading Teacher, 63*(4), 325–329.

National Reading Panel (NRP). (2000). *Report of the National Reading Panel: Teaching children to read.* Washington, DC: National Institute of Child Health and Human Development.

Nilsson, N. L. (2008). A critical analysis of eight informal reading inventories. *The Reading Teacher, 61*(7), 526–536.

Pressley, M. (2000). What should comprehension instruction be the instruction of? In M. L. Kamil, P. B. Mosenthal, P. D. Pearson, & R. Barr (Eds.), *Handbook of reading research* (Vol. 3, pp. 545–561). Mahwah, NJ: Erlbaum.

Reutzel, D. R., & Cooter, R. B. (2011). *Strategies for reading assessment and instruction: Helping every child succeed* (3rd ed.). Upper Saddle River, NJ: Merrill/Prentice Hall.

Salvia, J., Ysseldyke, J., & Bolt, S. (2009). *Assessment in special and inclusive education.* Florence, KY: Wadsworth/Cengage Learning.

White, D. (2008). *Assessment first.* New York: Scholastic.

Woodcock, R. W. (1997). *Woodcock Reading Mastery Tests–Revised (WRMT–R).* Circle Pines, MN: AGS.

Woodcock, R. W., Muñoz-Sandoval, A. F., Ruef, M., & Alvarado, C. G. (2009). *Woodcock-Muñoz language survey–revised (WMLS).* Rolling Meadows, IL: Riverside.

Woodcock, R., Mather, N., & Barnes, E. K. (1987). *Woodcock reading mastery tests–revised.* Circle Pines, MN: American Guidance Service.

Chapter 11

Anderson, N. A. (2007). *What should I read aloud?* Newark, DE: International Reading Association.

Anton, W. (1998). *Corn: From farm to table.* Boston, MA: Newbridge Educational Publishers.

Armbruster, B. B., Lehr, F., & Osborn, J. (2001). *Put reading first: The research building blocks for teaching children to read.* Washington, DC: U.S. Department of Education.

August, D., & Shanahan, T. (2006). *Developing literacy in second-language learners: A report of the National Literacy Panel on language-minority children and youth*. Mahwah, NJ: Lawrence Erlbaum.

Barrett, F. L. (1982). *A teacher's guide to shared reading*. Richmond Hill, Ontario, Canada: Scholastic-TAB.

Bear, D. R., Invernizzi, M., Templeton, S., & Johnston, F. (2012). *Words their way: Word study for phonics, vocabulary, and spelling instruction* (5th ed.). Upper Saddle River, NJ: Merrill/Prentice Hall.

Block, C. C., Oakar, M., & Hurt, N. (2002). The expertise of literacy teachers: A continuum from preschool to grade 5. *Reading Research Quarterly, 37*(2), 178–206.

Burns, M. S., Griffin, P., & Snow, C. E. (Eds.). (1999). *Starting out right: A guide to promoting children's reading success*. Committee on the Prevention of Reading Difficulties in Young Children, Commission on Behavioral and Social Sciences and Education, National Research Council. Washington, DC: National Academy Press.

Calkins, L. (1994). *The art of teaching writing*. Westport, CT: Heinemann.

Calkins, L. M., & Harwayne, S. (1987). *The writing workshop: A world of difference* [Video]. Portsmouth, NH: Heinemann.

Clicker 5 [Computer software]. (2006). Redmond, WA: Crick Software.

Dickinson, D. K., & Tabors, P. O. (Eds.). (2001). *Young children learning at home and school: Beginning literacy with language*. Baltimore: Paul H. Brookes.

Edwards, P. (2010). The role of family literacy programs in the school success or failure of African American families and children. In K. Dunsmore & D. Fisher (Eds.), *Bringing literacy home* (pp. 184–202). Newark, DE: International Reading Association.

Eldredge, J. L., Reutzel, D. R., & Hollingsworth, P. M. (1996). Comparing the effectiveness of two oral reading practices: Round-robin reading and the shared book experience. *Journal of Literacy Research, 28*(2), 201–225.

Elish-Piper, L., & L'Allier, S. K. (2010). Exploring the relationship between literacy coaching and student reading achievement in grades K–1. *Literacy Research and Instruction, 49*(2), 162–174.

Ford, M. P. (2005). *Differentiation through flexible grouping: Successfully reaching all readers*. Naperville, IL: North Central Regional Educational Lab.

Gambrell, L. B. (1996). Creating classroom cultures that foster motivation. *The Reading Teacher, 50*(1), 14–25.

Hoffman, J. V., Roser, N., & Battle, J. (1993). Reading aloud in classrooms: From the modal to a "model." *The Reading Teacher, 46*(6), 496–503.

Holdaway, D. (1979). *The foundations of literacy*. Exeter, NH: Heinemann.

Holdaway, D. (1984). *Stability and change in literacy learning*. Portsmouth, NH: Heinemann.

Kidspiration 2 [Computer software]. (2005). Beaverton, OR: Inspiration Software.

Labbo, L. D., & Teale, W. H. (1990). Cross age reading: A strategy for helping poor readers. *The Reading Teacher, 43*, 363–369.

Ladson-Billings, G. (2010). Making the book talk: Literacy in successful urban classrooms and communities. In K. Dunsmore & D. Fisher (Eds.), *Bringing literacy home* (pp. 226–244). Newark, DE: International Reading Association.

Lipson, M. Y., & Wixon, K. K. (2010). *Successful approaches to RTI: Collaborative practices for improving K–12 literacy*. Newark, DE: International Reading Association.

Lopez, O. S. (2010). The digital learning classroom: Improving English language learners' academic success in mathematics and reading using interactive whiteboard technology. *Computers & Education, 54*(4), 901–915.

Lovell, M., & Phillips, L. (2009). Commercial software program approved for teaching reading and writing in the primary grades: Another sobering reality. *Journal of Research on Technology Education, 42*(2), 197–216.

Malloy, J. A., Castek, J. M., & Leu, D. J. (2010). Silent reading: Different contexts, different readers. In E. H. Hiebert & D. R. Reutzel (Eds.), *Silent reading revisited: New directions for researchers and teachers* (pp. 221–240). Newark, DE: International Reading Association.

Martin, B. (1990). *Brown bear, brown bear, what do you see?* New York: Henry Holt.

Martin, B. (1991). *Polar bear, polar bear, what do you hear?* New York: Henry Holt.

Mathes, P. G., Denton, C. A., Fletcher, J. M., Anthony, J. L., Francis, D. J., & Schatschneider, C. (2005). The effects of theoretically different instruction and student characteristics on the skills of struggling readers. *Reading Research Quarterly, 40*(2), 148–183.

McCardle, P., & Chhabra, V. (2004). *The voice of evidence in reading research*. Baltimore: Paul H. Brookes.

McKenna, M. C., & Walpole, S. (2008). *The literacy coaching challenge: Models and methods for grades K–8*. New York: Guilford.

Meisinger, H., Schwanenflugel, P. J., Bradley, E., Kuhn, M. R., & Stahl, S. A. (2002). *Interaction quality during partner reading*. Paper presented at the Annual Meeting of the National Reading Conference, Miami, FL.

Morgan, D. N., Mraz, M., Padak, N. D., & Rasinski, T. V. (2009). *Independent reading: Practical strategies for grades K–3*. New York: Guilford Press.

Morrow, L. M. (1990). Preparing the classroom environment to promote literacy during play. *Early Childhood Education Research Quarterly, 5*, 537–554.

Morrow, L. M. (2002). *The literacy center: Contexts for reading and writing* (2nd ed.). Portland, ME: Stenhouse.

Morrow, L. M. (2005). *Literacy development in the early years: Helping children read and write* (5th ed.). Boston: Allyn & Bacon.

Morrow, L. M. (2009). *Literacy development in the early years: Helping children read and write* (6th ed.). Boston: Allyn & Bacon.

Morrow, L. M., Mendelsohn, A. L., & Kuhn, M. R. (2010). Characteristics of three family literacy programs that worked. In K. Dunsmore & D. Fisher (Eds.), *Bringing literacy home* (pp. 83–103). Newark, DE: International Reading Association.

Morrow, L. M., Reutzel, D. R., & Casey, H. (2006). Organization and management of language arts teaching: Classroom environments, grouping practices, and exemplary instruction. In C. Evertson (Ed.), *Handbook of classroom management* (pp. 559–582). Mahwah, NJ: Lawrence Erlbaum Associates.

Morrow, L. M., Tracey, D. H., Woo, D. G., & Pressley, M. (1999). Characteristics of exemplary first-grade literacy instruction. *The Reading Teacher, 52*(5), 462–476.

National Early Literacy Panel. (2008). *Developing early literacy: Report of the National Early Literacy Panel*. Jessup, MD: National Institute for Literacy.

National Reading Panel. (2000). *Report of the National Reading Panel: Teaching children to read*. Washington, DC: National Institute of Child Health and Human Development.

Neuman, S. B., & Cunningham, L. (2009). The impact of professional development and coaching on early language and literacy instructional practices. *American Educational Research Journal, 46*(2), 532–566.

Neuman, S. B., & Roskos, K. (1990). Play, print, and purpose: Enriching play environments for literacy development. *The Reading Teacher, 44*(3), 214–221.

Neuman, S. B., & Roskos, K. (1992). Literacy objects as cultural tools: Effects on children's literacy behaviors in play. *Reading Research Quarterly, 27*, 202–225.

Neuman, S. B., & Roskos, K. (1997). Literacy knowledge in practice: Contexts of participation for young writers and readers. *Reading Research Quarterly, 32*(1), 10–33.

Opitz, M. F. (1998). *Flexible grouping in reading: Practical ways to help all students become better readers.* New York: Scholastic.

Osborn, J., Lehr, M. A., & Hiebert, E. H. (2003). *Focus on fluency: Research-based practices in early reading series.* Honolulu, HI: Pacific Resources for Education and Learning.

Paratore, J. R., Krol-Sinclair, B., Brooke, D., & Schick, A. (2010). Writing the next chapter in family literacy: Clues to long term effects. In K. Dunsmore & D. Fisher (Eds.), *Bringing literacy home* (pp. 265–288). Newark, DE: International Reading Association.

Payne, C. (2005). *Shared reading for today's classroom.* New York: Scholastic.

Pearson, P. D., & Gallagher, M. C. (1983). The instruction of reading comprehension. *Contemporary Educational Psychology, 8*(3), 317–344.

Pressley, M., Allington, R. L., Wharton-McDonald, R., Collins-Block, C., & Morrow, L. M. (2001). *Learning to read: Lessons from exemplary first grade classrooms.* New York: Guilford Press.

Pressley, M., Dolezal, S. E., Raphael, L. M., Mohan, L., Roehrig, A. D., & Bogner, K. (2003). *Motivating primary-grade students.* New York: Guilford Press.

Reutzel, D. R. (2006). Hey teacher, when you say fluency, what do you mean? Developing fluency and meta-fluency in elementary classrooms. In T. V. Rasinski, C. Blachowicz, & K. Lems (Eds.), *Fluency instruction: Research-based best practices* (pp. 62–85). New York: Guilford Press.

Reutzel, D. R. (2007). Organizing effective literacy instruction: Differentiating instruction to meet the needs of all literacy learners. In L. M. Morrow, L. B. Gambrell, and M. Pressley (Eds.), *Best practices for literacy instruction* (3rd ed., pp. 313–343). New York: Guilford Press.

Reutzel, D. R., & Fawson, P. C. (2002). *Your classroom library—giving it more teaching power: Research-based strategies for developing better readers and writers.* New York: Scholastic Professional.

Reutzel, D. R., & Hollingsworth, P. M. (1993). Effects of fluency training on second graders' reading comprehension. *Journal of Educational Research, 86*(6), 325–331.

Reutzel, D. R., Hollingsworth, P. M., & Eldredge, J. L. (1994). Oral reading instruction: The impact on student reading development. *Reading Research Quarterly, 23*(1), 40–62.

Reutzel, D. R., & Morrow, L. M. (2007). Promoting and assessing effective literacy learning classroom environments. In R. McCormick & J. Paratore (Eds.), *Classroom literacy assessment: Making sense of what students know and do* (pp. 33–49). New York: Guilford Press.

Roberts, D. F., Foehr, U. G., & Rideout, V. (2005). Generation M: Media in the lives of 8–18 year-olds. Washington, DC: Henry J. Kaiser Family Foundation. Retrieved April 29, 2010, from www.kff.org/entmedia/upload/Generation-M-Media-in-the-Lives-of-8–18-Year-olds-Report.pdf

Rogg, L. J. (2001). *Early literacy instruction in kindergarten.* Newark, DE: International Reading Association.

Roskos, K., & Neuman, S. B. (2001). Environment and its influences for early literacy teaching and learning. In S. B. Neuman & D. K. Dickinson (Eds.), *Handbook of early literacy research* (pp. 281–294). New York: Guilford Press.

Samuels, S. J., & Farstrup, A. E. (2006). *What research has to say about fluency instruction.* Newark, DE: International Reading Association.

Shanahan, T. (2004). Critiques of the National Reading Panel report: Their implications for research, policy, and practice. In P. McCardle & V. Chhabra (Eds.), *The voice of evidence in reading research* (pp. 235–266). Baltimore: Paul H. Brookes.

Shanahan, T., & Lonigan, C. J. (2010). National Early Literacy Panel: A summary of the process and the report. *Educational Researcher, 39*(4), 279–285.

Shanahan, T., Mulhern, M., & Rodriquez-Brown, F. (1995). Project FLAME: Lessons learned from a family literacy program for minority families. *The Reading Teacher, 48*, 40–47.

Smith, M. W., Dickinson, D. K., Sangeorge, A., & Anastasopoulos, L. (2002). *Early language and literacy classroom observation (ELLCO) toolkit.* Baltimore: Paul H. Brookes.

Stahl, K. A., & McKenna, M. C. (2006). *Reading research at work: Foundations of effective practice.* New York: Guilford Press.

Stahl, S. (2004). What do we do about fluency? In P. McCardle & V. Chhabra (Eds.), *The voice of evidence in reading research* (pp. 187–211). Baltimore: Paul H. Brookes.

Taylor, B. M., Pearson, P. D., Clark, K. F., & Walpole, S. (1999). *Beating the odds in teaching all children to read* (Ciera Report No. 2-006). Ann Arbor, MI: Center for the Improvement of Early Reading Achievement.

Taylor, B. M., Pearson, P. D., Clark, K. F., & Walpole, S. (2000). Effective schools and accomplished teachers: Lessons about primary grade reading instruction in low-income schools. *Elementary School Journal, 101*, 121–165.

Taylor, B. M., Pearson, P. D., Peterson, D. S., & Rodriguez, M. C. (2005). The CIERA school change framework: An evidence-based approach to professional development and school reading improvement. *Reading Research Quarterly, 40*(1), 40–69.

Teale, W. H., & Martinez, M. (1986). Reading in a kindergarten classroom library. *The Reading Teacher, 41*(6), 568–573.

Toll, C. A. (2005). *The literacy coaches' survival guide: Essential questions and practical answers.* Newark, DE: International Reading Association.

Toll, C. A. (2008). *Surviving but not yet thriving: Essential questions and practical answers for experienced literacy coaches.* Newark, DE: International Reading Association.

Topping, K. J. (2006). Building reading fluency: Cognitive, behavioral, and socio-emotional factors and the role of peer-mediated learning. In S. J. Samuels & A. E. Farstrup (Eds.), *What research has to say about fluency instruction* (pp. 106–129). Newark, DE: International Reading Association.

Unsworth, L. (1984). Meeting individual needs through flexible within-class grouping of pupils. *The Reading Teacher, 38*(3), 298–304.

Van Allsburg, C. (1985). *The polar express*. Boston: Houghton Mifflin.

Vopat, J. (1994). *The parent project: A workshop approach to parent involvement*. York, ME: Stenhouse.

Vopat, J. (1998). *More than bake sales: The resource guide for family involvement in education*. York, ME: Stenhouse.

Vygotsky, L. S. (1978). *Mind in society*. Cambridge, MA: Harvard University Press.

Walpole, S., & McKenna, M. C. (2004). *The literacy coach's handbook: A guide to research-based practice*. New York: Guilford.

Wang, M., Haertel, G., & Walberg, H. (1994, December). What helps students learn? *Educational Leadership*, 74–79.

Wong, H. K., & Wong, R. (1998). *The first days of school: How to be an effective teacher*. Mountain View, CA: Harry K. Wong.

Wood, A. (1984). *The napping house* (Don Wood, Illustrator). San Diego, CA: Harcourt Brace.

Write: Outloud Solo [Computer software]. (2005). Volo, IL: Don Johnson.

Chapter 12

Adesope, O. O., Lavin, T., Thompson, T., & Ungerleider, C. (2010). A systematic review and meta-analysis of the cognitive correlates of bilingualism. *Review of Educational Research, 80*(2), 207–245.

Anders, P. L., & Bos, C. S. (1986). Semantic feature analysis: An interactive strategy for vocabulary development text comprehension. *Journal of Reading, 29*, 610–617.

Anderson, R. C., & Freebody, P. (1983). Reading comprehension and the assessment and acquisition of word knowledge. In B. Hutson (Ed.), *Advances in reading/language research* (pp. 231–256). Greenwich, CT: JAI.

Baldwin, R. S., & Kaufman, R. K. (1979). A concurrent validity study of the Raygor readability estimate. *Journal of Reading, 23*, 148–153.

Bass, L., & Woo, D. G. (2008). Comprehension window strategy: A comprehension strategy and prop for reading and writing informational text. *The Reading Teacher, 61*(7), 571–575.

Bintz, W. P. (2010). Singing across the curriculum. *The Reading Teacher, 63*(8), 683–686.

Blasingame, J. (2007). *Books that don't bore 'em: Young adult books that speak to this generation*. New York: Scholastic.

Bloom, B. (1956). *Taxonomy of educational objectives*. New York: David McKay.

Boulware-Gooden, R., Carreker, S., Thornhill, A., & Joshi, R. M. (2007). Instruction of metacognitive strategies enhances reading comprehension and vocabulary achievement of third-grade students. *The Reading Teacher 61*(1), pp. 70–77.

Brent, D. (1994). Writing classes, writing genres, and writing textbooks. *Textual Studies in Canada, 4*(1), 5–15.

Carr, E. (1985). The vocabulary overview guide: A metacognitive strategy to improve vocabulary comprehension and retention. *Journal of Reading, 28*(8), 684–689.

Cook, L. K., & Mayer, R. E. (1988). Teaching readers about the nature of science text. *Journal of Educational Psychology, 80*(4), 448–456.

Cooter, K. S. (2002). When mama can't read: Counteracting intergenerational illiteracy. *The Reading Teacher, 59*(7), 698–702.

Cooter, K. S., & Cooter, R. B. (in press). *Urban literacy education: Helping city kids in regular and special education classrooms*. Boston: Pearson/Allyn & Bacon.

Cooter, R. B. (2004). The pillars of urban literacy instruction: Prerequisites for change. In R. B. Cooter (Ed.), *Perspectives on rescuing urban literacy education: Spies, saboteurs, and saints*. Mahwah, NJ: Lawrence Erlbaum.

Cooter, R. B. (2009). *Research in academic literacy: Academic Word Walls or AW²*. Unpublished manuscript.

Cooter, R. B., & Flynt, E. S. (1996). *Teaching reading in the content areas: Developing content literacy for all students*. Upper Saddle River, NJ: Merrill/Prentice Hall.

Cooter, R. B., Mathews, B., Thompson, S., & Cooter, K. S. (2004). Searching for lessons of mass instruction? Try reading strategy continuums. *The Reading Teacher, 58*(4), 388–393.

Corpus, D., & Giddings, A. (2010). *Planning & managing effective reading instruction across the content areas*. New York: Scholastic.

Cox, C., & Zarillo, J. (1993). *Teaching reading with children's literature*. Upper Saddle River, NJ: Merrill/Prentice Hall.

Dale, E. (1969). *Audiovisual methods in teaching* (3rd ed.). New York: Holt, Rinehart and Winston.

Dalton, B., & Grisham, D. L. (in press). eVoc strategies: Ten ways to use technology to build vocabulary. *The Reading Teacher*.

Dana, C. (1989). Strategy families for disabled readers. *Journal of Reading, 33*(1), 30–35.

Diffily, D. (2004). *Teachers and families working together*. Boston: Allyn & Bacon.

Duke, N. K., & Bennett-Armistead, V. S. (2003). *Reading and writing informational text in the primary grades: Research-based practices*. New York: Scholastic.

Eldredge, J. L. (1990). Increasing the performance of poor readers in the third grade with a group assisted strategy. *Journal of Educational Research, 84*(2), 69–77.

Eldredge, J. L., & Quinn, D. W. (1988). Increasing reading performance of low-achieving second graders with dyad reading groups. *Journal of Educational Research, 82*, 40–46.

Epstein, J. L. (2001). *School, family, and community partnerships: Preparing educators and improving schools*. Boulder, CO: Westview Press.

Estes, T. H., & Vaughn, J. L. (1978). *Reading and learning in the content classroom*. Boston: Allyn & Bacon.

Fisher, D., Brozo, W. G., Frey, N., & Ivey, G. (2011). *50 instructional routines to develop content literacy*. Boston: Pearson.

Fisher, D., & Frey, N. (2008). *Improving adolescent literacy: Content area strategies at work*. Upper Saddle River, NJ: Pearson Merrill Prentice Hall.

Frayer, D., Frederick, W. C., & Klausmeir, H. J. (1969). *A schema for testing the level of concept mastery* (Working Paper No. 16). Madison: University of Wisconsin, Wisconsin Research and Development Center for Cognitive Learning.

Fry, E. (1977). Fry's readability graph: Clarifications, validity, and extension to level 17. *Journal of Reading, 21*, 242–252.

Gamberg, R., Kwak, W., Hutchings, M., & Altheim, J. (1988). *Learning and loving it: Theme studies in the classroom*. Portsmouth, NH: Heinemann.

Gladwell, M. (2002). *The tipping point: How little things can make a big difference*. New York: Back Bay Books.

Gregg, M., & Sekeres, D. C. (2006). Supporting children's reading of expository text in the geography classroom. *The Reading Teacher, 60*(2), 102–110.

Hall, L. (2004). Comprehending expository text: Promising strategies for struggling readers and students with reading disabilities? *Reading Research and Instruction, 44*(2), 75–95.

Harris, A. J., & Sipay, E. R. (1990). *How to increase reading ability: A guide to developmental and remedial methods* (9th ed.). New York: Longman.

Harris, T. L., & Hodges, R. E. (Eds.). (1995). *The literacy dictionary: The vocabulary of reading and writing*. Newark, DE: International Reading Association.

Heilman, A. W., Blair, T. R., & Rupley, W. H. (2001). *Principles and practices of teaching reading* (10th ed.). Upper Saddle River, NJ: Merrill/Prentice Hall.

Kang, H. W. (1994). Helping second language readers learn from content area text through collaboration and support. *The Journal of Reading, 37*(8), 646–652.

Kornblith, G. J., & Lasser, C. (2005). "The truth, the whole truth, and nothing but the truth": Writing, producing, and using college-level American history textbooks. *Journal of American History, 91*(4), 1380–1382.

Krashen, S. (1992). *The power of reading*. Englewood, CO: Libraries Unlimited.

Lapp, D., Flood, J., & Farnan, N. (2004). *Content area reading and learning*. New York: Lawrence Erlbaum.

Manz, S. L. (2002). A strategy for previewing textbooks: Teaching readers to become THIEVES. *The Reading Teacher, 55*(5), 434–435.

Martorella, P. H. (2000). *Teaching social studies in middle and secondary schools*. Upper Saddle River, NJ: Prentice Hall.

Martorella, P. H. (2008). *Teaching social studies in middle and secondary schools* (5th ed.). Columbus, OH: Pearson/Prentice Hall.

Marzano, R. J. (2004). *Building background knowledge for academic achievement: Research on what works in schools*. Alexandria, VA: Association for Supervision and Curriculum Development.

Marzano, R. J. (2007). *The art and science of teaching: A comprehensive framework for effective instruction*. Alexandria, VA: Association for Supervision & Curriculum Development.

McGee, L. M. (1982). Awareness of text structure: Effects on children's recall of expository text. *Reading Research Quarterly, 17*(4), 581–590.

McKeown, M. G., Beck, I. L., & Blake, R. K. (2009, July/August/September). Rethinking reading comprehension instruction: A comparison of instruction for strategies and content approaches. *Reading Research Quarterly, 44*(3), 218–253.

McLaughlin, M. (2010). *Content area reading*. Boston: Pearson.

Meyer, B. J. F., & Freedle, R. O. (1984). Effects of discourse type on recall. *American Educational Research Journal, 21*(1), 121–143.

Montelongo, J., Jiménez, L. B., Hernández, A. C., & Hosking, D. (2006). Teaching expository text structures. *The Science Teacher, 73*(2), 28–31.

Moss, B. (2004). Teaching expository text structures through information trade book retellings. *The Reading Teacher, 57*(8), 710–718.

National Center for Education Statistics. (2010). *The Nation's Report Card: Reading 2009* (NCES 2010-458). Washington, DC: Institute of Education Sciences, U.S. Department of Education.

National Institute for Literacy. (2007). *What content-area teachers should know about adolescent literacy*. Jessup, MD: Author. Retrieved from http://literacyacademy-edublogs.org.

Nichols, S. L., Glass, G. V., & Berliner, D. C. (2006). High-stakes testing and student achievement: Does accountability pressure increase student learning? *Education Policy Analysis Archives, 14*(1), 1–172.

Ogle, D. (2011). *Partnering for content literacy: PRC2 in action*. Boston: Pearson.

Paige, D. D. (in press). That sounded good! Rethinking whole-class choral reading. *The Reading Teacher*.

Palmatier, R. A. (1973). A notetaking system for learning. *Journal of Reading, 17*(1), 36–39.

Pappas, C. C., Kiefer, B. Z., & Levstik, L. S. (1990). *An integrated language perspective in the elementary school*. New York: Longman.

Paradis, E. E. (1984). *Comprehension: Thematic units* [Videotape]. Laramie: University of Wyoming.

Paris, S. R., Fisher, D., & Headley, K. (2009). *Adolescent literacy [field tested]: Effective solutions for every classroom*. Newark, DE: International Reading Association.

Pauk, W. (2000). *How to study in college* (7th ed.). Boston: Houghton Mifflin.

Raygor, A. L. (1977). The Raygor readability estimate: A quick and easy way to determine difficulty. In P. D. Pearson (Ed.), *Reading: Theory, research and practice* (pp. 259–263). Clemson, SC: National Reading Conference.

Reutzel, D. R., & Cooter, R. B. (2011). *Strategies for reading assessment and instruction: Helping every child succeed* (4th ed.). Boston: Pearson/Allyn & Bacon.

Salahu-Din, D., Persky, H., & Miller, J. (2008). *The Nation's Report Card: Writing 2007* (NCES 2008-468). Washington, DC: National Center for Education Statistics, Institute of Education Sciences, U.S. Department of Education.

Singer, H., & Donlan, D. (1989). *Reading and learning from text* (2nd ed.). Hillsdale, NJ: Erlbaum.

Stahl, K. A. D. (2008). The effects of three instructional methods on the reading comprehension and content acquisition of novice readers. *Journal of Literacy Research, 40*(3), 359–393.

Stahl, K. A. D., & Bravo, M. A. (2010). Contemporary classroom vocabulary assessment for content areas. *The Reading Teacher, 63*(7), 566–578.

Sun, Y. (2009). Voice blog: An exploratory study of language learning. *Language Learning & Technology, 13*(2), 88–103.

Vygotsky, L. S. (1986). *Thought and language*. Boston: MIT Press.

Wepner, S. B., & Feeley, J. T. (1993). *Moving forward with literature: Basals, books, and beyond*. Upper Saddle River, NJ: Merrill/Prentice Hall.

Wiseman, D. L. (1992). *Learning to read with literature*. Boston: Allyn & Bacon.

Name Index

591

Subject Index